Contemporary Canadian Business

THIRD EDITION

Contemporary Canadian Business

THIRD EDITION

Steven H. Appelbaum   Concordia University
M. Dale Beckman   University of Manitoba
Louis E. Boone   University of South Alabama
David L. Kurtz   Seattle University

Holt, Rinehart and Winston of Canada, Limited
Toronto

Canadian Cataloguing Publication Data

Main entry under title:
Contemporary Canadian Business, Third Edition

Bibliography: p.
Includes index.
ISBN 0-03-922655-7

1. Business. 2. Canada - Commerce. I. Appelbaum,
Steven H., 1941-

Director of Publishing: David Dimmell
Acquisitions Editor: Elio Ennamorati
Developmental Editor: Allan Dwyer
Publishing Services Manager: Karen Eakin
Editorial Co-ordinator: Jill Parkinson
Editorial Assistant: Tess Fragoulis
Copy Editor: Olive Koyama
Cover Design: Pronk and Associates
Interior Design: Peter Maher
Typesetting and Assembly: Trigraph Inc.
Printing and Binding: John Deyell Company

Printed in Canada
  2 3 4 5 94 93 92 91

To Barbara

and to the memory of
Marvin Beckman,
a wise businessman

Acknowledgements

A great number of people have made significant contributions to *Contemporary Canadian Business*. The third edition has been strengthened as a result of invaluable input from fellow instructors, students, and business practitioners. We extend special thanks to the following people who, by reviewing early stages of the manuscript, played an integral part in shaping this third Canadian edition:

Jan Charbonneau, St. Francis Xavier University
Michael Prince, University of Windsor
William Sinkevitch, St. Claire College
Dorothy Derksen, Red River Community College
John Terrell, Camosun College
John Redston, Red River Community College
Norman Bell, Seneca College
Margot Adams-Weber, Brock University

We also wish to express our thanks for the assistance of Vanessa Chio of the University of Massachusetts and Concordia University, Marilyn Howell of Concordia, and Carolyn Kryschuk of the University of Manitoba.

Last, but certainly not least, we are grateful to the many professionals at Holt, Rinehart and Winston of Canada: Dave Collinge, Publisher; Elio Ennamorati, Acquisitions Editor; and Allan Dwyer, Developmental Editor. We also extend our thanks to the members of the production staff: Karen Eakin, Jill Parkinson, and Tess Fragoulis.

S H A
M D B

Preface

The nineties are exciting times in which to begin the study of business. Never before have organizations—from the smallest businesses to the largest corporations—placed greater emphasis on business knowledge. This emphasis has created more employment opportunities in all aspects of business than ever before—a trend that is sure to grow.

Over a million students have begun the study of business with *Contemporary Business*, the American version of this text. During the first twelve years of its existence, *Contemporary Business* introduced more students to business administration than any other textbook published. It became the standard against which other textbooks were compared.

By drawing on the success of the American text, and by writing with a totally Canadian perspective, *Contemporary Canadian Business* has become the standard here in Canada, against which all other introductory business texts are compared.

User feedback has identified several factors that collectively explain the success of the text. *Contemporary Canadian Business* is both rigorous and lively; it satisfies the dual course objectives of providing a solid foundation for more advanced business courses, while communicating the challenges and opportunities of a career in business.

The Canadian business setting is truly reflected: readily identifiable cases and real-world examples are included to illustrate the application of fundamental business concepts discussed in the text. In addition, the text has several strengths not found in competing books, beneficial to both instructors and students.

Changes from the Second Edition

Several chapters have been reorganized or completely rewritten to reflect the current business scene. All of the chapter profiles and the majority of the cases and focuses have been replaced, and statistical data have been updated. There is increased coverage of topics such as international business, women in business, and the Canada-U.S. Free Trade Agreement. The particular focus on small business/entrepreneurship issues has been retained and updated in the third edition.

Stress on Pedagogical Soundness

Contemporary Canadian Business is written to help students learn about business. They are challenged to apply business concepts rather than to just memorize lists and definitions. The following features are designed to make this new edition of the text even more effective as a teaching/learning tool:

- Perhaps the most important feature that distinguishes this book from other texts is that students enjoy reading and studying it. Business concepts are presented in a lively manner, and hundreds of real-world examples breathe life into these concepts for students. Business profiles, controversial issues, boxed items, cases, and numerous current examples are designed to illustrate the application of business principles discussed in the text.
- Each chapter begins with a list of specific learning goals, along with a profile of a real businessperson in a relevant setting to illustrate the application of the chapter's subject matter in a novel fashion. Profiled business personalities include Bill Kelly, renowned and respected labour mediator; Pierre Péladeau, the Quebec publishing magnate; John Crow, Governor of the Bank of Canada; and Heather Reisman, an innovative Toronto management consultant.
- Vocabulary building—a critical concern in the first business course—is stressed by including definitions in the margin next to the introduction, and a discussion of the term in the text.

- Key terms are also included at the end of each chapter for quick reference, and highlighted where they appear in the index.
- Each chapter ends with a controversial issue, included to increase student involvement and discussion, and with two case studies. The concepts in each chapter must be applied to solve the questions that accompany the two cases.

A Complete Learning/Teaching Package in Business

Contemporary Canadian Business is a comprehensive teaching and learning package that is unparalleled in its completeness. While the textbook is undoubtedly the most important element in the package, it is only one part, and is supplemented by the *Study Guide*. Prepared by Mick Carney of Concordia University, the *Study Guide* reinforces the concepts learned in the text, and includes many other real-world situations that can be used in the classroom.

Expanded Resources for Instructors

Although it can be argued that the first business course is the most important in the business curriculum, it is often taught by instructors with large classes and heavy teaching loads. Because the authors recognize the challenges facing the instructor of this course, much of this challenge is met with the Integrated Resource Manual written by Ross Crane of Seneca College. It is a complete resource tool for the instructor which includes: lecture outlines, transparencies, answers to exercises and cases, supplemental cases and lectures, and a host of enhancement materials such as experiential exercises, enrichment items, and term paper suggestions—all of which are designed to make this course a pleasure to teach. A computer test bank, to help streamline the evaluation and grading process, is also available, and a set of Video Cases has been prepared as well. These short videos, featuring Canadian companies, are designed to stimulate class discussion and reinforce chapter concepts.

Publisher's Note to Instructors and Students

This textbook is a key component of your course. If you are the instructor of this course, you undoubtedly considered a number of texts carefully before choosing this as the one that would work best for your students and you. The authors and publishers of this book spent considerable time and money to ensure its high quality, and we appreciate your recognition of this effort and accomplishment.

If you are a student we are confident that this text will help you to meet the objectives of your course. You will also find it helpful after the course is finished as a valuable addition to your personal library.

As well, please do not forget that photocopying copyright work means the authors lose royalties that are rightfully theirs. This loss will discourage them from writing another edition of this text or other books; doing so would simply not be worth their time and effort. If this happens we all lose—students, instructors, authors, and publishers.

Since we want to hear what you think about this book please be sure to send us the stamped reply card at the end of the text. This will help us to continue publishing high-quality books for your course.

Contents

Part Two   Organization and Management of the Enterprise

Part Three   Management of Human Resources

Part Four   Marketing Management

Part Five   Information for Business Decisions

Part Six   Production

Part Seven   Financing the Enterprise

Part Eight   Additional Dimensions

Part One

Business and Its Environment

The Foundations of Business

Learning Goals

"I know of no money-making business in Canada except the law, store keeping, tavern keeping, and perhaps I may add horse dealing."
—*John Langton, letter to his brother, Oct. 21, 1844.*

"Modern business is a complex, fast moving thing. The fit and educated survive, the remainder go into politics."
—*Herb Surplis, business columnist,* Calgary Herald, in Liberty, *Feb. 1964.*

1. To explain what a business is and how it operates as part of the private enterprise system within a mixed economy

2. To define the role of competition and of the entrepreneur

3. To explain the role of government in the Canadian mixed economy

4. To explain the concepts of gross national product and productivity and why they are important

5. To analyze how the historical development of the Canadian economy influences contemporary business

6. To identify the different types of economic systems

7. To explain the roles of business, labour, and government in modern society

8. To recognize how to study business and why

9. To analyze how contemporary business operates as a system designed to satisfy the needs of society

Profile

Pierre Péladeau—*Bad Boy Made Good*

As founding president and controlling shareholder of Quebecor Inc., Pierre Péladeau is a media mogul. The company publishes daily newspapers in Montreal, Quebec City and Winnipeg—43 weeklies and seven magazines. It operates a vast commercial printing business, distributes books under its own imprint and those of a hundred other publishers, and sells books, records and photographic equipment.

With $446 million in annual revenue, Quebecor is in the second tier of the Canadian communications business. Its recently acquired stake in the paper maker Donohue Inc. will catapult it into the billion-dollar club of Maclean Hunter, Thomson Newspapers and Southam. And in publishing markets where they compete with him, the majors consider Péladeau a genuine threat. "He's a very dynamic and wilful entrepreneurial leader," says Clark Davey, publisher of Southam's Montreal daily, *The Gazette*.

Even as Péladeau struck up associations with the rich and powerful, his enduring image remained that of the p'tit Québécois bad boy who made good. His rags-to-riches story, enhanced by a street-tough style and a bawdy sense of humour have made him a regional folk hero and a local celebrity. In Quebec, he is both icon and iconoclast.

Péladeau credits his mother, Elmire, with firing up his motivation. She even lent him $1,500 to buy his first weekly newspaper, launching him into a business so engrossing that he put aside both a law career and his dreams of becoming an impresario.

While studying law at McGill University, Péladeau produced a parody of the law society debates—hiring radio entertainers to argue the merits of blondes versus brunettes or whether young women should date older men. Now he applies the same touch to producing newspapers that people want to buy. His first ventures were neighbourhood weeklies close to the people. Discovering the public's insatiable

appetite for entertainment news, he soon branched into tawdry French-language copies of US tabloids.

Launched in 1964 while the leading French-language daily, *La Presse*, was crippled by a strike, Péladeau's *Journal de Montréal* feeds readers a steady diet of sports, crime and celebrity columnists. He hired René Lévesque as a political columnist when the Parti Québécois won 250,000 votes in the 1970 provincial election. His sense of what sells has pulled the tabloid into the top ranks of Canadian newspapers, with a weekly circulation that tops 325,000 and is surpassed only by the *Toronto Star*.

Source: Harvey Enchin, "Bad Boy Made Good," *Report on Business Magazine*, September 1987, pp. 32, 33, 34.

Foothills Stadium, Calgary: a Saturday in May. In the bottom of the ninth, the Las Vegas Stars are leading the Calgary Cannons 4 to 3. There's one out and a Cannon pinch runner is on second. On the mound, Stars pitcher Todd Simmons, a lanky righthander with a mean side-arm delivery, faces Dave Hengel, an outfielder who has become a local hero since joining the Cannons in 1985.

Coming into today's game Hengel was on an eight-game hitting streak, batting a hefty .393; up to this moment, however, he has gone 0-for-4. With a base hit, he can keep his streak alive and drive in the tying run. But he is overeager; he makes a wild swing at the first pitch for strike one and fouls off the second pitch for strike two.

The Cannons are behind on the scoreboard, but the crowd is having a ball. The sun—for a change—is warm, the sky is blue, and almost all of the 6,000 seats at Foothills are filled. Hot dogs and peanuts are selling briskly. Bare-chested young men in shorts and baseball caps pick their way to their seats, a frothing beer in each hand. Children cavort on the stadium steps and in the playground behind the stands. As Hengel tenses for a mighty blow, the organist is pumping up the crowd while a peanut vendor, wearing a red plastic Cannons batting helmet, leads the cheers.

On spring nights, fans bundled in ski jackets sip hot coffee and watch Triple A baseball, an uneven variety of the sport played by hopefuls, has-beens and never-has-made-its. Neither the weather nor the play inspires poetry. But the Cannons do inspire profits. Unlike many minor league teams, the Calgary Cannons are a smashing financial success.

As Hengel and the other Cannons ply their trade on the diamond, one of the team's most valuable assets watches from the press box. He is Bill Cragg, assistant general manager and the leader of the Cannons' vigorous marketing team put together by owner Russ Parker, 46.

Before the Cannons played their first game in April, 1985, broadcast rights had been sold to Molson Breweries, and local and national advertisers were lining up to lease outfield-fence sign boards at $4,000 each. Every square centimetre of the fence has been leased and there is a waiting list for the next available space. The team has lined up dozens of corporate sponsors who participate in give-aways and promotions such as "Texaco T-Shirt Day" and "CFCN Helmet Night."

And the crowds have been showing up in droves. Parker says: "We have no control over our on-field performance because we do not own the ball players [they are owned by the Seattle Mariners], and we have no control over the weather. So our plan was to market baseball, the fun of going to the ballpark, the fun atmosphere." That meant selling baseball not as a sport, but as affordable family entertainment.

In Bill Cragg's words: "Russ saw a void in the family entertainment market in Calgary; nothing was truly affordable. He set out to grab a chunk of that market by providing a place where a family can be entertained for up to three hours, eat, have fun, and do it all on a tight budget." Cannons' ticket prices range from $3.50 for children's general admission to $5.50 for the best box seats at the park—less than a seat at the movies. There are the daily give-aways. There are zany stunts such as White Christmas Day on June 25, complete with Christmas carols, Santa Claus, and Styrofoam snowflakes dumped from the roof of the grandstand.

The Cannons don't just hire hawkers to sell peanuts in the stands, they audition them. Cragg says they look for kids who are gregarious, the class clowns, the"future vacuum cleaner salesmen of the world." Some have become as famous as the players.

The Cannons package what Cragg calls "a complete entertainment product that zeroes in on the family unit." A band sometimes serenades fans as they stand in line to buy tickets. When they walk through the gates on special occasions, they are handed T-shirts, or helmets or caps. As they wait for play to start, there are contests on the field, and more contests between innings and even during play. The crowd is kept amused no matter what happens on the field or how cold the weather.

The payoff at the box office has been dramatic. In 1986, the Cannons had the highest percentage of attendance of all teams in the minor leagues. They were among the top 10 minor league teams in attendance figures, and second in attendance in their league. Virtually all 2,200 box seats at Foothills are sold well before the season opens and the stadium is filled to capacity when warm weather arrives. In the closing game of the 1986 season, they jammed 7,432 fans into Foothills. At mid-May of 1988, the Cannons were almost 10 percent ahead of last year's attendance, and some nights hundreds are turned away.

Russ Parker purchased the Cannons for $1 million in 1984. He has recently put another $500,000 into renovations at Foothills (principally for a new electronic scoreboard) and he plans to put an additional $500,000 into expanding Foothills to 7,500 seats. Over the 72-game home schedule, he needs to average 3,000 people per game to break even; he attracted an average of 4,300 per game over the first two years, and 1988 promises to be the best year yet. The crowds come despite Calgary's erratic weather and less-than-winning ways. The team has played mediocre baseball in its two years at Calgary and in the second half of 1986 it finished dead last, 13 games out of first place.

Parker first moved into professional baseball in late 1976 when he acquired a franchise in the Pioneer League, a Class A summer league where newly signed rookies are paid pocket money to play under the discerning eyes of major league scouts. The franchise operated in the municipally owned Foothills Stadium, which at the time had poor lighting, splintered bench seats, a ramshackle concession stand operated by the city, and two smelly toilets beyond the outfield fence.

"The team became a family affair," Parker says. His sons cleaned out the clubhouse and retrieved foul balls.

When Peter Pocklington acquired the Triple A Edmonton Trappers in 1981, Parker was eager to follow suit; the Pacific Coast League shared his enthusiasm. The league was impressed with the Trappers' success and was looking to place another team in Alberta to share travel expenses. Besides, the famous Edmonton-Calgary rivalry needed another outlet. When a Salt Lake City team came up for sale in late 1983, Parker purchased the club. On April 22, 1985, the Cannons played their first game at Foothills after Parker sold the City of Calgary on a $750,000 renovation of the facility. The game was three days late; it had been delayed by a blizzard.

Success is as elusive in baseball as it is in the world of business. For those who make it, the rewards are whopping salaries (the average major league salary is about $400,000 a year), fame, and a lifestyle that rivals that of the tycoons of the Gilded Age. For those who don't, the dream ends in the minors and life is very different. Triple A salaries range from $15,000 to $40,000, covered for the most part by the major league parent club. (In the case of the Cannons, 90 percent of salaries is paid by the Mariners.) Players must play winter baseball in places such as Venezuela or the Dominican Republic to survive, or they must find off-season jobs. They dress in small, crowded clubhouses, eat cold cuts off paper plates after their games, and carry their own luggage through the airports. Most are virtually unknown in the cities in which they play. Each shares the same dream—a steady job in the major leagues, a chance to grab the brass ring and be somebody.

Dave Hengel, 25, thought he had grabbed that ring after hitting 27 home runs for Calgary in 1986. In September, when major league teams are allowed to carry 40 players on their rosters, he was called up to Seattle. He ended the season with a six-game hitting streak but at the end of spring training, the Mariners assigned him to Calgary once again.

On the diamond in Foothills Stadium, Hengel stares intently at Simmons, who checks the runner at second, then turns to home plate, kicks and fires a low, side-arm slider. In one fluid motion Hengel brings the bat back and up, steps toward the mound and brings the bat around in a mighty swing. As the ball reaches the plate, it falls down and away. Hengel swings over the top for strike three. The hitting streak is ended; the game is lost. But for Russ Parker and the Calgary Cannons, another successful season is just beginning.

Source: David Bercuson, "It's a Hit," *Report on Business Magazine*, August 1987, pp. 62–64.

Not all businesses are as hectic as Canadian minor league baseball, but contemporary business is every bit as dynamic and challenging. So let's begin our study of this fascinating subject by defining what the term "business" really means.

Mention the word "business", and you will get varied responses. Some people think of their jobs; others of the individual merchants they deal with as consumers; and still others of the thousands of firms, large and small, that make up this nation's economy. And rightly so, for this broad all-inclusive term can be applied to many kinds of enterprises. Business provides the bulk of our employment as well as the goods and services we seek.

What Is Business?

business
All profit-seeking activities and enterprises that provide goods and services necessary to an economic system.

profit
The difference between a company's revenues (receipts) and expenses (expenditures).

Business comprises all profit-seeking activities and enterprises that provide goods and services necessary to an economic system. Profits are a primary mechanism for accomplishing these goals. Accountants and business people define **profit** as the difference between a company's revenues (receipts) and expenses (expenditures).

Businesses must serve their customers in some way if they are to survive in the long run. Some businesses produce tangible products, such as automobiles, light bulbs, and aircraft. Others provide services, such as insurance, car rentals, and lodging.

A business has to be continually aware of new opportunities to satisfy customer needs. Often it must modify its traditional operating methods in order to remain competitive. Businesses are discovering that selling environmental health improves the earnings curve (Focus 1-1).

Focus 1-1

Greening the Profits

Patrick Carson, vice-president of environmental issues and supplies for the Loblaws supermarket chain, points to a copy of the Brundtland report on the environment, released last year by a United Nations commission. But he is not talking about its celebrated contents. Instead, he is noting that its pristinely white pages have probably been bleached with dangerous chemicals to make them more attractive. Carson expounds on his company's commitment to reduce waste and toxicity in the environment. The gigantic supermarket chain is considering a full line of so-called environmentally friendly products. For Loblaws, the environmental message is also good business. Said Carson: "If the market's there, let's take advantage of it."

Loblaws is not alone in capitalizing on this compatibility between the profit motive and environmental sensitivity. More and more Canadian companies are becoming sensitive to a tidal wave of consumer concern about the environment and dangerous chemicals present in products they use every day. For their part, businessmen are taking advantage of the fact that individuals are not only clamouring for change, they are willing to pay for it.

Retailers are promoting more all-natural products and encouraging customers to recycle bags and bottles. Makers of widely used foam-plastic products are now producing alternatives that do not use ozone-damaging chlorofluorocarbons (CFCs). The plastics industry is producing new compounds that disintegrate within a few months or years, instead of centuries. And behind the scenes, gigantic chemical producers, including DuPont Canada Inc., are spending millions looking for alternatives to a wide range of potentially dangerous substances. Other companies are switching back to paper-based packaging from plastics.

A study conducted by Winnipeg pollster Angus Reid Associates Inc. in September 1988 found that a staggering 83 percent of Canadians surveyed ranked the environment as very important, and four out of five said that they were willing to pay more for such items as hamburgers and candy in degradable wrappers. In a sharp rebuke to business, only 11 percent said that private industry contributes to solving environmental problems.

While many businesses have become involved with environmental issues as a marketing ploy, some businesses are moving at high speed to correct what spokesmen acknowledge are past mistakes. Moreover, reaction by individual companies has produced a snowball effect. Changes at one company often lead to changes at a competitor or supplier.

Food retailers have been particularly sensitive to changing consumer demands, and their mammoth size has been instrumental in forcing change. Provigo Inc., a Quebec-based grocery chain with about 1,500 retail-food outlets across Canada, was one of the first to reassess its practices. More than a year ago, Provigo responded to inquiries from the Ottawa-based environmentalist group Friends of the Earth by eliminating CFC-based coffee cups and egg cartons from store shelves and telling suppliers that they must find substitutes for other CFC-based packaging by the end of the year. The company's sheer buying power helped ensure cooperation.

While businesses have traditionally been seen as the arbiters of change in people's attitudes on what to use and what to eat, there are increasing signs that those roles are in the process of readjustment. More and more, consumers are exerting their own, far-reaching influence over the marketplace. And business is listening.

Source: Patricia Chisholm and John Daly, "Greening The Profits," *Maclean's*, November 7, 1988, pp. 40, 41.

Private Enterprise in a Mixed Economy

private enterprise system
The system under which firms operate in a dynamic environment where success or failure is determined by how well they match and counter the offerings of competitors.

Most Canadian businesses, large or small, belong to what is called the **private enterprise system**. This means that firms operate in a dynamic environment where success or failure is largely determined by how well they match and counter the offerings of competitors.

competition
The battle among businesses for consumer acceptance.

mixed economy
Economy consisting of a mix of socialism and private enterprise.

Competition is the battle among businesses for consumer acceptance. Sales and profits are the yardsticks by which this acceptance is measured. Canada, however, is a **mixed economy**. Government support, intervention, and control and even government-owned businesses are intertwined with the free enterprise system. Canada Post, Alberta Government Telephones, and Hydro-Québec are examples of government-owned enterprises.

The business world has abundant examples of firms that were once successful but failed to continue satisfying consumer demands. Competition assures that, over the long run, firms that satisfy consumer demands will be successful and those that do not will be replaced.

The private enterprise system requires that firms continually adjust their strategies, product offerings, service standards, operating procedures, and the like. Otherwise the competition will gain higher shares of an industry's sales and profits. Consider the following cases. Steinberg was long the largest supermarket chain in Quebec. Now Provigo is challenging that position. Ford was once the dominant automaker. Today, it is behind General Motors. Eaton's was for many years the leader in catalogue sales; its sales fell behind Sears and eventually Eaton's closed its catalogue operation. These events suggest the dynamic environment of the private enterprise system.

Competition is a critical mechanism for guaranteeing that the private enterprise system will continue to provide the goods and services that make for high living standards and sophisticated lifestyles. Few organizations that offer a product or service can escape the influence of competition. The Canadian Cancer Society competes for contributions with the Canadian Heart Foundation, your local university or art gallery, and other nonprofit enterprises. The armed forces compete in the labour market with private employers. Even Canada Post faces competition as courier services compete for package shipments.

The Entrepreneur's Role in the Private Enterprise System

entrepreneur
A risk taker in the private enterprise system.

An **entrepreneur** is a risk taker in the private enterprise system, a person who sees a profitable opportunity and then devises a plan and an organization designed to achieve the objective. Some entrepreneurs set up new companies and ventures; others revitalize established concerns.

Companies also assume an entrepreneurial stance even though they may be large corporations. Canadian subsidiaries such as A&P are among those who have seen local opportunities and have been more successful than their US parent corporations.

The entrepreneur is very important in the Canadian economic system. Without the willingness to take risks, there would be no successful businesses, and the private enterprise system could not exist.

Enterprise and Government

capitalism
The system founded on the principle that competition among business firms best serves the needs of society.

invisible hand of competition
Description by Adam Smith of how competition regulates the private enterprise system and assures that consumers receive the best possible products and prices.

The private enterprise system, or **capitalism**, is founded on the principle that competition among business firms best serves the needs of society. Adam Smith, often called the father of capitalism, first described this process in his book *Wealth of Nations*, published in 1776. Smith said that an economy is best regulated by the **invisible hand of competition**. By this he meant that competition among firms would assure that consumers received the best possible products and prices, because the less efficient producers would gradually be eliminated from the marketplace.

The invisible hand concept is the basic premise of the private enterprise system; competition is the primary regulator of our economic life. However, the Canadian economy is a mixed economy in which the private sector and the government both have significant roles to play. Private sector organizations provide the majority of Canada's employment, wealth, and productivity, while the government is responsible for balancing the economic equilibrium through strategy that ultimately aids private firms by accelerating economic growth. The government also protects workers of private firms by labour standards, health insurance, unemployment insurance, and workers' compensation. The consumers of products from the private sector are also protected by the government from unfair practices and safety problems. In essence, there is a loose partnership in the Canadian economy between private firms and government.

Basic Rights of the Private Enterprise System

Certain rights crucial to the operation of capitalism are available to Canadians, who live in a mixed economy based on the private enterprise system. They include rights to private property, to profits, to freedom of choice, and to competition.

Private Property

The private enterprise system is built on the assumption that people have the right to own, use, buy, sell, and bequeath most forms of property—including land, buildings, machinery, equipment, inventions, and various intangible properties. Most people in our society believe that they should have the right to own **private property** and to enjoy all benefits resulting from this ownership.

private property
Property that can be owned, used, bought, sold, and bequeathed under the private enterprise system.

Profits

The private enterprise system also guarantees the risk taker the right to all profits (after taxes) that are earned by the business. There is, of course, no guarantee that the business will earn a profit; if it does, the entrepreneur has a legal and ethical right to it.

Freedom of Choice

In a private enterprise system the people have the maximum amount of freedom of choice in employment, purchases, and investments. This means that people can go into (or out of) business with a minimum of government interference. They can change jobs, negotiate compensation levels, join labour unions, and quit if they so desire. Consumers can choose among different breads, furniture, television programmes, magazines, and so on. We are so used to this freedom of choice that we sometimes forget its importance: that the private enterprise economy tries to maximize human welfare and happiness by providing alternatives.

Competitive Ground Rules

Canada's mixed economy guarantees the public the right to set ground rules for competitive activity. Speaking for the public, the Canadian government has passed laws to prohibit the "cutthroat" competition—excessively competitive practices designed eventually to eliminate competition. It has also established ground rules that prohibit price discrimination, fraudulent dealings in financial markets, and deceptive practices in advertising and packaging.

Government involvement is intended to reduce the impact of the problems of a pure capitalistic system. It protects consumers, workers, and the privately-owned firm itself. The amount of power the government has and the way it exercises this power is often questioned, but its overview helps keep business, labour, consumers, and government in an equitable balance.

Factors of Production

factors of production
The basic inputs into the private enterprise system, including natural resources, labour, capital, and entrepreneurship.

natural resources
Everything useful as a productive input in its natural state, including land and everything that comes from the land.

labour
All individuals who work for a business.

capital
The funds necessary to finance the operation of a business.

entrepreneurship
The taking of risks to set up and run a business.

Businesses require certain inputs if they are to operate effectively. Economists call these inputs the **factors of production**. Not all enterprises require exactly the same combination of elements. Each business has its own mix of the four factors of production: natural resources, labour, capital, and entrepreneurship.

Natural resources refers to everything useful in its natural state as a productive input including agricultural land, building sites, forests, mineral deposits, and so on. Natural resources are basic resources required in any economic system.

Labour is critically important. The term refers to everyone who works for a business, from the company president to the production manager, the sales representative, and the assembly line worker.

Capital is defined as the funds necessary to finance the operation of a business. These funds can be provided in the form of investments, profits, or loans. They are used to build factories, buy raw materials, hire workers, and so on.

Entrepreneurship is the taking of risks to set up and run a business. As defined earlier, the entrepreneur is the risk taker in the private enterprise system. In some situations the entrepreneur actively manages the business; in others this duty is handed over to a salaried manager.

All four factors of production must receive a financial return if they are to be used in a private enterprise system. These payments are in the form of rent, wages, interest, and profit (see Table 1-1). The specific factor payment received varies among industries, but all factors of production are required in some degree for all businesses.

Table1-1
The Factors of Production and Their Factor Payments

Factors of Production	Factor Payments
Natural Resources	Rent
Labour	Wages
Capital	Interest
Entrepreneurship	Profit

The output of our economic system is crucial to the Canadian standard of living. In fact, this output literally determines the economic well-being of the nation.

Gross National Product: The Measure of National Output

gross national product (GNP) The sum of all goods and services produced in an economy during a year.

The overall measure of national output is called the **gross national product** (GNP), the sum of all goods and services produced in the economy during a year. This concept allows year-to-year comparisons that check the current status of the economy.

But things are not always the same. Inflation—defined as a rising price level—is one factor. It complicates the measurement process. Accurate comparisons of annual gross national figures must allow for inflation. Economists use the term **real gross national product** to describe inflation-discounted GNP figures.

real gross national product Inflation-discounted gross national product figures.

Productivity

productivity A measure of the efficiency of production. It relates to the amount of goods or services a worker produces in a given period of time.

The four factors of production just discussed contribute to the productivity of our economy. **Productivity** is a measure of the efficiency of production. It relates to the amount of goods or services a worker produces in a given period of time. The availability of the resources and capital needed to produce these goods and services is also an important factor.

In Canada annual productivity gains have been decreasing in recent years in comparison to countries like Italy, Japan, France, and West Germany. Productivity gains are what allow people to receive higher real wages—those that are rising faster than the cost of living. If wages go up 15 percent in a year and productivity only 2 percent, then prices will go up approximately 13 percent. Productivity increases must exceed wage increases if workers are to receive what are known as real wage increases. A more recent assessment of productivity indicated that increased levels of productivity depend on five factors: technology, labour, education, government policies and management. This five-pointed star for increased productivity is shown in Figure 1-1.

Various reasons have been given for the low rate of productivity growth in Canada. These include: high inflation, a decline in the work ethic or basic desire to work, failure to invest in new plants and equipment, the difficulty of increasing productivity in service-oriented industries, excessive government regulation, inadequate research and development of new products, the high cost of energy,

Figure 1-1

Five-pointed Star for Increased Productivity

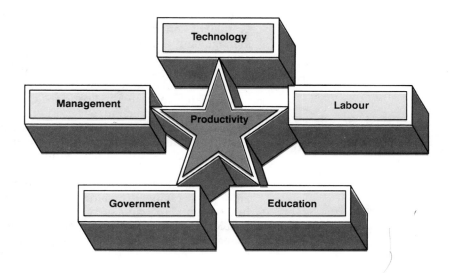

the lack of availability of capital, and high interest rates caused by uncertainty about the country's economic future. But perhaps the most damaging factor of all is that many Canadians do not realize that Canada is lagging behind in this crucial area. It is clear that productivity is a major responsibility of the total management system. Refer to Focus 1-2 for an assessment of why the Canadian manufacturing industry is lagging behind in its productivity.

Focus 1-2

Bridging the Productivity Gap

Economists call it the "productivity gap." It means that the average American has been working harder and creating more wealth in an hour on the job than the average Canadian. While other areas of the Canadian economy such as financial services and transportation have improved dramatically over the years, the manufacturing industry has not been as successful in bridging this difference.

The productivity gap in manufacturing reached 26 percent in 1986, wiping out a decade of gains Canada made during the 1970s and putting Canadian manufacturers back where they were in the 1960s. For every hour on the job, a US worker produced $19.40 US worth of manufactured goods, while the Canadian worker produced $14.35 US (figures in 1982 prices).

In a world where the secret to success is to produce more quality goods at lower prices, Canada's ability to compete internationally is impaired by high production and wage costs, inefficient plants and inadequate technology.

According to Judith Maxwell, chairperson of the Economic Council of Canada, the blame rests "squarely on the shoulders of management," which has been slow to innovate and reluctant to explore the opportunities offered by high technology.

Ultimately, the answer lies not only in new technology, but also in the adoption of new, more innovative ways of doing the job.

A research study by the Economic Council found that for many firms, technological change is most effective when it is accompanied by innovation in the way managers and employees perform their tasks. The study found that Canadian companies with innovative work rules saved large sums of money, reduced absenteeism, improved productivity and boosted employee morale.

The innovations include profit-sharing and rotating employees among several jobs. The latter allows them to perform a variety of functions and to gain a greater appreciation for the company's problems and needs. Perhaps the most radical approach is the growing use of semi-autonomous work groups, which handle all the planning and production in a specific area of a plant.

But these ideas are rarely put into practice in corporate Canada.

Council researcher Jacquie Mansell says management and unions need to break out of their traditional roles. Collective agreements that spell out detailed work rules and impose limits on what management can ask of its employees simply don't allow the joint control and shared responsibility that is needed for innovation to thrive.

Source: Peter Hadekel, "Bridging the Productivity Gap," *Quebec Business*, October 1988, p. 11-12.

Types of Competition

perfect competition
A situation where the firms in an industry are so small that none of them can individually influence the price charged in the marketplace.

law of supply and demand
An economic law that says market price is determined by the intersection of the supply and demand curves.

Four basic types of competition exist in a private enterprise system: perfect (or pure) competition, monopolistic competition, oligopoly, and monopoly. Firms fall into one of these categories on the basis of the relative competitiveness of their particular industry.

Perfect competition is a situation where the firms in an industry are so small that none of them can individually influence the price charged in the marketplace. Price is thus set by total market demand and total market supply—the **law of supply and demand.** *Supply* is a schedule of what sellers will offer in the market at various price levels; *demand* is a schedule showing what consumers will buy at various price levels. Supply and demand is the price level that will prevail (see Figure 1-2).

Perfect competition involves similar products, ones that cannot be differentiated from those of a competitor. Agriculture is probably the closest example of perfect competition (except for commodities regulated by marketing boards), and peaches, celery, and potatoes are examples of products that are similar from farm to farm. Finally, the small size of the firms involved in a perfectly competitive market makes it relatively easy for any firm to enter or leave that market.

monopolistic competition
A situation where somewhat fewer firms than would exist in perfect competition produce and sell goods that are different from those of their competitors.

Monopolistic competition arises in an industry where somewhat fewer firms than would exist in perfect competition produce and sell products that are different from those of their competitors. Monopolistic competition gives the firm some power over the price it charges. A good example is retailing, where the price can vary among, say, different brands of headache tablets, toothpaste, or gasoline. The relatively small size of these retailers also makes it easy for any firm to enter or leave the industry.

oligopoly
A market situation where there are few sellers.

Oligopoly is a market where there are few sellers. In some oligopolies (such as steel) the product is similar; in others (such as automobiles) it is different. The entry of new competitors is restricted by the huge investments required for market entry. But the primary difference between oligopoly and the previously mentioned markets is that the limited number of sellers gives the oligopolist substantial control over the product's price. In an oligopoly the prices of competitive

Figure 1-2
Supply and Demand Determine Price

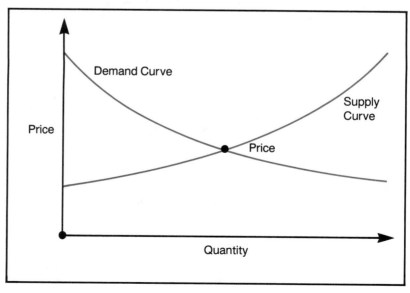

products are usually quite similar because substantial price competition would lessen every firm's profit. Price cuts by one firm in the industry are typically met by all competitors.

monopoly
A market situation where there are no direct competitors.

Monopoly is a market situation where there are no competitors. Since the Combines Investigation Act of 1975 prohibits attempts to monopolize markets, nearly all the monopolies that do exist are regulated monopolies, such as the public utilities. Firms selling electricity, natural gas, and telephone service are regulated by agencies of the federal and provincial governments. These agencies are concerned with many aspects of the regulated monopolies, including pricing and profits. In a pure monopoly the firm would have substantial control over pricing, but in a regulated monopoly pricing is subject to rules imposed by the regulatory body. There are no directly competitive products in a regulated monopoly, and entry into the industry is restricted by the government.

Table 1-2 summarizes the most important characteristics of the four types of industry structures.

Table 1-2
Major Characteristics of Perfect Competition,
Monopolistic Competition, Oligopoly, and Monopoly

Type of Competition	Characteristics			
	Number of Firms	Product	Control over Pricing	Ease of Entry
Perfect competition	Many	Similar	None	Easy
Monopolistic competition	Many	Different	Some	Relatively easy
Oligopoly	Few	Similar or different	Substantial	Difficult
Monopoly	One	No readily available substitute	Usually regulated by government	Virtually impossible

Development of the Canadian Economy

Canada has a unique business history. Business has significantly influenced customs, politics, and even family living. Economic development and industrial growth in Canada followed a very different path from development and growth in the United States, which was based upon private incentive with very little government interference. But in Canada business was forced from the beginning to depend upon government intervention, finances, and policy. This continues to affect the way business operates today.

Business and Enterprise to 1759

When the first colonies were established in the lands that became Canada, it was expected that commercial activity would be controlled from Europe. Fishing off the east coast was a seasonal operation run by businesses in Portugal, Spain, and England's west country. The colony of New France was expected to provide furs for the profit of the French court; trapping and trading operations were to be strictly licensed.

However, the entrepreneurial spirit of the *habitants* could not be limited by government order, and *coureurs de bois* like Pierre Radisson and Médard Chouart des Groseillers soon began to trade for furs on their own behalf. By the 1750s, the French had trading posts as far west as the Saskatchewan River.

From the Conquest to Confederation

After Quebec became a British colony, a consortium of French-Canadian and Scottish businessmen formed the Northwest Company from the network of trading posts and canoe routes that stretched west from Montreal. The Northwest Company soon found itself competing both for furs and territory with the Hudson's Bay Company (founded by English merchants at the suggestion of Pierre Radisson in 1670, after a particularly painful experience with French bureaucracy). In 1820, the two groups merged.

Thus in the West fur trading was the major business activity. The Atlantic zone of Nova Scotia and Newfoundland concentrated on fishing. In the early 1800s demand for lumber saw business increase in Quebec City and New Brunswick. After the American Revolution, new settlers from the United States and Britain demanded manufactured products from Europe. The desire for trade led the government to support the expansion of the St. Lawrence water system through the building of canals. However, great hopes for this waterway never came to fruition, and by 1867 it was severely under-utilized. Thus, at Confederation, the new country was already shouldering a large national debt.

The Era of National Policy (1867 to 1900)

National Policy
Policy of increased immigration, improved transportation, and protective tariffs to strengthen the Canadian economy.

Canada had great resources—timber in British Columbia, wheat in the prairie provinces, oil and timber in Ontario, timber and a commercial and manufacturing base in Quebec, and fish, iron, coal and timber in the Atlantic provinces. Shortly after Confederation, the government instituted the **National Policy,** which was intended to bring settlers to the western prairies; to increase the manufacturing of goods within the country by imposing high tariffs in order to slow the importation of goods, particularly from the US; and to build a railway (the Canadian Pacific Railway) to transport both goods and people.

Financing the building of the Canadian Pacific Railway was an early example of cooperation between private enterprise and government in Canada.

From Growth to Decline (1900 to 1930)

Wheat and mining exports at the turn of the century helped to stimulate the Canadian economy. Manufacturing still played only a small part: only 15 percent of the Canadian labour force worked in manufacturing in 1911 while agriculture occupied 35 percent of workers. But the amount of capital available for investment in manufacturing and the production capacity for consumer goods were growing all the time. By the close of the 1920s, every other Canadian household owned an automobile. New roads were being built. Mass production in all other areas followed the automobile boom. The refrigerator, washing machine, and radio became part of the family. Government continued to step in, as it had when it financed the CPR in the 1870s, to assist enterprises it considered vital to the economy: Ontario set up Ontario Hydro as a crown corporation; the western provinces built their own telephone networks; the federal government formed Canadian National Railways from a number of failing companies in order to ensure an adequate transportation system.

The Depression and the War (1930 to 1950)

The Depression following the stock market crash of 1929 led to lower demand for goods as consumers and businesses cut back. Farmers in the West suffered the double blow of lack of markets and severe drought. Government intervention was seen as a necessary antidote to the vicious cycle of lower demand and production. Following the example of US President Franklin Roosevelt, Prime Minister Richard Bennett offered unemployment insurance, higher old age pensions, and regulation of working conditions in the attempt to regenerate the economy. Many of the policies of the "welfare state" Canadians know today had their origins in the 1930s.

World War II led to new levels of employment and productivity in new industries such as shipbuilding and aircraft manufacturing. After the war, new exploration led to the development of vast resource industries, such as the first significant exploitation of Alberta's oil fields. This much-needed stimulation led to a new problem at the close of the 1940s. Almost one half of all Canadian manufacturing assets and many natural resources were owned or controlled by foreign investors, many of them from the United States.

Fifties to Now

Some people feel government has come to play too large a role in our economy in recent years. In addition, some Canadian industries are all but controlled by a few large and complex corporations. While this has sometimes led to reduced competition, large corporations have used their higher productivity to generate higher profits, employment, and wages. And yet in the face of the apparent domination of the business world by government and the giant firms, more and more Canadians are going into business for themselves, founding small companies that reflect the personality of the owners. Companies offering services rather than manufactured products form a growing sector of the Canadian economy.

Consumer concerns, occupational health and safety, environmental pollution, and higher fuel costs have all affected the way Canadian business has been run in recent years. Financial scandals, infrequent but spectacular, have led to greater government regulation as legislators try to protect consumers, workers, and businesses themselves from a loss of confidence in the system.

As a result of challenges like these, business has become more socially responsible; the impact on society of a business decision is now weighed in most management decision-making. Business has become more conscious of its operating costs, particularly energy costs. Management continues to struggle with the problem of predicting and then reacting to new government regulations and requirements. Business has found new markets abroad but has encountered increasing competition from foreign producers at home. Writers may some day describe the current era as one of the most challenging for Canadian business.

Since 1980 the Canadian economy has experienced faster and more productive growth than all other industrialized countries except Japan and the USA. We know that our largest firms do not create as much employment as the medium-sized and small companies. As an example, in Ontario there were about 46,000 new firms established in 1985 that created 69,000 new jobs, new investments of $212 million, sales of $1.5 billion, and $220 million in extra provincial tax revenue.

High technology has created a Canadian dependence upon information and service and altered our dependence on manufacturing. Our government's influence and role as an employer have also reduced the growth of industry. The Prime Minister in 1985 proposed a new position for his government, a "business to justify government" posture that has NOT been tested yet as has the other attractor of "free trade" with the US. To say the least, this era is one of excitement and challenge for Canada.

Other Economic Systems

A number of economic systems have developed in the modern world. In North America our way of life has developed from the private enterprise or capitalist system. The United States in particular considers itself to work under a private enterprise system. Other parts of the world live under socialist or communist systems. Still others, perhaps the majority of countries, use aspects of both the free enterprise and socialist systems to develop what we call mixed economies. Private enterprise has already been described. However, it is important to learn the primary features of the alternative economic systems. The concerns here are the economic aspects; political questions are beyond the scope of this book.

Communism

communism
An economic theory, developed by Karl Marx, under which private property is eliminated and goods are owned in common.

Communist theory began with Karl Marx, a nineteenth-century economist. Marx believed that the labouring classes were being exploited by capitalists, those who owned the means of production. He said that there would be a class struggle that eventually would develop into a working-class revolution, and a new form of society would emerge. Marx labelled his new order **communism.** He believed that all the people should own all of a nation's productive capacity. Marx recognized that the government would have to operate businesses at first, but felt that government structure would eventually "wither away" as a classless society evolved. An important principle of his system was that people should give according to their abilities and receive according to their needs.

A complete communist state does not exist, because even the Soviet Union and the People's Republic of China have social systems with managerial and professional classes, and because in practice the government owns the means of production. The people, in turn, work for the government. The government plays a major role in determining what kinds of work people will do, and determines what goods will be produced. Workers do not invest in business enterprises, because the government owns them all.

Communists feel that centralized management of all productive activity results in less waste than the competition of free enterprise. They hold that a consumer's freedom of choice has to be sacrificed in the interest of production efficiency. This is in contrast to the view of capitalists, who hold that government-operated industries soon become inefficient bureaucracies because of a lack of employee incentive. Capitalists believe that competition promotes efficiency by providing incentive to achieve and by eliminating inefficient producers from the marketplace.

Focus 1-3

Now Let Us All Laugh, Comrades

Officially, as the Russians and their East European satellites see it, inflation is a disease unique to capitalism. "With the exception of the war years," triumphs Nikolai Glushkov, chairman of the Soviet State Committee on Prices, "there has never been any inflation in the USSR, nor does any exist today. . . ." Now. . .the East bloc, like the West, is suffering a severe dose of rapidly rising consumer prices. It is not called inflation but "an adjustment in the state pricing structure. . . ."

Since 1977 Russia has ordered four waves of price increases covering everything from books and cut glass to gasoline, plane fares and chocolate. . . .Soviet cars jumped 18% and carpets and restaurant meals rose 50%. Czechoslovakia lifted its rate for children's clothing, fuel, postage, and rents, while Hungary raised the price of bread, flour, sugar, and some meats by up to 50%. . . .

Buyers also suffer from hidden prices that the state slides in without fanfare. A product—for example, a $45 electric razor— suddenly might be given a new model number, a different colour or a fresh package, and a new price: $58. . . .

Source: "How Communists Beat Inflation," reprinted by permission from *TIME, The Weekly News magazine*, Copyright Time, Inc., 1979.

Socialism

socialism
An economic system that advocates government ownership and operation of all basic industries (with private ownership continuing to exist in smaller businesses).

Socialism is an economic system that exists in countries where the government owns and operates all the basic industries, such as banking, transportation, and large-scale manufacturing. Private ownership still exists in smaller businesses such as shops and restaurants. Socialists believe that major industries are too important to be left in private hands. They argue that government-owned industries are more efficient and serve the public better.

Socialist economies usually follow some master plan for the use of the nation's resources. Workers are free to choose their employment, but the state often encourages people to go into areas where they are needed. As a result most citizens work for some government enterprise.

Mixed Economies

The "mix" in a mixed economy can vary a great deal, but the term, which has become popular in recent years, is useful to describe economies that contain elements of both socialism and free enterprise. Sweden and the United Kingdom are often given as examples of nations that have a traditional philosophy of private enterprise but that also have a high degree of government ownership. The United Kingdom's coal, steel, and communications industries are government enterprises.

Private enterprise proponents often classify these mixed economies as socialist because of the high degree of public ownership. But such countries still have a far greater degree of private ownership than is found in socialist nations. For example, Canada is usually classed as a mixed economy rather than a pure free enterprise system. Even the United States might be considered a mixed economy in that some public utilities are government-owned.

A Comparative Note

The mixed economic system has proven to be very effective for Canada and many other countries. It has provided a high degree of economic freedom, a low cost of living, substantial product choice, high earnings, considerable public welfare, and many other economic benefits. Government in Canada has influenced our freedom of choice, competition, and property rights in the attempt to balance the disadvantages of pure capitalism. We still have an incentive to produce, but the gap between rich and poor is narrowed under this philosophy.

Canada's standard of living, economic opportunities, and social services are the envy of people all over the world. The vast majority of Canadian citizens are proud of Canadian business and social accomplishments and thoroughly support the continuation of the mixed economic system.

The Study of Business: Why? And How?

Many people are actively involved in studying the Canadian business system. Senior business executives are constantly learning how to become more effective managers. Many consumers are examining how business decisions affect their daily lives. Many students are enrolled in business administration courses. With this much activity, it is fitting that attention be given to why and how people study business.

Why Study Business?

People study business for a number of reasons. Some plan a business career. Others want to learn how the business system affects them in their role of wage earner or consumer. Still others are curious about what business actually means. Certainly, business affects all of us in some manner, and the more we know about the subject, the better able we will be to cope with some of our most common everyday problems. Some specific reasons for studying business are given below.

Career selection. Most students do not spend adequate time in selecting their careers. Many drift from one curriculum to another and then from one kind of job to another. The study of business allows a student to consider various occupational possibilities. The bulk of career possibilities is in private industry, but many similar possibilities are available in government agencies and in other forms of public employment.

The study of business allows the student to consider various kinds of jobs—the work required, the available rewards, the necessary training, and the relative advantages and disadvantages of each. This text includes sections describing jobs that can be found in each major area of business. Chapter 24 is devoted entirely to careers in business. Employment trends, job sources, employment search strategies, résumé preparation, and other useful topics are explored.

Self-employment. Some students will decide to work for themselves and establish their own businesses. Since most business concepts and principles are the same regardless of the size of the firm, studying business in general can be an invaluable first step in setting up a business.

Self-employed persons are actively and personally involved in business. A knowledge of successful business practices becomes even more crucial for those who risk their own funds. The solution—study business!

Tackling the problems of society. Business puts people on the firing line for most of today's pressing social problems. Alternative energy sources, resource conservation, pollution, minority hiring and affirmative action programs, consumerism, and industrial safety are problems encountered on a daily basis by the businessperson.

A business career is likely to place an individual in a position of responsibility earlier than most other occupations. Many experts believe that business careers are an excellent choice for activists who want to improve their society.

Better consumer decisions. Business decisions create consumer decisions. A certain stereo comes with three options for accessory equipment. An executive decides to pass along a recent union wage increase to the consumer by raising a product's price. These are typical business decisions that call for related decision making by consumers.

The study of business provides an appreciation of the background for many consumer decisions. Consumer advocates often point out that an informed consumer is a better consumer.

Business is relevant. Students often argue that some fields of study simply are not relevant to life today. Perhaps this is so. But few students believe that business is not relevant. Regardless of opinions about business, executive behaviour, and the private enterprise system, the study of business is the study of what is happening today. Business is probably one of the most relevant and fascinating subjects the student will ever study.

How to Study Business

Business can be studied through formal programmes of instruction such as those offered at various colleges and universities. These programmes teach the basic concepts, methods, principles, and practices used in modern business. The formal study of business provides the framework for later experiences; together they build toward a well-rounded management education.

The study of business, or business administration as it is often called, has grown more formalized and systematic over the years. In the past, many managers achieved their positions on the basis of practical experience in a given area rather than through formal study. But times have changed, and formal education in business has become a recognized early step to a business career. Business leaders of earlier decades would be amazed to see the modern classrooms and instructional methods used by contemporary business students.

The study of business has become one of the most popular programmes at colleges and universities. More and more students want to enter this challenging career field.

Business programmes are usually organized around functional areas. Typically, courses are offered in such subjects as accounting, finance, management, personnel, marketing, sales, and data processing. Most business programmes require students to take at least one course in each major area of study.

This book, combined with an introductory business course, will give the student a broad overview of the field of business. The information acquired here will allow for a better selection of business courses in the future.

While students can learn the basics of business in a classroom setting, it is impossible to learn all that is needed in this manner. Informal study—reading and various job-related experiences—can further a business education. Meaningful part-time and summer work experiences can be invaluable. Internships, study tours, visits to manufacturers, and the like are also vital. Serious business students should pursue knowledge through extensive reading of authoritative sources such as *The Financial Post, Business Week, Fortune,* and *Canadian Business*. Much can be learned outside the classroom.

A Diagram of Contemporary Business

It is helpful to visualize contemporary business as a system designed to satisfy the needs of society. Business continues to function only if it achieves consumer acceptance for its products. Firms that fail in this objective soon disappear from the marketplace.

Figure 1-3 is a simplified diagram of contemporary business; it shows that a business's objective is to make a profit by serving the needs of its markets. The manager has several variables to control in operating the firm. These variables, the **five Ms**, are manpower, materials, money, machinery, and management.[2] The manager combines them into a proper mix to produce goods and services that satisfy markets.

five Ms
The basic resources of any firm—manpower, materials, money, machinery, and management.

There are four major markets for the products of industry—consumers, industry, government, and foreign markets. Some businesses serve all four markets; others serve only one or a few. In any case, the provision of satisfactory goods and services to the market means that the firm will receive funds necessary to operate the business, pay its taxes, and perhaps earn a profit. Focus 1-4 outlines some of the changes in the global market that confront Canadian exporters.

Figure 1-3
A Diagram of Contemporary Business: a business's objective is to make a profit by serving the needs of its markets.

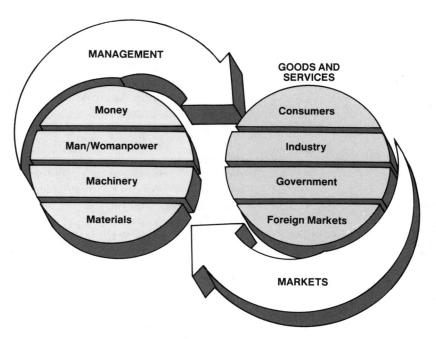

The diagram will be used throughout the text. As each part of the business organization is studied, it will be useful to relate it to the model shown here. This will clarify the complex but exciting world of business.

Focus 1-4

Foreign Markets an Opportunity for Quebec Exporters

The trade winds are changing.

With the passage of the free trade agreement, the move toward a single North American market is under way. Western Europe plans to further integrate its economic-trade alliance by 1992. Japan, Korea, and Hong Kong are expected to lead Pacific countries into their own consolidation—perhaps as a defensive move.

The current trend among Canada's major trading partners away from national economic frontiers towards enlarged trading blocs signals important changes in the foreign trade environment which will likely have a significant impact on Canada's export-import ratio in the next decade. While these developments could spell increased opportunities for Canadian exporters, the powerful new trading pacts could lead eventually to regional protectionism and damage the chances for improved multilateral trade.

Canadian companies are thus facing a costly question of commitment: market abroad or mark time.

For the first eleven months of 1988, Canada exported nearly $127 billion in goods and services, compared with $125 billion for all of 1987. For Quebec alone, total exports for 1988 are expected to exceed $22 billion. Since 1985, Quebec has exported more than $19 billion of goods each year. Paper and forest products, transportation and telecommunications equipment as well as engineering and aerospace expertise have made Quebec corporate names such as Bombardier, Consolidated-Bathurst, and CAE part of the global business vocabulary.

However, the US consistently buys more than 75 percent of Quebec exports, and Quebec business for the most part seems to have missed out so far on opportunities in the increasingly important Pacific Rim market. Unlike the rest of Canada, exports to the region from Quebec have not increased dramatically.

In Western Canada, the Asian impact is an economic reality. For 1988, Asia is expected to account for more than 30 percent of British Columbia's exports, compared with less than 6 percent for Quebec. Canadian trade experts expect that Asia will continue to be the fastest growing market for exports over the next decade, outstripping the European Economic Community.

As the trade winds change, so too must the flow of goods and services.

Source: Hyman Glustein, "Foreign Markets Provide Increased Opportunities for Quebec Exporters," *This Week in Business*, March 11, 1989, p. 15. Reprinted by permission.

Controversial Issue

Takeovers—The Invasion of the Frenzy-Feeders

Business headlines in 1989 have been dominated by what seems to be a favourite Canadian pastime, the takeover.

January marked a record in takeovers with the announcements that Imperial Oil Ltd. intended to take over Texaco Canada Ltd., Chicago's Stone Container Corp. would buy Consolidated-Bathurst Inc., PWA Corp. would absorb Wardair Inc. and The Molson Cos. Ltd. would bid for rival Carling-O'Keefe Breweries of Canada. The megatakeovers culminated in the announcement on January 27 that monolithic Bell Canada Enterprises would sell 49.9 percent of its $2.7 billion real estate empire to the billionaire Reichmanns.

That same month, a Statistics Canada report confirmed that concentration of economic power had risen dramatically: the top 25 corporate groups in Canada had increased their share of total corporate assets to 35 percent by 1986 from 30 percent in 1976.

Economists measure two types of concentration—aggregate concentration (more assets owned by fewer entities) and product or industrial concentration (market share in specific sectors or product lines).

Canada continues to have inordinately high levels of both.

A possible antidote to this trend towards greater concentration of power lies with Canada's Competition Act which has been attacking mergers that lessen competition substantially. Since the Act became law in June 1986, some 365 deals were investigated, nine were restructured, seven were abandoned and four were referred to the competition bureau.

Critics of the trend towards greater concentration believe the act to be long overdue. According to them, when competition thrives, prices are lower and quality higher. In turn, this translates into huge savings for consumers, leaving them with more disposable income to buy other things or to invest. Although such savings may amount to a few dollars per day per person, collectively they represent a redistribution of wealth out of the hands of wealthy conglomerates and into the "little guy's pocket."

While the new act provides some checks against product or industry concentration, there remain no checks on aggregate concentration. Only ad hoc political intervention could stop the Reichmanns from taking over the biggest Canadian-owned empire, Bell Canada Enterprises. The last time the country's two biggest empires talked takeover—Power Corp. and Argus Corp. in 1975—the proposed deal led to the formation of the Royal Commission on Corporate Concentration, even though their combined size was only a fraction of the Bell-Reichmann merger. In the absence of any public policy to arrest aggregate concentration, individual Canadians can only hope they form a benevolent economic dictatorship.

Source: Diane Francis, "The Invasion of the Frenzy-Feeders," *Maclean's*, March 20, 1989, p. 11.

Summary of Learning Goals

1. **Explain what a business is and how it operates as part of the private enterprise system within a mixed economy.**
   Business comprises all profit-seeking activities and enterprises that provide goods and services necessary to an economic system. Canadian businesses are part of a mixed economic system in which success is determined by competition among firms, capitalism and government intervention.

2. **Define the role of competition and of the entrepreneur.**
   Competition is at the heart of the private and Canadian (mixed economy) economic systems. It is the customer's needs that competing firms attempt to best satisfy. If a firm is not aware of its competitors, or minimizes the consumer's needs in terms of importance, long-term survival is threatened.

An entrepreneur is the risk taker in both the private and mixed economies. Whether due to family tradition, higher education, or work experience, the entrepreneur is the individual who sees a profitable opportunity and then sets up a business designed to achieve this profit. Society benefits from the rich diversity of new products and services brought to the marketplace by the entrepreneur.

3. **Explain the role of government in the Canadian mixed economy.**
   The Canadian economic system is a mixed economic one in which the private sector and the government have significant roles to play. The private sector organizations provide the majority of Canada's employment, wealth and productivity while the government is responsible for balancing the economic equilibrium via strategy that ultimately aids private firms by accelerating economic growth. The government also protects workers of private firms by social welfare, labour standards, health insurance, unemployment and worker's compensation. The consumers of products from the private sector are protected as well by government from exploitation and safety problems.

4. **Explain the concepts of gross national product and productivity and why they are important.**
   Gross national product—the sum of all goods and services produced in the economy during a year—is an overall measure of national output. Productivity is a measure of the efficiency of production; conceptually easy to define, it represents an extremely difficult concept to operationalize. At its simplest level, productivity is the output per worker. It is a serious problem in Canada, due to our declining position relative to Japan and other countries. While social and governmental factors have contributed to the problem, it seems that 85 percent of productivity problems are of managerial nature.

5. **Analyze how the historical development of the Canadian economy influences contemporary business.**
   Chapter 1 traces the development of the Canadian economy across five stages: Birth to Confederation; The National Policy; From Growth to Decline; The Depression and the War; Fifties to Now.

6. **Identify the different types of economic systems.**
   Mixed Economy: economies with a mix of socialism and free enterprise. While Canada is a relatively clear example of this type of economy, US government ownership of its public utilities shows that the classification "mixed economy" also applies to America.
   Communism: a term denoting both economy and society, Karl Marx defined communism as a new order; the society would be

classless, with the people owning all factors of production.

Socialism: the government owns all major industries, while private ownership remains intact in smaller enterprises.

7. **Explain the roles of business, labour, and government in modern society.**

   Large-scale business and smaller firms dominate many aspects of Canadian industry. Leading Canadian firms are among the world's largest companies. But big business has also led to the development of big labour and big government. As a result, economic size has become a crucial public issue. In addition, further complications arise as a result of Crown Corporations and our mixed economy system.

8. **Recognize how to study business and why.**

   Specific reasons for studying business include:

   a) Career selection.

   b) Self-employment.

   c) Tackling the problems of society.

   d) Better consumer decisions.

   e) Business is relevant.

   The study of business often begins in a classroom and continues in a less formal manner in the world of business.

9. **Analyze how contemporary business operates as a system designed to satisfy the needs of society.**

   Figure 1-3 shows that a business's objective is to make a profit by serving the needs of its markets. The manager has four variables—manpower, materials, money, and machinery—to control in operating the firm. There are four major markets for the products of industry: consumers, industry, government, and foreign markets. The provision of satisfactory goods and services to the markets means that the firm will receive the necessary funds to operate the business, pay its taxes, and, perhaps, earn a profit.

Key Terms

business	entrepreneurship
profit	Gross National Product
private enterprise system	real Gross National Product
competition	productivity
mixed economy	perfect competition
entrepreneur	law of supply and demand
capitalism	monopolistic competition
invisible hand of competition	oligopoly
private property	monopoly
factors of production	National Policy
natural resources	communism
labour	socialism
capital	five *M*s

Discussion Questions and Exercises

1. Comment on this statement: "All organizations must serve their customers or clients in some way if they are to survive."
2. Make a list of all the businesses that serve students on your campus. Then prepare a brief evaluation of how effectively they serve their customers.
3. Profit has sometimes been described as the regulator of the private enterprise system. What do you think people mean by this comment? Discuss.
4. What is the role of entrepreneurs in the private enterprise system?
5. Discuss the basic rights upon which the private enterprise system is based.
6. Why is productivity such an important public issue today?
7. The four basic types of competition are perfect competition, monopolistic competition, oligopoly, and monopoly. Match these types with the businesses listed below:
   a) Ontario Hydro
   b) The Bay
   c) General Motors of Canada
   d) Harold Clawson's Niagara fruit farm
8. Differentiate among private enterprise, communism, socialism, and mixed economies. Identify examples of each of these economic systems.
9. Identify and describe the inputs that are required by a private enterprise system. What payments are made to each of these inputs?
10. Discuss how the business curriculum at your institution reflects the current climate of the economy. Set up a panel discussion of instructors and advanced students.

Case 1-1

Delivering the Goods

From the outside, The National looks like any other neighbourhood grocery store. But there's something special going on inside.

Upscale Westmount ladies and suburbanites manoeuvre around each other filling their baskets with a cornucopia of prime fruit and vegetables. People come from all over Montreal to shop at the small store on Sherbrooke Street near Victoria, in Westmount.

Caterer Marni Craig sometimes spends $1,000 a week buying produce at the store. "Nothing comes close to the National," Craig says. "Their produce is perfect. You may spend a little more, but there's absolutely no waste." Customers can get virtually anything there, year round, from hard-to-find baby eggplants to kumquats and asparagus. Everything is always fresh.

Owner Mathew Cho, 56, says whereas large chain stores can only check samples of what they are buying, The National inspects every item in every box. And, after buying hand-picked fruit and vegetables, "we hand-pick them again."

Tucked away at the back of the store is one of the secrets to The National's success. Three people—the owner's wife, Susan Cho, her brother Carl Kim and their 74-year-old father—stand at the counter all day, sorting green beans, berries and exotic lettuce. Each family member puts in over 70 hours a week. "If you don't work hard like this, you won't succeed," says Cho.

For the first three years after buying the store, Cho and his wife worked from 4 a.m. to 6 p.m. without so much as a coffee break. Then, the store had four employees. Now it has 12, including seven family members. Employees know most customers by name. According to Sophie Cho, the owner's daughter who works in the family business, "I even know how they like things bagged. Some prefer paper, others like plastic bags."

Hard work has earned Cho annual sales of more than $1 million, 70 percent of which comes from produce sales. Gross profits are 30 percent. Because of the store's small size, its sales capacity has been reached. Cho would like to expand, but can't find a bigger place in the area and doesn't want to move. At 1,000 square feet, sales amount to about $1,000 per square foot, a figure retail analysts say is outstanding when compared to $600 per square foot for an average food store of comparable size. They say anyone doing $1,000 per square foot must be doing something special.

Source: Ellen Kom, "The National Delivers the Goods," *This Week in Business*, March 12, 1988, p. 12. Reprinted by permission.

Questions:
1. What are the primary factors behind The National's success? Explain.
2. What must The National do in order to stay competitive? Explain.
3. Should Mathew Cho expand his business to other areas of the city? What are some of the problems inherent in this alternative? Discuss.

Case 1-2

Launching a Revolution

Business is not going well for Mitel Corp. It has just laid off 410 employees, a 10 percent reduction of its staff across three countries. Within a decade, it went from being Canada's high-tech success story to one of its most ailing companies. Since 1983, when it last turned a profit, Mitel has lost more than $300 million. John Jarvis, Mitel's president and chief executive, has been vested with the task of turning the company around.

"Continued losses are unacceptable," Jarvis says. "Trying harder to make the old ways work is not the answer. We must take a new road and it won't be easy. Mitel must change."

Jarvis calls it a corporate cultural revolution.

To create a winner, Jarvis wants to turn an entrepreneurial company into a bastion of product planning and development and customer service. The new Mitel will concentrate on its major markets, and to effect the change, senior executives are being recruited into Mitel and the corporate structure reworked.

In the past, Mitel corporate structure included head office and four production divisions run by individual management groups. It will be replaced by a single corporate head office and a realignment of the divisions. Under the former system, says Jarvis, "people really didn't have a clear understanding of the scope of our problems." As a result, although individual divisions were all doing well, the corporation was losing money. In the new structure, head office will oversee divisions of marketing, business development, research and development, manufacturing and a professional services group to respond to customers' special needs.

In addition, Jarvis has just hired a new senior vice-president of human resources. A new head of worldwide marketing is also being recruited to improve customer service and focus on Mitel's main markets.

William Rich, an analyst with Northern Business Information Inc. in New York, says Mitel has lost touch with its customer base in the US because of the way it has sold its products through dealers. Since traditional private branch exchange (PBX) markets—Mitel's original business—began to decline in the early 1980s, the tele- communications industry has moved to selling more add-on features and improvements to their installed base. Many companies had tight arrangements with their dealers who kept them close to their customers. According to Rich, "At a time when Mitel should be farming their systems, they can't get a grip on them because they don't know where they are or who has them."

Mitel has already taken steps to keep track of its customers by requiring them to buy software directly from Mitel, although the hardware is bought through dealers.

Likewise, Mitel had neglected its main markets in favour of branching into new areas. Large amounts of money were poured into projects that took a long time to get off the ground. In the meantime, other companies like Northern Telecom Ltd. of Ontario, and American Telephone & Telegraph Inc. of New York were catching up, and the nature of the industry changed. "The floor fell out from under them," says Rich.

Source: Richard Siklos, "Addressing The Crises at Mitel by Launching a Revolution," *Financial Times of Canada*, April 4, 1988, p. 3. Reprinted by permission.

Questions:
1. According to the text, what was generally wrong with Mitel? Explain.
2. What changes have been undertaken to turn the company around? Refer to the diagram of contemporary business.

Chapter 2

Social Issues and Business

Learning Goals

There is nothing sinful about being rich.
—*Roy Thomson*

Canadian action is an assertion of the importance of the environment, of the sanctity of life on this planet, of the need for the recognition of a principle of clean seas, which is in all respects as vital a principle for the world of today and tomorrow as was the principle of free seas for the world of yesterday.
—*Pierre E. Trudeau, speech Annual Meeting, Canadian Press, Toronto, Apr. 15, 1970.*

1. To explain the concept of social responsibility as an accepted business policy

2. To discuss how social performance can be evaluated.

3. To describe the major social issues confronting business: inflation, people-oriented management, ecology and environmental protection, consumerism, and the energy crisis

4. To analyze the ethical questions facing management in its relations with consumers, with other company personnel, with business associates, and with investors and the financial community

Profile

George A. Cohon: *Keeping a Dream Alive—At Home and Abroad*

To the children who lined the chilly streets of Toronto early in November 1988, he was just another costumed figure in the city's 83rd annual Santa Claus parade. It is doubtful that any of the youngsters, or even many of their parents, realized that without the effort of George Cohon, the slim, smiling man in the top hat, there might not have been any parade at all. For the 51-year-old president of McDonald's Restaurants of Canada Ltd., the parade is just one reflection of the quiet philanthropy that he practises across the country each year.

Tough-minded and ambitious enough to build a nationwide chain of over 600 restaurants on the foundation of a single hamburger stand, Cohon is also a shrewd, energetic businessman. His acumen was on full display in April 1988 when McDonald's reached an agreement with the Soviet Union to open an outlet within lunchtime walking distance of the Kremlin—with at least 19 more units to follow. In the same month, his philanthropy was recognized with the award of the Order of Canada—the country's highest civilian honour.

Seven years ago, when the annual Toronto parade faced cancellation for the lack of sponsors, organizers asked Cohon to help save the Christmas institution. Said Cohon, who is Jewish: "I don't celebrate Christmas. I celebrate Hanukkah. But children are the greatest equalizer. You see 850,000 children, and they are not saying, 'I'm Jewish' or 'I'm Moslem' or Catholic or Protestant." Added Cohon: "I like to keep the dream alive that Santa Claus exists."

Cohon's life reflects the imprint of both sides of his character. Born in Chicago, he, like his father, became a lawyer in Illinois in 1961. In the same year, he helped found a club for boys struggling to escape the city's ghettos. In 1968, the young lawyer and his wife, Susan, borrowed heavily to finance the first McDonald's restaurant in Eastern Canada. On the day it

opened, in London, Ontario, he donated $1,200 to a local charity. "It was drummed into my head by my parents. You owe a duty to put something back into your community."

Within weeks of signing the agreement that will bring McDonald's to Moscow, Cohon joined the board of directors of the Lenin Soviet Children's Fund, a charity for disadvantaged young people.

Source: Carl Mollins, "Keeping a Dream Alive at Home and Abroad," *Maclean's*, December 26, 1988, p. 18. Reprinted by permission.

Johnson & Johnson's dedication to high product quality was put to the test in October 1982, when eight people in Chicago and Philadelphia died after ingesting Extra Strength Tylenol capsules laced with cyanide—a tragedy that caused the immediate collapse of one of Johnson & Johnson's most lucrative consumer markets.

Within days, it became clear that the poisonings did not start in the manufacturing unit: rather, someone had tampered with the Tylenol boxes already in stores, selectively opening capsules, adding the fatal cyanide doses, and returning the resealed bottles to the shelves.

Faced with this enormous tragedy, Johnson & Johnson chairperson James E. Burke had two priorities: first and foremost, he had to protect public safety. But he also had to reestablish Tylenol's reputation among consumers—a reputation that had made Tylenol the most popular nonaspirin pain reliever on the market. With poisoning scares continuing and an 80 percent immediate sales plunge for all Tylenol products, these tasks posed the most difficult challenge Johnson & Johnson had ever faced.

From the start of the tragedy, Johnson & Johnson took swift action on both the public safety and marketing fronts. As Burke put it: "We don't want to do anything to make it seem we haven't taken every step to ensure the public safety."

The concern translated into an almost immediate recall of more than 30 million bottles of Tylenol capsules. This move cost the company approximately $100 million, but it allayed the public's fears. In the immediate aftermath of the tragedy, Johnson & Johnson made its executives accessible to the press to answer questions, and established a toll-free telephone line which eventually handled more than 350,000 consumer calls. These public relations efforts gave Johnson & Johnson an important edge over its competitors (who felt obliged to refrain from any direct attacks that would make them seem to be capitalizing on Tylenol's misfortunes), and allowed the company to seize the moment and ask consumers to continue trusting Tylenol.

As the weeks passed, the efforts to rebuild Tylenol's reputation continued. By late November 1982, less than two months after the tragedy, Johnson & Johnson flooded some 40 million households throughout America with coupons for a free bottle of Tylenol—a move that encouraged consumers to return to the brand. Soon after, in a nationally reported press conference, Burke announced Tylenol's new triple-layer tamper-resistant packaging, which he described as "the best protection we could reasonably devise." The advertising campaign also concentrated on Tylenol tablets, which were not involved in the poisoning incidents.

These efforts paid off. Within months, Tylenol regained most of its lost market share—a feat that was due to the determination of company executives not to let the product die, and to the reservoir of trust and public responsibility built up over the years. "People just don't blame us," said chairperson Burke. "They feel we are being victimized just like everyone else."

The concept of **social responsibility** refers to management's consideration of the social as well as economic effects of its decisions. It applies to all businesses regardless of size, location, or industry. Social responsibility is a popular term in today's business vocabulary. In recent decades, society has increasingly called on private enterprise to be more socially conscious and to adopt a higher level of management ethics. Production managers are asked to make assembly-line jobs more meaningful. Personnel managers have been called on to revise many of their procedures. Retail executives are questioned about their store policies in low-income areas. And credit departments must answer charges concerning the invasion of personal privacy.

social responsibility
Management's consideration of social as well as economic effects in its decision making.

All organization levels must deal with these kinds of vital questions. Middle managers, production managers, district sales managers, and staff personnel must all be involved in a company-wide effort to raise the firm's level of business ethics and corporate responsibility.

Most companies have adopted social responsibility as the proper business philosophy. It has become standard corporate policy. But its acceptance at this level does not mean that it is always practised. A divergence between policy and practice is common in modern business. It can best be overcome by assuring that every policy adopted also contains a set of procedures for putting it into practice.

And once a programme is put into operation, there must also be provision for evaluating its results on a continuing and regular basis. New technology, new laws, and new ideas and attitudes present business with an environment that is often difficult to predict.

Self-Regulation or Government Regulation?

It is essential for the businessperson to realize that public outcry for increased social responsibility will not disappear. When industry fails to respond to the challenge posed by society, the public will is typically enforced through other means—namely, the government. Some children's toys have been banned because of their dangerous features. And government now regulates the type of information that can be requested on job applications. Intelligent managers realize the need for self-regulation by industry. It has become a prerequisite for corporate survival.

A federally financed study of recently retired middle-management executives found that over 70 percent believed that some degree of government regulation is necessary in contemporary business. Nearly all of these middle managers said that top management has an impact on corporate compliance with the law. It is apparent that the current mix of self-regulation and government regulation will continue in the foreseeable future.⟩

How Can We Evaluate Social Performance?

While critics demand higher levels of social responsibility for business, management is faced with the dual problems of implementation and evaluation. The implementation of socially oriented objectives requires a careful analysis to determine whether the benefits deriving from the action exceed the cost. A current public debate centres on whether Canada should strive for completely safe work and living environments. Many argue that such goals are unobtainable and that the related costs are prohibitive.

Business also faces the question of how to evaluate a firm's social performance. Critics readily point out that the private enterprise system is oriented toward quantity, not quality. In other words, modern society tends to confuse new houses, automobiles, dishwashers, vacation cottages, and the like with the true quality of life, however that is defined.

Historically, methods of evaluating social performance were usually based on the firm's contribution to national output and the provision of employment opportunities. Items such as weekly wage payments were often used as crude measures of social performance. However, such methods ignore the other areas of business responsibility—industrial safety, assembly-line drudgery, product safety, minority hiring, affirmative action, and pollution. Industry has traditionally been unable to answer its critics because it has lacked adequate measures of social performance.

Some companies are now developing means of assessing social responsibility. General Motors of Canada for example, distributes an annual *Public Interest Report* that outlines the corporation's accomplishments in areas such as improved fuel efficiency, minority contracting, vehicle safety, studying alternative fuels, quality of work life, industrial pollution control, and substance-abuse recovery programmes for employees. No generally accepted format has emerged, but the work is encouraging. Environmental, religious, and public interest groups are also attempting to create measures of corporate performance. For example, church groups monitor the amount of investment Canadian chartered banks have in white-supremacist South Africa. And it is important that this development continue and accelerate in the future. Accomplishing meaningful social goals may be retarded by the lack of an adequate evaluation system for corporate social performance.

What Are the Social Issues Facing Business?

Business today is confronted with five major groups of social issues: inflation, people-oriented management, ecology and environmental protection, consumerism, and the energy crisis. Nearly all specific social questions fall into one of these general areas. Some issues are interrelated. The energy crisis, for example, has led to concern over the use of petroleum resources, but it also has raised important consumer, ecological, and inflation issues.

Inflation: A Contemporary Business Issue

inflation
A decrease in the purchasing power of a nation's currency, often defined in terms of rising prices.

demand-pull inflation
A rise in prices caused when consumer demand for a product exceeds its supply.

cost-push inflation
Results when a rise in operating costs is passed along to the consumer.

Inflation can be defined in terms of either rising prices or the decreasing purchasing power of a nation's currency. Inflation has often been a critical economic problem for both consumers and businesses. The two traditional types of inflation are demand-pull and cost-push. **Demand-pull inflation** occurs when there is too much money relative to products available. In other words, if consumer demand for a product is greater than its supply, the price of the item will tend to go up. **Cost-push inflation** results from rising costs (labour, raw materials, interest rates, and the like) that are passed on to the consumer.

A Historical Perspective

Consider the situation in post-World War I Europe. Both victors and losers suffered the agony of unprecedented inflation. In Austria and Hungary the currency fell to a 15,000th of its former worth, and in Poland it fell to a 2,000,000th of its prewar value. The Soviet Union's currency dropped to a 50,000,000,000th of its former value. But the greatest inflation hit Germany, where the amount of money in circulation reached hundreds of trillions of marks. And because German industry and agriculture were unable to provide the food and other goods that people needed, prices skyrocketed. Consider these German prices: one egg for 80,000,000,000 marks, one match for 900,000,000 marks, and one newspaper for 2,000,000,000 marks. But when the German mark reached an unbelievable 1,000,000,000,000th of its prewar value, the government finally took measures to stabilize its worth.[1] Although the current situation has not reached these proportions, inflation is a serious economic problem throughout the modern world.

Inflation is an ongoing problem of businesses and consumers alike.

A Current Perspective

Compared to the German example cited above, price rises of recent years seem minuscule. Yet inflation remains a major problem for Canada and the rest of the world. To put the situation into perspective, let's assume inflation in Canada were to continue at a double-digit rate of say, 13 percent. By 1993 a ticket to a first-run movie would cost $17; the average North American car, $35,000; a stamp, $1.00; 500 g of bacon, $8.00 and a litre of gasoline, $1.65. In addition, McDonald's would be selling its Quarter Pounder for $5.00 and a shake for $2.55.

The problem of inflation in Canada is complicated by the problem of unemployment. A high level of unemployment means that many people do not have much money to spend. At the same time, rapid inflation eats at the purchasing power of earnings and savings. Cost pressures force prices up, even though demand decreases. This causes significant problems for the business community as well as for consumers. Economists now use the term **stagflation** to describe the dual economic problem of high unemployment and a rapidly rising price level.

stagflation
The dual economic problem of high unemployment and a rapidly rising price level.

Unfortunately, few people can agree on the causes of inflation. Public opinion poll after public opinion poll shows that Canadians consider too much government spending as a leading cause of inflation—usually closely followed by labour demands, energy costs, business profits, and excessive government regulations. Nor can they agree on ways of solving it.

Consumer Responses to Inflation

Rising consumer prices have forced people to make a number of changes in their daily lives. Soybeans became popular as meat extenders when meat prices went to record levels. High housing costs have forced many people to seek alternatives to single-family homes. Some housing experts now believe that single-family units will make up only one-third of all housing starts by 1990. Many people see borrowing as a means of countering inflation. Others argue that they should buy things now, because prices will be 10 to 20 percent higher next year. The increased use of credit has created even more economic problems, including a high rate of bankruptcy.

Inflation calls for adjustments on the part of consumers, who for the most part have reacted sensibly and blunted its worst effects. People have cut expenses where possible, and many have delayed purchases. They have also begun to take direct action where they see pricing abuses. For instance, consumer boycotts of various products and sellers became commonplace during the past decade. But producers have also boycotted the marketplace. Farmers, for example, have tied up traffic in several cities with their slow-moving tractors in an effort to get higher prices for their products.

Management Responses to Inflation

Businesspeople must also deal with the rising price spiral. Higher costs must be absorbed or passed on to the consumer in the form of higher prices. Management has had to adopt innovative responses to the problems of inflation and tight budgets.

Air Canada, CP, CN, Bell Canada, and other stalwart firms have pared down, cut back, reduced and even eliminated services which at one time were considered as dependable as the sun rising every morning.

Inflation does not have a negative impact on all firms. One firm sells giant chocolate-chip cookies that act as a combination greeting card and gift. Discount stores, do-it-yourself kits, energy-saving items, secondhand outlets, and generic drugs all do well in an inflationary economy. Consumers are adapting to inflation, and businesses must make similar adaptations to remain in operation.

People-Oriented Management

Business executives must strive to maintain a people-oriented philosophy of management. The daily press of commercial activity often makes it easier to deal with numbers, organization charts, interoffice memos, and administrative procedures. But industry is not the only segment of society that should pay greater attention to people. The federal and provincial governments have been under attack for treating people as "files" instead of human beings. Insensitivity to human needs is a critical problem in nearly all organizations; yet, a humanistic approach to management is always good business, regardless of the industry.

The special needs of some people have been neglected. The physically handicapped have had to overcome some managerial barriers in order to achieve occupational dignity. Individuals who have served time in jails or prisons need jobs that will keep them from returning to criminal activity. Asbestos miners are often affected by silicosis, an occupational disease of their industry.

These situations reflect dissatisfaction on the part of people involved in or affected by business organizations. Such people argue that business has been too concerned about short-run profitability, machinery, evaluation, and control of corporate personnel, and not concerned enough about the people involved. One of the aims of social responsibility is the achievement of a new concept of management that will take into account people-oriented concerns. (See Focus 2-1.)

Workers are more productive when they have a sense of participation in the decisions affecting them. Human resource development has thus become a major organizational objective for many businesses. West German firms have labour representation on management boards. Swedish automobile manufacturers have pioneered the concept of job enrichment for assembly line workers. Canadian companies have substantially upgraded their affirmative action hiring programmes, as will be described in Chapter 8.

People-oriented management requires a careful balance between productivity and profitability objectives on the one hand and employee desires on the other. Is the four-day workweek (four working days of 10 hours each) as productive as the traditional five eight-hour day workweek? This is the type of question that must be answered by management. Several human relations questions will be discussed in detail later in the book.

Focus 2-1

Towards Air That's Fit to Breathe

Consistent with the growing trend in business towards a greater concern for the employee and the environment, officials at Marathon Realty Co. Ltd. think they've found the hottest selling point yet: fresh air.

"You only have to pick up the newspaper to see that air quality is becoming a major social issue," says Toronto architect Murray Beynon. "We think it will become one of the major selling points for office buildings in the late 1980s and 1990s." His firm, Brisbin Brook Beynon, is designing a 700,000-sq.-ft. office complex in north Toronto called Atria North; its inhabitants will inhale air that's much fresher than what's available outdoors. Using electrostatic scrubbers and state-of-the-art humidifiers, Atria's internal atmosphere will be bracing as a mountain breeze—and contain three times as much fresh air as comparable energy-efficient buildings.

Ever since the 1973 oil crunch, developers have been building and retrofitting office towers that are virtually airtight: recirculating air that's already been heated is cheaper than piping in fresh air. The result has been an emergence of a new workplace issue: the Sick Building Syndrome.

Rampant in office towers, hospitals and many large new buildings, the sick building syndrome is a flu-like condition that causes irritation of the eyes, nose, throat, skin, and respiratory tract. Some people complain of headaches, dizziness, lack of concentration, and fatigue. Often the symptoms disappear upon leaving the building, notes Dr. Theodor Sterling, a fellow of the American College of Epidemiology who has researched this syndrome extensively.

According to Beynon, the ratio of fresh to recirculated air in some buildings is as low as one to twenty; in Atria North, the ratio will be one to six. The building will also feature 16 roomy balconies, accessible from the offices. Does this mean that fresh air could become a management status symbol? "What we're talking about," says Beynon, "is air quality for everybody. People regard fresh air as a right, and I think you'd have a backlash from employees if you tried to use that sort of thing as an executive perk."

The cost? "We're probably looking at 60 to 80 cents per square foot, maybe a dollar," says Beynon. For tenants, that works out to an extra 6 to 10 cents per square foot per year. He hopes most firms will recover the cost through lower absentee rates.

"When they breathe stale air all day, people feel lethargic," he says. "Some get headaches. It's just a general feeling of not feeling great. So there's absolutely no question that air quality is going to become one of the major driving forces in the design of new office buildings."

Source: "The Office Perk of the 1980s: Air That's Fit to Breathe," *Canadian Business*, March 1987, p. 14.

ℚ Ecology and Environmental Protection

In 1981 Ontario Hydro announced an agreement to sell power to General Public Utilities of New Jersey. The power was to be delivered by a cable running under Lake Erie. The plan was immediately assailed by environmentalists. Energy Probe of Toronto estimated that 60 Ontario lakes would be destroyed each year by the acid rain caused by the coal-fired generators the sale would require. Ontario

Energy Minister Robert Welch countered that if GPU did not buy power from Ontario it would get it from Ohio where all power was coal-generated.[2]

Eventually the deal fell through because of changes in the economy and the demand for energy, but the story shows what a vital issue ecology and environmental protection can be in modern business.

ecology
The relationship between people and their environment.

Ecology—the relationship between people and their environment—is an important managerial consideration from a legal as well as a social viewpoint.

Nearly everyone accepts the premise that we should maintain an ecologically sound environment. But the achievement of this goal requires tradeoffs that we are not always willing to make. For example, although we fear the oil spill danger of supertankers, we insist upon readily available supplies of gasoline at reasonable prices. Coal-burning boilers were once converted to oil-using furnaces in order to cut air pollution. But coal is relatively plentiful in Canada, so now some plants are switching back to it.

Ecological goals are important. However, the real issue is whether we can coordinate these goals with other social and economic objectives. No clear consensus has emerged on this matter.

pollution
The contamination of a natural environment.

Pollution—the contamination of a natural environment—is a major ecological problem today. We are constantly being reminded of the dangers of water and air pollution. Automobiles now have elaborate emission control devices. Smoke-belching factories are fined by environmental protection authorities. Municipal water and sewage treatment systems are being improved. Focus 2-2 provides an example of devastation caused by modern day pollutants.

Society faces two major questions about pollution. One is whether the benefits of cleaning up any particular form of pollution are worth the costs involved. The other is whether we are willing to pay now for a future ecological benefit. While most of us recognize the current pollution problems, our willingness to pay for corrections is sometimes doubtful. Gulf Oil, for example, had to withdraw unleaded gasoline when it first appeared because of low sales.

Disposable packaging (such as throwaway plastic bottles) has created a major ecological problem. Trash of this type continues to pile up, showing an amazing resistance to decomposition. Most provinces have taken action to reduce accumulations of trash. For example, many require deposits on soft drink and beer bottles and cans. But the most logical approach, recycling, remains under-utilized. It has been estimated that **recycling**—the reprocessing of used materials for reuse—could provide two-fifths of the materials required in the manufacturing sector.[3] While the recycling concept has received considerable public support, a comprehensive system has yet to be implemented. The basic question "Who is going to pay for it?" remains unanswered.

recycling
The reprocessing of used materials for reuse.

Focus 2-2

Acid Rain—An End to Sugaring-off Parties

The Quebec tradition of sugaring-off parties could soon be a thing of the past. Acid rain and air pollution are killing the province's trees. And if corrective measures aren't taken immediately, the forests will be ravaged and the maple syrup industry could be wiped out within ten years, scientists reported at a recent Montreal conference on acid rain.

"The areas where there is highest fallout definitely show the greatest amount of die-back," says Dr. Archibald Jones, director of the Morgan Arboretum at MacDonald College and professor of woodland resources.

The first cases of premature death of maple stands in Quebec were noted about ten years ago by maple syrup producers in the Beauce. Since 1978, the problem has spread to all Quebec maple stands and hardwood forests. Damage appears in such species as beech, wild cherry, basswood, white ash, walnut, red maple, and hemlock.

Provincial ecological stations in the Sutton-Brome region that measure the acid and alkaline levels (pH factor) show that the fog is at times more acidic than a lemon. This acidity coats the leaves of trees and is a paramount cause of die-back.

This trend prompted a local ecologist to launch an aerial fertilization company in 1988. Blair McDougall, president of Terra Tech Inc., says his firm will spread organic fertilizer by helicopter to raise the pH factor of the soil and restore nutrients that have been stripped from trees.

Source: Nancy McHarg, "Acid Rain Could Drown Out Sugaring-Off Parties," *This Week in Business*, March 12, 1988, p. 15. Reprinted by permission.

Air and water pollution present serious ecological problems.

Government and the Environment

There are few aspects of the environment of Canada that are not covered by at least one government department and quite comprehensive legislation. At the federal level, environmental protection is spread among four major departments: The Environment (1972); Fisheries; Health and Welfare; and Agriculture. Since 1970 the Department of the Environment and the Department of Fisheries have become responsible for 29 different acts affecting water, wildlife, clean air, fisheries, inspection, forestry, freshwater fish, migratory birds, ocean dumping, whales, Pacific fur seals, and international rivers. Other environmental protection mandates are spread among other government departments. Agriculture regulates animal health and parasites; Labour regulates industrial hygiene and safety; Energy, Mines and Resources controls mineral extraction processes and chemical uses; External Affairs deals with international air and water pollution. The provinces handle similar responsibilities.[4]

Consumerism

Consumer demands are another pressing issue facing business. Business-people often see the consumer as unpredictable, emotional, and sometimes irrational. Certainly, some consumer demands are unusual. For example, the Royal National Institute for the Blind once reported a demand by blind British men for pornographic magazines printed in Braille.[5]

consumerism
The demand that businesses give proper consideration to consumer wants and needs in making their decisions.

Consumerism—the demand that businesses give proper consideration to consumer wants and needs in making their decisions—has become a major social and economic movement within the United States, Canada, and other industrialized nations. Ralph Nader has been a leading contributor to this movement. His book *Unsafe at Any Speed* was one of many consumer criticisms leveled against industry. Some criticisms have been justified; others have not.

Since the emergence of consumerism in the 1960s, consumer groups have sprung up throughout the country. Some concentrate on an isolated problem such as excessive pricing by a local service industry, while others are more broadly based. The net effect has been the passage of consumer protection laws covering everything from unethical sales practices to the licensing of persons in the repair business. There is little doubt that more consumer protection laws will be passed in the years ahead, and business would be well advised to heed the comments of those in the consumerism movement.

The Consumer Affairs division of the federal Department of Consumer and Corporate Affairs is the main government agency concerned with consumer complaints and products. It administers four major acts:

1. Hazardous Product Act. This act gives the government the right to ban outright or to regulate sales, distribution, labelling and advertising of potentially dangerous products.
2. Consumer Packaging and Labelling Act. This act defines how ingredients, weight, and so forth are described on the labels of consumer products.
3. Food and Drug Act. The main purpose of this act is to protect the consumer from injuries, fraud, and other deceptive practices relating to food and drugs.
4. Weight and Measures Act. This act regulates weighing and measuring devices to ensure their accuracy and defines the measuring units that may be used in trade (for example, units of the metric system).

Comparable agencies operate in each of the provincial governments. The Combines Investigation Act prohibits price fixing, price discrimination, resale price maintenance, and mergers and monopolies. Deceptive advertising, fictitious sales, and provision of misleading information to consumers are criminal offences under this act.[6]

Bristol-Myers Canada was convicted under the misleading information section of the Combines Investigation Act for a Fleecy fabric softener advertisement in 1978. The television commercial stated that "Fleecy in the rinse softens right through the wash for three times more softness than any dryer product...Fleecy beats the best. It's the softest touch of all." The court ruled that Fleecy could not substantiate the claim of three times more softness even though Fleecy delivered three times more chemical softener.[7]

Energy: A Contemporary Challenge

In the early seventies numerous forecasters predicted that the demand for energy would exceed the supply by the 1980s. Little credence was given to those claims. The oil embargo of 1974 was thus a tremendous shock to the entire world, as people discovered that an oil shortage was both possible and very unpleasant. The public awakening and subsequent stocktaking have produced some truly disturbing findings.

Energy is an essential element in an industrial society. Although the energy supply in Canada is better than in most industrial countries, we import about 15 percent of our oil, mainly from Venezuela. We are self-sufficient in coal, uranium, natural gas, and hydroelectric power. Transportation is a lingering problem, with rail and pipeline capacity being insufficient to adequately service Quebec and the Maritimes with oil and natural gas.

According to the latest energy supply-and-demand study from the National Energy Board, oil and gas prices will rise and Canada could become a net oil importer by the early 1990s. The report indicates that gas exports will grow only slightly from 1988 levels, and it casts doubt on the prospects for many mega-projects, including new pipelines and offshore-oil developments.

The supply conclusions should be taken with a grain of salt, because the federal agency's biennial studies have invariably under-estimated the production capacity of Canada's oil and gas industry. Compared with earlier ones, this report contains substantially higher estimates for oil and gas output, but the projections may still be too low, partly because the study declines to anticipate policy changes.

In the 1970s, when the National Energy Board had a tight regula-tory grip on the oil and gas industry, such reports had a major impact on economic policy, because they were used to justify strict controls on oil and gas exports.

Because of what it terms ''considerable uncertainty about eco-nomic growth,'' the report makes two separate oil-price projections. The lower case shows crude rising by the year 2005 to $20 from the current level of about $15. The higher projection, which assumes higher world oil demand and economic growth, calls for the bench-mark-crude price to double to $30 by the year 2000, after which it remains steady to the end of the study period. The projections are in constant 1987 dollars, so that general consumer price inflation would further boost oil prices.

Net oil imports occur only in the low-price scenario, in which the board projects that Canadian crude output would drop steadily to about 1.2 million barrels daily by 2005 from a peak of 1.7 million barrels daily this year. In the high-price scenario, oil production rises to more than 2 million barrels daily in 2005, with net exports that year of 327,000 barrels daily, up from 245,000 barrels in 1987.

Figure 2-1
World Oil Prices

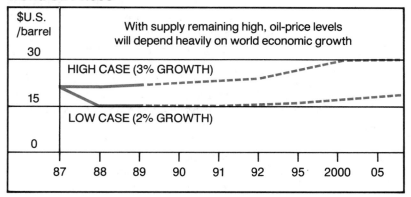

Source: National Energy Board

Figure 2-2
Crude Oil Capacity

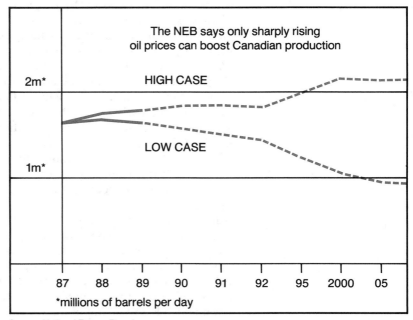

Source: National Energy Board

The low-price scenario would rule out such oil mega-projects as Newfoundland's $5.2-billion Hibernia off-shore development and as much as $1.4 billion of pipeline expansions from Alberta by Interprovincial Pipe Line Ltd. of Calgary and Trans Mountain Pipe Line Co. of Vancouver.

As in previous studies, the latest report assumes that "the existing framework of institutional practices and public policies would continue." That assumption could lead to unnecessarily low production estimates, since policy-makers tend to provide tax and royalty incentives to boost output when prices are weak. The study also assumes that finding and production costs will rise sharply over time, because undiscovered pools of oil and gas tend to get smaller. But in recent years, costs have actually been declining, and the oil and gas industry is working hard to continue the trend through technological advances and other means.

Still, the latest study represents a sea-change for the board because nearly all of its previous reports were even more pessimistic. This time, the study says projections of future oil output are higher mainly because of "various government and industry actions." In particular, it cites "the introduction of drilling, exploration and development incentives after the decline in oil prices in 1986, reduced regulation of production and exports, (and the) implementation by industry of cost-cutting measures that lowered operating costs in most areas."

In 1986, peak oil production in the high-price scenario was estimated at only 1,650,000 barrels daily. Moreover, the peak was to have occurred in the year the report was written. By the year 2005, output was projected to have dropped to 1,524,000 barrels daily, even with an oil price of $27 a barrel in constant 1986 dollars.

The low-price scenario was even worse, with projected output collapsing to 764,000 barrels daily at an oil price of $18 a barrel in 2005. In natural gas, the latest study forecasts that in the year 2005 Alberta prices will more than double to about $3.53 a thousand cubic feet from about $1.63 currently, even in the low-oil-price scenario. With high oil prices, gas would soar to $4.86 in the year 2005.

Like most observers, the energy board expects Canadian gas supply to be greater than domestic demand to the end of the forecast period, but the federal agency's export projections look conservative to some analysts. The gas industry is gearing for annual deliveries to the United States of at least 2 trillion cubic feet within a few years, compared with about 1.27 trillion cubic feet this year. But because of the competitive abilities of US producers, the board projects that future annual exports will remain between 1.32 trillion cubic feet and 1.45 trillion cubic feet until 2005.

That would be bad news not just for Canadian producers but for sponsors of various pipeline projects who hope to deliver large additional amounts of Canadian gas to the US. The board's regional US market projections are consistent with pipeline expansion to the US Northeast rather than the West, even though at least four projects have been proposed to boost gas deliveries to California. On the positive side, the board says steady gains in Canadian domestic demand will boost total annual Canadian gas production to between 4.4 trillion cubic feet and 4.8 trillion cubic feet in the year 2005, a 25 percent to 37 percent gain from about 3.5 trillion cubic feet this year. And, as with oil production, the board's new gas-output projections are extremely bullish compared with the previous outlook, when natural-gas exports were forecast to peak in 1990 at about 1.33 trillion cubic feet and wither to nothing by the year 2000.

Although its price projections are smooth, the study warns that "in reality, it is reasonable to expect that oil prices will fluctuate from time to time above and below the high and low paths." Also, fossil fuels assessment could be affected by environmental issues which may force governments to institute conservation measures or shift to renewable energy sources. But, as with oil and gas production incentives, the study says it doesn't attempt to anticipate environmental-policy changes in its projections. The NEB study, which also looks at electricity and coal production, concludes that Canada will remain a net energy exporter even in the low-price scenario. While many of its other conclusions are bad news, that at least provides some hope that the country's future as an energy producer is secure.[8]

Table 2-1
Crude Petroleum and Natural Gas Production in Canada,
1984-1987 ($000s)

PRODUCT	1984	1985	1986	1987
Crude Oil	15,399.40	15,553.00	7,886.90	9,921.30
Synthetic crude oil*	2,385.30	2,806.50	1,710.10	2,203.50
Condensate	28.40	35.60	14.90	16.30
Pentanes plus	1,155.90	1,257.90	730.40	907.40
Propane	629.80	579.30	426.90	322.00
Butanes	519.60	524.20	313.00	337.10
Ethane	544.60	448.50	332.10	309.80
Natural gas	7,225.90	7,344.40	5,645.90	4,615.10
Sulphur	419.30	730.70	700.60	493.80
TOTAL VALUE	28,308.20	29,280.10	17,760.80	19,126.30

*Includes crude bitumen

Source: *The Crude Petroleum and Natural Gas Industry 1987*, Statistics Canada, Industry Division, Energy Section, Ottawa: Supply and Services Canada, Table 4, pp. 24-25. Reproduced with permission of the Minister of Supply and Services Canada, 1989.

Table 2-1 summarizes Canada's crude petroleum and natural gas production from 1984 to 1987. While production fell drastically in 1986, Canada remains one of the main exporters of petroleum and natural gas in the world.

Canada's trade in petroleum and natural gas chalked up a favourable balance in 1987, for the 22nd consecutive year. Net exports in 1987 increased to a total of 27,928 million cubic metres—an increase of approximately 34 percent over the previous year.[9] Over the same period, total imports fell by approximately 58 percent, adding to the overall surplus.

Canada's domestic energy problems are as follows:

1. Dependence upon imported oil creates political vulnerabilities. The threat of cutting off supply might blackmail Canada into supporting some regimes and ceasing trade with others.

2. Canada's energy consumption is increasing at a rate of about 5.5 percent per year, which means that the domestic oil shortfall could grow severalfold by the year 2000, and the demand for electricity and other forms of energy will also compound. Therein lies a further problem. Nuclear power plants are expensive and pose certain serious risks, which has led to stiff resistance against their construction by concerned persons. Hydroelectric sites will be largely allocated. The use of coal involves health and environmental hazards. Alternative energy sources (solar, geothermal, wave power, etc.) are in their infancy. Reliance on oil to fill the gap will only hasten the exhaustion of oil reserves.

3. Energy pricing has become an acute political and economic issue. Canada's resource-based economy, dispersed population, and life-

style propects for economic growth are predicated upon abundant and inexpensive energy. But that in turn stimulates consumption, and raises the issue of who should pay the bills when energy prices rise. As an example, 60 percent of the oil used in Eastern Canada (east of the Ottawa Valley Line) is imported.

4. Domestic energy problems cannot be separated from the world energy situation. Canada's major foreign customers, the United States and Western Europe (which also supply many of our finished goods and much capital and own or control much of our industry), face still more pressing energy crises, and cannot be refused help in emergencies. Wars or political upheaval in a country like Iran can have serious effects on the supply of oil available on the open market.

5. Energy prospects, as noted earlier, depend upon technological progress in such fields as nuclear fusion and other alternative energy sources. However, these depend in turn upon a further chain of events, including public and private decisions to do and support the necessary research, and the managing of existing resources until those developments are operating.

Table 2-2 **A Statistical Summary of Electric Energy in Canada**

	1986	1987	% Change
Total Demand for Electricity (GWh)	423,198	439,689	3.9
Total Generation (GWh)	457,175	483,643	5.8
by: hydro	308,570	314,060	1.8
nuclear	67,232	72,883	8.4
conventional thermal	81,373	96,700	18.8
Total net exports (GWh)	33,977	43,954	29.4
total imports	4,957	3,471	−30.0
total exports	38,934	47,425	21.8
Total capacity at December 31 (MW)	91,498	94,667	3.5
hydro	56,953	57,005	0.1
nuclear	8,596	11,329	31.8
conventional thermal	25,949	26,333	1.5
Total net additions (MW)	1,107	3,169	186.3
hydro	390	52	−86.7
nuclear	32	2,733	8440.6
conventional thermal	685	384	−43.9

Source: *Electric Power Statistics*, Annual Electric Power Survey of Capability and Load (Vol. 1), Statistics Canada, Ottawa: Supply and Services Canada, November 1988, Table 1, p. 10. Reproduced with the permission of the Minister of Supply and Services Canada, 1989.

Table 2-3　　　　　**Generation Capacity for Electric Energy in Canada**

	Steam	Gas Turbine	Internal Combustion	Nuclear	Total Thermal	Hydro	Total
CANADA							
Total End 1986*	28,610.90	2,660.11	598.47	11,671.40	43,540.88	89,375.81	132,916.69
Additions 87	00.00	00.00	00.00	784.00	784.00	26.00	810.00
Total End 1987	28,610.90	2,660.11	598.47	12,455.40	44,324.88	28,401.81	133,726.69
Additions Proposed							
1988	400.00			881.00	1,281.00	0.75	1,281.75
1989	400.00			881.00	1,281.00	988.00	2,269.00
1990	380.00				380.00	256.00	636.00
1991	300.00			881.00	1,181.00	640.00	1,821.00
1992	750.00			881.00	1,631.00	1,017.00	2,648.00
1993	750.00				750.00	734.00	1,484.00
1994						736.17	736.17
1995							
1996	375.00						
1997	375.00				375.00	846.50	1,221.50
1998					375.00	1,168.50	1,543.50
1999	375.00					151.00	151.00
2000	750.00				375.00	130.00	505.00
2001		100.00			750.00	640.00	1,390.00
2002		200.00			100.00	710.00	810.00
2003	750.00				200.00	110.00	310.00
2004		100.00			750.00	165.00	915.00
					100.00		100.00
Total End 2004	34,215.90	3,060.11	598.47	15,979.40	53,853.88	97,694.73	151,548.61

Assumption: Actual additions are equal to additions proposed for 1985-1987.
Source: Derived from Statistics Canada.

The National Energy Board has been uncertain about the availability and quantity of natural gas and oil reserves in Canada. In 1977 the board believed that natural gas was in short supply and reduced exports and the amount shipped east. Subsequent information led the board to conclude that there was sufficient natural gas, and export permits were provided, but many potential consumers had by then switched to alternate fuels.

The energy problem includes not only oil, but also electricity. In 1976 one-third of Canada's primary energy demand was provided in the form of electricity.

The demand for Canada's electricity in 1987 is shown in Table 2-2. The generation capacity for steam, gas turbine, internal combustion, nuclear thermal, and hydro energy for 1987 and projected until the year 2004 is found in Table 2-3.

Although demand for electricity experienced a remarkable growth in 1987, the long-range demand forecasts were reduced for most of the electric utilities. For example, average annual growth for the period 1984 to the year 2000 was reduced by BC Hydro to 2.2 percent from the previous forecast of 3.2 percent; in Alberta the utilities forecast was reduced from 4.0 percent to 3.6 percent; Saskatchewan and Manitoba were reduced to 2.2 percent and 2.5 percent from the respective 2.6 percent and 3.0 percent; Ontario Hydro's forecast was slightly reduced from 2.5 percent to 2.4 percent; and Newfoundland reduced from 4.6 percent to 4.2 percent. Overall, the reduced major utility forecasts resulted in a national electricity demand forecast from 1984 to 2000 of 2.4 percent compound annual growth compared to the 1983 forecast of 2.8 percent. Interestingly enough, the total capacity for nuclear generation was increased by approximately 37 percent (Table 2-2) in 1987, resulting in a staggering change in net additions.

Historically, electricity demand has been very highly correlated with economic performance. Electricity intensity in the Canadian economy, i.e., the amount of electricity used for each dollar of real gross national product (GNP), has been steadily increasing over time. This was true even during the very turbulent period from 1974 to 1985. This seems reasonable, since Canada has low-cost electricity relative to other parts of the world. However, utility-based forecasts result in decreasing electricity intensity, based on the economic growth forecast used in the EMR forecast, from 2.74 kWh/\$GNP in 1984 to 2.49 in 2000. In assessing the reasonableness of such a forecast, it is necessary to question what factors would cause this change in a long-term trend, and whether such a change is reasonable in the Canadian situation.

This differing perception in the demand for electricity during the 1990s could result in inadequate capacity in that period, if the EMR forecast turns out to be more accurate than that of the utilities. However, it could be that the utility forecasts have reached a low point for this cycle, and the forecasts will tend to increase as demand picks up. Utility forecasts tend to be reduced during periods of slow growth, and to increase as demand picks up. Electricity demand has picked up in many areas during the economic recovery experienced through 1983-84, particularly during the period from May of 1983 to the end of the year. Utility forecasts have continued to increase as this new information is assimilated into the forecasting process.

Electricity demand is very highly correlated to the country's economic performance. Part of the reason why electricity demand has been much less than was forecast over recent years is that our economic performance has been much worse than forecast. Similarly, the magnitude of future electricity demand will depend critically on the level of economic performance, something that has proven to be very difficult to predict with a high degree of accuracy. Further work needs to be done to explain differences between the several forecasts that may result from a combination of methodology differences and ranges of assumptions on prices and other economic variables.

An increasing demand for energy creates an energy shortfall, which results in the building of additional capacity to supply the demand for electric power, which has, at times, increased at a rate of 6.6 percent per year. Canada has almost exhausted the available hydro sites and needs to look to coal or nuclear power as sources of energy. This of course has social implications with government and the people often holding opposite views.

The issues relating to electric power production are as follows:

1. The possible development of nuclear power and coal raises issues of environmental damage, safety, and health.
2. Electricity output needs to increase by 30 percent by 1990, with resultant utilization of resources and materials estimated at between $90–130 billion.
3. We may prove unable or unwilling to generate the additional electrical capacity required, in the event of a switch from oil to electricity for heating and industrial uses.

The Science Council as early as 1975, in its report *Canada's Energy*, concluded that "In the long term, we in Canada can be optimistic about the security of our energy supplies since we have an abundance of natural resources if we manage them wisely." Nevertheless, the council urged technologies that would use renewable resources rather than exhaustible ones, enhance the natural environment, emphasize efficiency in the utilization of energy, and expand the range of energy choices. The Department of Energy, Mines and Resources for Canada has pointed out that if "the demands for energy in Canada were to continue to grow at 5.5 percent per year, then in the year 2005 energy demands would amount to the equivalent of 14.3 million barrels of oil per day. Within this period of 30 years, energy use would increase 4 times."[10] These demands could be met by doubling hydroelectric capacity, and constructing four new nuclear plants the size of the Pickering generating station near Toronto over the next 30 years. By the end of the century other energy forms would still be required to supply 40 percent of energy demands. It is clear that Canada must develop alternative energy resources. Nuclear power, wind, sun, synthetic fuels, coal, even garbage and waste products all have been suggested as possible substitutes for oil and natural gas. Time will tell what the solutions will be.

Ethical Questions Facing Business

Social and ethical issues are closely related and similar in meaning and impact. Generally, however, social issues are somewhat broader in that they are usually directed at all areas of business enterprise. By contrast, it is possible to isolate specific ethical issues for various segments of a company.

Management is required to resolve specific ethical questions dealing with right and wrong that arise in any work environment. Sometimes a conflict exists between an ideal decision and one that is practical under certain conditions. But it is important that companies evaluate their ethical responsibilities in decision making. Many firms

*CORPORATE CODE OF
CONTINENTAL BANK
OF CANADA*

OUR RESPONSIBILITY TO SHAREHOLDERS

Shareholders and depositors enable the Bank to exist. Their confidence is essential to our business. It is the Bank's primary purpose therefore to increase the value of the shareholders' investment by carrying on the business of banking in a prudent, productive and profitable way.

Fair profits enable the Bank to provide

dividends to shareholders. It is our responsibility therefore to achieve a return on their investment which is equal to or better than the average of Schedule A banks.

OUR RESPONSIBILITY TO CUSTOMERS
It is the right of our customers to expect honesty from the Bank and its employees, integrity in the Bank's records and privacy in their dealings with the Bank.

Furthermore, it is the responsibility of the Bank to safeguard the deposits that are entrusted to it and to conduct business as a sound financial institution that is innovative, aggressive, flexible and responsive to its customers' needs.

These responsibilities are summed up in

the Bank's Credo, which is displayed in all Branches.

As a bank, we strive to bring together the strength of our depositors' capital and the dynamism of free enterprise so that both may prosper.

Although our business is banking, banking is not our only business. We recognize the need for corporate participation in societal concerns that go beyond the boundaries of the balance sheet.

Branch staff are encouraged to take leadership roles in the towns and cities across Canada, in which we do business. We recognize the need for and support the work of

non-profit organizations dedicated to improving the health and welfare of Canadians.

We also understand and support the benefits of creative expression in society whether it be through the arts, the sciences or on the playing field.

CREDO
When customers think of the Bank they believe it to be:

| a safe place to deposit money |
| staffed with competent people |
| long established with a successful history |
| aggressive in asking for business |

| innovative in pursuing new banking ideas |
| responsive to customers' needs and interests |

Everything we do will strengthen this belief or we will not do it.

OUR RESPONSIBILITY TO STAFF
The excellence of our service depends on the excellence of our staff. The Bank must therefore ensure that employees are given every opportunity to improve their existing skills, further their development as professional

bankers and be justly compensated for their performance.

Continental Bank of Canada is a 'first name' organization and endorses an open door policy. Staff members may discuss their views with any level of management and are encouraged to do so.

OUR RESPONSIBILITY TO THE PUBLIC
Continental Bank of Canada believes in a free society in which entrepreneurs may succeed on the merit of their ideas and enterprises. Initiative, inventiveness and the right to bring new ideas to the public form the basis for growth and progress in any society.

Some companies, such as the Continental Bank of Canada, have developed written codes of ethics to reflect their ethical responsibilities in decision making.

today have developed written codes of ethics. (See the corporate code of the Continental Bank of Canada above.)

How businesspeople deal with ethical questions was the subject of a study outline in the *Harvard Business Review*. Businesspeople were presented with hypothetical situations where some actions would normally be right, others wrong. Half the sample were asked, ''What would you do?'' while the other half were asked, ''What would the average businessperson do?'' The answers to the second question indicated more unethical behaviour than did responses to the first question. Businesspeople apparently think their peers are less ethical than they themselves are.[11]

Businesses face numerous ethical questions every day. Some of the more frequently encountered ones are discussed below.

Relations with Customers

The possibility of ethical abuses is quite evident in relations with customers. High-pressure sales tactics have led to cooling-off laws that allow consumers to cancel sales contracts within a certain period of time. The acceptable degree of advertising aimed at children is being questioned. A multitude of package sizes makes price comparison difficult for the consumer. When toothpaste manufacturers switched to metric packaging in Canada they agreed to reduce the confusing array of sizes to four: 25 g, 50 g, 100 g, and 150 g.

Promotional strategy is the basis of most ethical questions involved in relations with consumers. The personal sales process has always been open to some form of ethical criticism, but in recent years advertising has been subjected to close scrutiny because of its vast reach. Advertising has become an increasingly pervasive force in our lives.

Pricing is an area that has an immediate, direct effect on the consumer. It is also the most regulated of the firm's relations with consumers. Chapter 22 describes many of the laws that affect pricing strategy.

Relations with Company Personnel

Some of the most difficult ethical questions deal with companies' relations with their employees, because decisions in this area affect people's work environment for years to come. Managers are required to make hiring, promotion, transfer, compensation, and dismissal decisions. Consider the ethical dilemma of a manager who has to choose between promoting a rising young executive with potential for further development and a long-service employee nearing retirement who has performed faithfully, if not sensationally, over the years. Promotion of the older person may cause the younger one to move to a competing firm. Selection of the younger person may be regarded as breaking faith with senior people in the organization. Many complex and vital ethical questions are involved in such decisions.

Ethical questions also arise in the course of a manager's other relationships with people in the organization. For example, consider the situation where one executive keeps important information from a peer so as to enhance his or her own chances for promotion and to lessen the advancement opportunity of the other manager.

Relations with Business Associates

Relations with business associates are another area of possible ethical conflict. Many interpersonal relationships in business include important ethical considerations. For example, an executive may ask, "Am I Nancy's friend because I like her as a person or because she is sometimes a good source of competitive information?"

Another important question is: When does a gift and/or business entertainment become a bribe? Most firms have clear policies prohibiting the outright payment of bribes to purchasing directors, government officials, and competitors' employees. On some occasions these restrictions have not been effective in stopping ethical abuses, but most of the time they work. However, often a very fine line exists between a business gift and a bribe. Some organizations have prohibited their employees from giving or receiving *any* business gift; others have set limits on the value of gifts to their employees.

Relations with Investors and the Financial Community

Throughout history there have been financial scandals. The financial health of firms has been misrepresented, numerous land swindles have been perpetrated, savers have lost millions of dollars due to embezzlement, and nonexistent assets have been reported to the financial community.

Each of these types of financial abuse has been dealt with by the government, so that we now have a comprehensive, well-developed set of laws regulating financial affairs. (These laws will be outlined later in the text.) But business management has also moved to a higher level of ethical behaviour. Firms are now more alert to financial misconduct by their personnel. Professional organizations and societies such as the Canadian Institute of Chartered Accountants have also worked to improve financial ethics.

There is probably no place where the public expects a higher level of business ethics than in the arena of financial transactions. Public attention goes beyond the illegitimate activities identified by statutes. Financial executives such as bankers are expected to exhibit the highest standards of ethical behaviour in order to justify the public trust placed in them. (See Focus 2-3.)

The Scorecard on Social Responsibility in Business

We have briefly explored the various aspects of the social responsibility puzzle facing business, suggesting several areas where management needs to improve. But let us look at the overall scorecard for business.

Certainly there have been failures, particularly in earlier years when less exacting standards were commonplace. Even today critics can point to overseas payoffs and illegal political contributions as violations of contemporary guidelines for social responsibility. Yet the vast majority of business decisions are responsible, and the level of this achievement continues to climb each year. Most businesspeople know that socially responsible behaviour is simply good business. In many communities the Better Business Bureau, an association sponsored by businesspeople, acts as a watchdog monitoring fair and unfair business practices.

Social responsibility is an inherent part of a businessperson's job, because commercial decisions affect virtually all elements of society. Responsible actions are expected of everyone working in business today.

Focus 2-3

Are Business Ethics in Decline?

Leaders of Canada's financial services industry are taking a hard look at business ethics following a series of well-publicized financial scandals in which thousands of small investors got burned.

National associations representing 111 insurance companies and 36 trust companies have begun drafting codes of ethics for the guidance of their 80,000 employees across the country.

Major firms like Standard Life, The Royal Bank of Canada and London Life already have adopted their own codes, setting out principles that employees are expected to follow in their dealings with investors and depositors.

Other companies say they are tightening up their staff training and monitoring procedures to discourage conflicts of interest, misrepresentation, insider trading and other unsavoury practices.

And the Quebec Securities Commission, whose hard-pressed staff is investigating more than a dozen brokers accused of bilking investors, is preparing a tougher code of ethics for all investment dealers.

Although some brokerage houses and trust companies have been involved in major controversies across Canada, industry spokesmen insist that their standards remain high.

They say the new codes of conduct are not being implemented in response to wrongdoing at their own firms, but simply to entrench and clarify ethical principles.

Elaine Phénix, who heads the Quebec branch of the Investment Dealers' Association, says her group probes complaints against any of the 86 member companies across Canada.

"Most of the time," Phénix says, "complaints are due to misunderstandings between the client and the broker; 99 percent of the complaints are settled through the IDA."

But Stephen Jarislowsky, one of Canada's top pension fund managers and president of Jarislowsky, Fraser Investment Counsellors, takes a far more critical view.

He refers to the IDA as a "public relations operation" and says the brokerage industry is "filled with conflicts of interest and ethical problems."

While brokers are told the client's objectives should be their prime concern, Jarislowsky wonders to what extent this is really enforced. He says there's a built-in conflict for the sales person, who profits every time a client makes a transaction.

"Ethics are clear, but for most people, it's what the law permits them to get away with. At month end, the brokerage house looks at how much commission a broker made, not how much money he made for his client."

Jarislowsky says this is "penny ante" when compared with the situation of minority shareholders, whom he terms true victims of "rip-offs."

His firm sometimes stops dealing with brokerage houses that he feels are not acting in the best interest of shareholders.

In a recent commencement address at Queen's University, Jarislowsky urged the graduates to seek out and work for companies with ethical management.

At McLeod Young Weir, Chairman Austin Taylor says an internal compliance manual, detailing how brokers should and should not act, is updated and signed annually by employees.

"Over the years, securities regulations have become more strict. The types of suits seen at the courts in the US have heightened responsibility on people in the business."

He adds that ethical behaviour is in a company's own self-interest. "If you're labelled with unethical conduct once, you will never get rid of it [the stigma].

"But there are laws against murder and fraud, and people still do it. All the guidelines and rules can't guarantee ethical behaviour."

Since 1981, McLeod Young Weir's training program has included studies of actual cases of wrongdoing, to see "where the individual may have gone wrong," says Robert Guilday, director of sales training.

Recently, the firm invited a chaplain to its Toronto head office to discuss business ethics.

"We try to get an outsider's point of view, to see the broad picture," Guilday says. He believes insider trading and other unethical practices are less common in Canada than in the US.

Canadians are more wary of high pressure stock promotions and have been shocked by the vast scope of the Wall Street scandals involving Ivan Boesky and other takeover specialists.

Paul Guy, chairman of the Quebec Securities Commission, says his agency is working on a new code of ethics. He hopes the document will be issued by the end of the year.

"I've been concerned with ethics because of the changing environment," says Guy, referring to deregulation in the financial sector, where cross ownership among banks and brokerage firms can lead to potential conflicts of interest.

"The situation is changing, but the rules haven't yet changed," Guy says.

"There is some merit to developing a code where all the rules will be in one place for firms and brokers to follow," instead of being spread out in various regulations and stock exchange rules as they are now.

Guy says it's hard to say whether unethical behaviour is spreading. "There are more complaints now, but that is usual in a bear market. In a large industry based on trust, there are bound to be some problems."

At the Royal Bank, David Grier, vice president and chief advisor on public affairs, says employees sign a statement every year acknowledging they have read and understood the bank's Code of Conduct.

Various elements of an ethics program are being considered, such as discussion groups, role-playing sessions and guest speakers, he says. "Discussion of ethics makes a difference."

Source: Ellen Kom, "Are Business Ethics in Decline?" *This Week in Business*, June 25, 1988, p. 13. Reprinted by permission.

Controversial Issue

Big Firms Lack Social Values

From his perch on the tenth floor of a high-rise in east-end Montreal, Leo-Paul Lauzon watches big business like a hawk.

Lauzon is a pioneer in "social accounting." For more than a decade, he has been trying to make large companies think beyond profits to their social roles.

He pores over annual reports to check out a company's track record in such areas as the environment, and treatment of minorities, consumers and employees.

"Being an accountant is an excellent training to criticize big business," Lauzon said. "I know how corporate executives think because I have the same mentality myself.

"The only difference is that I have a social conscience and most of them don't."

His unsolicited advice—in the studies he publishes—is not always appreciated.

"It's a very insecure life," Lauzon admitted. "I receive enough money from teaching to live."

The wiry, bearded Lauzon, 42, is a chartered accountant with an MBA degree from the Université de Montréal and a Ph.D. in management sciences from the Université de Grenoble in France.

He has worked for a national bank and three accounting firms and he now lectures in the accounting sciences department at the Université du Québec à Montréal.

Lauzon's social conscience came, in large part, from growing up in a welfare family in Montreal with no father and a mother and two sisters to support.

"I didn't have the time or the luxury of being a political revolutionary when I went to school during the 1960s," he said. "There were no demonstrations or love-ins for me. You develop a very healthy respect for money when you don't have any."

Respect for money, and the way companies spend it, has led Lauzon to develop a system of evaluating the annual reports of this country's largest corporations.

He studies their public statements in such areas as environmental protection, human relations, equal opportunities, and consumer interests. Then he grades them in terms of their social responsibility.

Lauzon's study of the companies which create the most pollution in Canada stated that there were so few references to the environment in their annual reports that the issue "is a joke."

On the issue of women in upper management, he caustically observed that there are more and more women popping up in large corporations with the title of vice-president.

"But these titles usually carry no authority and no bottom-line decision-making power," he argued. "It's a farce."

Nor does Lauzon hesitate to criticize a company's economic performance.

In a study entitled *Steinberg Inc.: A list of the 26 biggest flops from 1968-88*, Lauzon concluded that the Montreal-based grocery giant "must be one of the worst-managed companies in Canada."

"Management's strategy had been to rush blindly in every direction like a chicken with its head cut off."

Lauzon has his share of critics in the business community.

Claude Garcia, executive vice-president of Standard Life Assurance Co. in Montreal, questioned Lauzon's method of only studying annual reports.

"The people who read these [annual] reports most closely are our competitors and we have no intention of telling them anything we don't have to," Garcia said. "Things like pollution control or hiring of women are internal corporate matters which are not really discussed in these kinds of documents."

On the other hand, Lauzon has supporters like François Renauld, president of the

Professional Corporation of Certified Management Accountants in Quebec.

"When he first started doing these studies ten years ago, Prof. Lauzon was considered an outsider or a radical by accountants and businessmen," Renauld said. "But its's amazing how corporate philosophy and public awareness of social accounting has changed in that time. Now large companies are talking about more than just money in their annual reports and you have to give Leo-Paul Lauzon a fair degree of credit for that."

Source: "Big Firms Lack Social Values: Accountant. Self-styled Watchdog Says Environment, Women's Issues Ignored," *The Gazette*, Montreal, February 27, 1989, p. B-7.

Summary of Learning Goals

1. **Explain the concept of social responsibility as an accepted business policy.**
   Social responsibility has become accepted business policy, but its actual implementation has often lagged. As a result, there is a real need to develop an effective method of evaluating a firm's social performance.

2. **Discuss how social performance can be evaluated.**
   Social performance had been traditionally measured by such factors as the firm's contribution to national output and employment opportunities. Today, we seek to measure social performance on a broader basis. While no generally accepted format has emerged, many firms are working on developing measures of social responsibility.

3. **Describe the major social issues confronting business: inflation, people-oriented management, ecology and environmental protection, consumerism and the energy crisis.**
   There are five major groups of social issues confronting business today: inflation, people-oriented management, ecology and environmental protection, consumerism, and the energy crisis. The rising prices caused by inflation are of concern to both consumers and businesses alike. In addition to economics, business must also be more aware of and responsive to the needs and problems of people in the workplace. At the same time, business cannot ignore the physical environment in which it operates, paying particular attention to pollution and its effects on the ecology of an area. Nor can business turn its back on its consumers, who are demanding to be treated fairly and to have their rights protected. Finally, business, like everyone else, must look for ways to conserve or to find alternate sources of energy on which to run.

4. **Analyze the ethical questions facing management in its relations with consumers, with other company personnel, with business associates and with investors and the financial community.**

Social and ethical issues are closely related and similar in meaning and impact. Social issues are somewhat broader in that they are usually directed to all areas of business enterprises. By contrast, it is possible to isolate specific ethical issues for various segments of a company. Ethical questions face management in its relations with consumers, company personnel, business associates, and investors and the financial community. A brief assessment of business's social responsibility scorecard shows that most business people today are socially responsible decision makers.

Key Terms

social responsibility
inflation
demand-pull inflation
cost-push inflation
stagflation

ecology
pollution
recycling
consumerism

Discussion Questions and Exercises

1. Discuss the need for social performance measures in business.
2. Outline the five major groups of social issues facing business.
3. What acts governing matters affecting consumers are administered by the Department of Consumer and Corporate Affairs?
4. Contrast the short-run and long-run components of the complex energy question.
5. Identify the various ethical questions facing business executives.
6. What are the major societal and ethical issues facing:
   a) automobile manufacturers
   b) real estate developers
   c) detergent manufacturers
   d) drug firms selling birth control products
   e) corporate attorneys?
7. Outline what you see as the moral of the Controversial Issue.
8. Explain the statement: "Businesspeople know that socially responsible behaviour is simply good business."
9. What is the role of the Better Business Bureau?
10. Identify two or three social issues facing business in your local area. How have local firms responded to them? How have local governmental agencies and officials responded?

Case 2-1

Caught in a Bind

What happens when what is ethically right is wrong from a business standpoint? If doing the right thing puts you out of business, is doing the wrong thing justifiable? Nora Pollard, president of Phoenix Industries Ltd. of Saskatoon, is wrestling with these questions now as she tries to pull her company from the brink of bankruptcy.

Although Phoenix got started as a maker of plastic hoses for householders, this side of the business accounted for only 20 percent of total sales in 1984. The rest of the company's sales were generated by its industrial water irrigation products division— some 90 percent of the revenues from this division come from exports. Markets include Mexico, Brazil, Argentina, Greece, Italy, France, Japan and Australia.

In 1983, Pollard had expanded her production facilities to meet anticipated contracts for the next three years. Her estimates were too optimistic. By 1986, Phoenix still hasn't been able to use its increased capacity. The company is just marginally profitable now.

In order to respond to Phoenix's poor financial condition, Pollard signed a $500,000 contract to supply industrial irrigation products to a firm in Brazil.

Everything went smoothly until hours before the order was to be shipped, when Pollard's inspectors discovered defects in the products. While the problems were not evident to the eye—and were paid for—they would cause difficulties for the customer in the field and would require repairs. However, if Pollard delayed shipment or informed the customer of the problem, Phoenix might lose the order. And if that were to happen, the company could be forced into bankruptcy.

Pollard has only a few hours to come up with a solution to her dilemma, and none of the alternatives she is considering is totally satisfactory. She believes she has four to choose from:

1. Not ship the order and not tell the customer the reason, which would place Phoenix Industries in voluntary bankruptcy.
2. Inform the customer of the quality problem, not ship the products, and declare voluntary bankruptcy.
3. Ship the order and inform the customer of the defects after receiving payment.
4. Ship the order and say nothing to the customer. (Pollard doubts the Brazilian firm could obtain any legal judgement against her in this event.)

Source: Daniel Stoffman, "Caught in a Bind," *Canadian Business*, November 1987, pp. 173-174.

Questions:
1. Why are the four alternatives listed not satisfactory? Explain.
2. What other alternatives are open to Pollard? What should she do?
3. Why should Pollard inform the customer of the defects? Discuss.

Case 2-2

AIDS in the Office

Jonathan Harnett, chairman and CEO of Harnett Advertising Ltd., had always considered himself a liberal-minded person until he began to suspect one of his employees had AIDS.

Last March Harnett hired a new creative director after a prolonged search. Anthony Granleese, 35, had recently immigrated from England, where he had acquired extensive experience and impressive credentials with several large multinational agencies. He had come to Canada to be nearer his two children. His ex-wife had remarried and moved to Toronto.

Granleese's first few months on the job were a crowning success. Not only did he produce brilliant campaigns for existing clients, but his imaginative concepts and passionate presentations helped Harnett Advertising win new business. In late summer, however, his health seemed to deteriorate dramatically. He was losing weight and his energy level was low. A serious bout of flu kept him off work for several weeks. Not long after his return to work, Granleese was absent again. When questioned about his health, Granleese told Harnett not to worry.

Granleese appeared to bounce back in the fall and scored a major triumph by masterminding the pitch that brought in a $1.5 million retail food account. During the victory party, Harnett overheard a conversation that troubled him deeply. A member of Granleese's creative team was gossiping to a secretary, saying that he thought Granleese was gay and had AIDS.

From that point on, Harnett could not get the idea out of his mind that Granleese had AIDS. He telephoned one of Granleese's former employers. The employer confided that rumour had it Granleese's wife had divorced him because he was bisexual.

The prospect that Granleese had AIDS disturbed Harnett in several ways. He was worried for himself. He also worried about the effect it could have on his employees and clients if his suspicions proved true and the information became public. Harnett wondered if someone with such a debilitating and apparently terminal disease could function effectively in the high-pressure advertising world.

A few weeks later, Harnett confronted Granleese in private. Breaking down in tears, Granleese admitted that he did have AIDS, but that he was undergoing various treatments and was determined to fight and defeat the virus. He emphasized that he was healthy and able to perform his duties and that he was no danger to anyone and would fight to keep his job. "What are you going to do?" Granleese asked. Harnett said he needed time to think and would meet with him again in a few days. In his mind, however, he knew what he was going to say. He felt it was impossible for Granleese to continue to work for the company and decided to ask for his resignation.

Source: Paul McLaughlin, "AIDS in the Office," Casebook #27, *Canadian Business*, March 1988, pp. 139, 140, 142. Paul McLaughlin is a Toronto writer and broadcaster.

Questions:

1. What are some potential problems connected with Harnett's decision at the end? Explain.
2. What are some of the questions Harnett should have considered before deciding to force Granleese's resignation? Discuss.
3. Why should the case outlined above be of concern to managers in general? Explain.

Chapter 3

Forms of Business Ownership

Learning Goals

"It has been difficult not to be impressed by the fact that the corporate form of business not only gives freedom from legal liability, but also facilitates the evasion of moral responsibility for inequitable and uneconomic practices."
—*Canadian Royal Commission on Price Spreads, Report, 1934.*

1. To identify and explain the three basic forms of business ownership

2. To outline the advantages and disadvantages of sole proprietorships

3. To compare the advantages and disadvantages of partnerships

4. To outline the advantages and disadvantages of corporations

5. To differentiate between general partnerships and limited partnerships

6. To discuss how a corporation is organized and operated

7. To explain the differences among private ownership, public ownership, and collective ownership (cooperatives)

Camille Dagenais—*The Stuff that Dreams Are Made Of*

When a small boy dreams of building dams and bridges, you'd expect him to become an engineer some day. What you might not expect is that he would also engineer the growth of a small consulting partnership into an international, employee-owned corporation ranked in the *Financial Post 500*.

That is exactly what became of the SNC Group's Camille Dagenais.

An engineering graduate from the University of Montreal's Ecole Polytechnique in 1946, Dagenais spent the first seven years after graduation working with Canadian Industries Ltd. and HJ Doran. In 1953, a consulting partnership called Surveyer, Nenniger & Chenevert hired Dagenais to do preliminary studies in Northern Quebec for the Daniel Johnson Dam. In 1959, he was made a partner, and in 1965, chairman of the board and general manager. In 1966, the partnership was incorporated with Dagenais as president.

On a fishing trip that year, Dagenais sketched the outline of a five-year company plan on a lunch bag; that plan included turning SNC into an employee-owned company. Believing that "knowledge is the ultimate world currency," Dagenais also planned on expanding geographically.

Today, SNC is one of four leading international engineering companies. The company has completed projects in 80 countries, and it takes roughly 50% of its consulting fees from outside of Canada.

Working in developing countries means financing has to be part of any proposal. In addition, SNC offers a complete package of diversified services—everything from design to project management. "Engineering has become 10 percent engineering and 90 percent other things," says Dagenais, and with that in mind, SNC has put a lot of effort and money into

helping technical employees develop management skills.

In spite of the many professional and business distinctions which had been conferred on him throughout the years—he has also been made an officer of the Order of Canada— Dagenais maintains that one of the greatest rewards has been proving Canadian engineers stand among the best in the world. Canadian engineers are better known than any other kind of Canadian, he says. "We are the diplomats and salesmen for this country."

Source: Janet Crocker, "The Stuff That Dreams are Made of," *The Financial Post*, March 21, 1988, p. 46.

When Joseph of Nazareth set up business as a carpenter he was what we would now call a sole proprietor. He would have owned his own tools, run his own workshop, kept all the profits from his business and been responsible for any losses. Many businesspeople in Canada today still do their business in this way. Most, however, find it is more practical to incorporate their businesses.

Business corporations come in many sizes, from the one-person music copying outfit to Canadian Pacific or General Motors of Canada. Their shares may be owned by a single person or family or by tens of thousands of people across the country or elsewhere in the world. They may be crown corporations, owned by the government. Nonprofit organizations, too, often find that incorporation is the most practical way of conducting their affairs.

Of course, some businesses, usually very small ones, are still run as sole proprietorships. Others are partnerships. Some people find it most convenient to come together to operate at least part of their businesses, or to provide mutually desired services in cooperatives.

Forms of Private Ownership

Each of the three forms of purely private ownership—sole proprietor-

Table 3-1
Advantages and Disadvantages of Each Form of Private Ownership

Form of Ownership	Advantages	Disadvantages
Sole Proprietorship	1. Retention of all profits 2. Ease of formation and dissolution 3. Ownership flexibility	1. Unlimited financial liability 2. Financing limitations 3. Management deficiencies 4. Lack of continuity
Partnership	1. Ease of formation 2. Complementary management skills 3. Expanded financial capacity	1. Unlimited financial liability 2. Interpersonal conflicts 3. Lack of continuity 4. Complex dissolution
Corporation	1. Limited financial liability 2. Specialized management skills 3. Expanded financial capacity 4. Economies of larger-scale operation 5. Ease transferability of ownership 6. Frequent tax advantages	1. Difficult and costly ownership form to establish and dissolve 2. Legal restrictions 3. Alienation of some employees 4. Lack of secrecy of operations

ship, partnership, and corporation—has its own unique advantages and disadvantages. A summary of these features appears in Table 3-1.

Sole Proprietorships

sole proprietorship
Ownership (and usually operation) of an organization by a single individual.

Sole proprietorship is the original form of business ownership. It is also the simplest, because there is no legal distinction between the sole proprietor as an individual and as a business owner. A **sole proprietorship** is an organization owned and usually operated by a single individual. Its assets, earnings, and debts are those of the owner. Today, sole proprietorships are used mostly by individuals offering freelance services.

Advantages of sole proprietorships. Sole proprietorships offer advantages not found in other forms of business ownership, such as retention of all profits, ease of formation and dissolution, and ownership flexibility. All profits—as well as losses—of a sole proprietorship belong to the owner (except, of course, that part going to the government for personal income taxes). If the business is very profitable, this can be an important advantage. Retention of all profits (and responsibility for all losses) provides sole proprietors with the incentive to operate the business as efficiently as possible.

A minimum of legal requirements makes it easy to go into (and out of) business. Usually the only legal requirements for starting a sole proprietorship are registering the business name (this guarantees that two firms do not use the same name) and taking out any necessary licenses (restaurants, motels, barbershops, retail stores, and many repair shops require certain kinds of licenses).

The fact that it is easy to discontinue a business set up as a sole proprietorship is an attractive feature for certain types of enterprises. This is particularly true for businesses that are set up for a limited time period and are involved in a minimum of transactions—for example, the business created by an individual to organize a rock concert at a local sports arena.

A sole proprietorship is a business owned and operated by a single individual.

Flexibility is another advantage of sole proprietorships. The owner has no one to consult about management decisions. He or she can take prompt action when needed and can preserve trade secrets where appropriate. Such flexibility can also contribute to the proprietor's personal satisfaction as exemplified by the common saying, "I like being my own boss." See Focus 3–1 for a profile of Chong-su Lee, an entrepreneur with a difference.

Finally, the sole proprietor pays taxes as a private individual, making it simpler than corporate accounting.

Disadvantages of sole proprietorships. Disadvantages associated with sole proprietorships include unlimited financial liability, limitations on financing, management deficiencies, and lack of continuity.

Because there is no legal distinction between the business and its owner, the sole proprietor is financially liable for all debts of the business. If the firm's assets cannot cover its debts, the owner is required to pay them with personal funds. A sole proprietor may even be forced to sell personal property—home, furniture, and automobile—to pay off business debts. The unlimited liability of a sole proprietorship can bring financial ruin to an owner if the business fails.

The financial resources of a sole proprietorship are limited to the owner's personal funds and money that can be borrowed. Sole proprietors usually do not have easy access to large amounts of capital, because they are typically small businesspeople with limited personal wealth. Banks and other financial institutions are often reluctant to risk giving loans to such small organizations. Financing limitations can sometimes retard the expansion of the sole proprietor's business.

Many sole proprietors eventually incorporate their business because of tax considerations. All the profits of a sole proprietorship are taxed as personal income. A small corporation can pay its chief executive officer (and owner) what he or she requires in personal income, and any further funds can be retained with the business where they may attract a lower rate of taxation. Revenue Canada rarely allows a sole proprietor to pay a spouse a salary, meaning that even though both may work, all the income must be declared by the proprietor. (An exception has recently been made for farming couples.) A corporation may employ and pay whom it wishes.

The manager of the sole proprietorship is usually the owner. This person has to be able to handle a wide range of managerial and operative activities. As the firm grows, the owner may be unable to handle all duties with equal effectiveness and may also be unable to attract managerial personnel. Sole proprietorships typically offer little hope of promotion (except for the owner's offspring), fewer fringe benefits than can be found in other organizations, and less employment security. But they do offer employees an excellent chance to learn about a particular type of enterprise.

Finally, sole proprietorships lack long-term continuity. Death, bankruptcy, retirement, or change in personal interests can terminate a business organized as a sole proprietorship.

Focus 3-1

Chong-su Lee—The King of Rock 'n' Roll

The strangest storefront along Toronto's Bloor Street belongs to a noisy rock club called Lee's Palace. Its mural of weird cartoon characters leaves visitors gaping. Just as remarkable is the entrepreneur inside. Three years ago, Chong-su Lee, 53, an immigrant from South Korea, knew nothing about rock music or the entertainment business. Ignorance did not deter him. Today he has managed to transform the site of several failed nightspots into one of the most successful rock clubs in Toronto.

Like other successful entrepreneurs, Lee knows how to exploit his strengths and how to compensate for his weaknesses. One of his strengths was the confidence he was able to inspire in Hanil Bank Canada, which lent him $600,000 of the $680,000 it cost him to buy the building in 1985. The Korean-owned bank was willing to gamble that a Korean-born businessman would succeed in a business where the failure rate is notorious.

Besides the required financing, Lee had the construction skills to renovate the building cheaply. The variety store he'd owned previously had ''taught him how to handle money.'' But he still knew nothing about nightclubs. He started by studying the competition. He decided there was a market for a big club offering an informal atmosphere, the city's best bands and a sunken dance floor allowing a good view of the stage. Lee compensated for his lack of rock expertise by hiring a student as his entertainment manager. Buoyed by the success of his first club, Lee has spent $1.1 million for another building he hopes to open as a neighbourhood bar.

One of the hazards of his line of work, says Lee, is that ''there are a lot of big mouths in the entertainment business.'' He is frequently approached by self-proclaimed experts who want to book his entertainment, manage his business and ''keep my profits.'' But Lee is having none of that. ''I learn something every day and use what I learn,'' he says. ''I stay in control.''

Source: Daniel Stoffman, ''The King of Rock 'n' Roll,'' *The Globe and Mail*, *Report on Business Magazine*, October 1988, p. 65.

A local Toronto band performs at Lee's Palace.

partnership
An association of two or more persons who operate a business as co-owners by voluntary legal agreement.

general partnership
A partnership in which all partners carry on the business as co-owners and are liable for the business's debts.

limited partnership
A partnership composed of one or more general partners and one or more limited partners (those whose liability is limited to the amount of capital contributed to the partnership).

joint venture
A partnership in which two or more people form a temporary business for a specific undertaking.

Partnerships

Partnerships are another form of private business ownership. As defined by the Partnerships Act, they are associations of two or more persons who operate a business as co-owners by voluntary legal agreement. Partnership has been a traditional form of ownership for professional service organizations of such people as doctors, lawyers, and dentists.

General partnerships are those in which all partners carry on the business as co-owners and all are liable for the business's debts. **Limited partnerships** are composed of one or more general partners and one or more limited partners. A limited partner is one whose liability is limited to the amount of capital contributed to the partnership as long as the limited partner takes no active role in the management of the partnership.

Joint ventures, another type of partnership, occur when two or more people form a temporary business for a specific undertaking—for example, a group of investors who import a shipment of high-quality wine from France and then resell it to restaurateurs in Canada. Joint ventures are often used in real estate investments. Focus 3–2 highlights some of the problems confronting Canadian companies involved in joint ventures in the Soviet Union.

A partnership is an association of two or more people who operate a business as co-owners by voluntary legal agreement.

Advantages of partnerships. Partnerships offer the advantages of ease of formation, complementary management skills, and expanded financial capability. It is relatively easy to establish a partnership. As with sole proprietorships, the legal requirements usually involve registering the business name and taking out needed licenses. Limited partners must also comply with provincial legislation based on the Partnerships Registration Act.

It is usually wise to establish written articles of partnership specifying the details of the partners' agreement. This helps clarify the relationship within the firm and protects the original agreement upon which the partnership is based.

A common reason for setting up a partnership is the availability of complementary managerial skills. If the people involved were to operate as sole proprietors, their firms might lack some managerial skills, but by combining into a partnership, each person can offer his or her unique managerial ability. For example, a general partnership might be formed by an engineer, an accountant, and a marketer who plan to produce and sell a particular product or service. If additional managerial talent is needed in the business, it may be easier to attract people as partners than as employees.

Partnerships offer expanded financial capability through money invested by each of the partners. They also usually have greater access to borrow funds than do sole proprietorships. Because the individual partners are subject to unlimited financial liability, financial institutions are often willing to advance loans to partnerships. Involvement of additional owners may also mean that additional sources of loans become available.

An added advantage is that employees of the firm who do well may be offered partnership interests. This is the practice in law and chartered accountancy firms. The possibility of becoming a partner in the business serves as an incentive.

Disadvantages of partnerships. Like other forms of business ownership, partnerships have some disadvantages. They include unlimited financial liability, conflicts between partners, lack of continuity, and complexity of dissolution. Each partner is responsible for the debts of the firm, and each is legally liable for the actions of the others. This holds true not only for debts in the name of the partnership but also for lawsuits resulting from any partner's malpractice. As with sole proprietors, partners are required to pay the total debts of a partnership from private sources if necessary. In other words, if the debts of a partnership exceed its assets, then creditors will turn to the personal wealth of the partners. If only one general partner has any personal wealth, that person may be required to pay *all* the debts of the partnership. Limited partners lose only the amount of capital they invested in the firm.

Conflicts between partners may also plague partnerships. All partnerships, from barbershops to rock groups, face the problem of personal and business disagreements among the participants. If these conflicts cannot be resolved, it is sometimes best to dissolve the partnership because continuation could adversely affect the business.

Continuity of a partnership may be disrupted when a partner is no longer able (or willing) to continue in the business. Then the partnership agreement is terminated, and a final settlement is made.

It is not as easy to dissolve a partnership as it is to dissolve a sole proprietorship. Instead of simply withdrawing the investment in the business, the partner who wants to leave must find someone (perhaps an existing partner or perhaps an outsider who is acceptable to the remaining partners) to buy his or her interest in the firm. Sometimes it is very difficult to transfer an investment in a partnership to another party.

Focus 3-2

Joint Ventures—Pitchmen in Russia

After almost eighteen months of negotiations, officials from Magna International Inc.—the Ontario auto-parts manufacturing giant—and the Soviet automobile industry ministry finally signed a $25-million joint manufacturing agreement. The Soviets, who are desperate for so-called hard Western currency to use alongside the country's nonconvertible rubles, welcome Magna's $5-million investment in the new deal. That represents the largest publicly announced stake invested by a Canadian company since the Soviets began permitting joint ventures in 1987.

Magna, which is contributing 20 percent of financing, will hold a 25 percent ownership in the project and will take its profit in the form of Soviet-made machinery. The venture involves the construction and operation of a factory in the Ukraine that will build moulds for the manufacture of Soviet automobile parts. As part of the exchange, 23 Soviet factory employees will go to Toronto to be trained in Magna management methods. The company operates without unions at more than 85 locations and rewards all workers through profit-sharing. When the plant opens in 1989, Soviet workers, like their Magna counterparts in Canada, will share in 10 percent of any profits the factory makes.

Despite such economic reforms, large stumbling blocks remain in the path toward such cooperation.

Although close to 100 Western firms have signed protocols of intention to engage in joint ventures with the Soviets, less than half of those ventures are now in operation. Many potential investors are wary of Soviet manufacturers' traditional problems with ensuring adequate supply and quality control. As well, business operations are often complicated by the Soviet Union's lack of basic office equipment. Many offices do not have switchboards, which means that unattended telephones can ring unanswered for long periods, and some Western observers estimate that fewer than 1,000 Soviets own personal computers. Photocopying and telefax machines are not in wide use, and most long-distance calls to Western countries must be booked hours in advance.

Business executives also complain that the country's joint venture law, which gives the Soviets a minimum of 51 percent control and the right to appoint the managing director of jointly-controlled companies, is one-sided and needlessly complex. Many investors balk because of the difficulty in taking profits made in rubles out of the country. "You can do tremendously well here if you know what you are doing," declared Emanuel Vorona, the Moscow-based vice-president of The Seabeco Group Corp., a Toronto-based international group of companies offering consulting and business development services in the Soviet Union. But, added Vorona, "if you do not, you can go crazy."

Source: Wilson Smith, "Pitchmen in Russia," *Maclean's*, July 25, 1988, p. 24. Reprinted by permission.

Corporations

corporation
An association of persons created by statute as a legal entity with authority to act and to have liability separate and apart from its owners.

A **corporation** is a *person* in the eyes of the law, that is, it is a *legal person.* To understand the nature of a corporation we must first comprehend the idea of legal person. A legal person is an entity recognized by the legal system as having rights and duties under that system.[1] Because corporations are legal persons apart from their owners, the liability of each owner is limited to the amount that owner invests.

Corporate charters are granted through federal and provincial legislation. Corporate ownership is represented by shares of stock in the firm. Types of stock and their issuance are discussed later in the chapter. Anyone who holds one or more shares of a corporation's stock is considered a part owner of the business. Shares of many corporations, large and small, can usually be bought and sold readily on the open market, such as the Stock Exchanges in Montreal, Toronto, and Vancouver.

Advantages of corporations. Corporate ownership offers considerable advantages, including limited financial liability, specialized management skills, expanded financial capability, and economies of larger-scale operation.

Because corporations are considered separate legal entities, the shareholders (owners) have limited financial liability. If the firm fails, they can lose only the amount of their investments. Personal funds of owners cannot be touched by creditors of the corporation. The limited liability of corporate ownership is clearly designated in the names used by firms throughout the world. Corporate enterprises in Canada and the United Kingdom usually use "Limited" or "Ltd." at the end of their names (Limitée or Ltée in French). In Australia, limited liability is shown by "Proprietary Limited" or "Pty. Ltd." This limited liability is the most significant advantage of corporate ownership over other forms of ownership.

The managerial skills of sole proprietorships and partnerships are usually confined to the abilities of the owners. Corporations can more easily obtain specialized managerial skills, because they offer longer-term career opportunities for qualified people. Employees may be able to concentrate their efforts in some specialized activity or functional area, because corporations are often larger than partnerships or sole proprietorships.

Expanded financial capability is usually another advantage of corporate ownership. This may allow the corporation to grow and become more efficient than it would if the business were set up as a sole proprietorship or partnership. Because corporate ownership is divided into many small units (shares), it is usually easier for a firm to attract capital. People with both large and relatively small resources can invest their savings in corporations by buying shares of stock. Corporate size and stability also make it easier for corporations to borrow additional funds. Large, financially strong corporations can often borrow money at lower rates than can smaller businesses. Of course, as we have seen, not all corporations are large; many small firms are also set up in the corporate form.

The larger-scale operation permitted by corporate ownership has several advantages. Employees can specialize in the work activities they perform best. Many projects can be internally financed by transferring money from one part of the corporation to another. Longer manufacturing runs usually mean more efficient production and lower prices, thus attracting more customers. The largest industrial corporations are listed in Table 3-2.

While corporate size may be an advantage from a business viewpoint, some economists, lawyers, political figures, and business executives have begun to question whether there should be limits on corporate size to protect the interests of society.

Disadvantages of corporations. Some disadvantages are also inherent in corporate ownership. Corporations are the most difficult and costly ownership form to establish; they often face a multitude of legal restrictions, and their impersonality can alienate some employees.

Table 3–2   **The 50 Largest Canadian Corporations Ranked by Sales and Earnings, 1988**

Companies	Rank by Sales	Sales $000	Rank by Earnings	Net Earnings
General Motors of Canada	1	19,310,538	11	359,373
Ford Motor of Canada	2	15,943,000	18	269,800
BCE	3	15,253,000	2	887,000
Canadian Pacific	4	12,016,300	4	774,500
George Weston	5	10,831,200	37	137,400
Alcan Aluminium	6	10,617,743	1	1,145,968
Campeau	7	10,600,964	569	(41,582)
Noranda	8	8,858,000	6	603,000
Brascan	9	8,813,000	19	262,800
Chrysler Canada	10	8,667,900	38	127,200
Loblaw	11	8,307,600	108	40,800
Provigo	12	7,378,500	78	60,200
Imperial Oil	13	7,105,000	7	501,000
Northern Telecom	14	6,656,092	25	225,501
Seagram	15	6,223,025	5	725,566
Imasco	16	6,000,554	16	314,310
John Labatt	17	5,107,034	36	140,579
Shell Canada	18	5,060,000	8	427,000
Hudson's Bay	19	4,671,740	89	49,172
International Thomson	20	4,609,720	17	281,876
Steinberg	21	4,584,685	559	(12,912)
Sears Canada	22	4,327,200	54	95,700
Oshawa Group	23	4,274,535	82	56,870
Inco	24	4,016,493	3	850,311
Nova Corp. of Alberta	25	3,941,000	9	424,000

dividend
Payment from earnings of a corporation to its shareholders.

Each province has different incorporation laws, some of which are quite technical and complex. Establishing a corporation can require the services of a lawyer, which means legal fees. Provinces also charge incorporation fees that add to the cost of setting up this type of business.

As separate legal entities, corporations are subject to federal and provincial income taxes. Corporate earnings are taxed, and any **dividends**—payments from earnings—to shareholders are also taxed on an individual basis. From the viewpoints of shareholders who receive dividends, this is effectively double taxation of corporate earnings. By contrast, the earnings of sole proprietorships and partnerships are taxed only once, because they are treated as personal income. As corporations can deduct numerous expense items that are not available to individuals, however, and as the rate of taxation on retained earnings above a certain amount is lower than it would be if those earnings were taxed as personal income, many small

Companies	Rank by Sales	Sales $000	Rank by Earnings	Net Earnings
IBM Canada	26	3,693,000	21	260,000
Air Canada	27	3,426,000	51	99,000
Abitibi-Price	28	3,304,500	30	188,200
MacMillan Bloedel	29	3,273,500	14	329,800
TransCanada PipeLines	30	3,268,700	554	(8,600)
Canada Packers	31	3,219,449	117	37,215
Moore	32	3,131,433	24	228,942
Mitsui (Canada)	33	3,127,894	401	2,853
Canadian Pacific Forest Products	34	3,005,900	15	323,400
Dofasco	35	2,982,400	26	222,000
Stelco	36	2,711,491	52	96,771
Varity	37	2,703,155	75	62,936
Domtar	38	2,703,000	43	112,000
Texaco Canada	39	2,662,000	13	333,000
Canadian Tire	40	2,640,709	39	124,873
Molson	41	2,427,574	63	78,685
Ensite	42	2,427,111	33	175,390
Core-Mark International	43	2,391,165	265	10,682
Consolidated-Bathurst	44	2,372,083	23	239,630
Total Petroleum (North America)	45	2,256,904	57	89,546
Ivaco	46	2,238,000	99	43,800
Metro-Richelieu	47	2,200,252	239	13,045
PWA	48	2,175,743	139	30,322
F.W. Woolworth	49	2,146,159	93	48,202
Falconbridge	50	2,123,837	12	341,103

businesspeople see tax advantages in incorporation.

Corporate ownership may involve a multitude of legal requirements. Corporate charters may restrict the type of business activity in which the corporation can engage. Corporations must also file various reports about their operations. The number of laws and regulations affecting corporations has increased dramatically in recent years. Since publicly owned corporations are legally required to supply shareholders with financial statements, it is difficult to keep this information confidential—from competitors, for example.

Big corporations, like other large organizations, sometimes suffer from the impersonality of management. Employees become alienated because they do not feel any close ties with the corporation or its management. By being limited to doing one of many specialized jobs within a corporation, employees often do not develop a sense of identity with the firm. Some managers lack the initiative and sense of self-achievement found in sole proprietorships and partnerships. Employee morale, productivity, volume, and profitability can all be affected if steps are not taken to reduce the problem.

Current Ownership Structure of Canadian Business

Figure 3-1 presents the actual ownership structure of Canadian business in the manufacturing sector. Corporations are far more common than the other forms of businesses, about 89 percent of the total. Because incorporation allows owners to divorce their personal financial status from that of the company, an advantage for tax purposes or in case of bankruptcy, most sole proprietorships and partnerships incorporate once they reach a certain size. Your corner grocer has probably registered the company as a corporation. Partnerships, the smallest segment, are used by only three percent of businesses.

Figure 3-1
Forms of Ownership of Registered Canadian Businesses in the Manufacturing Sector

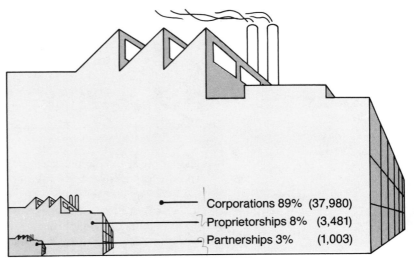

Corporations 89% (37,980)
Proprietorships 8% (3,481)
Partnerships 3% (1,003)

Source Statistics Canada 1982.

Organizing and Operating a Corporation

Suppose you decide to start a business and you believe that the corporation is the best form of ownership for your enterprise. How should you go about setting up this corporation?

Your first step should be to consult a lawyer. While it may be possible to incorporate the business by yourself, most people hire a lawyer so they can be assured that all necessary requirements are met.

Your second step should be to choose whether to incorporate federally or provincially. If you intend to operate your business in several provinces rather than just one, you should choose to incorporate federally. Regulations, incorporation costs and other fees, taxes and ownership rights vary widely among the ten provinces. If you intend to operate primarily within the province of Alberta, for example, you would probably incorporate in that province, but if your principal business will be in Hamilton, Ontario, you would probably become an Ontario corporation.

Incorporating the Business

Most provinces designate a certain official or agency to administer corporations. Blank articles of incorporation, corporation charters, or incorporation papers can be obtained from this official or agency. These forms must be filed with the appropriate provincial agency. This process must also be completed if the business is being incorporated federally.

Corporation charters of the various provinces usually include similar information. Saskatchewan articles of incorporation show the corporate name, corporate purposes, authorized capital stock, registered office and agent, and name of the incorporator.

Shareholders

shareholders
The people who acquire the shares (and therefore are the owners) of a corporation.

Shareholders are those people who acquire the shares of the corporation; they are its owners. Some corporations, such as family businesses like the T. Eaton Company, are owned by relatively few shareholders. In these firms—known as **closely held corporations**—the shareholders also control and manage the corporation's activities. But in larger corporations—sometimes described as **open corporations**—the ownership is widely diversified. Bell Canada, for example, has 675,000 shareholders. These people obviously have little individual control over the giant corporation. But there is a ready market for their shares if they decide to sell. Adequate markets are available for the stock of large corporations, so the individual shareholder can sell the stock more easily than if the shares held were in a small firm with no public market for its stock.

closely held corporation
A corporation owned by relatively few shareholders, who control and manage the corporation's activities.

open corporation
A large corporation where ownership is widely diversified.

Corporations usually hold an annual shareholders' meeting during which management presents reports on the firm's activities. If the firm is not a closely held corporation, the information presented at this meeting will become public knowledge. Any decisions requiring shareholder approval are put to a vote at this time. The election of certain directors (discussed in the next section) and the choice of an independent public accountant are two matters that must be voted on at nearly all shareholder meetings.

A major reorganization of the corporation's structure or the type of business it does must also be brought before the shareholders. However, in some cases such a change may also require government approval of one type or another.

Stock is usually classified as common or preferred. Owners of **preferred shares** have the first claim to the corporation's assets after all debts have been paid, but they usually do not have voting rights at the shareholder meetings. Owners of **common shares** have only a residual claim (after everyone else has been paid) to the firm's assets, but they do have voting rights in the corporate system. When a vote is taken, each common share is worth one vote; thus, a person with 225 shares has 225 votes. If people cannot attend the shareholder meetings, they can give their **proxy** (authorization to vote the shares as the owner has instructed) to someone who will attend.

Small shareholders generally have little influence on corporate management. A holder of 200,000 shares has 200,000 votes for each director, while a holder of 50 shares has only 50 votes for each director. As a result, the issue of cumulative voting has come before many shareholder meetings. **Cumulative voting** allows smaller shareholders to have a greater influence on the selection of directors by enabling them to combine their votes. If, say, three directorial positions are to be filled, cumulative voting allows the holder of 50 shares to cast 150 votes (50×3) for one person rather than 50 votes apiece for all three. The shareholder could, of course, allocate the votes any way desired.

Issues of corporate social responsibility have also come before recent shareholder meetings. Many religious organizations, labour unions, and college and university trust funds invest in common stock. The trustees of these organizations have sometimes used their voting power to raise questions about a corporation's social performance.

preferred shares
Shares whose owners have the first claim to the corporation's assets after all debts have been paid but who usually don't have voting rights at shareholders' meetings.

common shares
Shares whose owners have only a residual claim (after creditors and preferred shareholders have been paid) to the firm's assets, but who have voting rights in the corporation.

proxy
Authorization by shareholders for someone else to vote their shares, as instructed, at shareholders' meetings.

cumulative voting
The practice of enabling shareholders to combine their votes in selecting the board of directors.

Board of Directors

board of directors
The governing authority of a corporation (most provinces require at least one annual meeting of the board) elected by the shareholders.

The shareholders elect a **board of directors**, which becomes the governing authority for the corporation. These directors are not necessarily shareholders. The board elects its own officers—usually a chairperson, a vice-chairperson, and a secretary. Most provinces require a minimum of three directors and at least one annual meeting of the board. Most corporations, other than small or closely held ones, have large boards of directors that meet at least quarterly. Public corporations may have up to 20 directors.

The board of directors must authorize major transactions involving the corporation and must set overall corporate policy. It is concerned with changes in areas such as the firm's shares, financing arrangements, dividends, and major shifts in corporate holdings. But its most important role is that of hiring the corporation's top management. Even the company president is an employee of the board. Although the board hires the top executive officers, it usually leaves the selection of other managers to those executives.

In some corporations (particularly smaller ones) the board of directors plays an active role in the management of the organization, but in most corporations it acts more as a review panel for management decisions. Most boards are composed of both corporation executives and **outside directors** (people not employed by the organization). Sometimes the corporation president is also the chairperson of the board.

outside director
A member of the board of directors of a corporation who is not employed by the organization.

Top Management

Top management people, including the president and most vice-presidents, are responsible for the actual operation of the corporation, subject to board approval. They make most of the major corporate decisions and delegate other tasks to subordinate managers. They are responsible to the board of directors, and, indeed, they often sit on the board themselves. Provincial and federal legislation usually defines the duties of such corporate officers as president, secretary, and treasurer, but other executive posts are created by the board. Refer to Focus 3-3 for a list of characteristics common to the "average" CEO.

Subsidiary Organizations

subsidiary
A corporation with all or a majority of its shares owned by another corporation. Management is appointed by the chief executive of the parent company subject to the approval of the parent's board of directors.

parent company
A corporation that owns all or a majority of another corporation's shares (called a subsidiary).

Many corporations own other organizations called **subsidiaries**. Simpsons is a subsidiary of the Hudson's Bay Company. Harlequin Enterprises Limited, publishers of paperback romance novels, is a subsidiary of the Torstar Corporation which also publishes the *Toronto Star*.

When all or a majority of a corporation's shares of stock are owned by another corporation, it is a subsidiary of that corporation. The owner is usually called the **parent company**. Typically, the management of the subsidiary is appointed by the chief executive of the parent company, subject to the approval of the parent's board. Many well-known corporations are actually subsidiaries of other corporations. Among the companies listed in Table 3-2, Northern Telecom is a subsidiary of Bell Canada, and Loblaw's of George Weston.

Focus 3-3

What You Should Know About Your Basic CEO

A survey of top executives conducted by *The Financial Post* shows that CEOs work hard, are well paid, and love their jobs. They are conservative in their lifestyle—31 percent drive grey cars, 24 percent blue. And they are conservative in their politics, favouring the Progressive Conservatives over the Liberals by roughly four to one. They are well paid; the majority made over $200,000. Approximately 15 percent are in the half-a-million-plus category.

CEOs don't jump from company to company; the average number of companies worked for is 2.8. A number have been with the same company all their working life, and only a handful have worked for as many as six different firms.

More than half of those answering have at least a Bachelor of Arts degree. One third also have a Master's and nine have doctorates. The majority have a great deal of faith in education, and 78 percent say they would advise someone planning a business career to get an MBA. The remainder say they wouldn't.

One third say they read management books frequently, and almost two-thirds admit to reading them sometimes. A small 5 percent say they never do. For the best book read in the past year, the range is wide—all the way from the Bible to thrillers.

Nearly 80 percent believe competition is stiffer, only a handful feel it has lessened, and 19 percent say it's the same as always. The executives are fairly close on whether corporate concentration is a problem in Canada—45 percent say yes and 55 percent, no. But they aren't nearly as worried about the high degree of foreign ownership—78 percent say they aren't concerned. Just about 68 percent see free trade as an opportunity for their company, 8 percent expect problems from it, and the rest see little effect either way.

About 70 percent of the CEOs are Canadian-born and 55 percent are from a middle-income background. A third are from low-income families and the rest range from an upper-income background to 2 percent who come from wealthy families. The executives are overwhelmingly married, 96 percent, and have an average of three children.

The favourite spectator sports are hockey, baseball, football, golf and tennis—in that order. But rather than sit around, 74 percent of executives exercise regularly. Nearly 22 percent engage in workouts, often combined with some sport. Walking is next in popularity, followed by tennis and squash. Jogging and running are well down the track, as is golf. But golf is not forgotten; about 17 percent list it as their favourite hobby, second to reading.

Sailing, farming, gardening and wood-working also get mentions. One CEO says his hobby is model-ship building, and another opts for stamps. One says it's playing with his grandchildren, and one put down his wife (so to speak).

A few executives say work is their hobby. This is not surprising. These executives believe strongly in what they are doing. They enjoy their work, even love it.

How do you get to be a top executive? Not surprisingly, most of the written comments say the key ingredient was hard work. But it was also vital to have bosses that stimulated you and gave you challenges and responsibilities. And it helped to be lucky.

Source: Paul Rush, ''What You Should Know About Your Basic CEO,'' *The Financial Post 500/Summer 1988*, pp. 58, 59, 60.

Corporate Growth

Corporate growth has become a major economic, political, and social issue in recent years. Successful corporations traditionally have been able to expand through effective business management practices. In some cases, however, they have grown by acquiring other firms. A **merger** occurs when one firm buys the assets and liabilities of another company.

merger
The event that occurs when one firm buys the assets and liabilities of another.

Historically, corporate growth has been seen as desirable, provided it does not restrain competition. But today some people are questioning the need for such growth. Typically, these critics argue that further enlargement will not significantly improve the firm's productivity, and it may reduce competition in the marketplace. Corporate executives usually reply that significant economies are still available if the firm expands. No consensus has emerged on this question, and it is likely to remain a critical public issue in the decade ahead.

A Special Type of Business Ownership: The Crown Corporation

public ownership
The ownership and operation of an organization by a government unit or its agency on behalf of the population served by that unit.

One alternative to private ownership is some form of **public ownership**, where a government owns and operates an organization on behalf of the population it serves. When a corporation is owned by the federal or a provincial government, it is known as a **crown corporation**.

crown corporation
A form of corporation owned by a provincial or federal government to operate services such as broadcasting and electricity, with the intent of protecting and guaranteeing the service.

When is public ownership used? In Canada it is generally reasoned that certain activities are so important to public welfare that they should not be entrusted to private ownership. Roads and municipal water systems are examples. Some nations, including Canada, have used public ownership to foster competition by operating public companies as competitive business enterprises. Canadian National Railways (publicly owned) competes with Canadian Pacific Railway (privately owned) in a wide range of travel activities. In Australia Trans-Australia Airlines (publicly owned) competes with Ansett Airlines of Australia (privately owned). Sometimes public ownership replaces privately owned organizations that fail. The CNR was created from a number of companies in financial trouble. At other times it comes about when private investors are unwilling to make investments because they believe the possibility of failure is too high, or the investment may not provide an adequate return. Petro-Canada Ltd., for example, is a federal crown corporation established in 1975 to search for future oil and gas supplies and assist the federal government in the formulation of a national energy policy. Syncrude Canada Ltd. is a joint venture on the part of the federal government, the Ontario and Alberta governments, and major private oil companies to produce synthetic crude oil from Alberta's tar sands. In both instances the capital required for these undertakings was so large and the return on investment so uncertain that few private investors would be willing to participate.

Table 3-3
The 15 Largest Canadian Crown Corporations Ranked by Assets, 1988

Rank	Crown Corporation	Total Assets $000	Total Revenue $000	Net Earnings $000
1	Bank of Canada	24,319,141	2,109,705	1,937,662
2	Canada Mortgage and Housing Corporation	9,300,000	925,000	50,000
3	Petro-Canada	8,611,000	4,801,000	94,000
4	Canadian National Railway	6,906,035	4,676,194	282,665
5	Export Development	6,522,000	619,000	4,000
6	Farm Credit	4,307,191	384,018	(511,838)
7	Canadian Wheat Board	4,102,531	2,862,936	n.a.
8	Canada Post	2,573,995	3,138,552	(37,763)
9	Federal Business Development Bank	2,294,108	266,848	6,427
10	Atomic Energy of Canada	1,036,264	289,470	10,360
11	Canadian Broadcasting Corporation (CBC)	799,437	325,701	(51,226)
12	Canadian Deposit Insurance	731,946	233,724	90,458
13	Canadian Commercial	606,332	681,601	(1,948)
14	St. Lawrence Seaway Authority	602,956	60,539	(5,488)
15	Royal Canadian Mint	121,369	892,577	8,757

Source: *Canadian Business*, Top 500, June 1989. Reprinted by permission.

Crown corporations are also established to perform special functions for the public. The Bank of Canada is responsible for regulating credit and currency, while the Central Mortgage and Housing Corporation provides financial capital for private housing. In some cases federal or provincial governments may create a crown corporation to take over a private firm that has decided to close its operation, in the event that its closure might harm the region economically.

Crown corporations may also be established in order to assist economic development in particular regions of the country, to undertake basic research, to prevent a Canadian company from being taken over by a foreign firm, to ensure competition, or to provide service that otherwise might not be available.

Since crown corporations are often established for activities too risky for the private investor, they do not always make a profit; indeed, they may not break even. A crown corporation that loses money on its operation relies on the government that owns it to make up the loss. Government assistance often extends to the financing of fixed assets, if the crown corporation cannot raise the money on its own in the private money market. Approximately $2 billion a year is required to support federal crown corporations.[2] See Table 3-3 for a listing of the fifteen largest crown corporations.

Cooperatives

cooperative
An organization whose owners band together to operate collectively all or part of their company or industry.

Another alternative to private ownership is collective ownership of production, storage, transportation, and/or marketing activities. **Cooperatives** are organizations whose owners band together to collectively operate all or part of their industries. They are often created by large numbers of small producers who want to be more competitive in the marketplace. Farmers often use cooperatives to market their products or to buy equipment and supplies as can be seen from the list of the ten largest cooperatives in Canada (excluding financial cooperatives) in Table 3-4. In the US the cooperative Sunkist Growers uses the well-known Sunkist brand to identify its products.

Some cooperatives have become large economic units that exert considerable power. The Mesta was a Spanish sheep-owners' cooperative formed in the 1200s. By the sixteenth century it was the biggest economic organization in Spain, herding three million sheep. Its size allowed it to exert considerable influence on government policy.[3] Credit unions or caisses populaires are financial cooperatives. A credit union is often formed by a union, religious group, or other community organization with common aims to provide deposit and loan facilities for its members. In Canada, this type of cooperative is doing well, especially in Quebec and the West. Assets of credit unions and caisses populaires are so great today that they are capable of competing with the chartered banks across the country. There are also cooperative trust firms and cooperative insurance companies. Most extensive cooperatives are in agriculture (grains, dairy products and livestock), and perform production and buying activities.

Cooperatives can flourish in many areas of business. In Toronto, the Canadian Booksellers Cooperative has been quite successful in competitive bidding situations against the major bookstore chains such as Coles, W.H. Smith and Classic.

Although many cooperatives began as local small organizations, where members exercised control and accumulated profits as a return on their investment, today cooperatives are big business and must deal with the same challenges and constraints as those with whom they compete. They face problems in raising capital and hiring quality managers, and the membership is currently exercising less control over operations.

Table 3-4
The 10 Largest Canadian Cooperatives Ranked by Sales, 1988

Rank	Name	Sales $000
1	Saskatchewan Wheat Pool	1,804,099
2	Federated Co-operatives	1,442,144
3	Coopérative fédérée de Québec	1,268,618
4	Alberta Wheat Pool	926,834
5	United Grain Growers	880,359
6	Agropur, Coopérative agro-alimentaire	795,722
7	United Co-operatives of Ontario	567,643
8	Manitoba Pool Elevators	457,249
9	Calgary Co-operative Association	449,118
10	Co-op Atlantic	356,265

Source: *Canadian Business*, Top 500. Reprinted by permission.

Controversial Issue

Herb Pinder—On the Advantages of Privatization

If fads are temporary and transitory, and trends are enduring and persistent, then by any measure privatization is firmly established as a trend in the 1980s. More likely than not, privatization will remain on the public agenda well into the 1990s.

The airline business is an excellent example of a worldwide trend in an important industry. Whereas historically, airlines were proud pillars of national policy, privatization is now in motion. All British Airways PLC shares have been disposed of by the government. In Europe, Lufthansa, KLM, Finnair, and Air France have been partially sold to the private sector.

In Asia, the airlines of Japan, Singapore and Malaysia have been completely or partially sold to private investors. In Argentina, Mexico, Australia, and New Zealand, governments have or are in the process of reducing their ownership in their national airlines.

In Canada, the Alberta government successfully privatized PWA Corp. in 1983, creating the opportunity for an aggressive management team to expand the airline through acquisition and the purchase of additional modern aircraft. As with Air Canada, privatization opened the capital markets to the airlines—a necessity to compete both at home and abroad in this capital-intensive industry.

The forces that are driving privatization are powerful and worldwide. With the increase in international trade and competition, there is a renewed requirement for productivity and efficiency—skills in which government-owned enterprises have not excelled. Globalization drives entrepreneurialism which begets privatization.

Privatization gives individuals the right to decide whether or not to invest in a particular enterprise, rather than their government making the decision. This movement toward less government, on an individual basis, has also occurred in a business context, and is called deregulation.

With the privatization of numerous enterprises over the past few years, the Canadian government have been able to save taxpayers from picking up the tab for hundreds of millions of dollars to finance the losses of its Crown corporations.

Now, three years after de Havilland was bought from the Canadian government by Seattle-based Boeing, it cannot keep up with its orders from around the world for aircraft made in Canada by Canadian workers. Canadair's Challenger jet is also selling well, and the company—sold to Bombardier Inc. in 1986—is now considering a stretch model commuter plane. A major maintainance contract is expanding the business and creating more employment in Canada.

As these two examples illustrate, the opportunities abound for saving money, improving services, making institutions more responsive, making businesses more competitive, and improving the country. Moreover, these advantages are not limited simply to disposing of losing businesses.

The benefits of privatization at every level of the government can be immense. Many of the essential institutions in Canadian society such as the judicial system, the health care system, education, and municipal services can be a part of the process.

Source: Herb Pinder, ''Opportunity is Ripe to Push for More Gains through Privatization,'' *The Financial Post*, February 6, 1989, p. 16.

Summary of Learning Goals

1. **Identify and explain the three basic forms of business ownership.**
   There are three forms of business ownership. Sole proprietorships are organizations owned and usually operated by a single individual. A partnership is a business operated by two or more people as co-owners. A corporation is a legal entity separate from its owners.

2. **Outline the advantages and disadvantages of sole proprietorships.**
   The advantages of sole proprietorships are retention of all profits, ease of formation and dissolution, and ownership flexibility. Their disadvantages are unlimited financial liability, financing limitations, management deficiencies, and lack of continuity.

3. **Compare the advantages and disadvantages of partnerships.**
   The advantages of partnerships are ease of formation, complementary management skills, and expanded financial capability. The disadvantages are unlimited financial liability, interpersonal conflicts, lack of continuity, and complex dissolution.

4. **Outline the advantages and disadvantages of corporations.**
   The advantages of corporations are limited financial liability, specialized management skills, expanded financial capability, and economies of larger-scale operation. The disadvantages are the difficulty and cost of establishing the company, high taxes, legal restrictions, possible alienation of some employees, and lack of secrecy of operations.

5. **Differentiate between general partnerships and limited partnerships.**
   General partnerships are those in which all partners carry on the business as co-owners and all are liable for the business's debts. Limited partnerships are those composed of one or more general partners and one or more limited partners.

6. **Discuss how a corporation is organized and operated.**
   In organizing a corporation, consideration should be given to hiring a lawyer, selecting the province in which to incorporate, and following the correct legal procedures for incorporating. Registration as a domestic, foreign, or alien corporation is also important. Shareholders own the corporation, the board of directors govern it, and top management is responsible for its actual

operation. Subsidiaries are corporations owned by other (parent) corporations.

7. **Explain the differences among private ownership, public ownership, and collective ownership (cooperatives).**
Private ownership refers to organizations owned by individuals, regardless of whether they are set up as sole proprietorships, partnerships, or corporations. One alternative to private ownership of business organizations is public ownership, where a government unit or its agency owns and operates an organization on behalf of the population served by that unit. In Canada, publicly owned corporations can be crown corporations. Another alternative is the cooperative, where there is collective ownership of production, storage, transportation, and/or marketing activities.

Key Terms

sole proprietorship

partnership

general partnership

limited partnership

joint venture

corporation

dividend

shareholders

closely held corporation

open corporation

preferred shares

common shares

proxy

cumulative voting

board of directors

outside director

subsidiary

parent company

merger

public ownership

crown corporation

cooperative

Discussion Questions and Exercises

1. Discuss the major features of each of the three forms of business ownership.
2. Secure announcements of future stockholder meetings of corporations located in your area. Analyze the types of issues that are scheduled to be debated at these meetings. Can you make any generalizations about them?
3. Why are complementary management skills so important to a successful partnership?

4. Distinguish between a general partner and a limited partner.
5. What is the most commonly used form of business ownership? Why?
6. List the steps in the incorporation process.
7. What are some reasons for establishing a crown corporation?
8. What are some reasons for participating in cooperatives in Canada?
9. Assume that you are involved in establishing the following businesses. What form of business ownership would you employ?
   a) roadside fruit stand (assume you own an orchard)
   b) barbershop
   c) management consulting firm
   d) small foundry
10. Find earlier listings of the largest Canadian industrial corporations and compare Table 3-2 to them. What major changes have taken place over the past ten years or so?

Case 3-1

Parting Ways

For several months, Roger McIntyre and his partner, John Altman, have had trouble with their printing business, Central Decal Ltd. of Calgary. McIntyre thinks the problems are Altman's faults. He has just told Altman that either Altman has to leave the business or he will. Altman, shocked, wants to know why. McIntyre has told him that his handling of the company's finances is completely unsatisfactory and has put Central's future in jeopardy. Now McIntyre is wondering if he was justified in issuing this ultimatum.

Three years ago, McIntyre and another businessman, Bill Merrill, each put up $16,500 to start Central. They also received a $44,000 grant from the federal government after promising to create eleven new jobs. The company makes decals and displays for retailers and trade shows. Its primary markets are Canada and the northern US states, and it has never had any problems generating sales. Its successful production and marketing strategy is to specialize in a few high-volume areas of business.

A little more than a year after the start-up, Merrill left the firm for personal reasons. As a result, McIntyre began looking for someone to join the company to share the managerial responsibilities. Altman, a certified general accountant and management consultant for small business, agreed to join Central as an equal shareholder. He did so on the understanding that he would produce Central's financial statements, conduct its dealings with the bank, and share management duties with McIntyre, who would be primarily responsible for production and marketing.

But it wasn't long before problems developed.

Altman had difficulty delegating authority, which meant that many jobs weren't completed on time. There was also confusion among staff about who they should report to—McIntyre or Altman. It soon became clear that Altman was more interested in production and marketing than in finance and accounting. Cash-flow projections and financial statements were rarely done. Relations with the bank deteriorated. Several cheques were returned because of insufficient funds.

McIntyre believed Altman knew a cash-flow crunch was imminent but had made no plans to cope with it. When the crunch did come, Altman put $55,000 of his own money into the business to resolve the crisis, and after discussions with McIntyre agreed to improve his management of the financial side of business.

However, two months later, Central's finances were as disorganized as ever and McIntyre demanded that Altman either do the job properly or hire someone who could. Another crunch came, and Altman came up with another $55,000 to resolve the problem.

McIntyre now believes that Altman's actions have only hidden the company's real problems. He discovered that Altman hasn't increased Central's line of credit, though sales have tripled. Nor has he pursued further government grants, even though the company has more than fulfilled its job creation obligations. The bank has also sent a report to McIntyre outlining other flaws in Central's finances.

McIntyre feels he has three alternatives. Several individuals have agreed to put up $275,000 in exchange for becoming shareholders. McIntyre could use this money to buy Altman's shares and put the firm on a better financial footing. Secondly, he could sell Altman his shares and leave the company. His third option is to start another company.

Source: Daniel Stoffman, "Parting Ways," *Canadian Business*, September 1987, pp. 157, 159, 161.

Questions:
1. What are the basic problems confronting Central? Explain.
2. What might have been done to avoid the current situation? Explain.
3. What is wrong with McIntyre's solutions? What other alternatives are available to him? Discuss.

Case 3-2

A Whole New Ball Game

Common perceptions of a corporate director's life can be vastly different from what happens in actual reality. Irate shareholders are increasingly vigilant in holding corporate directors personally liable for their decisions on corporate policy and management selection.

"It has not been uncommon," says Andrew Waller of the Wyatt Co., a Toronto firm of consulting actuaries, "for a director and officer liability insurance premium to have increased, for example, by 1,000 percent in the last two years, combined in a ten-fold increase in the deductible and a lowering of the coverage from $50 million to $15 million. Some companies have had difficulty finding insurance coverage at any price."

In Sparling versus Royal Trustco, the director of corporations for the federal Department of Consumer and Corporate Affairs took Royal Trustco and its directors to court, alleging that shareholders were oppressed and unfairly treated in 1980 when the company fought off a takeover bid by Campeau Corp. The courts have already upheld Sparling's right to initiate an action of this type of behalf of shareholders—a significant finding that opens the doors for other groups of disgruntled shareholders to appeal to the federal government to sue on their behalf.

If liability is the concern, just who is the corporate director accountable for? The director is elected by the shareholders to direct the affairs of the company on their behalf. With the qualifications of independence, experience, and business acumen, he or she is responsible for establishing corporate policy and for ensuring appointment of the best possible senior management team. A large corporation in Canada might typically have 10 to 16 board members, of whom only two or three will be full-time employees of the company. The Canadian Business Corporations Act and its provincial equivalents state essentially that a director should act honestly and in good faith with a view to the best interests of the corporation, employing the care, diligence and skill that "a reasonably prudent person" would use in comparable circumstances.

But a series of court decisions and legislative actions over the years have extended the accountability of directors to the point where a director, depending on the circumstances, may now be accountable to employees, creditors, the government, or the general public.

According to Anthony Griffin, a semi-retired professional director who joined his first board in 1954 and has sat on 27 boards since that time, there have been some significant changes in boardroom behaviour over the years: "Appointment to a board of directors used to be viewed almost as an end in itself—a symbol of recognition of a successful and illustrious career. Constructive activity once on the board was almost secondary. An 'Establishment' atmosphere prevailed, and the director was expected to ply his wisdom in full support of management. As directors' performance has come under closer scrutiny from shareholders, the media and the general public, a more professional attitude has begun to emerge."

Source: Robin Cardozo, "A Whole New Ball Game," *The Financial Post Moneywise Magazine*, April 1987, pp. 46, 48.

Questions:
1. What are the responsibilities of a corporation's board of directors?
2. Who are the board of directors accountable for?
3. According to the case, why has a "more professional attitude" emerged among corporate boards of directors? Discuss.

Chapter 4

Small Business/ Entrepreneurship

I am a great believer in luck, and I find the harder I work the more I have of it.
—*Stephen Leacock*

In the long run the pessimist may be proved right, but the optimist has a better time on the trip.
—*Daniel L. Reardon*

Learning Goals

1. To explain the vital role played by small business in the economy

2. To define small business and to identify sectors of the economy in which most small firms are established

3. To define entrepreneurship and its importance in small business

4. To compare the advantages and the disadvantages of small businesses

5. To describe franchising and its advantages and disadvantages

6. To analyze the small business opportunities for women and to understand the special problems faced by these entrepreneurs

7. To describe how the federal and provincial governments support small business

Profile

Andrew Benedek—*Life After the Ivory Tower*

As a tenured academic, Andrew Benedek once enjoyed a lot of security and plenty of time off. As an entrepreneur, he doesn't have very much of either. Yet he has no regrets about the switch he made eight years ago.

Benedek was 37 when he left McMaster University in Hamilton to found Zenon Environmental Inc. in neighbouring Burlington. Zenon makes water purification systems used by the medical, electronics, pharmaceutical and cosmetics industries. As a researcher, Benedek became an expert in reverse osmosis, which purifies water by forcing it through a plastic membrane under pressure. Earlier Canadian researchers had pioneered other water-filtration technologies, only to see those advances commercialized in other countries. "I wanted to prove that it could be done in Canada."

He used his own savings, got backing from family members and mortgaged his house to the hilt. That raised almost $500,000. Later he got additional backing from the Ontario Development Corporation. He was able to attract highly qualified scientists from universities and government departments. Now Zenon trains its own people and has a staff of 100, including 60 engineers and scientists.

In addition to its Canadian head office and manufacturing plant, Zenon has a US sales office and has negotiated joint ventures and sales agreements with companies in Europe and Japan. Sales are approaching $10 million. Benedek says the water market is going to keep growing, and "we have some technologies that are very important to that market."

Canadian sailors will appreciate the technology too. The Navy's new frigates will have Zenon systems to turn salt water into fresh water.

Zenon's success is based on being at the leading edge of an increasingly important

technology. Benedek thinks more Canadian scientists will go into business for themselves in future. For years, they've been inventing products or processes without giving a thought to commercial development. Now, there's a new interest in turning technological advances into business opportunities. "We are definitely in a new entrepreneurial age in Canada," he says.

Source: Daniel Stoffman, "Life After the Ivory Tower," *Report on Business Magazine*, *The Globe and Mail*, October 1988, p. 74.

After his first year at university in 1971, Greig Clark needed a summer job, so he started painting houses. Despite having no experience he earned about $3,000 the first summer. Two years later, he had refined the techniques that formed the College Pro system, that employs about a dozen painters and earns about $11,000.

Following graduation, Greig went to work as a product manager for General Foods for a time. However, he continued testing College Pro franchises on the side, and developed a complete 600-page manual and training system. This system, along with the selection of entrepreneurial college students who work with him, has turned College Pro Painters Limited into a $13 million business. He has a network of 231 Canadian franchises and 85 in the US. The business is generally very profitable for student franchisees as well. For example, College Pro considers any franchisee who fails to earn $7,000–$10,000 for a summer's work "a failure."[1] Clark says, "We've never forgotten what made us great—the entrepreneurial spirit of the student-cum-businessman who wants to run his own firm."[2]

Importance of the Small Business Sector

Greig Clark is typical of many small businesspeople. The successful service provided to many homeowners by a small firm indicates the vital role small business plays in the economy. Canadians increasingly recognize that a strong small business sector is the backbone of the private enterprise system. Small businesses provide much of the competitive zeal that keeps the system effective. And much has been done to encourage the development and continuity of small firms. Anticombines legislation, for example, was designed to maintain the competitive environment and market structure in which small companies thrive. Also, Industry, Trade and Commerce Canada, through its regional offices and the Small Business Secretariat assists smaller firms in many ways. Provincial governments also have programmes to encourage the development of small business.

Small business is a vital segment of the Canadian economy. There are 1.2 million businesses in Canada, 95 percent of which are small businesses with annual sales of less than $2 million. They account for about one-third of total sales in Canada and close to half of total employment.[3] In general, small businesses in Canada are increasing at a faster rate than all other categories of business.[4] Figures in 1988 show that small firms constitute 97 percent of Canadian companies and employ 42 percent of the country's labour force.[5]

These statistics suggest the vital role that small business plays in contemporary business. Aside from the many services they provide to consumers, small businesses also help large businesses function efficiently. Many suppliers to large manufacturers are small firms attempting to offer a product or service better than that of their competitors.

Our private enterprise system started with the small shops and workrooms of pioneer days, and we still depend on such independent entrepreneurs today. They are the very heart of the private enterprise system.

How Do We Define Small Business?

Any definition of a small business is dependent on comparisons with other businesses. Sales, number of employees, assets, net worth, market share, and relationship to competitors have all been used to make the determination. There are probably as many ways to define *small business* as there are people wanting to run one.

There is probably no such thing as a "typical" small business. Probably the most workable concept of such a business is one suggested some years ago. To qualify as a **small business** under this definition, a business must have at least two of the following characteristics: (1) independent management with the managers often owning the firm, (2) the capital contribution coming from a limited number of individuals—perhaps only one, (3) the firm operating in a local area and (4) the firm representing a small part of the overall industry.[6]

small business
A business that is independently owned and operated, is not dominant in its field, and meets a variety of size standards.

Entrepreneurs: The Core of Small Business

To make a small business work requires a great deal of individual initiative, hard work and risk-taking. Most small businesses are started by a special type of person, the entrepreneur. Entrepreneurship begins with the recognition of an opportunity, a demand that needs to be satisfied. The entrepreneur is a person who not only sees the opportunity, but is willing to take the risk and make the effort to make it happen.

Entrepreneurs share certain psychological traits and are motivated by a similar set of values and needs.[7] Entrepreneurs tend to be independent, self-reliant individuals with a high need to achieve. They have a tremendous amount of energy and drive, with a capacity to work long hours. This is important for the success of a small enterprise that generally faces many crises.

Entrepreneurs tend to compete against standards of achievement they set for themselves rather than standards set for them by others. This need for personal achievement tends to be a main motivating force.

They have a high level of self-confidence and believe strongly in themselves and their own abilities to achieve the goals they set. Thus, they are willing to undertake ventures that others might thinks of as risky. However, psychological testing has shown that they are not reckless gamblers. Entrepreneurs tend to be positive, optimistic types who focus their attention on their chances of success rather than the chances of failure.

Entrepreneurs are often more driven by the challenge of building a business than the idea of simply getting in and out in a hurry and making a fast buck. They seem to be primarily interested in the creation of an entity. For some, profits are more a means of keeping score than an end in itself.

Entrepreneurs are the product of their family and environment. Parents and family have set high standards of performance, and served as role models in the creation of the entrepreneur.

These special individuals play a key role in the Canadian economy. They are opportunists who are able to recognize the existence of both a need waiting to be satisfied and a way of satisfying that need. They are thus creators of business enterprise. While it is obvious that entrepreneurship is at the core of small business, it should be also noted that entrepreneurial activity can be valuable in larger corporations as well. Table 4-1 provides a statistical profile of business owners in Canada.

Popular Small Business Ventures

Small businesses are found in nearly every industry in Canada. They often compete against some of the nation's largest organizations as well as against a multitude of other small companies. Retailing and service establishments are the most common small businesses. New-technology companies also often start as small organizations.

Retailing

While general merchandise giants like The Bay, Eaton's, Woolco, and K-mart are the most significant firms in this area of retailing, they are far outnumbered by small, privately owned retail enterprises. Small business, in fact, characterizes the retailing of shoes, jewellery, office supplies and stationery, apparel, flowers, drugs, convenience foods, and thousands of other products. In recent years, small business has provided the vast majority of new jobs.

Service Firms

Service-oriented industries and individuals—such as restaurants, funeral homes, banking establishments, movie theatres, dry cleaners, carpet cleaners, shoe repairers, lawyers, insurance agents, automobile repairers, public accountants, dentists, and doctors—also abound

Convenience stores are often franchise operations.

in our private enterprise economy. There are relatively few national sellers of services, except in the case of insurance. Seven out of ten of the nearly 1.7 million Canadians employed by small businesses are in service industries.[8]

Table 4-1
Statistical Profile of Small Business Owners in Canada

New Job Creation	Percentage
New jobs created 1978-85 by firms employing fewer than five people	59.6
New jobs created by firms employing more than 500 people	6.8

By Age	
Under 25	4.5
25-34	23.7
35-44	31.4
45-54	22.5
55-64	13.8
Over 65	4.2

By Gender	
In 1988:	
Men	76.3
Women	23.7
In 1981:	
Men	78.7
Women	21.3

By Origin	
Canadian-born	80.0
Immigrants	20.0
Business founders in 1987 whose fathers were business owners	35.0

By Education	
Less than secondary school	32.6
Secondary school diploma	10.6
Post-secondary	56.7

How Many People They Employ	
Less than five	77.3
5-19	16.6
20-49	3.8
50-99	1.2
100+	1.2

How They Got Into Business	
Founded	68.6
Bought	25.3
Inherited	5.0

Why They Got Into Business

Wanted a personal sense of accomplishment	81.4
Wanted to be own boss	73.4
Wanted variety and adventure	66.0
Wanted to make better use of training and skills	63.3
Wanted freedom to adopt own approach to work	61.8
Wanted to be challenged by the problems and opportunities of starting own business	60.7
Wanted to be able to develop a product or an idea	57.5
Wanted an opportunity to lead rather than be led	56.3
Wanted to make a direct contribution to the success of a company	55.7
It was a time when it made sense	55.5
Wanted to keep learning	55.5

Source: Daniel Stoffman, "Who are the Entrepreneurs?" *Report on Business Magazine*, the Globe *and Mail*, October 1988, p. 62. Statistical Sources: Statistics Canada, Department of Regional Industrial Expansion, and the Canadian Federation of Independent Business.

High-tech Firms

Many new-technology firms—those striving to produce and market some scientific innovation—typically start as small businesses, and many great inventors and technical geniuses began their businesses in barns, garages, warehouses, and attics. Small business is often the best (or only) option available to a scientist who seeks to make an idea into a commercial reality.

Although most new businesses, including a variety of retail and service enterprises, appear in industries that have limited capital requirements, some technical firms require substantial capital to get off the ground. Initial capital requirements of $1 million or more are not at all uncommon in such industries. The high cost is primarily due to the long time lag between start-up and receipt of sales revenue.

Advantages of a Small Business

Small firms are not simply smaller versions of large corporations. Their legal organizations, market position, staff capability, managerial style and organization, and financial resources generally differ from bigger companies, which gives them some distinct advantages and disadvantages. Small size may provide some unique competitive advantages over larger size, such as innovative behaviour, lower costs, and the filling of isolated market niches.

Innovative Behaviour

Small firms are often the ones to offer innovations, new concepts, and new products in the marketplace. In fact, there is a rapid growth in the formation of small high-technology firms.

Scientific innovations are not the only concepts offered by small business entrepreneurs. Rick Messina of Toronto started a Video on Wheels service to help the handicapped. After a year on the road, the store-in-a-van, which is stocked with feature films in cassette and disk form as well as related equipment, is becoming a familiar feature all over metro Toronto. Messina is franchising his idea, and has over 11 vans and is providing them as a turn-key operation (a completely equipped van ready to operate) for between $55,000 and $75,000.[9]

Lower Costs

Small firms can often provide a product or service cheaper than large firms. They usually have fewer overhead costs—those not directly related to providing the goods and services—than large firms. Thus, they may be able to earn a profit on a price lower than a large company can offer.

Small businesses have leaner organizations with smaller staffs and fewer support personnel. The lower overhead costs resulting from fewer permanent staff people can provide a distinct advantage to small businesses. Small businesses tend to hire outside consultants or specialists, such as lawyers and accountants, only during periods when their assistance is needed. Larger organizations tend to maintain such specialists on their permanent staffs.

Small businesses also often have the services of a great deal of unpaid labour. Entrepreneurs themselves are usually willing to work long hours on their pet projects, and no one pays them for overtime or holidays. And family members contribute a significant amount of unpaid labour as bookkeepers, labourers, receptionists, delivery personnel, and the like.

"I think it's fair to warn you, I'm with small business tax auditing."

Toronto Sun Syndicate

The entrepreneur should consider how taxation will affect a small business.

Filling of Isolated Niches

Big businesses are excluded from some commercial activities because of their size. High overhead costs force them to set minimum targets at which to direct their competitive efforts. Some large publishers, for example, have identified minimum acceptable sales figures that take into account their overhead costs. Editorial and production expenses for a certain type of book may not be justified unless the publisher can sell, say, 5,000 copies. This situation allows substantial opportunities for smaller publishers with lower overhead costs.

In addition, certain types of businesses lend themselves better to smaller firms. Many services illustrate this point. For example, Bon

Santé Catering specializes in preparing gourmet foods for small social gatherings. Finally, organizational factors may dictate that an industry consist essentially of small firms.

Disadvantages of a Small Business

A variety of disadvantages face smaller firms, including poor management, inadequate financing, and government regulation. While these problems often can be overcome, they should be considered by anyone contemplating a small business venture.

Poor Management

It is a simple fact that most people who start small businesses are ill-prepared to function as managers. Successful small businesspeople are almost always good managers, but they are a minority compared to the failures. Thousands of small businesses open every year. Thirty percent fail within the first year, and half within five years. Poor management is to blame for most failures. But that doesn't stop people. Many of those failing the first time around will try again, and again, if necessary. Eventually some will succeed. Figure 4-1 shows the number of births and deaths of small business in some recent years. It can be seen that they were particulary hard-hit in the 1982 recession. The figure also shows that there continue to be many who are optimistic about their chances to succeed. Focus 4-1 discusses the problems of family businesses.

Figure 4-1
Small business births continually outnumber small business deaths

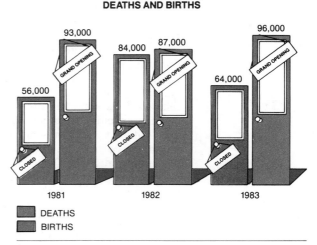

SMALL BUSINESS
DEATHS AND BIRTHS

- DEATHS
- BIRTHS

Source: "More start-ups than closures show small business's resiliency" by Douglas Lajeunesse. *Profit$*, vol. 4, no. 2, Autumn 1984

Family Business—Small but Tough

Pity the people who run family businesses. On top of all the special problems they have to face—and there are many—they have to deal with the fact that their long-term success depends on something that has a very nasty reputation: nepotism. The word itself has a nasty connotation. It's not quite up there in the same league as adultery or loansharking, but it's not far behind. People tend to say it with a bit of a sneer. Yet nepotism is what family business is all about; if you want to pass your business on to your children, you have to practise nepotism.

Practising nepotism diplomatically, finding the fairest way to bring a son or daughter (or an in-law) into the family company, is only one of the challenges that an organization called the Canadian Association of Family Enterprise (CAFE) is trying to meet. David Gallagher is its managing director, and when someone suggests that family businesses are akin to minefields, he agrees. "Family business is the toughest business in the world to run," says Gallagher. "There is no set formula because every family is different. There ain't nobody you can get mad at like your brother," he adds, using a little slang for emphasis.

Established in 1983, CAFE helps family businesses cope with a wide range of problems. It lobbies governments, and its members use it to share information and find solutions to their particular problems, such as the financial complexities involved in passing a business along to the next generation. Similar organizations have existed for years in other countries, but there was none in Canada until recently. CAFE is growing fast. Last year 100 new members joined, bringing the total to 350. Most of them are mid-sized businesses with about 100-plus employees.

You can see just how dangerous running a family business can be when you consider that only about 25 to 30 percent of all family businesses stay within the family to the second generation. And only 10 to 15 percent survive into the third generation. Lawyers and accountants by the score give up on passing along family businesses. It's easier to get rid of them, they say. And even when the businesses are not in transition, there are all sorts of prickly family relationships that can cause problems.

One particularly delicate matter is what many experts refer to as the "old goat" problem—the business boss, usually the founder, who hangs on and on and on and won't pass his authority along to his son or daughter. Or he may step aside and then keep coming back, poking into this or that. "The number of dads who are still running businesses in this country after age 65 is appalling," says Gallagher. Gail Regan (she is with Cara Holdings Ltd.), who is chairman of CAFE's research committee, says little is known about the overall operations of family business in Canada. But they do share the same concerns as family businesses in other countries— there are "old goats" everywhere.

Part of the difficulty, Gallagher points out, arises from the nature of the men (and women) who launch family businesses. They are entrepreneurs, and they're accustomed to doing things themselves—and doing things their own way. The idea of relinquishing power is distasteful, to say the least. Yet that is exactly what they have to do. And if the transition is to be smooth, the entrepreneur has to carry it out over a period of time, beginning early on, when he (or she) is still young and entirely active. In fact, the entrepreneur ought to have the transition of the business as a long-term goal over most of his (or her) business life, says Gallagher and adds, "He has 25 or 30 years to transform himself from star quarterback to coach and trainer."

The problems are infinite, and so are the possible solutions. The solution to the last of these questions, says CAFE's Gallagher, is—again—to plan well ahead, to invest in other assets outside the family business, so the children (or other relatives) who do not share in the business will receive these other assets as compensation.

When a family business comes into the hands of more than one successor, there can be strong rivalries—and sometimes bitter struggles. Gallagher tells of the way three brothers handled things when they inherited the family's service business. Their ages ranged from 35 to 50, and all three wanted to get actively involved in running the business. The oldest brother became the nominal president, and his two brothers took over separate operations of the company. And they hired an executive vice-president to make sure everything went smoothly. "He was a buffer manager," says Gallagher. And things did go smoothly—for a while.

Then, in 1982 when the economy tightened up, the business had to tighten up too, and the three brothers found themselves pushed much closer together. And they realized they weren't going to get along. So they took a bold step: They hired a consultant, a professor who's been teaching at an American university, to come into the Canadian company and decide which one of the three should run it. "They said, 'Test us,'" Gallagher explains, "and they promised they would abide by his decision." And they did. The consultant picked the youngest brother, and he took over. The oldest brother became chairman and kept out of things, and the middle brother left the firm. "It was a great victory for the Victorian ethic of fairness," says Gallagher.

Wall Street Journal reporter Jeffrey Zaslow wrote: "Nepotism seems to be on the rise, propelled by a a tight job market that makes it tougher for sons and daughters to find jobs outside the family business. But its face is changing. A decade ago, nepotists catapulted their children directly from the playroom to the boardroom, causing employee bitterness and other problems." Today, Zaslow reports, "It has become increasingly popular to farm out a fledgling to another company for an apprenticeship of several years so he or she can mature and learn away from the imperious gaze of dad and his employees."

There's another big plus that comes from working outside the family business: It builds confidence in executives who often tend to worry that the only reason they became president of the family company is because they have the same name as their predecessors. "We have members," says Gallagher, "who are 40 or 50 or older who never will have confidence in themselves." Sometimes, he adds, a sort of reverse attitude develops. A son or daughter rises quickly to the top then says, at age 35, "Well, I've done it all—now I'm going to look for another challenge."

In the matter of training, the *Wall Street Journal*'s Zaslow points out, experience outside the family company avoids "the 'intellectual incest' of learning business only from dad." And for a family member, training is specially important because other employees must be assured of the competence of the family member moving into the company.

CAFE holds forums aimed at helping members with the complexities of transition and with other problems—and it does its best to try to get them a better deal from government. The main problem in this area is, of course, taxes. The capital gains tax paid when businesses are passed along within families puts them at a disadvantage, says CAFE's Gallagher. "It represents a substantial tax every 30 years or so," he says. "Service stations, shoe stores, all sorts of family businesses, compete against the big multinationals, and the family businesses have to cough up this money."

CAFE presented a brief to Finance Minister Michael Wilson asking for a couple of pieces of relief: It would like the $200,000 deferral of capital gains tax on death with respect to the family business increased to something in the neighbourhood of $1 million, and it would like to be able to deduct the interest paid on deferred taxes. "We believe," the brief says, "it is reasonable to argue that there should be no interest on these deferred taxes as there is, in fact, no actual realization of gain on death."

There is a feeling among some people who run family businesses that they—both the businesses and the people—have had something of a bum rap. The truth is they do have a very tough time. There are pressures on family members who join the firm. Everyone watches them—and sometimes their own relatives take advantage of them. "A lot of family members figure they have to work twice as hard as anyone else," says Gallagher, "and their salaries are often low."

Though some executives may have qualms about working for family-run companies, Gallagher says they are often better businesses in which to work. Public companies tend to be impersonal. "They'll kick you out without a care in the world," he says. "You're just a cog in the wheel."

"In family businesses," Gallagher adds, "there isn't the pressure that there is in other companies to produce the levels of profit which will keep their directors and shareholders happy." Which is not to say—not for a moment—that family businesses ought to be easygoing when it comes to the bottom line. As one author says, "The purpose of any business is to generate profits for its owners."

Source: Ron Jarry, "The Toughest Business In The World," *Goodlife*, March 1988, pp. 26, 28, 29.

Since *poor management* is a vague term, it is important to look at the types of management shortcomings that characterize small business. Often people who start small firms have little, if any, training or education in running a business. They have an idea for a product or service and assume that they will learn about business matters as they carry on the business. Bankruptcy is often the result. A word of caution is in order: Any budding entrepreneur is well advised to acquire as sound a foundation in basic business principles as possible before initiating any small business venture.

Another cause of failure is that small businesspeople sometimes let their entrepreneurial optimism run wild. Kenneth Eaton, head of Associated Business Consultants, puts it this way:

> An entrepreneur is an optimist by definition, and over-optimism is what does companies in. When things are going well, the average businessman assumes they will continue to go well. When a problem arises, he assumes it will go away quickly by itself. By the time he wakes up to the fact that he really has a problem, it's often too late to do anything about it.[10]

A closely related cause of failure is not doing needed homework before starting the small business. Entrepreneurs may believe that others will see their product or service as unique or better than that of the competition, but basic research is needed before any action is taken on this assumption. Essentially, what the individual must find out is whether a market exists for the proposed product or service. This information can be secured in many ways: through published sources, surveys, in-depth interviews, competitive analyses, observation, or a number of other techniques.

Inadequate Financing

Inadequate financing is generally listed as a leading cause of small business problems. Many small businesses start with inadequate capital and soon run into a shortage of funds. They often lack the resources to carry them over rough spots or to expand if they are successful.

Banks, venture capitalists, and the Federal Business Development Bank (FBDB) are traditional sources of small business funding—after personal or family funding. Banks are usually quite careful about lending money to small businesses because of their high failure rate. Banks and most other small business lenders require detailed information in order to justify such loans.

However, almost every type of new or existing business in Canada that does not have other sources of financing available to it on reasonable terms is eligible for consideration for assistance from the Federal Business Development Bank. Since the government wishes to encourage the development of small businesses, the FBDB is more willing to support risky but promising new ventures.

venture capitalists
Groups of private individuals or business organizations that invest in promising new businesses. Sometimes they lend money, and sometimes they become part owners of the firm.

Venture capitalists are groups of private individuals or business organizations that invest in promising new businesses. Sometimes they lend the business the money; at other times they become part owners of the new or struggling firm. Venture capital has been an important source of funds, particularly for firms offering a creative new concept or product.

Government Regulation

Like most executives, small businesspeople complain bitterly of excessive government regulation and red tape. The cost of doing the paperwork the government requires is quite significant for small firms. Furthermore, the regulation of small companies accounts for a large portion of the government's own paperwork costs. A survey by the Canadian Federation of Independent Business found that one firm in ten identified regulatory paperwork as its most important problem. This subject ranked fourth among all problems encountered by small firms.[11]

Most small businesses are not equipped to handle the paperwork necessitated by government regulation. Larger firms with substantial staff can usually cope with the blizzard of required forms and reports, but for many small business owners, it is often the force that drives them back to salaried positions in larger companies. Many experts within and outside government believe that a major effort must be made to reduce the paperwork load for small businesses.

franchising
A contractual arrangement between a manufacturer or other supplier and a dealer that sets the methods to be used in selling a product.

Franchising

franchisee
The purchaser of a franchise operation; a small businessperson who is allowed to sell a product or service of a supplier, or franchisor, in exchange for some payment–usually a flat fee plus future royalties or commissions.

The **franchising** concept has played a major role in the growth of small business. Many people have become well off as a result of their decision to purchase a franchise. Consider the case of the student franchisees of College Pro Painters. Many earn over $10,000 during the summer months. Success lies, in large measure, in the franchise system that has been developed.

Franchising is a legally a contract between a manufacturer or other supplier and a dealer that sets the methods to be used in marketing a product or service. The dealer, or **franchisee,** is a small businessperson who is allowed to sell a product or service of a supplier, or **franchisor** in exchange for some payment—usually a flat fee plus future royalties or commissions. The franchisor typically provides building plans, site selection research, managerial and accounting procedures, and other services to assist the franchisee. The franchisor also provides name recognition for the small businessperson who becomes the franchisee. This image is created by national or regional advertising campaigns to which the franchisee typically contributes.

franchisor
The supplier of a franchise who typically provides building plans, site selection research, managerial and accounting procedures, and other services to assist the franchisee–and who receives payment, usually in the form of a flat fee and royalties or commissions.

The franchisee purchases tangible and intangible items from the franchisor. Most franchisors charge an initial franchise fee plus a percentage of sales or profits. Some also charge additional management fees. Still others require contributions to a promotional fund.[12] The highly successful McDonald's requires $140,000 of unemcumbered funds for the initial start-up plus a percentage of gross sales.

Franchising has come to dominate certain segments of retailing— fast-food restaurants, car rentals, motels, weight reduction programmes, health spas, and so on. Names like Avis, Holiday Inn, Weight Watchers, and Radio Shack are widely recognized today.

The franchises associated with some fast food chains are truly household words. Some, such as Kentucky Fried Chicken, have been around for a long time. Others are relative newcomers. Dozens of others have failed.

A franchise is like any other business property: it is the buyer's responsibility to know what he or she is buying. Poorly financed or poorly managed franchise systems are no better than poorly financed or poorly managed nonfranchise businesses. The advantages and disadvantages of franchises are compared in Table 4-2.

Existing franchises have a performance record on which the small businessperson can make comparisons and judgments. The likelihood of success in the proposed venture can be assessed by looking at earlier results. This requires careful study and hard work by the prospective franchisee.

In addition, a widely recognized name gives the franchisee a tremendous advantage. Car dealers, for instance, know that their brand name products will attract a given clientele. A franchise also gives the small businessperson a tested management system. The prospective franchisee usually does not have to worry about setting up an accounting system, calculating quality control standards, or designing employment application forms. These things are typically provided for in the franchise arrangement.

On the negative side, franchise fees and future payments can be very expensive. Good franchises with tested management systems,

Table 4-2
Advantages and Disadvantages of Franchises

Advantages	Disadvantages
Performance record on which to make comparisons and judgments.	High cost of obtaining a franchise.
Widely recognized name.	Consumer judgment of the business on the basis of other, similar franchises.
Tested management system.	Restrictions on business decisions.

proven performance records, and widely recognized names usually sell for more than those lacking these characteristics. The prospective franchisee must determine whether the expenses involved are fair compensation for what will be received. Another potentially negative factor is that a successful franchise can be "pulled down" by similar but less successful franchises. An inherent disadvantage of the franchise system is that the franchisee is judged by what his or her peers do. A strong, effective program of managerial control can offset any bad impressions given by unsuccessful franchises. Finally, the franchisor's management system restricts many decisions. The franchisee may not have the independence that most small businesspeople seek.

Purchasing a good franchise requires careful study of these advantages and disadvantages. The correct decision in one set of circumstances may be wrong under a different set of circumstances. The franchising concept does not solve all problems for someone considering a small business investment; it merely adds alternatives.

Small Business Opportunities for Women

Small firms offer excellent opportunities for women to enter the business world. Currently women have only a modest share of business ownership; yet they are making significant advances.

Focus 4-2

A Woman's Place Is on the Site

"Why," the banker asked Heather McLeod in 1984, "don't you open a boutique?" A 37-year-old woman selling skirts and blouses was something the banker could understand. A woman who wanted to start a manufacturing business to produce plywood forms for the construction industry wasn't.

Plywood forms are a specialized product used by builders to hold poured concrete while it hardens, but McLeod knew first-hand that nobody was meeting the demand for good quality forms in Nova Scotia. She had worked seven years, first as an accountant then in sales, for a company that made plywood forms, and her customers were telling her they weren't happy with the workmanship of the product they were getting.

With her background and knowledge, McLeod was dumbfounded that bankers should tell her she was in the wrong business. They were also unhappy that she wasn't married at the time, which meant no second income to support the new business. But she was able to get a mortgage on her house. She also "sold everything that wasn't tied down," including her car and her children's savings bonds, and got grants from the federal and Nova Scotia governments. Finally, she had a bankroll of $150,000.

In 1985, Superior Forming Systems and Supplies went into production in the village of Debert, near Truro. McLeod backed the quality of her product with a lifetime guarantee, and contractors— many of whom had encouraged her to go into business—were quick to place orders. Now she's expanding into New England and Ontario. Sales this year will pass the $1 million mark and she's investing more money in manufacturing. The company has ten employees, including her husband of three years, who is vice-president.

McLeod says she loves working at her own business. At the height of the summer construction season she puts in a staggering 16 hours a day. "If you want to work from 9 to 5, you won't be successful," she says.

To survive in a new business, says McLeod, "You have to monitor your costs and not get in over your head. We could have used more expensive equipment than we had at first, but we made do until we could afford better."

Now that she's a success, McLeod has a car again. It's a well-travelled Pony and it looks right at home on a Nova Scotia construction site.

Source: Daniel Stoffman, "A Woman's Place is on the Site," *Report on Business Magazine*, The Globe and Mail, October 1988, p. 71.

Women-Owned Businesses

Government statistics indicate that women own only about 23.7 percent of all Canadian firms.[13] Most such firms are relatively small. Most of the women in a recent study had started their business rather than buying existing firms or inheriting. Many, however, came from entrepreneurial families.[14] Although self-employment is much more prevalent among men than women, since 1975 the number of self-employed women has been rising three times as fast as the number of self-employed men: 117.6 percent compared with 39.1 percent.[15]

While women are beginning to make their mark in the world of small business, their advances have not been easy. Many prospective female entrepreneurs lack business training or experience. College-educated women have typically followed general arts courses or studied in traditional career areas for women such as teaching, nursing, and home economics. Today, many of these people are retraining themselves through programmes offered by community colleges, universities, and other groups interested in furthering female entrepreneurship. Future generations of small businesspersons should include better-prepared women, judging by the number of women now studying business administration.

Some argue that prejudice in varying degrees is a factor that women-owned firms must face. However, two-thirds of female owners would disagree. In a recent study they stated that female owners do not face problems that are any different from businesspeople in general.[16] Certainly businesswomen also encounter all the problems faced by businessmen. Like their male counterparts, the good entrepreneurs usually survive, and those who cannot adjust or satisfy their markets eventually fail. Focus 4-2 illustrates some of the problems encountered by women venturing into nontraditional areas of business ventures.

Government and Small Business

The government of Canada has had a strong commitment to assisting small businesses for many years. Within the Department of Regional Industrial Expansion (DRIE) there is a Minister of State for Small Business. A branch of the department, called the Small Business Secretariat, gives support to the minister. This has resulted in an increasing number of programmes of practical business assistance. Furthermore, DRIE maintains continuous contacts with the small business community through its regional offices. Provincial governments also actively assist small business. In fact, the federal and provincial governments provide services designed to meet the needs of small business in virtually every circumstance.

The primary services governments provide are financial assistance, assistance in selection of employees, and offering management training and consulting. There are programmes available designed to meet needs at all stages of development: from start-up to expanding regionally or internationally.

One notable organization that is part of the federal programmes is the **Federal Business Development Bank**. If a small business requires financial assistance, and has not been able to arrange financing from another source with reasonable terms and conditions, the FBDB often will help. The FBDB also conducts management training seminars designed to meet the needs of small businesses. These are conducted in many towns and cities across Canada. CASE (**Counselling Assistance to Small Enterprise**) is part of the FBDB service. CASE provides management counselling, using retired businesspeople selected for their management experience. Assistance is provided at nominal cost. In addition, the Enterprise Development Program (EDP) offers financing assistance to smaller and mid-sized firms in processing or manufacturing that are not reluctant to assume higher-risk and innovative activities. Loans and grants are available to applicants.

Federal Business Development Bank (FBDB)
An agency of the Department of Industry, Trade and Commerce providing financing, management training, and consulting to small business.

Counselling Assistance to Small Enterprise (CASE)
Group of retired businesspeople who offer consulting services to small businesses. A programme of the FBDB.

Some Concluding Thoughts on Small Business

Despite the many difficulties encountered by small business, owning and operating a business offers many promises and hopes beyond those of a financial nature. Independence, self-fulfillment, self-respect, and contributions to society are but a few.

Small business has long been an integral part of the private enterprise system, the cradle of great industries, great companies, and great business leaders. It remains a vital mechanism for the release of competitive energy. People who see a chance for personal achievement are usually more productive than those who see their work as boring or routine and with no chance of improvement. Small business offers the opportunity for personal achievement. It always has offered this opportunity, and it probably always will!

Controversial Issue

Bank Bias Against Businesswomen

In their book, *Head and Heart: Financial Strategies for Smart Women*, authors Arthur Drache and Susan Schneider discussed many of the problems women face in borrowing from financial institutions. On the basis of interviews with businesswomen, they observed that while attitudes towards women are changing in society, many banks are still biased against lending to women. Often, loans would only be made when a man, spouse or father, was prepared to act as a guarantor.

A recent study by the Canadian Federation of Independent Business (CFIB) has tended to confirm this observation. In light of the controversial nature of the subject matter, the study was done with scrupulous attention to achieving scientific accuracy. The report, "Banking on Women: The Relationship of Canada's Banks with Small Businesswomen," highlights two striking points.

First, the interest rate for an average female business owner for a line of credit was 1.59 above prime versus 1.51 over prime for a male in the same position. Second, collateral of 300 percent of the line of credit was required for almost 50 percent of female business owners versus fewer than 30 percent of men.

According to the study, there are several differences between the ways banks treat women and men when setting financing conditions, and in no case do women get getter treatment than men.

These biases occur at a time when 95 percent of new businesses operated as sole proprietorships are run by women. Moreover, studies have established that the failure rate of businesses started by women is only half of that for businesses started by men.

According to the CFIB study, another study should be undertaken to examine banks' financing policies for women business-owners. Why are these women forced to put up more collateral than men?

Banks are quick to deny the accuracy of the picture painted by the CFIB study. But whether they publicly accept the report or not, they may well have to consider the recommendations—if only as a means of generating new business. Financing policies aside, the study recommends that banks strengthen their ties with women business-owners by providing greater advisory services to them.

Women entrepreneurs are here to stay, and their success rate is impressive. It clearly will be beneficial to financial institutions and to

society to treat them as economic equals.

The ball is in the bankers' court.

Source: Arthur Drache, "Bank Bias Against Businesswomen," *The Financial Post*, January 14–16, 1989, p. 12.

Summary of Learning Goals

1. **Explain the vital role played by small business in the economy.**

   Small businesses play an important part in the private enterprise system. They provide independence and bring competitive fervour to the economy. Small firms account for the bulk of all commercial enterprises and provide a major portion of national output and employment.

2. **Define small business and identify the sectors of the economy in which most small firms are established.**

   A small business is one that is independently owned and operated and does not dominate its market. Most small companies are concentrated in the retailing and service sectors of the economy, although many new technology firms also began as small businesses. Most new companies have formed in industries with low entry-level capital requirements.

3. **Define entrepreneurship and its importance in small business.**

   The entrepreneur is a person who not only sees business opportunities, but is willing to take the risk and make the effort to make them happen. Entrepreneurs tend to be independent, self-reliant individuals with a high need to achieve. Most small businesses are started and run by such persons. Consequently, their importance to the economy is very significant.

4. **Compare the advantages and disadvantages of small business.**

   Small businesses have some distinct advantages over larger competitors, including innovative behaviour, lower costs, and filling of isolated market niches. They also have disadvantages, including the possibility of poor management, inadequate financing, and problems caused by government regulation.

5. **Describe franchising and its advantages and disadvantages.**

   Franchising is a contract between a supplier and a dealer that sets the methods to be used in producing and marketing a product. Franchising now dominates the retailing of some products. It has increasingly become a factor in the growth of the service sector. The advantages of the franchising approach to small business are performance records on which to make comparisons and judgments, a widely recognized name, and tested management systems. The disadvantages include the high cost of obtaining some franchises; consumer judgment of the business on the basis of other similar franchises; and restrictions on business decisions.

6. **Analyze the small business opportunities for women and the special problems faced by these entrepreneurs.**
   Women own 23.7 percent of all Canadian firms. In recent years, however, women have begun making significant advances in small firms, and greater growth is occurring.

7. **Describe how the federal and provincial governments support small business.**
   The federal government provides counselling assistance through the Department of Regional Industrial Expansion. Also, it sponsors the Federal Business Development Bank, which provides funding and counselling. Provincial governments have a range of programmes to support and counsel small businesses.

Key Terms

entrepreneur
small business
venture capitalists
franchising
franchisee

franchisor
Federal Business Development
  Bank (FBDB)
Counselling Assistance to
  Small Enterprise (CASE)

Discussion Questions and Exercises

1. Evaluate the pros and cons of the Controversial Issue that appears in this chapter.
2. Many people believe that Canada's industrial future is linked to high-tech firms. What role do you think small business will play in the future?
3. Why is financing such a problem for small businesses? Explain.
4. Explain why franchising is such a vital element of today's small business sector.
5. Describe the current status of women in small business and the reasons for it.
6. Explain why most small business is started by entrepreneurs.
7. Contact some small businesses in your area. Make up a list of the specific problems each faces. Are any of them common problems?
8. Visit the owners of one or more local franchise businesses. Ask these people why they decided to buy a franchise rather than start an independent business of their own. Find out what problems (if any) they are having with their franchisor.
9. Prepare a two-page report on the services available from the Small Business Secretariat and FBDB.

10. Would you prefer to own a small business, work in a small business, or work in a large one? What would be the advantages or disadvantages of each option for you personally?

Case 4-1

First Things First

Two would-be entrepreneurs had a wonderful idea. It was a sure thing, they thought; it couldn't miss. But they didn't quite know how to launch it. So they took it to Robert Wyckham, associate dean of the faculty of business administration at Simon Fraser University in Burnaby, BC—along with a substantial legal document swearing Wyckham to secrecy.

Wyckham signed, and they showed him a game—the next *Trivial Pursuit*, boasted the pair. Wyckham asked if they'd done any market research. Had they, perhaps, shown it to the buyers at department stores? "Oh no," chorused the inventors, "they'd steal it."

Without an accurate gauge of demand for the product, potential backers refused to put up any cash. Lacking any numbers, the cocky but paranoid partners promptly became a statistic of their own: their company joined the 80 percent of businesses that fail within five years of starting. "The world is full of wonderful ideas," sighs Wyckham. "But there are very few people who can turn them into commercial ventures."

However, there is help. Many provinces have set up small-business centres to counsel entrepreneurs on how to avoid the fate that felled Wyckham's gamesters. Latest on the scene are seventeen centres that the province of BC has quietly set up over the past two years at community colleges and universities under its Enterprise BC project. With a total annual operations budget of $1.36 million, the Enterprise Centres are meant to help small businesses get started and stay in the black. Counsellors point out what market research a client ought to do and where to go to get the figures. They show the neophyte how to set cashflows and budgets. In short, they provide the basic skills to effectively run a small business. And the advice is free.

Each centre provides the same basic services. They begin by assessing whether the individual has the necessary qualifications and characteristics for the business proposed. Next, they evaluate the viability of the idea. Only when both assessments have been analyzed will they proceed. Counsellors don't actually do the work; they just point out what is needed and where to look for it. Clients can come back to the centres with questions as often as necessary.

If clients do the homework, the reward is a solid, handsomely packaged business plan, a document that lays out what the plan is, why it's a good idea, who's involved and what skills are available. In addition, it also lays out a set of numbers for the first years of operation that show year by year how the owner stands financially, when he/she is going to need money, and how much.

Entrepreneurs need to be able to do the business plan themselves so that when they have to present it to bankers, they know it backward and forward.

According to Brian Hann, manager of independent business for BC at the Royal Bank of Canada, "Bankers don't have a lot of time to assess proposals. One that is done professionally, effectively, gets our attention. If we're satisfied after asking questions that they not only put the plan together themselves, but they know what the contents are, it gives us a lot of faith as lenders. Their chances of getting the money they need are substantially improved."

Source: John Masters, "First Things First," *Canadian Business*, May 1987, pp. 25, 26, 31.

Questions:
1. According to the case, why do many businesses fail within five years of starting? Explain.
2. What can be done to improve a business's ability to obtain the needed financing? Explain.
3. How do the centres help businesses survive once they have been established? Explain.

Case 4-2

Going Forward

The sound is an awful one—the raw snapping of threads through resisting cloth. "We try to destroy things here," says Mary Rose Ward, smiling as she pulls apart the waistline of the light, floral-print dress until it hangs, sagging. The Toronto-based designer and manufacturer thought the construction looked cheap and she wouldn't stand for it.

Saying no to imperfect garments, no to banks, rapid expansion, and even—sometimes—no to retailers, has given the 42-year-old Ward profits well above average in an industry that's seeing difficult times. Her six-year-old company, 535370 Ontario Ltd., which operates as Mary Rose, took in $3.2 million in sales in fiscal 1987 and had gross earnings of 41 percent. Industry average is around 27 percent.

Ladies' dresses, skirts and coordinates make up almost one quarter of the $6.2–billion domestic garment manufacturing industry. It's in this highly competitive sector that Ward does battle. Her comfortable, mid-priced, one-size knitwear is sold to small, independent stores and boutiques across the country, as well as to seven Mary Rose stores.

Ward believes in doing things the old way—doing things right. She is adamant that as corners are cut, quality suffers and consumers will notice.

But many Canadian manufacturers fear that lower-cost garments, mainly in the form of imports, are severely eroding the domestic market. Imports cover roughly 50 percent of the market today and will grow to about a 70 percent share within the next three years. In Ward's opinion, rivalry from US firms as a result of the free trade deal won't add much to the squeeze the industry is already experiencing. "I think in our industry, doing well means you can keep opening season after season," she says.

Ward is known for her business and creative instincts: one of these instincts was a feeling that she didn't ever want to deal with bank loans. "Most people use the bank rather than starting small and expanding like a big puddle of water," Ward says. "They set themselves up with lovely offices, lots of staff and buy a lot of machinery. I've seen people go right out the window in a year and a half."

Ward put up about $4,000 of her own cash for several pieces of cloth-cutting and production equipment when she set up in 1982. She moved the two industrial sewing machines that she already owned into a 72-square-metre factory space in the garment district. After years of freelance designing, Ward had established net 30-day credit terms with a fabric supplier. From her own customers she demanded a cheque on delivery, guaranteeing the cashflow to pay her labour costs—two sewing machine operators—and to make continuous fabric purchases. Within a year, her company had 10 employees and was housed in 288-square-metre space.

Now the approximately 140 styles that make up the Mary Rose line are produced by 40 employees, who turn out 600 units a day. Being familiar with every piece of equipment in her factory has allowed Ward to maximize production. She's also a believer in maintaining a steady presence on the production floor.

Ward insists that machinery and staff be employed to their potential and new markets be secure before considering expansion. Manufacturers can be tempted into rapid expansion by large orders from clothing chains and department stores, either on an entire design line or by asking for their own label to be put in the garment. Not Ward.

While selling to a large number of small retailers is one way to avoid overdependence on any single customer, Ward has circumvented this problem by integrating vertically, thus ensuring a marketplace for her own manufactured goods. She now has five retail outlets, which brought in a total of $1.5 million in 1988.

Source: Suzsi Gartner, "Executive Material," *Canadian Business*, January 1989, pp. 13, 14.

Questions:
1. Explain Ward's success in the garment manufacturing industry. Refer specifically to her product concept.
2. How did Ward circumvent financial problems normally associated with a small business? Explain.
3. What must Ward do to continue generating high returns? What factors must she account for? Explain.

Part Two

Organization and Management of the Enterprise

Chapter 5

Introduction to Management

Management
1. What ought to be done.
2. How should it be done.
3. Who should do it.
4. Has it been done.
—*Joseph E. Atkinson "Four things an Executive Should Know" in R. Harkness, J. E. Atkinson of the Star, 1963, p. 209.*

Learning Goals

1. To describe the three levels of managers in a firm and to analyze which functions are likely to be important to each level

2. To explain the skills required for managerial success

3. To explain the importance of objectives in establishing standards by which management performance is measured

4. To identify the steps in the decision-making process

5. To define the basic functions performed by all managers—planning, organizing, directing, and controlling

6. To explain the concept of leadership and three basic leadership styles

Profile

Jean Gaulin—*The Turnaround King of Quebec Energy*

According to Jean Gaulin, president of Ultramar Canada Inc., the management style he used to turn an ailing oil company into a dramatic success can be applied to any corporation. Gaulin advises managers to always remember two things: Trust the people, and keep the company on a strict diet.

"The problem with most companies is that they feel their employees are not capable," says Gaulin. "But the truth is, if you trust the employees, give them information and a common goal, they'll do a better job than you." Managers should not overspend and keep trim at all times, he adds.

Ultramar Canada, a wholly owned subsidiary of the British petroleum multinational, had been losing $70 million between 1982 and 1986 with its gas stations. When Gaulin, 45, took over as president in 1985, he knew he had only one option: Get more from the workers and rationalize.

To save the company, Gaulin immediately implemented some harsh medicine. He laid off 25 percent of the entire Canadian staff. And when he acquired the eastern division of Gulf Canada Ltd., he retained its 600 service stations in Quebec but closed Gulf's Montreal refinery. At the same time that he wielded the axe, however, he kept in close contact with workers and tried to keep morale going.

The layoffs and the closing of the refinery made Gaulin a disliked man. But the criticism soon subsided. By 1987, when profits hit $104 million, the highest in Ultramar's twenty-five-year history in Canada, praise was heaped on the company and its chief. He became more of a Quebec hero when he relocated the Ultramar head office from Toronto to Montreal in January 1987.

With the hardest tasks behind him, Gaulin now concentrates on being a good "people manager" and keeping the company trim. He

says Ultramar got into trouble by overspending and not looking at what the competition was doing. He vows that will never happen again. "It's my responsibility to the employees that I'll never have to lay off again."

In March of 1988, he surprised employees by giving each and every one at least $1,500 in cash bonuses and company shares, besides awarding the highest pay rises in the industry. While keeping costs down and handing out bonuses may seem contradictory, Gaulin defends the move: "If you want performance, you must recognize it."

Source: Linda Massarella, "Ultramar's Jean Gaulin Scores with Friendly Style, Descipline," *This Week in Business*, June 4, 1988, p.5. Reprinted by permission.

When Alan Ladd, Jr., son of the late movie actor, joined Twentieth Century Fox Corporation as head of the film division in the early 1970s, he joined an organization with an unenviable reputation for producing such costly turkeys as "Dr. Doolittle," "Tora! Tora! Tora!," and "Hello Dolly." Ladd's managerial talents coupled with the financial skills of his boss Dennis Stanfill quickly converted Fox from a consistent loser to a profitable company.

Ladd recognized the need for an appropriate blending of creativity and financial controls in filmmaking, and he followed the practice of using talented professionals in such areas as reviewing scripts, selecting stars, and maintaining overly tight controls over the director, but he held his producers and directors responsible for results.

Ladd would become involved with unusual problems or projects. When young George Lucas approached him in 1973 with a movie idea—a "Western" filled with spaceships, robots, villainous villains, and heroic heroes, and a theatre filled with special effects at a price tag of at least $10 million in production costs—Ladd listened and liked what he heard.

Although Ladd knew that Universal had already rejected the proposal, he realized that managers must sometimes take risks, and he convinced his boss that this one should be taken. The rest is history. Although the worldwide rental income continues to be counted, "Star Wars" is approaching $500 million in rentals and ranks as one of the most successful films made so far. Its successors are enjoying similar returns.

After a few years, Ladd left Twentieth Century Fox to start his own operation. He recognized the importance of effective management in the movie industry but was also convinced that creative people are often self-motivated and identify their work not with a company but with themselves. As patron-manager of his own firm, he felt it would be easier to provide his creative people with applause and rewards for good work and protection for failures. He understood management concepts, but he also recognized the importance of fitting them to the special characteristics of his organization.[1]

Different Problems, Different Goals...But All Managers

Dave King, Beverly Sills, and Jean Gaulin have at least one thing in common. They are all managers. King is head coach of the University of Saskatchewan's hockey team, Sills is the general director of the New York City Opera Company, and Gaulin is president of Ultramar Canada Inc. Other managers preside over organizations such as the local Red Cross office, city governments (many cities are run by a city manager), and colleges or universities.

What Is Management?

management
The achievement of organizational objectives through people and other resources.

Management is the achievement of organizational objectives through people and other resources. The manager's job is to combine human and technical resources in the best way possible to achieve these objectives. Managers are not directly involved in production; they do not produce a finished product. Instead they direct the efforts of others toward the company goals. As Figure 5-1 indicates, management is the critical ingredient in the five *M*s—management, manpower, materials, money, and machinery—the basic resources of any firm.

Management Principles Are Universal

The management principles and concepts to be discussed are applicable—even fundamental—not only to profit-seeking firms but also to nonprofit organizations. The local hospital administrator, the head of the United Way, and the president of a home and school association all perform managerial functions similar to those performed by their counterparts in industry.

Businesses are only distinguished from other forms of enterprise in terms of objectives. Businesses are profit-oriented, while nonprofit organizations such as hospitals, city governments, and charitable agencies are service-oriented. But both benefit from effective management.

Figure 5-1
The 5 Ms—Basic Resources of the Organization

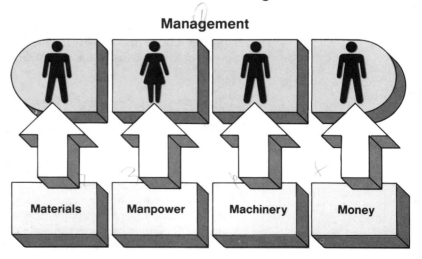

Management
Materials Manpower Machinery Money

The Management Pyramid

The local McDonald's franchise has a very simple organization—a manager and an assistant manager or two. In contrast, CTV has a president, several vice-presidents, department heads, plant managers, and supervisory personnel. Are all these people managers? The answer is yes. Since they are all engaged in combining human and other resources to achieve company objectives, they are all managers.

management pyramid
The various levels of management, or hierarchy, in an organization—supervisory, middle, and top management.

The various levels of management form a **management pyramid**, or hierarchy, in an organization. As Figure 5-2 indicates, a firm's management can be divided into three categories: top management, middle management, and supervisory management. Although all three categories contain managers, each level of the pyramid stresses different activities.

top management
The highest level of the management pyramid, comprising the president and other key company executives who develop long-range plans for the company and interact with the government and community.

Top management, the highest level of the management pyramid, is composed of the president and other key company executives. These people devote their time to developing long-range plans for the company. They make broad decisions such as whether to manufacture new products, to purchase other companies, or to begin international operations. A considerable amount of their time is directed to outside activities involving government and community affairs. Focus 5-1 provides some pointers on how executives can avoid losing sight of their company's long-term goals in the thick of daily operations.

middle management
The second level of the management pyramid, including executives, such as plant managers and department heads, who are responsible for developing detailed plans and procedures to implement the general plans of top management.

Middle management, the second level of the management pyramid, includes such executives as plant managers and department heads. Middle management is more involved than top management in specific operations within the organization. Middle managers are responsible for developing detailed plans and procedures to implement the general plans of top management. They may, for example,

Figure 5-2
The Management Pyramid

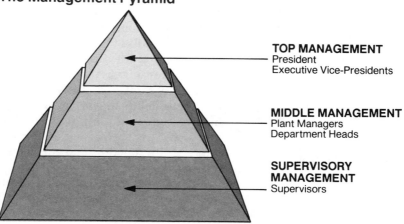

TOP MANAGEMENT
President
Executive Vice-Presidents

MIDDLE MANAGEMENT
Plant Managers
Department Heads

SUPERVISORY MANAGEMENT
Supervisors

determine the number of salespeople for a particular territory, operate a branch of a department store chain, select equipment for a new facility, or develop techniques for evaluating employee performance.

Supervisory management, the third level of the management pyramid, includes people who are directly responsible for details of assigning workers to specific jobs and evaluating daily—even hourly—performance. They are in direct and continuing contact with production personnel and are responsible for putting into action the plans developed by middle management.

At any level, managers need certain skills, including the ability to work in a team, the ability to formulate and carry out long-range plans, the courage to take risks, and the ability to get on well with others, in order to succeed. One important skill that is often forgotten is the ability to "manage" and communicate with one's own supervisor as well as one's subordinates. A manager's immediate boss links the manager to the rest of the organization. Lack of some of these abilities often prevents people from moving up the managerial ladder.

Organization and Management

Skills Required for Managerial Success

Every manager, regardless of level in the organization, must possess three basic managerial skills: technical skills, human relations skills, and conceptual skills. Although the importance of each skill varies at different managerial levels, managers use all three types at some time during their careers.

Technical skills refers to the manager's ability to understand and use techniques, knowledge, and tools of a specific discipline or department. Technical skills are particularly important for first-line managers who are frequently involved with production employees who operate machinery or with salespersons who must explain technical details of their firm's products, or with computer programmers working on a complicated assignment. These skills become relatively less important going up the manager hierarchy.

Human relations skills are "people" skills. They involve the manager's ability to work effectively with and through people. They involve communicating with, leading, and motivating workers to accomplish assigned activities. In addition, they involve the ability to interact with superiors and others outside the immediate department or work area.

The ability to create a work environment in which organizational members will contribute their best efforts to achieve objectives is a crucial managerial skill at every level.

---

supervisory management
The third level of the management pyramid, including people who are directly responsible for the details of assigning workers to specific jobs and evaluating performance.

technical skills
The ability of a manager to understand and use techniques, knowledge, and tools of a specific discipline or department.

human relations skills
The ability of managers to work with and through people in communicating, leading, and motivating workers to accomplish assigned activities.

conceptual skills
The ability of a manager to view the organization as a unified whole, while also understanding how each part of the overall organization relates to other parts.

Conceptual skills refer to the ability of the manager to see the organization as a unified whole while also understanding how each part of the overall organization relates to other parts. These skills involve the ability to "see the big picture" by acquiring, analyzing, and interpreting information. Such skills are especially important for top management, who must develop imaginative and analytical plans for the future direction of an organization. Although a manager may initially have held responsibility in a single functional area, such as engineering, his or her ability to be a successful top manager is greatly affected by the ability to understand the contributions of other departments, such as finance, marketing, human resources, industrial relations, and public relations. (See Chapter 8 for more information on management and development programmes.)

Conceptual and human relations skills may be transferred from one department, company, or industry to another. A number of major government officials have successfully switched from careers in the private sector. In addition, it is now common for the top managers at many firms to have held previous managerial positions at other companies. On the other hand, technical skills are more difficult to transfer from one industry to another due to the unique characteristics and requirements of many such skills.

Focus 5-1

Golden Getaways—Helping Executives Find Their Way Again

For the owner and senior management of Kadem Technology Inc., the thrill of seeing sales increase was dulled by a nagging concern about the firm's future. Rapidly changing technology had opened a vast array of options for the Windsor, Ontario-based manufacturer of tooling aids for the plastic-parts industry. Getting everyone to concentrate on the problem, however, proved virtually impossible. "I don't know how you can plan at the office," says Gene Dennis, vice-president of sales and marketing. "Half your life is spent on the phone. It's like trying to take a vacation at the office—you just can't do it."

The solution: Step back and get away.

When organizational problems demand too much of executives' time, clearing their schedules for an out-of-the-office planning session may be the biggest problem. With determination, however, it can be done. The fresh perspectives that arise when senior managers step back from the daily grind to look objectively at the business far outweigh the problems involved in organizing a getaway.

The first thing to keep in mind is to set the date for the planning meeting well in advance. The organizer needs time to find the right setting, and participants have to arrange for others to take over as well as prepare for the sessions. Timing is also critical. The site of the meeting should be remote enough to prevent unplanned interruptions and distractions. It should encourage informality.

Who attends these sessions is as important as the location. The chief executive must not only be present but also lend his or her active support. Other participants include senior managers from key departments such as finance, operations, and marketing.

Companies often find it useful to bring someone in as a discussion leader. The outsider, or facilitator, contributes objectivity, techniques for resolving issues, and experience with similar situations in other industries. Facilitators keep the discussions on track and help narrow down objectives and future scenarios to realistic numbers. He or she can introduce subjects that people on the inside might have shied away from.

While facilitators come from many backgrounds, most organizations turn to professional management consultants. Finding the right person can mean soliciting advice from outsiders and paying big bucks.

Participants and the organizer should come prepared with a broad agenda spanning at least two days. This often includes a detailed outline of the corporate mission, performance history, the global and competitive environment, the present course of the company, and the future as executives would like to see it. While dealing with basic issues, the programme should be flexible enough to deal with items of immediate concern and issues which keep recurring.

At the end of the meeting, some of the participants should commit themselves to tracking the progress of proposals and reporting back to the others. That, however, is just the start. Aside from the technicalities of implementation, everyone in the company needs to know what is now expected and what changes they should prepare for.

Source: Donald Wood, "Golden Getaways," *Canadian Business*, August 1987, pp. 21–22. Reprinted by permission.

Importance of Objectives

The old maxim "if you don't know where you are going, any road will get you there" applies to business as well as to individuals. Both need definite objectives in order to be successful. **Objectives** are guideposts used by managers to define standards of what the organization should accomplish in such areas as profitability, customer service, and social responsibility. Managers can continually evaluate performance in terms of how well the organization is moving in the direction of its objectives.

objectives
Guideposts used by managers to define standards of what the organization should accomplish in areas such as profitability, customer service, and social responsibility.

Objectives Serve as Standards

Objectives often become standards for the manager by their definition of excellence in organizational performance. Without such standards, the manager possesses no tools for evaluating performance—no means of deciding whether work is good or bad. Thus, objectives provide not only a definite statement of what the organization wants to accomplish but also a means of evaluating progress toward its goals: If performance appears unsatisfactory, management can take corrective action, refocusing the organization in the direction of its objectives.

Examples of Objectives

The belief that the purpose of a business is to make a profit is accepted by most people—whether they are defenders or critics of business. Newspaper accounts of the success of, say, Steinberg's or Domtar are typically stated in terms of annual earnings, which is the most straightforward measure of business performance.

Profits are obviously necessary for survival. A company must be profitable in order to attract additional capital and to satisfy its owners with an adequate return for their invested funds. But other objectives are equally important. The company must, for example, provide its customers with needed goods and services, or it will not make any profits.

A firm's mere existence usually results in the achievement of a number of social objectives as well. These include the provision of job opportunities, good wages, safe working conditions, job training (often for the hard-core unemployed), and good corporate citizenship within the community. See Focus 5-2 to envision how the CEO of Air Canada determines the objectives and purpose of his organization.

Focus 5-2

Report from the President and Chief Executive Officer

Air Canada's first year as a corporation with private shareholders was marked by a record profit of $96 million, with an operating income increase of $21 million over 1987. The results represent a strong achievement when it is noted that during the year the Corporation overcame two major challenges. The first was to restore market share to its previous level following the work stoppage in late 1987. Air Canada responded through aggressive fare action and innovative promotional programs. The action was fully effective, resulting in a restoration of market share during the first quarter.

The second challenge was to counter the intense pressure placed on our domestic operations by the dramatic increase in competitive capacity. This

Pierre J. Jeanniot, O.C.
President and Chief
Executive Officer

resulted in escalating price wars as carriers struggled for traffic growth and improved yields. Air Canada succeeded through intense concentration on cost controls, renewed emphasis on marketing initiatives and careful attention to service standards.

The airline faces 1989 and beyond with solid confidence. Air Canada is committed to achieving customer service, operational, technical and financial levels of performance which will result in maximum benefits for its shareholders. To accomplish this, the Corporation has developed a business strategy of remaining the premier airline in Canada, while expanding its major international passenger and cargo network. This will ensure that every customer is provided with world-class quality. Under the theme "The Bottom Line is Quality", the airline recognizes that corporate success rests with the skill and professionalism of all employees, and encompasses every discipline within the Corporation.

Operationally, the business strategy is based on a total dedication to customer service; and aggressive pursuit of profitable growth by extending the airline's domestic and international network through alliances and route expansion.

Air Canada's six Connector carriers increased their operations during the year with the addition of new routes, services and aircraft. This will continue during 1989.

As part of our international strategy two new destinations were added in 1988; Lisbon, Portugal and Madrid, Spain. In 1989 four destinations will be added, including Birmingham, England; Nice, France; Zagreb, Yugoslavia; and Athens, Greece. The pre-eminent Canadian carrier between Canada and Europe, Air Canada is also planning a transpacific network that will include destinations in Malaysia, the Republic of Korea, India, the Philippines, and Singapore. The airline is seeking the right to serve routes between Canada and Japan, recognizing the rapidly growing importance of Canada's trade with Pacific Rim countries, in particular Japan.

Technically, Air Canada is committed to operating a modern and efficient fleet. During the year we took delivery of one Boeing 747 passenger/cargo aircraft, and four Boeing 767 extended range (ER) aircraft. Orders were placed for 34 state-of-the-art technology Airbus A320's.

Financially, the Corporation has on-going programs to reduce unit operating costs, to achieve further productivity improvements, to redeploy assets to higher yield use, and to further strengthen its financial position.

These programs; customer service, technical and financial, have been committed to because Air Canada's management and its professional staff are dedicated to ensuring that our shareholders' confidence is well justified.

Against this background, however, some caution must be noted. For the immediate future air travel should grow steadily. Unfortunately, the facilities upon which convenient airline travel depends have not kept pace and many airports throughout the world are now overburdened with traffic.

It is the role of airport authorities, working in consort with the airlines, to respond to this urgent need for improvement in the ability of airport facilities to cope with worldwide passenger growth. This growth, along with the sector's continued globalization and the increasing move towards international liberalization will create an intensely competitive environment placing strong pressure on airline cost structures and profit levels. Air Canada has, and will continue to make the necessary adjustments. Our ability to provide reliable, dependable service, and our internationally recognized technical excellence ensure that the Corporation will have the capability to take full advantage of future domestic and international opportunities.

Three of the company's senior officers, G. Chiasson, G.G. Gauvreau, and R.W. Linder have retired. Tribute was paid for their outstanding dedication and contribution to the airline.

Decision Making: Vital Task of Every Manager

The most important task of managers is decision making. Managers earn their salaries by making decisions that enable their firms to solve problems as they arise. In addition, managers are continually involved with anticipating and preventing future problems. The decision-making process can be described in five steps. Figure 5-3 shows how the manager systematically progresses through each step ultimately to reach a decision aimed at solving a specific problem or taking advantage of a particular business opportunity.

The following hypothetical story illustrates a problem to which the decision-making process can be applied.

> The Flavourfest Meat-Packing Company is a leading firm in the meat-packing industry, with annual sales in excess of $80 million. Its brand name is well known in the areas of canned meat products and frozen meats. Although the brand is highly regarded by consumers, Flavourfest's management has recently become concerned about the growing price difference among domestic meat products. Large food chains are increasingly marketing meat products under their own brand names, often at prices as much as 10 to 15 percent lower than national brands because of their large purchases from countries such as Argentina. The imported meats are identical in quality with domestic meats, because Agriculture Canada controls grading.
>
> Consumers appear to be gradually turning away from the Flavourfest brand because of the price differential. Flavourfest has been approached by two South American meat suppliers to contract for future beef imports.

Figure 5-3
Steps in the Decision-making Process

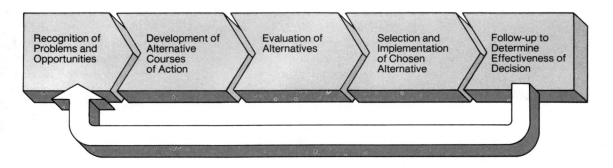

| Recognition of Problems and Opportunities | Development of Alternative Courses of Action | Evaluation of Alternatives | Selection and Implementation of Chosen Alternative | Follow-up to Determine Effectiveness of Decision |

Flavourfest probably first learned of its problem (and potential opportunity) when it compared company sales with organizational goals for the current year. Now that management is aware of the problem, it can list and evaluate alternative courses of action. It will want to consider such factors as consumer reaction to imported meats, labelling requirements, and dependability of the South American suppliers. Information on these factors will enable management to assess the merits of the various alternatives.

After this assessment, management can choose one of the alternatives and put it into action. It must also, of course, devise methods of follow-up to determine whether its decision will prove effective in solving the problem or taking advantage of the new opportunity. Feedback on the correctness of this decision will be extremely useful to management when it has to make similar decisions in the future.

decision making
Choosing among two or more alternatives by following these steps: recognizing the problem, identifying and evaluating alternatives, selecting and implementing alternatives, and obtaining follow-up on the effectiveness of the decision.

In a narrow sense, **decision making** is choosing among two or more alternatives—the chosen alternative being the decision. But in a broader sense, decision making involves problem recognition, identification and evaluation of alternatives, selection and implementation of an alternative, and follow-up (in the form of feedback) on the effectiveness of the decision. Whether the decision to be made is routine or unique (such as a decision to construct a major new manufacturing facility), the systematic step-by-step approach will be effective.

Management Functions

Management has been defined as the achievement of objectives through people and other resources. This definition implies that it is a process—a series of actions that result in a certain end. A manufacturer converts a series of inputs in the form of raw materials, machinery, workers, and other ingredients into finished products designed to satisfy the firm's customers. Completion of this process allows the firm to achieve its objectives.

Managers perform four basic functions—planning, organizing, directing, and controlling—and they must be skillful in performing them if they are to accomplish their goals. (Management writers differ on both the number of management functions and the specific lists of them. Writers who choose to define them more narrowly include such functions as staffing, communicating, motivating, innovating, coordinating, and evaluating—all of which must be accomplished by managers. The four functions listed here are broadly

Figure 5-4
The Functions of Management

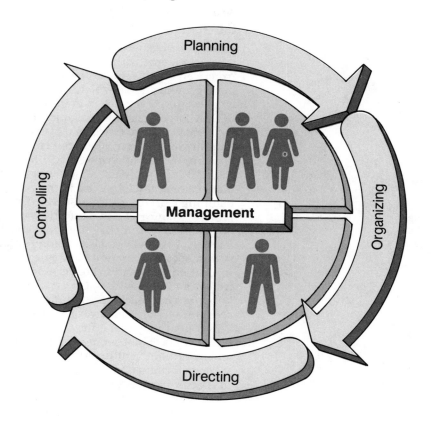

conceived and are assumed to include these more specific functions.)
Although Figure 5-4 shows these functions as separate, they really
are interdependent, and it is up to the manager to coordinate them.
(The arrows in the figure indicate that management is a continual
process.) Thus, as managers develop plans, they become involved in
organizing to carry them out. They also have to consider methods of
directing and controlling the operations during the planning process.
Careful coordination of these functions leads to effective decisions
and the accomplishment of organizational objectives. The four management functions are necessary for any enterprise to work successfully.

The basic management functions are performed at *all* levels of the
management pyramid, although top and middle managers devote
more time to the planning function and supervisory managers spend
more time on the directing function.

Focus 5-3

Making Strategic Management Work—The Coopers and Lybrand Approach

Strategic or business planning is a unique management discipline when compared with other management systems common to North American organizations. It is unique because it is the only management system which requires diverse inputs from a broad cross-section of managers in the organization in order to develop an overall corporate strategy, composed of distinct business unit strategic plans and functional plans. To accomplish such a feat, typically once a year, requires a closely coordinated, finely tuned planning system and work schedule.

The second principal reason why strategic planning is a unique management discipline lies in the very nature of the tasks involved. Planning is an imprecise, ill-defined and "soft" management process. Many argue that effective strategic planning requires both "right brain" or creative thinking, and "left brain" or analytical analysis. Few individuals, let alone organizations, are capable of both modes of operation. Strategic planning often deals with very inaccurate information concerning markets, political and economic trends, and competitors. Uncertainty abounds. It is an "unprogrammable" decision-making process. Strategy formulation continues to rely heavily on management intuition and judgement. This is not to say that efforts to apply analytical tools and planning frameworks do not serve a useful purpose.

Apart from the difficulties inherent in the characteristics of the strategy formulation process, as outlined above, there are a number of specific barriers to effective strategic planning. These include:

1. Lack of commitment by senior management
2. Conflict between short- and long-term planning
3. Lack of management time to devote to planning
4. Organizational conflict between line management and staff planners
5. Lack of quality data
6. Environmental uncertainties
7. Lack of understanding and skill in strategic planning
8. Too much paper
9. Lack of communication by middle management, and
10. Difficulty in achieving implementation of plans.

Strategic planning remains a management art. Many barriers continually challenge the establishment of effective strategic planning systems in organizations, be they large or small, public or private. However, given senior management commitment and leadership in the planning process, opportunities exist to overcome each barrier in order to establish an effective planning process which can contribute to outstanding corporate performance.

Source: Erik G. Rule, "Making Strategic Management Work," *Business Quarterly*, Winter 1987, pp. 33, 34. Published by the School of Business Administration, University of Western Ontario.

Planning

planning
The management function concerned with anticipating the future and determining the best courses of action to achieve organizational objectives.

Planning is the management function of anticipating the future and determining the best courses of action to achieve company objectives. It encompasses decisions about the activities the organization should perform; how big it should be; the production, marketing, and financial strategies it should use in reaching its objectives; and the resources it will need to accomplish its goals. Thus, planning involves the determination of courses of action to answer the questions of what should be done, by whom, where, when, and how. In the same way that an architect designs a blueprint, a manager constructs a plan for the organizational activities necessary to reach objectives.

Planning is a continual process. The statement "the only thing constant is change" is undeniably true in today's business world. Business conditions change; laws change; organizations change. Managers must continually monitor their own operations and the business environment and make necessary adjustments to their plans. This ongoing analysis and comparison of actual performance with company objectives allows the manager to adjust plans before problems become crises. Successful accomplishment of other managerial functions is unlikely without sound and continual planning.

Strategic Planning and Tactical Planning

Planning can be classified on the basis of scope or breadth. Strategic planning can be defined as the process of determining the primary objectives of an organization and adopting courses of action and allocating resources necessary to achieve those objectives. Strategic plans tend to be both broad and long-range, focusing on those organizational objectives that will have major impact on the organization over a time period of several years. An example of strategic planning would be IBM's introduction of the IBM PC and PCjr to compete with Apple, Texas Instruments, and other producers of microcomputers. Strategic planning has a critical impact on the destiny of the organization since it provides long-run direction for managers. Focus 5-3 reviews some of the barriers to effective strategic planning.

By contrast, tactical planning focuses on the implementation of activities specified by the strategic plans. Tactical planning tends to be shorter-term than strategic planning, and focuses more on current and near-term activities required to implement overall strategies. Although the two types of planning are different, both must be integrated into an overall system designed to achieve organizational objectives.

organizing
The means by which management blends human and material resources through the design of a formal structure of tasks and authority.

Organizing

Once plans have been developed, the next step typically is organization. **Organizing** is the means by which management blends human and material resources through the design of a formal structure of tasks and authority. It involves classifying and dividing work into manageable units by:

1. determining specific work activities necessary to accomplish the organizational objectives,
2. grouping work activities into a logical pattern or structure, and
3. assigning the activities to specific positions and people.

Included in the organizing function are the important steps of staffing the organization with competent employees who are capable of performing the necessary activities, and assigning authority and responsibility to these individuals. Organizing is discussed in more detail in Chapter 6, and staffing is dealt with in Chapter 8.

Directing

Once plans have been formulated and an organization has been created and staffed, the task becomes that of directing people toward achievement of organizational goals. **Directing** is the accomplishment of organizational objectives by guiding and motivating subordinates. It includes assigning work, explaining procedures, issuing orders, and seeing that mistakes are corrected.

The directing function is particularly important at the supervisory level, because the greatest number of employees are concentrated there. If supervisors are to accomplish the task of ''getting things done through people,'' they must be effective leaders. Directing—sometimes referred to as motivating, leading, guiding, or human relations—is thus the ''people'' function of management. It is discussed at length in Chapter 7.

directing
Guiding and motivating subordinates to accomplish organizational objectives.

A businessperson who directs others—by assigning work, explaining procedures, issuing orders, and so on—performs a role not unlike that of Andrew Davis conducting the Toronto Symphony.

Controlling

controlling
The management function
involved in evaluating the
organization's performance to
determine whether it is
accomplishing its objectives.

Controlling is the management function that evaluates the organization's performance to determine whether it is accomplishing its objectives. Controlling is linked closely to planning; in fact, the basic purpose of controlling is the determination of how successful the planning function has been. The three basic steps in controlling are:

1. setting standards,
2. collecting information to discover any deviations from standards,
3. taking corrective action to bring any deviations into line.

The temperature control system shown in Figure 5-5 provides a good illustration of the controlling function. Once the objective of a temperature setting, say 20°C, has been established, information about the actual temperature in the house is collected and compared with the objective, and a decision based on this comparison is made. If the temperature drops below 20°C, the decision is to activate the furnace until it reaches the established level. If the temperature goes too high, the decision is to turn off the furnace and start the cooling system.

**Figure 5-5
A Temperature Control System**

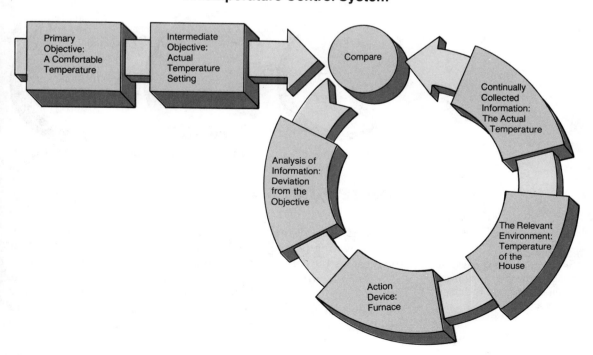

Deviation from a firm's goals about profitability, return on investment, or market share may require changes in price structures, new sources of raw materials, changes in production methods, new package design, or a number of other changes. The firm's control system must provide the necessary information from sales records, production cost figures, financial data, or market research studies to uncover deviations from organizational goals. This information then becomes the key ingredient for revisions in plans, and the cycle of planning-organizing-directing-controlling continues.

Earlier in the chapter it was pointed out that all four management functions are performed at all levels of management. But as Figure 5-6 indicates, the amount of time devoted to each function varies by management level. Top management performs more planning than does supervisory management, while supervisors at the third rung of the management pyramid devote more of their time to directing and controlling.

In order to be able to carry out their functions of planning, organizing, directing, and controlling, it is important for managers to use their time well. Time management is an essential part of any manager's job.

Figure 5-6
Relative Amount of Time Spent on Each Management Function by Different Levels of Management

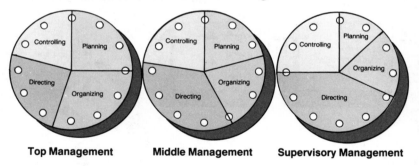

Top Management **Middle Management** **Supervisory Management**

Leadership

leadership
The act of motivating or causing others to perform activities designed to achieve specific objectives.

Managers achieve organizational objectives by being good leaders and motivating people to high levels of achievement. **Leadership,** the most visible component of a manager's responsibilities, is the act of motivating or causing others to perform activities designed to achieve specific objectives. Because of the importance of effective leadership in organizational success, it is not surprising that the search for such individuals has been in process for generations.

great man theory
Leadership theory emphasizing that only an exceptional person is capable of playing a prominent 突出 leadership role.

Early leadership concepts concentrated on the **great man theory**, which held that remarkable individuals—George Washington, Napoleon Bonaparte, Adolph Hitler, Mahatma Gandhi—emerged and were prepared to play important leadership roles. As a result, the early research attempted to focus on the traits of a good leader. Although the various listings differ, three traits were often mentioned: empathy, self-awareness, and objectivity in dealing with others. These traits are illustrated in Table 5-1.

Obviously these traits do not fit all of the leaders mentioned above. Empathy was hardly characteristic of Adolph Hitler. Other lists proved equally contradictory. Extroversion is an often-mentioned trait, but Prime Minister Mackenzie King was an introvert. Height may be characteristic of such leaders as Abraham Lincoln and Charles de Gaulle, but what about Napoleon? Leadership is often associated with the experience that often comes with age, but Alexander the Great won some of his most important victories at the age of 18.

Gradually leadership research began to focus on different styles of leadership and circumstances under which each style might prove more successful. By considering both alternative styles and a given set of circumstances, it is possible to determine the optimum type of leadership for a particular situation.

**Table 5-1
Frequently Listed Traits of a Good Leader**

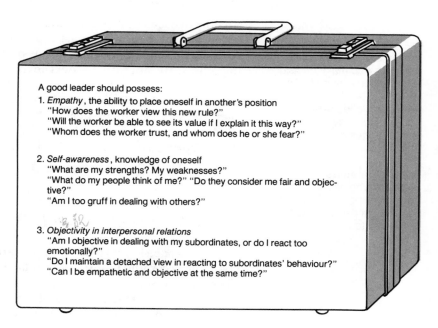

A good leader should possess:

1. *Empathy*, the ability to place oneself in another's position
   "How does the worker view this new rule?"
   "Will the worker be able to see its value if I explain it this way?"
   "Whom does the worker trust, and whom does he or she fear?"

2. *Self-awareness*, knowledge of oneself
   "What are my strengths? My weaknesses?"
   "What do my people think of me?" "Do they consider me fair and objective?"
   "Am I too gruff in dealing with others?"

3. *Objectivity in interpersonal relations*
   "Am I objective in dealing with my subordinates, or do I react too emotionally?"
   "Do I maintain a detached view in reacting to subordinates' behaviour?"
   "Can I be empathetic and objective at the same time?"

Figure 5-7
Continuum of Leadership Behaviour

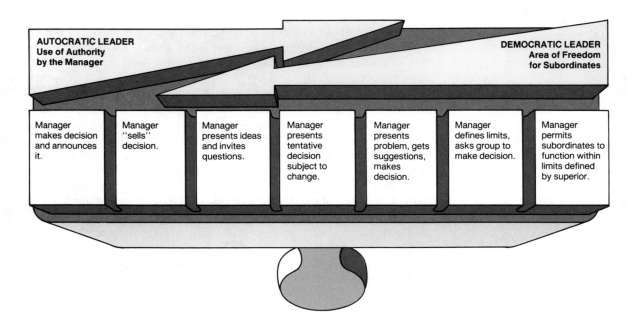

Leadership Styles

An effective leader recognizes that there are variations in leadership styles. The three basic styles are autocratic, free rein, and democratic. **Autocratic leaders** make decisions on their own, without consulting others. **Democratic leaders** involve their subordinates in making decisions. (An autocratic sales manager, for example, provides sales personnel with specific sales quotas, while a democratic manager allows them to participate in setting the quotas.) **Free-rein leaders** believe in minimal supervision, leaving most decisions to their subordinates. Figure 5-7 illustrates the continuum of leadership styles.

autocratic leaders
Leaders who make decisions without consulting others.

democratic leaders
Leaders who involve their subordinates in making decisions.

free-rein leaders
Leaders who believe in minimal supervision and who leave most decisions to their subordinates.

Which Leadership Style Is Best?

The best leadership style is one that varies with the circumstances, changing according to three elements: the leader, the followers, and the situation. Some leaders simply will not encourage or even allow subordinates to participate in decision making. And some followers do not have the ability or the desire to assume such responsibility.

Furthermore, the particular situation helps determine which style will be most effective. Problems requiring immediate solutions may have to be handled without consulting subordinates. With less time pressure, participative decision making may be desirable.

A democratic leader may be forced by circumstance to be autocratic in making a particular decision. For example, if there is to be a 10 percent reduction in staff, those subject to being laid off are not likely to be consulted on who should go.

Managers are increasingly moving toward a more democratic style of leadership. They find that workers involved in decision making tend to be more interested in the overall organization and may be more motivated to contribute to organizational objectives than those not involved in decision making.

After devoting many years of research into the best types of leaders, management professor Fred Feidler concluded that no single best style of leadership exists. Feidler feels that the most effective leadership style depends on the power held by the leader, the difficulty of the tasks involved, and the characteristics of the workers. He argues that extremely easy and extremely difficult situations are best handled by leaders who emphasize task accomplishment. Moderately difficult situations are best handled by leaders who emphasize participation and good working relations with subordinates.[2]

Controversial Issue

Sociotech—Towards an Innovative Management System

How well does your company trust its employees? Enough to allow them to run their own production teams?

In Bromont, Canadian General Electric does just that. By letting the plant workers manage the manufacturing of sensitive, high-precision blades for jet engines, the company has surpassed its goals.

"You have to trust people, that's the key here," says Pierre Bisaillon, the plant manager. "If you cannot delegate responsibility, you're in trouble." For CGE, that means abandoning the pyramid chain of command and treating the employees in each department as quasi-subcontractors.

Their work environment resembles a textbook model for a small business rather than a traditional assembly line. As a result, the staff has not organized any unions. The $100 million facility makes 16 types of blades and vanes for US plants in the GE Aircraft Engine Business Group. Last year, the Eastern Townships turned out over one million blades.

The innovative management system they used is called Sociotech, created by two Englishmen in the 1960s and introduced at Bromont in 1983 by consultants from the McGill University business school. More ambitious than so-called quality circles, the system enables the workers to form teams and to decide for themselves how to run each phase of production.

Like a subcontractor, teams of 60 to 90 workers are given product specifications and a budget. At frequent meetings, the teams then determine their own working hours, quality and cost controls. The teams even handle the hiring of new employees and evaluations of fellow workers' performance.

"This helps them develop a sense of entrepreneurship," says Luc Pellerin of the senior management team. "It shows in the initiative and hard work they put into their jobs."

The system has helped productivity immensely. The plant's original goal for last year was 500,000 engine blades, but output more than doubled. The target now is 1.5 million blades. Its annual sales to the GE engine group total $70 million at peak capacity. The assembled engines power airliners like the Boeing 737, the McDonnell Douglas DC-8 and the Airbus A-310.

The Bromont plant has twice won Canadian Business Excellence awards—for labour relations in 1987 and for production last year.

There are five production and ten support teams. Up to 12 percent of working hours are used for meetings and training sessions. Pellerin says all these meetings pay off. Team members exchange needed information, plan their work and solve problems. "All the employees know their job, know what to expect, and can adapt to change."

There are no punch clocks, no foremen, no big controls. Employees are paid by the week with no deduction for sick days. Absenteeism has never exceeded 3 percent per year.

The teams do have to follow strict quality control standards. They must also train their members in all the jobs within their operation. This multiple-skill system improves teamwork and no one is dependent on an absent member.

Source: Stephen McDougall, "Innovative Teamwork System Pays off at CGE's Expanding Plant in Bromont," *This Week in Business*, March 11, 1989, p. 11.

Summary of Learning Goals

1. **Describe the three levels of managers in a firm and analyze which functions are likely to be important to each level.**
   There are three levels of management in most firms: top management, which includes the president and vice-presidents; middle management, which includes plant managers and key department heads; and supervisory management, which includes the first-line managers such as supervisors. These three levels constitute the management pyramid.

2. **Explain the skills required for managerial success.**
   The three basic managerial skills are technical, human relations, and conceptual. Technical skills, which involve the manager's ability to understand and use techniques, tools, and knowledge of a specific discipline or department, are most important for first-level managers. Human relations skills, which involve working effectively with and through people in the accomplishment of assignments, are important for managers at every level. Conceptual skills, which involve the ability to see the "big picture" of the organization as a whole and how each part contributes to its overall functioning, are relatively more important for top management.

3. **Explain the importance of objectives in establishing standards by which management performance is measured.**

   Definite organizational objectives are needed by managers in performing their functions. These objectives serve as standards, and their pursuit is the basis of all management efforts. Common organizational objectives include profitability, market share, and social aims such as providing employment and being a good corporate citizen.

4. **Identify the steps in the decision-making process.**

   Decision-making is the most important task of the manager. The process can be described in five steps. The manager must recognize problems and opportunities, develop alternative courses of action, evaluate these alternatives, select and implement the chosen alternative and lastly, follow up to determine the effectiveness of the decision.

5. **Define the basic functions performed by all managers—planning, organizing, directing, and controlling.**

   Managers perform four basic functions in attempting to achieve company objectives: planning, organizing, directing, and controlling. Planning involves creating blueprints for future courses of action. Organizing involves grouping work into logical patterns and assigning tasks to specific workers. Directing (the people function of management) involves matching performance with organizational goals. Controlling deals with evaluating actual performance to determine whether the organization is accomplishing its objectives. It involves setting standards, collecting information to discover any deviations from standards, and taking corrective action to bring deviations into line. All four functions involve the manager in the task of decision-making. Although all management levels are involved in each of the managerial functions, top management devotes more of its time to planning and organizing, while the lower levels are more involved with directing and controlling.

6. **Explain the concept of leadership and three basic leadership styles.**

   Effective leaders often possess three traits: empathy (the ability to look at the situation from another's point of view), self-awareness, and objectivity. The three basic leadership styles depend on three elements: the leader, the followers, and the situation. The general trend is toward greater participation of subordinates in decisions that affect them.

Key Terms

management
management pyramid
top management
middle management
supervisory management
technical skills
human relations skills
conceptual skills
objectives

decision making
planning
organizing
directing
controlling
leadership
great man theory
autocratic leaders
democratic leaders
free rein leaders

Discussion Questions and Exercises

1. Explain the statement "Management principles are universal."
2. How do managers achieve objectives through people and other resources?
3. On what level of the management pyramid would each of the following persons be listed?
   a) department head
   b) executive vice-president
   c) supervisor
   d) branch manager
   e) mayor
   f) dean
4. Brisebois et Frères, a small electronics firm in eastern Ontario, has long observed St. Jean Baptiste Day as a paid holiday for its employees, 60 percent of whom live in Quebec. Jacques Brisebois, company president, has noticed that St. Jean Baptiste Day will fall on Tuesday during the next year. He wonders whether the Monday of that week should be declared a company holiday instead. Using each of the steps in the decision-making process, describe how you would make this decision.
5. Why are the functions performed by organizational objectives?
6. Briefly explain the four functions of management. Compare the relative importance of each function at each level of the management pyramid.
7. Classify each of the following as either primarily strategic plans or tactical plans. Defend your answer:
   a) registrar's office system for processing student requests for dropping and adding courses;
   b) IBM's development of the relatively inexpensive PCjr computer;

c) retail store manager's decision about the number of men's dress shirts to reorder;

d) hospital's procedure for admitting new patients;

e) Canadian Pacific Air Line's decision to relocate corporate headquarters to Quebec City;

f) student's choice of a university.

8. Relate the steps in the controlling process to the following: Although Air Canada has established the performance standard that at least 85 percent of its customers at an AC flight counter shall be waited on within five minutes, airport construction has reduced the available space of their flight counter at one terminal and limited the number of company personnel who can physically be available to assist customers. Construction is scheduled for completion in 90 days.

9. Give an example of strategic planning and tactical planning for each of the following:

a) off-campus bookstore

b) General Motors of Canada

c) *National Lampoon* magazine

d) local apartment complex

e) Pastaficio Pizza

f) local Canadian Army recruiting office

10. Identify the three basic leadership styles. Give an example of an instance in which each might be appropriate.

Case 5-1

WPP's Canadian Strategy

Purchase by the British marketing services group, WPP, of Toronto-based Public Affairs Resource Group in March 1989 was the conglomerate's first direct foray into Canada. Many observers believe it won't be the last.

WPP has had a commanding presence in Canada since it acquired J. Walter Thompson Canada, one of the largest advertising agencies in the country, as part of the deal to buy New York-based J. Walter Thompson Co. in 1987.

PARG's attraction lies in its highly visible research arm—Decima Research—and its neat fit with Hill & Knowlton, WPP's public relations arm. PARG's PR division operated both in Canada and the US. Hill & Knowlton, a subsidiary of JWT with an enormous US presence, had only a modest Canadian operation.

Combining all the companies under the umbrella of Hill & Knowlton Canada Ltd. allows WPP to tap a growing demand by clients for cross-referrals. Decima, for example, is one of Canada's leading public opinion research houses. It is thus well placed to do consumer research for clients of the new public relations subsidiary, Hill & Knowlton Communications.

David McNaughton, the co-founder of PARG, says "integration of communications services" is the key to future success. Since it bought JWT, the British company has snapped up at least 14 communications companies—from research houses and design firms to ad agencies on both sides of the Atlantic.

The push to integrate communications has also been driven home at JWT Canada. "WPP brought tremendous financial clout to JWT," says Andrew Krupski, executive vice-president and general manager. "They also brought an acute focus on managing the business and the ability to look at the communications game on a broader scale."

A direct marketing arm and a division that specializes in retail advertising have already been added.

JWT Canada wasn't weighed down by the corporate fat that encumbered its parent before the WPP purchase. And the emphasis on the bottom line has paid off. The agency's billings from all sources, including advertising, direct marketing and promotion, rose to $205 million at the end of last year from $162 million in 1987.

Source: Jamie Hubbard, "WPP's Canadian Strategy," *Financial Post*, March 27, 1989, p. 15.

Questions:
1. According to the case, why did WPP purchase PARG? Explain.
2. What does WPP's strategy of "integrating its communications services" imply about its top management's planning abilities? Explain.

Case 5-2

Leading Questions

According to consultant Douglas Bowie, businesses today must know what it is that they're trying to get done. Whereas managers of the 1970s could get by on plodding "management by objective," the leaner corporate structures of the 1980s require leaders who can imbue their subordinates with a grasp of a company's overall goals. "How can employees react quickly to changing conditions," asks Bowie, "if they don't understand what the company is about or what it's trying to accomplish?"

Bowie is executive president of The Niagara Institute, a nonprofit group based in Niagara-on-the-Lake, Ontario, working to improve the quality of leadership in Canadian society. He believes it's increasingly important for corporations to be guided not by nuts-and-bolts managers but by visionary leaders. Under the rationalizations of the early 1980s, corporate hierarchies were flattened out, and responsibility and authority were more widely distributed to employees. The employees taking on higher duties must have a good grasp of their company's broad vision for the future—which can only come from a special kind of corporate leader.

"Managers are caught up in the day-to-day running of a firm," says Larry Cash, a management career consultant with the Toronto firm Cash & Lehman. "Leaders are visionary, creative, and make things happen. The two roles are different, and too many companies are not going to the trouble of distinguishing between them among employees. What it costs a company is lost opportunities."

There is much evidence of an increasing yearning in North American business for the cultivation of better leaders. Some experts view lack of corporate leadership as part of the reason the Japanese have out-performed us in recent times. "Maybe we worried too much about the quick turnaround," says Bowie, "while the Japanese paid more attention to the longer-term direction they were taking."

While leaders see the big picture, and can inspire dedicated workers to achieve their top potential, they also have their limitations. They're apt to become bored with running the day-to-day affairs of a firm and are generally not tough enough at getting the best work out of employees who are misplaced or apathetic in their work. "My own research has shown that fully 80 percent of Canadians are not happy with their jobs," says Cash. "A good leader type, by this definition, just couldn't motivate them in most cases. You need someone who is satisfied just keeping the foot on the pedal—a manager."

Source: Michael Clugston, "Leading Questions," *Canadian Business*, June 1988, pp. 267–68. Reprinted by permission.

Questions:
1. How does Bowie's definition of the visionary leader coincide with the text's concept of leadership? Explain.
2. According to the case, why have North American companies fallen behind their Japanese counterparts? What implications does this have for top management's functions?
3. According to Bowie, what management combinations are necessary for a company to survive in the future? Explain.

The Role of Organization

Learning Goals

1. To explain the steps involved in the organizing process

2. To distinguish between organization and the organizing process

3. To identify the major forms of departmentalization

4. To explain the relationship between authority, responsibility, and accountability

5. To list the determinants of the span of management

6. To describe Parkinson's Law and how to avoid its effects

7. To evaluate each of the five basic forms of organization

8. To explain the function of the informal organization in a firm

Profile

Peter Widdrington—*Building an International Conglomerate*

As president, chief executive and chairman of giant John Labatt Ltd. of London, Ontario, Peter Widdrington has overseen the company's transformation from a domestic brewer into a huge food and beverage conglomerate that has made a major attack on the US and its first significant steps overseas as it strives to become a truly diversified international concern.

As a result of all this expansion, fiscal 1987 sales for the first time surpassed the $4 billion mark to hit $4.25 billion. And net earnings climbed to a record $125.2 million, 23 percent better than the year before.

Widdrington says Labatt's emphasis on diversification and globalization is not hard to understand.

Though highly profitable, beer is a static business and one which governments view as a "tax revenue haven." As long as there is a "tremendous tax burden imposed on breweries, there won't be room for growth in Canada. Therefore we must go to other things for growth possibilities," Widdrington says.

As for the assault south, Widdrington says the company finds itself in a number of businesses at a size where they really can't grow much bigger because of the Competition Act. "Unless we wanted to change our business mix, which we didn't want to, we were forced to look outside the country," he says.

If anyone should know what Labatt needs, it should be Widdrington. At age 57, the Toronto-born Queen's University and Harvard MBA grad is a Labatt "lifer," who started as a beer salesman in 1955 and has been promoted up the ladder ever since. He has been president and chief executive since 1973. Widdrington acknowledges spending an uninterrupted 32 years with Labatt has made a tremendous difference in his knowledge of the company.

Widdrington, who averages an 80-hour workweek, 40 percent of it in Toronto, 30

percent in London, and 30 percent on the road, takes little personal credit for the company's strategies, insisting "it's very much a cohesive team effort."

Delegating authority is seen as one of his major strengths by both analysts and subordinates. "This company is built on a very decentralized basis and senior operating people are given a lot of freedom and accountability," says Sydney Oland, president of Labatt Brewing Co. Ltd.

Source: Terry Brodie, "Labatt Builds an International Conglomerate," *Financial Times of Canada*, December 28, 1987, p.4. Reprinted by permission.

In 1961 US President John F. Kennedy committed his country to the goal of landing a person on the moon before the decade ended. The undertaking, Project Apollo, was an assault of unparalleled magnitude on the unknown. No one at the time knew if a human being could stand the strain of lunar flight or even if the moon could be landed on: many scientists believed its surface to be soft dust that would swallow a landing craft. If all the mysteries could be solved, and the goal achieved, the job of putting together the endeavour would be one of history's greatest organizational challenges.[1]

The trip to the moon would last eight days and cover nearly 400,000 km. Substandard work by any member of the organization was likely to produce tragic results. The project was coordinated by the Office of Manned Space Flight, a National Aeronautics and Space Administration (NASA) agency. Some 400,000 workers, 16 major industrial firms, and 20,000 subcontractors built rockets and controls, worked singly and jointly to train astronauts, conducted thousands of tests, and finally succeeded. But success was not without cost. A 1967 fire in an Apollo spacecraft killed three astronauts. The accident, a result of defective design and careless workmanship, served to bind the efforts of NASA and its contractors even more strongly to the goal.

The success of this unparalleled effort to organize people and resources in order to achieve specific objectives is summed up in the photo of the first footstep on the moon. On July 20, 1969, astronaut Neil Armstrong planted his boot in lunar dust, and the capabilities of organization were once again dramatically demonstrated.

Astronaut Neil Armstrong's first step on the moon is a dramatic symbol of the capabilities of organization.

What Is Organization?

We are constantly confronted with organization in a bewildering variety of activities. Sports teams and social organizations, religious groups and work activities—all include organization. Even other social species—ants, baboons, beavers—have organization.

Much of the success of any business depends on organization. Some kind of established structure is necessary to ensure that the manager's plans are carried out.

Organization is a structured process in which people interact to accomplish objectives. Managers must create a formal organization structure in which people and physical resources are properly arranged to carry out plans and achieve overall objectives. The definition of organization includes three key elements: human interaction, goal-directed activities, and structure.

For a small business, the organizing function is fairly simple. The owner-manager of the local dry-cleaning firm employs a few people to sell, to launder and dry-clean clothing, and to make deliveries. The owner usually handles purchases of detergents, plastic wrappers, and

organization
A structured process in which people interact to accomplish objectives.

**Figure 6-1
As the Number of Employees
Working in a Business Grows,
So Does the Need for Organization**

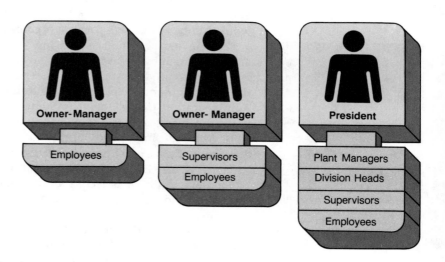

other materials; assigns jobs to employees; and personally directs the operation of the business.

But as a company grows, the need for organization increases, as Figure 6-1 illustrates. With increased size come specialization and a larger number of employees. Rather than a single salesperson, the organization employs a large sales force; rather than one bookkeeper, the firm has a sizable accounting department. The large number of personnel and accompanying specialization make it impossible for one person to supervise all operations. Some formal organization is necessary because the manager faces a larger number of specialized employees to supervise.

Organizational Structure

Although a small dry-cleaning firm experiences fewer organizational problems than a larger company, both have a formal structure to ensure that people perform tasks designed to accomplish company objectives. In the dry-cleaning company, for example, specific duties are assigned to wrappers, cleaners, and other personnel.

Organizational structure focuses first on the activities necessary to reach goals. Management analyzes the jobs that are to be performed. Then, people with both an interest in and the necessary qualifications for performing the jobs are employed. Coordination of the activities of each worker is another important responsibility of management, because employees must "pull together" if the firm is to operate smoothly.

Well-defined organizational structure should also contribute to employee morale. Employees who know what is expected on the job, who the supervisor is, and how the work fits into the total organizational structure are likely to form a harmonious, loyal work force.

Building the Organizational Structure

The structure of the formal organization is based on an analysis of the three key elements of any organization: human interaction, goal-directed activities, and structure. Management must coordinate the activities of workers to accomplish organizational objectives.

A company objective of "providing our customers with quality products at competitive prices" does not specifically spell out to the mechanic that production machinery should be regularly inspected and defects repaired. Company objectives are often broad in nature and do not specify individual work activities. Consequently, they must be broken down into specific goals for each worker in the organization.

Hierarchy of Objectives

hierarchy of organizational objectives
Levels of objectives that progress from the overall objectives of the firm to the specific objectives established for each employee.

A **hierarchy of organizational objectives** extends from the overall objectives of the firm to specific objectives established for each employee. The broader goals of profitability, sales, market share, and service are broken down into objectives for each division, each factory, each department, each work group, and each individual worker. Once this has been accomplished, each worker can see his or her contribution to the total organizational goals. The number of levels in the hierarchy depends on the size and complexity of the firm. Smaller firms usually have fewer levels than larger ones. Figure 6-2 illustrates this hierarchy of organizational objectives.

Figure 6-2

The Hierarchy of Organizational Objectives

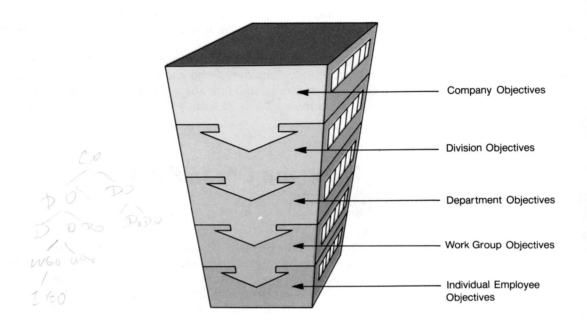

Company Objectives

Division Objectives

Department Objectives

Work Group Objectives

Individual Employee Objectives

Departmentalization

Building an organizational structure begins with an analysis of the major activities of the organization. In most firms these activities consist of production, marketing, and finance. Each activity is assigned to separate departments in the firm, to both managers and employees.

departmentalization
The subdivision of work activities into units within the organization.

Departmentalization is the subdivision of work activities into units within the organization. This subdivision allows individual workers to specialize in certain jobs and to become efficient in them. A marketing department may be headed by a marketing vice-president and may include sales, advertising, and market research. A personnel department may include recruitment, training, employee benefits, and industrial relations.

product departmentalization
Departmentalization organized on the basis of products.

geographic departmentalization
Departmentalization organized by regions of the country.

customer departmentalization
Departmentalization organized on the basis of customer segments.

functional departmentalization
Departmentalization based on the various functions (production, finance, marketing, and so on) of an organization.

Five major forms of departmentalization exist: product, geography, customer, function, and process. Maclean Hunter subdivides its organizational structure on the basis of **products**—the *Financial Post* division, the Business Magazines division (*Photo Canada*, *Canadian Interiors*, *Canadian Aviation*), the Consumer Magazines division (*Maclean's*, *Chatelaine*, *Flare*). Petro-Canada is subdivided on a **geographic** basis by regions of the country, as are CN, Canadian Pacific and the Bay. Many sporting-goods stores subdivide on a **customer** basis, with a wholesale operation serving school systems and a retail division serving other customers. Oil companies are sometimes divided on a **functional** basis, with departments in exploration, production, refining, marketing, and finance. Machinery manufacturers may departmentalize on the basis of **process**. Manufacturing a product may include cutting the material, heat-treating it, forming it into its final shape, and painting it—all these activities being included in one or more departments.

As Figure 6-3 indicates, a number of different bases for departmentalization may be used within the same company. The decisions on

Figure 6-3

An Organization Using Several Bases for Departmentalization

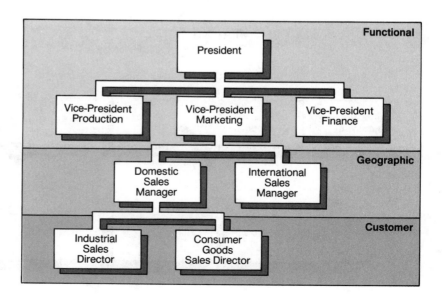

process departmentalization
Departmentalization based on the activities being performed (washing, heat treating, painting, packaging, and so on).

which bases to use are made by balancing the advantages and disadvantages of each. The experience and judgement of top management come into play in such decisions.

Authority and Responsibility

As the organization grows, the manager must assign part of his or her activities to subordinates in order to have time to devote to managerial functions. The act of assigning activities to subordinates is called **delegation.**

In delegating activities, the manager assigns to subordinates the responsibility to perform the assigned tasks. **Responsibility** is thus the obligation of a subordinate to perform assigned duties. Along with responsibility goes **authority,** the power to act and make decisions in carrying out assignments. Authority and responsibility must be balanced so that subordinates are capable of carrying out their assigned tasks. Delegation of sufficient authority to fulfill the subordinate's responsibility in turn makes the subordinate accountable to the supervisor for results. **Accountability** is the act of holding a person liable for carrying out activities for which he or she has the necessary authority and responsibility. This relationship is shown in Figure 6-4.

Even though authority is delegated to subordinates, the final responsibility rests with the manager. It is therefore incumbent upon that person to select qualified subordinates who are capable of performing the tasks. Focus 6-1 details the need for and the conditions guiding effective delegation in small companies.

delegation
The act of assigning part of a manager's activities to subordinates.

responsibility
The obligation of a subordinate to perform assigned duties.

authority
The power to act and make decisions in carrying out assignments.

accountability The liability of a manager for carrying out activities for which he or she has the necessary authority and responsibility.

Figure 6-4
The Delegation Process

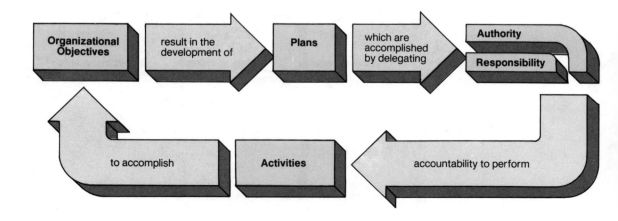

How Many Subordinates Can a Manager Supervise?

span of control
The optimum number of subordinates a manager can effectively manage.

One of the reasons for departmentalization is that managers are limited in the number of activities they can perform and the number of subordinates they can effectively supervise. The **span of control** is the optimum number of subordinates a manager can effectively manage.

Although the optimum number varies from one firm to the next, many management writers agree that top management should directly supervise no more than four to eight people. Supervisory managers, who direct workers performing relatively routine tasks, are capable of effectively managing a much larger number.

The critical factors in determining the optimum span of control are the type of work, the workers' training, the manager's ability, and the effectiveness of communications. An experienced supervisor who manages trained workers performing routine tasks with clear guidelines as to what is expected of them can effectively manage a much larger number of subordinates than can the vice-president of marketing or production. Focus 6-1 details the need for and the conditions guiding effective delegation in small companies.

Focus 6-1

Handing Over the Oars of Power

Coming to grips with the necessity of letting others share the workload can lead to substantial rewards. Studies have shown that a firm's performance increases significantly with the degree of delegation practised by its CEO. This recognition is particularly important among entrepreneurs who, by definition, like to be in control—making them poor team players and poorer delegators.

Most owner-managers follow a crisis-management style to delegation. These individuals seek assistance only when forced to do so in the face of their own inability to deal with the increasing demands of the company.

"It's difficult to be a two- or three-man operation in today's competitive market," says Ken Kirby, owner-manager of Kirby Floral Greens Inc., one of Vancouver's largest wholesale distributors of fresh flowers. By learning to share some of his work with his employees, Kirby has seen his firm grow over eight years to annual sales of around $5 million. "To grow and be successful—and not work 20 hours a day," he says, "you just have to learn to delegate."

Individuals should watch out for signals indicating a delegation problem. According to Wayne Hansen, a partner at Dunwoody & Co.

in Vancouver, it's usually time for a reassessment when things that can be done on a daily basis are not getting done, or when too much time is spent on the day-to-day activities, leaving no time for planning. Letting go through delegation doesn't mean opting out— an owner-manager still must maintain control.

A second key to effective delegation lies in knowing what to delegate. Individuals should stick with areas where they're strong and delegate in areas they're not. Prior to deciding on who should take on the duties to be handed over, thought must be given to the tasks and responsibilities of the job. Personality and educational requirements should be taken into account. And employers should start by looking inside for potential candidates. Employees will have a good motivational tool. Only when candidates are not available from the inside should employers look outside.

Another frequent problem confronting an employer who has always held the authority in the past lies in convincing employees that he/she is serious about delegating. Decisions to delegate certain responsibilities must be reinforced by a refusal to deal hands-on with those issues delegated.

Finally, the key to successful delegation lies in motivating the staff to be enthusiastic about accepting their new responsibilities. Employees should be encouraged to participate in company planning and given a piece of the action through profit sharing. If managers want employees to take on more responsibility, a coaching process that is corrective and not punitive should be instituted. Staff should be handled to the best of their abilities.

Source: Carla Furlong, "Handing Over the Oars of Power," *Canadian Business*, October 1987, pp. 100, 101.

Centralization versus Decentralization

How much authority are managers willing to disperse throughout the organization? Managers who emphasize **centralization** delegate only the smallest possible amount of authority. Proponents of a centralized management philosophy feel they can most effectively control and coordinate company activities by retaining most of the authority.

centralization
The practice of managers' dispersing very little authority throughout the organization.

Managers who emphasize **decentralization** disperse great amounts of authority to subordinates. Decentralization allows middle and supervisory management more leeway in making decisions than does centralization. For example, middle managers in a decentralized operation are likely to make many financial, production, and personnel decisions themselves rather than obtain approval from their superiors. When such decisions are made by subordinates, higher-level managers can devote their time to more important problems. But decentralization may be carried too far in some situations.

decentralization
The practice of managers' dispersing great amounts of authority to subordinates.

Avoiding Unnecessary Organizational Growth

As the size and complexity of an organization increase, the tendency is to add more supervisory personnel and specialists. This tendency is natural as decentralization occurs and managers recognize their limited span of control. However, the organizational planner should be certain that the new layers of managers and the dozens of technical advisors are really needed, or there will be little increase in production output or efficiency.

British historian-philosopher C. Northcote Parkinson explained this tendency in his book *Parkinson's Law*: "Work expands so as to fill the time available for its completion."[2] He applied his law to organizations by illustrating how the number of employees in a firm increases over a period of time regardless of the amount of work to be done. He pointed out, for example, that in 1914 the British navy, the most powerful in the world, contained 2,000 admiralty officials. In 1938 the number had increased to 3,569. By 1954 the "practically powerless" British navy was managed by 33,788 members of the admiralty staff. As the British Empire shrank in the period from 1935 to 1954, the number of officials in the British Colonial Office grew from 372 to 1,661—an average annual increase of nearly 6 percent.[3]

Why is there a tendency to add employees at a rate faster than the work is increasing? According to Parkinson, it can be blamed on (a) the selfish desire of managers to build empires by adding subordinates and (b) the paperwork created by the employment of additional workers.[4] Preventing (or minimizing) the occurrence of **Parkinson's Law** requires top management to be constantly vigilant and to give honest appraisals of the need for each proposed new position.

Parkinson's Law
A theory that claims "Work expands so as to fill the time available for its completion."

Forms of Organization Structure

Any group possessing common goals is an organization. But business organizations can be classified according to the nature of their internal authority relationships. Although five forms of organization structure will be discussed, only four forms are in common use today: line, line-and-staff, committee, and matrix. The line structure is the oldest form and is frequently used today in smaller organizations. The functional form uses specialist managers entirely responsible for their own fields within the operation. The line-and-staff form uses specialists to assist line officers. This is commonly used in medium- and large-sized firms. The fourth and fifth types, committees and the matrix organization, exist in many firms but only rarely as the sole types. They are typically used as a suborganizational form within a line-and-staff structure.

Line Organization

The line form of organization is the oldest and simplest form of organizational structure. Caesar's legions used this form; so does the Roman Catholic Church. Figure 6-5 illustrates line organization.

Figure 6-5
Line Organization Used by the
Roman Catholic Church

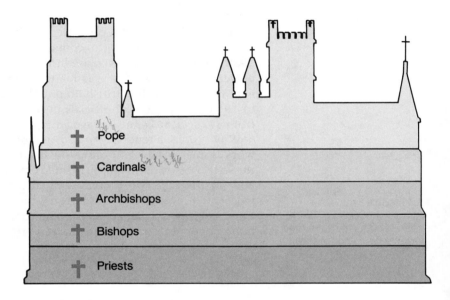

✝ Pope

✝ Cardinals

✝ Archbishops

✝ Bishops

✝ Priests

line organization
The organization structure based on a direct flow of authority from the chief executive to subordinates.

Line organization is the organization structure based on a direct flow of authority from the chief executive to subordinates. It is illustrated by the familiar story of the general who informs the colonel, who tells the major, who instructs the captain, who orders the lieutenant, who yells at the sergeant, who makes an unprintable request of the private, who carries out the order—or else.

The line form is simple. The chain of command is clear, and buck-passing is extremely difficult. Decisions can be made quickly, because the manager can act without consulting anyone other than an immediate superior. But an obvious defect exists within line organization. Each manager has complete responsibility for a number of activities and cannot possibly be an expert in all of them. The supervisor is therefore forced to become a jack-of-all-trades.

This defect is very apparent in medium- and large-sized firms, where the pure line form fails to provide the specialized skills so vital to modern industry. Executives are overburdened with administrative details and paperwork and have little time to devote to planning.

In evaluating the strengths and weaknesses of the line form, the obvious conclusion is that this structure is ineffective in all but the smallest organizations. Beauty shops, cleaning plants, "mom and pop" grocery stores, and small law firms can operate effectively with a simple line structure. The CBC, Eaton's, and Canadian General Electric cannot. Focus 6-2 shows the adjustment problems confronting COGNOS Inc. as the company grows from a small to a medium-sized enterprise.

Focus 6-2

Growing Pains Cramp Earnings at COGNOS

Ottawa-based software maker COGNOS Inc. is going through a turbulent transition. COGNOS executives maintain they can rein in escalating costs to make the company leaner and stronger. But outside analysts wonder how long this will take. Last year, COGNOS reported its first quarterly loss since going public in July 1986. It was a major setback for a company that had logged record revenues and earnings in the previous fiscal year.

Analyst Mark Sterling, president of International Data Corp., Toronto, remains optimistic about COGNOS' long-term prospects, but predicts "another couple of poor quarters" in the year ahead. Annual sales have grown to an estimated $80 million in the fiscal year ended February 29, 1988, from $10 million five years ago. The company has not yet come to grips with its size, Sterling says.

"We're going through some quite significant growing pains," COGNOS president Tom Csathy concedes. "We still do not have the management structure and productivity tools appropriate to a medium-sized company."

Csathy is a relative newcomer to COGNOS, although not to the computer industry. The former Burroughs Canada president was hired in July 1986. COGNOS' previous president, Michael Potter, stepped aside to become chairman.

Csathy's goal at COGNOS has been to lay the management groundwork for further growth.

First, the organization is being streamlined to trim administrative fat. Instead of separate product development and marketing organizations for each product line, Csathy has created one combined operation. This streamlining is long overdue. While sales during 1987's disastrous third quarter rose 9 percent from a year earlier, operating expenses soared 34 percent to $20.4 million.

Another bold about-face is the introduction of a direct sales organization to woo customers by mail and telephone. Previously, COGNOS relied on face-to-face selling, with representatives criss-crossing the globe in search of prospects. This worked well for products with price tags up to $100,000. But now that customers have smaller and cheaper computers, they are demanding less expensive software. COGNOS has obliged them this month by launching Powerhouse PC, a product designed for microcomputer networks.

One area where COGNOS is increasing spending is research and development. The research push is designed to take COGNOS into new areas of customer demand. In particular, users want to be able to develop custom software themselves, because programmers, to whom this task usually falls, do not necessarily have a good grasp of operations. COGNOS researchers are developing a new generation of software that can write other programmes. According to Potter, computer end-users with no knowledge of programming will be able to specify what programmes they need, and leave the writing to the software.

But in the short term, the company's fortunes will probably hinge on the success of its new PC product, and on the performance of US giant Hewlett Packard, whose microcomputer customers last year generated 60 percent of the Ottawa company's sales.

Source: Tamsin Carlisle, "Growing Pains Cramp Earnings at COGNOS," *The Financial Post*, March 14, 1988, p. 39.

Functional Organization

The functional organization form was developed by the father of scientific management, Frederick Taylor, who was attempting to overcome the basic weakness of the line organization form—the concentration of too many duties on a single manager. Taylor divided the work of a single supervisor into components similar to those shown in Figure 6-6. Then he made one supervisor responsible for each individual activity.[5]

Thus, workers become responsible to a specialist in each area such as repair and maintenance, routing, inspection, training, and time and credit. The functional organization does not increase the number of managers: it simply groups them differently. Under the line form each supervisor occasionally is responsible for training. Under the functional form a specialist is placed in charge of all training.

functional organization
The organization structure based on a direct flow of authority for each work activity or function.

The **functional organization** is the organization structure based on a direct flow of authority for each work activity or function. This form suffers from one critical deficiency. It creates a situation where workers have more than one boss at the same level. Even though each boss should possess authority only in the area of specialization, overlap and conflict are inevitable. And when problems occur, it is extremely difficult to locate the person at fault. With too many masters, production may be slowed rather than speeded up, and disciplinary problems may be difficult to handle. The problems of functional organization are so great that it no longer exists in most organizations. But it did serve a purpose in forcing management to focus on the need for developing an organization structure that would overcome the shortcomings of the pure line form.

Line-and-Staff Organization

line-and-staff organization
The organization structure that combines the direct flow of authority present in the line organization with staff departments that service, advise, and support the line departments.

The next logical step in organization structure is to combine the strengths of the line and functional organization forms. The **line-and-staff organization** is the organization structure that combines the direct flow of authority present in the line organization with staff departments that serve, advise, and support the line departments. Line departments are involved directly in decisions affecting the

Figure 6-6
The Functional Organization Form

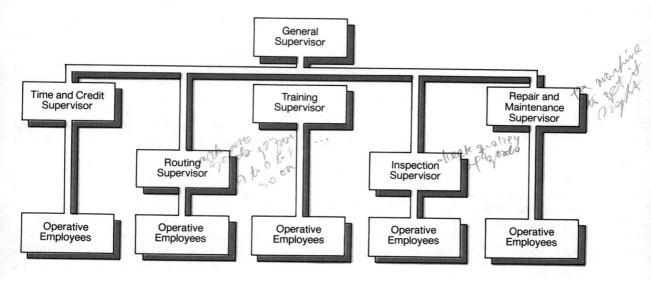

Figure 6-7
The Line-and-Staff Organization

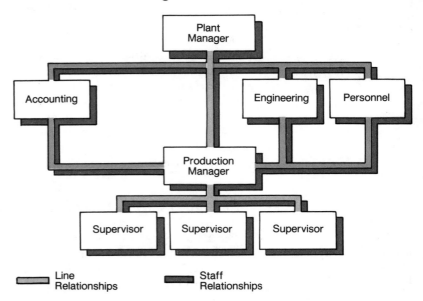

operation of the organization. Staff departments lend specialized technical support. As Figure 6-7 shows, workers receive daily supervision from a line manager and specialized advice and suggestions from staff personnel.

For all practical purposes the line-and-staff and the newer matrix structures (see page 173) are the only forms of organization capable of meeting the requirements of modern businesses. They combine the line organization's rapid decision making and effective, direct communications with the functional organization's expert knowledge needed to direct diverse and widespread activities.

The major difference between a line manager and a staff manager is in authority relationships. Staff managers are expected to make recommendations and to advise line managers. They do not possess the authority to give orders or to compel line managers to take action, although they do have the necessary line authority to supervise their own departments. Table 6-1 lists a few staff managers and their activities.

committee organization
The organization structure wherein authority and responsibility are jointly held by a group of individuals rather than by a single manager.

Committee Organization

Committee organization is the organization structure where authority and responsibility are jointly held by a group of individuals rather than by a single manager. It is proposed not as a separate

Table 6-1
Five Staff Managers and the Line Managers They Advise

Staff Manager	Duties and Line Managers Advised
Controller	Performs financial analyses and makes recommendations to the president and other high-level executives.
Advertising Manager	Assists the marketing director in developing the firm's advertising strategy.
Director of Research	Collects information and advises the firm's president, vice-presidents, and general managers.
Legal Counsel	Advises top management on legal matters.
Director of Engineering	Advises top management on technical and engineering matters.

structure for the entire organization but as part of the regular line-and-staff structure.

In the area of new product introductions, the most common organizational arrangement is the new product committee, which is typically composed of representatives of top management from such areas as marketing, finance, manufacturing, engineering, research, and accounting. In major corporations the inclusion of representatives from all areas involved in developing new products generally improves planning because diverse perspectives—production, marketing, finance—are considered. Company morale is also usually strengthened when all areas participate in decision making.

But committees tend to be slow and conservative, and decisions are often made through compromise based on conflicting interests rather than by choosing the best alternative. The definition of a camel as a horse established by a committee is descriptive of some committee decisions.

The Matrix Organization

matrix organization
The organization structure in which specialists from different parts of the organization are brought together to work on specific projects. It is usually used in conjunction with a traditional line-and-staff structure.

During the past two decades a growing number of organizations have utilized a new approach in adjusting their existing structures to changing requirements, particularly in the areas of research and development and new-product development. Operating in coexistence with traditional line-and-staff structures, this new form is referred to as **matrix organization** or project management organization, which may be defined as an organizational structure in which specialists from different parts of the organization are brought together to work on specific projects.

An identifying feature of such organizations is that some members of the organization report to two superiors instead of the traditional single boss.[6] This type of organization exists in companies as diverse as Canadian Marconi, Procter and Gamble, Canadian General Electric, NASA, Texas Instruments, Lockheed Aircraft, and the Harvard Business School. In each case, they attempt to focus the activities of several specialists from different functional areas of the organization on a specific problem or project.

Because this structure is designed to tackle specific problems or projects, the identification of such projects is followed by the selection of a team whose members have the appropriate skills. General Motors Corporation's decision to develop a line of economical, front-wheel-drive compacts was followed by the establishment of project teams consisting of specialists from design engineering, finance, marketing, research and development, and electronic data processing.

As Figure 6-8 indicates, the matrix organization produces a combination of dual authority—project members receive instructions from the project manager (the horizontal authority) and maintain their membership in their permanent functional departments (the vertical authority). In order to reduce the potential problems of two bosses, the project manager is typically granted considerable authority for the project and usually reports to the general manager.

The major benefits of the matrix structure lie in its flexibility and the ability to focus resources on major problems or projects. However, it requires coordination on the part of the project manager to mold individuals from diverse parts of the organization into an integrated team. Team members must be comfortable in working for more than one boss. To offset the temporary nature of the matrix team, the project manager is usually granted the authority to make salary decisions, promotion recommendations, and take other personnel actions for team members during the duration of the project.

Comparing the Five Forms of Organization

Although most large companies are organized on a line-and-staff basis, the line organization is usually the best form for smaller businesses. The committee form is also used to a limited extent in major corporations; and some departments (such as legal departments) may be organized on a functional basis. The matrix approach is increasingly used by large, multiproduct firms to focus diverse organizational resources on specific problems or projects. Table 6-2 compares the strengths and weaknesses of the five forms of organization.

Figure 6-8 The Matrix Organization

this president is on the top

if president

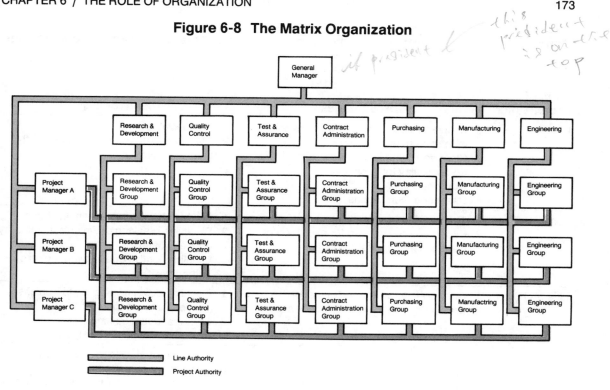

Line Authority

Project Authority

The Organization Chart as a Method of Formalization

organization chart
The formal outline of authority and responsibility relationships in an organization.

Most companies use an **organization chart** as their formal outline of authority and responsibility relationships. Such charts provide all employees with a visual statement of these relationships, enabling them to see how their work relates to the overall operation of the company and to whom they report. The organization chart is thus the blueprint of the organization, indicating lines of authority within it, including staff relationships, line relationships, and permanent committees.

Because the organization chart specifies each area of responsibility and authority, it can also help managers coordinate activities. But it reflects the organization at only one point in time, and it should, therefore, be updated periodically to reflect changing conditions.

Although most organization charts are constructed in the shape of a pyramid, extending downward from the board of directors or

Table 6-2
Comparison of Line, Functional, Line-and-Staff, Committee, and Matrix Organizations

Form of Organization	Advantages	Disadvantages
Line	1. Simple and easy for both workers and managers to understand 2. Clear delegation of authority and responsibility for each area 3. Quick decisions 4. Direct communications	1. No specialization 2. Overburdening of top executives with administrative details
Functional	1. The benefits of specialization 2. Expert advice available for each worker 3. Reduced managerial workload	1. Workers having more than one boss 2. Discipline breaking down unless authority is clearly defined 3. Possible conflict due to overlapping of authority
Line-and Staff	1. Specialists to advise line managers 2. Employees reporting to one superior	1. Conflict between line and staff unless relationships are clear 2. Staff managers making only recommendations to line managers
Committee	1. Combined judgement of several executives in diverse areas 2. Improved morale through participation in decision making	1. Committees slow in making decisions 2. Decisions that are the result of compromises rather than a choice of the best alternative.
Matrix	1. Flexibility 2. Provides method for focusing strongly on specific major problems or unique technical issues 3. Provides means of innovation without disrupting regular organizational structure	1. Problems may result, since this approach violates the traditional unit of command (one boss for each individual) principle 2. Project manager may encounter difficulty in developing cohesive team from diverse individuals recruited from numerous parts of the organization 3. Conflicts may arise between project managers and other department managers

"doughnut" structure
An organization chart made up of concentric circles that represent top management, staff personnel, and functional areas and that reflect a more flexible structure.

president, some firms have adopted the **"doughnut"** structure recommended by Robert Townsend, former president of Avis and author of the business satire *Up the Organization*. Townsend strongly endorses the need for flexible organization charts that reflect a dynamic organization.

In the best organizations people see themselves working in a circle as if around one table. One of the positions is designated chief executive officer, because somebody has to make all those tactical decisions that enable an organization to keep working.[7]

The doughnut design is made up of concentric circles, in which the centre ring consists of top management. The second ring is composed of important staff personnel, such as legal, personnel, research and development, and electronic data processing, whose services are used by all departments. The third ring consists of managers of functional areas, while remaining rings comprise department and other supervisory managers. Figure 6-9 shows the construction of a doughnut-shaped organization chart.

The Informal Organization

informal organization
A self-grouping of employees in the organization who possess informal channels of communication and contact.

In addition to the formal lines of authority and responsibility shown in the organization chart, informal channels of communication and contact also exist. The **informal organization** is a self-grouping of employees in the organization who possess informal channels of communication and contact. This type of organization is not formally planned; it develops out of the interactions of people.

**Figure 6-9
A Doughnut-Shaped
Organization Chart**

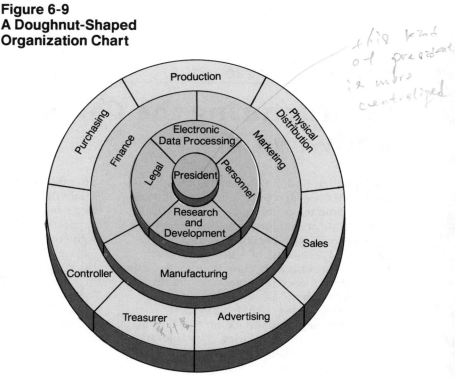

Formal organization is the creation of management; informal organization is the result of social and communications relationships. Groups of workers often cut across the formal organizational structure, and informal relationships exist at both managerial and lower levels. Supervisors from a number of departments may take coffee breaks together to discuss mutual interests and problems—both company and personal. Two machinists, a drill press operator, a receiving clerk, and a supervisor may form the company bowling team. As part of this regular interaction, they may discuss company operations and communicate the results of their talks to other workers in their areas.

Even though the informal organization is not shown on the organization chart, managers should be aware of its existence. It may even be possible to make use of some aspects of the informal organization in accomplishing organizational objectives such as through the use of the **grapevine**—the informal communications network found in most organizations. In his studies of the grapevine, Professor Keith Davis has found it to be 80 or 90 percent accurate in transmitting noncontroversial information. Because this information travels by word of mouth, the grapevine is faster than formal communications.[8] Recognition of its existence and how it works can enable managers to use the grapevine as a supplement to formal communications channels in dispersing information and in minimizing rumours and incorrect information.

grapevine
The informal communications network found in most organizations.

Controversial Issue

Restructuring the Canadian National Railway Co.

The Canadian National Railway Co. is a diversified Crown corporation, with holdings ranging from telecommunications to consulting to real estate, a conglomerate built up over 68 years. Before CNR's president and CEO, Ron Lawless, 63, can think of retiring, he must dismantle the unwieldy giant in order to bring it out of a very deep financial hole and save its essential rail division.

This restructuring includes selling off assets such as the telephone services in Newfoundland and the Northwest Territories, the exploration division, the steamships and even such landmarks as Toronto's CN Tower and the venerable railway hotels, including the Queen Elizabeth. Money raised this way will pay down the $3-billion debt that is draining the corporation of about $1 million in interest payments daily and crippling its ability to plan.

More difficult than selling off assets will be trimming the workforce. At its peak in 1962, the CNR carried 131,297 workers on its payroll. Today it has 41,000, and in five years it's expected to employ 26,000. Even Lawless, usually the optimist, admits that the job of trimming down might be too big and time too short.

Chief among his obstacles is a federal

government facing re-election and lacking the courage to give him a free hand to reorganize. A full corporate overhaul would do nothing to enhance the popularity of the ruling party. Unions would rise up in arms over the disappearing jobs and so would mayors and provincial politicians in towns that still rely on the CNR for their economic survival. Disappointed employees already feel that the spirit of railroading has been betrayed. These are the same disgruntled workers on whom the railway must rely for a successful reorganization.

The CNR has always been a political tool, as much a nation-builder as a transportation network. Born in 1919 from an amalgam of a handful of near-bankrupt railways across the country, it has two operating arms—the Canadian division, and three smaller US lines. A rail-transport network was essential to draw distant provinces into the infant nation of Canada. Fulfilling these promises, whatever the cost, fell to the CNR.

Ottawa allowed the CNR to run up deficits, which the government would eventually pay off by exchanging debt for equity. This did not sit well with private-sector competitors such as Canadian Pacific. Ottawa eventually bowed to their pressure. The modern mandate is based on three seemingly conflicting principles: that the CNR must be profitable; that without issuing shares to the public, it must raise money like any other company; that it should not stifle private-sector companies by growing too big.

The CNR Lawless inherited has the lowest productivity level of any major North American railway. It's top heavy with managers. It has no clearly defined decision-making centres, a cumbersome administrative process, too much track and not enough freight. For the past two decades, avaricious trucking companies have been eating into its business, and deregulation now allows larger US railways to bid for business that was once carried almost exclusively by the national railway.

For the future, Lawless foresees a stripped-down CNR that will also seek out new business relentlessly and offer the best rates and services. The key will be marketing, with regional managers having power to make decisions. To this end, he has essentially split the country in two with an imaginary line running through Toronto. Special rail cars for carrying manufactured goods will be based in and managed from Toronto while those for natural resources will operate in and be directed from Western Canada.

All plans to shake up the corporation must be approved by the CNR's board of directors, political appointees whose three-year hold on office depends on how well they look after the interests of the people who put them there. To succeed, Lawless must insulate his managers from the politicians. Former CNR president, Robert Bandeen, believes that Lawless has the skills and the personality to get the job done.

Source: Cecil Foster, "The Rule of the Lawless," *Report on Business Magazine, The Globe and Mail*, February 1988, pp. 40, 42, 44.

Summary of Learning Goals

1. **Explain the steps involved in the organizing process.**
   The act of organizing involves the blending of human and material resources through the design of a formal structure of tasks and authority. Once organizational objectives and plans have been developed, organizing involves the following five steps:

a) Determine specific work activities necessary to implement those plans and accomplish objectives.

b) Group work activities into a logical pattern or structure.

c) Assign activities to specific positions and people together with the necessary resources and authority to carry them out.

d) Coordinate activities of different groups and individuals.

e) Evaluate the results of the organizing process.

2. **Distinguish between organization and the organizing process.**

Organization refers to a structured grouping of people working together to achieve organizational objectives. Organizing involves the creation of an organizational structure. It is the process by which work activities are identified and assigned to specific individuals and departments. The result of the organizing process is the organizational structure.

3. **Identify the major forms of departmentalization.**

Departmentalization is the subdivision of work activities into units within the organization. This subdivision may be based on one of five major alternatives: products, geography, customers, functions, or processes. In addition, the same organization may use more than one basis for departmentalization.

4. **Explain the relationship between authority, responsibility, and accountability.**

Developing a formal organizational structure means that top management must delegate to subordinates the authority and responsibility to accomplish assignments. Responsibility is the obligation of a subordinate to perform those assigned duties. When subordinates are delegated such responsibilities, they must also be granted the necessary authority—the power to act and to make decisions in carrying out assignments. The individual who is granted such authority is also held accountable for carrying out these assigned tasks.

5. **List the determinants of the span of management.**

Determining the optimal number of subordinates a manager can effectively supervise involves a number of elements: the type of work performed, the workers' training, the amount of paperwork involved, the manager's ability, and the effectiveness of communication.

6. **Describe Parkinson's Law and how to avoid its effects.**

Parkinson's Law describes the unnecessary growth that frequently occurs over time in organizations. The law states, "Work expands so as to fill the time available for its completion." Such growth can usually be blamed on the selfish desires of some managers to build empires by adding subordinates, and by the paperwork created by the employment of additional workers. Auditing paperwork flows and requiring managers to justify additional employees can often minimize the occurrence of this phenomenon.

7. **Evaluate each of the five basic forms of organization.**

Five forms of organizational structure have been used: line, functional, line-and-staff, committee, and matrix. The line organization is the simplest form, but it suffers from a lack of specialization by management. The functional organization solves the problem of specialization by appointing managers for each specialized activity, but it suffers from the potential problem of multiple bosses for each worker. The line-and-staff form incorporates the strengths of both line and functional organization structures by assigning authority to line managers and adding staff specialists to provide information and advice.

The committee form of organization is rarely used as the sole organizational structure, but it is often incorporated to some extent within the line-and-staff structure. Because committees can be composed of representatives of a number of areas in the organization, they ensure that each area is represented in the decision-making process. The matrix form of organization, another subform of the line-and-staff structure, permits large, multiproduct firms to focus organizational resources on specific problems or projects. Because of its "team" approach and the fact that team members are accountable to more than one manager, conflicts can occur.

8. **Explain the function of the informal organization in a firm.**

The informal organization is a self-grouping of employees in a firm who possess informal channels of communication and contact. It grows out of social interactions and extracurricular relationships. Such informal contacts may serve as additional sources of information and may supplement the formal organization in serving the needs of its members.

Key Terms

organization
hierarchy of organizational
   objectives
departmentalization
product departmentalization
geographic departmentalization
customer departmentalization
functional departmentalization
process departmentalization
delegation
responsibility
authority
accountability

span of control
centralization
decentralization
Parkinson's Law
line organization
functional organization
line-and-staff organization
committee organization
matrix organization
organization chart
"doughnut" structure
informal organization
grapevine

Discussion Questions and Exercises

1. Contrast the terms *organizing* and *organization structure*. What are the purposes of a formal organization structure?

2. What is departmentalization? What are its major forms?

3. Give an example of a firm in your province that should use each of the following forms of departmentalization. Defend your answers.
   a) product
   b) geographic
   c) customer
   d) functional
   e) process

4. Why is it important that authority and responsibility be balanced in an organization?

5. Suggest some ways by which Parkinson's Law might be circumvented.

6. Identify the determinants of the optimal span of control.

7. Distinguish between centralization and decentralization. Under what circumstances might each be preferred?

8. Summarize the major strengths and weaknesses of each type of formal organization structure.

9. The typical professional sports team is owned by a wealthy individual who enjoys being involved with a particular sport. The owners usually make the major policy decisions, but a hired general manager handles other managerial duties. This person oversees facilities, equipment, vendors, and personnel matters, as well as usually having responsibility for player personnel decisions such as trades, new-player drafts, and assignment of players to minor leagues. The field manager, or head coach, is in charge of the team's actual performance. This person assists the general manager in matters concerning players. Other personnel employed by professional teams include physicians, assistant coaches, trainers, equipment managers, secretaries, scouts, and ticket sales personnel. Draw an organization chart for a professional sports team. Describe the strengths of this organizational structure.

10. The committee structure is rarely used as a separate structure for an entire organization. Suggest several specific ways of improving the committee form of organization structure.

Case 6-1

Hiram Walker—In High Spirits

Plant workers, executives and analysts watched anxiously for more than a year as multinationals waged a bitter battle for distiller Hiram Walker-Gooderham & Worts Ltd.—hoping for the best but anticipating the worst.

Most of them are now singing the praises of the eventual victor, Britain's food and drink group Allied-Lyons PLC, which wrested control of Hiram Walker from Gulf Canada in 1986. Allied-Lyons later bought the 49 percent it didn't already own and merged it with its own liquor business to create Hiram Walker–Allied Vintners Ltd.

More than a year after the merger, Canadian workers discovered that they have gained more than they lost. Senior sales and administrative executives are also breathing easier. Ron Dickson, a Canadian Autoworkers official who spoke for Hiram Walker employees during the takeover struggle, says Allied has lived up to, and exceeded, the commitments it made. Employment is up and Canadian-based management is still in place.

"You had two groups of rather concerned executives," says Michael Jackaman, chairman and CEO of the new company. "Put them together, give them some stability...and there's been a great upsurge in spirit and motivation. The future is more stable for both properties."

Windsor is still home to the finance and legal departments, human resources, communications and all North American operations. All other functions are based in Britain.

"We will always have more than one headquarters," says Jackaman. "Our operations are so spread out around the world that we can't possibly do it from one location." With head office functions now split between Windsor and Allied headquarters in Shepton Mallet, southwest of London, and with sales and distribution spread around the world, the facsimile machine has become the office workhorse.

Hiram Walker's North American sales force is busier than ever, with all of its leading brands showing sales gains. The wine and spirits division became Allied's biggest profit contributor in 1988, generating over $500 million. About 56 percent came from North American operations.

As a result of these changes, the company moved from eighth to fourth spot among wine and spirits producers, measured by volume, and second in profits.

Source: Barrie McKenna, "Spirits High at 'New' Hiram Walker," *The Financial Post*, April 3, 1989, p. 6.

Questions:
1. From the information in the case, what bases for departmentalization are evident for the newly merged company? Discuss.

2. Why must the company structure itself on such a diversified and decentralized basis? Explain.
3. What implications do this decentralized structure have on CEO Michael Jackaman's ability to delegate? How does this affect his responsibilities? Explain.

Case 6-2

Managing Line and Staff Relationships at Canadtronics Ltd.

Canadtronics Ltd., with operational headquarters in Winnipeg, is a large manufacturer of electronic component parts that operates 11 plants located throughout Canada. The company has three geographic divisions—Atlantic Provinces, Central, and West Coast— each of which is headed by a vice-president and general manager who is responsible for the sales and manufacturing functions within that division. The Central division's general manager is Cal Wyatt, a youthful, assertive executive who, according to himself, is destined to become the president of the company. He is involved in many decisions that affect the total company. Under his direction the profits and sales volume of the division have grown each year, mostly as a result of the successful operations of the Vancouver plant. The manager of the Vancouver plant, Jean Tracy, is a graduate engineer from the University of British Columbia who was brought into the company as part of a plan to bolster management talent. Plans are now being made to transfer her to corporate headquarters in Toronto, thus making it necessary to hire a new manager for Vancouver.

In Winnipeg, Rusty Hodge is the director of organizational strategy and also a member of general corporate staff. He reports directly to Adam Wilkinson who is president of the company and is also involved in many broad organizational decisions. Hodge has just completed a study of key personnel that indicates a need for technically trained managers. Normally Hodge operates as an adviser to the division vice-presidents. When he and the vice-president agree upon a proposed change of some important personnel, the move is made without consulting Wilkinson. However, when there is disagreement, the issue is referred to Wilkinson, who as president will make the final decision.

There is still a need for graduate engineers to fill top managerial positions that are presently available and positions that are expected to occur within the next five years as a result of growth and retirement of some of the present personnel. Corporate philosophy states that any preparation for a top management position should include three years as a plant manager. This forces the incumbent to learn the technical aspects of electronics manufacturing.

In regard to filling the important Vancouver position that will be vacated by Tracy, there are three possible choices: (1) a candidate could be recruited from outside the company. This move would allow for a period of training with subsequent assignment to a more responsible position in the corporation. (2) One of several younger assistant plant managers could be promoted. A number of them would benefit from the experience as manager of a large plant. It would take longer to train such a person, but he or she could be promoted to more responsible positions in time. (3) Philip Drummond, the present assistant plant manager in Winnipeg who has been with the company for 21 years, could be promoted. He has been largely responsible for the success of the plant since he directly supervises the operating departments and is familiar with the technical aspects of electronic component manufacturing. But he claims that he does not want to move from Winnipeg and wants to retire in nine more years when he reaches 55.

In discussing these three options with Cal Wyatt of the Central division, Rusty Hodge stated his preference for either of the first two. He felt that if the Drummond appointment were adopted it would tie up an important training position for about five years. He also felt that if Drummond elected to work until the retirement age of 65, it would mean an even longer period of time before the plant could be utilized for a training position. However, Elliot Lande, the West-Coast division vice-president, wants to promote Drummond, an old friend of his. He does not want to see any of the younger assistant plant managers in the Vancouver position nor will he approve the hiring of personnel from outside the company at this time. He feels options 1 and 2 lead to placing an unknown person into an important operating position that will affect the profitability of his division.

Hodge could not resolve the issue with Wyatt and Lande, and he decided to direct the question to Wilkinson for his decision.

Questions:
1. As president of the company, how would you decide the matter?
2. Should Hodge be given the authority to overrule Lande in the functional area of organizational planning? Support your answer.
3. Would you recommend a committee organization to solve the particular problem of Canadtronics Ltd.? Why or why not?

Part Three

Management of Human Resources

Chapter 7

Human Relations in Management

There's a lot of sentiment in Seagram.
—*Edgar Bronfman*

I don't care a rap *why* people do things in novels or real life. Working out motives is about as useful as a signboard on Niagara Falls.
—*Sir William Van Horne to a McGill English professor, in P. Newman, Flame of Power, 1959, p. 89.*

Learning Goals

1. To trace the development of the human relations movement in North America

2. To identify the different needs in Maslow's hierarchy

3. To distinguish between Theory X and Theory Y managers

4. To describe and differentiate the motivational factors and maintenance factors of a job

5. To identify the steps involved in a management by objectives (MBO) programme

6. To explain the "quality of work life" concept and identify the major categories of QWL programmes

7. To distinguish between job enrichment and job enlargement

8. To identify the alternative forms of flexible work schedules

9. To contrast the Theory Z organization with the typical North American firm

Profile

Roger Smith—*A Lesson in What to Avoid*

Roger Smith, chairman of General Motors, has been conferred the ignominious distinction of having "transformed the industry leader into a fallen giant."

The reason: Smith neglected his workforce.

Under his stewardship, the company went from holding 57 percent of the US car market in 1978 to only 35 percent in 1987. In the process, the company's break-even point went up by more than 30 percent. In 1986, during a booming decade, GM had to use creative accounting to justify paying common stock dividends. Today Ford gets all the credit for its new cars, and Chrysler all the attention for its sexy management style.

According to *Call Me Roger* author Albert Lee, Smith was a naive visionary who fundamentally misdiagnosed the dynamics of the new industrial age. He thought it was solely about technology. He did not see that it was about people in a new technical environment.

When Smith became chairman in 1981, he set out to revolutionize the making of cars. To this end, he would spend more than $6 billion a year through the 1980s. Computers and robotics would be the means to a "lights out" factory that would churn out high quality vehicles night and day at modest cost. Machines would replace people in GM factories.

Smith never found the key to productivity and success: trust between managers and workers. He regarded his workforce as an expensive substitute for technology, rather than a potentially productive companion.

This, despite GM's happy experience with a Toyota 50-50 joint venture in California, New United Motors Manufacturing Inc. The NUMMI plant is run by Japanese managers with emphasis on participation and responsibility for workers. It turned out 940 cars a day with the lowest costs and the highest quality, and with the most involved and satisfied workforce. Absenteeism was only 2-3 percent, a fraction of the absences at the vast majority of GM plants.

NUMMI produces 25 percent more cars per hour than GM has been able to do, with a third of the floor space.

Throughout, Smith continually expressed puzzlement that his workforce should take offence at large executive bonuses and stock options while assembly-line workers take pay cuts and see their earnings fall behind inflation. According to Lee, "far from motivating and inspiring, Smith's chairmanship was marred by an endless array of insensitive acts and public utterances that have devastated morale and turned cooperation into confrontation." His response to warning signals from Wall Street was a classically conservative combination of broad-swath cost-cutting and glitzy public relations.

Source: William Thorsell, "GM's Big Mistake," *Report on Business Magazine, The Globe and Mail*, October 1988, pp. 33-34.

Kockums, a Swedish company that builds supertankers, faced critical personnel problems a few years ago. Labour turnover was running at about 50 percent a year, and productivity was down. The firm's management at first turned to efficiency experts who pushed for greater worker output and angered Kockums' production workers.

In desperation, Nils-Hugo Hallenborg, the firm's chief executive officer, made an unusual decision. He turned the problem over to the union and asked union officials to work out a solution. They agreed to tackle the problem and produced a public report that was highly critical of Kockums' management. They also asked for specific changes in working conditions.

Hallenborg again startled observers by implementing the union's report. Wages based on the number of units produced were replaced by hourly rates. Additional medical personnel were hired. Safety standards were upgraded. Saunas were provided. Social workers were made available to deal with workers' personal problems. Vacation cabins were built in Scandinavia, Western Europe, and Africa.

Kockums also tried to give production workers more responsibility. Joint management-labour committees now schedule the construction of the approximately six supertankers built annually. The firm acknowledged that basically "dirty" jobs could not be changed. But management worked to improve nearly everything related to those jobs.

Kockums' employees have enthusiastically supported these reforms. Workers' output is up, and turnover is now under 20 percent a year. Kockums' personnel director puts it this way: "People like to work when they know why they are working."[1]

The Hawthorne Studies: Birth of a New Approach to Manager-Employee Relations

Although the changes in compensation programmes and the cooperative efforts of the Swedish shipbuilder may appear unusual (and perhaps impractical) even to workers and managers in the 1980s, striking changes in both the assumptions made by managers about their employees and in the approaches used by managers in motivating employee excellence have occurred over the past half century. The origin of many of these changes can be traced to a series of experiments that later became known as the Hawthorne studies.

In 1927 Elton Mayo and a group of researchers from Harvard University travelled to Chicago to explore the relationship between changes in physical working conditions and employee productivity. They chose the Hawthorne Plant of Western Electric as the subject of

Hawthorne studies
A series of investigations that revealed money and job security are not the only sources of employee motivation and that led to the development of the human relations approach to employee motivation.

their research. The **Hawthorne studies**, a series of investigations that revealed that money and job security are not the only sources of employee motivation, led to the development of the human relations approach to motivation.

The aim of the studies was to improve the output of factory workers responsible for assembling electrical relays. A group of workers were asked to act as subjects, and were assigned to a setting where they could be readily observed. Then, various changes were systematically introduced. Improved lighting had beneficial effects on productivity, as did better ventilation. Coffee breaks and snacks were introduced, and again output went up.

Eventually, the investigators became suspicious about the consistently positive effects of all these changes, and they began restoring the original conditions, even turning the lighting down gradually so that the workers did not notice it. Mayo and his colleagues were baffled to discover that reducing the light had no negative effect on productivity—in fact, in some cases output continued to rise! Productivity rose even when the light intensity was reduced to about that of moonlight.

> [Mayo and his colleagues] swooned at their desks. . . Because of some mysterious X which had thrust itself into the experiment. . .this group of six women was pouring 25 percent more relays into the chutes. . .
>
> What was this X? The research staff pulled themselves together and began looking for it. They conferred, argued, studied, and presently they found it. It wasn't in the physical production end of the factory at all. It was in the workers themselves. It was an attitude, the way the women now felt about their work and their group. By segregating them into a little world of their own, by asking their help and cooperation, the investigators had given their subjects a new sense of their own value. Their whole attitude changed from that of separate cogs in a machine to that of a congenial team helping the company solve a significant problem.
>
> They found stability, a place where they belonged, and work whose purpose they could clearly see. And so they worked faster and better than they ever had in their lives. The two functions of a factory had joined into one harmonious whole.[2]

What Motivates Workers?

The Hawthorne studies revolutionized management's approach to direction (or motivation) of employees. Prior to the Hawthorne investigation, most organizations had used money as the primary means of motivating workers. Satisfactory wages and job security were assumed to satisfy employees and motivate them to work faster and more efficiently in pursuit of overall organizational objectives. The importance of the Hawthorne findings lies not in denying the effect of money as a motivator but in emphasizing the presence of a number of other sources of employee motivation.

need
A lack of a useful or desired thing; a discrepancy between the actual state and a desired state.

Each individual is motivated to take action designed to satisfy needs. A **need** is simply a lack of a useful or desired thing. A **motive** is the inner state that directs the individual toward the goal of satisfying a felt need. The individual is moved (the root word for motive) to take action to reduce a state of tension and return to a condition of equilibrium. This motivation process is depicted in Figure 7-1.

motive
The inner state that directs the individual toward the goal of satisfying a felt need.

Figure 7-1
The Process of Motivation

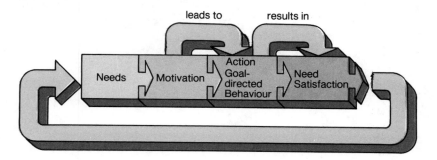

A Hierarchy of Human Needs

In the forties, psychologist Abraham H. Maslow developed a still widely accepted list of human needs based on two important assumptions:

1. People are wanting animals whose needs depend on what they already possess. A satisfied need is not a motivator; only those needs that have not been satisfied can influence behaviour.
2. People's needs are arranged in a hierarchy of importance. Once one need has been at least partially satisfied, another emerges and demands satisfaction.[3]

Figure 7-2 shows Maslow's hierarchy of human needs with the rungs arranged in order of importance to the individual. Priority is assigned to the basic physiological needs.

Figure 7-2
Maslow's Hierarchy of
Human Needs

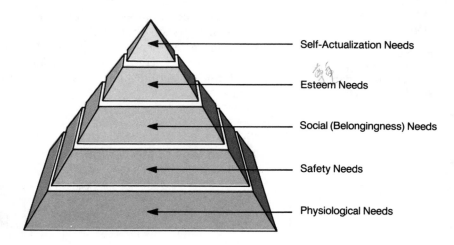

Self-Actualization Needs

Esteem Needs

Social (Belongingness) Needs

Safety Needs

Physiological Needs

Physiological Needs

physiological needs
The primary needs for food, shelter, and clothing that are present in all humans and that must be satisfied before higher-order needs can be considered.

Physiological needs are the primary needs for food, shelter, and clothing that are present in all humans and that must be satisfied before the individual can consider higher-order needs. A hungry person is possessed by the need to obtain food; other needs are ignored. But once the physiological needs are at least partially satisfied, the other needs come into the picture. Because minimum wage laws and union wage contracts have forced wage levels upwards so that most families can afford to satisfy their basic needs, the higher-order needs are likely to play a greater role in worker motivation today.

Safety Needs

safety needs
A second level of human needs, which includes job security, protection from physical harm, and avoidance of the unexpected.

The second-level **safety needs** include job security, protection from physical harm, and avoidance of the unexpected. In today's society gratification of these needs may take such forms as guaranteed annual wages, life insurance, the purchase of radial tires or the obeying of job safety rules.

Social Needs

social (belongingness) needs
The desire to be accepted by members of the family and other individuals and groups.

Satisfaction of physiological and safety needs leads to the third rung on the ladder, **social needs** (also known as **belongingness needs**)— the desire to be accepted by members of the family and other individuals and groups. The individual may be motivated to join various groups at the factory, conforming to the standards established and accepted by the informal organization, in order to fulfill these needs.

Esteem Needs

esteem needs
The human needs for a sense of accomplishment, a feeling of achievement, and the respect of others.

The needs near the top of the ladder, **esteem needs**, are more difficult to satisfy. At this level is the need to feel a sense of accomplishment, achievement, and respect from others. The need to excel is an almost universal human trait.

The esteem need is closely related to belongingness needs. However, at this level the individual wants not just acceptance but also recognition and respect—the desire to stand out from the crowd in some area.

Self-Actualization Needs

self-actualization needs
The needs for fulfillment, for realizing one's potential, and for totally using one's talents and capabilities.

The top rung on the hierarchy of human needs is **self-actualization needs**—the needs for fulfillment, for realizing one's own potential, for using totally one's talents and capabilities.

Robert Louis Stevenson was describing self-actualization when he wrote, "to be what we are, and to become what we are capable of becoming, is the only end of life."[4] For Rich Little, self-actualization may mean being the most popular comedian in Canada and the United States. The approximately 200 new entries in each revised edition of the *Guinness Book of World Records* represent individuals daring to accomplish what no person has done before.

Applying the Needs Concept

Maslow points out that a satisfied need is no longer a motivator. Once the physiological needs are satisfied, the individual becomes concerned with higher-order needs. There will obviously be periods when one is motivated by the need to relieve thirst or hunger, but interest is most often directed toward the satisfaction of safety, belongingness, and the other needs on the ladder.

Business organizations have been extremely successful in satisfying the lower-order physiological and safety needs. The traditional view of workers as ingredients in the productive process—as machines like lathes, drill presses, and other equipment—led management to motivate them with money. The Hawthorne studies showed that people are not like machines and that social and psychological needs are motivators as effective as money. Managers at that point had to reconsider their assumptions about employees and how best to motivate them. Focus 7-1 shows that managers everywhere are reconsidering these assumptions.

Focus 7-1

Motivating the Soviet Worker

Maslow's hierarchy of needs is not unknown in the Soviet Union.

There, getting people to *work harder* is a big test for managers. Soviet economic growth targets rely almost entirely on more output from labour. But productivity gains are lagging. Any remedy is *worth a try* —

Bonuses for beating production quotas are old hat in the Soviet Union but still useful. In addition, many factories now have special *"workers' brigades"* that, in theory, are paid wholly on results. They often set their own output goals. A new award has been adopted for *"shock" workers*, those employees who post outstanding results. Factories, too, may be pitted one against another.

The *Soviet stick* also is used. Workers who damage machinery must pay for repairs. Absentees and people persistently late to work may be shunted to jobs with low pay. Others may be dropped *down the waiting list* for new apartments.

Soviet labourers have their gripes, too. One is *"storming"* — having to work flat out at the end of every month to fulfill quotas. Disregard of health and safety rules also irks them. Authorities' advice: *Complain to your union.*

But Soviet unions see their main task as insuring that output meets goals.

Source: "World Business," *U.S. News & World Report*, Sept. 19, 1977, p. 54.

Theory X: Do People Hate Work?

Theory X
The traditional managerial assumption that employees dislike work and must be coerced, controlled, or threatened to motivate them to work.

Theory X is the traditional managerial assumption that employees dislike work and must be coerced, controlled, or threatened to motivate them to work. According to its author, Douglas McGregor, Theory X involves the following:

1. The average human being has an inherent dislike of work and will avoid it if possible.
2. Because of this characteristic, most people must be coerced, controlled, directed, or threatened with punishment to get them to put forth adequate effort toward the achievement of organization objectives.

3. The average human being prefers to be directed, wishes to avoid responsibility, has relatively little ambition, and wants security above all.[5]

If true, this traditional view of workers is a rather depressing indictment of human nature. Managers who accept the view may choose to direct their subordinates through close and constant observation, continually holding over them the threat of disciplinary action and demanding that they closely follow company policies and procedures.

Theory Y: Replacement for Theory X

Theory X appears to have a critical deficiency. It focuses strictly on physiological and safety needs while ignoring the higher-order needs. If people behave in the manner described by Theory X, the reason for their behaviour may be that the organization only partially satisfies their needs. If, instead, the organization enables them to satisfy their social, esteem, and self-actualization needs, new behaviour patterns should develop—and different assumptions should be made.

Theory Y
The newer managerial assumption that workers do not dislike work and that under proper conditions they accept and seek out responsibilities in order to fulfill their social, esteem, and self-actualization needs.

Theory Y offers a new managerial assumption—that workers do not dislike work and that, under proper conditions, they accept and seek out responsibilities in order to fulfill their social, esteem, and self-actualization needs. Under Theory Y, McGregor points out:

1. Workers do not inherently dislike work. The expenditures of physical and mental effort in work are as natural as play or rest.
2. Employees do not want to be rigidly controlled and threatened with punishment.
3. The average worker will, under proper conditions, not only accept but actually seek responsibility.
4. Employees desire to satisfy social, esteem, and self-actualization needs in addition to security needs.[6]

Unlike the traditional management philosophy that relies on external control and constant supervision, Theory Y emphasizes self-control and direction. Its implementation requires a totally different managerial strategy.

Maintenance Versus Motivational Factors

Over two decades ago, psychologist Frederick Herzberg conducted a study in human motivation of various job factors as sources of satisfaction and dissatisfaction. Based on his research, Herzberg reached two conclusions:

maintenance factors
Job-related factors, such as salary, working conditions, and job security, that must be present in order to prevent worker dissatisfaction but which are not strong motivators.

motivational factors
Job-centred characteristics, such as the work itself, recognition, responsibility, advancement, and growth potential, which are the key sources of employee motivation.

1. Certain characteristics of a job, called **maintenance factors**, are necessary to maintain a desired level of satisfaction. They include such job-related factors as salary, working conditions, and job security. They must be present in order to prevent worker dissatisfaction, but they are not strong motivators. If they are absent or inadequate, they are likely to serve as *dissatisfiers*.
2. Other job-centred characteristics are **motivational factors** such as the work itself, recognition, responsibility, advancement, and growth potential—the key sources of employee motivation.

Thus, although maintenance factors such as money are extremely important when they are lacking, they are of low motivational value when they are present in adequate amounts. Instead, the key motivational factors are related to the job itself. The supervisor motivates the worker not with an additional coffee break but with greater involvement in the job.[7] Focus 7-2 provides an example of factors and techniques used by Ultramar to motivate its employees, with success.

As Figure 7-3 shows, a great deal of similarity exists between Herzberg's two factors and Maslow's hierarchy of human needs. Herzberg's message is that the lower-rung needs have already been satisfied for most workers, and the manager must focus on the higher-level needs—the primary motivators.

Figure 7-3
Comparing Herzberg and Maslow

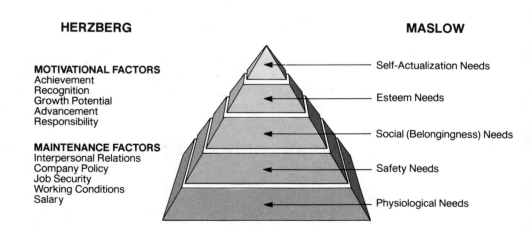

HERZBERG

MOTIVATIONAL FACTORS
Achievement
Recognition
Growth Potential
Advancement
Responsibility

MAINTENANCE FACTORS
Interpersonal Relations
Company Policy
Job Security
Working Conditions
Salary

MASLOW

Self-Actualization Needs

Esteem Needs

Social (Belongingness) Needs

Safety Needs

Physiological Needs

Focus 7-2

Ultramar—On Rewarding Employees

There were smiles all around at Ultramar Canada Inc. as 1,400 employees received $3 million in cash bonuses and company shares. "It's really like a holiday," says Pierre Martel, Ultramar's manager for compensation. "People got their cheques in the morning and they didn't stop smiling all day."

Ultramar decided to pay the one-time bonus to reward its staff for the company's strong performance in 1987. While the annual report is not yet out, the British-controlled, Montreal-based oil company earned profits for the first time in five years.

The amount awarded depended on the individual's performance over the year. A cheque for half the bonus was attached to the regular paycheques, while the rest came in the form of company shares. The bonuses came over and above salary increases.

The company, which moved its head office to Montreal from Toronto a year ago and operates a refinery in Quebec City, has launched other personnel programmes to improve morale and productivity. Ultramar asks each employee to work an extra half hour each day and in turn, the employees can take off one full day each month, in addition to regular paid vacation. The company has also introduced flex hours. In addition, a payroll savings plan launched in 1988 allows employees to save up to 18 percent of their weekly basic salary. For every dollar an employee puts into the plan, the company contributes 50 cents, up to a maximum of 6 percent of the base salary.

Martel says these new programmes have boosted morale and helped Ultramar to increase its share of gasoline sales in Quebec and the Atlantic region. When Ultramar took over the Gulf gas stations in Eastern Canada two years ago, a five-year plan was put forward to increase staff productivity. This plan plus management efforts to improve employee relations have helped bring the company out of the red.

Source: Linda Masse, "Ultramar Rewards Employees with Bonuses, Shares," *This Week in Business*, April 2, 1988, p. 12. Reprinted by permission.

What Factors Influence Employee Morale?

morale
The mental attitude of employees toward their companies and their jobs.

Morale is the mental attitude of employees toward their companies and their jobs. High morale is a sign of a well-managed organization, because the worker's attitude toward the job affects the quality of the work done.

One of the most obvious signs of poor manager-worker relations is poor morale. It lurks behind absenteeism, employee turnover, slow-downs, and wildcat strikes; it shows up in lower productivity, employee grievances, and transfers.

But often management's view of what leads to high employee morale is incorrect. One research study compared how managers and workers ranked the importance of various morale factors. Table 7-1 shows how managers ranked these factors.

Managers chiefly emphasized the lower-order needs of money and job security. But Table 7-2 reveals a quite different ranking by employees. Opinions varied significantly on the importance of such

Table 7-1
Managers' Assessment of Factors Leading to High Morale

Morale Item	Manager Ranking
Good wages	1
Job security	2
Promotion and growth with company	3
Good working conditions	4
Interesting work	5
Management loyalty to workers	6
Tactful disciplining	7
Full appreciation for work done	8
Sympathetic understanding of personal problems	9
Feeling "in" on things	10

Table 7-2
Workers' Assessment of Factors Leading to High Morale

Morale Item	Employee Ranking
Full appreciation for work done	1
Feeling "in" on things	2
Sympathetic understanding of personal problems	3
Job security	4
Good wages	5
Interesting work	6
Promotion and growth with company	7
Management loyalty to workers	8
Good working conditions	9
Tactful disciplining	10

Source: Lawrence Lindahl, "What Makes a Good Job," *Personnel*, p. 265. January, 1949. Reprinted by permission.

items as job security and appreciation for work done. Other differences included the importance of fair pay, promotion, and understanding of personal problems.

The maintenance of high morale means more than keeping employees happy. A two-day workweek, longer vacations, or almost continual coffee breaks could easily produce happy employees. But high morale results from an environment in which workers obtain satisfaction from their work and are motivated to excel in their assigned duties, which should lead to greater production. Management, therefore, should create a work environment that will result in high employee morale. (See Focus 7-3.)

Focus 7-3

Walt Disney—Making Customers and Employees Happy is Mickey Mouse's Job

Walt Disney Co., often singled out for its brilliant way of managing America's number one tourist attraction, is now peddling its success formula at Orlando's Walt Disney World in the form of seminars. Indoctrination in what Disney calls its ''Pixie Dust Formula'' isn't cheap, but the insights, if obvious, are often overlooked and thus bear repeating:

• Don't underestimate the personal touch. Disney employees, called ''cast members'' whether they're actors or janitors, are taught to compliment visitors to Disney World on their clothes and to check their birth dates when examining identification in order to wish them a happy birthday if the big day is near.

• ''Our philosophy is that if you take care of your employees, the dollars will take care of themselves,'' says Disney business seminar manager Jim Poisant. ''Cast members are treated as we expect them to treat guests. If we treat our people properly, they will turn around and treat our guests properly.''

• Employee rules won't work unless top executives set the example. ''Modelling is everything,'' Poisant says.

Most visiting executives are daunted as they emerge from the seminars by the huge task of trying to make their companies measure up to Disney. ''The Disney experience illustrates,'' says one recent lecturee, ''that you can't create a pleasant customer experience by wishing on a star.''

The same may be said of employees at work.

Source: David Olive, ''How To Make Customers Happy? Why, That's Just Mickey Mouse,'' *Report on Business Magazine, The Globe and Mail*, February 1988, p. 14.

"Why, thank you, sir, and I had it in mind to tell you
what a bang-up job I think _you're_ doing."

Showing full appreciation for work done is one way to motivate people.

Drawing by Mulligan; © 1975 The New Yorker Magazine. Inc.

Management Techniques Designed to Improve Motivation

Two management techniques are widely used today in an attempt to improve the overall motivation and performance of workers: management by objectives, and job enrichment.

Management by Objectives

The management by objectives (MBO) approach was first proposed nearly 50 years ago. It was popularized in the early fifties by Peter Drucker, who described it this way:

> The objectives of the district manager's job should be clearly defined by the contribution he and his district sales force have to make to the sales department, the objectives of the project engineer's job by the contribution he, his engineers and draftsmen make to the engineering department. . . . This requires each manager to develop and set the objectives of his unit himself. Higher management must, of course, reserve the power to approve or disapprove his objectives. But their development is part of a manager's responsibility; indeed, it is his first responsibility.[8]

management by objectives (MBO)
A programme designed to improve employees' motivation through having them participate in setting their own goals and letting them know in advance precisely how they will be evaluated.

Thus, **management by objectives** is a programme designed to improve employees' motivation through having them participate in setting their own goals and letting them know in advance precisely how they will be evaluated.

Five steps in an MBO programme. Figure 7-4 illustrates the five-step sequence of most MBO programmes:

1. Each subordinate discusses the job description with the manager.
2. Short-term performance goals are established.
3. The subordinate meets regularly with the manager to discuss progress toward the goals.
4. Intermediate checkpoints are established to measure progress toward the goals.
5. At the end of a defined period, manager and subordinate together evaluate the results of the subordinate's efforts.

Management by objectives involves mutual goal-setting by manager and subordinate. Both must reach an understanding about the subordinate's major area of responsibility and the acceptable level of performance. These understandings form the basis of the subordinate's goals for the next planning period (usually in about six months).

Goals should be in numerical terms whenever possible—for example, reducing scrap losses by 5 percent or increasing sales of pocket calculators by 15 percent. Once these goals are established and agreed upon, the subordinate has the responsibility for achieving them.

Figure 7-4
The Management by Objectives Sequence

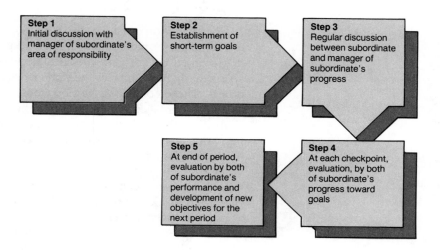

During the interim the subordinate may check often with the manager. At the end of the period a formal progress review is conducted. Both the subordinate and the manager discuss perform-ance and determine whether the goals were achieved. New goals are then established for the next period.

Benefits of an MBO programme. The chief purpose of manage-ment by objectives is to improve motivation of employees through their participation in setting their own goals. Workers thus know both the job to be done and precisely how they will be evaluated.

An MBO programme should improve morale by improving com-munications between individual employees and their managers. It should also enable workers to relate their performance to overall organizational goals. Finally, it should serve as a basis for decisions about salary increases and promotions.

MBO at all levels. MBO is not limited to any single level in the organization. It should probably begin with the president, who should set some personal job objectives in consultation with the board of directors. The process should then proceed throughout the organi-zation, extending to every employee.

Is MBO for everyone? Experience with MBO programmes indi-cates that they have merit if used with judgment and a great deal of planning. Because changes may have to be made in such areas as the degree of communication between managers and subordinates, MBO will succeed only where both managers and subordinates feel com-fortable with it and are willing to participate in it.

Management must also recognize that in many organizations workers' goals are constantly changing. In such situations it is much more difficult to measure results accurately.

Improving the Quality of Life

The participation of employees who meet with supervisors and agree to a set of performance goals in an MBO programme is a major step in improving the quality of work life. However, the typical worker with an assembly line job faces the same work conditions as do millions of others. These conditions can be traced to the investigations of the scientific management thinkers of the early part of the twentieth century. In their efforts to generate added productivity from subdivid-ing work activities and assigning them to specialized workers, they produced jobs with common characteristics; mechanically controlled work pace, repetitiveness, minimum skill requirements, predeter-mined tools and techniques, and minute subdivision of the product that, therefore, requires only surface mental attention.

What do these job characteristics add up to? In many cases, they lead to boredom—or to what is popularly called "the blue-collar blues." When workers cannot control their pace, cannot use judgement, and are not challenged to improve their skills above a minimal level, they are likely to be poorly motivated and will possibly suffer from alienation.

In addition to the boredom factor, the simplification and narrowing of tasks is becoming less applicable with technological changes and increased automation. Millions of manufacturing jobs—especially in such industries as automobile, steel, and rubber—are disappearing because of foreign competition and automation. The new jobs created frequently require more broadly trained employees with the knowledge and flexibility to adapt to an evolving workplace.

quality of work life (QWL)
Process of reshaping the workplace by permitting organization members to have input into job design and the overall work environment.

In recent years, the term **quality of work life (QWL)** has been used to describe a number of techniques currently being used to reshape the workplace. QWL is a process whereby all members of the organization, through appropriate channels of communication set up for this purpose, have some say about the work environment in general and the design of their jobs in particular. It involves recognition on the part of management that employees are unique, adult individuals and that their input is valuable and should be encouraged. As Bryon P. Crane, General Motors' director of labour relations, puts it, "There are many fancy definitions of QWL, but really they all boil down to treating people as adults when they are at work." Three major categories of QWL programmes are work restructuring to provide job enrichment, flexible work schedules, and Theory Z participative management. See Focus 7-4 for a report on employee participation and its positive impact on Donelly Corp.

Focus 7-4

Participative System Propels Donelly Corp. to the Top

Several executives and assembly line workers from Michigan flew to Montreal recently to describe how participative management has transformed their company into a leading auto parts maker. After their presentation, human resources director Kay Hubbard offered to send reports on the Donelly management system to all those who left their business cards. A hundred executives responded.

Based in Holland, Michigan, Donelly has become one of the most successful makers of rearview mirrors and modular windows for the automobile industry, with annual sales in 30 countries topping $100 million US.

One of the first companies to adopt a truly participative management and profit-sharing structure, Donelly employs 1,400 people across two countries. The company has also managed to break into the Japanese and Asian markets and has won auto industry awards for the high quality of its products.

Key to this success, the managers and workers agree, is that Donelly has a committed workforce that cares about its products and performance.

The Donelly Management System was first implemented in 1952, based on a concept developed back in the 1930s by Joseph Scanlon, then an accountant for the United Steel Workers of America. The plan is based on the belief that employees should have a voice in company management and a share in company profits. And while profit-sharing is an obvious drawing card, many Donelly employees feel that taking part in decision-making makes a big difference.

The [pay] bonus is really a by-product of the incentive programme," comments Bob Baird, manager for organizational development and training programmes. "The *real* incentive is the opportunity to participate and get involved."

Involvement at Donelly comes through work teams of 20 persons each. Everyone is encouraged to discuss all issues relating to fairness on the job. To tackle issues at the company-wide level, each work team elects a representative to management-labour committees that hash out staff problems, company expansion plans and production quotas.

To top off these perks, wages and benefits at Donelly are attractive. Bonuses tied to the company's net profits are paid out each month and average about 6 percent of an employee's salary. But the system does work two ways. When profits decline, the bonus payments are suspended until the balance sheet improves. Similarly, when the company makes a major decision about hirings or layoffs, the staff committees are consulted.

The grassroots committees—on which every employee is given the opportunity to serve—make the management structure truly innovative. The resulting sense of responsibility reinforces the feeling among employees that they make a difference, and keeps up the level of quality awareness.

To deter despondency, which can be a problem on assembly lines, team members rotate jobs. "Self-direction means a lot of commitment and flexibility," says Hubbard. Employees are expected to know all the jobs and all the skills in each committee.

Unlike many production workers, Donelly employees don't punch a clock or wear uniforms. Not too long ago, however, they decided on some common attire. They had T-shirts made with *We Do Windows* printed across the front.

Source: Nancy McHarg, "Donelly Corp. Gives Employees Management Voice, Share of Profits," *This Week in Business*, April 8, 1989, p. 13. Reprinted by permission.

Job Enrichment

Most assembly line jobs are likely to have certain common characteristics: mechanically controlled work pace, repetitiveness, minimum skill requirements, predetermined tools and techniques, and minute subdivision of the product that, therefore, requires only surface mental attention.[9]

job enrichment
Giving workers more authority to plan their work and to decide how it is to be accomplished and allowing them to learn related skills or to trade jobs with others.

Job enrichment means giving workers more authority to plan their work and to decide how it is to be accomplished, and allowing them to learn related skills or to trade jobs with others. Building on Herzberg's ideas, it focuses on motivational factors by designing work that will satisfy individual as well as company needs. Herzberg explains job enrichment this way:

> [It] seeks to improve both task efficiency and human satisfaction by means of building into people's jobs. . .greater scope for personal achievement and recognition, more challenging and responsible work, and more opportunity for individual advancement and growth. It is concerned only incidentally with matters such as pay and working conditions, organizational structure, communications, and training, important and necessary though these may be in their own right.[10]

How can jobs be enriched? A number of companies are using job enrichment with excellent results. For example:

> Chrysler assembly line workers now get the chance to road test cars to help spot quality defects. In one assembly plant, Chrysler formed a workers' "damage committee" to check welding operations of car bodies. One worker wrote management after his week of moving around the department. "Since that week, I see metal damage, missing welds, and forming fits I never noticed before. This. . .gives me a whole new outlook on body building. . .a sense of real satisfaction. . .using my eyes and mind instead of just my hands."[11]

Two Swedish automobile manufacturers, Volvo and Saab, began a programme of job enrichment in 1971. Rather than station each worker on an assembly line to perform one task or a few monotonous operations on each car as it passed by, they decided to have parts brought to the cars and then installed by semiautonomous groups of workers.

job enlargement
A method of increasing the number of tasks performed by a worker in order to make the job more psychologically rewarding.

In this instance, the enrichment process was accomplished by job enlargement. **Job enlargement** is a method of increasing the number of tasks being performed by individual workers in an attempt to make the job more psychologically rewarding.

An important application of job enrichment took place at the General Foods Corporation manufacturing facility in Topeka, Kansas. The plant, built to process and package Gaines dog food products, was designed specifically with job enrichment in mind. Workers are free to schedule their own hours for starting and stopping work. Production is built around three teams: one processes products, one packages and ships them, and one handles supporting office services. The members rotate jobs within their team. A worker on the packaging and shipping team may operate the forklift truck one day and bag "Gravy Train" the next. Undesirable jobs must be rotated so that each worker does them periodically. Executive parking spaces do not exist. Team members screen job applicants, make employment decisions, and draw up work rules. Because team members are expected to perform numerous functions normally expected of managers, a strong need for training exists. For instance, those team members making personnel decisions must be well versed on government regulations concerning hiring practices. Top management at the Topeka facility recognize the need to provide continual training and to maintain communication systems to keep up the enthusiasm workers bring to their jobs.

During the first years of the plant's operation total employment tripled, but the policy of job enrichment continued. In 1981, Randy Castelluzzo, General Foods' manager of personnel services, summarized the benefits of the Topeka "experiment": "higher product quality, lower operating costs, little absenteeism, and productivity per worker averaging 15 to 20 percent higher than similar, conventionally managed plants."[12] This classical experiment has had a major impact upon organizations in North America.

Is job enrichment for everyone? Like MBO programmes, attempts at job enrichment have not always been successful. After introducing job enrichment programmes in 19 areas at AT&T, management reported that nine were outstandingly successful, one was a complete flop, and the remaining nine were moderately successful.[13] A series of interviews with assembly line workers in an "unenriched" television plant revealed that they did not view their jobs as either frustrating or dissatisfying.[14] One researcher even discovered that some workers prefer routine jobs because it gives them more time to daydream or talk with their fellow employees without hurting their productivity.[15]

Prospects for job enrichment are good. Although job enrichment programmes continue to be relatively rare, their accomplishments in a number of industries and in companies of varying size are indications of their merits. Even though they are not always successful, their numbers will undoubtedly grow during the nineties. More and more managers are recognizing that such programmes allow an integration of individual and company goals.

Flexible Work Schedule

flexitime
A work-scheduling system that allows employees to set their own work hours within constraints specified by the organization.

The flexible work-scheduling plan in which employees set their own arrival and departure times within specified limits is called **flexitime**. This approach is extremely popular in Europe. An estimated 40 percent of the work force in Switzerland and 25 percent in West Germany use this approach.

About 12 percent of the North American labour force currently works on a flexitime schedule. Although the finance and insurance industries and the federal government use flexitime more than manufacturing companies do, all major industry groups are at least experimenting with flexible working hours.

Core Hours and Fringe Hours

Most organizations designate certain core hours, such as 9:30 a.m. to 3:30 p.m., when employees are required to be on the job. Beyond those hours workers can adjust their schedules to suit themselves by working additional hours in fringe hour periods before and after the core hours. Figure 7-5 shows how a flexitime schedule works.

**Figure 7-5
The Flexitime Concept**

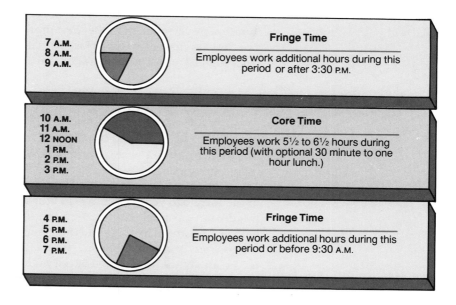

Strengths and Weaknesses of the Flexitime Concept

Proponents of flexitime cite numerous merits for the concept. Bill Batt, a labour management specialist with the National Centre on Productivity, sums up its strengths: "Flexitime gives people much more freedom to organize their lives, reduces pressure on transportation systems, and improves productivity. It just makes good sense. It would be my recommendation that more companies should try this."

Flexible work schedules have limited applicability in continuous production operations and in assembly line settings where worker presence at prescribed times is essential. In addition, flexible work schedules may result in increased energy use and problems in situations where key people are not available at crucial times.

Other Forms of Flexible Work Schedules

compressed workweek
Work-scheduling practice in which workers spend fewer days on the job, but work approximately the same number of hours.

job sharing
The division of one job assignment between two or more persons.

Two additional work-scheduling practices are compressed workweeks and job sharing. A **compressed workweek** is one in which employees work the same number of hours in less than the typical five days. A schedule such as a four-day, forty-hour week often results in energy savings for the firm and added time for personal pursuits by employees. **Job sharing** is the division of a single job assignment among two or more persons. This approach, which basically involves the regular use of part-time employees, is relatively rare in industrial settings. It is limited to tasks requiring limited training and is most frequently used in clerical positions and retailing. While job sharing and compressed workweeks may improve the quality of work life for some employees, the result is not likely to be unanimous. Although some employees may increase their productivity by working 10-hour days, others may experience fatigue. Still others may be tempted to "moonlight," and accept an additional job.

Theory Z: Participative Management

During the past ten years, North America has been importing more than automobiles, television sets, and videocassette recorders from Japan. In an attempt to explain the rapid strides of Japanese industry in the forty-odd years since World War II, a number of management writers have paid particular attention to the relationships that exist between Japanese workers and their employers. University of California business professor William G. Ouchi argues that part of the reason for Japan's extraordinary industrial success is not technology, but the Japanese corporation's special way of managing people—a style that

Table 7-3
Comparing Japanese and North American Organizations

Japanese Organizations	North American Organizations
Lifetime employment	Short-term employment
Slow evaluation and promotion	Rapid evaluation and promotion
Nonspecialized career paths	Specialized career paths
Implicit control mechanisms	Explicit control mechanisms
Collective decision making	Individual decision making
Collective responsibility	Individual responsibility

focuses on employee involvement in every phase of corporate life. The contrasts between the typical Japanese organization and the typical North American organization are shown in Table 7-3.

The Japanese approach involves lifetime employment, worker participation in decision making, and nonspecialized career paths. Unlike the high turnover in many North American corporations, large Japanese companies often hire workers for life. About 35 percent of all the workers in Japan will be employed by only one company.

Lifetime employment means that a major firm or government bureau hires once a year, in the spring, when young people graduate from junior high school, high school, and university. A major firm that hires only "rookies" takes on a large inventory of new employees all at once, although it typically does not have work for all of them immediately. Promotions are entirely from within, and a person with one, five, or twenty years at one company will not be hired or even considered by another. Once hired, the new employee is retained until mandatory retirement at age 55. An employee will not be terminated for anything less than a major criminal offense, and termination is a harsh punishment, since anyone who has been fired has no hope of finding employment in a comparable firm and instead must turn either to a minor firm that pays comparatively low wages and offers little security, or else must return to his or her hometown.

There is currently a tendency in North America to recommend implementation of Japanese management approaches as a "quick fix," but Ouchi warns that cultural differences must be taken into account. His approach to management has been labelled **Theory Z**. Theory Z views involved workers as the key to increased productivity and an improved quality of work life. Theory Z organizations would provide long-term employment for employees and a sharing of responsibility for making and implementing decisions. Evaluations and promotions would be relatively slow and promotions would be tied to individual progress rather than to the calendar. Employees would be provided with varied and nonspecialized experience to broaden their career paths. The result of this approach, according to Ouchi, would be increased productivity and improved worker satisfaction.

Theory Z
Approach to management that emphasizes involved workers as the key to increased productivity and an improved quality of work life.

The Theory Z approach does not require adoption of all Japanese management practices. Since highly qualified young managers in North America are likely to have numerous job alternatives with different firms, a rigid adherence to the Japanese practice of slow evaluations and promotions is likely to result in the loss of a North American firm's brightest talents. In addition, such Japanese practices as excluding most women from top management positions is both a waste of human resources and illegal in North America. Finally, although lifetime employment provisions are rare in North America, a growing number of firms are adopting a no-layoff philosophy. Eli Lilly has not laid off an employee in its 110-year history. Neither has IBM or Hewlett-Packard. Delta Air Lines has not laid off anyone since the fifties.

The Future of QWL Programmes

Although formal QWL programmes are not currently operating in many North American companies, their accomplishments in a number of industries and firms of varying size are indications of their merits. Even though some QWL programmes are not equally applicable in every industry, their numbers will undoubtedly grow during the remaining years of the twentieth century. More and more managers are recognizing that such programmes allow an integration of individual and organizational goals.

Controversial Issue

Sexism in Banking

Are the Canadian banks equal opportunity employers?

At first glance, the answer would appear to be yes, as far as women and visible minorities are concerned.

While women make up 42 percent of the national labour force, they hold 74 percent of the jobs at the Big Six banks and at their largest foreign-owned competitor, Lloyd's Bank of Canada, according to a new survey.

And members of visible minorities, who represent 4.9 percent of the workforce, now make up 10 percent of the bank employees.

However, a closer examination of the banks' employment statistics shows a stodgy pattern at the top.

Women hold a paltry 3 percent of senior executive posts and about 39 percent of the middle management jobs, according to figures issued by the Canadian Bankers' Association. About 80 percent of the female employees earn less than $30,000 a year, mostly working as tellers and clerks.

A little-known federal statute passed in June 1986, the Employment Equity Act, requires federally regulated companies with more than 100 employees to remove any discriminatory barriers which may be limiting the advancement of women, the disabled, visible minorities and natives.

Since the seven Canadian-owned banks employ 163,000 people in this country, including about 30,000 in Quebec, their hiring and promotion practices have a considerable impact on labour market trends.

Starting in 1988, the banks and other industries under federal jurisdiction (railways, airlines, broadcasting, telecommunications) were required to file reports on the four target groups to the Canadian Human Rights Commission, which will monitor their employment equity performance.

"The message from government is that they want the workforce within these companies to mirror society's structure," says Martine Linteau, assistant director of the employment equity programme at the National Bank of Canada, and a member of the Bankers' Association equity committee.

The Human Rights Commission has begun to examine detailed reports from the major employers in order to pinpoint barriers holding back women and minority groups. The federal agency has been empowered to consult with the 370 affected companies on how to correct imbalances.

Canadian Banker, the CBA magazine, reported recently that under the banks' own job categories (which differ from those in equity law), the ratio of women holding middle management positions has climbed from 4 percent in 1975 to 18 percent in 1986.

The CBA says its members are "committed to equal opportunity employment," and want to increase the representation of the target groups to reflect the composition of the labour force.

In an apparent bid to back up its claims about making progress in equity programmes, the Canadian Bankers' Association has chosen a woman president for the first time in its history.

Helen Sinclair has succeeded Robert MacIntosh as the full-time leader of the powerful Toronto-based lobby group, which has been pressing hard for wider powers under the Bank Act revision due this year.

Asked about the low representation of women at bank offices, she commented, "There's still some potential for improvement. But, banks are making a concerted effort to identify talent. It's important to say the problems are being addressed pro-actively."

The banks reject tokenism and will base all promotions on merit, she adds. "Merit keeps the numbers [of women executives] lower longer, but the long-term effect is much stronger."

Canada's biggest banks are still a long way from delivering equal treatment to women. According to two recent studies, they still underpromote women employees, and, when they're lending to female entrepreneurs, they demand stiffer terms than from men.

EthicScan Canada Ltd., a Toronto company that tracks the social performance of 1,500 Canadian companies, concludes in their newsletter that the six largest Canadian banks "are taking their social responsibilities seriously." But they give them lower grades on their performance in promoting women. Only two, the Bank of Montreal and the National Bank, have women occupying roughly half of all management positions. In senior management, women are seriously under-represented: only 3 percent at the Canadian Imperial Bank of Commerce and the Toronto-Dominion Bank, and 8 percent at the Bank of Montreal. "All six banks need to adopt a program of affirmative action if senior positions are to show a balanced picture between the sexes," says EthicScan.

According to the Canadian Federation of Independent Business, women fare even worse when borrowing money. Based on a nationwide sample survey of its membership, the CFIB has concluded that female entrepreneurs are, in effect, discriminated against by loan officers. "What we discovered," says CFIB chief economist and research director Catherine Swift, "is that for nearly one-half of the small businesswomen respondents, the banks demand collateral of at least 300 percent on lines of credit. This requirement was faced by only 20 percent to 30 percent of the male respondents."

Sources: "Sexism and The Banks," *Canadian Business*, March 1989, p. 11. Reprinted by permission.
Nancy McHarg, "Women Hold 74 Percent of the Jobs at the Banks but Only 3 Percent of Top Executive Posts," *This Week In Business*, February 25, 1989, p. 13. Reprinted by permission.

Summary of Learning Goals

1. **Trace the development of the human relations movement in North America.**

   Early scientific management researchers studied individual workers and groups in an attempt to increase their productivity. Jobs were subdivided into minute tasks in an attempt to determine the most efficient means of performing them. Motivation took the form of incentive wages for meeting and exceeding performance quotas. The birth of the human relations movement and the emphasis on employee motivation can be traced to the Hawthorne studies of the twenties, which revealed that employee attitudes are important sources of motivation. In recent years, technological advances have freed workers from the boredom that frequently results from the subdivided tasks of specialization. Various programmes aimed at improving the quality of work life are being implemented by a growing number of organizations.

2. **Identify the different needs in Maslow's hierarchy.**

   Psychologist Abraham Maslow proposed a hierarchy of needs. They include (1) physiological needs—food, shelter, and clothing, (2) safety needs, (3) social (belongingness) needs, (4) esteem needs, and (5) self-actualization needs. He pointed out that needs that are already satisfied are not motivators. Since union contracts, social security, and other benefits have contributed to the attainment of lower-order needs for many workers, the focus of most individuals is on satisfaction of higher needs.

3. **Distinguish between Theory X and Theory Y managers.**

   The traditional Theory X manager views workers as lazy, disliking work, and requiring close and constant supervision. More recent assumptions about workers, termed Theory Y, assume that employees want to satisfy social, esteem, and self-actualization needs through work as well as through other activities. Theory Y emphasizes employee self-control and direction.

4. **Describe and differentiate the motivational factors and maintenance factors of a job.**

   Certain job-related factors, such as salary, working conditions, and job security, have been called maintenance factors. In order to prevent worker dissatisfaction they must be present. However, they do not serve as strong motivators. The key to employee motivation and positive morale appears to lie in such job-centred motivational factors as the work itself, the potential for achievement, recognition, responsibility, advancement, and growth.

5. **Identify the steps involved in a management by objectives (MBO) programme.**

   Management by objectives (MBO) focuses on employee participation in establishing individual work goals. Managers and subordinates agree on goals, and each participates in evaluating the achievement of predetermined objectives. Employees thus know precisely what is expected of them and on what basis they will be evaluated.

The sequence of an MBO programme is as follows:
1. Each subordinate discusses his or her job description with the manager.
2. Short-term performance goals are established.
3. Subordinate and manager meet regularly to discuss progress toward the goals.
4. Intermediate checkpoints are established to measure progress toward the goals.
5. At the end of the predetermined period, manager and subordinate meet and both evaluate the results of the subordinate's efforts.

6. **Explain the "quality of work life" concept and identify the major categories of QWL programmes.**
   Quality of work life is a concept that gives all members of an organization some say about the design of the work environment in general and their jobs in particular. It involves management's acceptance of its employees as unique, adult individuals who should be encouraged to make meaningful input into the operation of the organization. The major categories of QWL programmes currently being used to reshape the workplace are work restructuring to provide job enrichment, flexible work schedules, and Theory Z participative management.

7. **Distinguish between job enrichment and job enlargement.**
   Job enrichment involves redesigning the work itself to give workers more authority to plan their activities and to decide how the work is to be accomplished, and allowing them to learn related skills or to trade jobs with others. Job enlargement, by contrast, is a similar expansion of a worker's assignments to include additional, but similar, tasks. Although increasing the number of tasks performed by a worker may result in making the job more psychologically rewarding, job enlargement does not necessarily result in job enrichment.

8. **Identify the alternative forms of flexible work schedules.**
   Three forms of flexible work schedules are flexitime arrangements, compressed workweeks, and job sharing. Flexitime is a flexible work-scheduling plan in which employees set their own arrival and departure times within specified limits. Employees may be required to be at work during certain core hours, but they may determine their own arrival and departure times within these constraints. A compressed workweek is one in which the employee works the same number of hours in less than the typical five-day workweek. Compressed workweeks may involve a four-day, ten-hour schedule or even longer hours over a three-day period. Job sharing is the division of a single job assignment among two or more persons.

9. **Contrast the Theory Z organization with the typical North American firm.**

The typical North American organization is often characterized by individual responsibility and decision making, specialized career paths, short-term employment, and rapid evaluation and promotion. By contrast, a Theory Z organization more likely includes long-term employment, shared decision making, relatively slow promotions and evaluations, and varied and nonspecialized job assignments. The Theory Z approach to management emphasizes involved workers as the key to increased productivity and improved quality of work life.

Key Terms

Hawthorne studies	motivational factors
need	morale
motive	management by objectives (MBO)
physiological needs	quality of work life (QWL)
safety needs	flexitime
social (belongingness) needs	job sharing
esteem needs	compressed workweek
self-actualization needs	Theory Z
Theory X	job enrichment
Theory Y	job enlargement
maintenance factors	

Discussion Questions and Exercises

1. How did the Hawthorne studies revolutionize management's approach to employee motivation?

2. Relate the process of motivation shown in Figure 7-1 to the following situation. Make any assumptions necessary.

   Gordon Chenowitz narrowly escaped injury yesterday when a 20-pound crate fell inches from his left foot. Gordon's supervisor reminded him of the requirement that all warehouse employees wear steel-toed safety shoes and warned him that he could lose his job if he were injured without required safety clothing. On his way home from work, Gordon stopped at a nearby shoe store carrying a line of safety shoes.

3. Based upon Maslow's hierarchy of human needs, which needs are being referred to in the following statements:

   a) ''The new General Motors labour agreement will guarantee the jobs of at least 80 percent of all GM workers through 1990.''

    b) "This is an entry-level job here at Marks Clothiers, and we pay minimum wage for the first six months."

    c) "We have just organized a company hockey team. Why don't you try out Thursday afternoon after work?"

    d) "Judy won our Employee of the Month award this month due to her exceptional performance."

    e) "We pay a 20 percent bonus for employees who work the midnight shift."

4. Consider your most recent (or current) job supervisor. Would you describe this person as a Theory X or a Theory Y manager? Why do you think your boss has adopted this management approach?

5. What does Frederick Herzberg mean by dissatisfiers? How do they relate to Maslow's hierarchy of human needs?

6. Outline the five steps in an MBO programme. Use these steps to design an MBO programme for the successful completion of a course you are now taking.

7. A survey of 2,010 workers performing 23 different jobs conducted by the Institute of Social Research of the University of Michigan gave the following "Most Boring" awards: assembly-line worker, forklift-truck drive, machine tender, and monitor of continuous flow goods. By contrast, these jobs were ranked at the bottom of the boredom scale: physician, professor, air traffic controller, and police officer. Identify some common characteristics of each group of jobs that appear to explain their rankings.

8. Identify several methods of work structuring that should result in job enrichment. Can you think of situations where job enrichment programmes would not be effective? List them, and explain your reasoning.

9. What are the strengths of the flexitime schedule? What are its major limitations? How do you account for the high percentage of employees using flexitime in European countries as compared with its relatively low usage in North America?

10. In the October 1980 issue of *Business Horizons*, J. Clayton Lafferty, president of Human Synergistics, made the following statement: When a three-engine Boeing 727 flying at 40,000 feet loses all three engines at once (under normal circumstances the plane could glide for over 130 miles), the captain has ample time for quickly consulting with the copilot and flight engineer to get their ideas about the cause and remedy, and to discuss emergency procedures with the flight attendants. However, if a similar power loss occurred at 500 feet during a takeoff climb, the captain would be ill-advised to practice such participative techniques.

Relate this statement to the Theory Z approach to management and point out the perceived strengths and possible problems with this approach.

Case 7-1

Keeping Your Distance

Dennis McIntyre loved his job as senior writer with Cullingham Associates Ltd., a large Toronto public relations agency. But he hated going to work. He hated the alarm that jolted him out of bed every morning at 6:30. He hated the 45-minute drive in rush-hour traffic that regularly put his nerves on edge. And he resented having to be at work by 9 o'clock, whether he felt creative or not.

Once at work, the constant interruptions from the telephone and fellow employees coming into his office often made it difficult to concentrate on his writing. Even more irritating and distracting were the frequent meetings he had to attend, most of which he considered a waste of time.

As his frustration grew, McIntyre became obsessed with the idea of working at home, where he had an office all set up. All he had to do was bring home his computer and get a modem, which would enable him to transmit and receive communications with his company. He was certain that if he made such a move, his productivity would improve.

However, McIntyre seriously doubted that the president of Cullingham Associates would ever agree to such a seemingly radical change. Edgar Slickman, 55, was a former high school principal who had built his company into a major success through the sheer dint of hard work and discipline. He was a stickler for punctuality, appearance, and teamwork.

But a cold and stormy day in February convinced him to give it a try. McIntyre, who had an extremely important project to finish that day, was stuck in bumper to bumper traffic for three hours. By the time he arrived at work, he was exhausted and in a panic to meet a late afternoon deadline.

During his meeting with Slickman, McIntyre used the snowstorm as a starting point, explaining how unproductive and stressful his day had been. He talked about a new trend called "telecommuting," an arrangement whereby employees worked at home and stayed in communication with the office primarily by telephone and computer. Naturally, he pointed out, only certain types of jobs were suited to this sort of arrangement.

The idea of McIntyre operating from his home without supervision greatly disturbed Slickman's sense of how a business should be run. He told McIntyre that he would consider the proposal. He wanted time to evaluate certain questions, the most important being whether McIntyre could be trusted to work efficiently at home without the discipline of an office environment.

Source: Paul McLaughlin, "Keeping Your Distance," *Canadian Business*, May 1988, pp. 133-34. Paul McLaughlin is a Toronto writer and broadcaster.

Questions:
1. What do you think Slickman should do? Why? Explain.
2. What are some of the considerations Slickman must account for, should he say "yes" to McIntyre's proposal? Discuss.
3. What are some of the potential drawbacks associated with saying "yes"? Discuss.

Case 7-2

Machine Schemes

When Harcourt Manufacturing Co. and Palmerston Production Inc., two financially sound Ontario firms, merged, their respective owners were confident the new organization would result in improved profits. Both companies expected a new manufacturing method to give them the corner on the market. They forgot one thing: the people using the new technology.

The merger centred on a technologically advanced plant, built at a cost of $75 million, that would replace the old assembly-line methods both companies had previously used. Senior managers were convinced that assembly-line manufacturing was behind lower productivity, more product defects, and higher employee absenteeism.

The Japanese and Scandinavian experiences reinforced their beliefs that when employees are involved in putting together a complete product, rather than just a part of it, they work harder, make fewer mistakes and take greater pride in their accomplishments. They designed the new plant so that employees worked in teams under the direction of a supervisor.

On the first day the plant opened, employees were assigned to their teams. Chaos predominated—workers were unsure of what they were supposed to do. Three months after the transition to the new plant, consumer demand outstripped production. Malfunctions led to an unprecedented rate of returns for repairs and adjustments. Accidents on the job were extremely high, as was employee absenteeism. Employees vandalized company property.

The director of manufacturing, Dennis Clarke, responded by imposing increasingly strict disciplinary procedures. Employees who did not appear to be busy were questioned, late-comers were interrogated, and those negligent with safety were docked pay. A security firm was hired to watch employees and try to identify those responsible for vandalism. Employees, in turn, initiated grievances.

The manager became anxious to appease the employees and approached Clarke for a solution. Clarke suggested that the move to a multidisciplinary team approach was the source of the problem. Team supervisors, who had been selected on the basis of seniority alone, did not know how to manage the work units. Clarke felt the only solution was to go back to the assembly-line, a move he knew the workers also wanted. But this would require major modifications, at a cost of $750,000. The executive committee was divided.

Source: Paul McLaughlin, "Machine Schemes," *Canadian Business*, January 1988, pp. 99-100.

Questions:
1. Why did things go wrong? Explain.
2. What action should the executive committee undertake? Discuss.
3. What could have been done to prevent the same outcome?

Chapter 8

Personnel: Managing Human Resources

Learning Goals

"I've always found that you can control people better if you don't see too much of them."
—*W. L. MacKenzie King, in* Hardy, MacKenzie King of Canada, *1949, pg. 94.*

"When you find a man about whom people speak no evil, it is evidence, not that the man, but that the people are unusual."
—*Peter McArthur, d. 1924, in* The Best of Peter MacArthur, *1967, pg. 172.*

1. To explain the functions of a specialized human resource department and the continuing responsibilities of all departments for the effective use of human resources

2. To describe the concept of human resource planning and to outline the major steps involved

3. To explain how each of the steps in the recruitment and selection process contributes to finding the right person for the job

4. To evaluate the different methods of training operative employees and present and potential managers

5. To relate performance appraisal to effective human resource management

6. To outline the different forms of compensation and to explain when each form should be used

7. To enumerate the different types of employee benefits and the changes that are likely to occur in future fringe benefit programmes

Profile

Bill Mulholland—*Managing by Fear at Bank of Montreal*

Sarasota, Fla.—The tourist in the deck chair squints slightly as he holds up his memories to the kind light of the evening sky.

Bill Mulholland, 62, is in casual mode: blue madras shirt, buff shorts, snowbird-white sneakers, shades clipped to his steel-grey frames. Just beyond his poolside suite at the Long Boat Key Club near Sarasota, Florida, the Gulf of Mexico shimmers slate blue.

His wife, Nancy, is combing the shoreline for seashells.

Back at poolside, Bill has other things on his mind. The day before they arrived, he had announced that after ten years as chairman of the Bank of Montreal he would soon step down. This is a holiday for reflection, rumination, psychic consolidation.

And, naturally, thoughts of the recent past, most specifically his choice of 44-year-old career banker Matthew Barrett as his successor. It was a good choice, he believes: experience is important, but it's crucial to look at the man—his character, his values.

The leader must be able to balance his own responsibility for the bank's future with lifetimes that others have invested in the 172-year-old bank.

Mulholland sees the role of chief executive as a sacred trust: "For a little period of time you hold in your hands the soul of the bank." A bank, he says, is a social organization as much as a profit machine. "And one thing you can't have is people who think they're bigger than the institution, who think that it's just sort of a pedestal for their greater glory."

These are strange words indeed, coming from a man who, in the past fifteen years, has become a legend that almost overshadows his staid old bank.

An iconoclast most often compared to the patrician Bank of Nova Scotia chairman Ced

Ritchie, Mulholland is a shy intellectual not given to visceral reactions. He simply can't comprehend the wellspring of emotion he provokes in others.

"I don't have many personal reactions to people," he says. "If I didn't work with people that I don't like, I'd have a hell of a hard time."

Some who have worked with him for years say they don't really know him. Others have kidded themselves that a cosy working relationship with Bill Mulholland is possible.

Executive vice-president Don Munford recalls one senior manager who assumed he and the chairman had a close rapport. "The conversation started out Bill, and it ended up Mr. Mulholland, sir."

Importing Bill Mulholland was a radical departure for Canada's oldest bank: he was American, he was an investment banker, and he was not, like the other bank chieftains, a lifer.

In 1974, when Mulholland became president, Bank of Montreal had plenty of bureaucracy, but no real accountability. "It was felt that some of the things that happened to us were acts of God," recalls Munford, "as opposed to acts of management."

There was no single system of ledgerkeeping, no control of portfolios, no matching of deposits and loans. "Profit," Munford adds, "was whatever was left in the till at the end of the year."

Mulholland immediately set to work, figuring out how the bank worked—and how to fix the parts that didn't work.

He had trouble communicating his vision. When he moved into the chairman's seat in 1979, the bank's real problem was people. But Mulholland didn't recognize that his lack of interest in personal relationships would translate into a disoriented, uncomfortable and bitter stream of ex-employees.

A decade and a day later, when he announced his retirement, staff turnover had become an embarrassment to the bank. And the legend of Mulholland the career-destroyer grew.

Says bank director Peter Bentley, chairman of Canfor Corp.: "He brought that on himself. And once that reputation is there, it's very hard to get rid of. Whether it is deserved is somewhat in question, but I can well imagine how it developed."

Bill Mulholland fitted comfortably into the world of Morgan Stanley, the New York investment bank that he joined in 1952, straight out of Harvard Business School.

It was a natural environment for him: cerebral, unstratified, hard-driving.

A five-year veteran of the Bank of Montreal board, Mulholland took command at one 1974 meeting after hearing that the bank had just lost a pot of money because of a foreign trading position that top management hadn't even known about.

Impressed by his performance, bank chairman Arnold Hart and president Fred McNeil approached Mulholland to see if he would take a more active role.

But when Mulholland became president of the Bank of Montreal, any successful strategy rested on adjusting the mindset of the employees. At first, their reaction to the new president was shock.

With Mulholland's arrival, the bank started running on overdrive: no holidays, managers on constant call, 20-hour days in the executive suites in both Montreal and Toronto.

Mulholland's nine children rarely saw him. A few of the older children used to make appointments with him at the bank.

Before he arrived at the bank, the only measurement of staff was an incomprehensible sheaf of salary lists, updated erratically by the chief executive himself.

Today there is a sophisticated set of staff levels and performance reviews. "We tried to get away from the system where a guy can be a victim of one man's prejudices." But there were inevitable victims of the shift to credit ratings from old-style relationship banking.

Mulholland had long planned to leave by the age of 62. By the time he does retire as chairman, he will be 18 months behind schedule.

He had vowed that his successor would come from within, and in Matt Barrett he found a real bankers' banker (see Focus 8-1).

At 44, Barrett is also about the oldest manager on the fast track; the stream of departures has left a 15-year gap in the ranks between him and the bank's senior statesmen.

With a successor chosen, Mulholland says he plans to relax in retirement.

Others say he isn't likely to leave the stage forever. Mulholland curled up with two books during his week in Sarasota.

One was *The Predators' Ball*, a sizzling inside account of high-risk Wall Street. The other was a paperback titled *The Charm School*.

Source: Ann Shortel, "Scaring Up Profits," *Montreal Gazette*, February 19, 1989, p. B-8. Reprinted by permission.

Help Wanted: Professional hockey team seeks
general manager. Must be US citizen.

Detroit Red Wings General Manager Jim Devellano, a Canadian citizen, had applied for permanent resident alien status in the United States, and the Labor Department had turned him down. Under Labor Department regulations, an employer must demonstrate that no qualified US citizen is available before hiring a foreigner, and that's why the Red Wings had to advertise.

Red Wings fans were up in arms at the idea that anyone might harass their beloved general manager. After all, Devellano helped build the New York Islanders, who had won four straight Stanley Cups. And the Red Wings made the National Hockey League playoffs for the first time in several years, thanks in part to Mr. D, as Devellano is called.

The general manager took it all in stride. "Some days with this franchise, I might have been happy to let anybody do my job," he joked, referring to the Red Wings' former problems. As for aspiring general managers, they shouldn't get their hopes too high—since the Red Wings were sticking with Mr. D.

Things would be a lot simpler if Devellano were a player. In a policy that dates back to the days when there weren't many top-flight Americans in the sport, the Labor Department waived its rules for NHL players. Six or seven Red Wings players have permanent resident green cards, and there's also an exception for coaches. But not general managers.

Mr. D thinks the whole business was a bit silly. He owned a residence in Florida and since he earned a good salary and was single, he's in the 50 percent tax bracket. "I'm a good citizen," he said. But of course, that's the problem. He was not a citizen. Not in the United States, at least.[1]

People—The Critical Resource in Every Organization

human resource management
The process of acquiring, training, developing, motivating, and appraising a sufficient quantity of qualified employees to perform necessary activities; and developing specific activities and an organizational climate conducive to producing maximum employee efficiency and worker satisfaction.

The emphasis of this chapter is on people—the human element—accomplishing the goals of an organization. The acquisition, training, motivation, and retention of qualified personnel is a critical factor in determining the success or failure of a business firm or a nonprofit organization. As a consequence, most organizations devote considerable attention to the management of human resources.

Human resource management can be defined as the process of acquiring, training, developing, motivating, and appraising a sufficient quantity of qualified employees to perform the activities necessary to accomplish organizational objectives; and developing specific activities and an overall organizational climate to generate maximum worker satisfaction and employee efficiency. While the owner-manager of a small organization is likely to assume complete responsibility for human resource management, most medium- and large-sized organizations use company specialists called "human resource managers" to perform these activities in a systematic manner. These human resource, or personnel, managers assume primary responsibility for forecasting personnel needs and recruiting and aiding in selecting new employees. Personnel managers also assist in training and evaluation, and administer compensation, employee benefits, and safety programmes.

A hundred years ago companies hired workers by posting a notice outside the gate stating that a certain number of workers would be hired the following day. The notice might have listed skills, say welding or carpentry, or it might simply have listed the number of workers needed. The next morning people would appear at the front gate—a small number in prosperous times, large crowds in periods of unemployment—and the workers would be selected. The choices were often arbitrary; the first four in line might be selected or the four people who looked the strongest.

Table 8-1
Rules for Clerks—in 1882

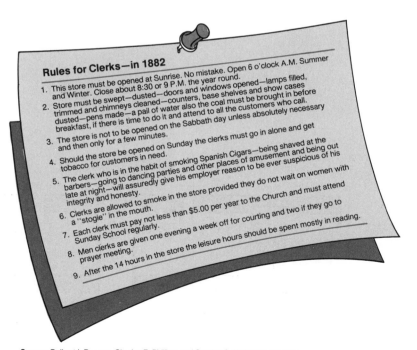

Rules for Clerks—in 1882

1. This store must be opened at Sunrise. No mistake. Open 6 o'clock A.M. Summer and Winter. Close about 8:30 or 9 P.M. the year round.

2. Store must be swept—dusted—doors and windows opened—lamps filled, trimmed and chimneys cleaned—counters, base shelves and show cases dusted—pens made—a pail of water also the coal must be brought in before breakfast, if there is time to do it and attend to all the customers who call.

3. The store is not to be opened on the Sabbath day unless absolutely necessary and then only for a few minutes.

4. Should the store be opened on Sunday the clerks must go in alone and get tobacco for customers in need.

5. The clerk who is in the habit of smoking Spanish Cigars—being shaved at the barbers—going to dancing parties and other places of amusement and being out late at night—will assuredly give his employer reason to be ever suspicious of his integrity and honesty.

6. Clerks are allowed to smoke in the store provided they do not wait on women with a "stogie" in the mouth.

7. Each clerk must pay not less than $5.00 per year to the Church and must attend Sunday School regularly.

8. Men clerks are given one evening a week off for courting and two if they go to prayer meeting.

9. After the 14 hours in the store the leisure hours should be spent mostly in reading.

Source: Delbert I. Duncan, Charles F. Phillips, and Stanley C. Hollander, *Modern Retailing Management* (Homewood, Ill.: Richard D. Irwin, 1972), p. 184. Reprinted by permission.

Workers operated under a set of specific rules. One such list is shown in Table 8-1.

What Is Personnel Management?

Personnel management can be viewed in two ways. In a narrow sense it refers to the functions and operations of a single department in a firm—the personnel department. Most firms with 200 or more employees establish a separate department and assign to it the responsibility and authority for selecting and training personnel. A typical personnel department is illustrated in Figure 8-1.

In a broader sense personnel management involves the entire organization. Even though a special staff department exists, general management is also involved in the process of training and developing workers, evaluating their performances, and motivating them to do their jobs. **Personnel management** is thus the recruitment, selection, development, and motivation of human resources.

personnel management
The recruitment, selection, development, and motivation of human resources.

Focus 8-1 describes the personnel management skills necessary and practised by the new CEO of the Bank of Montreal who inherited many problems from his predecessor (described in the PROFILE of this chapter).

Figure 8-1
Organization of a Typical Personnel Department

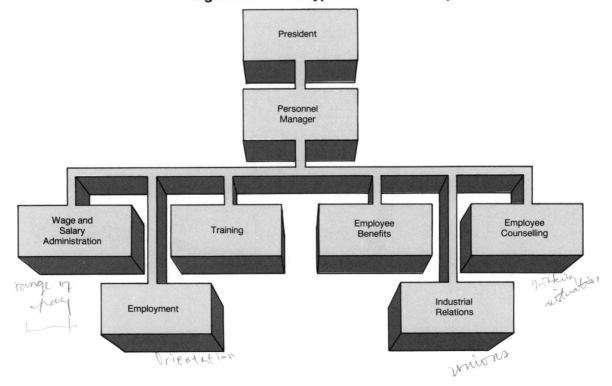

Focus 8-1

Picking up the Pieces at Bank of Montreal

When Matthew Barrett was formally crowned heir to the throne by Bank of Montreal chairman William Mulholland at last week's annual meeting, there was a sudden, transparent swing in the mood at the podium. Mulholland—announcing that as of June 30, he would relinquish the mantle of chief executive officer to Barrett—was clearly relieved; he giddily choked back laughter at private jokes and skipped ahead to shareholders' questions before requesting a vote on the board of directors' slate. Barrett, for his part, immediately felt the weight of his inheritance. As he slipped into the shareholders' buffet luncheon, he said that his pride in reaching the top rung after 26 years at the bank was balanced by a realization of the responsibilities he will soon be shouldering. With the slightest trace of an Irish lilt, he quoted Oscar Wilde: "You know the gods are punishing you when they answer your prayers."

That fey reaction is understandable. At 44, Barrett is assuming leadership of the country's third-largest bank during an industry upheaval that is prompting daily redrafting of the rules of operation. At the same time, the Bank of Montreal has a shortage of seasoned executives, and the highest exposure level to Third-World debt in the industry. And the bank's cost of doing business is high—a crucial factor in a sector that fears price-war tactics from new and eager foreign competition.

Barrett's challenge may, in fact, equal that faced by Mulholland when he took over the top job. Mulholland, 62, a former partner at investment bank Morgan Stanley in New York, joined Bank of Montreal as president in 1975 and assumed the chief executive's title exactly ten years and one day before announcing Barrett's succession. His hiring was a desperation play by a bank that was fast losing ground to its competitors. During his tenure, operations were streamlined and costs cut substantially; innovative computer systems were developed; and the bank purchased Harris Bankcorp of Chicago and stockbroker Nesbitt Thomson Inc. Asked to list his accomplishments, Mulholland says: "We have a sense of discipline and due process which never existed—no more 'ad hocery,' no more patronage."

But Mulholland's wide swath—and his often ruthless managerial style—cut down a number of executives over the years. One senior group left shortly after Mulholland arrived and another group has departed in the past few years.

In choosing Barrett, Mulholland and his board picked a career banker whose strengths lie in retail banking and people management. The decision is seen as a recognition that the bank makes most of its money from retail lending. And Barrett's personnel expertise is regarded as the beginning of a new era in executive cooperation. Still, while many praise his management talents, insiders emphasize that he must develop the leadership qualities of a chief executive. At this point, Barrett still feels there is an "aura of unreality" about the appointment. "It's an Oh-Me-God feeling," says Barrett. "There will come a day when there isn't Bill to go to with the tough ones." He had his first taste of the future last week: after setting in motion his plan of succession, Mulholland promptly went fishing in Florida.

Source: Ann Shortell, "Can Matthew Barrett Revive the Ailing Bank of Montreal?" *Financial Times of Canada*, January 23, 1989, p. 5. Reprinted by permission.

Human Resource Planning

human resource planning
Developing a comprehensive strategy for meeting the organization's future human resource needs.

Although the formulation of organizational objectives results in clear guideposts for evaluating performance, resources—human and other—are necessary for their achievement. **Human resource planning** is the development of a comprehensive strategy for meeting the organization's future human resource needs. It is the process by which management makes certain that it has the right number of people with the right number of appropriate skills at the right places at the right time.

Human resource planning involves three steps. First, present human resources must be assessed. At this stage, management determines whether the present work force is appropriate for the firm's current needs and whether it is being used properly. Second, the

Figure 8-2
Steps in the Human Resource Planning Process

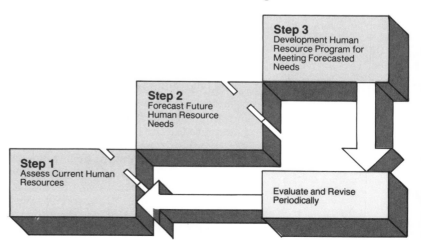

Step 3
Development Human Resource Program for Meeting Forecasted Needs

Step 2
Forecast Future Human Resource Needs

Step 1
Assess Current Human Resources

Evaluate and Revise Periodically

human resource forecast
Determining a firm's personnel needs, in terms of both numbers of individuals and their required skills.

human resource forecast of future personnel needs must be conducted. This forecast compares current employee skills and their expected projected skills at some future date with the expected organizational needs at that date. Finally, a programme must be developed for meeting future human resource needs. The forecast serves as a blueprint for training current employees and recruiting new employees to meet organizational needs as they occur. Figure 8-2 identifies the steps involved in the development of the human resource planning sequence.

Figure 8-3
Steps in the Employee Selection Process

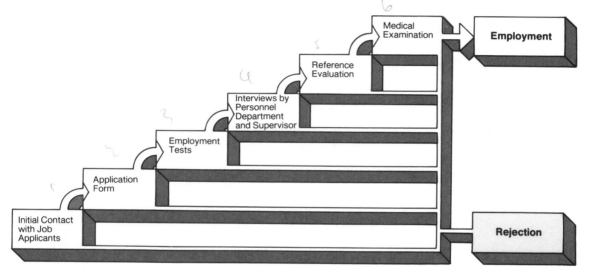

Employee Selection

The personnel manager plays a crucial role in selecting employees. The selection process is based on the philosophy: don't fit a square peg into a round hole! Adding new employees is an expensive process. Recruitment costs alone are high. Various interviews and tests are often conducted before new employees are selected. Medical examinations at company expense are often required for applicants. Training new people is also costly, and an inefficient worker wastes money. The personnel manager must ensure that potential employees possess the necessary qualifications for the job. The steps in the selection process are shown in Figure 8-3.

Job Analysis, Job Description, and Job Specification

job analysis
A systematic, detailed study of jobs based on identification and examination of job characteristics and the requirements of the person assigned the job.

job description
A document specifying the objectives of a job, the work to be performed, the responsibilities involved, the skills needed, the relationship of the job to other jobs, and the working conditions.

job specification
The written description of the special qualifications required of a worker who fills a particular job.

In order to match jobs effectively with qualified people, the personnel manager uses three techniques: job analysis, job description, and job specification.

Job analysis is a systematic, detailed study of jobs; it consists of identifying and examining the elements and characteristics of each job and the requirements of the person to the job. From the job analysis, the personnel department develops a **job description**, which is a document specifying the objectives of a job, the work to be performed, the responsibilities involved, the skills needed, the relationship of the job to other jobs, and the working conditions. Next, the **job specification**—the written description of the special qualifications required of a worker who fills a particular job—is prepared. The specification lists experience, education, special skills, and other requirements.

The job description and job specification are typically combined into one document. This type of document is invaluable to personnel departments seeking qualified applicants for job openings. First used in factory jobs, such combination documents are common today in retail stores, offices, banks, and almost all large organizations.

Avoiding Sexism in Job Specifications

Numerous laws—both federal and provincial—have been passed to prohibit the use of job specifications that limit employment to one sex. Employers are not allowed to exclude persons of either sex from job consideration, though physical requirements such as strength may, in practice, bar many women from some jobs.

In many countries women are widely employed in occupations that some would label "men's jobs." For example, 90 percent of the physicians in the Soviet Union are women; so too are 70 percent of the overhead crane operators in Sweden. Women are now being hired in greater numbers to fill organizational positions. A reason for this event is that the federal government through the Advisory Council for the Status of Women has set mandatory guidelines requiring that a proportion of women must work on federally funded projects.

One result of job specification laws is the elimination of sex distinctions in the "positions available" sections of newspapers. A second result is the change in job titles. Employment and Immigration Canada has updated its *Canadian Classification and Dictionary of Occupations* with a *Manual of Sex-free Occupational Titles*. Table 8-2 shows some of the changes.

Recruitment

After the job description and job specification are prepared, the next step in the selection process is the recruitment of qualified employees. Personnel departments use both internal and external sources to find candidates for specific jobs.

hiring from within
A policy whereby a firm first considers its own employees for new job openings.

Most firms have a policy of **hiring from within**—first considering their own employees for new job openings. Because the personnel department maintains a file on all employees, its records can be quickly screened to determine whether any employees possess the necessary qualifications for a new opening.

The use of current employees to fill new job vacancies is a relatively inexpensive method of recruitment that also contributes to good employee morale. One personnel manager summarized the policy of filling job vacancies with existing workers whenever possible this way: ''When a president retires or dies, we hire a new office helper.''

All firms must go outside to some extent to fill vacancies or to add employees for newly created jobs. A company may not have qualified employees to fill a certain position, or better-qualified people may be available elsewhere. Sources for potential job applicants outside the company include university and college placement offices, advertisements in newspapers and professional journals, Canada or Quebec Employment Centres, private employment agencies, vocational

Table 8-2 Changes in Job Titles

Nursemaid / Nursery Attendant

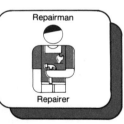
Repairman / Repairer

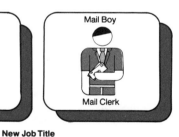
Mail Boy / Mail Clerk

Former Job Title	New Job Title
Brakeman	Brake Worker
Cameraman	Camera Operator
Cowboy	Cowhand
Driver-Salesman	Route Driver
Egg Poultryman	Egg Farmer
Longshoreman	Longshore Worker
Mail Boy	Mail Clerk
Nursemaid	Nursery Attendant
Policeman	Police Officer
Prison Matron	Correctional Officer
Public Relations Man	Public Relations Agent
Repairman	Repairer
Saleswoman	Salesperson
Sound Effects Man	Sound Effects Technician
Stewardess	Flight Attendant

Source: *Manual of Sex-free Occupational Titles*, Occupational and Career Analysis Branch, Department of Employment and Immigration, 1976. Reprinted by permission.

Equal opportunity legislation has eliminated the "male only" specifications for many jobs.

schools, labour unions, unsolicited applications, and recommendations by current employees. For finding candidates to fill top management positions, a firm may use specialized executive recruiting agencies or advertise in *The Globe and Mail Report on Business* or *The Financial Post*.

The Screening Process

evaluate job applicants

Once job applicants have been located, the next step is screening them to determine which candidate is best fitted for the job. Often the first step of the screening process is to have the applicant complete an application form, which is used to determine whether he or she meets the general qualifications for the position. The form requests information such as type of work desired, education, experience, and personal references.

Human Rights Legislation and Affirmative Action

> Every individual should have an equal opportunity with other individuals to make for himself or herself the life that he or she is able and wishes to have, consistent with his or her duties and obligations as a member of society, without being hindered in or prevented from doing so by discriminatory practices based on race, national or ethnic origin, colour, religion, age, sex, or marital status, or conviction for an offence for which a pardon has been granted or by discriminatory employment practices based on physical handicaps.
>
> *The Canadian Human Rights Act*, paragraph 2, subsection (a)

Canadian Human Rights Commission
The agency that oversees fair employment practices for workers who come under federal jurisdiction. Most provinces have similar agencies.

affirmative action programme
A programme whereby a firm makes special efforts to hire or advance members of groups—for example, physically challenged individuals—that previously experienced discrimination.

Personnel managers must not be influenced by prospective employees' sex, religion, race, physical condition, national origin, or age. The legislation governing human rights is a combination of federal and provincial acts with the goal of providing equal employment opportunities for all. This legislation does allow employers to reward outstanding performance and not reward unacceptable productivity. The basis for rewards, however, must be directly related to the work and not to an individual's age, sex, race, or other irrelevant issues.

The Canadian Human Rights Act of 1977 permits the **Canadian Human Rights Commission** to enforce the act by improving equal employment opportunities for special groups. The act encourages **affirmative action programmes** as a legal way to improve opportunities for a special group that may previously have suffered from discrimination. The Canadian Charter of Rights of 1982 recognizes affirmative action programmes as nondiscriminatory. Affirmative action does not necessarily involve quotas but is a deliberate structured approach to improve work opportunities for women and minorities by removing barriers to their advancement.

The principles of employment equity and non-discrimination are entrenched in the human rights legislation of every Canadian jurisdiction. Individual rights are also protected in the Charter of Rights and Freedoms, although its application to employment equity has not yet crystallized. This section begins with an overview of the statutes and the Charter, the prohibited grounds of discrimination, and the human rights complaint process. A careful examination of the legal concepts and principles that affect management of human resources follows. It is important to understand that each province and territory as well as the federal government currently has its own human rights code or act to prohibit discrimination in employment and the delivery of services to the public. In each of these 13 jurisdictions, the appropriate human rights statute is administered by a human rights commission or council. In addressing the employment issue, human rights legislation can prohibit various types of discrimination found in recruitment, selection, training, compensation, promotion, and working conditions. These standards apply to employers as well as employer associations, labour unions, and professional associations.

Each human rights statute specifies the grounds upon which individuals should not be recognized as being different. Figure 8-4 lists these issues for each of the 13 Canadian jurisdictions. Every statute prohibits discrimination on the basis of race, colour, marital status, and sex. Except for the Yukon, every jurisdiction also includes age and disability status as prohibited grounds. Protecting extremes in age groups is important since it affects mandatory retirement. Other factors in Figure 8-4, such as ancestry and place of origin, have similar meaning but differ from one statute to the next.

Companies often voluntarily develop affirmative action programmes to correct earlier discriminatory practices and also to avoid any future infractions. The existence of such a programme helps guard against both intentional and unconscious discrimination. See Focus 8-2 for affirmative action and women.

Equal employment opportunity legislation and affirmative action plans affect the activities of personnel departments in the following ways:

1. Job descriptions cannot contain irrelevant requirements that are only intended to exclude certain individuals.
2. Human resource plans must state the firm's affirmative action commitment.
3. Performance evaluation cannot contain biases intended to discriminate against special individuals.
4. The recruitment process cannot exclude any prospective applicants and must attract all.

Figure 8-4
Prohibited Grounds of Discrimination in Employment*

Jurisdiction	Federal	British Columbia	Alberta	Saskatchewan	Manitoba	Ontario	Quebec	New Brunswick	Prince Edward Island	Nova Scotia	Newfoundland	Northwest Territories	Yukon
Race	●	●	●	●	●	●	●	●	●	●	●	●	●
National or ethnic origin[1]	●				●	●	●	●	●	●	●		●
Ancestry			●	●		●		●				●	●
Nationality or citizenship				●	●	●						●	
Place of origin			●	●	●	●		●				●	
Colour	●	●	●	●	●	●	●	●	●	●	●		●
Religion	●	●		●	●		●	●	●	●			●
Creed[2]			●	●		●		●	●	●	●	●	●
Age	●	● (46-65)	● (18 +)	● (18-65)	●	● (18-65)	●	● (19 +)	●	●	● (40-65)	● (19-65)	●
Sex	●	●	●	●	●	●	●	●	●	●	●	●	●
Pregnancy or childbirth	●		●	●			●						
Marital status[3]	●	●	●	●	●	●	●		●	●	●	●	●
Family status[3]	●				●	●	●					●	
Pardoned offence	●						●					●	
Record of criminal conviction			●			●	●						
Physical handicap or disability	●	●	●	●	●	●	●	●	●	●	●	●	
Mental handicap or disability	●	●			●	●	●	●	●	●	●	●	
Dependence on alcohol or drug	●												
Place of residence												●	
Political belief			●			●		●		●	●	●	
Assignment, attachment or seizure of pay[4]												●	
Source of income													
Social condition[4]							●						
Language							●						
Social origin[4]												●	
Sexual orientation[5]						●	●						
Harassment[5]	●					●	●					●	

This chart is for quick reference only. For interpretation or further details, call the appropriate commission.

*Any limitation, exclusion, denial or preference may be permitted if a bona fide occupational requirement can be demonstrated.

[1]New Brunswick includes only "national origin."

[2]Creed usually means religious beliefs.

[3]Quebec uses the term *civil status*.

[4]In Quebec's charter, "social condition" includes assignment, attachment, or seizure of pay and social origin.

[5]The federal, Ontario, and Quebec statutes ban harassment on all proscribed grounds. Ontario, Nova Scotia, and Newfoundland also ban sexual solicitation.

Source: Canadian Human Rights Commission, *Dossier 87-3*, March 1987. Reproduced with permission.

5. The selection process cannot use screening mechanisms that are not related to the job.
6. Compensation must be related to performance, skills, and seniority and must not discriminate against individuals in special classifications.
7. Training must be available to all individuals without regard to factors external to the work.

Focus 8-2

Who's Practising Affirmative Action for Women?

Affirmative action doesn't necessarily involve quotas. Basically it is a structured approach to improving work opportunities for women or minority groups by removing barriers to their advancement.

The first step is to ensure a company doesn't practise systemic discrimination; that is, biases built into their way of doing business. For example, a company may advertise jobs in publications read mainly by men, or use culturally biased job qualification tests that men are more likely to do well on, but have little to do with the skills required for the job.

To start, a company forms a committee to examine its personnel policies. Are hiring and promotion procedures and selection for training and development programmes biased against women? Does it discriminate between men's and women's salaries? Do clauses in benefits plans discriminate as to sex?

The next step is to compare how many women the company has in each job category with the number of women in the work force in similar areas. The company then takes steps to bring more women into job categories where they are under-represented.

A program to explain affirmative action to all employees is also necessary. As many experts point out, changing attitudes is half the battle.

Some firms might choose to set a quota, and set a time limit in which to attain this goal. The rationale for setting quotas is that since women as a group have had to surmount discriminatory practices, they should be advanced more quickly than men to redress previous wrongs.

Toronto-based Warner-Lambert Canada Inc., a pharmaceutical and health-care products manufacturer, started an affirmative-action programme in 1975.

The company's greatest success has been in increasing the number of women in its supervisory/management group. As of 1983, 32 percent of this group were women, up from 18 percent in

1976. The number of women in sales, however, has hovered between 4-6 percent of the total since the late seventies. In the management/executive group, comparable figures are 4-10 percent.

President Bob Serenbeta, 40, thinks the age of top management is a factor in whether a company accepts affirmative action. Younger CEOs are far more amenable to the idea, since many women of their age are college educated and have jobs. Older CEOs are more reluctant to take steps in this direction.

Air Canada started an equal opportunity programme in 1973. The federally regulated airline then had no female pilots, mechanics, or station attendants. Women were in clerical or service positions, and represented only 6 percent of management. Currently, 12.5 percent of the management group are women, and there are now five female pilots—out of 1,800—and a few female mechanics and cargo agents.

Given that 30 percent of Air Canada's work force are women, "the numbers are not significant," says Margaret Hamilton, manager, human resources and organizational programmes. "But we have cracked the barriers. It took four years, for instance, to get our first woman pilot. We will consider setting targets for getting women into nontraditional jobs," she adds. "Quotas have their own backlash, but some people feel that nothing will happen without them."

Ottawa-based Bell Northern Research, the research arm of Northern Telecom Ltd. and Bell Canada, pursues equal opportunity but has no official policy in this area, says spokesperson Brian Fraser.

"Employees are measured against their technical performance, and that is a nondiscriminatory goal."

BNR does, however, track the percentage of women in each graduating class of electrical engineers—from where it draws many new employees—and tries to make sure it hires a comparable percentage. This year, for example 7 percent of graduating electrical engineers in Canada were women, and 11 percent of BNR's new research employees were women.

Bank of Nova Scotia's personnel planning programme evaluates and identifies all high-performers—and then lists high-performing women separately. It's one way of promoting people only according to their skills, but at the same time ensuring women receive a special look. Women make up 50 percent of management trainees in areas for which university degrees are needed to qualify. As well, 70-75 percent of the employees in entry-level administrative training positions are women.

A good job evaluation system can ensure that women are not discriminated against when it comes to pay, says Diane Barsoki, director of employee and labour relations.

Source: Michael Salter, "Moving on Affirmative Action," *Financial Post*, September 8, 1984, p. 18.

Employee Testing

Employee testing makes the selection process more efficient. Careful studies determine the tests to be used in measuring the aptitude and abilities required for each job. Some companies with testing programmes also administer personality tests.

Testing serves two main purposes. It helps eliminate those applicants who are not suited for a particular job, and it helps predict which candidates are likely to become successful employees.

Employee testing becomes a controversial issue since it has been found that some tests are culturally biased and do not predict job success. Considerable effort is being made to evaluate the objectivity of tests currently being used and to design bias-free tests.

Interviewing

The job applicant's first formal contact with a company is usually an interview with a company representative. This face-to-face contact is another step in the screening of candidates for a job. Trained interviewers are able to obtain considerable insight into the prospective employee's goals, attitudes toward others and self, and motivations.

The line manager for whom the prospective employee is to work may also interview the candidate at this stage. Because the line manager will make the ultimate hiring decision (or at least participate in the decision with the personnel department), it is sound practice to involve that person in the screening process.

The Physical Examination

Most firms include a medical examination as part of the employee selection process for certain jobs. The examination determines whether the applicant is physically capable of performing the job; it also helps to protect the company against future claims for disabilities that were already present at the time of employment and, therefore, did not happen on the job. In certain European countries—France, Belgium, and the Netherlands, for example—pre-employment physical examinations are required by law.

Orientation of Employees

The applicant who is hired after the screening process goes through an orientation programme, which is the joint responsibility of the personnel department and the department in which the employee will work. Orientation is likely to include a tour of the building and a meeting with the department head and the new employee's immediate supervisor. The personnel department explains company policy on vacation, absenteeism, rest periods, lunch breaks, and so on, and describes the employee benefits offered. The supervisor is responsible for introducing the new employee to fellow workers, explaining the operations of the department, and how the job the worker will be doing fits into these operations.

A new employee in a large firm should be put at ease by the supervisor and shown that he or she is needed. The lonely, isolated feelings that often accompany the first days on a new job may lead to frustration, negative attitudes, and poor job performance. The orientation programme is designed to convey a sense of belonging. While the personnel department provides information about company history, products, and benefits, the responsibility for developing a new employee's sense of importance and involvement is primarily that of the immediate supervisor and the other employees in the department.

Employee Training and Counselling

A second major function of the personnel department is the development of a well trained and productive labour force. An employee's training should be viewed as an ongoing process that lasts as long as that person is with the company. Two types of training programmes are common—on-the-job training and classroom training. Many companies also conduct management development programmes.

On-the-Job Training

on-the-job training
An employee training program in which the worker actually performs the required tasks under the guidance of an experienced employee.

For relatively simple jobs, **on-the-job training** is most often used, so workers can learn by doing. In this kind of training, the new employee actually performs the work under the guidance of an experienced worker. The experienced worker, through advice and suggestion, teaches the new worker efficient methods for handling the job.

A variation of on-the-job training is apprenticeship training, which is used in jobs requiring long periods of training and high levels of skill. In **apprenticeship training** programmes, the new worker serves for a relatively long period as an assistant to a trained worker—for example, a carpenter, welder, electrician, or plumber. Community colleges provide training facilities and provincial governments establish criteria, cooperating with employers to ensure that skill standards are maintained in these trades.

apprenticeship training
An employee training program in which the new worker serves as an assistant to a trained worker for a relatively long time period.

Classroom Training

In many jobs, some form of classroom training is appropriate. In this kind of training, employees can acquire the necessary skills at their

classroom training
An employee training programme that uses classroom techniques to teach employees difficult jobs requiring high levels of skill.

vestibule schools
Company-established schools where workers are given instruction in the operation of equipment similar to that used in their new jobs and are exposed to facsimiles of their actual work areas.

management development programmes
Employee training programmes designed to improve the skills and broaden the knowledge of present managers as well as to provide training for employees with management potential.

job rotation
A management development programme that familiarizes junior executives with the various operations of the firm and the contributions of each department through temporary assignments in various departments.

coaching
A management development programme in which a junior executive works directly under a senior executive.

own pace, without the pressures of the actual job environment. This prior training also minimizes the possibility of wasting materials and time on the job.

Classroom training programmes use classroom techniques to teach employees jobs requiring high levels of skill and knowledge. The training may involve lectures, conferences, films and other audiovisual aids, programmed instruction, or special machines. Some companies establish **vestibule schools**, where workers are given instruction on the operation of equipment similar to that used in their new jobs. Vestibule schools are facsimiles of actual work areas: they duplicate the jobs and machinery found in the plant. New employees are trained in the proper methods of performing a particular job and have an opportunity to become accustomed to the work before actually entering the department.

Management Development Programmes

While job training is at least as old as recorded history, most management development programmes have been established only within the last 35 years. These programmes are designed to improve the skills of present managers and to broaden their knowledge; they also provide training for employees who have management potential.

Management development programmes, which usually include formal courses of study, are often conducted off the company premises. General Motors and Texaco, for example, have established college-like institutes that offer specific programmes for current and potential managers. New managers for McDonald's Corporation are required to complete an intensive three-week programme at Hamburger University, the McDonald's training facility.

Two other forms of management development programmes are job rotation and coaching. **Job rotation**, through temporary assignments in various departments, familiarizes junior executives with the various operations of the firm and the contributions of each department. **Coaching** involves a junior executive working directly under a senior executive.

The type of management development programmes used will vary with different levels of management. While such programmes for supervisory-level managers are likely to emphasize basic technical and human skills, middle-management development programmes are more likely to focus on human and conceptual skills and analytical abilities. Management development programmes for top-management personnel tend to be oriented toward conceptual skills and strategy.

Assessment Centres

One method for training managers and identifying employees with management potential—the **assessment centre**—traces its roots to

assessment centre
Special career development programmes that use simulation techniques to identify employees with management potential and to aid in making promotion decisions.

the shadowy world of World War II espionage. The US Office of Strategic Services—a forerunner of the Central Intelligence Agency—used this technique to screen and select undercover agents. Assessment centres have since been used by business firms to identify employees with management potential.

The typical assessment centre is actually a programme, not a place. It uses a variety of simulation techniques, leaderless discussions, and group problem-solving exercises to measure an individual's ability to perform job-related assignments. One such technique, the "in-basket simulation," places management candidates in the role of the manager and asks for responses to such scenarios as a customer complaint letter, a telephone call from a superior, or a problem facing the department. Trained evaluators, or "assessors," observe the candidate's responses and make judgements about them.

Empirical research studies indicate that assessment centres are highly effective in predicting job performance. Firms currently using assessment centres include AT&T (which pioneered their use in private industry in 1959), Canadian General Electric, J.C. Penney, Boise Cascade, American Airlines, Sears Canada, and IBM Canada. In addition to identifying management candidates, assessment centres are used as recruiting tools for firms hiring sales personnel and by such brokerage firms as Merrill Lynch.

Performance Appraisal

performance appraisal
The process of defining acceptable performance levels, evaluating the performance levels of employees, and comparing actual and desired performance in order to make objective decisions about additional training needs, compensation, promotion, transfers, or terminations.

Performance appraisal is the evaluation of an individual's job performance by comparing actual performance against desired performance for the purpose of making objective decisions about compensation, promotion, additional training needs, transfers, or terminations. Such appraisals are not confined to business in today's era of evaluation. Driver's license departments evaluate the written and physical capabilities of potential drivers. Professors appraise student performance through homework assignments, quizzes, and examinations. Students, in turn, appraise instructors by completing written evaluations of instructional effectiveness.

In 1800, Robert Owen implemented a performance appraisal system in a Scottish factory through the use of "character" books and "character" blocks. Daily worker output was recorded in Owen's character books, and the following day Owen placed coloured wooden character blocks at each worker's station to inform fellow workers of performance. Different colours represented different levels of performance levels, ranging from poor to excellent.

Performance appraisal serves three important purposes:

1. *Information for employees* By providing employees with information about their relative level of performance, they learn about their strengths, weaknesses, and areas needing improvement.

2. *Information for management* Managers use such information to make decisions concerning compensation, promotion, additional training needs, transfers, and terminations.
3. *Employee motivation* Performance appraisals permit managers to identify superior employees and to reward them with promotions, praise, and pay increases.

It is important to devise objective systems to accomplish these objectives. While appraisals are the responsibility of the line supervisor, specialists from the human resource department may be able to help in devising special forms and rating instruments and comparing appraisals in individual departments with overall organizational scores.

Employee Counselling

Usually employees with personal problems that may adversely affect their job performance will discuss them with their immediate supervisor. But personnel departments are now adding trained specialists to assist workers in solving certain problems—typically family or financial problems.

Another aspect of employee counselling is performance evaluation. While this task is the chief responsibility of the line supervisor, workers occasionally feel that they have been treated unfairly or that the performance standards are too high. In such instances, dissatisfied employees may discuss their objections with a personnel counsellor.

One of the chief advantages of the management by objectives programme discussed in Chapter 7 is that it provides the employee with specific information on how performance will be evaluated. Because the employee participates in goal setting, there is little uncertainty about what constitutes satisfactory performance.

Promotions, Transfers, and Separations

promotions
Upward movements in an organization to positions of greater authority and responsibility and higher salaries.

seniority
The privileges attained as a result of the full length of time an employee has worked at a particular job or in a particular department.

Many business organizations experience employee movement over a period of time. This movement involves promotions, transfers, and separations.

Promotions are upward movements in an organization to positions of greater authority and responsibility and higher salaries. While most promotions are based on employee performance, some companies and many labour unions prefer to base them on **seniority**—the length of time the employee has worked at a particular job or in a particular department. Managers, however, generally agree that seniority should be the basis for promotion only when two candidates possess equal qualifications.

transfers
Horizontal movements in the organization at about the same wage and the same level.

separations
Employee movements resulting from resignations, retirements, layoffs, and terminations.

layoffs
Temporary separations due to business slowdowns.

terminations
Permanent separations resulting from inability to perform the work, repeated violations of work rules, excessive absenteeism, elimination of jobs, or the closing of work facilities.

Transfers are horizontal movements in the organization at about the same wage and the same level. They may involve shifting workers into new, more interesting jobs or into departments where the workers' skills are required. Focus 8-3 outlines potential problems associated with transfers in the workplace. As two-career families become the norm, ensuring a smooth transition for a company's transferred employees will constitute a growing personnel issue.

Separations include resignations, retirements, layoffs, and terminations. Resignations result when employees find more attractive jobs, better-paying positions, or when they move to other cities. Many large firms have had compulsory retirement programmes that required employees to retire at age 65.

Layoffs form terminations in that they are considered temporary separations due to business slowdowns. Most employers lay off workers on a seniority basis, letting the newly hired employees go first. When business conditions improve, these workers are the first to be rehired. Some companies help laid-off workers find new jobs.

Terminations, or discharges, are permanent separations resulting from inability to perform the work, repeated violations of work rules, excessive absenteeism, elimination of jobs, or the closing of work facilities. Well-run personnel departments have specific disciplinary policies that are explained to all workers. The violation of work rules typically results in an oral reprimand for a first offense. Further violations lead to written reprimands and, ultimately, to discharge. Figure 8-5 illustrates some typical penalties.

**Figure 8-5
Typical Penalties for
Violating Work Rules,
in Order of Increasing Severity**

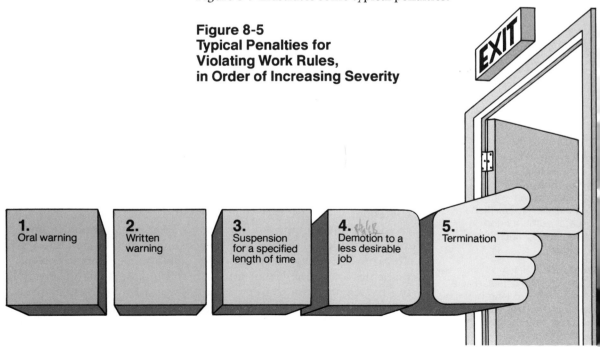

1.
Oral warning

2.
Written warning

3.
Suspension for a specified length of time

4.
Demotion to a less desirable job

5.
Termination

Focus 8-3

Transfers—Bridging the Continental Rift

The days are long gone when a husband, told he was being transferred, would simply go home and tell his wife to pack up the kids for a move. During the 1980s, many career women have moved into jobs that get equal or greater billing in a marriage. And many women are now asking their husbands to give up their jobs to follow them in a transfer.

Moving across the country is stressful enough for an employee without the additional worry of how a working spouse is going to relocate. Some resentment from the spouse is almost inevitable.

Personnel managers are often unaware of the family stress that a transfer can cause an employee with a career-minded spouse. Managers who become aware of such problems are often confused about what to do. On the one hand, what the spouse does can be considered a private family matter. On the other hand, a disgruntled spouse can easily sabotage a move. While managers may be limited in what they can do to address this problem, they can help by simply being more sensitive to it.

A manager could avoid the problem by either (1) transferring only single people or those with spouses who don't work outside the home, or (2) simply choosing to ignore the problem. The first is unrealistic, the second reactive—if a spouse's unhappiness with a move causes so much stress on the family at home that a transferred employee is unable to cope with his/her new job, mending the situation could be an expensive lesson in human relations for the company.

Despite this growing need to smooth the transfer process in two-career families, most Canadian firms are not doing much about it. While no company can guarantee that a transferred spouse will find a new job, some experts think an employer should help ease the transition. Attention to employee needs is simply good business practice. As two-career families become the norm, more and more companies will likely formalize some form of spousal assistance policies. The following are examples of some programmes:

- While transferring a manager, Toronto-based Procter & Gamble Inc. will reimburse the spouse's expenses up to a maximum of $3,500. In some cases, the company will reimburse the spouse for a portion of wages lost as a result of the transfer. IBM Canada Ltd. has a similar programme that covers a spouse's job-search expenses up to $500.

- When Shell Canada Ltd. relocated its headquarters from Toronto to Calgary in 1984, it moved 425 employees. To help ease the transition, Shell's personnel department gave working spouses access to word-processing facilities, offered help with résumé preparation, and counselled them on where they might best fit into the Calgary job market. Similarly, Digital Equipment of

Canada Ltd. offered help to spouses when it moved 115 jobs to Toronto from its headquarters in Kanata, Ontario. DEC hired a placement firm to help working spouses find employment and also reimbursed employees for expenses their spouses incurred on job-search trips.

• For employees about to make international moves, the Bank of Montreal uses the services of a counselling and consultant firm in Toronto to help prepare a family for its adjustment to a different culture, including how the spouse will spend his/her time if continuing a career in the new country is impossible.

Source: Tim Falconer, "Continental Rift," *Canadian Business*, April 1988, pp. 132-33.

Many personnel managers view the termination of an employee as a failure of the selection process for that individual. Because terminations represent substantial cost to the company, most firms investigate each termination and separation to uncover the cause of failure and improve the personnel selection process.

Employee Compensation

One of the most difficult functions of personnel management is the development and operation of a fair and equitable compensation system. Because labour costs represent a sizable percentage of total product costs, wages that are too high may result in products that are too expensive to compete effectively in the marketplace. But inadequate wages lead to excessive employee turnover, poor morale, and inefficient production. A satisfactory compensation programme should attract well-qualified workers, keep them satisfied in their jobs, and inspire them to produce.

The terms *wages* and *salary* are often used interchangeably, but they do have slightly different meanings. **Wages** are employee compensation based on the number of hours worked or on the amount of output produced. They generally are paid to production employees and maintenance workers. **Salary** is employee compensation calculated on a weekly, monthly, or annual basis. It is usually paid to white-collar workers such as office personnel, executives, and professional employees.

The compensation policy of most companies is based on five factors: (1) salaries and wages paid by other companies in the area that compete for the same personnel, (2) government legislation, (3) the cost of living, (4) the ability of the company to pay, and (5) the workers' productivity.

wages
Employee compensation based on the number of hours worked or on the amount of output produced.

salary
Employee compensation calculated on a weekly, monthly, or annual basis.

Job Evaluations Determine Compensation Levels for Different Jobs

job evaluation
A method of determining wage levels for different jobs by comparing each job on the basis of skill requirements, education requirements, responsibilities, and physical requirements.

In developing compensation programmes the personnel department conducts a **job evaluation**—a method of determining salary and wage levels for different jobs by comparing each job on the basis of skill requirements, education requirements, responsibilities, and physical requirements. A monetary scale is then determined for each job. A monetary scale is a quantitative procedure that involves assigning points for different responsibilities and functions. The points are then translated into money. This process attempts to eliminate compensation inequities that exist among jobs. Although the personnel department does not set the specific compensation of employees, it does recommend to line officials rates based on the job evaluation and on surveys of comparable wages and salaries paid by other firms in the area.

Alternative Compensation Plans

piece wage
Employee compensation based on the amount of output produced by a worker.

time wage
Employee compensation based on the amount of time spent on the job.

Employee compensation may be based on the amount of output produced by the worker (a **piece wage**), the amount of time spent on the job (a **time wage**), or some incentive added to a salary or to a time wage or piece wage to reward the employee with extras (such as time off or bonus money) for exceptional performance.

Time wages are usually paid to assembly line workers, clerks, and maintenance personnel. These wages are easy to compute, quickly understood, and simple to administer. Time wage plans assume a satisfactory performance level but include no incentive for outstanding performance by the employee.

Skilled craftworkers are often paid on a piece-rate basis for each unit of output produced. Their wage may be based on individual output or on the production of an entire department. The practice of compensating salespeople with commissions based on sales is an example of the piece-wage form of compensation. This kind of payment plan not only includes an incentive for increased output but also encourages workers to supervise their own activities. It operates well in departments where the work is standardized and the output of each employee or department can be accurately measured.

incentive compensation
Rewarding an employee for exceptional performance by adding something extra to a salary or to a time or piece wage.

bonuses
Additions to a salary or time or piece wage that are intended as incentives to increase productivity or as rewards for exceptional performance.

Incentive compensation refers to programmes designed to reward salaried employees and wage earners for superior performance. Salaried personnel, such as salespersons, may receive a base salary and a commission designed as an incentive. Other types of incentive compensation programmes include bonuses and profit-sharing plans.

Bonuses are a type of addition to a salary or time or piece wage. Intended as an incentive for increased productivity, they are occasionally used to reward employees for exceptional performance.

profit sharing
A type of incentive compensation program where a percentage of company profits is distributed to employees involved in producing these profits.

employee stock ownership plans
Plans that allow employees to receive shares of stock in the company as part of their compensation.

fringe benefits
Nonmonetary employee benefits such as pension plans, health and life insurance, sick-leave pay, credit unions, and health and safety programmes.

Some employees, for example, receive annual bonuses equal to the amount of dividends paid to company shareholders.

Profit-sharing plans are a type of incentive compensation programme where a percentage of company profits is distributed to employees involved in producing those profits, and are used more and more to increase the feeling of belongingness for employees. This kind of partnership between employees and the firm increases employee morale and helps create harmonious working relationships between management and labour.

Employee stock ownership plans give the worker an incentive to perform well. As owners, the workers actually work for themselves and take less supervision. This helps to develop a more positive industrial relations climate since sharing of resources is encouraged.

Employee Benefits

The typical business organization furnishes many benefits to employees and their families, in addition to wages and salaries. These benefits are typically administered by the personnel department. **Fringe benefits** are nonmonetary employee benefits such as pension plans, health and life insurance, sick-leave pay, credit unions, and

Table 8-3
Average Employee Benefits Costs in Canada in 1986

Employee Benefit	Cost as a Percentage of Gross Annual Payroll
Vacations	6.5%
Holidays	3.7
Coffee breaks, rest periods	3.9
Other paid time off	1.1
Subtotal: Paid time off	15.2
Disability plans	1.6
Provincial medical insurance	1.4
Unemployment insurance	2.3
Workers' compensation	2.0
Other insurance-based benefits	2.4
Subtotal: Insurance-based benefits	9.7
Employer pension plans	4.1
Canada/Quebec pension plan	1.3
Subtotal: Pension plans	5.4
Subtotal: Employee services	1.4
Subtotal: Cash benefits	4.6
Total benefits cost	36.3%

Source: Stevenson Kellogg Ernst & Whinney, *Employee Benefit Costs in Canada, 1986* (Toronto Stevenson Kellogg Ernst & Whinney, 1986).

health and safety programmes. Many large companies employ doctors and nurses to investigate working conditions and treat minor illnesses and job-related accidents. Some companies sponsor recreation programmes including hobby groups and golf, baseball, and bowling teams, all with separate recreational areas. The cost of benefits to Canadian companies is shown in Table 8-3.

Industrial Safety

Of vital importance to all workers are safe working conditions. An industrial accident results in both suffering for the injured worker and major costs for the employer, who may lose an experienced employee, suffer from poor morale among other workers, and be subject to increased insurance premiums. Provincial workers' compensation acts and the Canada Safety Code help provide for a safe working environment.

workers' compensation acts
Make compensation available to workers for injuries sustained in the course of their work. Each province has such an act.

Workers' compensation acts provide compensation for workers who are injured in accidents at their work. A provincial compensation board administers the act in each province. Employers contribute to workers' compensation funds at rates based on their total annual payroll and on the safety record of their particular industry. For example, a mining company will pay a higher rate than an advertising agency. The benefits falling under this legislation include protection against industrial accidents, first aid and hospitalization costs beyond those paid by medicare, rehabilitation services, cash benefits for the period of disability, and for a pension for life in the case of permanent disability. Workers' compensation programmes are not preventative; they only come into effect after accidents have happened.

Canada Safety Code
Occupational safety regulations incorporated in the Canada Labour Code and administered by the provinces.

The Canada Labour Code, proclaimed in 1978, includes the **Canada Safety Code** of 1968. The safety code spells out the basics of industrial safety programmes and makes regulations to handle occupational safety problems in various industries and related occupations. The provinces are responsible for the administration of the programme. Safety inspectors with powers and responsibilities laid down by the Canada Labour Code usually inspect industrial firms yearly. Each province sets occupational health standards with regard to smoke, chemicals, gases, and other forms of pollution associated with industrial activities. The code requires all employers to operate their businesses in a manner that will not endanger the health and/or safety of employees. Employers must also enforce reasonable procedures designed to prevent or reduce the risk of injury on the job.

The key element in these government programmes is the commitment of business to cooperate in good faith and enforce all safety procedures.

Human Resources in the Future

Currently most people work about 240 days out of the 365. By 1994 the 240 workdays may be reduced to 175 through shorter workweeks, longer vacations, and additional paid holidays. Other future fringe benefits may include retirement programmes that can be transferred from one company to another, the option of early retirement at age 55, guaranteed lifetime employment, educational benefits for both employees and their families, and a guaranteed annual wage.

Controversial Issue

Mandatory Drug Testing in the Workplace

A Gallup poll released in November 1986 alleged that 75 percent of Canadians were convinced that there was a "drug epidemic" in Canada. Two out of three favoured mandatory drug testing in the workplace. A few days later, American Motors (Canada) Inc. revealed its decision to conduct urine tests on all job applicants. This was followed by an Air Canada announcement conceding that it had been screening job applicants for illegal drug use "for at least a few months."

Spurred by the ensuing publicity, attitudes toward drug use in the workplace polarized rapidly. Upper management saw it as a safety and productivity crisis that calls for a reasoned and effective programme of detection and rehabilitation. Unions and workers interpreted these measures as another managerial club to be used against employees.

Currently, most drug testing is practised in the industrial sector, where the nature of the job dictates that employees must be in constant control over their work and its environment.

As the question of mandatory drug testing takes on greater momentum, troubling issues remain. Just how big is the drug problem? How do concerned managers reach a compromise between their reasonable desire to keep the shop floor safe and the rights and dignity of their employees? Added to these concerns is a pervasive distrust of the tests themselves. How accurate are they? What do "false positives" imply?

According to Bhushan Kapur, director of laboratories at the Ontario Addiction Research Foundation, when the tests are conducted properly and cross-checked against each other, they are never wrong. "It is not enough just to find a drug in the urine. The point of all drug testing is *how* it got there."

There must be expert medical supervision of any drug test programme. "You are dealing with human beings here. It's not just a matter of employment issues. It takes the skills of a physician to take and interpret the test results accurately. There are a lot of factors that have to be taken into account to accurately interpret those results."

The unreliability of the tests and the improper administration of drug testing programmes aside, fundamental issues of principle and individual liberty are involved. According to Gordon Wilson, president of the Ontario Federation of Labour, "the problem with mandatory drug testing is that it is nothing but McCarthyism." To him, across-the-board drug testing is a violation of some very important principles that govern the way people in civilized societies have agreed to deal with one another. It's unreasonable search, a presumption of guilt. "They force people to incriminate themselves."

Sandra Chapnik, chairperson of the constitution and civil liberties section of the Canadian Bar Association of Ontario concurs. "It's probably against the Charter of Rights and Freedoms. The trouble with mandatory drug testing is that at this time there is no legislation that requires the employer to relate the drug testing to safety in the workplace or to prove that there are 'reasonable and probable grounds to believe' the drug is there."

What then is to be done with drug users in the workplace? According to Wilson, there are alternatives aside from mandatory drug testing. One such alternative is to look at the drug abuser as a person with a sickness, not unlike the alcoholic. Employees who are performing unsatisfactorily are questioned about their drug problem. If they cooperate, the company may offer help in overcoming the problem. If they refuse, they are fired—not for drug abuse, but for substandard performance.

As the issue of mandatory drug testing continues, corporate managers who are, rightly, concerned about the safety and harmony of their employees must ask themselves if they really want to act as policemen in their own firms.

Source: Carsten Stroud, "Do What's Fair," *Canadian Business*, April 1987, pp. 68, 70, 101.

Summary of Learning Goals

1. **Explain the functions of a specialized human resource department and the continuing responsibilities of all departments for the effective use of human resources.**

   Human resource management can be viewed in two ways. One approach is through the human resource department, which is responsible for such matters as development of job descriptions, screening of applicants, development and administration of training programmes, and administration of compensation benefits and safety programmes. A more complete approach includes the role of line managers, for ultimate responsibility for selection, motivation, appraisal, and retention of qualifed workers remains with them.

2. **Describe the concept of human resource planning and outline the major steps involved.**

   Human resource planning is the process by which management ensures that the appropriate number of people with the appropriate skills are available at the appropriate place at the appropriate time. It involves an assessment of current resources, a forecast of future requirements, and the development of a programme for meeting these forecasted needs.

3. **Explain how each of the steps in the recruitment and selection process contributes to finding the right person for the job.**

   Specialists in human resources are involved with all aspects of employee selection, training, and development. This involves locating, interviewing, and evaluating potential employees, administering employment tests, and taking some responsibility for orientation.

4. **Evaluate the different methods of training operative employees and present and potential managers.**

   On-the-job training by an experienced worker is typically used for jobs that are relatively simple, while more complex jobs may be taught off-the-job, through a formal classroom training programme or through the use of vestibule schools. Human resource management also involves creating and administering management development programmes for current and potential executives. Such programmes include job rotation, coaching, specialized courses, and assessment centres.

5. **Relate performance appraisal to effective human resource management.**

   Performance appraisal compares actual and desired employee performance, for the purpose of making objective decisions about compensation, promotion, additional training needs, transfers, or terminations. In addition, it serves to provide information to employees concerning their relative strengths and weaknesses and suggest areas for improvement, and it serves as a source of motivation by permitting managers to identify superior employees and to reward them with promotions, praise, and pay increases.

6. **Outline the different forms of compensation and explain when each form should be used.**

   Employee compensation can be classified as wages or salaries. Wages can be based on output (piece wage) or the amount of time worked (time wage) and are usually paid to production or maintenance workers. Salaries are calculated on a weekly, monthly, or annual basis and are usually paid to white-collar workers, including office personnel, executives, and professionals. Incentive compensation programmes, such as bonuses or profit-sharing plans, are often added to a salary or wage in order to reward superior performance and to boost employee morale.

7. **Enumerate the different types of employee benefits and the changes that are likely to occur in future fringe benefit programmes.**

   An increasingly important function of human resource management is in the area of employee benefits, such as pension plans, insurance programmes, health and safety programmes, credit unions, and sick-leave pay. Portable benefit programmes that can be transferred from one firm to another, early retirement options, and guaranteed annual wages are possible employee benefits of the future.

Key Terms

human resource management
personnel management
human resource planning
human resource forecast
job analysis
job description
job specification
hiring from within
Canadian Human Rights
   Commission
affirmative action programme
on-the-job training
apprenticeship training
classroom training
vestibule schools
management development
   programmes
job rotation
coaching
assessment centre

performance appraisal
promotions
seniority
transfers
separations
layoffs
terminations
wages
salary
job evaluation
piece wage
time wage
incentive compensation
bonuses
profit sharing
employee stock ownership
   plans
fringe benefits
Workers' Compensation Act
Canada Safety Code

Discussion Questions and Exercises

1. Explain the primary functions of a human resource department. Which of these responsibilities are most likely to be shared with line departments?
2. Explain the concept of human resource planning. What are the major steps involved?
3. Identify the steps in the employee recruitment and selection process.
4. Why do many firms follow the policy of hiring from within? What are the problems involved in following such a policy?
5. Compare and contrast the various types of employee training programmes. What are some major differences between training programmes and management development programmes.
6. Explain the primary purposes for conducting performance appraisals.
7. Distinguish between promotions, transfers, layoffs, and separations.
8. Give an example of a job in which of the following employee compensation alternatives would be most appropriate:
   a) piece wage,
   b) incentive wage,
   c) salary,
   d) time wage.

9. Discuss the type of compensation plan you would recommend for each of the following:
   a) watch repairs,
   b) retail salespeople,
   c) assembly line workers in a home air-conditioner factory,
   d) professional athletes.
10. Describe the typical fringe benefits offered to employees in a large company. What unique types of benefits might each of the following companies offer their employees, and what are the problems connected with each type?
    a) Domtar,
    b) Air Canada,
    c) The Bay,
    d) Bell Canada,
    e) Royal Bank.

Case 8-1

Downsizing—Beyond Survival

When industry in North America was hit by the deep recession of 1981-82, the managers of many companies adopted a survival strategy known as downsizing—the planned reduction of staff, through early retirement programmes, layoffs, and hiring freezes.

After several decades of growth and prosperity, many businesses—and governments—found under the stress of recession that they were carrying more fat and deadweight than they could afford. In this context, reduction of the workforce was a necessary response.

According to a study by Appelbaum, Shapiro and Simpson, "Downsizing became a new permanent philosophy with employers realizing that they can get by with less." Job security is no longer a workable concept. Competitive considerations, both nationally and internationally, have caused companies to stay "lean and mean" in the interest of efficiency. The result has been an erosion of both job security and employee loyalty.

The Appelbaum-Simpson-Shapiro analysis notes that, while layoffs may be necessary for a company to remain competitive, downsizing the corporate staff is only one of many responses that may be open to a company. Because a major downsizing programme is expensive and not easily reversible, it is of strategic importance to the corporation to review all the options thoroughly.

"One of the key steps to successful downsizing," the study said, "lies in defining the future organization."

Before making a decision to downsize, management should satisfy itself that the condition the layoffs are meant to correct does not come from temporary market aberration; and before proceeding with the programme, management should develop a comprehensive plan for turning the company around.

Damage control should be part of the programme. Although increased efficiency and cost competitiveness are two common results of downsizing, there may be some unfortunate consequences. Downsizing can have a traumatic effect, not only on those employees who are laid off, but on the surviving employees. Research has shown that after downsizing, a company frequently goes into a depressed and lethargic state.

According to the study, it is essential for a company undergoing downsizing to make a serious effort to help displaced workers through the provision of counselling seminars, job search workshops and placement services. "It is an important part of the healing process for the company—not to mention the preservation of its reputation as a responsible employer within the community."

Source: Ronald Anderson, "Damage Control Key to a Firm's Downsizing," *The Globe and Mail*, November 25, 1987, p. B7.

Questions:
1. How is downsizing a component of the organization's human resource planning function? Explain.
2. Why is it strategically important that an organization review all its options before downsizing? Elaborate.
3. Why should an organization undertake "damage control"? Explain.

Case 8-2

Spelling Disaster

When Sherbourne Manufacturing Ltd., an Ontario company that produces machinery parts, announced it would soon be introducing new technology on its assembly line, foreman Stan Vandenburg knew that many of the 500 employees would not be able to cope with the change. A 20-year veteran of the firm, Vandenburg was well aware that a significant percentage of the workers possessed minimal reading and writing skills.

The new technology required the ability to read manuals and type on a keyboard. It also increased the number of workers who would be placed in a position of responsibility, for along with the new machinery came new management techniques. Workers would be organized into small teams with supervisors appointed from within each unit.

Vandenburg was certain that his bosses had no idea how many of the workers were functionally illiterate. He feared that many would be fired when it became apparent they could not operate the new equipment. Some of the workers had already resigned. Also, he knew how adept many were at faking their reading and writing skills. If they attempted to cover up their inability to comprehend the new technology in a similar manner, accidents could occur and the new machinery could be damaged.

Although these concerns bothered him, Vandenburg was hesitant to approach management. He wasn't sure they would respond with sufficient understanding. What if they ordered everyone to take literacy tests and laid off those who failed; the workers might feel that he had betrayed them. Over the years, he had seen how sensitive they were about their educational skills.

About three months before the technology was to be implemented, Vandenburg made the decision to bring the issue into the open. He spoke with Jack Hollingsworth, director of human resources. Following their discussion, they presented their concerns to Brian Buckley, the general manager of the plant.

Buckley's initial reaction was defensive. He assumed first of all that the workers who had English as a second language—approximately 50 percent—were the only ones involved. He found it hard to believe that many of the native English speakers, some with high school diplomas, could barely read or write. By the end of their lengthy meeting, he accepted the disturbing news that a significant portion of his workforce could not adapt to the forthcoming transition at the plant.

Buckley wondered what action to take. The thought of universal testing, followed by dismissals and a long and expensive hiring process, didn't appeal to him. The last thing he wanted was a significant staff turnover and a potentially serious drop in morale among those who stayed.

Source: Paul McLaughlin, "Spelling Disaster," *Canadian Business*, August 1988, pp. 83-84. Paul McLaughlin is a Toronto writer and broadcaster.

Questions:
1. What should Buckley do? Explain.
2. Why should Buckley agree to a training programme? Discuss.
3. What type of training would be most appropriate in this case? Explain.

Chapter 9

Labour-Management Relations

Learning Goals

1. To explain why labour unions were first organized and what their chief objectives are

2. To identify the major federal laws affecting labour unions and to understand the key provisions of laws

3. To explain how collective bargaining agreements are established, and what roles are played by arbitrators and mediators

4. To analyze the tools of labour and management and describe how each is used

5. To describe who the union members of the 1990s will be

Profile

William (Bill) Kelly—*Blessed Is the Peacemaker*

The warring parties checked into Montreal's Queen Elizabeth Hotel three weeks before Christmas in 1968. On one side were representatives of Canada's two national railway companies; on the other, delegates from eight unions representing 80,000 of the railway industry's 120,000 employees. In the unenviable middle was William (Bill) Kelly, the director of the federal labour department's then two-year-old conciliation branch. Even while that conciliation unit was being set up, Kelly had been active in another role: leading the 24,000-member Brotherhood of Railroad Trainmen into a strike against the same two railway companies—a strike that ended only when Parliament passed back-to-work legislation. But in 1968, after only 21 days in his first major mediation role, an exhausted Kelly emerged early on Christmas Eve to announce that he had accomplished the all-but-impossible: a memorandum of settlement. There would be no strike. Since then, he has exercised his patient pragmatism to resolve close to 70 major disputes. His intervention has brought to an end—or avoided altogether—strikes in every major unionized industry under federal jurisdiction. Now the peacemaker, who turns 65 in March, retires on New Year's Eve.

Over the years, Kelly's appearance at the negotiating table has signalled the resumption of such critical services as air travel, mail delivery, grain shipments, and the news provided by The Canadian Press, the national news agency. Kelly, a warm, intense man behind a brusque exterior, says that he was often guided by a belief in human flexibility: "I have a little saying—'When someone says no to me, it means not yet.'" That approach worked again in 1988 when Kelly negotiated a settlement in a strike by 19,500 Bell Canada workers that had disrupted telephone service in Ontario, Quebec, and the Northwest Territories for 17 weeks. And

in 1984 his sterling record led the federal cabinet to name Kelly to the Order of Canada, a highly unusual honour for a civil servant.

Kelly has been an unusual public servant from the outset of his career in government. A native of Toronto, he was trained as an RCAF pilot near the end of the Second World War and became a railway brakeman in Toronto in peacetime. Kelly was an active unionist and by 1960 he had become the youngest international vice-president in the Brotherhood of Railroad Trainmen's history. Six years later, Prime Minister Lester Pearson's government asked the gravel-voiced, chain-smoking union leader to head its newly reorganized labour mediation service. What seemed at first to be an unlikely choice turned out to be inspired.

Kelly quickly won the confidence of negotiators for both management and labour. "You can trust him," said Frederick Pomeroy, president of the 40,000-member Communication and Electrical Workers of Canada, the union that struck Bell. Added Pomeroy: "He is very logical, very intelligent and he has a lot of street smarts." He is also tough. Said Kelly of his approach to bargainers:

"I like to keep their feet to the fire and make them decide."

Kelly's tenacity and his wisdom have been models for other mediators in both the federal and provincial fields of labour-management relations. But Bill Kelly's special talents will be missed the next time a national union and its employer become locked in a destructive dispute. Men of his stature cross the national stage too seldom.

Source: "Blessed Is the Peacemaker: William (Bill) Kelly," *Maclean's*, December 26, 1988, p. 25. Reprinted by permission.

The union was formed for the same reasons that most worker collectives have developed throughout history. The workers faced a deteriorating quality of life as supplies of meat, sugar, and flour became difficult to acquire—even for those with sufficient funds. In addition, they wanted the workweek shortened to a 5-day 40-hour week from its present 6 days and 48 hours.

Government officials warned that a reduction in the workweek would be devastating to the already shaky economy. They also pointed, none too subtly, to the thousands of military personnel of an adjacent nation assigned to the border region. But still the workers continued to swell the ranks of the new union, and its members grew to eight million members within four months of its formation. Periodic work stoppages were called to demonstrate the union's power.

Although the above description reads like the script for an over-dramatized documentary film on the history of unionism, the description is both real and current. The union is Solidarity, the first independent trade union in a communist nation. Of the eight million Poles who joined the union headed by Lech Walesa, it is estimated that some one million were also members of Poland's Communist Party. Amid government warnings, Soviet troop concentrations at the Polish border, and domestic rationing programmes, the new union took actions designed to accomplish objectives shared by the founders of other unions organized over the past century.[1]

In December 1981 the Polish government declared martial law and banned Solidarity. The unionists must have felt frustrations similar to those of Canadian workers after government intervention in the Winnipeg General Strike of 1919, the Oshawa Strike in the late thirties, the Asbestos Strike of 1949, and the 1950 loggers' strike against the Anglo-Newfoundland Development Company.

What Is a Labour Union?

labour union
A group of workers who have banded together to achieve common goals in the key areas of wages, hours, and working conditions.

craft union
A labour union consisting of skilled workers in a specific craft or trade.

industrial union
A labour union consisting of all of the workers in a given industry regardless of their occupations or skill levels.

A **labour union** is a group of workers who have banded together to achieve common goals in the key areas of wages, hours, and working conditions. Two types of labour unions exist in Canada: craft and industrial. A **craft union** is a union consisting of skilled workers in a specific craft or trade such as carpenters, painters, machinists, and printers.

While a craft union focuses on a trade, an **industrial union** is a union consisting of all of the workers in a given industry, regardless of their occupations or skill levels. Industrial unions include the United Auto Workers, the International Woodworkers of America, and the Amalgamated Clothing and Textile Workers Union.

Why Are Labour Unions Needed?

During the late 1800s, young children made up a large part of the labour force, especially in textile mills.

The Industrial Revolution brought the advantages of specialization and division of labour. The factors produced increased efficiency, because each worker could specialize in some aspect of the production process and become proficient. Bringing together numerous workers also resulted in increased output over the individual handicraft methods of production. The factory system converted the jack-of-all-trades into a specialist.

But industrial workers of the nineteenth and early twentieth centuries discovered that the Industrial Revolution had produced a more sinister impact on their lives. Specialization had resulted in dependence on the factory for their livelihood. In prosperous times they were assured of employment. But when depressions came, they were out of work. Unemployment insurance was a subject for dreamers, and poorhouses represented reality for unemployed workers.

Working conditions were often bad. Workdays were long and safety standards nonexistent in many factories. Young boys and girls were pressed into the work force to earn a few pennies to help their families. In 1889, eight-year-old children in a Montreal textile mill worked six days a week from 6 a.m. to 6 p.m. for $92 a year. In the coal mines of Nova Scotia and Manitoba, small boys worked for 60¢ a day on their hands and knees in shafts and tunnels too small for a grown man to enter.

By the end of the nineteenth century, the workweek was typically 60 hours, but in some industries, such as steel, it was 72 or even 84 hours—seven 12-hour days a week. Working conditions were still frequently unsafe, and child labour was still common.

Workers gradually learned that through bargaining as a unified group they could obtain improvements in job security and better wages and working conditions. The sweeping changes in labour-management relations that occurred during the past century produced profound changes in wages, hours of work, and working conditions. A visible sign of the success of the labour movement is the presence of Douglas Fraser, the head of the United Auto Workers, on the board of directors of Chrysler Corporation.

The History of Labour Unions in Canada

To a large extent, the development of trade unionism in Canada was a reflection of the development of industrial relations in the United States. The growth was, however, considerably slower. An agriculturally based society, a scattered population, little industrialization, and poor communication in Canada sharply limited the scope of labour organizations.

Until the mid-nineteenth century, unionism was limited to small loosely knit local organizations among a small number of skilled craft workers in a few major urban centres. The first union recorded was in Montreal in 1827 among the boot and shoe workers.

Encouraged by the rapid progress of trade unionism in both the United States and Great Britain, unions developed more rapidly during the 1850s to 1870s. Increased mobility between Canadian and American workers led local organizations to join international unions.

However, the common law prohibited "restraint or any activities that prevented a company from carrying out its business." This was interpreted in the courts as rendering union activities illegal, and union organizers were jailed for conspiracy. Membership in a union often meant dismissal and blacklisting. In the 1870s, the Canadian government finally passed legislation, modelled on British law, removing legal barriers to unionism.

The depression of the mid-1870s to mid-1890s and the growth of manufacturing combined to create inhuman working conditions: workers were disciplined by beatings, imprisonment, and fines; factories were unsanitary; and a 60-hour workweek was the norm. These conditions stimulated the growth of unions and led to the establishment of an umbrella organization, the Trades and Labour Congress (TLC). In many cases these unions were affiliated with their American counterparts, thus forming international unions. The first half of the twentieth century saw unionism in Canada grow by leaps and bounds: membership went from 50,000 in 1900 to 250,000 in 1919 to 912,000 in 1947. The conservative TLC and the equivalent body in the US, the American Federation of Labor (AFL), were made up almost entirely of "craft" unions serving skilled workers. They largely ignored the needs of the unskilled and semi-skilled workers. New groups, including "industrial" unions serving all workers within an industry, were formed. These organizations, which often had broader social and political objectives, came together in the Canadian Congress of Labour (CCL) in Canada and the Congress of Industrial Organizations (CIO) in the United States. The rivalry between AFL-TLC and the CIO-CCL persisted for almost 20 years until 1955 when the AFL and the CIO were united under the presidency of George Meany. The following year the Canadian groups came together as the **Canadian Labour Congress** (CLC). Figure 9-1 shows the organization of the Canadian Labour Congress.

Canadian Labour Congress
The national organization to which most unions in Canada belong.

The only major group of unions not affiliated with the CLC are those affiliated with the Confederation of National Trade Unions and the Congress of Democratic Trade Unions, both Quebec-based organizations.

Figure 9-1
Organization of the Canadian Labour Congress

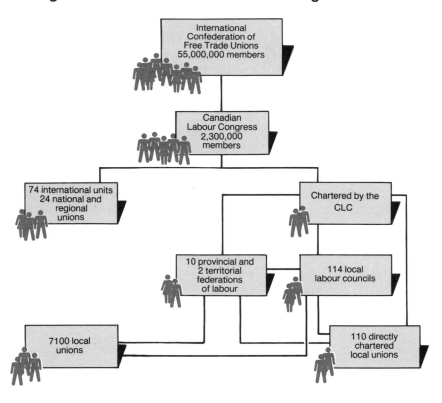

However, although membership has expanded considerably, only one-third of Canadian workers belong to unions. The largest unions in Canada according to membership are listed in Table 9-1. Table 9-2 shows statistics on union membership for 1960-1988. Table 9-3 shows union membership by congress affiliation for 1988.

The total number of union members in Canada increased to 3,841,000 as of January 1988, compared with 3,782,000 a year earlier, according to figures released by Labour Canada.

Union membership in 1988 represented 36.6 percent of Canada's non-agricultural paid workers.

The Canadian Labour Congress remains the largest central labour organization, with 2,231,697 members, or 58.1 percent of the total union membership (see Table 9-3).

The ten largest unions (see Table 9-1) have generally maintained or increased their membership with one exception: a decrease of 4,200 members registered by the Public Service Alliance of Canada.

Focus 9-1 examines the new role that could be taken by the CLC.

Table 9-1
The 10 Largest Unions in Canada Ranked by Membership, 1988

Unions and Affiliations	Membership (000s)
1. Canadian Union of Public Employees (CLC)	342.0
2. National Union of Provincial Government Employees (CLC)	292.3
3. Public Service Alliance of Canada (CLC)	175.7
4. United Food and Commercial Workers International Union (AFL-CIO)	170.0
5. United Steelworkers of America (AFL-CIO)	160.0
6. National Automobile, Aerospace and Agricultural Implement Workers Union of Canada (CLC)	143.0
7. Fédération des affaires sociales inc. (CSN)	96.5
8. International Brotherhood of Teamsters, Chaffeurs, Warehousemen & Helpers of America (AFL-CIO)	91.5
9. Commission des enseignantes et enseignants des commissions scolaires (CEQ)	75.0
10. Service Employees International Union (AFL-CIO)	70.0

Source: *Directory of Labour Organizations in Canada 1988*, Labour Canada, Bureau of Labour Information, Ottawa, 1988, Table 4, p. 16.

Table 9-2
Statistics on Union Membership in Canada, 1960-1988

Year	Union Membership (000s)	Total Non-Agricultural Paid Workers (000s)	Union Membership as a % of Civilian Labour Force	Union Membership as a % of Non-Agricultural Paid Workers
1960	1,459	4,522	23.5	32.3
1961	1,447	4,578	22.6	31.6
1962	1,423	4,705	22.2	30.2
1963	1,449	4,867	22.3	29.8
1964	1,493	5,074	22.3	29.4
1965	1,589	5,343	23.2	29.7
1966	1,736	5,658	24.5	30.7
1967	1,921	5,953	26.1	32.3
1968	2,010	6,068	26.6	33.1
1969	2,075	6,380	26.3	32.5
1970	2,173	6,465	27.2	33.6
1971	2,231	6,637	26.8	33.6
1972	2,388	6,893	27.8	34.6
1973	2,591	7,181	29.2	36.1
1974	2,732	7,637	29.4	35.8
1975	2,884	7,817	29.8	36.9
1976	3,042	8,151	30.6	37.3
1977	3,149	8,243	31.0	38.2
1978*	3,278	8,413	31.3	39.0
1980	3,397	9,027	30.5	37.6
1981	3,487	9,330	30.6	37.4
1982	3,617	9,264	31.4	39.0
1983	3,563	8,901	30.6	40.0
1984	3,651	9,220	30.6	39.6
1985	3,666	9,404	30.2	39.0
1986	3,730	9,893	29.7	37.7
1987	3,782	10,066	29.8	37.6
1988	3,841	10,483	29.6	36.6

*Figures not available for 1979.
Source: *Directory of Labour Organizations in Canada 1988*, Labour Canada, Bureau of Labour Information, Ottawa, 1988, Table 1, p. 13.

Labour Legislation

In Canada judicial decisions over the years have established that the federal government has jurisdiction in labour relations matters only over the federal public service, crown corporations, airlines, most railways, communication companies, and federal government agencies. The public service accounts for 5 percent and federally regulated industries for approximately 10 percent of the labour force. All other organizations fall under the jurisdiction of the provinces.

Table 9-3
Union Membership by Congress Affiliation, 1988

Congress Affiliation	Membership	%
CLC-CTC	2,231,697	58.1
CNTU-CSN	204,637	5.3
CFL-FCT	207,736	5.4
AFL-CIO	224,305	5.8
CEQ	99,114	2.6
CSD	50,379	1.3
CCU-CSC	31,407	0.8
CNFIU	3,476	0.1
Unaffiliated International Unions	15,386	0.4
Unaffiliated National Unions	662,876	17.3
Independent Local Organizations	110,478	2.9

CLC-CTC:	Canadian Labour Congress/Congrès du travail du Canada
CNTU-CSN:	Confederation of National Trade Unions/Confédération des syndicats nationaux
CFL-FCT:	Canadian Federation of Labour/Fédération canadienne du travail
AFL-FAT:	American Federation of Labour/Fédération américaine du travail
CIO-COI:	Congress of Industrial Organizations/Congrès des organisations industrielles
CEQ:	Centrale de l'enseignement du Québec
CSD:	Centrale des syndicats démocratiques
CCU-CSC:	Confederation of Canadian Unions/Confédération des syndicats canadiens
CNFIU:	Canadian National Federation of Independent Unions

Source: *Directory of Labour Organizations in Canada 1988*, Labour Canada, Bureau of Labour Information. Ottawa, 1988, Table 2, p. 14.

The Canada Labour Code and the labour codes of each province reflect the same general policies: the right of employees to form and join labour unions; protection against unfair labour practices by either employers or employees; the right for employees to strike and for employers to lock out employees when no agreement can be reached. The Canada Labour Code and provincial employment standards acts regulate minimum wages, the minimum age for employment, hours of work, overtime pay, vacations with pay, statutory holidays, and maternity leave. Other forms of legislation prohibit discrimination in employment on the basis of race, ethnic origin, colour, religion, and sex.

Focus 9-1

The New Role of the CLC!

The Canadian Labour Congress is currently rethinking its national role. The labour central has plans to become less of a "business union"—concerned only with issues that affect its members—and focus more on issues that affect all of society.

Canadian Auto Workers leader Bob White, as Canada's most prominent labour leader, is on the forefront of this re-evaluation. According to him, "There's no question that the congress has an important role to play as a force of progress in Canadian society."

A few years ago, this desire for progress and a strong Canadian identity led White and the CAW to their David-vs-Goliath fight for greater autonomy within, and eventually complete independence from, a large US-based union.

Taking on the US is never an easy task. It's probably even tougher in the automobile industry, where production in the two countries is so closely linked. The first big dispute came when the US government ordered Chrysler workers to accept major wage rollbacks before it would bail the automaker out of its financial problems.

The Canadians wouldn't make these concessions. White argued that the US government couldn't order Canadians to do anything, but was confronted by US colleagues who said things like, "If the American Congress had meant to exempt Canadians, it would have said so."

From then on the Canadian and US groups faced continual ideological and personality conflicts which culminated in the cessation of the Canadians' 50-year membership in the powerful, Detroit-based United Auto Workers and into an independent union.

When White stood before the Canadian Auto Workers' founding convention in September 1985, the US union was taking legal action against the Canadians to try to prevent them from using not only the title "United Auto Workers" but any acronym using the letters AW. Nor had the parent union given the Canadians a cent, even though it had promised to hand over $36 million—barely half of the 10 percent of the UAW's total assets to which the Canadian wing believed it was entitled.

The Canadians eventually got their money and settled on the acronym CAW.

Source: John DeMont, "Canadian Labour Congress Rethinks its National Role," *The Financial Post*, March 28, 1988, p. 5.

The Union in the Workplace

closed shop
A business that can only hire union workers; employees must join the union and must remain members of the union throughout their employment.

A **closed shop** is a business having an employment agreement under which management may offer jobs only to members of the union. Only if no union members are available may management look beyond the union ranks, and even then before being hired, workers must become union members, and remain such while they are employed. Unions regard the closed shop as important to union security. If all workers are union members, the union is assured of recognition of wages and working conditions. Unions also feel that because all employees enjoy the benefits of union contracts, they should all support the union.

Many employers and some employees have argued that a fundamental principle of freedom is violated if people are forced to join an organization as a condition of employment. If only union members can be hired, some qualified workers may be excluded. A guaranteed membership may allow union leaders to become irresponsible and to deal dishonestly with their members. Employers maintain the closed shop is open to abuse. One common complaint is that in the interests of job protection, unions may impede technological change by requiring a certain number of workers to conduct an operation even though they may not all be needed. This practice is known as **featherbedding**.

featherbedding
A practice of requiring more workers than necessary in order to provide more jobs.

union shop
A business that can hire any qualified workers, but the workers must join the union within a specified time.

In the United States the closed shop has been made illegal. In Canada, it is legal where both parties have agreed to it. A **union shop** answers some of the criticisms of the closed shop. It is a business having an employment agreement whereby all qualified workers may be hired, but if they do not belong to the union, they must join it within a specified time period. The union shop is widely practised in Canada.

Another compromise is known as maintenance of membership. No new worker is forced to join the union but those who are already members must remain members as a condition of employment.

In an arbitration award handed down in 1946 following a strike of employees of the Ford Motor Company in Windsor, Ontario, Supreme Court Justice Ivan Rand set up a system that has served as the basis for many union-management agreements in Canada. Instead of a closed or union shop, Rand provided for the compulsory checkoff of union dues from the wages of all workers under the agreement. In other words, workers were not to be required to join the union, but as they all benefited from the union contract, they were all to contribute to union funds. This arrangement has become known as the **Rand formula**.

Rand formula
A security plan for unions requiring the employer to deduct union dues from the pay of all employees who qualify for membership and remit them to the union.

Legislation at both the federal and provincial levels requires an employer to "checkoff" union dues from an employee's wages, when checkoff is part of the collective agreement—or if there is no collective agreement, when the employee has agreed to it.

Towards a New Labour-Management Order

A breakthrough deal signed between Bob White's Canadian Auto Workers and Suzuki Motor Co. Ltd. will ensure that the vehicles rolling off the brand new assembly lines at Ingersoll, Ontario, in 1989 will carry the union label. The Suzuki agreement marks the first time a Japanese automaker has agreed to recognize the adversarial-minded Canadian auto union. But perhaps more significantly, it is also the first time the CAW has accepted at least some aspects of Japanese-style plant management and work practices.

The 2,000 workers at the plant—a joint venture between Suzuki and General Motors of Canada Ltd.—will work in a Japanese-style "team concept," under which small, semi-autonomous work groups will have little supervision and are given responsibility for quality and efficiency. This is a marked departure from the traditional North American approach where workers perform only specific tasks and are never confused with their bosses.

The plant will retain North American features: Workers will have a grievance procedure and be paid in the same way as other Canadian auto workers. They will not work under a scheme of productivity bonuses that are the rule in Japan.

While the CAW was able to talk Suzuki out of its original proposal for a totally Jananese-style plant, it is still taking a chance. The union may only encourage heavier demands from the domestic Big Three, which are hungry for the kind of increased management flexibility the Suzuki agreement appears to offer.

More fundamentally, the new plant will test whether a tough and traditional Canadian union can maintain its vitality in an atmosphere where workers are treated as part of the "team." Canadians working in a Japanese-owned auto plant are unlikely to be singing the company song every day, but increased loyalty to the company many effectively undermine the union.

"It's a bit of a gamble, but I think it's worth it," White said in an interview.

The CAW leader is confident he can build an effective local at the Suzuki plant with a strong shop-floor presence. Besides, the union might never have had its foot in the door without such an agreement. According to White, the agreement gives him an opportunity to put pressure on Toyota and Honda, the two other Japanese auto giants that are setting up Canadain plants but which have shown no interest to date in dealing with his union.

For Suzuki, a company that prides itself on its good staff relations, the deal fits into its corporate philosophy. "Our basic relationship is cooperative," said Gary McGugan, a senior official of Suzuki Canada. "We want to encourage assembly-line workers to work as a team, to have a team effort turn out a quality product. Those are the kinds of things we're going to try to instill in our workforce in Ingersoll."

Source: Lorne Slotnick, "Will Canadian Workers Accept Japanese Ways?" *The Globe and Mail*, September 6, 1986, p. F1.

The Collective Bargaining Process

collective bargaining
A process of negotiation between management and union representatives for the purpose of arriving at mutually acceptable wages and working conditions for employees.

The primary objective of labour unions is the improvement of wages, hours and working conditions for its members. This goal is achieved primarily through **collective bargaining**, a process of negotiation between management and union representatives for the purpose of arriving at mutually acceptable wages and working conditions for employees.

Once a union is accepted by a majority of the workers in a firm, it is certified by the Canadian Labour Relations Board or the provincial equivalent and must be recognized by the firm's management as the legal collective bargaining agent for all employees. The stage is then set for representatives of the union and management to meet formally at the bargaining table to work out a collective agreement or contract.

Union contracts, which typically cover a one-, two- or three-year period, are often the result of days and even weeks of discussion, disagreement, compromise, and eventual agreement. Once agreement has been reached, union members must vote to accept or reject the contract. If the contract is rejected, union representatives may resume the bargaining process with management representatives, or the union members may strike to obtain their demands.

Bargaining Patterns

Bargaining patterns—and the number of unions and employers involved—vary for different industries and different occupational categories. Most collective bargaining involves agreements between a single plant and a single employer. Agreements between several plants and one employer bind all plants of the employer. Terms and conditions approved in the bargaining agreement between Westinghouse Electric and the International Brotherhood of Electrical Workers apply to all Westinghouse plants. Coalition bargaining involves negotiations between a coalition of several unions representing the employees of one company. In the case of industry-wide bargaining, a single national union would engage in collective bargaining with several employers in a particular industry.

In general, manufacturers would prefer to bargain with each local union representing its various employee groups on an individual basis rather than deal with a coalition of several unions. The influence and power of smaller, separate unions are likely to be less than that of a coalition.

The Bargaining Zone

Issues covered in bargaining agreements include wages, work hours, benefits, union activities and responsibilities, grievance handling and arbitration, and employee rights and seniority. As is the case in all types of negotiations, the collective bargaining process is one of demands, proposals, and counterproposals that ultimately result in compromise and agreement. Figure 9-2 illustrates a contract negotiation by focusing upon a single wage issue and two security issues—a union shop provision and a seniority rule. The vertical lines represent the outcomes for both the union and for management according to desirability. Thus, the best outcome for the union—and its initial demand—will be a 14 percent wage increase (based upon productivity increases and increases in the cost of living) and the addition of a union shop provision. Management's initial offer will be a 6 percent wage increase and the elimination of current seniority rules.

As Figure 9-2 shows, the initial demands of each party will ultimately result in a "final" offer from the union representative of a 12 percent pay increase and removal of its demand for a union shop. Management's "final" offer will be an 8 percent increase and an elimination of seniority rules. However, if the union is forced below its 8 percent wage increase demand, a strike will occur. Management's outer boundary in the bargaining zone is a 12 percent wage increase and maintenance of present security rules. These are the maximum terms it will accept without closing the plant. The solid areas indicate the range of possible terms within the **bargaining zone**. The negotiations should fall within this zone, with the final agreement dependent upon the negotiating skills and relative power of management and union representatives.

Once ratified by the union membership, the contract becomes the legally binding agreement for all labour-management relations during the period of time specified. Contracts typically include such areas as wages, industrial relations, and methods of settling labour-management disputes. Some are only a few pages in length, while others run more than 200 pages. Table 9-4 lists topics typically included in a union contract.

bargaining zone
The range of collective bargaining, in which one limit is defined as the point above which management will not go without closing the plant, and the other limit is defined as the point below which the union will not go without a strike.

Settling Union-Management Disputes

Although strikes make newspaper headlines, almost all union-management negotiations result in a signed agreement without a work stoppage.

Figure 9-2
The Bargaining Zone

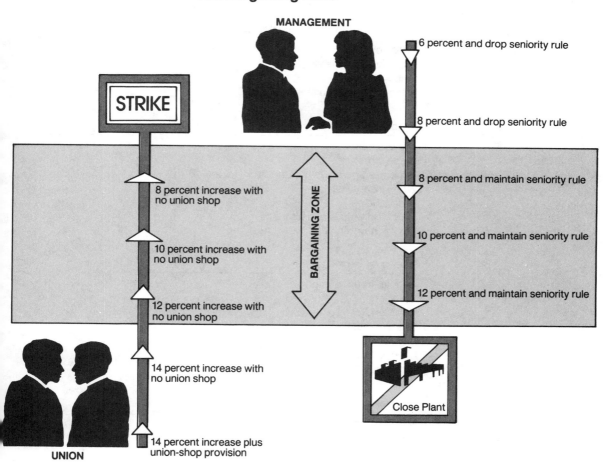

MANAGEMENT

6 percent and drop seniority rule

8 percent and drop seniority rule

8 percent and maintain seniority rule

10 percent and maintain seniority rule

12 percent and maintain seniority rule

Close Plant

BARGAINING ZONE

STRIKE

8 percent increase with no union shop

10 percent increase with no union shop

12 percent increase with no union shop

14 percent increase with no union shop

14 percent increase plus union-shop provision

UNION

Mediation

mediation
The process of bringing in a third party to make impartial recommendations for the settlement of union-management differences.

When negotiations do break down, disagreements between union and management representatives may be settled by **mediation**—the process of bringing in a third party, called a mediator, to make recommendations for the settlement of differences.

Although the mediator does not serve as a decision maker, union and management representatives can be assisted in reaching an agreement by the mediator's suggestions, advice, and compromise solutions. Because both sides must give their confidence and trust to the mediator, that person's impartiality is essential. Mediators are often selected from the ranks of community social or political leaders, lawyers, professors, and distinguished national figures.

Table 9-4
Topics Usually Included in a Union Contract

Union Activities and Responsibilities

Dues collection
Union bulletin boards
Union officers
Wildcat strikes and slowdowns

Wages

Job evaluation
Wage structure
General wage adjustments
Wage incentives
Time studies
Shift differentials and bonuses
Pay for reporting and calling in

Hours of Work

Regular hours of work
Vacations
Holidays
Overtime rules
Rest periods
Leaves of absence
Sick pay

Insurance

Medical and life insurance
Pensions
Supplemental unemployment benefits

Employee Job Rights and Seniority

Seniority regulations
Transfers
Promotions
Layoffs
Recalls

Grievance Handling and Arbitration

Discipline, Suspensions, and Discharge

Health and Safety

Arbitration

arbitration
The process of bringing an impartial third party, called an arbitrator, into a union-management dispute to render a binding, legally enforceable decision.

Arbitration is the process of bringing in an impartial third party who renders a binding decision in the dispute. This person must be acceptable to the union and to management, and by law his or her decision is final. In essence, the arbitrator acts as a judge, making a decision after listening to both sides of the argument. No special form of arbitration is required by statute: it is left to the discretion of the parties and most collective agreements contain explicit arbitration procedures.

voluntary arbitration
Arbitration where both union and management representatives decide to present their unresolved issues to an impartial third party.

Voluntary arbitration occurs when union and management representatives make a joint decision to present any issues that they have been unable to resolve through negotiation to an impartial third party.

compulsory arbitration
Arbitration to which both union and management representatives must submit, usually required by a third party (such as the federal government).

Occasionally, the government will require management and labour to submit to **compulsory arbitration**. Few contract disputes ever need to go to compulsory arbitration. However, the procedure can be imposed by the government in order to prevent or end prolonged strikes affecting major industries and threatening to disrupt the economy.

Grievance Procedures

The union contract serves as a guide to relations between the firm's management and its employees. The rights of each party are stated in the agreement. But no contract—regardless of how detailed it is—will completely eliminate the possibility of disagreement.

Differences of opinion may arise on how to interpret a particular clause in the contract. Management may interpret the layoff policy of the contract as based on seniority for each work shift. The union may see it as based on the seniority of all employees. Such differences can be the beginning of a grievance.

grievance
An employee or union complaint that management is violating some provision of the union contract.

A **grievance**—whether by a single worker or by the entire union—is a complaint that management is violating some provision of the union contract. Because grievance handling is the primary source of contact between union officials and management from the signing of one contract to the next, the way grievances are resolved plays a major role in the relationship between the employer and the union. Because grievances are likely to arise over such matters as transfers, work assignments, and seniority, almost all union contracts require that these complaints be submitted to a formal grievance procedure. Figure 9-3 shows the five steps involved in a typical grievance procedure. As this figure indicates, the employee's grievance is first submitted by the union representative (the shop steward) to the

Figure 9-3
The Five Steps Involved in Carrying Out a Grievance
Procedure. Any grievances not settled at one level are
carried to the next level

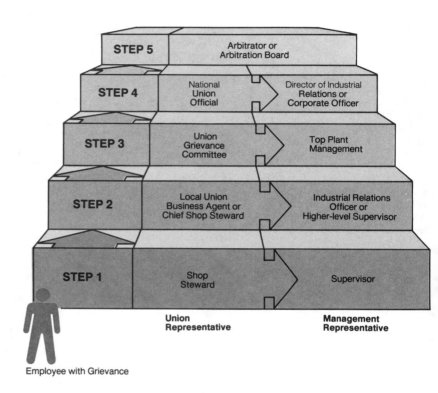

immediate supervisor. If the problem is solved, it goes no further. But if no satisfactory agreement is reached, a higher union official may take the grievance to a higher manager. If the highest company officer cannot settle the grievance, it is submitted to an outside arbitrator for a final and binding decision.

Tools of Unions and Management

Although most differences between labour and management are settled through the collective bargaining process or through a formal grievance procedure, both unions and management occasionally resort to tools of power to make their demands known.

Union Tools

strike
A temporary work stoppage by employees until a dispute has been settled or a contract signed.

picketing
Workers marching at the entrances of an employer's plant as a public protest against some management practice.

The chief tools of unions are strikes, picketing, and boycotts. The **strike**, or walkout, is one of the most effective strategies of the labour union. It involves a temporary work stoppage by employees until a dispute has been settled or a contract signed. Since striking workers are not paid by the company, unions generally establish strike funds to pay them so they can continue striking.

Although the power to strike is the ultimate weapon, it is not used lightly. In many cases the threat of a strike is almost as effective as an actual work stoppage.

Another effective form of union pressure is **picketing**—workers marching at the entrances of the employer's plant as a public protest against some management practice. By virtue of the Criminal Code, picketing is illegal except for the purpose of communicating or obtaining information. Some provincial labour codes have legislated specifically on the matter of picketing and permit picketing only when the workers are legally on strike or have been locked out. The signs carried by the union members usually outside the plants are intended to inform the public that a labour problem exists and also give other companies the message to not deal with the picketed firm.

During a strike, employees organize picket lines to impose a temporary work stoppage until a dispute has been settled, or a new contract signed.

boycott
An attempt to keep people from purchasing goods or services from a company.

A **boycott** is an attempt to keep people from purchasing goods or services from a company. There are two kinds of boycotts—primary and secondary. In the case of a primary boycott, union members are told to not patronize the boycotted firm. Some unions even fine members who buy from such a firm. A secondary boycott is a boycott or work stoppage intended to force an employer to stop dealing in the product of another firm involved in a labour dispute. In general, secondary boycotts are illegal in Canada, except in British Columbia. Boycotts, of course, may also be used by the general public as political weapons. For example, in the early eighties many Canadians boycotted Nestlé products in protest against the methods used by the company to market infant formula in underdeveloped countries.

Management Tools

lockout
A management method to bring pressure on union members by closing the firm.

injunction
A court order prohibiting some practice.

Management also has means for dealing with problems. In the past it used the **lockout**—in effect, a management strike to bring pressure on union members by closing the firm. The lockout is rarely used today, except when a union strike has already partially shut down a plant.

Injunctions—court orders prohibiting some practice—may be obtained by management to prevent an illegal strike, excessive picketing, or certain unfair union practices.

When unionized employees go out on strike, management personnel sometimes fill in for striking workers.
Drawing by Weber; © The New Yorker Magazine, Inc.

"Ma Bell at your service, Madam."

employers' associations
Cooperative efforts on the part of the employers to present a united front in dealing with labour unions.

Some employers come together in cooperative efforts to present a united front in dealing with labour unions. These **employers' associations** may even act as negotiators for individual employers who want to reach agreements with labour unions. In industries characterized by many small firms and a single large union, there is an increasing tendency for industry-wide bargaining between the union and a single representative of the industry employers. Although it does not negotiate contracts, the Canadian Manufacturers' Association is an example of an employers' association. It presents the views of its members on key issues.

The Future of Organized Labour

Unions now represent approximately one-third of the nonagricultural paid work force. Though union membership has increased in terms of numbers, recently labour unions have grown little in terms of the proportion of workers who are members.

In the past, union strength has been derived from workers in traditional blue-collar occupations and industries. The prospect of increasing union membership from these sources is bleak for two reasons.

First, most blue-collar workers have already been organized. Most employees of the automobile, steel, paper, mining, transportation, and many manufacturing industries are union members. The days of masses of unorganized blue-collar workers are gone even though some companies have resisted unionization.

Second, job-growth projections indicate that blue-collar ranks—until now the source of union membership strength—will be less important in the future. As factories become more automated, the demand for blue-collar workers will decrease.

Unions are likely to increase their efforts to recruit white-collar workers and agricultural labourers. Of white-collar workers, only public employees are unionized on a large scale. Workers in other white-collar occupations have so far resisted unionization. Also, agricultural workers have not joined labour unions largely because many of them come from outside Canada on temporary work permits. Also, organizing is difficult among workers who move from job to job. In contrast, many agricultural workers in the United States are now union members.

The success of organization attempts in these areas—white-collar and agricultural workers—may ultimately determine whether Canadian labour unions will continue to grow or whether their membership has already peaked. Focus 9-3 details the efforts of major public-sector unions to organize white-collar and service workers in the private sector.

Focus 9-3

Public Sector Unions Make Foray into Private Ranks

Faced with government cutbacks, privatization and the growing use of nonunion part-timers, public-sector unions are aggressively recruiting members in the private sector.

The Canadian Union of Public Employees, the National Union of Provincial Government Employees, and the Public Service Alliance of Canada are among the most powerful and militant in Canada. Their efforts to widen their influence may lead to more confrontation in some areas of private enterprise—especially in the service sector, where many companies are renowned for their tough anti-union views.

As well as trying to sign up new members, public-sector unions are fighting hard to retain members now working for newly privatized companies. They have also mounted organizing drives among part-time government workers.

John Fryer, NUPGE president, sees rich opportunities to expand union membership among workers who feel that they are not sharing in the prosperity of the past few years. According to him, it is easier to organize when the economy is in an up-swing. When there is a recession, "the you-should-be-lucky-you've-got-a-job syndrome takes over."

Michael Martin, assistant to PSAC president Daryl Bean, says PSAC is also planning an intense organizing campaign in the service sector. PSAC, representing federal government workers, has been hardest hit by contracting out. It has lost 66,300 members in the past two years. According to Martin, the federal government spent $3 billion on contract labour in 1987, compared to $700,000 in 1980. He claims the government is not saving any money by contracting; it is just using fewer employees and lowering work standards.

Jeff Rose, CUPE president, is confident his union will continue to grow despite the pressures. CUPE has had some success in retaining workers in the newly privatized sector, and is carrying on extensive organizing in areas it considers its "legitimate sphere of influence." That includes nonprofit agencies that receive government funding. CUPE is trying to organize private daycare workers, nursing home employees, and workers in other government-regulated areas.

While big industrial unions are railing against the free trade agreement as a threat to jobs, leaders of the public-sector unions agree the accord's impact will be less direct. However, Martin says pressures on Canadian public employees are already appearing.

Fryer expects the political atmosphere for unions in Canada to harden as a result of the free trade agreement. He points out that "in the US the hostile environment has almost beaten the trade union movement." To most labour leaders, the strength of the Canadian labour movement lies in its militancy—the ability to organize workers in the private sector without losing current members.

Source: Sheila Arnott, "Public Sector Unions Make Foray into Private Ranks," *The Financial Post*, January 14–16, 1989, pp. 1 and 4.

A New Generation of Workers

A major change required of Canadian labour leaders is the recognition that the work force of the nineties is increasingly the product of the baby boom years—a generation that has no memory of the Great Depression and economic hardship. These workers grew up in the affluent and permissive fifties and sixties. They often bring to the workplace a demand for challenging work and a dislike for both union and management bureaucracies.

Labour-Management Relations

As employment in goods-producing industries continues to decline, the stereotype of the blue-collar industrial worker becomes less valid. For nearly half a century the dominant pattern of bargaining over wages, hours, and working conditions has been set by the blue-collar unions. Studies forecast that by 1990 eight of every ten workers may be employed in providing services rather than products, particularly in information-processing industries such as finance, education, and communications.

The new workers will be better educated than their predecessors. They will also be more militant on the issues of environmental concerns, flexible working patterns, and shared decision making. The future of organized labour will be greatly affected by its responses to these workers.

Controversial Issue

Free Trade—The Labour Law Factor

Although the free trade agreement makes no mention of Canadian labour laws, many in the labour movement and business community alike concede that Canada's relatively advanced body of labour and employment legislation will face intense downward pressure from the new economic order spawned by free trade.

According to them, the threat comes from the competitive forces that Canadian business will face in the enlarged North American marketplace. Location decisions for investing in new plants and offices, or simply maintaining existing ones, depend in part upon a wide range of labour cost factors. Given the increasing

mobility of capital to uproot and relocate, factors such as minimum wages, levels of unionization, unemployment rates, and unobstructive labour laws are likely to become even more critical to a company's investment decisions.

With the implementation of a continental free trade pact, the push to erode labour laws—or at least to stem the tide of further reform—is most likely to come from Canadian corporations. The weaker labour laws in the US will be used as a yardstick to argue for less protection as the existing work rights in Canada, without the protection of tariffs, will render Canadian business less competitive.

According to the Grocery Products Manufacturers of Canada, "some product sectors in Canada are at a disadvantage because the comparative US industries are not as unionized. Therefore, some fundamental realignment of legislated benefits programmes and labour organizations will be required. Likewise, Canadian workers' income expectations will have to be substantially lowered."

The consequence: Bidding wars between American states as to who has the cheapest workforce and the most restrictive labour laws will spread to Canada. Provinces stripping labour laws to attract new business investments will become commonplace, leading to "forced harmonization."

A comparison between labour law standards in Canada and the US reveals some startling disparities in workplace rights. According to Lane Kirkland, president of the AFL-CIO, American labour laws provide workers with so little protection that they have become "a dead letter." Canadian labour laws are the envy of American trade unionists.

Particularly disturbing is the much weaker body of American laws to protect the right of workers to organize and to bargain with employers on a relatively equal footing. American labour law makes organizing in a workplace much more difficult than in Canada. The American stipulation of a mandatory certification vote, together with a lengthy campaign period, has meant that coercive and illegal employer tactics to keep unions out of their workplace have become much more widespread, and much more successful, than in Canada.

According to Paul Weiler, former chairperson of the British Columbia Labour Relations Board and now professor of law at Harvard University, at least one American worker in 20 who exercised his or her right to vote for a union in a representation election was fired for doing so; and this did not take into account unlawfully fired employees who did not pursue the legal remedies available to them. Because of the stronger legal remedies and the "automatic" certification process in Canada, the per capita number of wrongful dismissal complaints

arising from organizing campaigns are much higher compared to the US.

Another difference stems from the widespread existence of so-called "right-to-work" laws in the US. These laws permit workers in a unionized workplace to opt not to belong, or even to pay dues, to the certified union, despite the fact that the union must legally bargain for, and represent, all of the workers of the bargaining unit. The effect has been to undermine the unions' financial strength and organizational stability, and, ultimately, to increase union decertifications. Comparative 'right-to-work" laws currently do not exist in Canadian labour legislation.

Besides labour relations legislation, the "level playing field" that free trade is designed to create will also erode other employment-related laws. Canada's worker compensation, unemployment insurance, pension, and pay equity programmes have been cited by the Canadian business lobby for free trade as unacceptably expensive employment costs. According to Laurent Thibault, president of the Canadian Manufacturers' Association, "as industries are asked to compete toe-to-toe with American ones, Canadians will be forced to create the same conditions in Canada that exist in the US, whether it is the unemployment insurance scheme, workmen's compensation, the cost of government, the level of taxation...."

One employment standards area that will face substantial employer resistance to future reform after free trade is Canadian minimum wage legislation. While minimum wage laws are found in all Canadian jurisdictions, this is not the case in the US, where approximately 20 percent of the states have no such legislation. The higher minimum wage levels in Canada will provide Canadian employers with a compelling argument that the need to maintain a competitive edge requires curtailment of minimum wage improvements until American levels have caught up with us. As the pro-business Canada West Foundation has argued, "...free trade between our two countries will inevitably lead to wages being equalized between Canada and the US. This will occur since a high cost producer will not be able to compete against a lower cost producer if goods are traded freely.''

The passage of the free trade agreement poses a significant challenge to the Canadian industrial relations system: how to reconcile the coming downward pressure upon Canadian labour laws and collective bargaining with the upward expectations of unionized workers for continued legislative reform and bargaining table improvements.

With or without compensating effects arising from the agreement, a particularly tumultuous period in industrial relations is just around the corner.

Source: Michael Lynk, ''The Labour Law Factor,'' *Canadian Labour*, Spring 1988, pp. 18, 19, 20.

Summary of Learning Goals

1. **Explain why labour unions were first organized and what their chief objectives are.**

   Early attempts at employee organization began with the purpose of improving wages and working conditions. The Trade Union Act (1872) legalized unions, and their growth took off. Major disruptions occurred occasionally, such as the 1919 Winnipeg General Strike.

   Craft unions (workers in the same craft) and industrial unions (workers in the same industry) originally had separate associations. In 1956, the Trade and Labour Congress and the Canadian Congress of Labour came together to form the Canadian Labour Congress.

2. **Identify the major federal laws affecting labour unions, and understand the key provisions of laws.**

   Parliament has jurisdiction over labour relations in federally regulated industries, and the provincial legislations oversee all others.

   Every jurisdiction has its own labour relations board that is responsible for enforcement of its law. Management has the responsibility to work with unions and government.

3. **Explain how collective bargaining agreements are established, and what roles are played by arbitrators and mediators.**

   Generally, only a certified union can negotiate with management on wage and working conditions. A collective bargaining agreement, or contract, is the basis of communication. The contract is the result of negotiations between management and labour. Occasionally, if negotiations break down, a third party—a mediator or arbitrator—will join. The mediator offers advice; the arbitrator listens to both sides and then makes a binding decision. The collective bargaining process must be carried out in accordance with government regulations.

4. **Analyze the tools of labour and management and describe how each is used.**

   Although most differences are settled through collective bargaining or formal grievance procedures, both unions and management have other resources open to them. The chief tools of unions are strikes, picketing, and boycotts. The chief tools of management are the lockout, and employer associations for industry-wide bargaining.

5. **Describe who the union members of the 1990s will be.**

   Future union growth will result primarily from public employees, agricultural workers, and white-collar employees. These three relatively unorganized groups represent the greatest source of future union members, because most blue-collar workers are already involved.

Key Terms

labour union

craft union

industrial union

Canadian Labour Congress

closed shop

featherbedding

union shop

Rand formula

collective bargaining

bargaining zone

mediation

arbitration

voluntary arbitration

compulsory arbitration

grievance

strike

picketing

boycott

lockout

injunction

employers' association

Discussion Questions and Exercises

1. Trace the development of labour unions in industrialized society.
2. Briefly outline the history of labour unions and labour legislation in Canada.
3. What is the Canadian Labour Congress?
4. What is the Canadian Labour Code?
5. Describe the collective bargaining process and relate it to the concept of bargaining zones.
6. Distinguish between mediation and arbitration.
7. Outline the steps in the grievance procedures. What role does the shop steward play in a typical grievance?
8. Describe the major tools of union and management. Suggest instances in which each might be used.

9. Discuss the likely changes in union operations and objectives that may result from the entry of the baby-boom generation with the labour force.

10. Secure a collective bargaining agreement from a firm. Then divide the class into management and labour bargaining teams and conduct a simulated bargaining session for the next contract. The instructor will act as moderator and set ground rules for the bargaining.

Case 9-1

The Parrot Factor

After almost twelve years at the helm of the Canadian Union of Postal Workers, Jean-Claude Parrot has lost little of the single-minded intensity that has earned him so much opprobrium from colleagues and contenders alike.

Early in January 1989, his career was very nearly terminated in a representation vote that pitted his 23,000 mail sorters against an equal number of letter carriers, technicians and postal clerks. Parrot won by the slimmest of margins, emerging as the head of a new postal super-union.

His victory could spell trouble for Canada Post's ability to generate its first profit. Other union leaders simply do not believe Parrot has the bargaining skill to cut a deal on behalf of a vastly expanded CUPW, reasoning that his hardline tactics are too inflexible. The net result could be a costly strike and a consequent delay in the company's break-even plans.

Unlike most other union leaders, Parrot tends not to make distinctions about whether grievances are winnable. He forces Canada Post to fight them anyway. Similarly, he has stuck to contract demands until cabinet ministers themselves have shown up to negotiate, or until the government legislated his union back to work and imposed a deal.

Under the Liberals, this tenacity was rewarded by some of the best union contracts in the business. But the Conservatives have so far refused to get directly involved in wage talks, compelling Parrot to deal directly with Canada Post.

This tactic is designed to force Parrot into making the tough tradeoffs generally required of other union leaders. Parrot, much to the disdain of fellow union leaders, often tries to go for it all. A common point of departure between Parrot and other top union leaders is the latter's willingness, at some point, to make an accommodation with the economic establishment. Unlike Parrot, most of them recognize that modern employers are a source of wealth for workers, as well as a source of employee oppression.

"We all have our disputes with employers and sometimes you've got to have a showdown," says Jack Munro, president of the International Woodworkers of America. "But whatever the outcome of negotiations, most sensible people let the world continue. It isn't a constant showdown."

Parrot has only a few months to put together a new union constitution and bargaining strategy that will accommodate letter carrier concerns. Meantime, Canada Post is preparing contract offers that will stress further changes in work rules. Regardless of the probable outcome, Canada Post still likes the idea of having only one large group to deal with. Now, at least, the 46,000-member CUPW will be a single, albeit concentrated, source of militancy.

Source: James Bagnall, "Postal Leader Parrot Lives to Fight Another Day," *The Financial Post*, January 23, 1989, p. 34.

Questions:
1. According to the case, why do other union leaders doubt Parrot's ability to "cut a deal" on behalf of the vastly expanded CUPW? Explain.
2. How does the concept of a bargaining zone as outlined in the chapter explain why Parrot's bargaining strategy is a potential problem for a settlement? Explain.
3. From Canada Post's viewpoint, why is the newly consolidated union preferable to what had existed before?

Case 9-2

Unions—Saying No

In November 1986, about 65,000 strikers returned to work after the adoption of Bill 160 in the Quebec National Assembly. The legislation immediately put an end to a series of 24-hour walkouts initiated by the Confederation of National Trade Unions (CNTU).

Quebec unions vowed to use the courts to challenge the new law which imposes tough penalties for illegal strikes in hospitals and other health centres.

"We have already advised our legal advisers to take the necessary steps to contest the law," said Louis Laberge, president of the Quebec Federation of Labour. "It is really immoral and illegal."

Under Bill 160, individuals participating in these strikes may be fined up to $100 a day (in addition to lost wages) and face a reduction in their seniority. Unions could be fined up to $100,000 a day and their sources of income blocked by the government refusing to collect union dues from employees. The law also provides for the hiring of strikebreakers.

In an address to students at John Abbott College in St. Anne de Bellevue, Monique Simard, vice-president of the CNTU, described the new legislation as "the most regressive anti-worker, anti-labour law in the last 25 years in Canada."

Quebec unions weren't the only ones outraged by the law.

"It's unduly draconian," said John Fryer, president of the National Union of Provincial Government Employees—which has members in eight provinces. "It's certainly the most heavy-handed legislation we've ever seen. If the Quebec government succeeds, their other more timid colleagues will try the same thing; the political waters will have to be tested."

Source: "We Will Challenge New Anti-Strike Law in Court," *Montreal Gazette*, November 13, 1986, pp. A1, A2.

Questions:
1. Why were union leaders across Canada so vehemently against Bill 160? Explain.
2. Given the lack of a right to strike, what are the possible recourses available for settling union-management disputes? Explain.

Part Four

Marketing Management

Chapter 10

Marketing: Providing for Consumer Needs

In our business, we are forever trying to see what lies around the corner. We study the ever-changing consumer and try to identify new trends in tastes, needs, environment, and living habits. We study changes in the market place and try to assess their likely impact on our brands. We study our competition. Competitive brands are continually offering new benefits and new ideas to the consumer, and we must stay ahead of this.
—*Edward G. Harness, Chairman of the Board, Procter & Gamble Company*

Learning Goals

1. To discuss how marketing's role in the exchange process creates utility
2. To explain the marketing concept
3. To identify the functions of marketing
4. To identify the four strategies that make up the marketing mix
5. To show how a marketing strategy is developed
6. To explain the concept of a market
7. To discuss why the study of consumer behaviour is important to marketing
8. To explain the concept of market segmentation

Profile

Michael Bregman—*The Mmmuffin Man Finding New Market Opportunities*

Through the window of a Toronto shop called the Coffee Tree, a woman was gesturing to Michael Bregman, the 34-year-old creator and chairman of mmmuffins Inc., enticing him inside to sample her brew. Bregman went in and was instantly impressed. Unlike other stores that sell coffee by the cup or the pound, the Coffee Tree was roasting its beans right on the premises.

As Bregman well knew, today's consumers are willing to pay extra for freshness: baking goods in full view of customers had been a crucial ingredient in the success of his own chains, mmmarvellous mmmuffins and Michel's Baguette French Bakery Cafe. Bregman acted fast. Within weeks, he had entered into a partnership with the woman in the window, Denise Shearer, and her three partners. Now there are four Coffee Tree stores in Toronto, one in London, Ontario, and more to come in other parts of the country. Adding these to his two other chains, Bregman will have a total of 120 outlets in his rapidly growing food empire.

Building and buying food companies wasn't always what Bregman envisioned for himself, despite growing up around the business. Both his father and grandfather had been involved. But following in his father's footsteps did not initially appeal to Bregman: "My attitude was that the bakery business was a declining one," he says. As a Harvard MBA student he pictured a career in management consulting or perhaps investment banking.

During the 1970s, Bregman worked as an assistant to Dave Nichol, then president of Loblaw Companies Ltd. One of his assignments was in Loblaw's bakery departments. Witnessing the customer response to such new items as over-sized muffins, Bregman sensed an opportunity. "The consumer had never stopped demanding high-quality baked goods, but the industry had forgotten how to provide them," he says. "That meant there was a big niche that hadn't been exploited."

With the help of his wife, Barbara, who tested recipes, loans of around $425,000, and some good advice from his father, Bregman opened his first mmmarvellous mmmuffins store in Toronto's Eaton Centre in 1979. Business was slow during the first few weeks but within six months he had achieved twice his projected weekly sales for the first year.

Bregman quickly launched a second concept, the Michel's Baguette chain, which specialized in French bread and croissants. By the end of 1988 mmmuffins Inc. boasted a total of 115 stores. Of these Bregman owns 10; the rest are franchises. Sales were approximately $40 million.

Bregman intends to be a major player in the Canadian food industry. Undoubtedly, there will be more developments like the Coffee Tree. And he sometimes thinks about overseas expansion. A clear focus on understanding the customer and his or her needs plus having an obsessive commitment to execute in the best way possible are some of the main reasons for the success of mmmuffins.

Source: Daniel Stoffman, "Michael Bregman, Meet the mmmuffin man now hungering for a jumbo bite of a big-time US food empire," *Canadian Business*, August 1988, p. 53.

A thorough approach to marketing has shown Canadelle Ltd. of Montreal that it can profitably commit $8.2 million on a new bra merchandising system under its WonderBra brand label. In fact, the company predicts that the system will revolutionize how women shop for brassieres.[1] The new system is the product of extensive company marketing research, and embraces changes that include staff, product packages, display stands, store sales education, promotion, and advertising.

Central to the changes is a unique style-selection system based on colour coding. Under the system, WonderBra brings all its bra styles together on one free-standing display and groups all its secondary brands under its WonderBra brand.

Two years of consumer research led to the development of the boutique display system. It revealed that more than 70 percent of women found bra shopping a frustrating experience, and 90 percent indicated that because fit varies among styles and brands, they would prefer to have similar fitting styles of the same brand merchandised together. Further, the research showed that most women already know to which bra-support category they belong, and that 85 percent would most likely try various styles if organized by degree of support.

Based on this and other research, a new package was developed made of semi-rigid clear plastic with colour-coded inserts identifying each support level. A new modular chrome fixture was designed that holds 240 packages. Further research showed that there was high consumer acceptance of the fixture.

The system was test-marketed in Winnipeg. Results showed the new system's ease of selection was preferred by 87 percent of customers, and sales increased significantly.

Increased market acceptance and sales were *not* the result of new products or product changes. They were brought about by applying a sophisticated marketing approach to the problem of serving consumer needs and thereby generating business.

What Is Marketing?

Marketing
The process of planning and executing the conception, pricing, promotion, and distribution of ideas, goods, and services to create exchange.

Marketing is the link between the organization and the consumer. All organizations—profit-oriented or nonprofit—must serve consumer needs if they are to succeed. Perhaps one retailer expressed it best when he told his store managers: "Either you or your replacement will greet the customer within the first 60 seconds." But marketing is also used to advocate ideas or viewpoints, such as the United Way or a political campaign. Therefore, marketing has a broad scope. **Marketing** is the process of planning and executing the conception, pricing, promotion, and distribution of ideas, goods, and services to create exchanges that satisfy individual and organizational objectives.[2]

Marketing Creates Utility

utility
The want-satisfying power of a product or service.

form utility
Utility created when a firm converts raw materials into finished products.

time utility
Utility created by having the product available when the consumer wants to buy it.

place utility
Utility created by having the product available at a convenient location when the consumer wants to buy it.

ownership utility
Utility created by arranging for the transfer of title from seller to buyer.

An organization must create **utility**—the want-satisfying power of a product or service or idea—for its consumers. There are four kinds of utility—form, time, place, and ownership (see Figure 10-1).

Form utility is created when the business firm converts raw materials into finished products. This operation is part of the firm's production function (see Chapter 16). The other three kinds of utility are created by marketing.

Time utility—having the product available when the consumer wants to buy it—requires effective marketing research to determine what items the consumer will desire at some future date. **Place utility** is created by having the product available at a convenient location when the consumer wants to buy it. **Ownership utility** is created by arranging for the transfer of title from seller to buyer.

Marketing is a value-creating function in any organization. Saturday morning classes at a community college, a symphony performance in the park, and a toll-free telephone order system are all marketing activities that provide utility to the consumers involved. (See Focus 10-1 for other examples of utility created by marketing.)

Figure 10-1
The Four Types of Utility

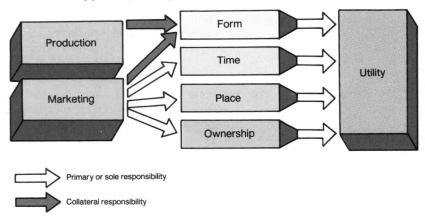

The Marketing Concept

marketing concept
An organization-wide consumer orientation with the objective of achieving long-run success.

The **marketing concept** is a managerial philosophy. It can be defined as an organization-wide consumer orientation with the objective of achieving long-run success. Both profit-oriented and nonprofit organizations have adopted the marketing concept as a guide to operating their enterprises. The basic goal is to target all of the organization's efforts at satisfying consumer needs.

How did the marketing concept evolve? There is a tendency for organizations to be production-oriented: their primary concern is

seller's market
A market situation characterized by shortages.

buyer's market
A market situation characterized by adequate or even excess supplies.

with the production and supply of their product or service. A firm with such an orientation may achieve limited success, especially in a **seller's market**—one characterized by shortages. In a **buyer's market**—one characterized by adequate or even excess supplies—the focus must be on serving customer needs. This focus results in more effective marketing. This is true in all conditions.

The shift from a seller's market to a buyer's market is illustrated by the immediate post-World War II era. Industry shifted from wartime production to consumer goods. The vast increase in products available allowed consumers a great range from which to choose. It resulted in a change in the way many firms conducted their business. Their emphasis on the marketing concept increased significantly during this period.

General Electric's annual report for 1952 gave a landmark description of the marketing concept:

> [The concept] introduces the marketing person at the beginning rather than at the end of the production cycle and integrates marketing into each phase of the business. Thus marketing, through its studies and research, will establish for the engineer, the design and manufacturing man, what the customer wants in a given product, what price he is willing to pay, and where and when it will be wanted. Marketing will have authority in product planning, production scheduling, and inventory control, as well as sales, distribution, and servicing of the product.[3]

Through the years, organizations which have adopted the marketing concept have found greater success in developing marketing programmes. Therefore, the discussion of marketing that follows focuses on consumers and how their needs can be satisfied. The starting point is to look at the exact functions performed by marketers.

Focus 10-1

The Quest for a Better Mousetrap

Well over 100 years ago, philosopher Ralph Waldo Emerson said: "If a man can write a better book, preach a better sermon, or make a better mousetrap than his neighbour, though he builds his house in the woods the world will make a beaten path to his door."

Inventors of all kinds have taken Emerson's words to heart as they have tried by the millions to satisfy consumer wants and needs. The following examples show that none has tried harder than mousetrap builders themselves.

- Australian inventor Brian Gardner designed a one-piece trap made of cardboard that is powered by the simple but dependable rubber band. Billed as "the most humane, hygienic mousetrap ever invented," the jaw of Gardner's device snaps down to kill unsuspecting rodents. This disposable trap is marketed under the name "Killer Katz."

- Aware of the squeamishness of consumers, inventors of the Blackhole devised a mousetrap that doubles as a coffin. After the mouse is lured to its death by a peanut-oil bait, a door closes, allowing consumers to dispose of the mouse without ever handling it. The company assures that the rodent "dies in its sleep, without pain or suffering."
- Environmentally Safe Products, a small California pest control products company focuses on parents' concern about keeping children and pets away from mousetrap pesticide. The company claims that its product, COUNT-DOWN, attracts mice, but is child- and pet-resistant.

As long as there are mice, the quest for a better mousetrap will continue, as will the effort to market these contraptions to anticipating and hopeful consumers.

The Functions of Marketing

Marketing is more than just selling or advertising! It is a very complex activity that reaches into many aspects of the organization and its dealing with its consumers. There are eight traditional functions of marketing: marketing information, risk taking, buying, financing, grading, storing, transporting, and selling (see Figure 10-2). Some are performed by manufacturers, some by wholesalers, still others by retailers. Let's look at how marketing is involved in each of these activities.

Marketing Information. Marketing research is a primary marketing activity. Marketers are constantly seeking out information on what will sell and who will buy it. Marketers are also concerned with the behaviour of buyers, or how they buy.

**Figure 10-2
The Eight Basic Functions of Marketing**

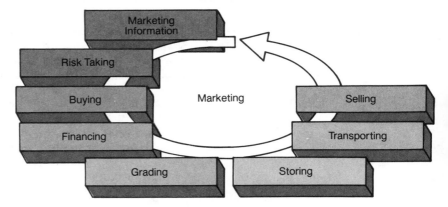

Risk Taking. Risk taking is part of the marketing process. Wholesalers and retailers acquire inventory for resale on the basis of their predictions of what consumers will buy. This action rewards the manufacturer's risk and gives it to middlemen. Manufacturers also accept risk when they schedule speculative production of a product before customers have entered orders.

Buying. Buying is important to marketing on several levels. Marketers must study how and why consumers buy certain products and services. The study of consumer or buying behaviour is crucial to the overall success of the firm. Industrial marketers have to purchase component parts and raw materials to complete their products. And retail buyers have to choose the styles and designs that will sell the next season. They have to be knowledgeable of what consumers are buying in order to make their own purchase decisions.

Financing. Marketers are also involved in financing. A merchant wholesaler buys products from a producer, thus providing the money the manufacturer needs to produce additional output. Retailers increase total sales by financing the purchases of consumers through credit arrangements.

Grading. Grading is a traditional marketing function. It deals with standardizing the description of products. Many industries, like the tire industry, have set up grading standards for their products. The government also requires some grading, as in the marketing of agricultural products.

Storing. Warehousing is another function of physical distribution. Some warehouses are set up to hold products for a lengthy period of time, such as cold storage warehouses for apples. Other warehouses receive shipments from manufacturers and then quickly redistribute the items to retailers.

Transporting. Transporting is part of the overall physical distribution function. It involves the physical movement of the product from the seller to the buyer. Transportation is expensive, so it is of prime importance to modern marketers. Manufacturers, wholesalers, and retailers can all be involved in transporting products.

Selling. All organizations must "sell" their goods or services to someone if they are to succeed. Selling is usually done through the organization's promotional strategy. Advertising, personal selling, and sales promotion are the standard sales tools.

The marketing functions identified above are as important to nonprofit organizations as they are to profit-seeking business firms. Nonprofit organizations can be classified as either public or private.

Humber College in Toronto, Ontario, is a public, nonprofit organization, Trinity Western University in Langley, British Columbia is a private, nonprofit organization open to the public.

Nonprofit Organizations and the Broadening Concept

broadening concept
The extension of marketing to nontraditional areas such as nonprofit organizations.

The term **broadening concept** refers to the extension of the marketing concept to nontraditional areas such as nonprofit organizations. It was originally described by marketing educators Philip Kotler and Sidney Levy. This extension has been obvious since the seventies, and gradually nonprofit organizations are beginning to utilize marketing in their management and operations.

Public transit systems research the market for their services. Hospitals have revamped some of their services in line with changing consumer needs. The pricing of on-street parking is a marketing issue faced by many municipalities. Colleges and universities have altered their distribution methods by offering in-plant classes, educational television, even courses inside prison walls. And promotional strategy plays a major role in recruiting efforts for the Armed Forces.

Developing a Marketing Strategy

All organizations need to develop a marketing strategy to effectively reach consumers. This is a two-step process:

1. Select the organization's market target.
2. Develop a marketing mix designed to satisfy the organization's market target.

Selecting Market Targets

The key to effective marketing lies in locating unsatisfied customers or potential customers which you can serve better. Such customers may not be purchasing goods because the goods are not currently available, or they may be buying products that give them only limited satisfaction. In the latter case they are likely to switch quickly to new products that offer greater satisfaction. These consumers should be the targets of consumer-oriented companies. Honda expected and found a ready market for its 4-wheel all-terrain vehicle in certain industrial and sports applications.

Selecting a target is the first step in developing a marketing strategy. The regional foods that sell well in this supermarket in the Northwest Terriories might not sell well in southern Ontario.

market target
A group of consumers toward which a firm decides to direct its marketing effort.

A **market target** is a group of consumers toward which a firm decides to direct its marketing effort. Sometimes the firm has several market targets for a given product. For example, WonderBra understands that there are several distinct groups with particular needs which can be served by their product. The selection of such targets requires considerable research and analysis. These activities will be discussed later in the chapter.

Focus 10-2

Airlines Battle for the Business Dollar

Competition is stiff among airlines to woo business-class clients. At 35,000 feet it is easy to be a hero these days. Simply book business class on almost any airline and you will be accorded the adulation once reserved for the victors of great battles. When it comes to catering to the commercial traveller, there is almost no limit to giveaways and special services.

In a very real sense, the business traveller is regarded by airlines as their potential saviour in the great battle to fill seats and remain profitable.

Business-class advance-seat selection and priority check-in are routine. Even the baggage of the business traveller is accorded special treatment by most carriers, with special tags ensuring that his or her luggage gets put on the conveyor belt before that of the folks in the cheap seats. Meals, too, are invariably a great improvement over the usually pallid provender dealt out in economy. And while awaiting departure, the business traveller is offered the shelter of special airport lounges.

The biggest trend seems to be the creation of what amounts to flying offices; on some planes, executives of extraordinary diligence can make phone calls, send and receive documents, and even give slide presentations to a captive group of colleagues or clients high above the clouds.

This focus on customer needs shows that airlines understand the cardinal marketing principle, that more business is generated from being customer-oriented. Those airlines that do the best job of understanding and serving customer needs will be the most successful with this market segment.

Source: "The Battle for the Business Dollar," *Financial Times of Canada*, October 13, 1985, p. A4.

The Marketing Mix

marketing mix
The blending of a firm's product, pricing, distribution, and promotion strategies focused on satisfying chosen consumer segments.

The second step in the development of a marketing strategy is the formation of a marketing mix to reach the firm's market targets. Decisions must be made concerning products, pricing, distribution and promotion. The combined decisions about these four elements form the **marketing mix**—the blending of product, price, distribution and promotion strategies focused on satisfying chosen consumer segments. It is the total combination (or mix) and its congruence with the market target that determines the degree of marketing success (see Figure 10-3).

Figure 10-3
A Marketing Strategy Involves Selecting a Market Target and Developing a Marketing Mix to Satisfy That Market Target

product strategy
Deals with package design, brand, trademarks, warranties, guarantees, product cycles, and new product development.

pricing strategy
Deals with the methods of setting profitable and justifiable prices. Consideration is given to government regulations and public opinion.

distribution strategy
Involves the physical distribution of goods and the selection of marketing channels, and the organization of wholesalers and retailers who handle distribution.

promotion strategy
Involves blending personal selling, advertising, and sales promotion tools to produce effective communication between the firm and the marketplace.

Product strategy includes decisions about product development, package design, brand name, trademarks, warranties, guarantees, and product life cycles. **Pricing strategy**, one of the most difficult parts of marketing decision making, deals with the methods of setting profitable and justifiable prices. Market response, government regulations and public opinion must be considered in pricing decisions. **Distribution strategy** involves the physical distribution of goods and the selection of marketing channels—the organization of wholesalers and retailers who handle the product's distribution. **Promotion strategy** involves personal selling, advertising and sales promotion tools. These elements must be skilfully blended to produce effective communication between the firm and the marketplace.

The marketing strategist is actually a "mixer" of these four basic elements. Just as a chef works with various basic ingredients to create many different outputs, the marketer skilfully blends the ingredients of the marketing mix to develop a marketing programme that is unique. Thus, the marketing mixes for two similar products such as automobiles at first may seem to be similar; examined more closely, they are found to be quite different. Hyundai entered the Canadian market using a low price as the main sales-generating element in its mix. Chrysler came back from the verge of elimination on the basis of finely crafted cars. Long-term warranties were given to prove their claims.

Each marketing mix is developed to be the best fit for the needs of the target market which the company seeks to serve. The process of developing a marketing mix that will serve the needs of the market better than competitors is a highly creative process. This is one of the aspects which make marketing so interesting.

The marketing mix is a mechanism that allows business to match consumer needs with product offerings. This chapter will discuss how marketers go about assessing consumer needs and classifying the various segments of consumers.

What Is a Market?

market
People with the necessary authority, financial ability, and willingness to purchase goods and services.

A **market** consists of people, whether they are consumers, company purchasing agents, or purchasing specialists for a government (local, provincial, or federal).

But people alone do not make a market. Many students may desire a new Porsche 928 but don't have the $60,000 needed to complete the transaction. A market requires not only people but also purchasing power and the authority to buy. One of the first rules the successful salesperson learns is to determine which person in a firm has the authority to make purchase decisions. Too many hours have been wasted convincing the director of purchasing about the merits of a particular product or group of products when the ultimate buying decision actually rests with the design engineer.

Industrial goods such as these huge pipes for an oil pipeline are products purchased for use in the production of other items.

Consumer and Industrial Markets

Markets can be classified by the type of products they handle. The two major categories of products are consumer and industrial goods. **Consumer goods** are those products and services purchased by the ultimate consumer for his or her own use. **Industrial goods** are products purchased to be used, either directly or indirectly, in the production of other goods for resale. Most of the products you buy—such as pizza, toothpaste, and cassette tapes—are consumer goods. Steel is an industrial product. Services can also be classified as consumer or industrial services.

Sometimes the same product has different uses, creating a classification dilemma. The bottle of ketchup purchased by a supermarket shopper clearly is classified as a consumer good; yet ketchup bought by McDonald's is considered an industrial good. Proper classification of products should be based on the purchaser and the reasons for buying the item. A calculator purchased as a back-to-school gift is a consumer good, but a calculator used by the manager of a nearby Burger King is an industrial good.

consumer goods
Products and services purchased by the ultimate consumer for his or her own use.

industrial goods
Products purchased to be used either directly or indirectly in the production of other goods for resale.

Consumer Behaviour

Pizza Hut knew it had a problem. Its lunchtime business constituted only 15 to 18 percent of total sales, compared to 35 percent for other restaurants. Pizza Hut's study of its customers also indicated that its lunchtime and evening customers were different. Lunchtime business was more likely to be singles or pairs, while families and other larger groups came to Pizza Hut in the evening.

Pizza Hut invested a great deal of time, effort and resources in introducing its personal pan pizza. The 6-inch pizza was a single-serving entree that came with a guaranteed 5-minute serving time for hurried lunchtime eaters. Each Pizza Hut offered a choice of a single-topping pizza or a supreme pizza with five toppings. Consumer behaviour research on regional tastes determined the topping selected for each city. For example, one city could get a sausage topping, but another might get anchovies.[4] The study of consumer behaviour played a major role in Pizza Hut's decision to launch its new product.

Figure 10-4
Steps in the Consumer Decision-Making Process

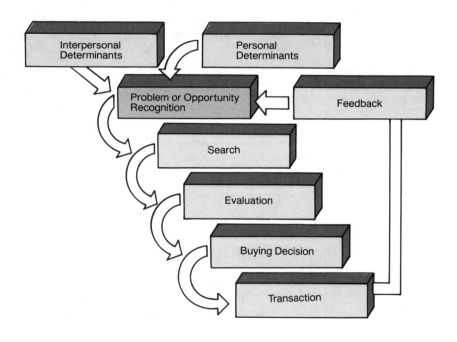

What Is Consumer Behaviour?

consumer behaviour
The acts of individuals in obtaining and using economic goods and services, including the decision processes that precede and determine these acts.

Consumer behaviour can be defined as "the acts of individuals in obtaining and using economic goods and services, including the decision processes that precede and determine these acts."[5] Both consumers and industrial purchasers are included under this definition. However, the industrial purchaser is subject to additional organizational influences that do not impact ultimate consumers.

Influences on Consumer Buying Behaviour

There are both interpersonal and personal influences on consumer behaviour. The Hudson's Bay Company recognizes this, and uses research data to profile market units. It not only looks at demographic data such as income and age, but also takes into consideration the activities, interests, and opinions of potential customers. Each store is profiled on what to carry, and also on where to place the emphasis in certain areas of the store. Buyers and sellers select each item of merchandise by comparing customer criteria with the merchandising goals of the company. Barry Agnew, marketing manager of The Bay, says, "Find your desired consumer and then effectively market to her."[6]

The personal influences on consumer behaviour are needs and motives, perceptions, attitudes, learned experiences, and the consumer's own self-concept. Interpersonal determinants include cultural influences, social influences, and family influences.

Industrial purchasers also face a variety of organizational influences. Many people play a role in an industrial purchase. A design engineer may be instrumental in setting the specifications which potential vendors must satisfy. A purchasing manager invites selected companies to bid on the purchase. A production supervisor is responsible for evaluating the operational aspects of the proposals that are received. And the vice-president of manufacturing might make the final purchase.

Consumer Decision Making

Consumer decision making follows a sequential process that is shown in Figure 10-4. The sequence begins with the recognition that a consumer behaviour problem or opportunity exists. Examples would include a consumer who is out of milk, or a student who just received a gift of money to buy a personal computer.

The second step is search, during which the consumer seeks out information about the contemplated purchase. The alternatives—such as different brands—are delineated and evaluated. The consumer attempts to get the best response to his or her perceived problem or opportunity.

Finally, a decision is reached, and the transaction completed. Later, consumers evaluate their experience with the purchase. This postmortem then becomes the feedback that is considered in repeat purchase decisions. Both interpersonal and personal determinants of consumer behaviour impact the various steps in the sequence.

Marketing Research

marketing research
The systematic gathering, recording, and analyzing of data about problems relating to the marketing of goods and services.

Marketing research refers to the study of marketing problems and opportunities. It is defined as "the systematic gathering, recording and analyzing of data about problems relating to the marketing of goods and services."[7] It is what allows marketers to select market targets and assess consumer behaviour. Market researchers use a variety of approaches in their work. These include surveys, consumer panels, direct observation of buying behaviour, personal interviews and analysis of published data.

Some market research is very sophisticated, using complex data collection procedures and computer-based analysis. Other market research is fairly simple. One retail chain asks its customers their postal codes. When they make a purchase, this simple piece of information gives the firm an idea of the area being served by each store and helps make its direct mail advertising more effective.

Market Segmentation

No marketer can devise a plan to satisfy all consumers. Henry Ford lost his number one position in the automobile industry because he failed to provide the options and colours offered by competitors. Now cars are targeted to a variety of consumers—those seeking fuel efficiency, those with families, the affluent, second-car buyers, and the like.

The construction company that decides to build and market only one style of house to satisfy all home buyers quickly encounters problems concerning floor plans, exteriors, flooring, and so on. In attempting to satisfy the "average" consumer, the builder ends up satisfying no one. Competitors with floor plans appealing to larger families will capture those customers. Other builders may adopt specialized strategies to capture submarkets that have significant similarities among members. This process of taking the total market and dividing it into groups with similar characteristics is called **market segmentation**. (See Focus 10-2.)

market segmentation
The process of dividing the total market into groups with similar characteristics.

Factors like age, income, place of residence and relative product use have all been used to segment consumer markets. Marketers continue to develop new and sophisticated ways of segmenting markets. The more precisely this can be done, the more accurately a marketing mix can be developed to service these market segments.

It is also possible to use market segmentation in industrializing markets. The procedure is similar to what is employed in consumer markets, where the bulk of the research has been done.

Focus 10-3

Marketing Lures Millions to the Slopes

"Gone are the days of bearded employees in overalls who aren't there to work but are out for what, in reality, is a paid vacation," says John Gow, president, Silver Star Mountain Resorts Ltd. in Vernon, BC. "The expectations for service are higher today in the marketplace and I think the industry is meeting them. You have to know your market in order to survive."

Advertising campaigns are important, but there is much more to marketing a ski area than that. Furthermore, ski areas have discovered it is no longer enough to have hills with snow. They are in the resort and entertainment business too. They must know and serve the market.

Today's skiers want well-groomed slopes with lots of snow, and faster chairlifts so they don't have to waste any precious time waiting in line. They demand better food and special lessons for the kids, all served up more efficiently and with lots of smiles. And, if they don't get it in one place, they can always go next door, or hop on a plane across the country or venture south of the border.

Careful attention to proper marketing is worth while. Skiing is a $5-billion-a-year business in Canada. This includes $500 million-plus spent on equipment and clothing and $900 million on lift tickets.

About 4.3 million Canadians have tried alpine skiing at least once, and 2.1 million of them have become sufficiently converted to ski at least six times a year. Similarly, 5.8 million have cross-country skied once, while 2.8 million have become enthusiasts. Because many people do both, the tally of regular skiers in Canada is put at about three million.

Source: Jamie Wayne, "Investment Paying Off for Ski Resorts," *The Financial Post*, January 23, 1989, p. 11.

Controversial Issue

The Practice of Social Responsibility

In late 1970, General Foods commenced an annual seminar on nutrition. Furthermore, it sponsored several awards to journalists and writers of outstanding articles on nutrition, and ran regional symposia on nutrition.

Bombardier has an active social involvement programme through the J. Armand Bombardier Foundation. This nonprofit institution was founded in 1965. It is located in Valcourt, Quebec, where many projects have been carried out with the assistance of the foundation: installation of a park, construction of a cultural centre, and founding of a ski-mobile museum which attracts 12,000 visitors each year. The foundation also provides financial assistance to a number of missions around the world, Canadian universities, and many charities in Quebec, Canada, and worldwide.

It has been suggested that all firms should regularly publish a balance sheet of their social behaviour as the foregoing have done. There are several reasons why some are reluctant to do so voluntarily. First, the absence of universally accepted scales and standards of evaluation dissuades many from making the results of their actions public. Second, since there has been no major study of the impact of disclosing social responsibility, some companies are hesitant to assume this additional risk. They don't know what the reactions of their shareholders will be, and fear that pressure groups, unions, the media, and others might use these data to tarnish the company image or

harm its interests in some way. Moreover, some companies are well aware of how unattractive their social performance is, and realize that disclosing it may lose them more points than they would gain.

Firms are linked to the environment largely through their marketing programmes. Some, like General Foods, have related valuable social contributions to the marketing of their products. Others have not done so. Their attitude seems to be, "Our job is to produce the best goods and services we can. It is not necessary to develop social programmes in relation to our marketing programme."

Source: Louis Demers and Donald Wayland, "Corporate Social Responsibility: Is No News Good News?—Part 2," *CA Magazine*, Feb. 1982, pp. 59-60. Reprinted by permission.

Summary of Learning Goals

1. **Discuss how marketing's role in the exchange process creates utility.**

   Exchange is the process by which two or more parties give something of value to one another to satisfy felt needs. Marketing is closely linked with the exchange process. It creates utility—the want-satisfying power of a good or service—by having the product available when and where the consumer wants to buy and by arranging for an orderly transfer of ownership. While production creates form utility, marketing creates time, place, and ownership utility.

2. **Explain the marketing concept.**

   The marketing concept is a managerial philosophy that requires an organization-wide consumer orientation with the objective of achieving long-run success. The marketing concept is used by both profit-oriented and nonprofit organizations.

3. **Identify the functions of marketing.**

   Marketing is more than just selling. In fact, there are eight basic functions of marketing: marketing information, risk taking, buying, financing, grading, storing, transporting, and selling.

4. **Identify the four strategies that make up the marketing mix.**

   The marketing mix is a unique combination of product strategy, price strategy, distribution strategy, and promotion strategy.

5. **Show how a market strategy is developed.**

   The development of a marketing strategy is a two-step process:

1. Select the organization's market target—the group of consumers toward which a firm decides to direct its marketing efforts.
2. Develop a marketing mix that will reach the organization's market target. A marketing mix is the combination of the firm's product, pricing, distribution, and promotional strategies.

6. **Explain the concept of a market.**

A market consists of people with purchasing power and the authority to buy. Markets can be classified on the basis of the types of products they handle. Consumer goods are those products and services purchased by the ultimate consumer for his or her own use. Industrial goods are products purchased to be used, either directly or indirectly, in the production of other goods for resale.

7. **Discuss why the study of consumer behaviour is important to marketing.**

Consumer behaviour deals with the reasons people buy things and the way they do so. This information is crucial to marketers if they are to successfully market a product or service. Marketers must understand the personal and interpersonal influences on consumer behaviour, as well as the organizational influences that impact industrial purchasers. It is also important that marketers understand the steps involved in consumer decision making: problem or opportunity recognition, search, evaluation, buying decision, transaction, and feedback.

8. **Explain the concept of market segmentation.**

Since few organizations can adequately serve all potential customers well with a single marketing mix, marketers segment the market into relatively homogeneous groups called "market segments." Consumer markets can be segmented on demographic, geographic, psychographic, or benefit factors. Bases for dividing industrial markets include geographic segmentation, product segmentation, and segmentation by end-use application.

Key Terms

utility	product strategy
form utility	pricing strategy
time utility	distribution strategy
place utility	promotion strategy
ownership utility	market
marketing concept	consumer goods
seller's market	industrial goods
buyer's market	consumer behaviour
broadening concept	marketing research
market target	market segmentation
marketing mix	

Discussion Questions and Exercises

1. Evaluate the pros and cons of the controversial issue that appears in this chapter.
2. How successfully do you think the following organizations have adopted the marketing concept:
   a) McCain's Foods?
   b) The college or university you are now attending?
   c) Petro-Canada?
   d) The telephone system serving your community?
3. List various examples of marketers who are performing each of the eight basic functions of marketing. What, if anything, does this list suggest?
4. Identify the likely market targets of each of the following:
   a) The Toronto Blue Jays.
   b) Professional wrestling in a local arena.
   c) A Mercedes-Benz 380 SL.
   d) Supercuts hair salons.
5. Develop a hypothetical marketing mix for each of the foregoing listed in the previous question.
6. How might the movement of the population from east to west affect the purchasing behaviour of those who moved?
7. Outline how the concept of market segmentation might be used in the marketing of:
   a) stereo component systems.
   b) a headache remedy.
   c) pocket calculators.
8. Prepare a case history of a firm that has successfully matched consumer needs with a new product offering. Also prepare a case history of a firm that has failed in this objective.

Case 10-1

Atlantique Electronics

Hard-nosed competition in electronics retailing will get even tougher, judging from the ambitious expansion plans of Atlantique Video & Sound Inc.

"Our objective is to double our [sales] volume in the next three to four years," says Michael Haberman, president and chief executive of Canada's largest specialty retailer in consumer electronics.

Haberman, 42, a former president of Consumers Distributing Co. Ltd., joined Atlantique just over a year ago, replacing the company's founder as president. Since then, he has shown a determination to move in new directions.

In December, Atlantique acquired an archrival in the tough Montreal market, the ten-store J.M. Saucier Ltd. chain.

It is also implementing a fresh marketing strategy whereby Atlantique stores will cover the full spectrum of tastes—from the mass market to the "Cadillac set"—and of store sizes, from 200 to 30,000 square feet.

With 189 stores under five names, Atlantique is a major player in the $4-billion consumer electronic industry. The company has been expanding furiously, doubling the number of locations every two years, Haberman says.

From its roots as a small shopping centre store, Atlantique is now in most major malls in Ontario and Quebec; in fact, about 30 malls have two outlets. Outside central Canada, it has four stores in Manitoba and one in New Brunswick.

But fast expansion and stiff competition have been costly. The company lost $1.6 million for the first half of fiscal 1989 (ended August 31, 1988) compared with net income of $177,000 a year earlier.

Still, Haberman maintains Atlantique is in good shape and will end the fiscal year profitably.

"We had a loss because we competed aggressively and intentionally with J.M. Saucier [before the takeover] and also opened 27 stores in low-volume months," says Haberman.

The loss is "irrelevant," agrees Jean-Pierre De Montigny, vice-president of corporate finance at Merrill Lynch Canada Inc. "They [the industry] always lose money in the first six months. The faster you grow, the more money you lose. But you make more once the right season comes around."

Revenues for the most recent fiscal year, ending February 27, 1988, reached $166.3 million, up from $146.6 million in 1987. Profits rose to $2.67 million (34 cents a share) from $2.26 million (32 cents).

Besides the financial costs, Haberman says one of the serious consequences of Atlantique's rapid growth was that "the company lost a little bit of focus."

So, the chain has embarked on a sophisticated marketing programme to capture all segments of this lucrative market. "We want to cover the spectrum from low ticket to high ticket, from brand A to brand Z," Haberman explains.

To do this, they have developed new kinds of stores to complement the traditional Atlantique outlets, which are 1,200-square-foot (111.4 m^2) outlets catering mainly to women aged 25 to 49. The approach in the old stores, Haberman says, is middle of the road and mass-marketing oriented.

One of the new wrinkles is Fuzzle, a chain of kiosks in malls, selling gift and impulse items such as Walkmans, calculators and electronic games. So far, there are five units in Quebec and one in Ontario.

Also new are the five Circuit stores in Quebec, designed to appeal to older, more affluent consumers. These stores carry the "Cadillacs and Rolls-Royces" of the industry, like televisions ranging up to $5,000 and expensive stereos.

Last August, Atlantique opened its first HQE (High Quality Electronics) store in Mississauga, Ontario. The gigantic outlet, the first of 20 HQEs planned in a 50 percent joint venture with Computer Innovations Distributions Inc., offers more than 3,500 items from audio and video equipment to home security systems.

In Quebec, the December acquisition of the troubled J.M. Saucier chain (in a share exchange valuing Saucier at about $1.6 million) gives Atlantique a foothold in areas like Granby and Drummondville where it had a poor presence.

Haberman says the combined sales of Atlantique and Saucier will generate fiscal 1990 revenues of around $225 million.

Saucier competed with Atlantique's Le Marché de L'Electronique stores, free-standing 6,000-square-foot units targeting 18- to 34-year-old-men, with double the assortment of the shopping centre stores. (Even the Le Marché stores are only one-fifth the size of the HQE outlets, which Atlantique calls "superstores.")

"The Saucier acquisition should help consolidate Le Marché's market," De Montigny says.

Le Marché de L'Electronique was started by Robert Fragman, Atlantique's founder and former chairman, after he left the company in 1984. Several years later, Atlantique, which already owned 50 percent of Le Marché's shares, bought the other half and Fragman returned to the helm of Atlantique shortly before the company went public in 1986.

"Fragman was good at spotting trends," says De Montigny. "He developed the shopping centre stores and made inroads in the superstore market."

In November, Fragman again resigned from Atlantique, although he remains a director and consultant.

"The company was very entrepreneurial-driven under Robert [Fragman]," says Haberman. "As a company goes through explosive growth, its needs change and the style of management must change too."

Source: Ellen Kom, "Growing Atlantique Electronics Chain Redefining Market Focus," *The Financial Post*, January 2, 1989, p. 6.

Question:
Evaluate the marketing strategy of Atlantique. In particular, consider the multiple target approach.

Case 10-2

The Challenge of the Youth Market

The quest for self-gratification and pleasure by young Canadians makes them compulsive buyers—and they'll spend even more in the next decade, a new study indicates.

These young people, aged 15 to 24, are already enthusiastic

consumers who like to live life to its fullest and are used to buying on credit, according to the study, conducted under a research program—3SC Monitor—that measures social change in Canada and abroad.

Young people, struggling to find an identity, want to make a personal statement with the objects they buy, the study said. "They wear products as 'badges' of the social identity they wish to project to their peers," said an analysis of the study, released yesterday.

The analysis was presented by Environics Research Group Ltd. of Toronto and the Centre de Recherches en Opinion Publique Inc. of Montreal, which have joined forces to launch the Canadian application of the international 3SC study.

The information is useful to marketers, retailers and manufacturers of everything from clothes to music tapes, Michael Adams, president of Environics, said in an interview.

"If you've got somebody who is looking for an identity and is using consumption to define themselves, that is very different from other consumers who may be looking for value and high quality," Mr. Adams said.

Young people "are looking for things for their symbolic value."

The study shows that the need by young people to project an image with the things they buy leads them to purchase products on other than strictly rational grounds.

"In this regard, young people are on the cutting edge of a modern trend that is pushing all of society toward materialism," an Environics statement said.

These young people, described as "a willing and lucrative market," place a greater value on saving money than those in slightly older age groups, the study found.

But rather than use their nest egg as a cushion against disaster, these young people plan to spend their savings on future indulgences.

Canada's young people are highly individualistic and don't seem to question themselves or the world around them, the research showed.

And even in the age of acquired immune deficiency syndrome, they are extremely sexually permissive, it found.

Environics researchers said packaging and presentation by companies will assume added importance in the years ahead.

Source: Marina Straus, "Young Pleasure Seekers Born to Shop, Study Says," *The Globe and Mail*, January 27, 1989, p. B6.

Questions:
1. What are the marketing implications of this study for:
    a) The clothing buyer at Eaton's?
    b) The sports equipment buyer at Eaton's?
    c) The hardware buyer at Eaton's?
    d) A local theatre group?
2. Name some totally new marketing opportunities which may result from these findings.

Chapter 11

Product and Pricing Strategy

Learning Goals

How much does it cost? A question heard throughout the world:
Combien est-ce? In Quebec.
Wieviel kostet es? In Germany.
Quanto costa? In Italy.
¿Quanto vale? In Spain.
Skol'ko eto stoit? In Russia.
Ikura desu ka? In Japan.

1. To discuss product mortality, and the new-product development process

2. To explain the product classification system

3. To describe the product life cycle concept

4. To explain how products are identified

5. To discuss pricing objectives

6. To discuss how prices are set in the marketplace

7. To show how breakeven analysis can be used in pricing strategy

8. To differentiate between skimming and penetration pricing strategies

9. To discuss the concept of price lining

10. To describe price-quality relationships and psychological pricing, and their impact on price perception

Profile

Sylvia Rempel—*Creator of Sun Ice Designs, Products to be Shown to the World*

As a teenage refugee from Kassel, West Germany, in the early 1950s, young Sylvia Rempel and other members of her family worked in the sugar beet fields of Alberta to help repay their ocean fare from Europe. Rempel has worked hard ever since. In the ensuing years she married, raised four children and found time to create a multimillion-dollar sportswear company—Sun Ice Ltd.—whose sports clothes and leisure wear are now stocked by stores throughout Canada and the United States. Sun Ice was chosen to provide outfits for about 10,000 Canadian athletes, officials, and volunteers at the Calgary Winter Olympics.

Rempel's achievement demonstrates that a well-designed and well-marketed product can surmount the distance from major markets. An important factor in marketing Sun Ice products has been the national pride shown by the company. It has supplied top Canadian athletes with the company's distinctive gear. The members of three climbing teams on Mount Everest wore Sun Ice clothing, and the outstanding Canadian downhill skiing team of Steve Podborski, Ken Read and Gerry Sorensen displayed the Sun Ice logo on the slopes of the international circuit.

The origins of Sun Ice were modest. Married at 20 to Calgary schoolteacher Victor Rempel, Sylvia began making outfits for her family and a growing number of neighbourhood clients. Then a local ski shop owner stocked some of Rempel's outfits. As sales grew, she moved the fledgling company from her basement through a series of locations, and finally expanded into a modern $3 million factory where 200 employees work on a computer-controlled production line.

After penetrating the US market the company has plans for Japan and Europe. In the

meantime, the company's president is as dedicated to work as ever. She still designs most of the styles in the Sun Ice collection and personally makes sure that the company's reputation for quality is upheld. "I'm always around the production floor," says Rempel. "They call me Eagle Eye."

Source: "I Was Brought Up for Work," *Maclean's*, December 28, 1987, p. 25. Reprinted by permission Maclean's Magazine.

Competition in the car rental business is tough, and the number of competitors has led to various strategies to try to gain more customers. One of the first competitive tools is price. If two or more firms have a similar sized car, the one who offers the lower price will have a competitive advantage. If business flows to the lower priced competitor, others are forced to meet the price. This is a process that has been occurring in the Canadian industry for some years. It is likely that all firms would abandon this competition if they could, but all it takes is for one to break ranks and the rest must follow.

However, such competition has an obvious negative impact on profits, and firms are forced to look at other means of competing. One way is through differentiating their products, which can be done in various ways. Increased service enhances the product. So do extra options. Tie-ins with airline frequent flier bonus programmes have also been used as a tool to increase the value offered. Auto rental firms have now begun stocking specialty-type cars such as convertibles and mini-vans to move some of their product assortment away from directly comparable products. Whatever competitive move is made by one firm, others try to meet or beat it. This is the reality of the marketplace.

The previous chapter outlined the importance of determining one's market target before initiating a marketing strategy. But once this target has been identified, the marketer needs to formulate an appropriate marketing mix to reach these consumers.

This chapter deals with the first two components of a marketing mix, product strategy and pricing strategy. Marketers broadly define a **product** as a bundle of physical, and/or service, and symbolic attributes designed to produce consumer want satisfaction. Therefore, product strategy is considerably more than producing a physical product or service. It includes decisions about package design, brand name, trademarks, warranties, guarantees, and new product development (see Focus 11-1).

The second element of the marketing mix is pricing strategy. **Price** is the exchange value of a good or service. An item is worth only what someone else is willing to pay for it. Pricing strategy deals with the multitude of factors that influence the setting of a price.

product
A bundle of physical, and/or service, and symbolic attributes designed to produce consumer want satisfaction.

price
The exchange value of a good or service.

Product Strategy

Product strategy is concerned with the development of physical, service, and symbolic attributes that satisfy consumers. It goes beyond the physical or functional characteristics of a product or service. Figure 11-1 shows that the marketer's total product concept also includes the brand, product image, warranty and service, and the package and label.

Figure 11-1 Components of the Total Product Concept

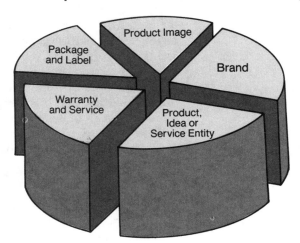

How to Develop New Products

The creation of new products or services is the lifeblood of an organization. Products do not remain economically viable forever, so new ones must be developed to assure the survival of the enterprise. Most products today are aimed at satisfying specific customer needs. Sony's Diskman was designed to improve upon the ubiquitous Walkman. It will likely be successful because it serves user needs better. Canada Packers researches emerging needs, and how they can develop products to serve them. Clearly, new products are very important to marketers. In fact, a recent survey by Booz Allen & Hamilton, a consulting firm, indicated that management thought that new products would account for a sizable part of the eighties' growth in sales and profits.

The Product Idea Mortality Curve

Booz Allen & Hamilton is also responsible for the concept of the product idea mortality curve, shown in Figure 11-2. The consultants' original survey in 1968 found that it took 58 new product ideas to get one commercial success. Figure 11-2 shows that it currently takes 50 ideas to generate a new product.

Booz Allen did a follow-up study in 1981. The consultants concluded that current new-product development was also more cost effective. Booz Allen says that product ideas are now eliminated more quickly. Commercially successful products comprised 54 percent of all new-product development expenditures, up from 30 percent in 1968.[1] The process of new-product development has become more efficient and cost effective.

Figure 11-2 The Product Idea Mortality Curve

MORTALITY OF NEW PRODUCT IDEAS

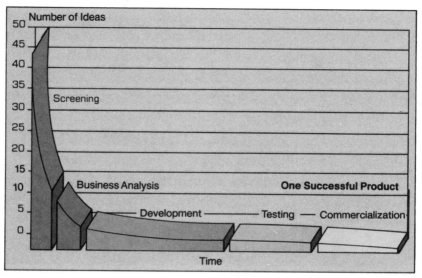

Focus 11-1

Product Opportunities from Biotechnology

Freshness indicators that change colour as food gets stale, a "salmonella dipstick" to replace complex tests for food-poisoning bacteria, and the grading of fruit and vegetables in terms of taste rather than just size and shape.

These are three of the many potential applications of biotechnology in the C$80-billion British food market, according to a study commissioned by the Department of Trade and Industry.

The report is intended to tell financiers and commercial managers of the scope for diversification and product improvement through applying biotechnology in the food and agriculture sectors.

Many applications are ripe for small companies and need not cost millions, the report says. One example—the development of a quick, enzyme-based sensor for B vitamins in food—could be developed within a year.

The 40 specific business opportunities suggested by the counsulting firm include:

• A freshness indicator for individual packs of supermarket food. It would have a sensor with a membrane sensitive to specific biological molecules, which would detect the "spoilage organisms" that build up when fresh food begins to go off—and change colour.

- Grading fruit and vegetables by quality and flavour. Develop a technique for analyzing the natural acids and sugars in a tiny sample of juice. This would show whether the fruit or vegetable is ripe and how it tastes.
- Developing micro-organisms which extend the shelf life of fresh foods. Some microbes excrete substances which are highly toxic to the organisms responsible for food spoilage.

Source: Clive Cookson, "Biotech Projects Can Help Spot Food Going Bad, "*The Financial Post*, October 3, 1988, p. 47.

Classifying Products

Marketers have found it useful to classify products, because each type requires a different competitive strategy. Products and services are classified as either consumer or industrial, depending on the purchaser of the particular item. Each of these categories can be subdivided.

Consumer Goods

A variety of classifications have been suggested for consumer goods, but the system most typically used has three subcategories: convenience goods, shopping goods, and specialty goods. This system, based on consumer buying habits, has been used for more than 50 years.[2]

convenience goods
Products that consumers seek to purchase frequently, immediately, and with a minimum of effort.

shopping goods
Products purchased only after the consumer has compared competing goods in competing stores on bases such as price, quality, style, and colour.

specialty goods
Products particularly desired by the purchaser who is willing to make a special effort to obtain them and is familiar with the items sought.

Convenience goods are products the consumer seeks to purchase frequently, immediately, and with a minimum of effort. Items stocked in 24-hour convenience stores, vending machines, and local newsstands are usually convenience goods. Newspapers, chewing gum, magazines, milk, bread, and gasoline are all convenience goods.

Shopping goods are products purchased only after the consumer has compared competing goods in competing stores on bases such as price, quality, style, and colour. A young couple intent on buying a new colour television may visit many stores, examine perhaps dozens of television sets, and spend days making the final decision. The couple follows a regular routine from store to store in surveying competing offerings and ultimately selects the most appealing set.

Specialty goods are particular products desired by the purchaser who is very familiar with the item sought and is willing to make a special effort to obtain it. A specialty good has no reasonable substitute in the mind of the buyer. The nearest Mercedes dealer may be twenty miles away, but the driving enthusiast might go there to obtain what he or she considers one of the world's best-engineered cars.

This classification of consumer goods may differ among buyers. A shopping good for one person may be a convenience good for another. Majority buying patterns determine the item's product classification.

Industrial Products

The industrial market is comprised of manufacturers, utilities, government agencies, contractors, mining firms, wholesalers, retailers, insurance and real estate firms, and institutions such as schools and hospitals that buy goods and services to use in producing other services or items for resale. The industrial market is a significant part of the total economy. Industrial markets are often concentrated geographically, such as the automobile industry. There is also typically a limited number of buyers. The aircraft industry is a good example. Industrial markets also consist of professional buyers and people who specialize in procurement.

capital items
Relatively long-lived industrial products that usually cost large sums of money.

Industrial goods can be classified as capital and expense items. **Capital items** are industrial products that are relatively long-lived and that usually involve large sums of money, such as factories, machinery, airplanes, and locomotives. **Expense items** are usually less costly than capital items and are consumed within a year of their purchase. Light bulbs, pencils, and lubricating oil are examples.

expense items
Usually less costly industrial products than capital items, consumed within a year of their purchase.

Industrial products are sometimes further classified into five additional categories: 1) installations, such as factories, 2) accessory equipment, such as microcomputers, 3) component parts and materials, such as an engine installed on a Bombardier snowmobile, 4) raw material, such as iron ore, and 5) supplies such as paperclips.

Installations, accessory equipment, and some component parts and material are considered capital items. Supplies, raw materials and some component parts can be classified as expense items.

Services Are Different

service
A product with no physical characteristics; it is a bundle of performance and symbolic attributes designed to produce consumer want satisfaction.

A **service** is a product with no physical characteristics; it is a bundle of performance and symbolic attributes designed to produce consumer want satisfaction. Services can be classified as either consumer or industrial services. A haircut by a local stylist is a consumer service. The Barnes security patrol at a nearby plant is an industrial service. In some cases a service can accommodate both industrial and consumer markets. For example, when an accounting firm prepares your personal income tax return, it is a consumer service. When it prepares financial statements for the corner laundromat, it is offering an industrial service.

The Product Life Cycle

product life cycle (PLC)
A series of stages in the life of all successful products: introduction, growth, maturity, and decline.

Humans grow from infants into children, then into adults who gradually move to retirement age and eventually death. Products, like people, pass through a series of stages: introduction, growth, maturity, and decline. This is known as the **product life cycle**. The typical path of products from their introduction to their eventual demise is depicted in Figure 11-3. Examples of consumer products in various stages of their life cycles are also shown.

Figure 11-3
Stages in the Product Life Cycle

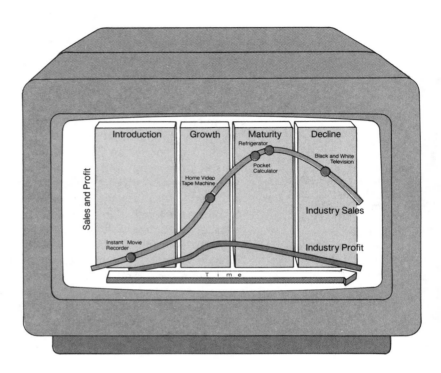

"Is this the new Coke or the old Coke that's now the new Coke?"

Creating new products or services is the lifeblood of an organization.

The introductory stage. In the early stages of the product life cycle the firm attempts to promote demand for its new market offering. Because neither consumers nor distributors are aware of the product, marketers must use promotional programmes to inform the market of the item's availability and explain its features.

New product development and introductory promotional campaigns are expensive and commonly lead to losses in the first stage of the product life cycle. Yet these expenditures are necessary if the firm is to profit later.

The growth stage. Sales climb quickly during the product life cycle's growth stage, as new customers are added to the early users who may now be repurchasing the item. Person-to-person referrals and continued advertising by the firm induce others to make trial purchases.

The company also begins to earn profits on the new product. But this success encourages competitors to enter the field with similar offerings.

The maturity stage. Industry sales first increase in the maturity stage, but eventually they reach a saturation level where further expansion is difficult. Competition also intensifies, increasing the availability of the product. Firms concentrate on capturing competitors' customers, often dropping prices to further their appeal. Sales volume fades late in the maturity stage.

The decline stage. Sales continue to fall in the decline stage of the product life cycle. Profits also decline and may become losses as further price cutting occurs in the reduced market for the item. The decline stage is usually caused by a product innovation or a shift in consumer preferences. The decline stage of an old product can also be the growth stage for a new product which the same company has introduced to take its place.

Focus 11-2

Products That Never Die

The product life cycle is often not as clear-cut as the PLC model seems to imply. Many products have long lives. In 1923, the following brands were market leaders. They still are today:

Swift Premium bacon   Gillette razors
Eastman Kodak cameras   Life Savers mint candies
Ivory soap   Wrigley chewing gum
Campbell's soup   Del Monte canned fruit
Coca-Cola   Eveready flashlight battery
Lipton tea   Singer sewing machines
Goodyear tires

Their success, says Murray Lubliner, president of a marketing research company, is due in part to the hold brand loyalty has on the consumer psyche. Manufacturers of these old standbys have made history work for them rather than against them by keeping their products up to date, positioning them to meet the needs of a changing market, and conducting effective promotional campaigns. As a result, these products have been passed on from generation to generation like fine heirlooms.

All the brands that have held onto their number-one positions have capitalized on their brand name, and continually updated their products as necessary rather than allow them to become obsolete.

With products like Tide, Ivory, Crest, Crisco, and Pampers (combined product age 250 years; oldest product, Ivory at 103 years), Procter & Gamble refuses to base product strategy on the theory that all products eventually die. "We don't believe in it," said former P & G chairman Edward G. Harness.

"The fellow who succeeds," continued Harness, "is the one who is the first to identify emerging consumer needs and to offer product improvements which satisfy those needs." Using Tide as an example, Harness points out that even though the detergent was first introduced in 1947, it has kept up with the changing market. "It is different in its cleaning performance, sudsing characteristics, packaging. In total, there have been 55 significant modifications in this one brand during its...lifetime."

Extending the Product Life Cycle

The marketer's objective is to extend the product life cycle as long as the item is profitable. Sometimes it is possible to extend a product's life cycle considerably beyond what it would otherwise be. Some useful strategies include the following:

- Increase the frequency of use. For example, persuading consumers that they need to have additional smoke alarms, flashlights, and so on may result in increased purchases by each household.
- Add new users. Introducing the product abroad might accomplish this.
- Find new uses for the product. Arm & Hammer baking soda is a classic example. Its original use in baking has been augmented by its newer uses as a refrigerator freshener, flame extinguisher, first-aid remedy, denture cleaner, cleaning agent, and pool pH adjuster.
- Change package sizes, labels, and product quality. Offering smaller, portable colour televisions led to many households acquiring two or more models.[3]

brand
A name, term, sign, symbol, design, or some combination used to identify the products of one firm and to differentiate them from competitive offerings.

brand name
That part of the brand consisting of words or letters that make up a name used to identify and distinguish the firm's offerings from those of competitors.

trademark
A brand that has been given exclusive legal protection—protection includes not only the pictorial design but also the brand name.

Identifying Products—Brands, Brand Names, and Trademarks

Products are identified by brands, brand names, and trademarks. A **brand** is a name, term, sign, symbol, design, or some combination used to identify the products of one firm and to differentiate them from competitive offerings. A **brand name** is that part of the brand consisting of words or letters included in a name used to identify and distinguish the firm's offerings from those of competitors. A **trademark** is a brand that has been given legal protection; the protection is granted solely to the brand's owner. Thus a trademark includes not only the pictorial design but also the brand name.[4] Any five-year-old can spot McDonald's golden arches among other fast-food franchises. Sunkist Growers, a cooperative, brands its oranges with the name *Sunkist*. An industrial purchasing agent can examine a piece of sheet steel and find the name and symbol, for, say, Dominion Steel. Brand identification of the firm's products is often a critical strategic decision for the marketing manager.

Brands are important in developing a product's image. If consumers are aware of a particular brand, its appearance becomes advertising for the firm. The RCA trademark of the dog at the phonograph, for example, is instant advertising to shoppers who spot it in a store. Successful branding is also a means of escaping some price competition. Well-known national brands often sell at a considerable price premium over their competition.

Selecting a Good Brand Name

Good brand names are easy to pronounce, recognize, and remember.[5] Short names like JVC, Crest, Bic, and Kodak meet these requirements. Multinational marketing firms face a real problem in selecting brand names, in that an excellent brand name in one country may prove disastrous in another. Every language has "o" and "k" sounds, and *okay* has become an international word. Every language also has a short "a," so that Coca-Cola and Texaco are pronounceable in any tongue. But an advertising campaign for E-Z washing machines failed in the United Kingdom because the British, like Canadians, pronounce *z* as "zed." Kodak, Styrofoam, Kleenex, Scotch tape, Fiberglas, Band-Aid, and Jeep are also often used by consumers as descriptive names.

Brand names should give the right image to the buyer. Accutron suggests the quality of the high-priced and accurate timepiece of Bulova. Diet Pepsi creates an image of a cola that can be enjoyed by those who are weight conscious.

Avoiding Generic Terms

Brand names cannot contain words in general use such as *television, automobile*, or *suntan lotion*. These are generic words—words that describe a type of product—and they cannot be used exclusively by any company.

Conversely, if a type of product becomes generally known by a certain brand name, it can be ruled generic, and the company that successfully developed the name can lose exclusive rights to it. The generic names *cola, nylon, kerosene, linoleum*, and *shredded wheat* were once brand names.

There is a difference between brand names legally judged generic and those viewed as generic by many consumers. Xerox is a brand name; yet many consumers use the term generically to refer to all photocopying processes. The legal brand names Aspirin, Formica, Kodak, Styrofoam, Kleenex, Scotch tape, Fiberglas, Band-Aid, and Jeep are also often used by consumers as descriptive names.

In order to keep their brand names from being ruled generic, most brand owners take specific steps to inform consumers of their exclusive ownership. The Coca-Cola Company uses ®, the symbol for registration, immediately after the names Coca-Cola and Coke. It also sends letters to newspapers, novelists, and nonfiction writers who use the name Coke with a lower-case first letter, informing them that the name is owned by Coca-Cola.[6] Firms of this sort face the task of attempting to retain exclusive rights to a brand name that is known throughout the world.

Private Brands

private brands
Products that are not identified as to manufacturer but instead carry the retailer's label (often known as house, distributor, or retailer brands).

generic product
One with no brand name that sells at a considerable discount from manufacturer and private brands; has plain packaging, minimal labelling, and little if any advertising; and meets minimum quality standards.

Not all brand names belong to manufacturers. Some are the property of retailers or distributors. **Private brands** (often known as house, distributor, or retailer labels) are products that are not identified as to manufacturer but instead carry the retailer's label. Some examples are: *Viking* (Eaton's), *Life* (Shoppers Drug Mart), and *St. Michael* (Marks & Spencer).

Many retailers now offer a third option to manufacturers' and private brands: generic products. These items have plain packaging (often yellow or white with black printing), minimal labelling and little if any advertising, and meet minimum quality standards. **Generic products** generally do not have individual brand names, and sell at a considerable discount from manufacturers' and private brands. Generics were developed in Europe and first appeared in Canada about 1977.

The Stages of Brand Loyalty

Although branding is very important, the degree of brand loyalty varies widely from product to product. In some categories, consumers are insistent on a specific brand. For other purchases they might readily accept a generic product. Brand recognition, brand preference, and brand insistence are the three stages used to measure brand loyalty.

brand recognition
The stage of brand loyalty at which the consumer is familiar with the product or service.

Brand recognition simply means that the consumer is familiar with the product or service. Free samples and discount coupons are often used to build this familiarity. A brand that is recognized is more likely to be purchased than one that is unknown.

brand preference
The stage of brand loyalty at which the consumer will be loyal if the brand is available.

Brand preference is the stage of brand loyalty at which the consumer will be loyal if the brand is available. Many consumer products like beer and soft drinks fall into this category. A considerable portion of all marketing expenditures are intended to build brand preference.

brand insistence
The stage of brand loyalty at which consumers will accept no substitute for their preferred brand.

Brand insistence is a stage of brand loyalty at which consumers will accept no substitute for their preferred brand. If it is not readily available locally, the consumer will special-order it from a store, or turn to mail-order or telephone buying. Brand insistence is the ultimate degree of brand loyalty, and few brands obtain it.

"Green" Products

Boyle-Midway, the maker of PAM, a spray product designed to eliminate the sticking of foods being cooked, recently unpacked hundreds of cases of their product and sent the cans back through the packaging line again. The purpose was to add one small sticker which said, "ozone safe."

In various parts of the country, the blue garbage recycling box has become famous. Companies are changing their behaviour. Soft drink companies such as Coca-Cola and Pepsi at first resisted, then jumped on the recycling bandwagon.

The reason for these activities is that companies have discovered that consumers are serious about the effect of products on the environment. Massive droughts, heatwaves, and the discovery of holes in the ozone layer around the earth have raised strong concerns.

The makers of PAM and many other spray product producers had actually changed to ozone-safe propellants much earlier, but consumers were not aware of this, and sales dropped.

Just as many stores now carry a line of "generic" products, we may see more "green" (environmentally safe) product lines being promoted.

Service and Warranties

Service programmes are vital aspects of the total product concept. Consumers want to know that an adequate service programme is available if something goes wrong. Products with inadequate service backing quickly disappear from the market as a result of word-of-mouth criticism. Warranties are also important. A **warranty** is simply a promise to refund or replace a product if it proves unsatisfactory.

warranty
A promise to repair a product, to replace it, or to refund its purchase price if it proves unsatisfactory.

Packaging and Labelling

Packaging also plays an important role in product strategy (see Figure 11-1). The original purpose of packaging was protection against risks like damage, spoilage, and theft. But over the years, packaging also acquired a marketing function.

Good packaging helps to sell the product. Marketers pay much attention to how a package will be perceived in the marketplace. Marketing research is commonly done on both product and package.

Packaging is now responsible for one of the biggest costs in many consumer products. As a result, marketers are now devoting more attention to it. Cost-effective packaging is one of industry's greatest needs.

Labelling

Labelling is now often part of the packaging process. Soft drinks, frozen vegetables, milk, and snack foods are examples. Labelling must meet a number of federal requirements. The intent is to provide the consumer with information that will assist in making an informed purchase decision. Labels must be printed in both official languages.

Pricing Strategy

After a product or service has been developed, identified, and packaged, it must be priced. This is the second aspect of the marketing mix. As noted earlier, price is the exchange value of a good or service. Pricing strategy has become one of the most important features of modern marketing.

The value of any item—consumer product, industrial product, or service—is its **exchange value** in the marketplace. An item is worth only what someone else is willing to pay for it. In a primitive society the exchange value may be determined by trading a good for some other commodity. A horse may be worth ten sheep; 12 apples may be worth two loaves of bread. More advanced societies use money as the medium of exchange. But in either case, a product's or service's **price** is its exchange value.

All goods and services offer some utility, or want-satisfying power. Individual preferences determine how much utility a consumer will associate with a particular good or service. One person may value leisure-time pursuits, while another assigns a higher priority to acquiring real assets (property, automobiles, and household furnishings).

Consumers face an allocation problem. They have a limited amount of money and a variety of possible uses for it. The price system helps them make allocation decisions. A person may prefer a new colour television to a vacation; if the price of the television set rises, that person may reconsider and allocate funds to the vacation trip instead.

Prices help direct the overall economic system. A firm uses various factors of production (such as natural resources, labour, and capital) based on their relative prices. High wage rates may cause a firm to install labour-saving machinery. Similarly, high interest rates may lead management to decide against a new capital expenditure. Prices and volume sold determine the revenue received by the firm and influence its profits.

Everyone recognizes the importance of prices in daily living. Early philosophers struggled with the issue of how to define a just price. As

exchange value
The value of any item—consumer product, industrial product, or service—in the marketplace.

price
The exchange value of a product or service in the marketplace.

consumers, we want lower retail prices, yet often complain of the lack of retail services. All such services—for example, gift wrapping, delivery, and credit—have costs associated with them, and these costs must be covered by higher prices. The continuing question is: how do we balance prices and costs?

Pricing Objectives

Management attempts to accomplish certain objectives through its pricing decisions. Research has shown that multiple pricing objectives are common among many firms. Some companies try to maximize their profits by pricing a new technological innovation very high. Others use low prices to attract new business.

The airline industry illustrates pricing policies that attempt to utilize both low and high prices for different target groups. There has been a significant increase in discount prices to try to attract more people to purchase unused airline seat space. To remain profitable, an airline must then cut services and other costs. Another option is to also attract a clientele that is prepared to pay a higher price for extra benefits and services. Air Canada has attempted to do this by providing up to three different categories of service. In the automobile industry Rolls-Royce does not sell great volumes of cars, but a few Corniche convertibles at a price of about $175,000 apiece generate considerable sales volume.[7]

There are three basic categories of pricing objectives—profitability objectives; volume objectives; and a group of other objectives, including social and ethical considerations, status quo objectives, and image goals.

Profitability Objectives

Most firms have some type of profitability objective for their pricing strategy. Management knows that

$$\text{Profit} = \text{Revenue} - \text{Expenses}$$

and that revenue is a result of the selling price times the quantity sold:

$$\text{Total Revenue} = \text{Price} \times \text{Quantity Sold.}$$

Some firms try to maximize profits by increasing their prices to the point where a disproportionate decrease appears in the number of units sold. A 10 percent price hike that results in only an 8 percent volume decline increases profitability. But a 5 percent price rise that reduces the number of units sold by 6 percent is unprofitable.

profit maximization
A pricing strategy whereby management sets increasing levels of profitability as its objective.

Profit maximization is the basis of much of economic theory. However, it is often difficult to apply in practice, and many firms have

target return goals
A pricing strategy whereby the desired profitability is stated in terms of particular goals such as a 10 percent return on either sales or investment.

turned to a simpler profitability objective—**target return goals**. For example, a firm might specify the goal of a 9 percent return on sales or a 20 percent return on investment. Most target return pricing goals state the desired profitability in terms of a return on either sales or investment.

Volume Objectives

sales maximization concept
A concept under which management sets an acceptable minimum level of profitability and then tries to maximize sales.

Another description of pricing behaviour is the **sales maximization concept**, under which management sets an acceptable minimum level of profitability and then tries to maximize sales. Sales expansion is viewed as being more important than short-run profits to the firm's long-term competitive position.

market share
The percentage of a market controlled by a certain company, product, or service.

A second volume objective is **market share**—the percentage of a market controlled by a certain company, product, or service. One firm may seek to achieve a 25 percent market share in a certain industry. Another may want to maintain or expand its market share for particular products or product lines.

Market share objectives have become popular for several reasons. Perhaps one of the most important is the ease with which market share statistics can be used as a yardstick for measuring managerial and corporate performance. Another is that increased sales may lead to lower production costs and higher profits. On a per unit basis, it is cheaper to produce 10,000 pens than it is to manufacture just a few dozen.

Other Objectives

Objectives not related to profitability or sales volume—social and ethical considerations, status quo objectives, and image goals—are often used in the pricing decisions of some firms. Social and ethical considerations play an important role in some pricing situations, that is, the prices of some products and services are based on the intended consumers' ability to pay them. For example, public transportation, union dues, and retirement fund contributions are often related to the income of the payers.

status quo pricing objectives
Objectives that reflect management's efforts to seek stable prices, enabling the company to channel competitive efforts into other areas such as product design or promotion.

Many firms have **status quo pricing objectives**; that is, they are inclined to follow the leader. These companies seek stable prices that will allow them to put their competitive efforts into other areas, such as product design or promotion. This is most common in oligopolistic markets.

image goals
Goals that are coordinated with pricing strategies to reflect an integrated company image.

Image goals are often used in pricing strategy. The price structures of major department stores, for example, are set to reflect the high quality of the merchandise. Discount houses, however, may seek an image of good value at low prices. Thus, a firm's pricing strategy may be an integral part of the overall image it wishes to convey.

Prices and Inflation

inflation
An economic situation in which there are rising prices or decreased purchasing power of a nation's currency.

Inflation can be defined in terms of rising prices or the decreased purchasing power of a nation's currency. Consumers became accustomed to high rates of inflation in the late seventies. The rise in consumer prices peaked in 1980 at an annual rate of over 12 percent, then began to decline.

When inflation was high, consumers were conditioned to further price hikes. Once inflation trended downward, this perception remained for a period of time. Now Canadians are more concerned with other economic issues than they are with inflation. What does this mean for marketers?

Consumers recognize that inflation is not the primary culprit in price increases anymore. This suggests that buyers will be more sensitive to price hikes than they were a few years ago. Marketers must work to keep prices at reasonable levels if the nation's economic progress is to continue.

While pricing is usually regarded as a function of marketing, it also requires considerable input from other areas in the company.

Focus 11-4

The Wheels of Justice Grind Slowly on Price Fixing

Coke Fined $65,000 for Winnipeg Price Fixing: Nearly nine years after the event, Coca-Cola Ltd. of Toronto has been fined for its role in a price-fixing conspiracy in Winnipeg.

The company pleaded guilty in the Manitoba Court of Queen's Bench yesterday. It admitted conspiring with the local bottler of Pepsi-Cola to raise prices by 22 percent for a six week period in 1980.

The two companies controlled 90 percent of the soft-drink market in Winnipeg at the time.

The general manager of Blackwoods Beverages Ltd., the bottler of Pepsi-Cola and several other soft drinks in Winnipeg, approached the local manager of Coca-Cola during a time of fierce competition in 1980, the court heard.

T.F. Kinahan, the general manager, suggested the two companies should agree to increase their prices. However, the local Coca-Cola manager rejected the idea.

Mr. Kinahan then travelled to Toronto to meet R.B. Ramsden, manager of Coca-Cola's bottling operations in Western Canada.

The two men agreed to a "damage control" plan that would end the price war. They agreed to raise the wholesale price of their soft drinks in the 750-millilitre size from $4.50 to $5.50 a case. They also agreed to limit their discount pricing.

The agreement lasted from the beginning of May to the middle of June 1980.

Federal Crown counsel Peter Kremer said there was "clear criminal intent" on the part of Coca-Cola.

Blackwoods already has been fined $75,000 for its part in the conspiracy.

Mr. Kremer said Coca-Cola should pay a larger fine because it is a high-profile national company and it should be a model corporation. He sought a $100,000 fine.

Coca-Cola lawyer Edgar Sexton said Blackwoods was more culpable because it was the instigator of the price-fixing deal. He said the two companies had a "vague" and "fragile" agreement that lasted only six weeks.

Mr. Sexton said Coca-Cola's profit for the 750-millilitre bottles during the six-week period in Winnipeg was only $13,000.

It is debatable whether the consumers felt the effect of the increase in the wholesale price, he said. He noted the wholesale price for the same product in other cities was not much different.

There is no evidence that the president or any of the vice-presidents of Coca-Cola were aware of the agreement, Mr. Sexton said.

He attributed the price-fixing to "over-zealous" employees trying to meet fierce competition.

Blackwoods controlled 50.5 percent of the soft drink market in 1980, while Coca-Cola controlled 39.5 percent, Mr. Sexton said.

Mr. Justice Theodore Glowacki was "somewhat persuaded" by Mr. Sexton's argument. He imposed a $65,000 fine to deter other corporations.

Coca-Cola also agreed to a prohibition order, requiring it to promise never to fix prices again.

Coca-Cola was the bottler of Coke and Canada Dry in 1980 in Winnipeg, and Blackwoods bottles Pepsi, Seven-Up, Orange Crush and other brands.

Source: Geoffrey York, "Coke Fined $65,000 for Winnipeg Price Fixing," *The Globe and Mail*, January 14, 1989, p. B5.

When business is slow, raising prices may not always be the most effective pricing strategy.

Price Determination

Accounting and financial managers have always played a major role in the pricing task by providing the sales and cost data necessary for good decision making. Production and industrial engineering personnel play similarly important roles. Computer analysts may generate data that provide up-to-date information needed in pricing. It is essential for managers at all levels to realize the importance of pricing and the contribution that can be made to determine appropriate prices. Marketing managers usually have a special role in price determination, as they are usually closest to the market.

Figure 11-4
Demand and Supply Curves

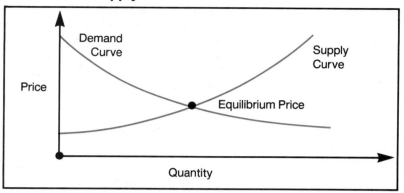

Price determination can be viewed from various perspectives. Economic theory provides an overall viewpoint, while cost-based pricing looks at the critical numbers that should be considered. A further dimension is added when marketers relate the former variables to the realities of the marketplace in setting the actual price.

Economic theory, assuming a profit maximization objective, says that the market price will be set at the point where the amount of a product desired at a given price is equal to the amount that suppliers will provide at that price—where the amount demanded and the amount supplied are in equilibrium. In other words, there is a schedule of amounts that will be demanded at different price levels— the **demand curve**. At $3 per pound, 5,000 pounds of an industrial chemical might be sold. A price increase to $4 per pound might reduce sales to 3,200 pounds, and a $5 per pound price might result in sales of only 2,000 pounds, as some would-be customers decide to accept less expensive substitutes or to wait for the price to be reduced. Correspondingly, there is a schedule that shows the amounts that will be offered in the market at certain prices—the **supply curve**. Theoretically, the intersection of these two curves is the **equilibrium price** that will exist in the marketplace for a particular good or service (see Figure 11-4).

Practical Price Setting

Although this economic analysis is correct in regard to the overall market for a product, managers face the problem of setting the price of individual brands based on limited information. Anticipating the amount of a product that will be bought at a certain price is difficult, so business has tended to adopt cost-based pricing formulas. While these are simpler and easier to use, executives have to be flexible in

demand curve
A schedule of amounts of a good or service that will be demanded at different price levels.

supply curve
A schedule of amounts of a good or service that will be offered in the market at certain prices.

equilibrium price
The price that exists in the marketplace for a particular good or service, determined by the intersection of the supply and demand curves. This is the point where the amount of a product desired at a given price is equal to the amount that suppliers will provide at that price.

applying them to each situation. Marketers begin the process of cost-based pricing by totalling all costs associated with offering an item in the market—including production, transportation, distribution, and marketing expenses. Then they add an amount for profit and expenses not previously considered—the **markup**. The actual amount may vary in accordance with the demand for the product. The total of this amount and the cost of the item determines the selling price. The **markup percentage**, then, is the markup divided by the price of the item:

markup
The amount added to cost for profit and expenses not previously considered. The total determines the selling price.

markup percentage
The markup divided by the price of the item.

$$\text{Markup Percentage} = \frac{\text{Amount Added to Cost (Markup)}}{\text{Price}}$$

If a game in a toy store is priced at $3, and its invoice cost (the amount the store has paid for it) is $2, then the markup percentage is $33\frac{1}{3}$:

$$\text{Markup Percentage} = \frac{\$1}{\$3} = 33\frac{1}{3}$$

The firm's markup should be related to its **stock turnover**—the number of times the average inventory is sold annually (using sales figures if the inventory is recorded at retail value and cost of goods sold if the inventory is recorded at cost):

stock turnover
The number of times the average inventory is sold annually.

$$\text{Stock Turnover} = \frac{\text{Sales or Cost of Goods Sold}}{\text{Average Inventory}}$$

Markups are generally lower for products with high stock turnover figures (e.g., groceries) and higher for items with low turnover figures (e.g., jewellery).

Marketers must be flexible, willing to adjust their markups and prices according to the demand for their products. While costs are a useful place to start, market demand must be considered in arriving at an appropriate price.

breakeven analysis
A method of determining the minimum sales volume needed to cover all costs at a certain price level. A breakeven analysis considers various costs and total revenue.

Breakeven Analysis—An Aid to Pricing Decisions

variable costs
Costs that change with the level of production such as labour and raw materials.

Marketers often use **breakeven analysis** as a method of determining the minimum sales volume needed at a certain price level to cover all costs. It involves a consideration of various costs and total revenue. Total cost (TC) is composed of total variable costs (TVC) and total fixed costs (TFC). **Variable costs** are those that change with the level of production (such as labour and raw material costs), while **fixed costs** are those that remain stable regardless of the production level

fixed costs
Costs that remain stable regardless of the production level achieved.

e.g. Insurance

achieved (such as the firm's insurance costs). Total revenue is determined by multiplying price by the number of units sold.

Figure 11-5 shows the calculation of the **breakeven point**—the level of sales that will cover all of the company's costs (both fixed and variable).

Figure 11-5
Breakeven Analysis

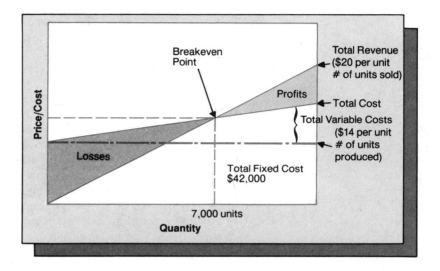

Sales beyond the breakeven point will generate profit. Breakeven points can also be found by using a simple formula:

$$\text{Breakeven Point (in Units)} = \frac{\text{Total Fixed Costs}}{\text{Per Unit Contribution to Fixed Costs}}$$

A product selling for $20 with a variable cost of $14 per item, produces a $6 per unit contribution to fixed costs. If total fixed costs are $42,000, then the firm must sell 7,000 units to break even:

$$\text{Breakeven Point (in Units)} = \frac{\$42,000}{6} = 7,000 \text{ Units}$$

Marketers can use breakeven analysis to compare the results of various prices. Different prices produce different breakeven points, which can then be compared with estimates of likely sales volume based on an analysis of various actual and potential characteristics of the market such as competition, needs of channels of distribution, and other consumer characteristics. This comparison will give an indication of a realistic market price.

New Product Pricing

Pampers, the disposable diaper, failed in its original market test because of pricing. With reduced pricing, it became Procter & Gamble's second best-selling item (behind Tide detergent). When first introduced, Pampers was a relatively new product concept and sold for considerably more than the per use cost of buying and washing a cloth diaper. When Pampers failed in the marketplace, Procter & Gamble redesigned production equipment and managed to reduce production costs to the point where per unit retail price was slashed 40 percent. This reduced cost brought it more into line with cloth diapers, making the convenience aspect worth considering. Since then, the product has become a household word for families with infants. Pricing strategy was a key determinant in this change in baby care.[8]

Procter & Gamble's experience with Pampers shows how difficult it is to select a price for a new product line. Because pricing decisions are risky, it is usually best to field-test alternative prices with sample groups of consumers. Once the product is actually launched, it is difficult to modify its price during the introductory period.

Pricing a new product involves important decisions for the firm. It can choose to price the product competitively—that is, to match the competitors' prices. Or, new-product pricing can be based on one of two strategies: the skimming price strategy or the penetration price strategy.

The Skimming Price Strategy

skimming price strategy
The strategy of setting the price of a new product relatively high compared to similar goods and then gradually lowering it.

The **skimming price strategy** involves setting the price of the new product relatively high compared to similar goods and then gradually lowering it. This strategy is used where the market is segmented on a price basis—that is, where some people may buy the product if it is priced at, say, $10; a larger group may buy it at $7.50; and a still larger group may buy it at $6. A skimming price strategy has been used effectively on such products as pocket calculators, home computers and videocassette recorders.

A skimming price policy allows the firm to recover its costs rapidly by maximizing the revenue it receives. But the policy's disadvantage is that early profits tend to attract competition, and this puts eventual pressure on prices. Today most ballpoint pens sell for less than $1, but when the product was first introduced after World War II, it sold for about $20.

The Penetration Price Policy

penetration price policy
The strategy of pricing a new product relatively low compared to similar goods in the hope that it will secure wide market acceptance.

The second strategy, the **penetration price policy**, involves pricing the new product relatively low compared to similar goods in the hope that it will secure wide acceptance. Soaps and toothpastes are often introduced this way. Penetration pricing discourages competition because of its low profits. It is most often used when the firm expects competition with similiar products within a short time and when large-scale production and marketing will produce substantial reductions in overall costs.

Price Lining

price lining
The offering of merchandise at a limited number of prices instead of pricing each item individually.

Price lining occurs when a seller decides to offer merchandise at a limited number of prices rather than price each item individually. For instance, a boutique might offer lines of women's sportswear priced at $90, $120, and $150. Price lining is a common marketing practice among retailers. The original five-and-ten-cent stores are an example of its early use.

As a pricing strategy, price lining prevents the confusion common to situations where all items are priced individually, and manages the pricing function more easily. But marketers must clearly identify the market segments to which they are appealing. Three "high-price" lines might not be appropriate to a store located in a low- to middle-income area.

A disadvantage of price lining is that it is sometimes difficult to alter the price ranges once they are set. This may be a crucial factor during a period of inflation, when the firm must either raise the price of the line or reduce its quality. Consumers may resist either of these alternatives. While price lining can be useful, its implementation must be considered carefully.

Price-Quality Relationships

Research has shown that the consumer's perception of product quality is related closely to the item's price. The higher the price of the product the better its perceived quality. Most marketers believe that the price-quality relationship exists over a relatively wide range of prices, although extreme prices may be viewed as either too expensive or too cheap. Marketing managers need to study and experiment with prices because the price-quality relationship can be of key importance to a firm's pricing strategy.

Psychological Pricing

Many retailers believe that odd prices are more appealing to consumers than even ones.

Many marketers feel that certain prices are more appealing than others to buyers. Psychological pricing is used throughout the world. The image pricing goals mentioned earlier are an example of psychological pricing.

Have you ever wondered why retailers use prices like $39.95, $19.98 or $9.99 instead of $40, $20, or $10? Years ago, before the age of cash registers, this practice of **odd pricing** was employed to force clerks to make change, thereby serving as a cash control technique for retailers. It is now a common practice in retail pricing because many retailers believe that odd prices are more attractive than even ones to consumers. In fact, some stores have begun to use prices ending in 1, 2, 3, 4, 6, or 7 to avoid the look of ordinary prices like $5.95, $10.98, and $19.99. The new prices are more likely to be $1.11, $3.22, $4.53, $5.74, $3.86, or $9.97.

Controversial Issue

Can "Price" Flexibility Improve the Health System?

In Canada, the cost of maintaining a "free" public health system is one of our most serious problems. We don't seem to have the funds to provide as many services and as much equipment as we would like. Britain faces even greater problems. Excerpts from a recent article concerning Britain's approach to the problem appear below. It appears that Prime Minister Thatcher has decided to allow some price flexibility in the hope that it will cause desirable changes in the system. Do you agree?

London (AP)—The government has proposed the biggest shake-up in Britain's free health system, boosting private health insurance and allowing big hospitals to charge fees.

Prime Minister Margaret Thatcher, in a statement introducing a government policy document yesterday, called the plan the "most far-reaching reform of the National Health Service in its 40-year history."

The opposition Labour party, which introduced free health care after the Second World War, accused her Conservative government of setting out to wreck the system.

The plan was seen by some as an attempt to borrow from the US health system, with its emphasis on private care, without increasing spending.

"In other words, excellent care, eventually, for perhaps as much as three-tenths of the population, but deteriorating health care for the remainder," said Dr. David Owen, a physician who leads the centrist Social Democratic party.

Government officials said the reforms would streamline the health bureaucracy and give the public wider choice, while denying no one access to free treatment.

It is a "change of pace, rather than a change of direction," Health Secretary Kenneth Clarke said.

"The National Health Service is and must remain open to all regardless of income, financed mainly out of general taxation," he told the House of Commons.

Under the plan, the 320 biggest and most sophisticated of the 2,000 state-run hospitals in Britain can become self-governing in 1991, taking fee-paying private patients and billing local authorities for the others.

Breaking another postwar tradition, the self-governing hospitals will charge patients for extras such as choice of meals, private telephones, or television.

For the first time, too, private health insurance for the elderly, the biggest burden on the state system, will be tax-deductible.

Self-governing hospitals will be able to attract

higher-quality staff, from consultants to cleaners, by setting their own pay scales.

Other changes planned over three years include fining general practitioners who resort too readily to prescribing medicines.

Family doctors with big practices will get separate state budgets to buy drugs and hospital treatment from private, state, or self-governing hospitals for elective surgery. They will be allowed to keep half of any savings on the drugs budget.

Consultants and general practitioners will have their costs independently audited and, like hospitals, will be encouraged to compete for patients.

Labour's parliamentary spokesman on health, Robin Cook, said the plan was the work "of people who will always put a healthy balance sheet before healthy patients."

The National Health Service, which with a staff of one million is second only to the Soviet army as the biggest employer in Europe, has been a major frustration for Thatcher since she won power in 1979.

Spending has increased in real terms by nearly one-third since 1979 to the equivalent of C$46.4 billion a year.

Source: "Thatcher Steps Away from Public Health Care," *The Winnipeg Free Press*, February 1, 1989, p. 52.

Summary of Learning Goals

1. **Discuss product mortality, and the new-product development process.**

   The product idea mortality curve is a concept that shows the various steps of the product development process. The stages are (1) new product ideas, (2) screening, (3) business analysis, (4) product development, (5) test marketing, and (6) commercialization.

2. **Explain the product classification system.**

   Products can be classified as consumer or industrial. Consumer products are those purchased by ultimate consumers for their own use. Industrial products are those purchased for use, either directly or indirectly, in the production of other goods for resale. Both consumer and industrial products can be subclassified.

   Consumer products can be classified as either convenience goods, shopping goods, or specialty goods. Industrial products can be classified as capital items or expense items, and can be further broken down into installations, accessory equipment, component parts and materials, raw materials, and supplies. Services can be classified as either consumer or industrial.

3. **Describe the product life cycle concept.**

   All products pass through four stages in their life cycle. In the introductory stage, the firm attempts to secure demand for the product. In the growth stage, sales climb and the company earns profits on the product. In the maturity stage, sales reach a saturation level. In the decline stage, both sales and profits decline. Marketers can sometimes employ strategies that will extend the length of the product cycle.

4. **Explain how products are identified.**

Products are identified by brands, brand names, and trademarks, which are important in developing the products' image. Good brand names are easy to pronounce, recognize, and remember, and they present a desired image to the buyer. Brand names cannot contain generic words; conversely, under certain circumstances, companies can lose exclusive rights to their brand name, which can be ruled generic. Some brand names belong to retailers or distributors rather than to manufacturers. Many retailers now offer a third option: no-brand generic products.

5. **Discuss pricing objectives.**

Prices can be viewed as the exchange value of goods and services in an economy. They are important because they help determine society's allocation of economic resources. Pricing goals include profitability objectives (profit maximization and target return goals); volume objectives (sales maximization and market share objectives); and other objectives, which include social and ethical considerations, status quo objectives, and image goals.

6. **Discuss how prices are set in the marketplace.**

Price determination is based on demand and supply considerations and is cost based. This involves determining costs and a markup on each product which is added to the cost. The markup is related to the stock turnover and should be higher for lower turnover figures and lower for high turnover figures.

7. **Show how breakeven analysis can be used in pricing strategy.**

Breakeven analysis is an aid in making pricing decisions. It involves studying the total costs and total revenues. The breakeven point is determined by dividing total fixed costs by the per unit contribution to fixed costs. Anything beyond the breakeven point is profit.

Breakeven points can be calculated for various prices. The resulting breakeven volumes can then be compared to marketing research estimates of likely volume in determining a final price based upon both consumer needs and the firm's need for a satisfactory return on its investment.

8. **Differentiate between skimming and penetration price strategy.**

New-product pricing can be based on skimming price strategy or penetration price strategy. The skimming strategy involves setting the price relatively high compared to similar goods and then gradually lowering it. The penetration price strategy involves pricing the goods lower than similar goods and eventually raising the cost after the product gains wide market acceptance.

9. **Discuss the concept of price lining.**

Price lining refers to sellers offering merchandise at a limited number of prices. Its value lies in preventing confusion; its disadvantage is that price levels are difficult to alter once they are set.

10. **Describe price-quality relationships and psychological pricing and their impact on price perception.**

Consumers tend to perceive a close relationship between product quality and price. The higher the price of a product, the better its perceived quality. The price-quality relationship can be of key importance to pricing strategy.

Psychological pricing such as odd pricing can also influence the consumer's perception of prices. Odd pricing is the practice of using uneven prices to make them more appealing to consumers.

Key Terms

convenience goods	warranty	equilibrium price
shopping goods	exchange value	markup
specialty goods	price	markup percentage
capital items	profit maximization	stock turnover
expense items	target return goals	breakeven analysis
service	sales maximization	variable costs
product lifecycle	concept	fixed costs
brand	market share	breakeven point
brand name	status quo pricing	skimming price
trademark	objectives	strategy
private brands	image goals	penetration price
generic product	inflation	policy
brand recognition	demand curve	price lining
brand preference	supply curve	odd pricing
brand insistence		

Discussion Questions and Exercises

1. Discuss the concept of a product idea mortality curve. Relate your comments to the steps in the new-product development process.
2. List the last five items you purchased. Then classify them as convenience, shopping, or specialty goods. Explain why you categorized each product as you did.

3. Classify each of the following as a capital item or expense item:
   a) Sharp fax machine.
   b) office stationery.
   c) a new assembly plant in St. John's, Newfoundland.
   d) iron ore from Labrador.
4. Identify each of the product life cycle stages. Suggest a number of products in each stage.
5. Suggest a brand name for each of the following new products, and explain why you chose each name:
   a) a development of exclusive home sites.
   b) a low-priced, term life insurance policy, sold by mail.
   c) an extra-durable, single-edged razor blade.
   d) a portable drill that is considerably more powerful than its competition.
6. List and identify the various pricing objectives used by companies. Which ones do you think are most important to marketers? Why?
7. If an automobile has a sticker price of $11,000, and the dealer paid $8250 for the product, what is the dealer's markup percentage?
8. Assume that you have been appointed marketing manager for a new hockey franchise. Your team will be using an arena with 3,000 first-class seats, 5,000 regular seats, and 2,000 seats behind the nets. How will you go about setting the seat prices?
9. Assume that a product selling for $10 has a variable cost of $6 per unit. If total fixed costs for this product are $38,000, how many units will the firm have to sell to break even?
10. Contrast the skimming and penetration policies of new-product pricing. Can you make any generalization about the types of products or market situations most suitable to each strategy?

Case 11-1

Market Police Service Stations

Shortly after the proposed takeover of Texaco by Imperial Oil, the following proposal was published in the *Winnipeg Free Press*.

How to Cut High Price of Gasoline

'Market Policemen' Could Keep Oil Giants in Line

Once again, developments in the Canadian oil industry are causing grave concern to the Consumers' Association of Canada and to the Federal Bureau of Competition Policy. The trigger this time: Imperial Oil, the largest integrated oil company in Canada, whose parent US company is the largest in the States, has announced it is buying Texaco Canada for almost $5 billion. The purchase will bring the number of Canada's oil giants down to three. These national integrated companies span the whole range from crude oil extraction to crude oil refining to pump sales of gasoline.

Concerns about high gasoline prices and collusion among oil companies re-surface with predictable regularity in this country. Almost every province and the federal government have, at one time or another, set up a commission to study the industry and to recommend corrective measures. But for one reason or another, little action has resulted.

The industry likes to present this lack of action as indirect proof that gasoline prices are competitive, and that consumers are served as well as can be. But, leaving aside complex indicators, even the simplest comparisons with prices in the US belie these claims. The Commission of Inquiry into Gasoline Pricing in Manitoba. . .found that gasoline prices not only did not fall fast enough and low enough in response to plummeting crude, but that gasoline prices are non-competitive on a more permanent basis. This sluggishness and permanent non-competitiveness cost Manitobans almost $3.7 million per month in 1986.

Taxes alone do not explain the higher Canadian prices. If, for example, we had bought our gasoline wholesale from Grand Forks, North Dakota, trucked it to Winnipeg and paid all federal and provincial taxes, we would have saved about 3.33 cents per litre or 15 cents per gallon at the pump, on average. This means that during the years 1986-88 the oil companies overcharged Winnipeggers by $62 million, a hefty sum by any standard!

Concentration in the oil industry is already high, and has been found to cost consumers millions of dollars. The purchase of Texaco by Esso means more concentration and probably more overcharges at the pumps. Can we do anything at all to rid ourselves of our misfortune?

Both consumers and government have a number of options in their defence against non-competitive business practices. Consumers can boycott; or they can search for bargain gasoline; or they can form cooperatives to get their gasoline cheap. Government can watch and block anti-competitive moves; or it can set up a Crown corporation as a "window to the industry"; or it can regulate; or it can attempt to enhance competition where possible.

Neither consumer action nor government intervention through legislation is a complete solution to the disease of non-competitive markets. These routes have their uses, but they simply do not go all the way to ensure that markets behave competitively, and they may even produce results opposite to the original aims. Nova Scotia, for example, has come to regulate the highest gasoline prices in the country. Petro-Canada, which was initially established to help shape government policy, has now been instructed to operate like any other major. It is least ironical that taxpayers' money was used to set up a corporation that would eventually overcharge consumers like the rest of the oil giants do!

The Manitoba commission avoided both the consumer and the legal routes and chose to recommend the option of market improvement, or market correction through policing. Let us see what this means.

To set the stage we must first ask: Why is the Winnipeg market itself not forcing the oil companies to price gasoline competitively? Simply put, our market is incomplete; if it had a few "market policemen" prepared to sell at competitive prices, everyone would follow, sooner or later, and prices would be proper. Not 44.5 cents/L in December 1988, but about 41.2 cents/L on average, for example. The lack of such market policemen has cost us an average of about $400,000 each and every week since January 1986.

But, welcome as they may be, these market policemen will not be forthcoming by themselves in our city; this is why the commission recommended that the government establish five of them, in the form of strategically located gasoline stations, and let them enforce competition through market action, not through legal procedure.

Contrary to reports that the commission suggested setting up a mini-Petro-Canada, the recommendations do not send the government into the gasoline business; on the contrary, they are explicitly designed to keep the government out of the market, where it does not normally belong. But, in the same way that governments set up a police force to make sure that no one breaks the law, the government would set up a small market police force to make sure that the market behaves. The police force would not be operated by the government, but by private lessee operators who would pay all federal and provincial gasoline taxes, and would also pay the government rent for the stations, in exchange for pricing gasoline competitively. The government would set up the stations to make sure that small competitive operators have a place to sell gasoline, without the risk of price wars that would be set off to teach them a lesson.

The extent of the government's involvement would be to select location, to set up the stations, and to lease them to businessmen or perhaps to such groups as the Manitoba Motor League or the Consumers' Association of Canada, which have the interests of motorists in mind. There its role would end. As for supply of competitive wholesale gasoline, this is easy and almost costless to organize, and it would ensure that the market policemen would not depend on the majors for fuel.

The plan involves two types of costs, which together amount to a maximum of $5 million. First, setting up these market policemen would cost no more than $1.75 million. Second, if the oil companies decided to declare a price war, these policemen would have to withdraw from their leases, at least temporarily. There would be little else for them to do, faced with the awesome financial power of the oil giants who can price the product below cost for any length of time without a dent in their overall profits. Because consumers would be enjoying the spoils of the war, the government would be left to cover basic expenses of the unrented station lots, like insurance and municipal taxes.

To cover these costs during price wars the government would need a maximum of $3.75 million. This is an absolute maximum, that would be put in a reserve to produce interest income to cover expenses. Only under the impossible condition of continuous price war year in, year out would the whole interest income be needed. And if so, consumers would be continuously enjoying low prices.

This, then, was a recommendation involving $5 million once-and-for-all costs and bringing $20 million of continuous benefits year after year with minimal government interference.

When the Manitoba report was released, concerns were expressed that the implementation of the recommendations involved risking taxpayers' money.

But there is a way to make this market police force pay for itself, very soon after it is in place. There is no risk in this procedure. This would mean that no taxpayers' money would have to be put up from regular budgetary sources, but the project would be funded by itself, first collecting the initial setup costs and returning them to government coffers, and then putting away the reserve amount.

This is easy to see when we recall that Winnipeggers, at 44.4 cents/L, are currently being overcharged by 3.2 cents/L, or by about $400,000 per week, or by over $1.5 million per month. If this money could be diverted away from the oil companies and to the government it would take just over three months to collect the necessary $5 million.

To do this the government would set up and lease the stations, so that they are ready to operate, and would at the same time place a temporary tax of 3.2 cents/L on Winnipeg gasoline for three months and a week. The gasoline policemen would then sell gasoline at 44.4 cents/L (since without the tax, they would have sold it at 41.2 cents/L) and the rest of the market would soon have to follow them. Consumers would be paying as much as before, but the overpayment which previously went to oil company coffers would now go to finance their market police. Once the amount was collected the tax would be repealed and prices would drop by 3.2 cents/L to 41.2 cents/L. Thereafter, consumers would go on enjoying continuously competitive gasoline prices.

These recommendations, then, go all the way towards permanent cure of the Winnipeg market from the non-competitive disease, mergers and other oil company strategies notwithstanding. Their implementation would cost nothing to the government and would lower gasoline prices soon after. The recommendations just require the political will to implement them. Or, shall we say that they need consumers to persuade the government to do so?

Source: Costas Nicolau, "How to Cut High Price of Gasoline," *The Winnipeg Free Press*, January 29, 1989, p. 7.

Questions:
1. Evaluate the service station proposal as a business venture.
2. If these stations were able to stay in business, would they have an effect on prices in the market?

Case 11-2

The Great Grey Wave

Seniors are an increasing proportion of the Canadian market. And businesses are finding that they are purchasers of many more products than medications and rocking chairs.

Consider the following facts:

- The size of the over-50 group jumped by 26 percent over the past 12 years and now represents 6.5 million customers.
- Customers over the age of 50 now control more than 50 percent of Canada's discretionary income.
- Canadians over 50 control 80 percent of the country's total personal wealth.
- They are among the largest consumers of magazines and newspapers.
- Older people tend to be shrewd and careful shoppers, but—once convinced that a product or service fits their needs—they will pay high prices with little hesitation.
- Canadians over 50 are among the heaviest consumers of expensive lifestyle products.
- 95 percent of advertising is directed at those under 50.
- Those over 50 spend more time examining the benefits and drawbacks of a product than their children do.
- Most people perceive themselves as being younger than they are. The over-50s do not perceive themselves as "old."
- 55 percent of those over 50 travel two or more times a year, often by plane.
- Second and third careers are common among older Canadians.
- It is estimated that by the year 2006—10 years after the oldest of the baby boomers begin turning 50—there will be 9.5 million Canadians over the age of 50.

Source: Patricia Chisholm, "Postponed Pleasures," *Maclean's*, January 9, 1989, pp. 24-25.

Questions:

1. Assume that you are a marketing consultant who specializes in market opportunities for the above market.
   a) What product strategies would be most appropriate?
   b) What kind of pricing strategies would you recommend?
2. List 10 products that you would make special efforts to market.

Chapter 12

Distribution Strategy

Learning Goals

I found the greater the volume the cheaper I could buy and the better value I could give customers.
—*Frank W. Woolworth*

1. To explain the value created by the distribution function

2. To identify the major components of a distribution strategy

3. To outline the various types of distribution channels

4. To describe how a vertical marketing system differs from a traditional distribution channel

5. To identify the various types of wholesaling middlemen

6. To discuss the role of retailing in the Canadian economy

7. To describe the different degrees of market coverage

8. To explain the role of the physical distribution function

Larry St. Cyr—*Building a Business Through Better Distribution*

He took the call on his cellular phone. "Larry, would today at 10 be okay?" she asked. "No problem," he replied. "Fine," she said, "the key will be in the usual place."

For Larry St. Cyr, class A mechanic and proprietor of Mobile Tune in Ottawa, this sort of request is all in a day's work. Another regular client has just confirmed an appointment for on-the-spot auto maintenance. When she returns from work in the evening, St. Cyr will have driven his specially outfitted van to her home, cast a trained eye over the whole car, changed the oil and filter, adjusted the tire pressure, and topped up all the fluids, for a total cost of $28.50.

No wonder demand for Mobile Tune is growing. Because of his low overhead, St. Cyr handles all the nagging necessities of car ownership at rates that are 30 to 40 percent less than those charged by regular garages—and saves his customers the trip. St. Cyr estimates that 40 to 50 percent of vehicles are left at home during the working day so it makes sense that home is a good place to service them. However, he adds that some of his clients, many of them salespeople, have him fix their cars in the parking lot at work. "They need a car that performs reliably, and they haven't got time to wait for maintenance to be done at a garage."

St. Cyr now services between 300 and 400 clients within a 60-km radius of Ottawa, and can usually meet requests within 24 hours. As well as his full schedule of regular appointments (a full winter tune-up, including new spark plugs and fuel filter, costs less than $60), he also does emergency work.

Eight years in the armed forces gave 33-year-old St. Cyr time to learn his trade. After leaving the military, he spent five years in the service bays of two large dealerships. In 1985, he set up Mobile Tune from the trunk of his '78

Fairmont, and began working nights and weekends, while keeping his day job. Although he inquired about a start-up loan through the provincial government's New Ventures programme, he didn't qualify because he had no plans to employ any other staff immediately. So St. Cyr and his wife, Vickie, expanded the business with a $10,000 personal loan. After 18 months, he had a new van and was on the road full time.

When the year showed a profit, St. Cyr took the next step. He hired Len Vanier, another class A mechanic, and outfitted a leased van for him. With two men on the job, Mobile Tune grossed about $150,000 in 1988, and netted about $30,000. So St. Cyr is considering franchising, or establishing a permanent garage where he can also deal with the major problems he often diagnoses on his rounds.

Communication is what's made Mobile Tune a success in just three years, says St. Cyr. "I'm happy to have someone leaning on a fender talking to me while I work. In large dealerships, the service adviser is not a mechanic, and often the details the owner tells him get lost on the way to the mechanic." St. Cyr adds that his direct contact with his customers makes him more accountable. "Say a water pump goes. There's a three-month warranty on the part, but it shouldn't need replacing for years. If something happened to it, I'd replace it. I need that customer." A rare statement indeed to hear from a mechanic.

Source: Jackie Robertson, "Winners: He'll Fix Your Wagon on the Spot," *Financial Post Moneywise Magazine*, January 1989, p. 6.

The marketer of consumer products has to be very careful that the firm's carefully designed and priced products are marketed in the correct channel of distribution. Years ago, the choice of channels was relatively easy. Today, the development of shopping behaviour to match retail channels requires careful attention.

Shrewd shoppers speeding off in their BMWs from a ritzy boutique to the discount store for a door-crasher special on detergent are contributing to the widespread changes affecting Canadian channels of distribution.[1] Store designs are being revamped, companies are changing hands, and the newer upstarts have become a force to be reckoned with. One example is the marketing of toys. A toy manufacturer who does not have good representation in the relatively new Toy City specialty toy chain will be missing a substantial portion of the market. Similarly, producers of building supplies, clothing, and hi-tech products must understand the nature and dynamics of the distribution system.

After products are produced and priced, they must be distributed to the marketplace. All organizations perform a distribution function. McCain's products are distributed in supermarkets and convenience stores across Canada. Tickets for the symphony, rock concerts, or other types of entertainment are distributed through Ticketron and other ticket outlets. Public libraries use bookmobiles to distribute their services to residents in outlying areas and to others who cannot get to the library.

Objectives of Distribution Strategy

The distribution function is vital to the economic well-being of society, because it provides the products and services desired by the consumer. Economists often use the terms place, time, and ownership utilities to describe the value of distribution. They mean that the marketer contributes to the product's value by getting it to the right place at the time the consumer wants to buy it and by providing the mechanism for transferring ownership. Firms that do not perform the distribution function effectively usually become business failures.

Distribution also provides employment opportunities. Salespeople, check-out clerks, truck drivers, stevedores, and forklift operators are all involved in distribution. Others service the products through a distribution network. Most people involved in distribution are classified as service personnel: their role is to provide service to some other sector of the economy. A considerable part of the labour force is now involved in service-related occupations.

Distribution strategy is comprised of decisions about two major components: distribution channels, and physical distribution. Physical distribution is the actual movement of goods and services from the producer to the user. This involves many activities, including transportation, inventory control, materials handling, order processing, warehousing, and customer service standards. This topic will be discussed in more detail later in the chapter. Distribution channels are defined and discussed in the following section.

Distribution Channels

distribution channels
The paths that goods and title to them follow from producer to consumer; the means by which all businesses and public organizations distribute the products or services they are producing and marketing.

Distribution channels are the paths that goods—and title to them—follow from producer to consumer. They are the means by which all businesses and public organizations distribute the products or services they are producing and marketing.

They are constantly changing. New channels and marketing institutions replace older methods of wholesaling and retailing. An example of shifting distribution patterns in Canada is gasoline retailing. The number of service stations has dropped as a result of distribution shifts by major oil companies. Because of the valuable locations, the buildings left by these stations offer considerable marketing opportunities to other forms of retailing. Consumers now find garden shops, used-car dealers, fruit and vegetable sellers, animal hospitals, real estate offices, and fast-food outlets occupying these sites.

Hundreds of different channels are used to distribute the output of Canadian manufacturing and service industries. Canned food products usually go through wholesalers and retailers to reach the consumer. Some vacuum cleaners and encyclopaedias are sold directly to the consumer. No single channel is always the right one: channel selection depends on the circumstances of the market and on consumer needs. Channels for reaching the consumer may vary over time: for example, the channel for distributing vitamins has changed from drugstores only to include supermarkets. Channels shift, and effective marketers must be aware of consumer needs so they can keep their distribution methods up to date.

middlemen
Persons or firms, including wholesalers and retailers, that operate between the producer and the consumer or industrial purchaser.

wholesalers
Persons or firms who sell primarily to retailers and to other wholesalers or industrial users.

retailers
Firms that sell products to individuals for their own use rather than for resale.

industrial distributors
Wholesalers of industrial goods.

Middlemen are persons or firms that operate between the producer and the consumer or industrial purchaser. Such firms perform some type of distribution function and assist in the operation of the channel. Their distribution functions include buying, selling, transporting, and warehousing. The two main categories of middlemen are wholesalers and retailers. **Wholesalers** are persons or firms who sell primarily to retailers and to other wholesalers or industrial users; they do not sell significant amounts to ultimate consumers. **Retailers** are firms that sell products to individuals for their own use rather than for resale.

The primary channels of distribution are shown in Figure 12-1. Channels 1 to 4 are typically used to distribute consumer goods, while channels 5 and 6 are commonly used for industrial goods. Wholesalers of industrial goods are are often called **industrial distributors**.

Figure 12-1 The Primary Channels of Distribution

Consumer Goods and Services

1	Manufacturer			Consumer
2	Manufacturer		Retailer	Consumer
3	Manufacturer	Wholesaler	Retailer	Consumer
4	Manufacturer	Wholesaler / Wholesaler	Retailer	Consumer

Industrial Goods

5	Manufacturer		Industrial User
6	Manufacturer	Wholesaler	Industrial User

Fish wholesalers often buy fish from fishermen and then sell the fish to retailers and restaurants.

Channel 1. A direct channel from producer to consumer is used for all services but relatively few products. Users, in the case of products, include Avon, Fuller Brush, Electrolux, Amway, and many encyclopaedia publishers.

Channel 2. Some manufacturers distribute their products directly to retailers. The clothing industry has many producers who sell directly to retailers through their own sales forces. Some manufacturers set up their own retail outlets in order to maintain better control over their channels.

Channel 3. The traditional channel for consumer goods, distribution to wholesalers, is used by thousands of small manufacturers who cannot afford to maintain an extensive field sales force to reach the retailing sector. Some of these manufacturers employ technical advisors to assist retailers and to secure marketing information, but they are not directly involved in the selling effort.

Channel 4. A succession of wholesalers is common in the distribution of agricultural products—canned and frozen foods—and petroleum products—gasoline. An extra wholesaling level is required to divide, sort, and distribute bulky items.

Channel 5. The direct channel from producer to user is the most common approach to distributing industrial goods. This channel is used for nearly all industrial products except accessory equipment and operating supplies.

Channel 6. The indirect channel from producer to wholesaler to user is used for some industrial goods. It is also used for small accessory equipment and operating supplies that are produced in large lots but sold in small quantities.

Multiple channels. The selection of a particular channel of distribution depends on the market segment the manufacturer is attempting to reach. If the product can be marketed to more than one segment, then multiple distribution channels may be required. In fact, multiple marketing channels have become increasingly popular in recent years.

Tire manufacturers attempt to reach part of the replacement tire market by using wholesalers to distribute their products to service stations and independent garages. At the same time, they may operate their own chain of retail outlets to reach the rest of the replacement market. The original equipment market (OEM) is the automobile manufacturer, which is typically reached through the tire manufacturer's own specialized sales force. Still another direct channel is the institutional market, which includes government motor pools, taxi companies, and motor vehicle fleet operators.

Channels should be chosen on the basis of the markets they serve, with great care used in making this crucial marketing decision. Multiple distribution channels are likely to become even more widespread as marketers try to obtain a competitive advantage within selected consumer segments.

Channel Members Perform Vital Marketing Functions

Channel middlemen—including both wholesalers and retailers—perform various marketing functions. They store, transport, and distribute products, and they are often involved in grading and classifying bulk products. Middlemen also perform both a buying and a selling function. By buying a manufacturer's output, they provide the necessary cash flow for the producer to pay workers and buy new equipment. By selling, they provide consumers or other middlemen with want-satisfying products.

Middlemen are able to enter a channel of distribution because they can perform some activities more efficiently than the manufacturer or other channel members. Sometimes their efficiency wanes, and they are replaced by other channel forms. But the important thing is that someone must perform these vital marketing functions. Marketers considering a channel change should study the functions being performed in the channel and then assess how they would be handled in a revised distribution channel.

Table 12-1
Examples of Vertical Marketing Systems

Type of VMS	Description	Examples
Administered	Channel dominated by one powerful member who acts as channel captain	Kodak General Electric Corning Glass
Corporate	Channel owned and operated by a single organization	Tip Top Tailors Firestone Sherwin-Williams
Contractual	Channel coordinated through contractual agreements among channel members	Canadian Tire IGA Aamco Transmissions

Vertical Marketing Systems

vertical marketing system
Planned distribution system.

Distribution channels have traditionally evolved over time. For the most part, they were unplanned systems that changed to meet consumers' needs. In recent years, however, vertical marketing systems have become a popular distribution strategy concept. The **vertical marketing system**, or VMS, is a planned distribution system. Three formats are prevalent today: administered, corporate and contractual. Examples of each are shown in Table 12-1.

channel captain
A channel member who dominates the activities of a distribution channel.

Administered VMS. An administered VMS is a distribution system dominated by one channel member. This member, often called **channel captain**, can be either a manufacturer, wholesaler, or retailer. Traditionally, the channel captain has been the manufacturer who provides the promotional budget to support a brand. In other instances, giant retailers such as The Bay or Canadian Tire serve as channel captains.

Corporate VMS. A corporate vertical marketing system is one in which the channel members are owned by one enterprise. Consider the distribution channel for office equipment sold to small business. Both Xerox and IBM have selected a corporate VMS in this instance. Both have opened retail outlets to serve this market.

Contractual VMS. Contractual vertical marketing systems have had the greatest impact on distribution strategy. A contractual VMS is one in which the members are bound together by contractual agreements. A franchise like Century 21 real estate is a contractual VMS. So is a wholesaler-sponsored chain of retail stores like IGA Food Stores. A retail cooperative, in which retailers set up their own wholesalers, is another contractual VMS. Associated Grocers is an example.

Regardless of whether a traditional distribution channel or a vertical marketing system is utilized, middlemen are usually involved. The marketing intermediaries can be categorized as either wholesaling middlemen or retailers.

Wholesaling

Wholesaling is crucial in the distribution channel for many products, particularly consumer goods. Wholesaling middlemen perform a variety of marketing activities: storing, transporting, financing and the like.

Before we examine the different aspects of wholesaling, some important terminology needs to be defined. The term wholesaler refers to wholesaling middlemen who take title to the goods they handle. This marketing intermediary will more specifically be identified in the sections that follow as a merchant wholesaler. It is important to distinguish *wholesaler* from *wholesaling middlemen* because the latter category includes various agents and brokers who perform the wholesaling functions, but never legally take title to the goods. Figure 12-2 outlines the various categories of wholesaling middlemen.

Figure 12-2 Categories of Wholesaling Middlemen

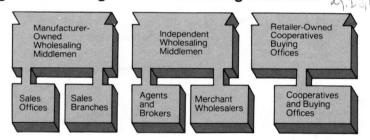

Manufacturer-Owned Wholesaling Middlemen

sales branches
Manufacturer-owned wholesaling operations that stock the items they distribute and process orders from their inventory.

sales office
Manufacturer-owned office for salespeople that provides close local contacts for potential purchasers.

Manufacturers' sales offices and branches tend to be large-volume middlemen specializing in complex, perishable, or intensely competitive products requiring considerable promotional efforts. **Sales branches** stock the items they distribute, and process orders from their inventory. They are common in the chemical, petroleum products, motor vehicle, and machinery and equipment industries. A **sales office** is exactly what it seems: an office for salespersons. Sales offices do not maintain inventories. They do provide a localized sales effort, with distribution being handled from warehouses located elsewhere.

Independent Wholesaling Middlemen

The second category of wholesaling middlemen, independent wholesalers, can be classified as either merchant wholesalers or agent

merchant wholesaler
Independent wholesaler who takes legal title to goods.

agent
Independent wholesaler who takes possession of the goods but not legal title.

full-function merchant wholesaler
Merchant wholesaler who performs many services in addition to taking legal title to goods.

rack jobber
A full-function merchant wholesaler who sets up and services a particular section of a retail store, e.g. magazines.

limited function merchant wholesaler
Merchant wholesaler who takes legal title to goods, but provides fewer services.

drop shipper
A limited-function merchant wholesaler who forwards orders directly to the producer for shipment to customers; holds legal title to goods, but never physically handles the product.

wholesalers. A **merchant wholesaler** takes legal title to the goods; an **agent** can take possession of the goods but not legal title. Agents usually perform fewer services than merchant wholesalers; they often act as sales agents.

Merchant wholesalers can be classified by the functions they perform. A **full function merchant wholesaler** performs a variety of services in addition to taking legal title to the products handled. A good example is a **rack jobber**, a firm that sets up and services a particular section of a retail store, e.g. magazines. A rack jobber sets up the displays, stocks the inventory, handles pricing, and completely services the rented space. A **limited-function merchant wholesaler** also takes legal title to the products handled, but performs fewer services. The ultimate example of a limited-function merchant wholesaler is a **drop shipper**. This wholesaler forwards orders directly to the producer for shipment to customers. Drop shippers who operate in industries like lumber and coal never physically handle the product, although they do hold legal title.

The second major category of independent wholesaling middlemen uses agents and brokers. Although these middlemen sometimes have possession of the products being sold, they never have legal title. Examples of these independent wholesaling middlemen include real estate brokers; sales agents of various types; manufacturers' agents, who sell noncompeting lines of several producers on a commission basis; commission merchants, who sell agricultural products for farmers; and auction houses.

Retailer-owned Cooperatives and Buying Offices

Some retailers have joined together to form their own wholesaling organization or buying offices. The objective is to reduce costs or to provide some special service not already available in the marketplace. These cooperatives were classified in the previous section as contractual VMSs.

Retailing

In the early sixties Kresge (K Mart since 1977) was a variety-store chain that faced the problem of deciding what direction to take in the years ahead. Kresge's president decided to take this firm down the discount-department-store path. Today K Mart is a leading retailer in Canada and abroad.

Many retailers seem to have had difficulty in matching the needs or keeping up with the constant changes that occur in the marketplace. Canada Safeway has had difficulty penetrating the central Canadian market. Department stores have lost ground to independent outlets and the chains specializing in clothing, furniture, and hardware. The result has been huge losses for companies like Hudson's Bay Co., which also operates Simpsons department stores.[2] Dominion has fallen prey to the rejuvenated Loblaws stores, which have opened super-combination stores that include large drug and hardware sections.

Retailers are the final link in the distribution chain. Because they are normally the only channel members with direct customer contact, it is essential that they change with the times and the environment in which they operate. Retailers are part of one of business's most dynamic settings, and special vigilance is required if they are to remain competitive.

Focus 12-1

Adaptability—The Key in Fashion Wear

When Alberta women's wear retailer B.J. Radomski faces an economic downturn, his firm seems to be able to adapt his nine-store Dori Lynn Fashions chain.

The secret to Dori Lynn's resilience, Radomski says, is adaptability. In a downturn, he believes women haven't stopped buying clothes—they're just buying fewer. A bargain is more important to them, he says, and retail outlets must respond.

Instead of Boxing Day sales, Dori Lynn has run store Boxing Week sales over the past couple of years. The traditional post-Christmas sales have turned into a "pre-Christmas markdown festival" that starts in mid-December.

By anticipating buyers' bargain-hunting, "you can work with it and buy for it," Radomski explains.

"Rather than reacting and being caught in the position where you have stock to the rafters, you pro-act and change your buying patterns."

The chain, which sells mid- to slightly higher-priced women's wear, also improved its efficiency three years ago by installing a computer system. The system links all nine stores with the main warehouse in St. Albert, northwest of Edmonton, where Dori Lynn opened its first outlet 17 years ago.

Radomski says the link allows the chain to adjust immediately to buying trends, re-ordering "hot" items and avoiding "clearance" items. It now buys fewer items, but makes more frequent purchases.

With the computer, Radomski says he can identify which store is having trouble selling a certain look. The chain can then move those items to another outlet where they will be more popular.

Such fast reactions are particularly crucial in highly competitive Edmonton, where Dori Lynn operates eight of its nine stores. Radomski says 300 new Edmonton stores have opened in the past three months, many of them selling women's apparel.

Radomski says that the Dori Lynn store in Fort McMurray is particularly sensitive to oil prices. "If I want to know what oil prices are, I just go to Fort McMurray and check my daily receipts. It's a fairly volatile market. You can't downplay the effect on the economy."

However, fluctuations in the oil price don't appear to have the same impact on the economy they did a few years ago.

"I still believe there are dollars being spent. It's not the 1970s again. We're not going through that boom, but we're working hard at what we're doing and we're seeing some positive results."

Source: Johanna Powell, "Adaptability: The Key in Fashion Wear," *The Financial Post*, November 21, 1988, p. 4.

Table 12–2
The Top 20 Retailers in Canada

rank by earnings

Rank by Net Income 88	87	Retailing	Net Income $000	% Change	500 Rank
1	1	Canadian Tire	124,873	26.4	40
2	2	Sears Canada	95,700	16.6	22
3	4	Provigo	60,200	−10.4	12
4	6	Oshawa Group	56,870	14.0	23
5	40	Hudson's Bay	49,172	n-p	19
6	7	F.W. Woolworth	48,202	44.6	49
7	3	Loblaw	40,800	−44.6	11
8	8	Finning	37,067	39.3	133
9	10	InterTAN Canada	35,388	60.7	243
10	41	Dylex	29,785	n-p	75
11	11	K Mart Canada	28,458	32.6	70
12	9	Gendis	25,821	15.2	151
13	35	Peoples Jewellers	16,888	n-p	470
14	13	Westfair Foods	16,460	9.5	66
15	15	Groupe Jean Coutu	15,467	39.2	229
16	14	Leon's Furniture	14,822	19.5	341
17	12	Kinney Canada	12,292	−25.9	185
18	17	Henry Birks & Sons	9,172	13.3	239
19	38	Grafton Group	8,334	n-p	158
20	16	Reitmans (Canada)	8,103	−14.2	253

Notes
n-p Net income negative in 1987, positive in 1988

Source: *The Canadian Business 500*, June 1989, p. 157.

Size of the Retailing Sector

There are approximately 166,000 retail stores in Canada.[3] Most of these stores are small, often having no paid employees other than the owner/manager. But others are big businesses, with millions of dollars in sales. The 20 largest are shown in Table 12-2, ranked by sales.

The Wheel of Retailing

Retail institutions are subject to constant change as new stores replace older establishments. This process, called the **wheel of retailing**, suggests that the retail structure is continually evolving as new retailers enter the market by offering lower prices through reductions in service.[4] Supermarkets and discount houses, for example, gained their initial market footholds through low-price, limited-service appeals. The new entries gradually add services as they grow, and they then become targets for competitive assault.

Today's attractive K Mart stores, for instance, offer good lighting, wide aisles, adequate paved parking, and services such as credit card purchasing. They are totally unlike those early discounters that often operated from Quonset huts set on unpaved lots in declining factory districts. Some retailers, however, do not survive the evolutionary processes inherent in the wheel of retailing.

wheel of retailing
Hypothesis explaining the evolution of retailing based upon new types of retailers gaining competitive footholds by emphasizing low prices in exchange for limited services. Over time, such retailers add more services, resulting in higher prices and vulnerability to new low-priced retailers.

Scrambled merchandising affects a variety of firms.

Source: Copyright 1983 Universal Press Syndicate. All rights reserved.

Scrambled Merchandising

scrambled merchandising
Practice of retailers who carry dissimilar product lines in order to preserve or increase sales volume.

Another factor that makes it difficult to classify retailers is the trend toward **scrambled merchandising**. Many retailers have sought to preserve or increase their sales volume by diversifying the products they offer for sale. Drugstores added soda fountains and then such items as magazines and newspapers. Now they are major retailers of cameras, greeting cards, cosmetics, and toys. Service stations offer an extensive array of products ranging from ice, soft drinks, candy, and milk to a complete mini-market. Some discount stores have added pharmaceutical departments. Supervalue is a grocery store that also carries hardware, automotive products, cameras, watches, and radios, as well as outdoor and yard-care products. In addition, dry cleaning outlets and opticians are located within the stores. The trend toward scrambled merchandising continues in all types of retailing (see Focus 12-2).

Focus 12-2

Cross-Merchandising Books and Food?

Doug Murphy started Chapters Bookstore Cafe in December 1986, with no food-service experience.

Set back from Toronto's Yonge Street in a streetfront-style mall, his unusual bookstore cafe did not catch the attention of the literati clientele he and his partner, Tim Snelgrove, meant to attract. A succession of one-customer nights led to a $150,000 loss on 1987 sales of close to $1 million.

But today, Chapters' 52-seat restaurant is jammed to capacity every Monday night with customers who've paid $14.95 for dinner and a chance to hear their favourite author speak. Even on an ordinary evening, 60 percent to 65 percent of the tables are filled. What has brought customers into Chapters are the books. They're on every wall and crammed spine to spine along the shelves. And although there are discreet signs discouraging customers from bringing tomes into the restaurant, restless browsers can page through "sticky-finger copies" at the bar.

Why the transformation? Murphy was so busy learning how to drive down high food and labour costs that he had little time to promote Chapters. It wasn't until he began cross-merchandising—using author events to attract restaurant clientele—that the business began to turn around. Buying a state-of-the-art computer to streamline book inventories and rallying staff also helped the cause. "A double business is complicated to run," says Murphy. "It's a definite liability unless you play one part of the operation off against the other." Adds Snelgrove: "There are six bookstores within three blocks of us. We'd never have made it in this area if we hadn't stuck a cappuccino bar in and served a lot of fettuccine and chicken."

Source: Joanne Sisto, "Catch 22," *Canadian Business*, Dec. 1988, pp. 23-24.

Focus 12-3

Retail Trends and Strategies in the Eighties

The following retail trends and strategies are forecast for the next decade.

- **Better market positioning**. This involves more careful identification of market segments and providing service superior to that of competition.

- **Market intensification**. This involves clustering more stores in the same metropolitan area and contiguous markets.

- **Secondary markets**. Expansion will be increasingly focused on secondary markets of under 100,000 population because there may be less competition from larger retailers, and costs, such as wages, may be lower.

- **Differences in store sizes**. Retailers will have a more flexible portfolio of different sized stores depending on the size of the community and existing retail competition. More use of second-hand space will occur because this can result in a savings of 30 percent or more in rent.

- **Productivity increases**. The application of central checkout, self-selection, and low gross margins to areas of trade where these techniques have not been used before. Look now at toy supermarkets, home-decorating centres, and self-service shoe stores.

- **Fewer product options**. Product lines will increasingly be consolidated, and new product development will be cut back.

- **Services growth**. Services retailing will continue to grow as a percentage of total retail sales. Services already represent about 50 percent of the gross national product.

- **More mergers**. Increasingly, smaller and weaker firms will be absorbed as more retail outlets struggle to survive.

Types of Retailers

While it is becoming more difficult to classify stores, the following general categories are usually acknowledged.

General stores.   The earliest type of retailers, general stores can still be found in some localities; they offer a wide variety of general merchandise.

Specialty stores, such as this stereo and sound equipment store, offer customers a wide selection of a particular type of product.

Department stores. Timothy Eaton opened his first store in 1869. He is known as the department store pioneer in Canada. The primary strength of department stores has always been the variety of products they offer. Large department stores provide over 200,000 items in many departments.

Specialty stores. Some retailers follow a marketing strategy of offering a complete selection in a narrow range of merchandise. By specializing their product offerings, they can concentrate on particular consumer segments and provide technical knowledge and/or services to those segments. Camera and jewellery stores are examples.

Convenience stores. Some retailers focus on convenient locations, long store hours, rapid checkout service, and adequate parking facilities. Local food stores, such as Mac's Convenience Stores, gasoline retailers, and some barber shops may be included in this category.

Chain stores. Chain stores are defined as two or more centrally operated stores that offer the same product lines. Chain organization is common among shoe stores, department stores, and variety stores such as the traditional five-and-ten-cent stores. Many major chain store organizations operate on an international basis.

Discount houses. Most retail discounters have emerged since World War II, traditionally offering lower prices and fewer customer services than other retailers. But, following the wheel of retailing pattern, some of yesterday's discount houses are beginning to resemble general merchandise retailers. Statistics indicate that discount houses are not a major segment of retailing.

Catalogue showrooms. Catalogue retailers send catalogues by mail to their customers who then may come to a showroom in which are displayed samples of some of the products. Customers select the product or products they wish to buy, and orders are filled from a backroom warehouse. Consumers Distributing is one such firm.

Supermarkets. Supermarkets are large-scale departmentalized stores offering a variety of food products including meats, produce, dairy products, canned goods, and frozen foods in addition to various nonfood items. Supermarkets operate on a self-service basis and emphasize low prices and adequate parking facilities. The largest supermarket chains in Canada are Provigo, Loblaws, Safeway, and Steinberg's.

Hypermarkets. Hypermarkets are giant food and general merchandise discount stores. These outlets offer one-stop shopping at discount prices. A typical hypermarket is like a shopping centre in a single store. The Hypermarché Laval outside Montreal was the first to open in Canada. There are more hypermarkets in Europe than in North America. This is probably because we already had many large, well-developed shopping centres before the hypermarket concept was developed.

Vending machines. Vending machines are an excellent method of retailing various types of consumer goods. Candy, cigarettes, soft drinks, ice, fruit, ice cream, chewing gum, sandwiches, coffee, milk, hot chocolate, and soup are all available through vending machines. Even entertainment has been packaged for vending operations, beginning with jukeboxes and pinball machines and progressing to the coin-operated video games found in a variety of settings today.

Selecting a Retail Strategy

Like other firms, retailers have to establish an effective strategy to reach the consumer. Retailers face a unique marketing environment since they have direct contact with consumers.

The starting point in developing a retail strategy is to identify the market target, the customers the firm wishes to attract. Various decisions must then be made about the firm's product/service strategies. These include product lines that will be carried, specific product selection, the level of merchandise assortment, and depth of backup stock. Pricing is another consideration. The firm's pricing strategy must be compatible with its market target and product decisions.

Location is the primary distribution decision made by retailers. Will they locate outlets in the downtown business district, major regional shopping centres, or smaller neighbourhood centres? Good location is often the difference between success and failure in retailing.

atmosphere
The image, amenities, and impression of a retail store that influence a shopper's behaviour.

Promotional strategy is also very important to retailers. Advertising must be correctly targeted, and sales personnel need to be well trained. But retailers also need to be concerned with **atmosphere**, the image, amenities, and impression that influence a shopper's behaviour. Again, these must be consistent with the rest of the retailing strategy. For example, the "flashing blue light" specials used by K Mart would be inappropriate for a retailer like Birks.

Market Coverage

There is probably only one Chevrolet dealer in your immediate area, but there may be several retail outlets that sell General Electric products. Coca-Cola can be found everywhere—in supermarkets, neighbourhood convenience stores, service stations, vending machines, restaurants, and coffee shops. Different types of products require different kinds of distribution coverage. Three categories of market coverage exist—intensive distribution, selective distribution, and exclusive distribution.

Intensive Distribution

intensive distribution
A strategy used to achieve saturation market coverage by placing a product in nearly every available outlet.

Intensive distribution is a strategy used by the marketer who tries to place a product in nearly every available outlet. Bread, chewing gum, newspapers, soft drinks, popular magazines, and other low-priced convenience products are available in numerous locations convenient to the purchaser. This kind of saturation market coverage requires the use of wholesalers to achieve a maximum distribution effort.

Exclusive Distribution

exclusive distribution
A strategy of giving a retailer or wholesaler the exclusive right to sell a product in a specific geographical area.

Exclusive distribution, the opposite of intensive distribution, occurs when the manufacturer gives a retailer or wholesaler the exclusive right to sell its products in a specific geographical area.

An exclusive distribution contract requires the retailer to carry an adequate inventory and provide the service facilities that might not be possible if competitive dealers existed in the area. Because the dealer has a guaranteed sales area, he or she is likely to make expensive investments in the business. In return, the manufacturer helps the dealer develop a quality image and promote its products effectively. For example, automobile companies give exclusive distribution rights to dealers.

Selective Distribution

selective distribution
A degree of market coverage somewhere between intensive and exclusive distribution; occurs when a limited number of retailers are selected to distribute a firm's product lines.

Selective distribution, a degree of market coverage somewhere between intensive distribution and exclusive distribution, occurs when a limited number of retailers are selected to distribute the firm's product lines. Television and electrical appliances are often handled in this manner. Manufacturers hope to develop a close working relationship with their dealers and often split advertising expenses with them. Extensive servicing and training facilities are also usually maintained by the manufacturer to help the retailer do a good job of distributing the product.

Physical Distribution

physical distribution
The actual movement of goods from producer to user; covers activities such as transportation, warehousing, and materials handling.

Physical distribution is the second of the two major components of distribution strategy. It involves the actual movement of goods from the producer to the user, which covers a broad range of activities including transportation, warehousing, materials handling, inventory control, order processing, and the establishment of customer service standards. Figure 12-3 shows the components of a physical distribution system.

The Physical Distribution Concept Helps Avoid Suboptimization

The study of physical distribution should include all factors involved in moving goods rather than concentrating on individual aspects of the process. Because the objective of physical distribution is to optimize the level of customer service, total costs should be considered.

Figure 12-3 The Physical Distribution System and its Interconnecting Components

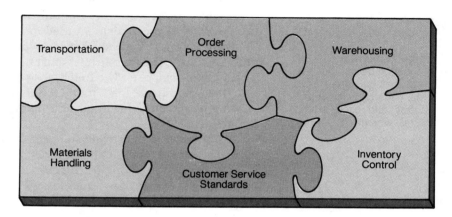

Physical distribution costs are often interrelated; a change in one element may affect other elements. Low inventory levels may reduce warehousing costs, but they can result in increases in transportation and order-processing costs. The total cost approach emphasizes the interrelationship of these costs in any physical distribution strategy.

Transportation

The form of transportation used to ship products depends primarily on the kind of product, the distance, and the cost. The physical distribution manager has a number of companies and modes of transportation from which to choose.

Transportation companies. Transportation companies can be classified into four basic types—common carriers, contract carriers, private carriers, and freight forwarders. A **common carrier** offers to perform services within a particular line of business for the general public. One example is a trucking company that handles general merchandise. Their trucks are available to serve all the people in the area who offer it general merchandise to haul. (It may decline to handle such dangerous items as liquid petroleum or aviation gas.) Examples of common carriers are Air Canada and Reimer Trucking.

Contract carriers transport goods for hire by individual contract or agreement. They do not offer to perform services for the general public; instead they usually offer services that meet the special needs of their customers. Contract carriers are most frequently engaged in business as owner/operator motor carriers. Usually they solicit large shipments from a particular shipper to a particular recipient.

common carrier
A transportation company that performs services within a particular line of business for the general public.

contract carrier
A transportation company that carries goods for hire by individual contract or agreement and not for the general public. Their services meet the special needs of their customers.

private carrier
A company that carries its
own property in its own
vehicles.

freight forwarder
A common carrier that
purchases bulk space from
other carriers by lease or
contract and resells this space
to small-volume shippers.

Private carriers transport their own property in their own vehicles. Examples are Safeway Stores, Petro-Canada, and mines that operate their own railways or ships.

Freight forwarders differ from the other carriers in that they do not own any of the equipment used in intercity carriage of freight. They are common carriers that lease or contract bulk space from other carriers such as the airlines and railways and resell this space to small-volume shippers. The freight forwarder picks up the merchandise from the shipper, loads it into the equipment of whatever carrier is being used, delivers it to its destination, and takes care of all the billing involved.

Freight forwarders provide shippers the advantage of better, less expensive service, and the carriers do not have to handle many small shipments and the billing for them. A further advantage of freight forwarding is that the forwarder knows at all times just where each piece of freight is while it is in transit. The addition of this middleman saves money for everyone and makes for improved service.

Transportation modes. The cost of using a particular transportation mode is usually related to the speed at which it operates. Fast modes typically cost more than slower ones.

Railroads. Of all domestic intercity freight, a little over 35 percent is carried by the railways, most of which are common carriers.[5] None are contract carriers. Railways are the most efficient mode for transporting bulk commodities over long distances.

Carload freight is the kind of freight railways prefer to handle. It is provided in shipper-loaded cars that are delivered to someone who will unload the cars, and thus costs less because railway personnel do not have to do the loading and unloading. Companion services to carload freight are containerization and trailer-on-flatcar (piggyback) services. Railways also offer trainload services to shippers of bulk commodities like coal and iron ore. Some trains of this type never stop: they use continuous loading and unloading equipment.

In their recent drive to improve standards and to capture more of the market, railways have put into effect some new services including run-through trains, which completely bypass congested terminals, and unit trains, which are used exclusively by a single customer who pays lower rates for each shipment.

Trucks. Highway transportation accounts for just under 25 percent of domestic freight shipping.[6] The principal advantage of highway transportation over the other modes of transportation is flexibility. A truck carrier can operate wherever there is a road, while trains depend on rails and aircraft on airports large enough to accommodate them. Highway carriers are divided into common carriers, contract carriers, and private carriers.

A number of highway carriers move freight thousands of kilometres. However, highway carriers are most efficient for distances up to about 500 to 700 km. For longer distances, railways are generally more advantageous.

The typical highway common carrier, with its own pickup and delivery equipment, picks up freight at the shipper's door and delivers it to a freight terminal, where it is loaded into larger trucks for delivery to a terminal in another city. There it is unloaded and delivered by smaller vehicles.

Contract highway carriers can frequently offer lower rates than common carriers because they serve a limited number of customers, deal in volume shipments, and operate only when they have a profitable load.

There are many private highway carrier operations. Wholesale grocery companies, supermarket chains, department stores, manufacturing establishments, and mining companies all engage in private-carrier operations when they transport their goods.

Water Carriers. Water transportation is one of the least costly of all modes of transportation. Great Lakes traffic is handled by specially built steamers, some of which are 300 m long. This low-cost type of transportation lends itself mainly to the hauling of bulky commodities. Ocean-going ships also operate on the Great Lakes, between Canadian port cities, and in international commerce.

Pipelines. Pipelines are second only to the railways in the number of tonne-kilometres transported. Pipelines convey primarily petroleum products ranging from crude oil to highly refined products and natural gas. They can transport many liquids and gases cheaper and faster than other modes of transportation. Focus 12-4 discusses possible future applications of pipelines.

Air Freight. While still dwarfed by other transportation modes, domestic air freight has become increasingly important in recent years. Air freight is usually limited to valuable and/or perishable products because of the mode's relatively high cost. For example, live lobsters are flown daily from the seashore to inland cities. Manufacturers ship critical parts to assembly plants by air. In some cases air freight costs are offset by lower inventory costs and more efficient manufacturing operations.

The certified airlines of Canada are all common carriers. Some of them (as well as a group of carriers known as supplemental carriers) engage in charter work, which is a form of contract carriage. Many business organizations own or lease aircraft that are operated to transport their personnel or, in some situations, their freight; this is defined as private carriage.

Warehousing

warehousing
The storage of products.

Warehousing is another important part of physical distribution and is involved in the storage of products. There are two types of

storage warehouse
A place used to store products for a relatively long period of time; usually used for seasonal products.

distribution warehouse
A place used to store products for a short period of time; usually used to gather and redistribute products.

warehouses: storage and distribution. **Storage warehouses** keep products for relatively long periods of time and are used most often for products that are seasonal in supply or demand such as farm products.

Distribution warehouses are used to gather and redistribute products. They try to keep products for as short a period of time as possible. They are mainly used by manufacturers that have several small customers in various, distant locations or by firms that have several suppliers in one area. Because the per unit cost of shipping small orders can be quite high, it is cheaper to ship a large quantity to a central distribution warehouse to be broken down into several smaller shipments and delivered to individual customers in the area.

Focus 12-4

Pipelines—An Alternative Distribution Mode

Liquids and gases have been the main commodities transported by pipeline. However, pipelines have the potential of distributing many other items as well. This basic idea is not new. Theoretically, any large bulk material such as coal, iron ore, sulphur, wood chips or grain can be adapted to a slurry pipeline system. The commodity concerned is pulverized and mixed with some liquid and moved in suspended state.

The various studies that have been done show that such a distribution system is possible but very expensive. The capital cost of building the pipeline would be in the billions. An Alberta government report, for example, estimated that the capital cost of a coal pipeline to the West Coast would cost $1.6 to 1.9 billion during the eight- to ten-year period from concept to operation. There are other technical problems to solve as well. On the other hand the idea still is attractive to some. For one thing, the western rail system can suffer unexpected capacity and bottleneck problems.

A variation on the concept is an urban freight pipeline system. The idea is to create a small pipeline using miniature carts to transport packaged goods and materials within a city. Propulsion would be provided by pressurized air. Optical scanners would identify a code on each package and then route it to a particular store's loading dock. This could be used in urban areas where traffic congestion is a problem.

Source: "Future Watch: A Look at What Might Someday Come Down The Pipe," *Canadian Business*, May, 1982, pp. 121-122.

Materials Handling

materials handling
The moving of items within the customer's warehouse, terminal, factory, or store.

Once a product has been transported from its place of manufacture to the customer, the physical distribution task involves moving the item within the customer's warehouse, terminal, factory, or store. This is known as **materials handling**.

Unitization and containerization have improved materials handling in many firms. **Unitization**—combining as many packages as possible into one load that can be handled by a forklift truck—is sometimes done with steel bands or shrink packing. In the latter case, packages are covered with a plastic sheet and then heated. When the plastic cools, it shrinks and binds the packages together.

unitization
Combining as many packages as possible into one load that can be handled by a forklift truck.

containerization
Putting packages, usually made up of several unitized loads, into a form that is relatively easy to transfer.

Containerization—putting packages, usually made up of several unitized loads, into a form that is relatively easy to transfer—has significantly reduced transportation costs for many products by cutting materials handling time, theft, insurance costs, damage, and scheduling problems. Containers are designed to be carried via rail, truck, or ship.

Inventory Control

inventory control
A physical distribution activity dealing with the controlling of inventory costs.

Inventory control is another physical distribution activity. It deals with the controlling of inventory costs such as insurance, taxes, storage, handling, and so on. The costs of holding inventory are now estimated at 25 percent annually.[7]

Order Processing

order processing
A physical distribution activity dealing with the actual preparation of an order for shipment.

Order processing concerns the actual preparation of an order for shipment. It is also included as an activity of the physical distribution function. Order processing is closely linked to the customer service standards that are set by the firm.

Establishing Customer Service Standards

customer service standards
The quantitative guidelines set by management for customer services.

Customer service standards are the quantitative guidelines set by management for customer service. For example, a firm may require that all orders be processed within 48 hours of receipt. Customer service standards like this are useful in measuring the effectiveness of the physical distribution system.

Controversial Issue

Keeping Control of Your Distributors?

A manufacturer develops a distribution system and associated policies as part of its marketing strategy. As time passes, competitive circumstances and business opportunities tend to change the focus of activities. As outlined below, Microsoft has chosen to cut off a top dealer and potentially forego its sales in order to maintain its distribution system. Might another company make a different decision? After all, a sale is a sale. Or is it?

Microsoft severs Businessworld ties over violation of distribution agreement.

The largest software company in Canada has cut off one of its top dealers, and its $2-million in annual sales, after learning that the dealer violated its distribution agreement.

Microsoft Canada Inc., a Toronto-based subsidiary of Microsoft Corp. of Redmond, Wash., did not renew its contract with Businessworld, a Toronto software dealer, when it expired on December 31. Businessworld projected $2-million in 1989 sales of Microsoft products.

The company was licensed to sell Microsoft software to corporate users but, in violation of their agreement, also sold to software dealers— in the process undercutting other companies in Microsoft's distribution system.

Microsoft Canada has contracts with 12 key dealers, allowing them to sell to users. It also has contracts with four major distributors, allowing them to sell to a network of about 2,000 resellers.

"Either it's good business or it's no business," said Malcolm MacTaggart, general manager of Microsoft Canada. Microsoft Corp. does not break out Canadian revenue in its financial reports, but Mr. MacTaggart acknowledged that Businessworld's $2-million estimate of 1989 Microsoft sales was an accurate number and made the company one of Microsoft's largest

Canadian dealers.

"The problem with Businessworld is that they were using their discounts to undercut distributors," Mr. MacTaggart said. "Because their overheads were considerably less, they were able to undercut the distributors in selling to those 2,000 reseller accounts."

Businessworld, which has total annual sales of about $50-million, halted the practice at Microsoft's request, Businessworld president Rod Hunter said.

"In the contract it is outlined that we are resellers to end-users, but it never explicitly said they'd discontinue the contract if we didn't follow the guidelines," Mr. Hunter said.

But Mr. MacTaggart said Businessworld was a repeat offender.

"We met with them in September and pointed out to them that type of activity wasn't permitted and if it didn't stop would be grounds for termination," he said.

Distributors and some dealers complained again in November that Businessworld was continuing the practice, Mr. MacTaggart said.

"We investigated again and got copies of invoices from various dealers, and the invoices were from Businessworld, so it was obvious Businessworld had continued to sell to the [resellers]," Mr. MacTaggart said.

Mr. Hunter said Businessworld got no warning "before they hit us with this bombshell.

"They never told us of this until they decided to do it," he said. "We were one of Microsoft's top resellers."

But Mr. MacTaggart said: "It's not so much the size or amount of revenue they were providing as the fact that some things are just basically right and wrong."

Source: Geoffrey Rowan, "Microsoft Severs Businessworld Ties Over Violation of Distribution Agreement," *The Globe and Mail*, January 19, 1989, p. B13.

Summary of Learning Goals

1. **Explain the value created by the distribution function.**
   The distribution function creates time, place, and ownership utilities. Marketers contribute to the product's value by getting it to the right place at the time the consumer wants to buy it and by providing the mechanism for transferring ownership.

2. **Identify the major components of a distribution strategy.**
   The major components of a distribution strategy are distribution channels (wholesalers and retailers) and the physical distribution function.

3. **Outline the various types of distribution channels.**
   Distribution channels are the paths that goods—and title to them—follow from producer to consumer or final user. Some channels are direct from manufacturer to consumer; others involve middlemen such as retailers and wholesaling middlemen.

4. **Describe how a vertical marketing system differs from a traditional distribution channel.**
   A vertical marketing system is a planned distribution system. This contrasts with traditional distribution channels, which were unplanned and evolved over time. There are three types of vertical marketing systems. An administered VMS is dominated by one channel enterprise. A corporate VMS is owned by a single enterprise. A contractual VMS is one in which the members are bound together by contractual arrangements.

5. **Identify the various types of wholesalers.**
   Wholesaling middlemen can be classified into three major groups. Manufacturer-owned wholesaling middlemen consist of sales offices and sales branches. Independent wholesaling middlemen consist of merchant wholesalers, who take title to the goods, and agents and brokers, who do not. Merchant wholesalers can be further classified into full-function or limited-function. Agents and brokers consist of brokers, selling agents, manufacturers' agents, commission merchants, and auction houses.

6. **Discuss the role of retailing in the Canadian economy.**
   Retailers are firms that sell products to persons for their own use rather than for resale. Retail institutions are constantly changing. Two factors make it difficult to describe and classify them: the wheel of retailing and the trend toward scrambled merchandising. Retailers fall into several general categories: general stores, department stores, specialty stores, convenience stores, chain stores, discount houses, vending machines, supermarkets, and hypermarkets.

7. **Describe the different degrees of market coverage.**
   Three categories of market coverage exist: (1) intensive distribution, in which products are placed in many outlets; (2) exclusive

distribution, in which a firm has exclusive marketing rights in a certain geographical area; and (3) selective distribution, in which a limited number of retailers distribute a firm's products.

8. **Explain the role of the physical distribution function.**
Physical distribution is an important part of distribution strategy. Because its objective is to maximize the level of customer service, marketers must consider total costs. There are various elements in physical distribution. They include transportation, warehousing, materials handling, inventory control, order processing, and customer service standards.

Key Terms

distribution channels
middlemen
wholesalers
retailers
industrial distributors
vertical marketing systems
channel captain
sales branches
sales office
merchant wholesaler
agent
full-function merchant wholesaler

rack jobber
limited function merchant wholesaler
drop shipper
wheel of retailing
scrambled merchandising
atmosphere
intensive distribution
exclusive distribution
selective distribution
physical distribution
common carrier
contract carrier

private carrier
freight forwarder
warehousing
storage warehouse
distribution warehouse
materials handling
unitization
containerization
inventory control
order processing
customer service standards

Discussion Questions and Exercises

1. Which distribution channel would you select for the following:
   a) an infant car seat?
   b) an income tax preparation service?
   c) Mack trucks?
   d) pears?
2. Describe a situation in which a company would decide to use multiple distribution channels. What generalizations can you draw from this example?
3. How can middlemen improve the efficiency of distribution channels?
4. Identify and discuss the various types of vertical marketing systems.

5. Differentiate between a wholesaling middleman and a wholesaler.

6. Identify some recent examples of the wheel of retailing and scrambled merchandising.

7. Explain how a retail firm develops its competitive strategy. Apply this discussion to a local retailer.

8. Which types of market coverage would be best for the following products:
   a) Rolls-Royce?
   b) bubble gum?
   c) men's cologne?
   d) bulldozers and other earth-moving equipment?

9. Outline the components of physical distribution. How are they related to each other?

10. Which transportation mode would you suggest for the following:
    a) sheet steel?
    b) natural gas?
    c) premium electronic components?
    d) breakfast cereal?

Case 12-1

Copp Builders Supply

Brayl Copp had a decision to make. He was paying more and more to stock the shelves of his four Copp Builders Supply Co. Ltd. stores in London, Ontario, and that meant his customers were paying more too. As a result, he was feeling the squeeze of competition from chains such as Beaver Lumber Co. Ltd., which, with 200 stores from coast to coast, could buy more cheaply than he could. Copp needed to do something to squeeze back. He could try to negotiate better deals with suppliers on his own but, with only four stores, he wouldn't have much leverage. Or he could join a buying group, an organization designed to give small operators the buying clout of the giants.

Buying groups are formed when entrepreneurs in the same field feel they can compete better by purchasing together. Some groups are big, some are small. Some only buy for their members, others provide a wide range of services. Whatever form they take, their popularity is increasing. "In this era of big chains and franchises, joining a buying group is becoming a common defence for smaller operators," says Kennedy Hardy, a professor of marketing in the business school at the University of Western Ontario in London. "Sometimes it's the only way they can compete. It's a matter of survival."

But, as Copp knows, the life of a buying group can be a hazardous one. A number of years ago, he paid $2,500 to become a shareholder in a building-supply group called Allont Ltd. Established in the mid-60s, the group prospered for more than a decade, even expanding into the manufacturing of interior doors and mouldings. Allont became a large concern, but the expansion-minded entrepreneurs running it reached too far. In 1979, with interest rates exploding and some members in dire financial straits, the overextended Allont collapsed.

Copp lost his $2,500 and more in the aftermath, enough to make him cautious when it came to joining another group.

Source: Marie Clarke, "Pulling Together," *Canadian Business*, November 1988, p. 28.

Question:
What should Mr. Copp do?

Case 12-2

William Neilson Ltd.

Every Jersey Milk or Sweet Marie chocolate bar consumed in Canada and abroad is manufactured in a factory with no warehouse space for storage. The chocolate factory is located in the centre of an old residential section of Toronto on a narrow street. Because there is no space, William Neilson Ltd. had to establish a warehouse 30 miles away in Georgetown.

Not surprisingly, transportation accounts for a significant slice of Neilson's costs. President Tom Lamont estimates that it accounts for six to eight cents of every sales dollar. Every working day the company must ship its finished product from the downtown factory to the outlying warehouse, which doubles as a distribution centre both for finished products and the raw materials needed to make the chocolate bars.

Gordon Ramm, vice-president of transportation, feels that the key to reducing costs and saving money in the trans-shipment of goods is "reducing all those empty miles," when a truck returns to the dispatch yard empty. The alternative is to back-haul; to make sure the company's transportation fleet does double duty. When the trucks go out with chocolate bars from the factory, they come back laden with sugar, cocoa, and milk.

This concept is not new in the transporation business, but whereas some companies might use it as an afterthought, Neilson has recognized that it is essential. This can be seen in the fact that Ramm holds one of the senior positions in the company, and meets regularly with the other vice-presidents of marketing, purchasing, finance, and personnel.

At one monthly management meeting, Ramm discovered that the marketing department was going to a firm in Syracuse, NY to test several brands of chocolate bars. Rather than simply expediting a shipping order, he pointed out that the company had a supplier in Syracuse who shipped cereals to Neilson by common carrier. Instead of looking at the problem from a sales standpoint, Ramm examined it from the company's total-cost point of view. The result was that Neilson's trucks delivered the chocolate bars and returned, whenever possible, with raw materials from their Syracuse supplier. By combining the two efforts they were able to save 40 percent on distribution costs.

Ramm realizes that he has to make the best of an inadequate system.

Source: "Neilson Sweetens The Margins by Slimming Down Transport Costs," *Canadian Business*, May 1982, pp. S117 and S121.

Questions:
1. Suggest other ways that Ramm might improve his physical distribution system.
2. Would it be possible for Neilson to continue developing transportation economies to the extent that it would be detrimental to profits? Explain.
3. Will Neilson's distribution strategy be appropriate in the long run? Explain.

Promotion Strategy

Learning Goals

1. To define the promotion mix concept
2. To identify the factors that influence the selection of a promotion mix
3. To contrast pushing and pulling promotion strategies
4. To discuss the objectives of promotion
5. To describe the different types of advertising
6. To identify the different advertising media
7. To discuss the various sales tasks
8. To describe the personal selling process
9. To identify the tools of sales promotion

Profile

Dave Nichol—*From the Worst Price Image to the Best*

Dave Nichol hadn't made a television commercial for Loblaw Companies Ltd. in four years, yet many viewers thought he still appeared regularly. It's a measure of the power of the medium. Of course, both Nichol and his French bulldog, Georgie Girl, were appearing in every issue of *Dave Nichol's Insider's Report*, an occasional advertising newsletter from the company.

It was Nichol's idea to go on television in the mid-70s. "The advertising agency," he says, "thought the CEO should be kept in reserve for a crisis situation." Nichol believed it was a crisis. "Loblaws had come out of the price wars of the early 70s with a high-price image. I viewed my key task as convincing consumers they were wrong about the Loblaws image."

Nichol's first script became a classic: "If you were president of Loblaws, would you go on TV and say you had the lowest prices if it weren't

true?" In subsequent ads he introduced No Name and President's Choice products. Georgie Girl first appeared in 1983. "Everybody just started talking about her," he says.

Loblaws eventually stopped using its ad agency and even built a small studio next to Nichol's office. "I would write an ad and go in and shoot, and we'd be all done within an hour," he says.

Nichol became somewhat of a celebrity. At one point, in a restaurant, he had to show his birth certificate to a couple squabbling over whether or not he was the real Dave Nichol. Then in 1984, the company promoted him and he stopped doing the ads. By then, he says, "we had gone from having the worst price image to having the best."

Source: Gerry Blackwell, "We went from the worst price image...," *Canadian Business*, November 1988, p. 100.

When news broke in February, 1986 that a suburban New York woman had died after taking a cyanide-laced Tylenol capsule, Canadian reporters rushed to their phones. Less than four years had passed since poisoned Tylenol capsules killed eight people in Chicago and Philadelphia—and threatened to kill the product as well until its manufacturer, Johnson & Johnson, quickly introduced much-publicized, tamper-resistant packaging. Could Tylenol survive a second disaster?

In two frantic weeks, Paul Mitchell, President of McNeil Consumer Products, Johnson & Johnson's Guelph, Ontario-based subsidiary, gave more than 300 interviews, carefully answering questions and highlighting decisive corporate action. Johnson & Johnson not only recalled all Tylenol capsules—some 850,000 in Canada alone—but also sacrificed an estimated $150 million (US) with its decision to stop manufacturing over-the-counter capsules entirely. In addition to the interviews, the company developed an extensive advertising campaign to tell the public what it was doing about the problem.

If past experience is any indication, the media blitz will pay off in consumer loyalty. Tylenol's share of the painkiller market plunged from a commanding 35 percent to just 7 percent after the 1982 deaths, but climbed back to 29 percent within a year—thanks largely to the candor of Johnson & Johnson executives, and their willingness and ability to communicate with the public.[1]

Most organizations use some type of promotion strategy to reach their goals. **Promotion strategy** is the function of informing, persuading, and influencing a consumer decision. It is as important to nonprofit organizations as it is to a profit-oriented company like Colgate-Palmolive. Some promotion strategies are aimed at developing *primary demand*—the desire for a general product category. For example, the suppliers and a retail jewellers' association might promote diamonds ("diamonds are forever") without reference to any particular manufacturer or retailer. But most promotion strategies are aimed at creating *selective demand*—the desire for a particular product or product line. Royal Trust's "What a financial partner should be" campaign is an example.

promotion strategy
The function of informing, persuading, and influencing a consumer decision.

advertising
A nonpersonal sales presentation usually directed at a large number of customers.

personal selling
A promotion presentation made on a person-to-person basis with a potential buyer.

sales promotion
A form of promotion other than advertising and personal selling that increases sales through one-time selling efforts such as displays, product samples, and demonstrations.

The Promotion Mix

Promotion strategy consists of three distinct components: advertising, personal selling, and sales promotion. Each of these components is important in developing a promotion strategy.

Advertising is a nonpersonal sales presentation usually directed at a large number of customers. **Personal selling** is a promotion presentation made on a person-to-person basis with a potential buyer. The third component of promotion strategy is called **sales promotion**. It is the form of promotion other than advertising and personal selling that increases sales through one-time selling efforts such as contests, cents-off coupons, product samples, and in-store displays.

promotion mix

A firm's combination of the three elements of promotion strategy.

A firm's combination of these three elements is referred to as its **promotion mix**. Different organizations employ different promotion mixes, but all are targeted at the consumer. For example, Great West Life does some advertising, but the bulk of its promotion mix is concentrated in its large sales force. By contrast, 7-Up concentrates its promotion effort in advertising around a pre-selected theme.

Selecting a Promotion Mix

Selecting the appropriate promotion mix is one of the toughest tasks confronting marketers. There are four considerations in determining the relative allocations of promotion efforts and expenditures among advertising personal selling and sales promotion. The first is the decision on whether promotion monies will be spent mainly on advertising or personal selling. (Sales promotion tools are used primarily to enhance and supplement the firm's sales and advertising efforts.)

A second consideration is the market served by the good or service. For instance, a drill press is sold to the industrial market (relatively few firms), so the manufacturer's strategy will likely emphasize the sales force. By contrast, Scope mouthwash is sold to consumers (too many customers to call on). Therefore an effective advertising campaign is necessary to consumer products like Scope.

The third consideration deals with the value of the product. Most companies cannot afford to emphasize personal selling in marketing a low-priced item, and instead choose advertising to promote goods like toothpaste, cosmetics, soft drinks, and candy. Higher-priced items in both industrial and consumer markets rely more on personal selling. Examples include time-sharing vacation condominiums and Boeing aircraft.

Finally, the marketer needs to consider the time frame involved. Advertising is usually used prior to a sales presentation. An effective and consistent advertising theme may favourably influence individuals when they are approached by a salesperson in a store. But except for self-service situations, a salesperson is typically involved in completing the actual transaction. Advertising is often used again after the sale to assure consumers of the correctness of their selection and to encourage repeat purchases.[2]

Alternative Promotion Strategies

The selection of a promotion mix is directly related to the promotion strategy that the firm will employ. The marketer has two alternative strategies available to meet these goals: pushing strategy or pulling strategy.

pushing strategy
A sales-oriented promotion strategy designed to motivate middlemen to push the product to their customers.

cooperative advertising
A sharing of local advertising costs for a product or line of products between the manufacturer and the middleman.

pulling strategy
A promotion strategy utilizing advertising and sales promotion appeals to generate consumer demand for a product as a means of exerting pressure on channel members to handle the product.

A **pushing strategy** is a sales-oriented approach designed to get promotion of the product, product line, or service through the efforts of middlemen (wholesalers and retailers). Sales personnel push the product by explaining to middlemen why they should carry and push it. Middlemen are usually offered special discounts, promotion materials, and **cooperative advertising** allowances to encourage them to do it. In the last case, the manufacturer shares the cost of local advertising of the product or line. All these strategies are designed to motivate the middlemen to push the product or service to their customers.

A **pulling strategy** attempts to generate consumer demand for the product, product line, or service, primarily through advertising and sales promotion appeals. Most advertising is aimed at the ultimate consumer, who then expects the retailer to carry the product or service; the retailer in turn requests the item or service from the supplier. The marketer hopes that strong consumer demand will pull the product or service through the marketing channel by forcing middlemen to carry it.

Most marketing situations require the use of both strategies, although the emphasis can vary. Consumer products are often heavily dependent on a pulling strategy, while most industrial products are sold through a pushing strategy.

Objectives of Promotion Strategy

Promotion strategy objectives vary among organizations. Some use promotion to expand their markets, others to hold their current positions, still others to present a corporate viewpoint on a public issue. Promotion strategies can also be used to reach selected markets. Chemical companies who produce fertilizer use farm magazines to reach farmers. An organization can have multiple promotion objectives. Most sources identify the specific promotion objectives or goals of providing information, increasing sales, positioning the product, and stabilizing sales.

Providing Information

In the early days of promotion campaigns (an era characterized by short supply of many items), most advertisements were designed to simply inform the public of a product's availability. Criers made public announcements of the cargo carried by vessels newly arrived in local ports. General stores on the frontier of a nation advancing westward inserted advertisements in weekly newspapers. These advertisements essentially listed the contents of the latest shipment from the East.

Today, a major portion of advertising in Canada is still informational. A large section of the daily newspapers on Wednesdays or

Thursdays consists of advertising that tells consumers which products are being featured by stores, and at what prices, for weekend shopping. Industrial salespeople keep buyers aware of the latest technological advances in a particular field.

Providing information about product availability, prices, and other details has always been of primary importance to marketing and promotion strategy. Marketers realize that nearly all promotion messages must have some educational role.

Focus 13-1

Positioning—A Means of Making a Product Relevant

Listerine Antiseptic, the solution that built an entire product category as the foe of that dreaded conversation-stopper—halitosis— is taking on a new mouth menace, dental plaque.

This new positioning of Listerine by Warner Lambert marketers is the latest wrinkle in the history of a product that began more than 100 years ago as a surgical antiseptic.

Throughout its century-long development, Listerine has depended almost entirely on advertising and marketing to keep itself up to date. Formulation of the product has changed slightly. (In fact, rumour has it that the word *halitosis* was invented by the advertising agency J. Walter Thompson to give an identity to the "ailment" Listerine was out to correct.)

"For a long-lasting product to remain successful, you need tangible reasons to keep using it," says product manager Katherine Macmillan. "Listerine is still first and foremost a mouthwash, and the fact that it helps prevent plaque formation is a secondary benefit." However, with the new plaque prevention claim, Warner Lambert hopes to get those people who know they don't floss and brush their teeth as often as they should to think of Listerine as a supplement to proper oral hygiene.

This latest repositioning of Listerine comes 106 years after it was formulated in St. Louis by a doctor and his pharmacist assistant, Jordan Wheat Lambert, a founder of Warner Lambert. It was distributed mostly by dentists as an oral antiseptic for use by patients until about 1914 when it became widely available to consumers.

Positioning strategies have gradually evolved over the years. It was positioned as an oral antiseptic until after World War II. In the late fifties and through to the seventies, as personal hygiene products grew, Listerine let in a newly developed mouthwash category. It was advertised as the product that "kills the germs that cause bad breath."

Source: Mark Smyka, "Listerine Takes a New Stance to Fight Dental Plaque," *Marketing*, May 27, 1981, p. 1.

Positioning the Product

positioning
The promotion strategy that concentrates on specific market segments rather than on trying to achieve a broad appeal.

Promotion strategy has been used to "position" a product in certain markets. **Positioning** is the strategy of concentrating on specific market segments rather than on trying to achieve a broad appeal. It requires the marketer to identify the market segments that will be likely users of the product. Promotion strategy is then brought into play to differentiate the item from others and to make it appealing to these market segments.

Positioning is also often used for products that are not leaders in their particular fields. Faced with a mouthwash widely accepted for control of bad breath but characterized by medicinal flavour, Scope offered itself as providing "minty fresh breath" instead of "medicine breath." Listerine's latest positioning strategy is that of mouthwash and reducer of dental plaque (see Focus 13-1). S.C. Johnson's handwarming product Hotshots has been positioned as an all-family product with a primary target of adults aged 18 to 49.

Increasing Sales

The ultimate promotion goal for most firms is increased sales, but there are other bases for positioning a product. In a classic promotion campaign Avis positioned itself against Hertz with the theme: "Avis is only number two in rent-a-cars, so why go with us? We try harder." More recently, Hertz has countered by stressing the advantages of its leadership position. It is difficult to contend that a particular ad itself created a sale, but these ads certainly contribute to the marketing programmes that ultimately result in sales.

Stabilizing Sales

Sales stabilization is another promotion strategy goal. Sales contests offering prizes (such as vacation trips, colour televisions, and scholarships) to sales personnel who meet certain goals are often held during slack periods of the year. Sales promotion materials—calendars, pens, and the like—are sometimes distributed to stimulate sales during off-periods. Despite shortages of antifreeze a few years ago, Union Carbide still advertised its Prestone brand heavily. Robert Cassidy, Union Carbide's marketing director, pointed out that a company should advertise when times are difficult: "We have a valuable consumer franchise and we don't intend to give it up as long as we can supply the product."[3]

A stable sales pattern allows the firm to do better financially in purchasing, and in market planning; even out the production cycle; and reduce some management and production costs. The correct use of promotion strategy can be a valuable tool in accomplishing these objectives.

Promotion strategy consists of three distinct elements—advertising, personal selling, and sales promotion. Each of these elements is important in developing a promotion strategy.

Advertising

Advertising was described earlier as a nonpersonal sales presentation usually directed to a large number of potential customers. It uses various media—newspapers, magazines, television, radio, direct mail, and outdoor advertising—to relay promotion messages to widespread markets. Newspapers receive the single largest share of total (national and local) advertising revenues. The leading national advertisers in Canada include the familiar names of the Government of Canada, General Foods, Procter & Gamble, Labatt's, and McDonald's (see Table 13-1).

Table 13-1
The Top 25 Advertisers in Canada

1987	1988	Company	Total ($000s)
1	1	Government of Canada	91,317.2
2	2	Procter & Gamble	58,624.2
3	3	General Motors of Canada	52,512.1
102	4	Gulf & Western	44,627.7
8	5	RJR	42,291.3
5	6	John Labatt Limited	42,106.0
9	7	The Molson Companies	41,172.1
4	8	The Thomson Group	40,184.5
337	9	Cineplex Odeon Corporation	38,851.5
10	10	Ontario Government	37,935.7
6	11	Unilever	36,254.9
14	12	McDonald's Restaurants of Canada	32,187.7
7	13	Chrysler Canada	32,056.1
11	14	BCE	31,831.0
12	15	PepsiCo	29,809.3
16	16	Imasco Holdings Canada	27,356.3
19	17	Coca-Cola	23,809.6
13	18	IXL Holdings Canada	22,986.0
22	19	Kellogg Canada Inc.	22,352.4
21	20	American Home Products	22,006.9
17	21	Ford Motor Co. of Canada	21,235.6
15	22	Kraft Limited	20,405.4
20	23	General Foods	20,045.6
29	24	PWA Corporation	19,193.7
18	25	Warner-Lambert Canada	19,130.4

Source: *Marketing*, April 10, 1989, p. 2.

Table 13-2
Percentage of Sales Invested in Advertising By Major Industry Groups

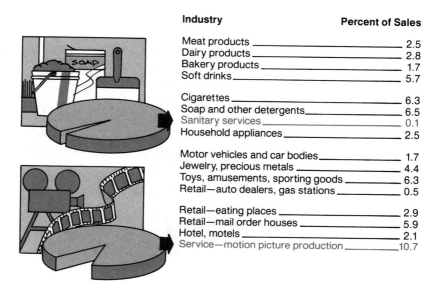

Industry	Percent of Sales
Meat products	2.5
Dairy products	2.8
Bakery products	1.7
Soft drinks	5.7
Cigarettes	6.3
Soap and other detergents	6.5
Sanitary services	0.1
Household appliances	2.5
Motor vehicles and car bodies	1.7
Jewelry, precious metals	4.4
Toys, amusements, sporting goods	6.3
Retail—auto dealers, gas stations	0.5
Retail—eating places	2.9
Retail—mail order houses	5.9
Hotel, motels	2.1
Service—motion picture production	10.7

Source: Schonfeld and Associates. Reprinted by permission.

Total Canadian advertising expenditures are estimated to exceed $4.8 billion annually.[4] This means that about $200 is spent in advertising each year for every person in Canada. The advertising expenditures for major industry groupings vary considerably, as Table 13-2 shows.

As can be seen from the table, advertising spending can range from one-tenth of 1 percent of sales in an industry like sanitary services to over 10 percent of sales in the motion picture production industry.

Types of Advertising

product advertising
The nonpersonal selling of a good or service.

institutional advertising
The promotion of a concept, an idea, a philosophy, or the goodwill of an industry, company, organization, or government entity.

There are two basic types of advertising—product and institutional. **Product advertising** involves the promotion of a good or service. Examples are advertisements by Pentax camera, Holiday Inn, or IBM Computers.

Institutional advertising involves the promotion of a concept, an idea, a philosophy, or the goodwill of an industry, company, organization, or government entity.

The challenge

In Brazil a tree is grown, and harvested after seven years. Sweden devalues its currency to improve the competitive position of its export industries. Other countries such as Chile, New Zealand, Argentina and Mexico increase their ability to make enough pulp and paper to serve their own needs and, in some cases, to sell to other nations. These new realities challenge the ability of Canadian producers to compete successfully in international markets.

But this is the world of pulp and paper in the 1980s; a setting radically different from the one so familiar to Canadian producers twenty years ago, when competition was less vigorous than it is today.

The need to be cost competitive internationally is the most important challenge facing Canadian pulp and paper producers, now and in the years to come. And the challenge is being met.

Research, advanced technology, and sophisticated equipment strengthen our competitive position. But these elements alone do not guarantee our success. We must also call on our ability to employ these tools in the most productive, efficient and skillful ways. And we must look to industrial, labour and political leadership to help create an economic climate that will foster the growth of industry through investment and, in the process, help to meet the competition worldwide.

These are decisive years for Canada's pulp and paper industry – our largest manufacturer and the leading contributor to Canada's balance of international payments.

To learn more about Canada's pulp and paper industry, write to Louis Fortier, Public Information Office, Canadian Pulp and Paper Association, Sun Life Building, 23rd Floor, 1155 Metcalfe Street, Montreal, Que., H3B 2X9.

⚠ The Pulp and Paper Industry of Canada

Some institutional advertising promotes the philosophy of an industry.

This is what insurance is all about.

Within hours after a series of tornadoes swept across Ontario Friday, May 31, a team of insurance people had put into effect the Claims Emergency Response Plan. This all-industry program, coordinated by Insurance Bureau of Canada, is designed to expedite handling of multiple claims.

By Monday morning a temporary office was functioning in Barrie to assist the representatives of individual insurance companies, who were already on the scene, coordinate the activities of adjusters, liaise with municipal officials and communicate with news media and the public.

Special facilities were established to appraise damage to automobiles. Agreements were reached with municipal officials to meet bylaw provisions. Lists of contractors were established. Special arrangements were made with moving companies for storage of furniture and appliances.

The result: within a few days, 22,000 individual claims were in process. By month end, final settlements had been made in thousands of cases and interim payments begun in most. Cost: $98 million for damage to property and $17 million for automobiles…a total of $115 million.

Canada's insurance companies, agents and brokers compete hard for your business. When emergencies arise, they cooperate to provide the help you need.

That's what insurance is all about.

Insurance CLAIMS EMERGENCY RESPONSE PLAN
COORDINATED BY INSURANCE BUREAU OF CANADA

Canadian Pacific Enterprises purchased a two-page advertisement showing all the different business sectors in which it is involved, and stating that "Canadian Pacific Enterprises is one of North America's largest resource asset management companies."[5] The Canadian Egg Marketing Agency spends considerable funds on advertising eggs, using the theme, "get cracking."

Advertising and the Product Life Cycle

informative advertising
The advertising approach intended to build initial demand for a product in the introductory phase of the product's life cycle.

Advertising strategy for a product varies according to its stage in the product life cycle (see Figure 13-1). **Informative advertising**, intended to build initial demand for a product, is used in the introductory phase of the product life cycle. The Australian Tourist Commission used an informative promotion campaign to get young Australians to explore their country. The campaign was based on a free, youth-oriented booklet, *Australia—A Land of Things to Do*, that listed hostels, places to crash, surfing beaches, and the like.

Figure 13-1
Relationship Between Advertising and the Product Life Cycle

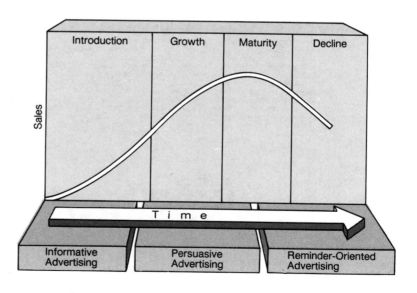

persuasive advertising
The advertising approach used in a product's growth and maturity stages to improve the competitive status of the product, institution, or concept.

comparative advertising
A trend in persuasive product advertising in which direct comparisons with competing products are made.

Persuasive advertising attempts to improve the competitive status of a product, institution, or concept. It is used in the growth and maturity stages of the product life cycle. "Save Money With a Carrier Heat Pump...Now!" is a persuasive advertising theme.

One of the latest trends in persuasive product advertising is to make direct comparisons with competitive products. The use of **comparative advertising** has grown very substantially. The Pepsi Challenge is an example of comparative advertising. Pepsi ads showed blind taste tests in which a majority of consumers chose Pepsi over Coca-Cola. Although Coca-Cola still leads the market, sales of Pepsi have increased considerably. It is uncertain at this point what the long-run status of comparative advertising will be in Canada and abroad, but its use has certainly changed forever the veiled comparisons that used to be made with Product X.

Reminder-oriented advertising is an attempt not to let a product name slip from consumers' minds.

reminder-oriented advertising
The advertising approach utilized in the late maturity and decline stages of the product life cycle that attempts to keep the product's name in front of the consumer.

Reminder-oriented advertising, used in the late maturity and decline stages of the product life cycle, attempts to keep a product's name in front of the consumer or to remind people of the importance of a concept or an institution. Soft drinks, electronics manufacturers, toothpaste, and oil companies are only a few products for which reminder-oriented advertising is used. Many ads seen on billboards are reminder advertisements. They are well-suited to dramatically present such a message. "Panasonic long life," and Safeway's "We bring it all together," are examples of reminder-oriented themes.

Advertising Media

All advertisers have to face the question of how to best allocate their expenditures. Cost is an important consideration. But it is equally important to choose the medium best suited for the job. All media have advantages and disadvantages.

Newspapers. Newspapers also account for 23 percent of total advertising revenue. Because newspaper advertising can be tailored for individual communities, local advertising is common. Newspapers also reach nearly everyone in the community. Another advantage is that readers can refer back to them, and that can be coordinated with advertising and merchandising efforts. The disadvantages include a newspaper's short life span, the speed at which they are read, and the relatively poor reproduction quality.[6]

Magazines. Magazines account for about 6 percent of advertising revenue. *Chatelaine* is the nation's largest magazine in terms of paid subscriptions. Advantages of magazines include selectivity, quality reproduction, long life, prestige, and the extra services that are offered to advertisers. The traditional disadvantage of magazines has been that they lacked the flexibility of other media, but the appearance of local advertising in various regional editions of national news magazines suggests that this problem is being overcome.

Television. Television ranks third behind newspapers (with 16 percent of total advertising revenue), but it is the leader in national advertising. Television advertising can be classified as network, national spot, and local. Television has significant impact on potential customers despite its high cost. Mass coverage, repetition, flexibility, and prestige are other advantages. In addition to high cost, its disadvantages include the temporary nature of the message, some public distrust, and lack of selectivity. Television is particularly effective in using the visual appeals of print media in combination with the sound of radio. McDonald's is famous for a continuous series of outstanding commercials.

Radio. Radio accounts for 9 percent of total advertising revenue. Advertising in this medium can also be classified as national or local. Radio's advantages are immediacy, low cost, practical audience selection, and mobility. But the radio audience is also highly fragmented. A radio message is only temporary and little research information is available to potential advertisers.

Outdoor Advertising. Outdoor advertising such as billboards accounts for approximately 8 percent of total advertising expenditures. Its strength is in communicating quick and simple ideas. Other advantages are repetition and the ability to promote products available for sale nearby. However, the message is limited by its brevity, and public concern has been expressed over the aesthetics of billboards in the environment.

Direct Marketing. Direct marketing includes direct mail, catalogues, telemarketing, and videotape "brochures." In total, it is now the leading advertising medium. Direct mail is its largest component and represents about 23 percent of total advertising. Its advantages include selectivity, intense coverage, speed, flexibility, complete information, and personalization. On the other hand, direct mail is an extremely costly medium. It is also dependent on effective mailing lists, and sometimes meets consumer resistance.

narrowcasting
Advertising on selected cable TV channels aimed at a particular audience.

Other Media Options. Marketers can also turn to some other more specialized media for their advertising programmes. One of the most popular is **narrowcasting**—advertising on selected cable TV channels aimed at a particular audience. For example, as TV channels are designed to specialize in sports, country music, etc., advertisers will be able to target their messages to these audiences.

Other media include advertising in movie theatres and on airline movie screens. Transit advertising is another important option in cities and regions with good transit systems. All of the alternative media can be employed separately or in conjunction with advertising campaigns using more traditional media.

Focus 13-2

Direct Marketing Takes Over

Direct marketing (DM) advertising expenditures in Canada have now surpassed those of newspapers, and have made DM the largest advertising vehicle in the country.

Although net advertising revenues in newspapers totalled $1.69 billion in 1987 (up 2 percent over the previous year), revenues in catalogues and direct mail had grown to $1.698 billion—up 8.1 percent over 1986.[1]

In fact, the Canadian DM industry is now growing at an average overall rate of 15 percent annually. Sales in the industry, which totalled $1.3 billion in 1981, had reached a new high of $5.4 billion by 1986.

Two major trends in the direct marketing industry are the rapid growth of business-to-business (B-to-B) DM and of telemarketing. Business-to-business DM now constitutes about 35 percent of the total market, and continues to grow steadily. Telemarketing is an organized information or selling campaign conducted by telephone and directed at specific target markets.

B-to-B direct marketing uses the new technology of telemarketing and video tape brochures in addition to the more traditional media of mail and catalogues to overcome the increasing costs of personal sales calls, and to approach a large and increasingly receptive market of businesspeople.

Telemarketing is itself one of the fastest-growing segments of the DM industry. With the new and rapidly advancing technology available to business, the potential of telemarketing is enormous.

Source: Terry Belque, "Telemarketing The Latest Trend," *Marketing*, July 18, 1988, p. 14.
[1]*Marketing*, February 8, 1988.

Personal Selling

personal selling
A promotion presentation made on a person-to-person basis with a potential buyer.

Personal selling is a promotion presentation made on a person-to-person basis with a potential buyer. Personal selling, the original method of promotion, continues to be essential in many fields.

The sales function of most companies is constantly changing. The image of the fast-talking, thick-skinned, glad-handing salesperson is passé. Companies have made significant changes in their sales forces. Sales duties have been expanded and in some cases the function itself has actually changed. The primary trend is toward increased professionalism on the part of sales personnel. Today's professional salespeople often know more about certain aspects of their customers' business than their customers. They act as advisers, helping their customers utilize more efficiently the items they buy.

Sales Tasks

A salesperson's work can vary significantly from one company or situation to another, but it usually includes three basic tasks—order processing, creative selling, and missionary selling.

order processing
The sales function of simply receiving and handling an order.

Order processing. **Order processing** involves the simple receipt and handing of an order. Customer needs are identified and pointed out to the consumer, and the order is processed. Route sales personnel for such consumer products as bread, milk, and soft drinks are examples of order processors. They check a store's stock, report the inventory level to the store manager, and complete the sale.

Most sales jobs have at least a minor order-processing function. It becomes the primary duty in cases where needs are readily identified and acknowledged by the customer. Consider Danny McNaughton's sales position in Belfast, Northern Ireland. McNaughton, while working for the Combined Insurance Company, sold 208 new personal accident income protection policies in a week, averaging one sale every 12 minutes of his working day, during one period of civil unrest.[7] Belfast residents readily acknowledged the need for McNaughton's product!

creative selling
A persuasive type of promotion presentation used when the benefits of a product are not readily apparent and/or its purchase is being based on a careful analysis of alternatives.

Creative selling. Sales representatives for most industrial goods and some consumer goods are involved in **creative selling**, a persuasive type of promotion presentation. Creative selling is used when the benefits of a product are not readily apparent and/or its purchase is being based on a careful analysis of alternatives. New product selling is a situation where the salesperson must be very creative if initial orders are to be secured.

missionary selling
An indirect form of selling where the representative markets the goodwill of a company and/or provides technical or operational assistance to the customer.

Missionary selling. **Missionary selling** is an indirect form of selling where the representative markets the goodwill of a company and/or provides technical or operational assistance to the customer. For example, many technically based organizations, such as IBM and Xerox, provide systems specialists who consult with their customers. These people are problem solvers and sometimes work on problems not directly involving their employer's product.

A person who sells a highly technical product may be doing 55 percent missionary selling, 40 percent creative selling, and 5 percent order processing. By contrast, some retail salespeople may be doing 70 percent order processing, 15 percent creative selling, and 15 percent missionary selling. Marketers often use these three sales tasks as a method of classifying a particular sales job. The designation is based on the primary task performed by the salesperson.

The Sales Process

canned sales presentation
A memorized sales talk intended to provide all the information that the customer needs to make a purchase decision.

Years ago sales personnel memorized a sales talk provided by their employers. Such a **canned sales presentation** was intended to provide all the information that the customer needed to make a purchase decision. The entire sales process was viewed as a situation where the prospective customer was passive and ready to buy if the appropriate information could be identified and presented by the representative.

Contemporary selling recognizes that the interaction between buyers and sellers usually rules out canned presentations in all but the simplest of sales situations. Modern sales personnel typically follow a sequential pattern, but the actual presentation varies according to the circumstances. Seven steps can be identified in the sales process—prospecting and qualifying, the approach, the presentation, the demonstration, handling objections, the closing, and the follow-up. Once again the type of sales work will affect the importance of each stage.

prospecting
The task of identifying potential customers.

prospects
Potential customers.

qualifying
A function of the sales presentation that enables the salesperson to identify those prospects with the financial ability and authority to buy.

Prospecting and qualifying. **Prospecting** is the task of identifying potential customers. They may come from many sources, such as previous customers, friends, business associates, neighbours, other sales personnel, and other employees in the firm. **Prospects**—the potential customers—must then be **qualified** with respect to their financial ability and their authority to buy. Those who lack the necessary financial resources or who are not in a position to make the purchase decision are given no further attention.

The approach. Salespeople should carefully prepare their approaches to potential customers. All available information about prospects should be collected and analyzed. Sales representatives should remember that the initial impression they give will often affect the prospects' future attitudes.

The presentation. The presentation is the stage where the salesperson transmits the promotion message. The usual method is to describe the products' or services' major features, highlight their advantages, and cite examples of consumer satisfaction with them.

The demonstration. Demonstrations allow the prospect to become involved in the presentation. They reinforce the message that the salesperson has been communicating to the prospective buyer.

Handling objections. Many salespeople fear objections from the prospect because they view them as a rebuke. Actually, such objections should be welcomed, because they allow the salesperson to present additional points and to answer questions the consumer has about the product or service.

The close. The close is the critical point in selling—the time when the seller actually asks the prospect to buy the product. The seller should watch for signals that the prospect is ready to buy. For example, a couple who start discussing where their furniture would fit in a house they are inspecting would be giving the real estate agent a clear signal to attempt to close the sale.

Several effective closing techniques have been identified. The salesperson can ask the prospect directly or propose alternative purchases. Or the salesperson may do something that implies the sale has been completed such as walking toward a cash register. This forces the prospect to say no if he or she does not want to complete the sale.

The follow-up. After-sale activities are very important in determining whether a new customer will buy again at a later date. After the prospect has agreed to buy, the salesperson should complete the order processing quickly and efficiently and reassure the customer about the purchase decision. Later, the representative should check with the customer to see that the product or service is satisfactory.

Sales Management

Consider a management problem faced by Great-West Life Assurance. It has a field sales force of about 900 representatives. The sheer size of this sales force triggers numerous questions about organization, personnel selection, training, motivation, supervision, and evaluation. But all sales forces, regardless of size, face similar problems, which must be solved if the sales force is to be truly effective and achieve the firm's promotion strategy objectives.

A company's sales function is supervised by multiple layers of sales managers. People are usually advanced to such positions from the field sales force. The sales management organizational structure follows a format along the lines shown in Figure 13-2.

Sales managers are required to perform various managerial tasks (see Figure 13-3). They must, for example, analyze the organization's sales personnel needs and recruit the appropriate number of candidates, who are then screened for eventual selection. Sales managers

**Figure 13-2
Typical Sales Management Organization for a Large Company**

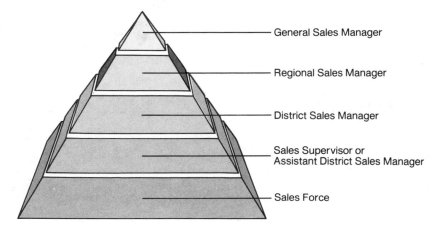

- General Sales Manager
- Regional Sales Manager
- District Sales Manager
- Sales Supervisor or Assistant District Sales Manager
- Sales Force

are closely involved in the training and development of sales personnel and in the organizational structure. Leadership and supervision are a natural part of the sales management role. Finally, sales managers must be involved in the evaluation of their sales forces and in making decisions on salaries, promotions, and dismissals. All sales management tasks are subject to the environmental influences that exist in competitive business surroundings.

Figure 13-3
The Sales Management Tasks

Environmental Influences

Analysis of Personnel Needs and Recruitment

Evaluation

Selection

The Sales Management Tasks

Leadership and Supervision

Training and Development

Organization of the Sales Force

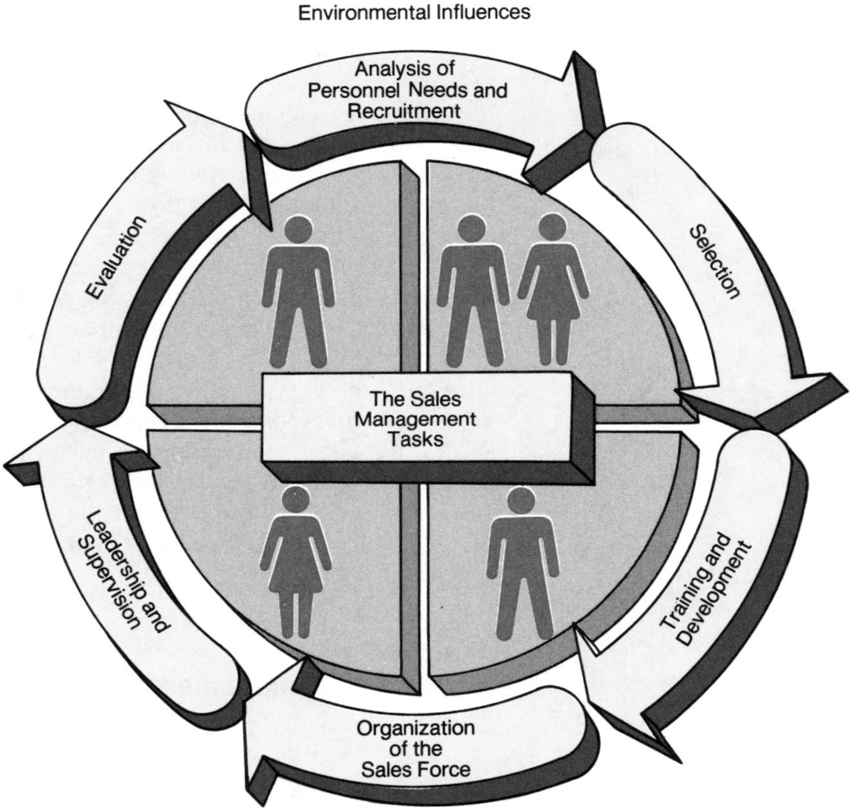

Focus 13-3

Revealed—Why People Say Yes

Psychological experiments have validated two of the oldest gimmicks in the salesperson's bag of tricks: (a) getting your foot in the door and (b) getting prospects to reject a Cadillac in order to sell them a Volkswagen.

In one classic 1966 experiment, homeowners were asked to display a Drive Carefully sign on their front lawn. Only 17 percent consented. A second group was asked to display tiny signs (the size of a business card) in their front windows. Later, this second group was asked to display Drive Carefully signs on their lawn; primed by the foot-in-the-door strategy of the window sign, 76 percent agreed.

In a similar experiment in 1976, researchers asked a group of college students to work a couple of hours at a community health centre; 29 percent volunteered. A second group was asked to spend two hours a week for the next two years at the centre. None volunteered. But when this group was asked to spend "a couple of hours, at your convenience," 76 percent agreed.

Alex Biel, executive director of San Francisco's Ogilvy Center for Research & Development, cited both experiments in a paper entitled "Why People Say Yes."

"The foot-in-the-door theory," he says, "is demonstrated by the fact that the best prospects for direct-mail solicitations are people who have responded to previous direct-mail campaigns."

The second experiment, Biel says, validates what he calls the door-in-the-face theory. One common application: retail markdowns. "The markdown is effective not only because it's less of an economic bite," says Biel, "but because it's perceptually seen as being a lot more attractive because the price was higher before."

Conclusion: social scientists are still asking the questions, but P.T. Barnum knew all the answers.

Source: Alexander Ross, "Revealed: Why People Say Yes," *Canadian Business*, October 1988, p. 12.

Sales Promotion

Sales promotion consists of the forms of promotion other than advertising and personal selling that increase sales through one-time selling efforts. Sales promotion techniques are used to enhance and supplement the firm's sales or advertising efforts. They are supporting aspects of a firm's promotion strategy.

Point-of-Purchase Advertising

point-of-purchase (POP)
A sales promotion that displays and demonstrates an item at a time and place close to where the actual purchase decision is made.

Point-of-purchase advertising (POP) includes displays and demonstrations promoting an item at a time and place near the location of the actual purchase decision, such as in a retail store. POP can be very effective in continuing a theme developed in some other aspect of the firm's promotion strategy. For example, the L'eggs displays in supermarkets revolutionized the pantyhose industry.

Specialty Advertising

specialty advertising
A sales promotion that consists of giving away items of nominal value imprinted with the donor's company name.

Specialty advertising is the giving away of items such as pens, calendars, and ashtrays—usually valued at less than $4—that are imprinted with the donor's company name. Specialty advertising has been around for centuries. Artisans in the Middle Ages gave knights wooden pegs bearing the artisan's name on which to hang their armour.[8]

Trade Shows

trade shows
A sales promotion that uses exhibitions designed to promote products or services to retailers, wholesalers, international buyers, and other resellers in the distribution channel.

Trade shows are often used to promote products or services to resellers in the distribution channel. Retailers and wholesalers attend trade conventions and shows where manufacturers exhibit their different lines. Such shows are very important in the toy, furniture, and fashion industries. They have also been used to promote the products of one nation to buyers from another. Eastern European countries have done this very effectively in recent years.

Samples, Coupons, and Premiums

samples
A sales promotion that uses distribution of free product gifts to gain public acceptance and future sales of a new product.

coupons
A sales promotion that uses advertising inserts or package inclusions that are redeemable for cash or a small price discount.

premiums
A sales promotion that offers small gifts to the consumer in return for buying a product.

trading stamps
A sales promotion that offers stamps that are redeemable for additional merchandise.

promotion contests
Sales promotion activities that offer cash or merchandise as prizes and are useful in getting consumers to consider new products.

Samples are free gifts of a product. They are an attempt to gain public acceptance of the product that will result in future sales. Samples are particularly useful in promoting new products. **Coupons** are advertising inserts or package inclusions that are redeemable by the customer for cash. Offering what amounts to a small price discount, they can be helpful in getting a consumer to try a new or different product. (See Focus 13-4.) **Premiums** are small gifts to the consumer for buying a product. They, too, are helpful in introducing a new product or getting consumers to try a different brand. **Trading stamps** are similar to premiums in that they are redeemable for additional merchandise. Historically, they have been used to build loyalty to a certain retailer or supplier. In Canada legal restrictions have rendered trading stamps virtually nonexistent.

Promotion Contests

Promotion contests offering cash or merchandise as prizes are also considered sales promotion techniques. Usually designed by specialists in this field, they are useful in getting consumers to consider new products.

Focus 13-4

A Marketer's Guide to Couponing—In and On Pack Coupons

Any in/on pack coupon redeemable on a product or brand that is different from the carrier product is classed as an in/on pack cross coupon.

The cross coupon has several very important advantages, the most important of which is that it is a very efficient and effective method of promoting product trial and inducing brand switching. In addition, with the possible exception of regular in/on pack couponing, in-pack cross couponing is probably the most cost efficient method of couponing available, in terms of cost per coupon redeemed.

In general, most cross coupons tend to achieve relatively high redemption rates and have low distribution costs. Since the cross coupon adds extra value to the carrier product in store at the shelf level, these coupons also give the potential buyer an extra reason to buy the carrier brand rather than a competing brand.

Because of these major advantages, many marketers actively look for other products to carry their brands' coupons, as well as for coupons for non-competing brands to carry on their own products.

The in/on package coupon's redemption rate is affected by the carrier product, as well as by other factors such as the coupon's face value, the couponed product and brand, and the valid term.

Typical redemption rates:

By Product Grouping	In-Pack Cross Ranges	Median Rates	On-Pack Cross Ranges	Median Rates
All Products	2.8%–20.2%	7.7%	0.8%–15.7%	4.4%
Grocery Products	2.9%–22.6%	10.5%	0.7%–15.5%	4.4%
Personal Care Products	1.2%–16.3%	4.8%	1.0%– 7.8%	3.3%
Pet Food Products	3.0%–16.2%	9.5%	2.7%–35.0%	10.9%

Controversial Issue

AIDS Ads—Is It Time to "Talk Dirty"?

Should government advertising "talk dirty" to get across its message on AIDS? AIDS advertising in Europe, aimed at "junkies," prostitutes and the rest of the "street" sub-culture, is far more explicit than anything seen so far in Canada.

The advertising used in some European settings is so explicit that in our setting it would be considered "coarse." Little is left to the imagination. Canadian authorities might argue that such explicitness is offensive to the Canadian public, and that Canadian ads are clear enough as they are.

Derek Cassels, editor of *The Medical Post*, disagrees with the Canadian approach.

"We hope that when the federal dollars are spent they are spent effectively and aimed at the proper targets—the young, the illiterate, and the poor.

"We need to be reminded there are thousands of people who have difficulty reading, who are strangers to terms we take for granted. To be faced with the possibility that a 14-year-old girl doesn't really know what the

term 'sexual intercourse' means amazes us. Yet we tell the same kid to be aware of 'body fluids.' If she doesn't know what 'sexual intercourse' means, how can she be expected to know that sweat is safe, but blood and semen are not. Does she know what semen really is?

"So as we move to educate the public about AIDS it would be better to assume that a high percentage of people don't have much of an education, medical or otherwise."

Question:
Mr. Cassels is familiar with medical issues and terminology since he is editor of a medical publication. Has he gone too far in his recommendations? Is it appropriate to break well-established principles of media propriety for such issues as AIDS education? If yes, what will be next? If no, are you satisfied with the way Canadian advertising is addressing the AIDS information problem?

Source: Derek Cassels, "AIDS Ads: Is it Time to 'Talk Dirty'?" *Marketing*, July 25, 1988, p. 4.

Summary of Learning Goals

1. **Define the promotion mix concept.**
   A promotion mix is a unique combination of the three elements of promotion strategy: advertising, personal selling, and sales promotion.

2. **Identify the factors that influence the selection of a promotion mix.**
   The first decision is whether to use advertising or personal selling. Sales promotion is a supplement to either strategy. The factors that influence the selection of a promotion mix are the type of product (industrial or consumer), value of the product, and the timing of its use.

3. **Contrast pushing and pulling promotion strategies.**
   A pushing strategy is a sales-oriented strategy designed to motivate middlemen to "push" the product to their customers. A pulling strategy utilizes advertising and sales promotion appeals to generate consumer demand for a product or product line.

4. **Discuss the objectives of promotion.**
   The objectives of promotion are providing information, positioning the product, increasing sales, and stabilizing sales.

5. **Describe the different types of advertising.**
   Product advertising involves the selling of a good or service. Corporate advertising—the major category—involves the promotion of a concept, idea, philosophy, or the goodwill of an industry, company, organization, or government entity. A special category of corporate advertising is advocacy advertising, which supports a specific viewpoint on a public issue. Both product and corporate advertising can be subclassified as informative, persuasive, or reminder-oriented.

6. **Identify the different advertising media.**
   Newspapers are the leading advertising medium in terms of advertising revenue. They are followed by television, magazines, direct mail, radio, and outdoor advertising. Other media include cinema and transit advertising. Each medium has specific advantages and disadvantages.

7. **Discuss the various sales tasks.**
   The three sales tasks are order processing, creative selling, and missionary selling. Order processing involves the simple receipt and handling of an order. Creative selling is a persuasive type of promotion presentation. Missionary selling is an indirect form of selling in which the representative markets the goodwill of a company and/or provides technical or operational assistance to the customer.

8. **Describe the personal selling process.**
   Personal selling is a promotion presentation made on a person-to-person basis with a potential buyer. There are seven steps in the sales process: prospecting and qualifying, the approach, the presentation, the demonstration, handling objections, the closing, and the follow-up.

9. **Identify the tools of sales promotion.**
   Sales promotion consists of the one-time selling aspects of a firm's promotional strategy. It includes point-of-purchase advertising (POP), specialty advertising, trade shows, samples, premiums, trading stamps, and promotion contests.

Key Terms

promotion strategy
advertising
personal selling
sales promotion
promotion mix
pushing strategy
cooperative advertising
pulling strategy
positioning
product advertising
institutional advertising
informative advertising
persuasive advertising
comparative advertising
reminder-oriented advertising
narrowcasting

order processing
creative selling
missionary selling
canned sales presentation
prospecting
prospects
qualifying
sales promotion
point-of-purchase (POP)
specialty advertising
trade shows
samples
coupons
premiums
trading stamps
promotion contests

Discussion Questions and Exercises

1. Suggest a product in each stage of the product life cycle and an appropriate type of advertising for each.
2. What promotion mix would be appropriate for the following products:
   a) arc welder?
   b) personal computer?
   c) specialty steel products sold to manufacturers?
   d) legal services?
3. Differentiate between a pushing and a pulling strategy. Under what circumstances should each be employed?
4. Not all promotion efforts are aimed at increasing sales. What other goals can be accomplished with promotion? Why?
5. Relate the various types of advertising used in modern business to the product life cycle. When is each type of advertising used?
6. How would you allocate the advertising budget for the following to the various media:
   a) IBM personal computer?
   b) American Express Gold Card?
   c) Liberal candidate seeking election to Parliament?
   d) Sony Walkman?
7. What is the primary sales task involved in the following occupations:
   a) office supply salesperson selling to local business firms?
   b) counter person at Wendy's?
   c) representative for an outdoor advertising firm?
   d) industrial salesperson representing Dow Chemical?

8. Divide the class into three groups. Then set up a role-playing exercise in which the student in Group A sells a product to someone in Group B. Group C is responsible for providing a critique of each of the sales interviews. Then rotate the roles among the three groups. Continue this process, for three rounds, so everyone will have a chance to play each role.

9. Discuss some ways in which the following companies might use a coupon promotion combined with its other promotion activities:
   a) Avis rent-a-car.
   b) Black and Decker (electric drills).
   c) Window manufacturer.
   d) Stereo set manufacturer.

10. What type of sales promotion technique, if any, would you use in the following businesses:
   a) independent insurance agency?
   b) Saab dealership?
   c) pizza restaurant?
   d) hardware wholesaling?

Case 13-1

Meadowlands Investments

Meadowlands Investments specializes in shopping centre developments. They are well financed, and have formulated a strategy of developing mid-sized shopping centres. These are modern facilities, with enclosed malls. The company has always been able to attract a large grocery chain, as well as a department store of the nature of Woolco, Zellers, etc. as anchors to create a good traffic flow.

In addition to these main stores, the malls have a variety of clothing stores, eating establishments, and service outlets. The developers also include a cinema complex in the mall.

Three new malls are in the completion stages in the lower BC mainland, suburban Toronto, and Halifax. Since each is relatively near to universities or community colleges, it is felt that such students might be an important target market. This was reinforced by a recent market study which described the nature of the student market.

A Current Profile of the Student Market

Today's university/college student is the quintessential consumer—educated, brand-selective, image-conscious and somewhat materialistic. They're more concerned with their financial futures than were students of past generations, and are pursuing the degrees that will give them the most promising futures, the majors being business, marketing, engineering, and computer sciences.

According to Statistics Canada, full-time enrolment in Canadian universities during the 1986-87 academic year totalled 470,330 and in community colleges 319,360, a market segment of 789,960, the majority of which is between the ages of 18-24 years, composing 5 percent of the adult population.

A 1985 survey for Campus Plus (Canadian University Press Media Services, Toronto, representing a network of campus newspapers across Canada) indicates an average personal income per Canadian university student of $5,809. Most are employed part time (75 percent during the summer and 44 percent during the academic year).

Three out of five students reside away from their parents' home (64 percent of university and 40 percent of college students). This, of course, varies on a regional basis: Maritimes 74 percent, Quebec 50 percent, Ontario 62 percent, Prairies 59 percent, and BC 50 percent.

Their dorm rooms and off-campus apartments/rooms are in effect "mini-households," where students first enter the world of independent decision-making, purchasing goods and services such as food, clothing, personal care products, sporting goods, travel, and banking. They are more consumer-conscious than students in the past.

Almost nine out of 10 look after their own food shopping (32 percent 1-7 times a week and 27 percent 2-3 times per month); 95 percent prepare meals (78 percent three times a week or more); 65 percent do their own laundry; and 72 percent purchase their own personal-care products.

Almost half shop around to take advantage of specials/bargains, and 54 percent have redeemed coupons in the past three months.

One-fifth of the students spend between $500 and $1,000 yearly on clothes, and about half spend between $200 and $500.

Milk is a popular beverage with students (91 percent drink it daily), as are soft drinks (consumption of regular 80 percent, and diet 70 percent). The typical Canadian university student is as likely to be a regular drinker of liquor (60 percent) as beer (60 percent), and 75 percent quaff white wine on occasion.

Students take pride in their appearance: 91 percent use a deodorant/anti-perspirant, 75 percent hair conditioner, 57 percent medicated skin care products and 54 percent facial moisturizer.

Social life centres around frequent attendance at movies (97 percent), parties (92 percent), pubs/taverns (87 percent) and friends' homes (74 percent visit once a week or more).

And they're an active group: 86 percent swim, 85 percent bicycle, 69 percent jog or run, 55 percent play tennis and 40 percent squash/racketball, 51 percent go downhill skiing and 49 percent cross-country skiing. Photography is a popular hobby with 63 percent, and 40 percent own 35mm cameras.

In terms of mobility, 84 percent have a driver's licence, 32 percent own their own car/van, 40 percent made one or more plane trips in the past year, and 40 percent have a passport. Slightly more than one-third have their own credit card(s).

Peer communication has consistently proven most successful in reaching this market, and print media, direct mail and promotion help create a buzz on campus.

Because of their active lives, students are harder to reach by conventional advertising media. TV viewing is light (average hours tuned per week 10.6), as is radio listening (average hours tuned per week 14.2). However, seven out of 10 students read a daily newspaper, and almost two-thirds read their campus newspaper.

Consumer magazines do not fare as well, with *Chatelaine* having 22.2 percent coverage, *TV Guide* 18.2 percent, *Maclean's* 16.3 percent, *Time* 14.9 percent, and *Flare* 8.6 percent.

Source: Jo Marney, "Students—A Market Growing Up," *Marketing*, September 19, 1988.

Question:
Design a promotional campaign to attract university/college students to the new shopping malls. In your campaign suggest appropriate target markets, advertising themes, and advertising media. The firm has allocated a budget of $40,000 for the campaign in each region.

Case 13-2

Roberta Fashions

Roberta Morton was the owner of a ladies' clothing store in Penticton, BC. The store catered to a broad range of middle-income women over 20. Normally, Roberta advertised in the local paper, and on radio. The theme of the advertisements was normally "new items available," or "sales." Recently the following article challenged her to reconsider her current advertising strategy.

Raise That Consciousness

Adding value at the retail level will become one of the critical marketing factors of the next few years, a senior advertising executive says.

Peter Swain, president of Media Buying Services, Toronto, told a recent retail advertising seminar sponsored by *Flare* magazine, that adding value means adding satisfaction, enjoyment and reliability to the product, as well as adding comfort with the store to make a pleasurable experience out of purchasing.

Adding value, Swain said, is an "element that advertising happens to be quite good at."

But advertising must change to reflect an older, better educated and smarter public, and consumers are applying added "confidence increasingly to purchase evaluation," he said.

"The Canadian consumer is becoming more value-conscious. This seems to be a residual effect of post-recessionary thinking. This value consciousness and greater skepticism applies directly to advertising in a new attitude of 'Show me, don't snow me,' " he said.

Swain also told the seminar that the dramatic increase in working women was having a dramatic increase in retailing. Value consciousness for this group, he said, is derived from convenience and reliability.

Swain stressed consistency of communication as the most important factor in successful retail advertising. He also said that to work, the communication must reflect corporate strategy, be clear, be present at the right time and place, be distinct, be relevant, be "relatable" to the consumer and be believable.

He added that even the best advertising suffers from one major problem.

"It is extremely difficult to measure its effect at the retail level," he said. "As a result, it is often mistrusted and misrepresented.

"In most retailing, cause and effect is readily apparent. Advertising often cannot provide this direct linkage in an easily understood manner. It does require an inferential leap of faith, but not without some ability to measure progress."

Source: Margaret Bram, "Raise That Consciousness," *Marketing*, July 4, 1988, p. 16.

Questions:
1. How could Roberta apply the points made to her advertising programme? Be specific.
2. How might she "add value" through advertising?

Part Five

Information for Business Decisions

Chapter 14

Obtaining and Using Information

Learning Goals

Information is of two kinds:
we know a subject ourselves
or we know where we can find
information upon it.
—*Samuel Johnson*

1. To show the basis of information for management decisions

2. To distinguish between primary and secondary data

3. To outline the marketing research process

4. To identify the methods of collecting primary data and to indicate when they might be used

5. To explain some common methods of statistical analysis in the analysis of information

6. To outline the role of computers in management

7. To show the evolution of computers in processing and transmitting information

Profile

Ivan Fellegi—*Managing Canada's Largest Database*

The first Canadian census was conducted in 1666 by Jean Talon, the Intendant responsible for administering New France. Aside from tallying the results and keeping up with his other duties in the colony, Talon had to do most of the knocking on doors himself. More than 300 years later, the legions at Statistics Canada record and process amounts of information that would be almost unimaginable to Talon. And while the head number-cruncher isn't obliged to knock on doors any more, Chief Statistician Ivan Fellegi is hard at work bringing the agency into step with its modern clients.

StatsCan manages the census, and annually conducts some 500 surveys and releases hundreds of publications. Under Fellegi's leadership, the agency has evolved a new "corporate philosophy" that finds it leaner and more efficient, more willing and eager than ever to do business with decision-makers in the private sector. As a result of Fellegi's efforts, managers whose job it is to look forward for their firms are looking to StatsCan for accurate and objective information that counts on the bottom line.

Fellegi's drive to position StatsCan as a resource for business has been accompanied by his accomplishments on the global statistical front. He has helped shape the agency into a world leader and model for other countries such as China, which has sent six delegations to Ottawa in the past four years to see how it's done. A career civil servant, he joined StatsCan (then the Dominion Bureau of Statistics) as a self-confessed "superclerk" in 1957. He studied nights at Ottawa's Carleton University, where he earned his M.Sc. and Ph.D. while he worked his way up through the ranks. To him, running StatsCan is like managing any business. "When I took up my position as chief statistician, one of my first acts was to tell employees that they shouldn't feel threatened despite a drive to increase efficiency."

The bulk of StatsCan's raw data comes from telephone interviews and written surveys. The agency is keen to reduce the paperwork burden on respondents: since 1978 the number of questionnaires sent to small businesses has fallen by 50 percent and continues to drop. This is part of the drive to increase efficiency: better interviews with fewer respondents improve the quality of the sample. Quality, not quantity, provides a better product.

Fellegi is excited about the growing interchange between the private sector and the agency that has immersed itself in Canadian lives for almost 70 years. The federal government buys more than $15 billion a year in services from the private sector. Fellegi says he'd be happy to sell back information worth 1 percent of that amount. His message to the StatsCan legions from Ottawa headquarters is simple: "We run a world-renowned shop here. Talk to business and tell them we've got a great product."

And he's got numbers to prove it.

Source: Evan Thompson, "The Add Man," *Canadian Business*, December 1988, pp. 129-132.

The Basis of Management Decisions

Information comprises the building blocks of management decisions. Answers to such questions as "how will consumers like our product?" "where should we locate the new Harvey's franchise?" or "what price should we charge?" can be found through **marketing research**.

Accounting information is vital to the life of a business. It provides a scorecard of the financial transactions which have occurred, and enables managers to understand the current position and plan for future activities.

Statistical information must be organized and analyzed for optimum decisions. Management decisions are vastly improved by collecting, organizing, and analyzing pertinent information. This is no easy task. In each of the foregoing situations, considerable expertise is required. The entire process is facilitated by the many applications of computer technology.

Marketing Research

marketing research
Systematic gathering, recording, and analysis of data relating to marketing of goods and services.

Because business success hinges on positive market response to its offerings, marketing research has become an indispensable tool for many organizations. Marketing research is the systematic gathering, recording, and analysis of data about problems relating to the marketing of goods and services. After the research problem has been defined, the marketing research process starts with a search of **secondary data**. This is followed by the collection of **primary data**, then all data are analyzed and normally presented in a final report.

Secondary Data

Secondary data offer an extremely important source of management information. Secondary data are comprised of internal data and external data that have already been collected for other purposes. Although considerable amounts of data are available internally, even more are available from external sources.

Internal Secondary Data

internal data
Data generated within the organization.

Internal data are data generated within the organization. A tremendous amount of useful information is available from financial records. Data can be obtained on changes in accounts receivable, inventory levels, loans outstanding, cash on hand, customers, product lines, profitability of particular divisions, or comparisons of sales by territories, salespeople, customers, or product lines. These records provide important insights into business operations. And because they are collected on a regular basis, the information can be added to the firm's management information system (MIS) at a low cost (see Focus 14-1).

Although much of the internal information is financial, other kinds of information input are also available. The personnel department can supply data on employee turnover and on worker attitudes and suggestions. Quality control can supply information on the quality level of materials purchased and the rejection rate of products produced by the firm. Customer complaint letters can serve as another information input.

Focus 14-1

The StatsCan Catalogue—Order by Number

A trip to one of the Statistics Canada regional offices in St. John's, Halifax, Ottawa, Toronto, Winnipeg, Regina, Calgary, Edmonton or Vancouver can be like a trip to a nicely laid out, price-smart retail operation: one generally leaves with more goodies than orginally intended. It's best first to purchase the Current Publications Index. This guide briefly describes almost 950 publications on statistics ranging from demographics to sales of running shoes and is available for $10.

The Daily is the menu or official release vehicle of StatsCan data and publications. At a glance it provides important statistical information in advance of, or in conjunction with, its publication in full. A subscription costs $100 per year. *Infomat* costs the same and is published every Friday. It runs six to eight pages and complements *The Daily*, providing more in-depth analysis that focuses on recent trends.

A subscription to the *Canadian Economic Observer* is $200 for 12 issues, or $40 off the single issue price of $20. The *Observer* is a monthly compendium of up-to-the-minute data and includes all major statistical series up to two weeks before publication. The culmination of StatsCan's efforts is the *Canada Yearbook*. A Herculean feat of compilation, it is targeted at schools, universities, and businesses with library facilities. There is no area of Canadian endeavour not measured or documented in this tome, which sells for $49.95. The *Canada Handbook*, more general in scope and not as large, costs $51.

If your eyes tire after scanning the multitude of information, the telephone is a useful alternative. There is no charge for data gathered by phone, so long as the request can be filled in 15 minutes. A call to Advisory Services (found in the phone book's federal blue pages under Statistics Canada) may be all that's required to support sales projections or a request for a raise. The Teledaily, another free service, gives recorded information on labour force surveys, the consumer price index and new publications.

When the information is more difficult to track down and assemble, the agency's new cost-recovery plan kicks in. The minimum charge for researching and supplying relevant information is $25.

Another telephone service is Info Express, which for a minimum of $25 per month provides a dedicated phone line. It's as if you have your own consultant inside StatsCan, billing you at that $25-per-hour rate. You're billed once a month for their time and incidentals such as photocopying.

For more detailed needs, a StatsCan consultant can plug you into the Canadian Socio-Economic Information Management system. You can gain quick access to customized information on complex economic or demographic data and have it downloaded into your own system.

Regional offices offer another, very personal service. They will prepare an official letter on behalf of anyone hammering out a salary contract or moving arrangement with an employer (minimum charge: $10). It will confirm changes in the consumer price index, for example, to support a pay increase. In the eyes of most Canadians, when StatsCan puts its name at the bottom of a page of information, the debate on its accuracy ends there.

Source: Evan Thompson, "The StatsCan Catalogue," *Canadian Business*, December 1988, p. 130.

External Secondary Data

This is information generated outside the firm by sources other than the company itself.

Although considerable amounts of secondary data are available internally, even more are available from external sources. So much is available at little or no cost that the information manager faces the problem of being overwhelmed by the sheer quantity.

Government sources. The various levels of government are the nation's most important sources of secondary data; one of the most frequently used is census data. Although Statistics Canada spends large sums in conducting each census of population, as well as other statistics, the information is available for use without charge at local libraries, or it can be purchased on computer tapes for a nominal fee. The census of population is so detailed that population characteristics for large cities are available by city block. Data are available on age, sex, race, citizenship, educational levels, occupation, employment status, and income.

Statistics Canada also collects and publishes data on finance, commerce, manufacturing, construction, primary industries, transportation, employment, education, culture, health and welfare, and prices.

To help users find the right information the agency produces a guidebook, the *Statistics Canada Catalogue*. Businesses can subscribe to its publications in their particular area of concern. Firms may also subscribe to CANSIM (Canada Socio-Economic Information Management System). CANSIM uses government statistics and other data to create a computerized database that provides much significant information for business decision-making in such matters as overall size and regional distribution of the market, and trends in various segments. (See Focus 14-1.)

Provincial and city governments are still other important sources of information on employment, production, and sales activities within a particular province or city.

Private sources. A number of private organizations provide information for business decision-makers. Trade associations are excellent resource centres for their members. They often publish journals or newsletters containing information on production costs and wages in the industry and suggestions for improving operations. Advertising agencies continually collect information on the audiences reached by various media such as magazines, television, and radio.

Several national firms offer information to businesses on a subscription basis. The A.C. Nielsen Company collects data every 60 days on the sales of most products stocked in food stores and drugstores. The Conference Board of Canada publishes the *Handbook of Canadian Consumer Markets*. *The Financial Post* publishes an annual *Survey of Markets*, which provides extensive demographic and business data on provinces, cities, and counties. *Sales and Marketing Management* magazine publishes an annual *Survey of Buying Power*, which provides detailed information on population, income, and retail sales in cities and counties for each Canadian province and each state in the United States. Moody's, Dun & Bradstreet, and Standard & Poor's provide financial information about companies on a subscription basis.

Primary Data

Primary data are facts collected for the first time. Most primary data are collected by one of three methods—survey, experimentation, or observation. The choice depends on information needed, costs, and time.

Considerable expertise is required in collecting primary data. Many firms have research departments staffed with specialists in designing questionnaires, training interviewers, developing representative samples, and interpreting the findings of the research study. Other organizations hire specialized research firms to handle specific projects.

Survey Method

Three different techniques can be used in the **survey method**: telephone, mail, and personal interview. Each has its advantages and disadvantages.

The personal interview is the most expensive and time-consuming survey method. It calls for well-trained and well-paid interviewers and involves the expense of travelling to the respondents' locations. (In fact, the costs are so great that officials at Statistics Canada collected the majority of the 1986 census of population by mail.) Still, the personal interview is typically the best means of obtaining detailed information, particularly because the interviewer can explain to the respondent any questions that are vague or confusing. The flexibility and detailed information offered by this method often more than offset the time and cost limitations.

Telephone interviews are cheap and fast for obtaining small amounts of relatively impersonal information, but they must be limited to simple, clearly worded questions. Because many firms have leased Wide Area Telephone Service (WATS) lines, a survey of suppliers' opinions on, say, a proposed payment plan could be conducted quickly and at little expense. (WATS is a telephone company service that allows a firm to make unlimited numbers of long distance calls for a fixed rate per province or region.) Telephone interviews have two major limitations: (1) it is extremely difficult to obtain personal information from respondents, and (2) the survey may be biased because two important groups are omitted—those without telephones and those with unlisted numbers.

In order to develop a representative sample of all telephone subscribers, telephone researchers frequently resort to using random numbers. Here is how it might work. If, for example, a sample of 100 respondents was to be chosen from an area with a 269 phone number prefix, the researcher would develop a list of perhaps 125 four-digit random numbers. Such lists may be obtained from a relatively simple computer-programmed number-generator or from published lists of random numbers. The telephone interviewer would then dial the prefix and the first four-digit number on the list. If that number proved to be busy, the interviewer would simply move to the next number on the list.

Mail interviews allow the researcher to conduct national studies at reasonable costs. Personal interviews with a national sample may prove too costly, but mail interviews allow the researcher to reach each potential respondent for the price of postage. Costs can be misleading, however, because the rate of return of questionnaires in such a study may average only 15 to 25 percent, depending on the length of the questionnaire and on respondent interest. Unless additional information is obtained, through a telephone interview or other method, from those not responding the results could be biased; there may be important differences between the characteristics of the nonrespondents and those who took the time to complete and return the questionnaire.

Companies using mail questionnaires to collect data often try a variety of techniques to increase response rates. Some firms include research questions on warranty cards. TI Corporation received a 60 percent response to its questionnnaire to shareholders by printing the questions on the back of dividend cheques. Others use a coin to attract the reader's attention.

Questionnaires are used to record responses from mail and telephone surveys as well as personal interviews. Considerable care should be taken in designing the questionnaire in order to minimize respondent confusion. Most researchers pretest questionnaires to detect and correct problems before administering the questionnaire.

Focus 14-2

Research Report Translator

The failure to achieve a "meeting of the minds" between research specialists and users is often best seen in the technical jargon appearing in research reports. The following report "translator" has been circulating in business and academia for the past several years. Many of the phrases are quickly recognizable:

WHILE IT HAS NOT BEEN POSSIBLE TO PROVIDE DEFINITE ANSWERS TO THESE QUESTIONS...
The experiment didn't work, but I felt that I could still get "brownie points" out of it.
IT HAS LONG BEEN KNOWN...
I haven't bothered to look up the original reference.
IT IS COMMON KNOWLEDGE...
I heard it through the grapevine.
OF GREAT THEORETICAL AND PRACTICAL IMPORTANCE...
Interesting to me.
IT IS BELIEVED THAT...
I think.
IT IS GENERALLY BELIEVED THAT...
A couple of other people think so, too.
IT IS CLEAR THAT MUCH ADDITIONAL WORK WILL BE REQUIRED BEFORE A COMPLETE UNDERSTANDING...
I don't understand it.
CORRECT WITHIN AN ORDER OF MAGNITUDE...
Wrong.
MY APPRECIATION IS EXPRESSED TO BEVERLY KATZ FOR ASSISTANCE WITH THE RESEARCH PROJECT AND TO DAVID LEE FOR VALUABLE DISCUSSION...
Katz did the work and Lee explained it to me.

Experimental Designs

Information from all the foregoing methods can be influenced by extraneous variables, such as the surroundings in which the data were gathered (e.g. receiving a request for a telephone interview when eating dinner), or the interviewer's interpretation of an answer.

Experimental research designs attempt to overcome these problems. An experimental design might assess price sensitivity through simulating purchases of various items in a laboratory using a given amount of money. Such designs are difficult to set up in a realistic manner, and to control. Where they can be used, the information obtained is some of the most reliable primary data available.

Observation Method

observation method
A method of collecting primary data that involves studies conducted by actually viewing the actions of respondents either directly or through mechanical devices.

The **observation method** involves studies that are conducted by actually viewing the actions of the respondents either directly or through mechanical devices. Researchers sometimes watch the pattern grocery shoppers travel in a supermarket. Traffic counts are used to determine the best location for a new fast-lube station. Television ratings are determined by use of an "audiometer," a device that is attached to television sets to record when the set is turned on and which channels are being viewed.

Sampling in Marketing Research

census
A primary data survey in which all possible data sources are contacted.

sample
A representative group from which data are gathered.

probability sample
A representative group selected in a random way so that every member of the population has an equal chance for inclusion in the study.

Information is rarely gathered from all possible sources because the costs are too great. (If all sources are reached, the results are called a **census**.) Instead, the researcher selects a representative group called a **sample**. If the sample is chosen in a random way so that every member of the population has a known chance of being selected, it is called a **probability sample**. A quality control check of every hundredth item on an assembly line may give production control engineers a representative sample of the overall quality of the work. A random selection of student names from the list at the registrar's office will provide a probability sample of students at a college.

Comparing Secondary and Primary Data

The use of secondary data offers two important advantages over the use of primary data: lower cost and less time for collection and use. Even though some secondary data may require fees paid to the firm involved in the data collection, the cost is invariably less than if the user-firm has to collect the data itself. A considerable amount of time must be spent in determining information needs, identifying sources of data, preparing collection instruments, training researchers, and collecting and interpreting the data—all activities that are performed in obtaining primary data.

But the use of secondary data is subject to a number of important limitations. First, the information may be obsolete. The data provided by the 1986 Census of Population is already obsolete in many areas due to substantial population shifts since then. Second, the classifications of secondary data were originally collected for a specific purpose, and they may not be in an appropriate form for a particular decision-maker. For example, a retail merchant who is deciding whether to open a new store in a shopping mall may require information on household income for a ten-kilometre area, but the only available data may have been collected on a county basis. In still other cases, available facts may be of doubtful accuracy. Errors in collecting, analyzing, and interpreting the original data may make the information inaccurate. In all such instances, a firm may be forced to collect primary data. Even the accuracy of the 1986 census has been questioned on the grounds that data were not obtained from all members of the population.

Analysis of Information

The world is filled with statistics. The average family has 2.1 children. Heart disease is the number one cause of death. The last episode of the M*A*S*H series attracted the largest audience ever to see a single television programme.

When viewed as individual items such as hockey scoring averages or the quarterly earnings per share of a corporation, the term "statistics" refers to a collection of numerical data about some event, object, or individual. More broadly, **statistics** is the collection, analysis, interpretation, and presentation of information in numerical form.

statistics
The collection, analysis, interpretation, and presentation of information in numerical form.

It is not an overstatement to say that statistics, like accounting, is a language of business. Although business executives are not expected to be statistical experts, they must possess some familiarity with the basic concepts and terms used in this field.

Statistical analysis is used in interpreting data obtained from research investigations. There are many methods for analyzing statistical information. Among the most often used are array and frequency distribution and measures of mean, median, and mode.

Array and Frequency Distribution

array
A listing of items by size, from either the smallest to the largest or the largest to the smallest.

Table 14-1 is an example of secondary data from an auto manufacturer. The table shows total production of each auto model during a recent year. It is an example of an **array**—a listing of items by size, from either the smallest to the largest or the largest to the smallest.

Table 14-1
Passenger Car Production by Watuzi Motor Company

Rank	Model	Number of Units Produced (in thousands)
1	A	290
2	B	187
3	C	179
4	D	126
5	E	124
6	F	107
7	G	107
8	H	94
9	I	91
10	J	77
11	K	73
12	L	31
13	M	25
	Total	1,511

frequency distribution
The common practice of grouping data in a listing or graph to show the number of times each item appears in the data.

In order to increase the meaning of the statistics, it is common practice to group the data into a **frequency distribution**, which shows the number of times each item appears in the data. Figure 14-1 is based on data in Table 14-1; it graphically displays the frequency distribution of auto models and production levels. It helps summarize the data, pointing out that fewer than 150,000 units were produced for most of the auto models.

Figure 16-2
Frequency Distribution of Ford Motor Company Passenger Car Models

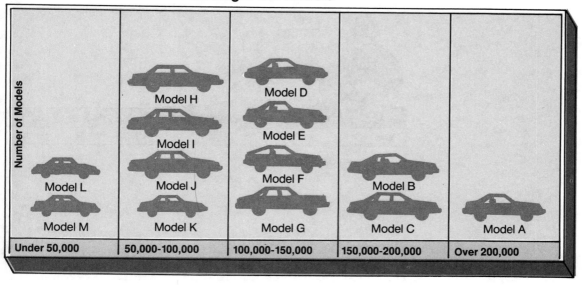

Averages

A useful method of summarizing a large number of observations or responses is through the use of averages. By reducing these data to a single summary statistic, a common denominator is created for use in making comparisons with other data. The three most commonly used averages are the mean, median, and mode.

Perhaps the most widely used statistical measure, the arithmetic **mean** (or average) is calculated by adding together all the observations and dividing by the number of observations. The mean number of units produced for each model in Table 14-1 is 116,231 (the 1,511,000 total divided by the 13 different auto models).

A second commonly used measure is the **median**, the middle score in the distribution. The median is the value that lies above half the observations in the distribution and below the other half. Because Table 14-1 contains 13 observations, the median is the seventh observation—the Model G line with 107,000 units produced.

A third measure is the **mode**, which represents the most frequently occurring value. As Table 14-1 indicates, two production lines—the Model F and the Model G—had identical production levels of 107,000 units.

Using Mean, Median, and Mode

Each of these measures has its limitations. Although the mean is the most commonly used, it is subject to distortions when extremely low or high numbers appear. Consider the data shown in Table 14-2. Six of the seven BC farms contain approximately the same number of hectares. When the mean number of hectares for all farms in this area is calculated, the large farm distorts the average size.

mean (average)
A statistical measure calculated by adding together all the observations and dividing by the number of observations.

median
The middle score in the distribution of observations.

mode
The most frequently occurring value in a series of observations.

Table 14-2

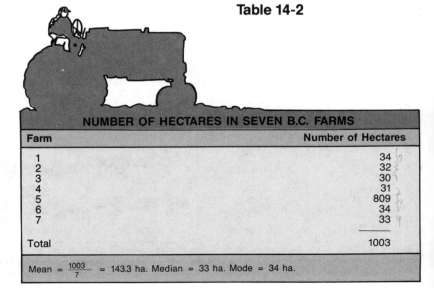

NUMBER OF HECTARES IN SEVEN B.C. FARMS	
Farm	Number of Hectares
1	34
2	32
3	30
4	31
5	809
6	34
7	33
Total	1003

Mean = $\frac{1003}{7}$ = 143.3 ha. Median = 33 ha. Mode = 34 ha.

The median and the mode can provide useful approximations of a "typical" measure in cases where extreme scores might distort the mean. For instance, the median is frequently used to estimate average income figures because of the presence of a few millionaires.

The mode is employed to determine the most commonly occurring measure. A travel agent may want to use the mode to plan a package vacation tour for the next season. By knowing last year's most popular vacation area, the agent is most likely to meet the desires of the firm's clients.

Focus 14-3

How to Lie with Statistics

Darrell Huff, the author of *How to Lie with Statistics*, argues that statistics can be used to sensationalize, inflate, confuse, mislead, oversimplify, and downright misrepresent information. He warns of four major pitfalls:

The Misleading Average. The word *average* may refer to the statistical mean, the median, or the mode. Suppose an executive claims that the average worker in the firm earns $25,000 a year. If $25,000 is the median salary, half of all employees earn more and half earn less. A $25,000 modal salary also provides some telling details, for it reveals that more employees earn that amount than any other. But if the average is the statistical mean, the true wage picture of the firm may be distorted. A few executives with $100,000-plus salaries will boost the lowly wages of most employees to the $25,000 average.

The Biased Survey. Statistics based on an unrepresentative sample are usually worthless. A classic presidential polling fiasco occurred in the United States when the *Literary Digest* conducted a survey of 10 million voters and concluded that Alf Landon would oust Franklin D. Roosevelt in a two-to-one landslide. How could they have been so wrong with such a large sample size? The *Digest* chose respondents from two sources: telephone directories and subscribers to the magazine. Apparently both sources were overrepresented by Republicans, since the Democratic incumbent was an easy winner.

Misleading Correlations. Correlations cause problems when cause and effect are read into them without supporting evidence. A children's breakfast cereal company may believe, for example, that its increased sales are produced by an attractive new package design. The true cause may be a large population increase or a growing trend to avoid other traditional breakfast foods (both bacon and eggs have received bad press in recent years).

Graphs that Fool. Graphs can be manipulated by the unscrupulous. When most trends are plotted on a graph, they form a modest-looking increase or decrease. But let's say the graph drawer wants to impress the viewer with the profit growth of a small firm that had seen profits increase by 10 percent per year over four years, then remain static for one year before again returning to the 10 percent profit growth for the previous year. If only the past two years of profit increases are depicted on the graph, the result is a stunning profit growth.

How can these distortions be uncovered? Huff recommends asking five simple questions:

1. Who says so? Examine whether the people creating the statistics have some vested interest—conscious or unconscious—that may distort the findings.
2. How do they know? Was the sample too small for conclusive results and were misleading averages used?
3. Did someone change the subject? Make certain that a proper conclusion is made from the data.
4. What is missing? Unreported facts can distort the meaning of any statistic.
5. Does it make sense? Application of a little common sense will often show a phony statistic for what it is.

Index Numbers

index number
Statistical tool for measuring the changes that take place in business activity or other variables over time.

An **index number** is a commonly used statistical tool for measuring the change that takes place in business activity or other variables over time. Index numbers are used to answer such questions as:

- How do this year's May 24th weekend traffic fatalities compare with those of 1975?
- How have prices changed over the past five years?
- How does the 1990 volume of stock traded compare with the 1980 figure?

Index numbers are useful in permitting the decision-maker to compare a complex set of current data with that of a previous time.

Although the construction of an index number is a complicated undertaking, the theory is relatively simple. A specific year or time period is chosen to serve as the *base* from which other comparisons are made. The base year is usually set at 100 and corresponding data for other years are expressed as a percentage of the base year. If, for example, 1985 was chosen as the base year and total company sales amounted to $200,000, changes in the sales in future years are reflected as a percentage of 1985 sales. An index number of 130 for 1990 indicates that 1990 sales are $260,000, or 30 percent greater than those for 1985.

Government statistics are often reported in terms of index numbers. Probably the most important single government index is the **consumer price index (CPI)**, reported monthly by Statistics Canada. The CPI is an index that measures the percentage change over time in the cost of a constant "basket" of goods and services purchased by the average urban Canadian family.

consumer price index (CPI)
Index developed by Statistics Canada to measure the average price changes for selected goods and services from month to month.

The index is based upon analysis of some 300 goods and services. Separate indices are available for major components, such as food, and for sub-components, such as dairy products. It uses 1981 as the base year, and is used as the Canadian inflation indicator.

Like any index number, the consumer price index is only as good as the components used to develop it. The choice of items in the "basket" is based on information gathered on the spending habits of Canadians through periodic Family Expenditure Surveys (FAMEX). If the FAMEX results indicate a shift to greater spending on a certain item, such as recreation, this item gains relative importance in its representation in the CPI. This process enables the CPI to be kept as relevant as possible.

The CPI has a direct or indirect effect on nearly all Canadians. Some of its uses include determining personal income tax exemptions, setting labour contracts, increasing unemployment insurance benefits, defining rental agreements, insurance coverage, maintenance, and child support payments.

Time Series Analysis

time series (trend) analysis
Statistical technique used in identifying and interpreting changes in business activity over time in order to serve as a basis for forecasting future business activity.

In attempting to determine the cause of changes in business activity over time, managers examine data in order to identify and interpret relationships. This process, called **time series**, or **trend analysis**, frequently becomes the basis for forecasting future business activity. Three types of fluctuations include seasonal trends, cyclical trends, and secular trends.

seasonal trend
Variations in sales or other business activities during the year.

A **seasonal trend** results from varying sales, output, or other activity during the year. Retail sales tend to increase prior to such holidays as Christmas and Easter. New-car purchases tend to be higher in October when most new cars are introduced. Sales of Campbell's soup tend to be higher in the winter than in the summer.

cyclical trend
Variations in sales or other business activities during the various stages of the business cycle.

A **cyclical trend** is a variation that takes place over a longer period of time and is related to periodic changes in economic activity. Periods of high economic activity, or prosperity, may be followed by recessions. Production tends to slow during recessionary periods and layoffs sometimes occur as manufacturers attempt to reduce costly inventories to match reductions in sales and new orders. As North America experienced in the thirties, recession may be followed by an economic depression. This low point of the economic cycle is characterized by high unemployment, low production, low wages, and a stagnant economy. As the economy begins to turn around, recovery occurs. Production begins to grow, laid-off workers are recalled, new employees are hired, and sales begin to increase.

secular trend
General long-term growth or decline of specific firms, industries, or the nation as a whole; may extend over several business cycles.

The final type of fluctuation, the **secular trend**, is a general long-term growth or decline of specific firms, industries, or the nation as a whole. Secular trends may extend over several business cycles, as was the case in the decline of rail transportation, which has been declining over the past fifty years. During the same period, the growth in air passenger service has continued. Such trends are particularly useful in developing future forecasts and in making plans designed to take these expected changes into account.

Correlation Analysis

While the mean, median, and mode are useful in summarizing data, and index numbers and time series analysis are effective in measuring, interpreting, and predicting changes in economic activity over time, managers need methods of determining variables that can be used in predicting events such as sales. What is the relationship between television advertising and sales? Will relocation in a shopping centre result in more store customer traffic than a freestanding store? Answers to these and other important questions may be found by using a technique called correlation analysis.

Correlation analysis is a statistical technique used to measure the relationship between two or more variables. If a firm finds that sales increase with increases in television advertising, this would indicate *positive correlation*. A cable television company research study reporting that people who regularly attend movies are less likely to be cable TV subscribers than those who only rarely go to movies would indicate *negative correlation* between these two variables. Other studies may indicate *zero*, or *no, correlation* between such variables as the relationship between the amount of carrot consumption and night vision. Figure 14-2 illustrates the different types of correlation.

correlation analysis
Statistical technique used to measure the relationship between two or more variables; can be positive, negative, or nonexistent.

Figure 14-2
Examples of Positive, Negative, and Zero Correlation

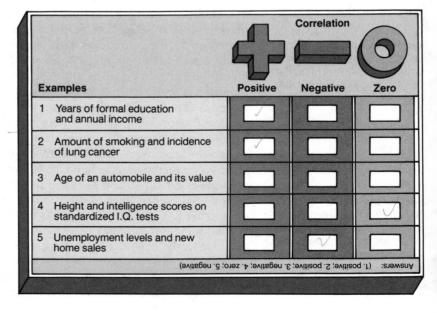

Examples	Positive	Negative	Zero
1 Years of formal education and annual income	✓		
2 Amount of smoking and incidence of lung cancer	✓		
3 Age of an automobile and its value			
4 Height and intelligence scores on standardized I.Q. tests			✓
5 Unemployment levels and new home sales		✓	

Answers: (1. positive; 2. positive; 3. negative; 4. zero; 5. negative)

Computers in Management

The previous section showed that information is only valuable if it can be put in some form which can be processed. If the processing of information is difficult and limited, the kinds of analyses available for management decision-making are severely restricted. Imagine the problem of analyzing by hand a survey of 1,000 automobile owners' preferences and buying behaviour. If and when you got through all the manual organization and tabulation of data, another survey would not follow very quickly! The task is trivial for a computer. And managers have found many other invaluable applications of computer technology to virtually every corner of a business.

The Transition in Information Processing

The transformation of business from the manual era of pencils, hand calculations, and mechanical tabulating machines to the computer era was accelerated by war. In 1944, IBM Corporation, working closely with the US Navy, built the Mark I, the first real computer. This electromechanical computer—14 metres long and 2.5 metres high—was controlled by punch cards and paper tapes and could perform both arithmetic and logical operations.

The first truly electronic computer was developed two years later. It was called ENIAC (Electronic Numerical Integrator and Computer). By using vacuum tabes rather than the Mark I's electronic relay switches, the ENIAC's calculating speed was increased 1,000 times. In 1954 General Electric became the first business organization to buy a computer (the Sperry UNIVAC I).

If the aircraft industry had evolved as spectacularly as the computer industry over the past 25 years, a Boeing 767 would cost $500.00 today, and it would circle the globe in 20 minutes on five gallons of fuel.[1] With such progress, it is no wonder that the computer has become *the* essential business tool. Its underlying technology has been adapted to applications as diverse as analyzing huge research studies to controlling a production line, or sending information from office to office or around the world in an instant.

Business Applications of Computers

Handling Data

Accounting. One of the earliest and most widespread uses of computers in business has been storage and processing of records. In repetitive work such as payroll accounting, inventory management, and billing, the speed and accuracy of the computer has been put to good use. The computer's memory can also assist management by supplying data on performance. For example it can report on sales for each geographic region, for each product and brand, and for each type of customer, and so forth.

Analysis. The speed of the computer makes its use mandatory in the analysis of marketing research data. The availability of highly sophisticated software enables complex analyses, and opens the door to new research methods. The main challenge for the user is to understand the strengths and limitations of the statistical procedures available.

Spread sheet analysis is a special business application which has found universal use in management. An electronic spread sheet is created that allows the manager to array numerical information in columns and rows, and then to apply mathematical operations to the data. For example, once a column of figures is listed, simple commands are available to add, subtract, or otherwise manipulate the figures.

The features of such electronic spread sheets allow the manager to ask "what if" questions by means of a few key strokes. For example, in a spread sheet portraying next year's budget projections for product A, you could ask, "What would be the effect on our returns of cutting price by 5 percent?" By changing one number, the entire budget would be recalculated almost instantly.

Word Processing

The volume of written communications is massive, and costly. Currently, the average typewritten business letter costs approximately $7 to prepare and send. Consequently, there is always a need for more efficient methods of handling communications. Other business communication needs include routine letters to customers; reports and other documents; business proposals needing specific modifications for a particular client; and various other paperwork. All of these activities have been made much more productive by the use of word processing systems.

Word processing is the use of computers to store, retrieve, view, edit, and print text material. By typing information into a computer using word processing software, the operator can easily revise sentences, correct errors, and print out individual letters or reports as needed. Personalized letters designed to respond to customer inquiries or to remind credit purchasers of overdue accounts can be created by combining stored sentences and paragraphs.

Production

Computers have also taken over many production jobs that formerly were performed by hand. Continuous-process operations, such as petroleum refineries, are often run entirely by computers. At each stage of the refining process, information on pressure of flows, temperature, and the like is fed into a computer. This information is then used by the computer to send instructions to machinery that will change the temperature, increase or decrease the pressure, or take whatever action is needed to control the refining process.

Ford, General Motors, and Chrysler use hundreds of computers in their production operations. Each automobile can have as many as 12,000 component parts, and computers are used to make certain that the right part is in the right place at the right time. Other computers test the engines, carburetors, distributors, and other machine parts.

In other industries, computers are also at work, monitoring glass-manufacturing plants, blast furnaces, paper machines, pulp digesters, nuclear power plants, and warehouse inventory.

Retailing

In many stores you wait while the cashier punches in a bunch of numbers. This enters the sum of the transaction and the inventory number into a computer, enabling the retailer to know immediately the sales and inventory position. Supermarket scanner checkout systems are even more efficient (and more expensive—costing between $100,000 and $150,000 per store). Despite the costs, this system is supposed to cut food costs by millions of dollars each year.

In many clothing stores an unusual price tag is attached to suits, dresses, and sportswear. The tag shows the price, but it also includes several punched holes and numbers. When the article of clothing is sold, the salesperson tears off the tag and deposits it in a special box. The tags are actually computer cards identifying the article of clothing and its cost and colour as well as the store and department. At the end of the day these tags are collected and taken to the computer centre. Processing them allows inventory in the store to be automatically controlled. When inventory reaches a certain level, new shipments can be made to stores, minimizing the possibility of running out of popular items.

Transfer of Information

Most business information now resides within computers, allowing easy analysis, formulation, and production of information for further business decisions. Why should this information be transferred to paper, and follow the sometimes-tortuous mail system? This question is now being addressed by business and the computer industry. Originally, computers were designed to stand alone and perform their functions. Consequently, the industry is now having to work to overcome compatibility problems between computers and other connecting hardware, problems which are now being rapidly overcome.

Within organizations, local area networks (LAN) connect various types of computers and enable information to be readily transferred by means of electronic mail. Any member of a LAN can instantly alert all other users—"There will be a Department meeting tomorrow at 9:00 a.m."

Between organizations, **networking** figures prominently in computer makers' future plans. It is becoming increasingly easy to sit down at your computer, press a few keys, and transmit pages of information from one city to another, or around the world, in a matter of seconds. For example, Peter Maurice, president of Canada Trustco Mortgage Co., says, "With our system I can sit at my cottage and access almost all of the information at Canada Trust."[2] This author communicated regularly by computer with his secretary in Winnipeg while visiting Australia. Networking is here, but its development is not yet complete. As business reaches around the globe, the demand for easier access to more networking facilities is also growing.

Focus 14-4

What Is It Like to Talk to a Computer?

Until recently, 18 harried operators in a small room in downtown Toronto answered telephone inquiries from Household Financial Corporation's 350,000 credit card holders across Canada. It was not an efficient operation—nor was it a pleasant place to work. "The office was a pressure cooker," admits Malcolm Thornley, HFC's vice-president of information systems. "We'd answer questions and complaints from 7 a.m. until midnight. As soon as an operator hung up, the next call was waiting."

A few months ago, HFC turned to **interactive voice technology (IVT)**—a talking computer. Now each cardholder can check on his or her account balance, line of credit, or last three transactions by calling into HFC's computer facility. After a security check, the customer is offered a menu of responses by the computer, each keyed to a number on the keypad of a touch-tone telephone: "Press one for your account balance, two for your record of payments..." and so forth. The computer then digs into the database to obtain the information. The company can now service customers 24 hours a day. Operators can take more time to handle the calls not appropriate for routinization.

Many university students have also benefited from IVT. Frustrated students no longer have to shuttle between buildings when confronted with the closing of a desired course. The entire process can be done through interacting with the computer on the telephone. Almost all major universities in Canada either have or are shopping for a system. "I can't think of a single innovation that had such a happy impact on campus," says Hugh King, associate registrar of schedules at the University of Alberta.

Source: Howard Druckman, "Chatter Boxes," *Canadian Business*, November 1988, pp. 199-200.

Controversial Issue

Has Market Research Gone Too Far?

From the standpoint of operating a business, there is no question that market research can be a vital source of information to improve the effectiveness of management decisions. For this reason, the means of collecting data about people's behaviour have been varied and ingenious.

A brassiere manufacturer, intent on improving its products, was reported to have installed one-way mirrors in selected store fitting rooms, so it might learn more about the use of this product. Other researchers have sought to learn about the behaviour of customers through a detailed analysis of people's garbage in the cans outside their homes. Other researchers have been reported to identify so-called "confidential" questionnaires with invisible ink so that they could match responses to individuals. Even the intrusion of researchers into the privacy of the home or office by telephone to ask questions has been criticized.

The boom in computers, the use of identification numbers, and instant access to information has created an era when individuals are feeling more insecure about their privacy. On the one hand, the efforts of market researchers, credit granting agencies and others, are being viewed with great concern. On the other, consumers expect quick and instant service at any bank, and they will not buy products and services that are not designed to satisfy their current needs and behaviours. This dilemma will become increasingly salient in the coming years.

Summary of Learning Goals

1. **Explain the basis of information for management decisions.**
   Management decisions are based on marketing research, accounting information, and statistical information generated both internally and externally.
2. **Distinguish between primary and secondary data.**
   External data collected outside the firm can be divided into two types: primary and secondary. Secondary data are those previously published. Primary data are collected for the first time for use in solving a business problem or taking advantage of an opportunity.
3. **Outline the marketing research process.**
   The process of marketing research involves the definition of the research problem, a search of secondary data, the collection of primary data, and the analysis of relevant data gathered.
4. **Identify the methods of collecting survey data and explain when each might be used.**
   Surveys can be conducted by personal interviews, mail questionnaires, or telephone. Personal interviews tend to be slow and expensive, but are effective in obtaining detailed information,

especially since interiewers can explain complex or potentially confusing questions to the respondent. Mail interviews are another relatively inexpensive method of gathering survey data, but poor response rates may be a problem. Telephone surveys are swift, inexpensive methods of obtaining small amounts of relatively impersonal information.

5. **Explain the common methods of statistical analysis in the analysis of information.**

Data are often listed in an array or grouped into a frequency distribution. Three commonly used methods of indicating the "average" values in a group of observations are the mean (arithmetical average), median (central value), and mode (most frequently appearing value). Index numbers such as the consumer price index measure changes that take place in business activity or other variables over time. Time series analysis involves an examination of data in an attempt to identify and interpret changes in business activity over time in order to forecast future activity. Fluctuations involved in time series analysis include seasonal, cyclical, and secular trends. Correlation analysis is a statistical technique used to measure the relationship, if any, between two or more variables.

6. **Outline the role of computers in management.**

Computers have become an omnipresent part of most businesses. The main applications are handling data, word processing, production, retailing, and transfer of information.

7. **Show the evolution of computers in processing and transmitting information.**

Computers have evolved quite quickly from large, limited ability electromechanical machines to powerful stand-alone computers which can process masses of data in a matter of seconds. Computers are now being networked over telephone lines to transmit information virtually instantaneously.

Key Terms

marketing research	array	cyclical trend
internal data	frequency distribution	secular trend
external data	mean (average)	correlation analysis
primary data	median	networking
secondary data	mode	local area network
observation method	index number	(LAN)
survey method	consumer price	interactive voice
census	index (CPI)	technology (IVT)
sample	time series (trend)	spread sheet analysis
probability sample	analysis	word processing
statistics	seasonal trend	

Discussion Questions and Exercises

1. Discuss the implications of the increasing use of networking in business.

2. Identify the major internal and external sources of information.

3. Distinguish between primary and secondary data and explain the strengths and limitations of each.

4. Identify the three methods of collecting survey data. Give an example of when each method might be used.

5. Assume that a class of fifteen students received the following grades on a business examination:

100	88	82	76	76
96	86	82	76	72
92	84	78	76	66

  a) What is the mean grade for this class?
  b) What is the median grade?
  c) What is the mode?

6. Assume that a local supermarket reported the following monthly sales figures during 1990:

Month	Sales	Month	Sales
January	$ 90,000	July	$ 70,000
February	85,000	August	80,000
March	90,000	September	105,000
April	100,000	October	100,000
May	105,000	November	130,000
June	105,000	December	140,000

  a) What is the mean monthly sales figure for this store?
  b) Would the median and mode be useful figures for the supermarket manager to calculate? Explain.

7. Refer to Question 6 above. Explain the types of trends present in the data shown.

8. Explain the statistical techniques of index numbers, time series analysis, and correlation analysis. Given an example of how each technique might be used in decision making.

9. A group of twenty-five students were enrolled in an introductory business class where *Contemporary Canadian Business* was the assigned textbook. They took a 50-item objective question examination. Consider the following scores achieved by these students:

Student	Score	Student	Score
Student 1	100	Student 14	72
Student 2	98	Student 15	70
Student 3	92	Student 16	70
Student 4	88	Student 17	70
Student 5	86	Student 18	68
Student 6	84	Student 19	66
Student 7	82	Student 20	66
Student 8	78	Student 21	64
Student 9	74	Student 22	60
Student 10	74	Student 23	56
Student 11	74	Student 24	48
Student 12	74	Student 25	46
Student 13	72		

    a) Calculate the mean, median and mode for this distribution of scores.

    b) What letter grade would you assign to each of these scores?

    c) Present the data using the following techniques: line chart, bar graph, pie chart, pictograph.

10. Identify the three methods of collecting survey data. Give an example of when each method might be used.

Case 14-1

Fisher-Price

Fisher-Price is a leading maker of toys for children under the age of six. For this reason it is not surprising to discover that its research and development building is actually a licensed nursery school located at the firm's headquarters. The nursery school is run by trained teachers paid by the company. As in any nursery school, the kids finger paint, sing, eat snacks, and read stories.

And they do other things. For Fisher-Price, the most important part of the school is the free-play time, where the three- and four-year-olds become toy testers for the firm's proposed new toys. There they bang, poke, kick, accept—and sometimes reject—the new toys dreamed up by the firm's designers.

A new group of kids comes in every six weeks to make certain that one group's whims aren't forced on a nation of toy buyers. In the nursery, the kids are never asked such direct questions as "How do you like this toy?" or "Isn't this a cute doll?" Instead, teachers make elaborate notes during free play and sometimes call designers to observe through one-way windows.

Children's input often initiates changes in successful toys. One such toy is the jack-in-the-box, a toy business staple item. Fisher-Price built one a few years ago and tested it in the nursery school. But the teachers reported an unusual occurrence. After pressing the button to make "Jack" pop out of his box, the children invariably would gather round and talk to him. "Is it dark in the box?" they would ask; then, assuming the role of Jack, they would give each other answers. So the teacher suggested making Jack's jaws move. Designers spent another year building a lever-operated mouth, a squeaky voice, a turntable head for the figure.

Questions:
1. What type of data are obtained by Fisher-Price, and through what method are they gathered?
2. What are the major advantages of this novel approach to obtaining management information? Suggest some other firms that might profitably utilize a similar approach to collecting information.
3. What are the potential disadvantages of this approach?

Case 14-2

Applying Statistical Analysis

In January a group of business students discussed the jobs they had held and the money they made during the holiday break. They tabulated their findings as follows:

Job	Hours Worked	Money Earned
Child care at local community centre	30	$180
Delivering flowers	24	108
Lead guitar player at New Year's Eve party	5	150
Retail salesperson	50	200
Security guard	40	220
Shopping mall Santa Claus	30	180
Shovelling snow	22	88
Swimming pool lifeguard	32	160
Temporary office help	28	210
Tutoring math	17	170

Questions:
1. Calculate the mean, median, and mode for the hours worked, the money earned, and the hourly rate of pay.
2. How would you present these data to:
   a) an instructor who is inclined to assign time-consuming research projects;
   b) a government policy maker on student grants and loans;
   c) a group of high school students considering the advantages of further education.

Chapter 15

Accounting

Learning Goals

Never ask of money spent
Where the spender thinks it
went.
Nobody was ever meant
To remember or invent
What he did with every cent.
—*Robert Frost*

Annual income twenty
pounds, annual expenditure
nineteen six.
Result: happiness.
Annual income twenty
pounds, annual expenditure
twenty pounds
ought and six.
Result: misery
—*Charles Dickens*
David Copperfield

1. To explain the functions of accounting and its importance to the firm's management and outside parties such as investors, creditors, and government agencies

2. To distinguish between public and private accountants and to explain the roles played by CAs, CMAs and CGAs

3. To explain the steps in the accounting process

4. To identify the accounting equation and its components and to explain the equation's relationship to double-entry bookkeeping

5. To explain the function of the balance sheet and to identify its major components

6. To explain the function of the income statement and to identify its major components

7. To identify the major financial ratios used in analyzing a firm's financial strengths and weaknesses and to explain the purpose of each

8. To explain the role of budgets in business

Profile

Ron Osborne—*An Accountant Who Demands Tight Financial Management and Diligent Planning*

Ron Osborne, Chief Executive Officer of Maclean Hunter, is a chartered accountant by training, a detail man with a reputation for asking perceptive questions and relentlessly second-guessing anyone who comes within range with an idea. Osborne is also considered a communicator who is able to motivate his managers with clear ideas and consideration. "If you give him something to sign, you'd better make sure it is right," says one associate. "But he never makes you feel like a dummy. He just gives you the impression that he's improving on your already good product."

A languages graduate from Cambridge in 1968, Ron Osborne quickly concluded that teaching and translating were not for him. Recalling a summer in Canada as a construction worker and fruit picker, he lined up a job as a junior clerk articling at Clarkson Gordon & Co. in Toronto.

By 1976 he had done so well that he was seconded to Clarkson's Brazilian affiliate, and when he returned three years later, he was made a full partner. In 1980, he became involved in supervising Maclean Hunter's yearly audit. Maclean Hunter were so impressed that they pirated him away, and he was hired as vice-president, finance, in March 1981. Within three years he was president and within five years CEO.

From the moment he took over there was no question about the blueprint for Maclean Hunter's growth. The communications business, in North America and Europe, is the company's designated turf, and the target for after-tax return on net assets employed is a minimum of 15 percent on average.

Founded 102 years ago, Maclean Hunter has grown into a diversified communications

company with interests in broadcasting, cable television, business forms and printing, and newspaper and periodical publishing. Over the past decade the company's revenues have grown on average by 22 percent a year, while profits have jumped an even more impressive 24 percent annually.

Source: Charles Davies, "The Two Ronnies," *Canadian Business*, February 1989, pp. 38-42.

Checkpoint Systems is a firm that developed an electronic tag that can be attached to library books and merchandise in retail stores to prevent theft. Tremendous growth has occurred over the years as product modifications resulted in an increased market acceptance.

But the growth brought problems. Checkpoint's old accounting system was adequate for a small operation, but could not accommodate the company's rapid growth. Moreover, the old system proved inadequate in providing managers with decision-oriented information to assist them in spotting trends, making pricing decisions, and controlling cash flows. As Jerry Klein, Checkpoint's vice-president of operations, stated: "Lacking timely data, the whole system had begun to collapse. Invoices lagged shipments by as much as 30 days; accounts payable ran 60 to 90 days." The importance of an adequate accounting system finally became obvious.

What Is Accounting?

The stereotype of the accountant—a pale, bookish male dressed in a white shirt and narrow tie, seated behind a desk in a small office, pencil in hand, poring over invoices and making notations in a dusty ledger—describes virtually none of the thousands of men and women in Canada who list their occupation as "accountant." In fact, never before have accountants been in such demand. The availability of jobs and the relatively high starting salaries for talented accounting graduates have lured thousands of students into accounting classes in Canada's colleges and universities. Today, accounting represents 50 percent of all student majors in the typical business programme.

accounting
The process of measuring and communicating financial information to enable interested parties inside and outside the firm to make informed decisions.

Accounting, like statistics, is a language of business. It is the process of measuring and communicating financial information to enable interested parties inside and outside the firm to make informed decisions. Accountants are responsible for gathering, recording, reporting, and interpreting financial information that describes the status and operation of a firm and aids in decision making. They must accomplish three major tasks: scorekeeping, calling attention to problems and opportunities, and aiding in decision making. These are essential aspects of keeping a business healthy (see Focus 15-1).

Accounting for Whom?

Who are the interested parties—inside and outside the firm—aided by accounting? Inside, management uses accounting information to help plan and control both daily and long-range operations. Owners rely on accounting data to determine how well the firm is being operated. Union officials use the data in contract negotiations.

Outside the firm, potential investors use accounting information to help them decide whether to invest in the company. Bankers and other creditors find that it helps them determine the company's credit rating and gives them insight into its financial soundness. Revenue Canada uses it to evaluate the company's tax payments for the year.

Focus 15-1

Five Warning Signals for Business

There are early warning signals that can tell a businessperson whether or not the operation is heading toward failure. These have been put together by a Vancouver accountant named Donald J. Henfrey, who should know about these things. He is president of the Canadian Insolvency Association, and his firm, Henfrey Samson Belair Ltd., is one of western Canada's leading trustees in receiverships.

Sad to say, his business has been brisk for several years. It may not be in his best interests to tell us how to avoid becoming one of his clients, but it is in the greater interest of the economy. A healthy economy generates plenty of business for accounting firms as well— and the business is more enjoyable to transact.

These are Henfrey's five warning signals:

One-man rule. "We've liquidated many companies which have a problem as a result of one-man rule," he says. This can be recognized when the owner and founder of the business works excessive hours, fails to hire competent staff and fails to delegate. Such an individual becomes busier and busier until the firm's problems become overwhelming. One solution might be to find a partner to invest in the company sharing both the risks and the load.

Cash-flow problems. These are cited by businesspeople who think their companies are running at a profit—or would be, if only their customers paid the bills on time. Often, that reasoning contains a large element of self-delusion.

Inadequate accounting. This failure feeds the self-delusion. "When a company recognizes it has financial difficulties," Henfrey says, "one of the first things it does is fire the bookkeeper." This may reduce salary costs, but it also reduces the quantity and quality of vital information that management needs.

Inventory imbalances. When a business has invested in a product which then does not sell, it is an error to tie up expensive warehouse space and other costs just storing the dud. "Get rid of obsolete stock," Henfrey advises. "Get it out of your warehouse; get it out of your office; get it off your balance sheet."

Failure to modernize. This is basic. One need only look to the American steel industry or British shipyards to recognize that poorly maintained or obsolete machinery and plants are unable to compete with modern facilities.

Source: *Skyword Magazine*, June, 1984.

Accounting Versus Bookkeeping

Too many people make the mistake of using the terms *accounting* and *bookkeeping* interchangeably. But they are not synonymous.

Bookkeeping is the chiefly clerical phase of accounting. Bookkeepers are primarily responsible for the systematic recording of company financial transactions. They provide the data that the accountant uses. Accounting is a much more creative area. Accountants are responsible for developing systems to classify and summarize transactions and for interpreting financial statements.

Accountants are decision-makers, while bookkeepers are trained in the largely mechanical tasks of record-keeping. Accountants hold positions as chief executives in many of the largest companies and in top-level government offices.

People in the Accounting Profession

chartered accountant (CA)
An accountant who has met national certification requirements involving university degrees and experience and who has passed a comprehensive examination (Uniform Final Examination) covering law, accounting theory and practice, and auditing.

audit
An independent appraisal of the effectiveness and reliability of financial reports.

Accountants in Canada are employed in a variety of areas in business firms, government agencies, nonprofit organizations, and as self-employed individuals. (See Focus 15-2 for a listing of some of the activities of an accounting firm.) Approximately 30,000 accountants are **chartered accountants (CAs)**. These CAs have proven their skills by successfully completing a number of rigorous examinations in accounting theory and practice, auditing, and law in order to meet the legal requirements of their province. CAs have the same professional status within their field as do attorneys in law and physicians in medicine. CAs can officially express an opinion on whether a firm's financial statements present fairly and accurately that company's financial position. Such **audits** of financial records are required of all publicly held corporations and are usually required by any lending agency. The Canadian CAs' national association is The Canadian Institute of Chartered Accountants (CICA).

Focus 15-2

Inside a Large Accounting Firm

To see exactly how a major public accounting firm operates, let's take a look at Price Waterhouse, the fifth largest public accounting firm in Canada, with 26,000 employees generating annual revenues of about $500 million. It is operated as a partnership with offices in more than 95 countries and territories around the world.

As the figure below indicates, most revenues are generated through three services provided for Price Waterhouse clients: auditing, tax services, and management consulting. A small but growing component of the firm focuses upon specialized services for small business and for firms operating in more than one country.

Price Waterhouse

Auditing
Provides independent opinions of its clients' financial statements; opinions are used in reports to stockholders and other interested parties.

Source of two-thirds of total fee income.

Tax Services
Provides comprehensive tax planning, tax preparation, and representation before tax officials in case of tax audits of its clients.

Source of about 20 percent of total fee income.

Management Consulting
Provides objective evaluations of decisions in such areas as manufacturing, marketing, and finance; attempts to increase productivity; and recruiting of key executive personnel.

Source of about 12 percent of total fee income.

International Services
Offers professional accounting advice to assist multi-national corporations in meeting their host countries' special accounting, taxation, and reporting requirements.

Services for Small Businesses
Offers wide range of financial, tax, and auditing services.

certified general accountant (CGA)
A professional accountant who has passed the CGA national examination and satisfied all other requirements for admittance.

certified management accountant (CMA)
An accountant who has met specific educational and professional requirements and has passed a series of examinations established by the Society of Management Accountants of Canada.

Another important type of public accountant is the **certified general accountant (CGA)**. There are about 10,000 certified general accountants in Canada. Many CGAs specialize in management and government accounting. The CGA serves to coordinate the work and opinions of the various provincial bodies in matters of national concern, such as the submission of briefs to the federal government and its agencies.[1] CGAs are members of the Canadian General Accountants' Association. Depending on the province, CGAs can officially express an audit opinion on the financial statements of a company.

Business firms usually employ a **certified management accountant (CMA)**. This individual has met the specific educational and professional requirements and passed a series of examinations established by the Society of Management Accountants of Canada and has been awarded the CMA designation. The key responsibilities of the CMA are developing, generating, and analyzing information to assist management in making sound decisions.

The Accounting Process

The basic data used in accounting are financial transactions between the firm and its employees, suppliers, owners, bankers, and various

Figure 15-1
The Accounting Process

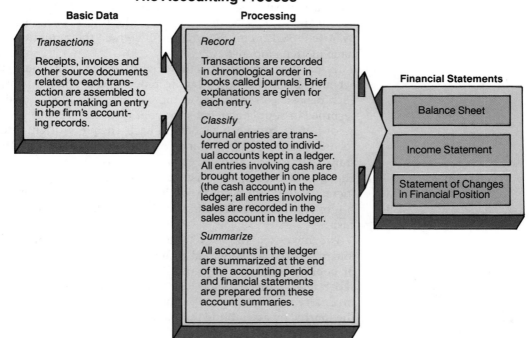

government bodies. Weekly payroll cheques result in cash outflows for the compensation of employees. A payment to a supplier results in the receipt of needed materials for the production process. Prompt payment of bills preserves the firm's credit rating and its ability to obtain future loans. This procedural cycle used by accountants in converting individual transactions to financial statements is called the **accounting process**.

As Figure 15-1 indicates, these transactions must be recorded, classified, and summarized in order to produce financial statements for the firm's management and other interested parties.

Accounting Journals and Ledgers: Storehouses of Financial Transactions

The first step in the processing of transactions by the firm is to record each of them in chronological order in a book called a **journal**. The journal can consist of a hand-prepared list, or a computer printout in firms with computerized accounting systems. A sample page from a journal is shown at the top of Figure 15-2.

The accounts listed on the journal page represent sources and uses of funds by the firm. The July 5 purchase of furniture from Oakleigh Furniture Company cost $8,000. The firm agreed to pay $5,000 of the total cost in ten days and the remaining balance at the end of the month. The payment made to Oakleigh on July 15 reduced the cash account by $5,000. On the other hand, the July 22 payment of $1,000 by Arlene Wilson on her account increased the amount of cash on hand by that amount.

In practice, the transactions work much like your chequing account. Each cheque you write reduces your balance. Conversely, each deposit you make raises the balance. The cheque or deposit is recorded in your chequebook for your records. The bank also keeps a record of each deposit made and each cheque written. The bank's records are usually maintained by computers, and a monthly bank statement is provided to each depositor. Journal entries reflect changes in a company's accounts in the same way. A cash sale increases the cash account while reducing inventory. Purchases of stationery, for instance, increase the supplies account and reduce cash.

The next step involves transferring the data contained in the journal entries to individual accounts in the firm's ledger. A **ledger**, or book of account, is a specialized accounting book that contains separate accounts for such items as cash, accounts receivable, sales, inventory, and salaries. It summarizes the listing of transactions in the journal by assembling them into specific accounts.

accounting process
Procedural cycle used by accountants in converting individual transactions to financial statements.

journal
The accountant's book of entry; an accounting book listing all business transactions in chronological order.

ledger
The book of account; a specialized accounting book containing separate accounts for items such as cash, accounts receivable, sales, and inventory.

Figure 15-2
Sample Pages of an Accounting Journal and Ledger Accounts

Accounting Journal

Genenal Journal				PAGE 1
DATE 1985	ACCOUNT TITLES AND EXPLANATION		DEBIT	CREDIT
July 1	Accounts Receivable - Arnold Wilson		1,800.00	
	Sales Revenue			1,800.00
	To record sale of merchandise on account			
July 5	Office Furniture and Equipment		8,000.00	
	Accounts payable - Oakleigh Furniture Co.			8,000.00
	To record purchase of furniture on account.			
July 15	Accounts payable - Oakleigh Furniture Co.		5,000.00	
	Cash			5,000.00
	To record payment on account.			
July 22	Cash		1,000.00	
	Accounts Receivable - Arnold Wilson			1,000.00
	To record collection on account.			

Accounting Journal

Ledger accounts

Cash				Account Number 1	
DATE 1985	EXPLANATION	DEBIT	CREDIT	BALANCE	
July 1				7,000.	00
July 15	Oakleigh Furniture Co.		5,000 00	2,000	00
July 22	Arnold Wilson	1,000.00		3,000	00

Ledger Accounts

Accounts Receivable				Account Number 3	
DATE 1985		DEBIT	CREDIT	BALANCE	
July 1				25,000	00
July 1	Arnold Wilson	1,800 00		26,800	00
July 22	Arnold Wilson		1,000 00	25,800	00

posting
The process of transferring journal entries to specific ledger accounts and recording them.

The bottom half of Figure 15-2 shows two ledger accounts: cash and accounts receivable. The process of **posting**, or recording, the individual transactions to specific ledger accounts is illustrated using these two accounts. At the end of the accounting period, the data in each ledger accounts are summarized and used as the basis for preparing the firm's accounting statements.

The Accounting Equation and Double-Entry Bookkeeping

assets
Everything of value owned or leased by a business.

equities
Claims against the assets of a business.

liabilities
Claims of the firm's creditors.

owners' equity
Claims of the proprietor, the partners, or the stockholders against the assets of the firm, or the excess of all assets over all liabilities.

Four fundamental terms are involved in the accounting equation: assets, equities, liabilities, and owners' equity. **Assets** are everything of value owned or leased by the business. Cash, accounts receivable and notes receivable (amounts owed to the business through credit sales), land, buildings, supplies, and marketable securities are all assets.

Equities are claims against the assets of a business. The two major classifications of individuals who have equities in a firm are creditors (liability holders) and owners. The **liabilities** of a business are everything owed to creditors—that is, the claims of the firm's creditors. When the firm makes credit purchases for inventory, land, or machinery, the creditors' claims are shown as accounts payable or notes payable. Wages and salaries owed to employees also represent liabilities (known as wages payable). The **owners' equity** represents the proprietor's, the partners', or the stockholders' claims against the assets of the firm or the excess of all assets over all liabilities.

$$\text{Equities} = \text{Liabilities} + \text{Owners' Equity}$$

Because equities by definition represent the total claims against assets, then assets must equal equities:

$$\text{Assets} = \text{Equities}$$

accounting equation
Fundamental concept upon which accounting is based; the equation showing that assets (things of value) are equal to liabilities (claims of creditors) plus owners' equity (claims of owners).

The basic **accounting equation** reflects the financial position of any firm at any point in time:

$$\text{Assets} = \text{Liabilities} + \text{Owners' Equity}$$

Double-Entry Bookkeeping

double-entry bookkeeping
Method of bookkeeping that requires two entries for every transaction, thereby keeping the accounting equation in balance.

The method for maintaining the balance of the accounting equation is to use two entries for every transaction affecting the equation. This procedure, first described in a book written in 1494 by an Italian monk named Pacioli and in use since then, is called **double-entry bookkeeping**. By offsetting one side of the accounting equation with a change on the other side, the equation remains in balance.

An example from the journal shown in Figure 15-2 illustrates the use of double-entry bookkeeping. On July 5, the firm made a $5,000 office furniture purchase and agreed to repay Oakleigh in two installments. The accounting equation would show:

$$
\begin{array}{llll}
Assets & = & Liabilities & + \ Owners'\ Equity \\
+\$5,000 & = & +\$5,000 & + \qquad \$0 \\
(office & & (accounts\ payable) \\
furniture)
\end{array}
$$

Debits and Credits

The bookkeeping entries made to reflect transactions are referred to as debits and credits. Although these terms have become a part of our language, their meaning is often misunderstood. Debits and credits do not necessarily refer to increases and decreases; they indicate on which side of the journal or ledger account an amount is to be recorded. A **debit** is a bookkeeping entry that records an increase in an asset, a decrease in liability, or a decrease in owners' equity. A **credit** indicates a decrease in an asset, an increase in a liability, or an increase in owners' equity.

debit
Bookkeeping entry recording an increase in an asset, a decrease in a liability, or a decrease in owners' equity.

credit
Bookkeeping entry recording a decrease in an asset, an increase in a liability, or an increase in owners' equity.

Accounting Statements

The relationship expressed by the accounting equation is used to develop two primary accounting statements prepared by every business large or small: the balance sheet and the income statement. (Many firms also prepare a third financial statement: the statement of changes in financial position. It is explained briefly on page 446.) These two statements reflect the current financial position of the firm and the most recent analysis of income, expenses, and profits for interested parties inside and outside the firm. They provide a fundamental basis of planning activities and are used in attracting new investors, securing borrowed funds, and preparing tax returns.

The Balance Sheet

balance sheet
A statement of a company's financial position as of a particular date.

The **balance sheet** shows the financial position of a company as of a particular date. It is like a photograph in that it captures the status of the firm's assets and equities at a moment in time.

Balance sheets should be prepared at regular intervals to provide information to management concerning the financial position of the firm. Balance sheets are provided for external users at least once a year; more typically, quarterly. Managers are likely to receive such statements on a more frequent basis.

Figure 15-3 shows the balance sheet for The Ski Patrol, an imaginary Alberta retailer marketing ski equipment, ski clothing, group ski tours, and ski instruction. The basic accounting equation is illustrated by the three classifications on The Ski Patrol's balance sheet. The assets total must equal the total of the firm's liabilities and the owners' equity.

Assets

The typical balance sheet classifies assets on the basis of *conversion time*: the ease with which they can be turned into cash. The three categories of assets are current assets, fixed assets, and intangible assets.

Current assets. Certain items are always listed first in the asset section of the balance sheet. These **current assets** include cash and those items that can or will be converted to cash within one year.

current assets
Cash and other items of value that can or will be converted to cash within one year.

Figure 15-3
Balance Sheet for the Ski Patrol

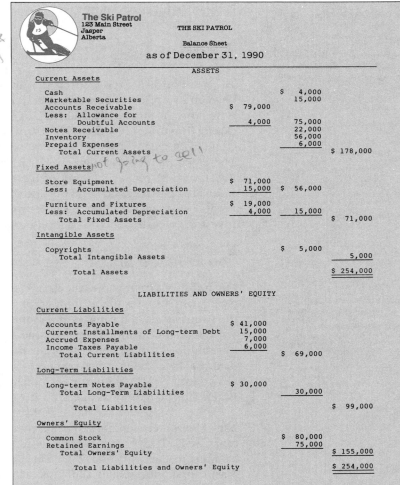

liquidity
The speed at which items can be converted to cash.

They are listed in order of their expected **liquidity**—the speed at which they can be converted to cash. For The Ski Patrol, the current assets include the following:

- Cash—funds on hand or in bank deposits that can be withdrawn immediately as needed.
- Marketable Securities—temporary investments of surplus funds in shares, bonds, or other investments that can be quickly converted to cash.
- Accounts Receivable—credit purchases by the firm's customers. In certain cases, the amount of outstanding accounts receivable is reduced to reflect management's belief that certain of these receivables will either be partially repaid or not repaid at all. As Figure 15-3 illustrates, an allowance for doubtful accounts is included to notify interested parties of this possibility.
- Notes Receivable—funds owed the company as described by a written document called a *note* that specifies the amount of funds owed and the time and place of repayment.
- Inventory—merchandise on hand for sale by the business. For manufacturers, inventory may also consist of raw materials, component parts, and goods in process as well as finished goods ready for sale.
- Prepaid Expenses—include services such as insurance, prepaid rent, and supplies on hand that have been paid for but not used. Benefits from these services and supplies will be received during the following operating period.

Items that will or can be converted to cash in one year are considered current assets.

fixed assets
Relatively permanent assets
expected to be used in the
operation of the firm for
periods longer than one year.

depreciation
Noncash expense involving
the allocation of the cost of a
long-term asset over the years
in which it is used to generate
revenue for the firm.

intangible assets
Items of value such as
copyrights, patents, goodwill,
and trademarks that have no
tangible, physical properties.

Fixed assets. Relatively permanent assets that are expected to be used in the operation of the firm for periods longer than one year are considered **fixed**—or plant—**assets**. Included in this category of long-term assets are land, buildings, machinery, transportation equipment, computers, and furniture and fixtures. All of these, except land, are considered depreciable assets since they wear out over time from use or age and must eventually be replaced. The cost of this wearing out of valuable assets is reflected on the balance sheet by an accounting procedure called depreciation. **Depreciation**, or cost recovery, is the allocation of the cost of a long-term asset over the years in which it is used to generate revenue for the firm. While no actual cash outlays are involved, charging a portion of the total cost of a machine or a piece of furniture or equipment to each of the years it is used results in a more accurate determination of the total costs involved in the firm's operation.

Intangible assets. Unlike current and fixed assets, **intangible assets** have no tangible physical properties. They include patents on inventions, designs, or processes; copyrights and trademarks protecting written or recorded materials; and goodwill. Although they are difficult to convert into cash, they frequently represent important assets for the firm. In some instances, they may be licensed for use by others or sold outright. Many of the items in the nation's toy stores—Smurf characters, Snoopy toys, Star Wars videogame cartridges—are the result of licences provided by copyright owners in exchange for royalty payments. As Figure 15-3 indicates, the copyrights held on The Ski Patrol name and distinctive logo are valued at $5,000.

Liabilities

The financial obligations of the business to other businesses and individuals are called liabilities. Like assets, liabilities are typically listed on the balance sheet in the order in which they will come due. They are classified as either current or long-term liabilities.

current liabilities
Claims of creditors that are to
be repaid within a one-year
period.

Current liabilities. Those claims that will be repaid within a one-year period are called **current liabilities**. For The Ski Patrol, current liabilities include accounts payable, current installments of long-term debt, accrued expenses, and income taxes payable.

Accounts payable and notes payable are the liability counterparts of accounts receivable and notes receivable. Accounts payable represent credit purchases by the firm that must be repaid within a one-year period. Notes payable are loans represented by a written and signed document specifying the amount to be repaid and the time and place of repayment. In many instances, notes payable extend beyond a single year. The installments payable on the note in the current year are current liabilities and the additional funds that are payable after

long-term liabilities
All debts that come due one year or more after the date of the balance sheet.

one year are included on the balance sheet as **long-term liabilities**. Accrued expenses are obligations incurred by the company for which payments have not been made. They include such items as utility services, interest on loans, labour, and taxes. Since tax payments represent a substantial accrued expense that must be paid, The Ski Patrol lists the $6,000 in taxes owed as a separate item on its balance sheet.

Comparing current assets and current liabilities. Because they will require repayment within the next year, current liabilities can quickly provide a cash crisis for a business with inadequate reserves of cash or other liquid assets that can be converted to cash. Consequently, most firms closely monitor the relationship between current assets and current liabilities. The term **working capital** refers to the difference between current assets and current liabilities. It reflects the ability of the firm to meet its short-term payment commitments. Any excess of current assets over current liabilities can provide a cushion against unexpected reductions in assets or increases in liabilities and serves as the means to finance such decisions as increasing inventory or credit sales to take advantage of unexpected situations.

working capital
The difference between current assets and current liabilities.

Long-term liabilities. All debts that come due one year or more after the date of the balance sheet are classified as long-term liabilities. These include such items as bonds, long-term notes payable, mortgages, and other business loans from banks or other financial institutions that are not scheduled for repayment during the coming year.

Owners' Equity

The final major category on the firm's balance sheet is also the final component of the accounting equation. Owners' equity represents the investment in the business. It is comprised of two elements: investments made by the owners of the firm and retained earnings that are left in the business rather than distributed to the owners.

The specific listings in the owners' equity section of the balance sheet varies according to the form of business organization. Unincorporated businesses record the direct investment of the owners in a *capital account* with the name of the proprietor or partners. For partnerships, the capital account reflects the exact amount invested by each partner. Corporate investment is reflected by issuing common shares to the owners (or shareholders). In the case of The Ski Patrol, the corporation was formed by issuing 80,000 common shares of stock to the firm's shareholders at a price of $1 per share. This direct investment of $80,000 is listed on the firm's balance sheet as *common shares*.

The profits of the corporation can be distributed to the shareholders in the form of cash dividends, or they can be retained by the corporation and reinvested in the business. Retained earnings can be used for expansion and growth and can be invested in such assets as land and buildings. The Ski Patrol's retained earnings of $75,000 represent the accumulated earnings that have been left in the firm.

Unincorporated businesses do not distinguish between the initial investment of their owners and subsequent earnings retained in the business. The capital account of a proprietorship or partnership includes not only the initial direct investment, but also subsequent additional investments, withdrawals, and retention of earnings. Unlike the corporate balance sheet, the owners' equity section of a proprietor's or partnership's balance sheet combines retained earnings and direct investments of owners into a single account.

The Income Statement

income statement
The financial statement that reflects the income, expenses, and profits of a company over a period of time.

Earlier, the balance sheet was compared to a photograph in the way it reflects the financial position of the company at a specific point in time. Using this comparison, the **income statement** would resemble a motion picture, because it shows the income, expenses, and profits of a company over a *period* of time.

The purpose of the income statement (also called an *operating statement* and a *profit and loss statement*) is to show the profitability or unprofitability of a firm during a period of time, usually a year, a quarter, or a month. In addition to reporting on the amount of profit or loss, it is particularly useful for decision makers in focusing on overall revenues and the costs involved in generating these revenues. For nonprofit organizations, this statement provides specific indications of the ability of the organization's revenues and contributions to cover the costs involved in its operation. Finally, the income statement provides much of the basic data needed to calculate numerous ratios used by management in planning and controlling the organization. Figure 15-4 shows the 1990 income statement for The Ski Patrol, an incorporated company.

Major Components of the Income Statement

The income statement summarizes the income and expenses of the firm over a period of time. The basis format shows the deduction of costs and expenses, including taxes, from income in order to determine the net profit of the firm for that time period. The equation for the income statement is:

$$\text{Income} - \text{Expenses} = \text{Net Profit (or Loss)}$$

Figure 15-4 may be divided into the following major sections:

Net Sales	$292,000
Minus: Cost of Goods Sold	−132,000
Equals: Gross Profit	$160,000
Minus: Expenses	−123,000
Equals: Net Income Before Taxes	$ 37,000
Minus: Income Taxes	−7,000
Equals: Net Income	$ 30,000

Figure 15-4
Income Statement for the Ski Patrol

```
                    The Ski Patrol
                    123 Main Street
                    Jasper, Alberta
                              THE SKI PATROL


                              Income Statement
                    For the Year Ended December 31, 1990


    Revenues

      Gross Sales                              $ 300,000
      Less:  Sales Returns and
                    Allowances                     8,000
            Net Sales                                         $ 292,000

    Costs of Goods Sold

      Beginning Inventory                      $  65,000
      Purchases during Year          $ 127,000
      Less:  Purchase Discounts          4,000
      Net Purchases                             123,000
      Cost of Goods Available for Sale        $ 188,000
      Less:  Ending Inventory, Dec. 31          56,000
            Cost of Goods Sold                                $ 132,000

    Gross Profit                                               $ 160,000

    Operating Expenses

      Selling Expenses
        Sales Salaries and Commissions  $  51,000
        Advertising                        16,000
        Depreciation:  Store Equipment      5,000
        Miscellaneous Selling Expenses      3,000
            Total Selling Expenses       $  75,000

    General Expenses
        Office Salaries                 $  35,000
        Office Supplies                     8,000
        Depreciation:  Office Equipment     3,000
        Miscellaneous General Expenses      2,000
            Total General Expenses          48,000

        Total Operating Expenses                              $ 123,000

    Net Income Before Taxes                                   $  37,000
      Less:  Income Taxes                                         7,000

    Net Income                                                $  30,000
```

revenues
Funds received by the firm from sales of products and services from interest payments, dividends, royalties, and rents.

Revenues. For most businesses, **revenues** are generated by the sale of products or services. In addition, some firms receive additional revenues from interest earned on investments; sale of property; rents; royalties earned on patents, copyrights, or trademarks; and dividends. Nonprofit organizations may generate substantial revenues from grants and donations from individuals, businesses, and government agencies. These revenues provide the funds necessary to operate the organization and earn a profit for its owners.

The Ski Patrol produces revenues by selling both products (ski equipment and clothing) and services (ski instruction and group ski tours). As Figure 15-4 indicates, total 1990 gross sales amounted to $300,000.

The gross sales figure is reduced by $8,000 as a result of a number of returns and allowances provided for Ski Patrol customers. Some reductions occur when a portion of the sales price is refunded on an item that is damaged or partially defective (a sales allowance). In other instances, returned merchandise must be subtracted from the gross sales figure to accurately reflect net sales.

cost of goods sold
Cost of the merchandise or services that generate the firm's revenue.

Cost of goods sold. This section of the income statement reflects the cost of the merchandise or services that generates the firm's revenue. These items vary directly with revenue. Since The Ski Patrol is a retailer, a subsection is included called *net purchases*. In the case of a manufacturer, an entry labelled *cost of goods manufactured* would be included in addition to purchases of raw materials and component parts. Otherwise, the income statements for manufacturers and inter-mediaries such as retailers and wholesalers are similar.

Cost of goods sold for The Ski Patrol is calculated in the following manner. At the beginning of the year, total inventory of $65,000 was on hand. In addition, The Ski Patrol managers purchased $127,000 in inventory during 1990 to add to the beginning inventory, but received a purchase discount of $4,000 from one firm for quantity purchases, resulting in net purchases of $123,000. When this was added to the cost of beginning inventory, the total cost of goods available for sale amounted to $188,000.

At the end of the year, $56,000 in unsold inventory was still on hand, indicating that the cost of goods sold during 1990 was $132,000 ($188,000 minus $56,000). Total *gross profit* ($292,000 net sales less $132,000 cost of goods sold) amounted to $160,000.

operating expenses
All business costs other than those included in the cost of goods sold.

selling expenses
Expenses incurred in marketing and distributing the firm's products and services.

Operating expenses. In addition to the costs of acquiring or producing goods to be sold, firms typically incur a number of **operating expenses** in the course of running the business. These consist of selling expenses and general expenses. **Selling expenses** are those resulting from marketing and distributing the products or services of the firm. They include salaries and commissions paid to sales personnel, advertising, sales supplies, delivery expenses, and such miscellaneous selling expenses as telephone charges, depreciation, insurance, and utilities allocated to sales. Total selling expenses for The Ski Patrol amounted to $75,000.

general expenses
Expenses incurred in the overall operations of the business that are not directly related to the acquisition, production, or sale of the firm's products or services.

General expenses are those resulting from the overall operations of the business. They include those expense items that are not directly related to the acquisition, production, or sale of the firm's products or services. General expenses include salaries of office personnel; supplies; special services such as consultants, accounting services, or legal fees; insurance; postage; and depreciation on office equipment. In 1990, The Ski Patrol incurred total general expenses of $48,000.

Focus 15-3

Are Accountants Ready for JIT?

Accountants are scrambling to catch up with the just-in-time (JIT) manufacturing systems being adopted in many companies. (Discussed in Chapter 16, on production; see page 487.) Managers complain that current accounting practice actually hinders implementation of a JIT system. The JIT concept rejects the concept that there is a tradeoff between quality and cost, and that there is a tradeoff between high inventory level and cost.

The new concept results in some significant differences between traditional and JIT costing systems:

- JIT continuous costing differs from traditional process costing in that direct labour and manufacturing overhead costs can be charged directly to finished goods. This is because direct labour costs are an insignificant portion of total costs, and because manufacturing overhead moves directly into cost of goods sold in the same period in which it is incurred.
- Direct labour hours may no longer be useful for allocating indirect overhead, because overhead costs are not as directly related.
- With a low inventory level, the inventory recording method can be simpler and more standardized.
- Traditional performance evaluation measures for factory workers (e.g. cost minimization or efficiency) do not consider some important elements in JIT such as quality improvement, inventory reduction, and set-up and lead time reduction.

This focus illustrates the interconnection between systems. Adopting a new system in production may have a profound effect on the accounting subsystem.

Source: Il-woon Kim, Hai G. Park, and Lance J. Besser, "Are You Ready for JIT?" *CMA Magazine*, July-August 1988, pp. 44-47.

net income
Actual profit or loss incurred over a specific time period; determined by subtracting all expenses from revenues.

bottom line
The overall profit or loss earned by a firm.

statement of changes in financial position
The financial statement that explains the financial changes that occur in a company from one accounting period to the next.

Net income or loss. Total operating expense is determined by combining selling expenses and general expenses. In the case of The Ski Patrol, total operating expense amounted to $123,000 (selling expenses of $75,000 plus $48,000 in general expenses). The Ski Patrol's *net income before taxes* amounted to $37,000 in 1990 ($160,000 gross profit minus $123,000 total operating expenses). After subtracting $7,000 for taxes, the firm earned a total **net income** of $30,000 for 1990. In instances where total expenditures exceed total revenues, a net loss occurs.

The final figure on the income statement is the famous **bottom line**—the overall profit or loss earned by the firm. Profit or loss statistics are perhaps the most commonly quoted measures of a firm's performance. When compared with profits of previous years and with the earnings of other firms in the industry, the bottom line permits comparisons and allows shareholders, lenders, and potential investors to make general assessments of a company's performance.

Statement of Changes in Financial Position

In addition to the income statement and the balance sheet, a third accounting statement is prepared by many firms. As the name indicates, the **statement of changes in financial position** explains the financial changes that occur in a company from one accounting period to the next. It is sometimes referred to as the "where got, where gone" statement because it presents the operating, financing and investing activities of the firm from period to period.

This statement acts as a link between the present and preceding year's accounting statements. It provides interested parties with an insight into how the firm's operations are being financed and how its funds are being used.

Interpreting Financial Statements

Once financial statements have been produced from the accounting data collected for a period, an accountant must interpret them. The fact that a firm earned a profit for the past year is of interest; of equal interest is the profit it *should* have earned. A number of techniques have been developed over the years for interpreting financial information in order to aid management in planning and evaluating the day-to-day and on-going operations of the company. Two commonly used techniques are percentage of net sales and ratio analysis.

Percentage of Net Sales

Figure 15-5 reveals how The Ski Patrol income statement can be converted from dollar amounts to percentages of net sales. Cost and expense items shown in percentage form can quickly be compared with those of previous periods or with other companies in the industry. In this way, unusually high or low expenses become immediately apparent to management, and corrective action can be taken if necessary. In addition, the percentage figures assist investors and financial analysts in making such comparisons.

Ratio Analysis

A second method of interpreting financial statements is ratio analysis. By comparing the company ratios to industry standards, problem areas can be pinpointed and areas of excellence can be identified. Moreover, by comparing ratios for the current accounting period with those of previous periods, developing trends can be detected. Four categories of ratios exist: liquidity ratios, profitability ratios, activity ratios, and debt ratios.

Heading

liquidity ratio
Financial ratio measuring a firm's ability to meet its short-term obligations.

Liquidity ratios. A **liquidity ratio** measures a firm's ability to meet its short-term obligations. Highly liquid firms are less likely to face emergencies in raising needed funds to repay loans. On the other hand, those firms with less liquidity may be forced to use high-cost lending sources to meet their maturing obligations or face default. Two commonly used liquidity ratios are the current ratio and the acid-test ratio.

Figure 15-5 Percentage of Net Sales for The Ski Patrol

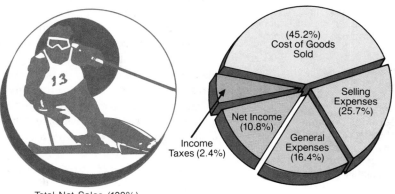

Total Net Sales (100%)

current ratio
A ratio that measures the company's ability to pay its current debts as they mature, calculated by dividing current assets by current liabilities.

The **current ratio** compares current assets to current liabilities. It measures the company's ability to pay its current debts as they mature. The current ratio of The Ski Patrol is computed as:

$$\text{Current Ratio} = \frac{\text{Current Assets}}{\text{Current Liabilities}} = \frac{\$178,000}{\$\ 69,000} = 2.6 \text{ to } 1$$

This means that the company has $2.60 of current assets for every $1 of current liabilities. In general, a current ratio of 2 to 1 is considered to be financially satisfactory. This rule of thumb must be considered along with other factors such as the nature of the business, the season of the year, and the quality of the company's management. The Ski Patrol's management and other interested parties are likely to compare this 2.6 to 1 ratio to previous operating periods and to industry averages to determine its appropriateness.

acid-test ratio
A ratio that measures the ability of a firm to meet its current debt on short notice, calculated by dividing quick assets by current liabilities.

The **acid-test ratio**, or quick ratio, measures the ability of the firm to meet its current debt on short notice. It calculates quick assets against current liabilities. It does not include inventory or prepaid expenses; only cash, marketable securities, and accounts receivable—all highly liquid assets—are considered.

The current balance sheet of The Ski Patrol lists the following "quick" assets: cash ($10,000), marketable securities ($15,000), accounts receivable ($75,000), and current installments of notes receivable ($22,000). The Ski Patrol's acid-test ratio is computed as:

$$\text{Acid-Test Ratio} = \frac{\text{Quick Assets}}{\text{Current Liabilities}} = \frac{\$122,000}{\$\ 69,000} = 1.8 \text{ to } 1$$

Because the traditional rule of thumb for an adequate acid-test ratio is 1 to 1, The Ski Patrol appears to be in a good short-term credit position. However, the same cautions as for the current ratio should be applied here. This ratio should be compared with industry averages and with previous operating periods in determining its appropriateness for a particular company.

profitability ratio
Financial ratio designed to measure the overall financial performance of the firm.

Profitability ratios. A **profitability ratio** measures the overall financial performance of the firm. It is designed to indicate just how successful a firm really is in terms of its earnings as compared with its total sales or investment. Over a period of time, profitability ratios may also reveal the effectiveness of management in operating the business. Three commonly used profitability ratios are earnings per share, return on sales, and return on equity.

One of the most frequently quoted and commonly watched ratios in business is **earnings per share**. This ratio indicates the amount of profits earned by a company for each common share of stock outstanding. Such earnings represent an important means by which firms can continue to grow if they are reinvested in the company. They also are the basis for dividends paid to the firm's owners. Earnings per share for The Ski Patrol in 1990 are calculated as follows:

earnings per share
The amount of profits earned by a company for each share of common stock outstanding, calculated by dividing net income after taxes by the number of common shares outstanding.

$$\text{Earnings per Share} = \frac{\text{Net Income after Taxes}}{\text{Common Shares Outstanding}} = \frac{\$30,000}{80,000}$$
$$= \$0.375$$

The 37½ cents earnings figure can be compared with earnings per share in previous years to provide some indication of The Ski Patrol's performance. It can also be compared with the earnings per share of other firms in the industry to evaluate the relative performance of the firm.

return on sales
Financial ratio that measures company profitability by comparing net income and net sales.

Return on sales is a financial ratio that measures company profitability by comparing net income and sales. For The Ski Patrol, the ratio is computed as:

$$\text{Return on Sales} = \frac{\text{Net Income}}{\text{Net Sales}} = \frac{\$\ 30,000}{\$292,000} = 10.3 \text{ percent}$$

This profitability ratio is a critical indicator for any profit-seeking firm. In the case of The Ski Patrol, it indicates that a profit of 10.3 cents was realized for every dollar of sales. Although this ratio varies widely among business firms, The Ski Patrol compares very favourably with retail stores in general, which average about a 5 percent return on sales. However, it should be compared with profit forecasts, past performance, and/or more specific industry averages in determining its appropriateness.

return on equity
Financial ratio that measures company profitability by comparing net income and total owners' equity to assess the returns owners are receiving for their overall investment.

Return on equity focuses specifically on the returns the firm's owners are receiving on their investment in the business. It is the ratio between net income earned by the firm and total owner's equity. Both financial statements provide data used to calculate this ratio.

$$\text{Return on Equity} = \frac{\text{Net Income}}{\text{Total Owners' Equity}} = \frac{\$\ 30,000}{\$155,000} = 19.4 \text{ percent}$$

While The Ski Patrol's return of almost 20 percent on equity appears to be satisfactory, the degree of risk present in the industry must also be considered. Shareholders use this ratio to determine whether their funds invested in the business are generating the returns they expected when they made their initial investment.

activity ratio
Ratio measuring the effectiveness of the firm's use of its resources.

inventory turnover ratio
A ratio that measures the number of times merchandise moves through a business, calculated by dividing the cost of goods sold by the average amount of inventory.

Activity ratios. The third category of ratios, the **activity ratio**, measures the effectiveness of the firm's use of its resources. The most frequently used activity ratio is the inventory turnover rate.

The **inventory turnover ratio** indicates the number of times merchandise moves through the business. It is calculated by dividing the cost of goods sold by the average amount of inventory. If the amount of inventory on hand varies considerably from month to month, all twelve of the end-of-month inventories should be totalled and divided by twelve to determine the average inventory for the year. Since The Ski Patrol inventory is relatively constant throughout the year, average inventory is determined by using the January 1 beginning inventory of $65,000 and the December 31 ending inventory of $56,000 as shown on the income statement and dividing by two. The average inventory of $60,500 is then divided into the firm's cost of goods sold using the following equation:

$$\text{Inventory Turnover Ratio} = \frac{\text{Cost of Goods Sold}}{\text{Average Inventory}} = \frac{\$132,000}{\$\ 60,500}$$
$$= 2.2 \text{ times}$$

The turnover rate can be compared with industry standards and used as a measure of efficiency. For retailers such as furniture and jewellery stores, an annual turnover rate of 1.5 times is about average. For a supermarket, however, the turnover rate is 14 to 18 times.

Receivables collection period. In our example, accounts receivable are $79,000. *If* sales are roughly equal per month, i.e., $25,000 per month, three months of sales on account are uncollected. This *could* indicate that the credit and collections are being handled too casually. The ratio is computed as:

$$\frac{\text{current accounts receivable}}{\text{sales on account for the previous year}}$$

The ratio is only informative when there is a worthwhile basis for comparison. This is especially true when a business has cyclical sales patterns.

Debt ratios. The final category of financial ratios, the **debt ratio**, measures the extent to which a firm relies on debt financing. Debt ratios are of particular interest to potential investors and lenders. If too much debt has been used to finance the firm's operations, problems may arise in meeting future interest payments and repaying outstanding loans. In addition, both investors and lenders may prefer to deal with firms whose owners have invested enough of their own money into the firm to avoid over-reliance on borrowing. The debt to owners' equity ratio provides answers to these questions.

The **debt to owners' equity ratio** measures the extent to which the operations of the company are financed by borrowed funds. It indicates the amount of funds contributed by creditors as compared with the total funds provided. The debt to owners' equity ratio for The Ski Patrol is computed as:

$$\text{Debt to Owners' Equity Ratio} = \frac{\text{Total Liabilities}}{\text{Owners' Equity}} = \frac{\$\ 99,000}{\$155,000} = 0.64$$

Since a debt-to-equity ratio of greater than 1 would indicate that the firm was relying more on debt financing than on owners' equity, it is clear that The Ski Patrol owners have invested considerably more than the total amount of liabilities on the firm's balance sheet. However, the specific ratio, like all the other financial ratios discussed earlier, should be evaluated only by comparing it with average industry ratios (the ratios of other firms in the area, if such data are available), previously calculated ratios for the firm, and management expectations.

debt ratio
Financial ratio designed to measure the extent to which the firm relies on debt financing in its operations.

debt to owners' equity ratio
Financial ratio that measures the extent to which company operations are financed by borrowed funds, calculated by dividing total liabilities by owners' equity.

Focus 15-4

Is Reporting of Financial Information Enough?

Corporate annual reports are normally expected to contain a full disclosure of financial information. From an analysis of such a report the health of a firm can be determined. However, as one of the major institutions in our society, a corporation cannot expect to operate without regard for its total impact.

Governmental agencies and social groups contend that corporations not only should accept responsibility for their actions but also should provide a public accounting of those non-economic aspects of corporate operations—product safety, pollution control and equal employment opportunities. This is known as corporate social measurement.

This subject has received increasing attention in accounting literature. There is a trend towards increased disclosure of social responsibility data. The banking and petroleum industries have

An analysis of annual reports showed that banks emphasized information on human resources, product information, and fair business practices. The petroleum industry tended to also include information regarding the environment and energy issues.

Will pressures for greater social responsibility cause more companies to include social responsibility reporting in their annual financial reports? It will be interesting to observe whether the expectation of such reporting will affect behaviour.

Source: Sandrudin A. Ahmed and Daniel Zeghal, "Social Responsibility and Information Disclosure," *CGA Magazine*, November 1988, pp. 25-31.

Budgeting

Although the financial statements discussed in this chapter focus on what has occurred in the past, they are the basis for planning the future. A **budget** is a financial blueprint for a future time period that reflects expected sales revenues, operating expenses, and cash receipts and outlays. It is the quantification of the firm's plans for a future period of time. Since it requires management to specify expected sales, cash inflows and outflows, and costs, it serves as a planning and control tool. The budget serves as the standard by which actual performance is compared.

Budget preparation is frequently time-consuming and involves many people in various departments. The complexity of the process tends to vary with the size and complexity of the organization. Giant

budget
Financial blueprint for a future time period that reflects expected sales revenues, operating expenses, and cash receipts and outlays, used as a planning and control tool.

corporations such as Petro-Canada, Canada Packers and Canadian Pacific tend to have complex and sophisticated systems; their budgets serve as a means of integrating the numerous divisions of the firm in addition to planning and control tools. But budgeting by both large and small firms plays the same role as household budgeting. In both instances, the purpose is to match income and expenses; to accomplish objectives; and to correctly time inflows and outflows.

Since the accounting department is the financial nerve centre of the organization, it provides much of the data used in budget development. The overall master, or operating, budget is actually a composite of numerous sub-budgets for each of the departments or functional areas of the firm. These typically include the production budget, the cash budget, the capital expenditures budget, the advertising budget, and the sales budget, among others. These budgets are typically established on an annual basis, but may be divided monthly or quarterly for control purposes. Since some activities, such as the construction of new manufacturing facilities or long-term purchasing contracts, tend to involve activities extending over several years, longer-term budgets may be used.

Figure 15-6 shows a sample cash budget for a six-month period. This company follows the common practice of establishing a minimum required cash balance each month to cover expected cash needs.

Figure 15-6
Sample Cash Budget

The Ski Patrol 123 Main Street Jasper Alberta	SAMPLE CASH BUDGET JANUARY - JUNE 1991					

	Month					
	January	February	March	April	May	June
Beginning Monthly Balance	$ 3,000	$ 3,000	$ 3,000	$ 3,000	$ 3,000	$ 3,000
Add: Cash Receipts (collections from customers, interest receipts, and other cash inflows)	6,000	5,000	2,000	7,000	4,000	9,000
Cash Available for Firm's Use	$ 9,000	$ 8,000	$ 5,000	$10,000	$ 7,000	$12,000
Deduct: Cash Disbursements (for payroll, materials, income taxes, utilities, interest payments, etc.)	5,000	6,000	5,000	4,000	3,000	4,000
Preliminary Monthly Balance	$ 4,000	$ 2,000	$ -0-	$ 6,000	$ 4,000	$ 8,000
Minimum Required Cash Balance	$ 3,000	3,000	3,000	3,000	3,000	3,000
Excess or Deficiency	1,000	(1,000)	(3,000)	3,000	1,000	2,000
Short-term Investment of Excess	1,000				1,000	2,000
Liquidation of Short-term Investment		1,000				
Short-term Loan to Cover Deficiency			3,000			
Repayment of Short-term loan				3,000		
Ending Monthly Balance	$ 3,000	$ 3,000	$ 3,000	$ 3,000	$ 3,000	$ 3,000

The $3000 minimum balance is determined on the basis of past experience. As the figure reveals, the cash budget identifies months when excess cash funds will be generated. In January, May and June these excess funds will be invested to earn interest rather than remain idle. The cash budget also indicates periods in which temporary loans will be required to finance operations (during March, in this example). Finally, it provides a tangible standard for comparing actual cash inflows and outflows.

Controversial Issue

What are the Responsibilities of Providing Information on the Health of an Organization?

Mr. Macdonald, Chairman of the Commission to Study the Public's Expectations of Audits, put the issue clearly when he said, "[There] is a 'we–they' syndrome." Most people feel "that 'we' are ordinary people trying to cope in the world and that there is a small group known as 'they' who are specially positioned and able to look after themselves. And when you apply that to the role of the auditor, I think that the public feels that 'they' are the people running the companies and that the auditor has to be the public's 'guy' on the job—looking after their interests; looking after us."[1]

At first glance, the conclusion is that it is the auditor's responsibility to look after the public's interest by free and full disclosure of information obtained in the course of an audit. The issue may be a bit more complicated, however. For example, what should the nature of reporting be when an enterprise is having financial difficulty? On the one hand, reporting the danger of a business failure might encourage it to actually happen. For example, investors might decide to put their money elsewhere, or banks could face a run on deposits. On the other hand, the argument is that there is an obligation to disclose any risks to the operation.

Another expert notes that both the external and internal auditor would be put in a difficult position by having to make such a drastic disclosure as doubting a going concern. He questions how much subjective judgement auditors should use, since they are not trained to predict the future, but to examine the past.[2]

Still another expert says auditors have every right to comment on the danger of a company going under, provided there is significant probability of this happening. Rather than predicting failure, the auditor would highlight serious problem areas that could create a potential risk.[3]

[1]William A. Macdonald, interview with *CA Magazine*, July 1988, p. 20.
[2]Rob Orr, quoted in "Macdonald Commission: CMAs Consider Auditors' Proposals," *CMA Magazine*, November 1988, p. 62.
[3]Eldon Gardner, quoted in "Macdonald Commission: CMAs Consider Auditors' Proposals," *CMA Magazine*, November 1988, p. 62.

Summary of Learning Goals

1. **Explain the functions of accounting and its importance to the firm's management and outside parties such as investors, creditors, and government agencies.**

   Accounting involves the measurement, interpretation, and communication of financial information to enable interested parties both inside and outside the firm to make informed decisions. Accountants are responsible for gathering, recording, reporting, and interpreting financial information. Their tasks include bookkeeping, calling attention to problems and opportunities, and aiding in decision making. In addition to assisting management, they supply financial information that describes the status and operation of the firm for use by such outside parties as government agencies and potential investors and lenders.

2. **Distinguish between public and private accountants and explain the roles played by CAs, and CMAs, and CGAs.**

   Chartered accountants (CAs) are independent organizations or individuals who provide accounting services to others. They may perform such services as tax statement preparation, independent audits of financial records, and management consulting, and provide specialized assistance in accounting systems design, filing loan applications, and securities registration documents. Private, or management, accountants (CMAs and CGAs) are responsible for collecting and recording financial transactions; preparing financial statements; and interpreting statements for managers in their own firm, nonprofit organization, or government agency. All have met certification requirements and passed comprehensive examinations.

3. **Explain the steps in the accounting process.**

   The accounting process involves the recording, classifying, and summarizing of accounting transactions; and utililizing these summaries to produce financial statements for the firm's management and other interested parties. Transactions are typically recorded in chronological order in a book called a journal. They are then posted, or transferred, to individual accounts kept in accounting ledgers. At the end of the accounting period, these accounts are summarized and the summaries are used to develop accounting statements.

4. **Identify the accounting equation and its components, and explain the equation's relationship to double-entry bookkeeping.**

   Accounting data are grouped into assets and equities, including liabilities and owners' equity. Assets are things of value owned or leased and used in the business. Cash, accounts and notes receivable, inventory, land, buildings, and machinery are all assets.

Liabilities are claims against the assets by the creditors of the firm. The owners' claims on the assets are called owners', or shareholders', equity. The relationship between the assets of a firm and the claims against those assets is shown by the basic accounting equation:

$$\text{Assets} = \text{Liabilities} + \text{Owners' Equity}$$

Double-entry bookkeeping is the accounting practice of using two entries for every transaction. An increase in assets (the left side of the accounting equation) results in an increase in liabilities or owners' equity (the right side of the equation). As a consequence of these changes offsetting one side of the accounting equation with a change on the other side, the accounting equation remains in balance.

5. **Explain the function of the balance sheet and identify its major components.**

The balance sheet is like a financial photograph, showing the financial position of a company as of a particular date. The three major classifications on the balance sheet represent the components of the basic accounting equation: assets, liabilities, and owners' equity.

6. **Explain the function of the income statement and identify its major components.**

The income statement is like a financial movie of the operations of a firm over a specific time period. It focuses on the firm's activities—its revenues and expenditures—and shows the profitability or unprofitability of the firm during this time period. The major components of the income statement are revenues, cost of goods sold, expenses, and profits or losses.

7. **Identify the major financial ratios used in analyzing a firm's financial strengths and weaknesses and explain the purpose of each.**

Ratios can be divided into four categories. Liquidity ratios measure a firm's ability to meet its short-term obligations. Examples include the current ratio and the acid-test ratio. Profitability ratios assess the overall financial performance of the firm. Earnings per share, return on sales, and return on owners' equity are frequently used profitability ratios. Activity ratios, such as inventory turnover rate, measure how effectively a firm uses its resources. The final category, debt ratios, measures the extent to which the firm relies on debt to finance its operations. The debt to owners' equity ratio is a commonly used debt ratio. Each of these ratios assists the manager and other interested parties by enabling a comparison of current company financial information with that of previous years and with industry standards.

8. **Explain the role of budgets in business.**

Budgets are financial blueprints for future time periods reflecting expected sales revenues, operating expenses, and/or cash receipts and outlays. They represent management's expectations of future occurrences based upon plans that have been made, and serve as important planning and control tools by providing standards against which actual performance can be compared. In addition to an overall master budget, many firms develop specific budgets for production, cash inflows and outflows, advertising, sales, and other functional areas.

Key Terms

accounting
chartered accountant (CA)
audit
certified general
  accountant (CGA)
certified management
  accountant (CMA)
current liabilities
long-term liabilities
working capital
income statement
revenues
operating expenses
selling expenses
owner's equity
accounting equation
double-entry bookkeeping
debit
credit
balance sheet
current assets
liquidity
fixed assets
depreciation
intangible assets
cost of goods sold

accounting process
journal
ledger
posting
assets
equities
liabilities
general expenses
net income
bottom line
statement of changes in
  financial position
liquidity ratio
current ratio
acid-test ratio
profitability ratio
earnings per share
return on sales
return on equity
activity ratio
inventory turnover
  ratio
debt ratio
debt to owners' equity
  ratio
budget

Discussion Questions and Exercises

1. Differentiate between accounting and bookkeeping.
2. Explain the steps involved in the accounting process and the use of accounting journals and ledgers.
3. Explain the concept of double entry bookkeeping. How is it related to the accounting equation? What role do debits and credits play?

4. Identify the three types of assets and the two types of liabilities that appear on a typical balance sheet. Categorize the following account titles:
   a) Bruce Jacobson, Capital
   b) Mortgage Payable
   c) Patent
   d) Buildings
   e) Common Stock
   f) Prepaid Expenses
   g) Accounts Payable
   h) Marketable Securities
5. Why do firms include depreciation on their accounting statement when it involves no cash outlays?
6. What are the major differences between the balance sheet and the income statement?
7. For each of the accounts listed below, check the appropriate columns:

Account	Current Asset	Fixed Asset	Intangible Asset	Current Liability	Long-term Liability	Owners' Equity	Rev.	Exp.
Net Sales								
Accounts Receivable								
Copyrights								
Advertising Expenses								
Common Stock								
Equipment								
Marketable Securities								
Long-Term Notes Payable								
Salary Expenses								
Retained Earnings								

8. What are the major advantages of showing the various items on a firm's income statement in percentages based upon net sales rather than showing the actual figures involved?
9. The financial ratios discussed in the chapter were divided into four basic categories. Identify these categories and describe specific ratios included in each one.
10. Explain the similarities and differences between budgeting and the development of accounting statements. What are the primary purposes of budgets?

Case 15-1

Delgado Amusement Company

The following account balances have been taken from the accounting books and records of Delgado Amusement Company on December 31, 1990. Exhibit 1 lists balance sheet items and Exhibit 2 lists income statement items.

EXHIBIT 1

Accounts Payable	$ 60,000	Current Installments of	
Accounts Receivable	60,000	Long-Term Debt	$ 10,000
Accrued Expenses	5,000	Equipment	150,000
Accumulated Depreciation		Furniture and Fixtures	30,000
on Equipment	40,000	Inventory	65,000
Accumulated Depreciation		Long-Term Debt	35,000
on Furniture and Fixtures	6,000	Marketable Securities	20,000
Allowance for Doubtful		Patent	6,000
Accounts	10,000	Prepaid Expenses	5,000
Cash	10,000	Retained Earnings	130,000
Common Shares (50,000			
shares @ $1)	50,000		

EXHIBIT 2

Advertising Expenses	$ 3,000	Income Taxes	$ 5,000
Beginning Inventory,		Miscellaneous General Expenses	1,000
January 1, 1987	50,000	Miscellaneous Selling Expenses	1,000
Depreciation: Sales		Net Purchases	125,000
Equipment	4,000	Office Salaries	9,000
Depreciation: Office		Office Supplies	2,000
Equipment	1,000	Sales Returns and Allowances	20,000
Ending Inventory,		Sales Salaries and Commissions	24,000
December 31, 1987	65,000		
Gross Sales	200,000		

Questions:
1. Prepare an income statement and balance sheet for Delgado Amusement Company. Use Figures 15-3 and 15-4 as guides for preparing these statements.
2. Calculate each of the financial ratios explained in the chapter, using the information presented above. What conclusions can you make about Delgado Amusement Company based upon these ratios?

Case 15-2

Mortgage Payments—Weekly or Monthly???

When a homeowner takes out a mortgage, his or her main concern should be negotiating a repayment schedule that will minimize the amount paid in interest. Recently financial institutions have been offering mortgagers a new scheme: repayment by the week instead of by the month. Does payment by the week cut interest payments? Consider the following example:

Assume that a mortgage of $50,000 is under consideration. Also assume that the rate is a constant 17.5 percent. In a standard 25-year mortgage paid on a monthly basis each payment will be $714.70. If only the scheduled payments are made and they are made on the due date, the total amount repaid will amount to $214,421.

Now consider the effects of changing the payment schedule from monthly to weekly. The normal way of determining the weekly payment is to divide the monthly payment by four, creating in this case a payment of $178.68. Payment weekly, however, means 52 payments a year, or the equivalent of 13 of the $714.70 payments under the monthly schedule. In other words, over the year the weekly payments of $178.68 x 52 come to $9,291.36, or $714.70 more than the monthly payments of $714.70 x 12, which total $8,576.40. Thus an additional $714.70 is paid yearly toward the mortgage. As interest is charged on the reducing principal balance, and this balance is being reduced more rapidly, the mortgage will be paid in full in 16 years and 14 weeks. The total repaid will be $151,185, which is a saving of $63,236 over the 25-year mortgage paid on a monthly basis.

There is, however, another matter to consider: how interest is compounded and collected. When payment is made weekly the interest is compounded weekly. This is more expensive than when the interest is compounded and collected half-yearly. This means there is a better way still of saving money on interest: making monthly payments, and on each mortgage anniversary date repaying an extra $714.96 (approximately one month's payment). This will bring the total annual payment to $9,291.36, as in the case of weekly payments. This approach will pay off the mortgage in 14 years and 34 weeks. The total repaid will be $136,138, a saving of $78,283 over the original 25-year mortgage.

If a weekly schedule can be afforded, it is still recommended that a homeowner choose a monthly plan, divide the payments by four, and place this amount weekly into a daily interest savings account. Each month the mortgage payment should be withdrawn, leaving the interest earned on the daily balances, plus the payments for the extra four weeks of the year until the anniversary date. The entire sum (deposits plus interest) may then be applied against the mortgage principal. The more paid to reduce the principal, the less will be paid in interest.

Source: *The Royal Bank Report (Manitoba Edition)*, Nov./Dec. 1982, Vol. 1, Issue 4, p. 3.

Questions:
1. The total amount paid out on a mortgage is affected by three variables: principal, interest rate, and period of time, which are being manipulated in Case 15-2. How else might they be manipulated to affect total payout?
2. Explain why a general knowledge of accounting is important for people in all walks of life.
3. Explain the terms *equity, principal,* and *interest*. How are these related to one another?

Chapter 16

Production and Operations Management

Learning Goals

Production is not the
application of tools to
materials. It is the application
of logic to work.
—*Peter F. Drucker*

1. To explain how production creates utility for a firm's customers

2. To explain the roles of standardization, specialization, and mechanization in mass production

3. To describe the contributions and problems involved with the use of assembly lines, automation, and robots in producing products and services

4. To identify the three components of production and operations management

5. To list the major factors involved in making plant location decisions

6. To compare the alternative designs for production facilities

7. To identify the steps involved in the purchasing process

8. To compare the advantages and disadvantages of maintaining large amounts of inventory

9. To identify each step in the production control process

Profile

Albert DeFehr—*From Chicken Barn to World Leader in Wood Furniture Products*

In 1944 Albert A. DeFehr started Palliser Furniture in the basement of his home. Two years later, in 1946, he moved to a chicken barn and in 1948 he built his first factory.

Today, Palliser is Canada's largest wood furniture manufacturer, serving between 300 and 400 retailers in Canada and the United States. The company has grown consistently over the last 25 years without a single year of loss, and is doubling every three to four years.

While founder Albert is still Chairman of the Board, his three sons now run the business. They are equal shareholders and work with a consensus on all issues.

Palliser has spread its wings to four buildings with nearly a million square feet and 1,100 employees in Winnipeg alone. On the national scene, Palliser has an upholstery factory of 13,000 square metres in Airdrie, Alberta, and a distribution centre in Vancouver of about 1,900 square metres. It also has a 13,700-square-metre factory in Fargo, North Dakota.

Technically, Palliser has developed a very modern production operation. It can hold its own and compete with furniture factories throughout North America. In fact, it is one of North America's most computerized operations, producing its own show-wood, upholstery frames, melamine panels, and plastic components. The company has just built a new particle board plant—the only one in the prairie provinces. To provide greater efficiency, the company has developed single-technology plants.

Although most of Palliser's business is done outside Winnipeg, Art DeFehr says it is important to the family to be based in that city. "We've got strong family, church, and community ties here. Winnipeg is a good manufacturing centre. It is not dominated by one or two cyclical industries, so there is a varied skilled labour force," he says.

Palliser works cooperatively with the city of Winnipeg and the provincial government in programmes designed to hire physically and mentally handicapped persons. As a result of the family's refugee background and continuing connections, it has become a corporate policy to hire refugees and immigrants. "I've brought Central American refugees here and have personally sponsored them. Co-workers are sensitive and we have strong employee loyalties," says DeFehr.

"In the next five years, our strength in the US should increase and we will have energy for the world market. Palliser Worldtrade, for example, is negotiating to market products in the US that are built in Asia" he says.

Future projections look bright for Palliser Furniture. "In the first half of this year, sales were very good," Art DeFehr says. "Other US and Canadian companies slowed down or had layoffs. Palliser's sales were up 42 percent in Canada in the first five months."

Not bad for a company that started in the basement of a residential home less than 45 years ago.

Source: Joan Rusen, "From Humble Beginnings," *Manitoba Business*, September 1988, pp. 6-8.

Ford's advertising slogan, "At Ford, Quality is Job One," reflects the reality of the marketplace and the firm's production situation in the late seventies and early eighties. Why did Ford have to mount a campaign of this type and magnitude? Simply stated, in the years leading up to the late seventies, the company had created some of its own problems and been caught up in others not of its making. Many of these were production related.

Quality was not as good as it might have been. Consumer acceptance of Ford vehicles had been slipping for some time. In addition, the firm had problems in costs and productivity, as did other members of the North American auto industry.

In its turnaround plans, the company set product quality as its first requirement. The second commitment was to take a new approach to product function and appearance. Third, long-range planning was strengthened, and fourth, major efforts were made to get costs in line and find ways to be more efficient. While this list covered many aspects of the company's operations, a great deal of it centred around the design of an efficient production system. Without this, chances for recovery were slim.[1]

Society allows businesses to operate only so long as they make a contribution. By producing and marketing desired goods and services, businesses satisfy this commitment. They create what economists call utility—the want-satisfying power of a product or service. There are four basic kinds of utility—form, time, place, and ownership.

Time, place, and ownership utility are created by marketing—by having products available to consumers at convenient locations when they want to buy and at facilities where title to the products can be transferred at the time of purchase.

form utility
Utility created through the conversion of raw materials and other input into finished products or services.

Form utility is created through the conversion of raw materials and other input into finished products or services. For example, glass, steel, fabrics, rubber, and other components are combined to form a new Nissan or Fiero. Plastics are moulded to produce a Frisbee. Fabric, thread, and buttons are converted into Arrow shirts. The creating of form utility is the responsibility of the firm's production function and the subject of this chapter.

What Is Production?

production
The use of people and machinery to convert materials into finished products or services.

Production is the use of people and machinery to convert raw materials into finished products or services, creating form utility. Figure 16-1 illustrates the production process.

Although the term production is sometimes used interchangeably with manufacturing, it is a broader term and includes a number of non-manufacturing processes. For example, it encompasses such extractive industries as fishing, lumber, and mining, as well as

Figure 16-1
Manufacturing coins at a mint is an example of a production system.

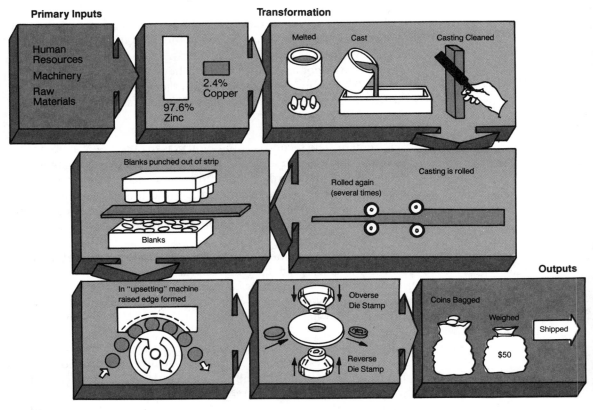

including the creation of intangible services. Table 16-1 lists ten examples of production systems for a variety of goods and services.

The conversion process may involve major changes in raw materials or a simple combining of finished parts. The butcher performs a production function by reducing a side of beef to ground beef, steaks, chuck roasts, and so on. General Motors combines tires, spark plugs, a battery, and thousands of other components to complete a new Pontiac Grand Am. All these processes result in the creation of form utility.

In many instances, the production system generates services rather than goods. Services are intangible outputs of the production system. They include outputs as diverse as trash hauling, education, haircuts, tax accounting, public and private health care systems, mail services, transportation, lodging, and hundreds of others. In addition to being intangible, services are often more difficult to standardize than are goods. While the output of equipment-based service producers such as dry cleaners, automatic car washes, airlines, and computer time-

Table 16-1
Some Typical Production Systems

Example	Primary Input	Transformation	Output
Pet food factory	Grain, water, fish meal, personnel, tools, machines, paper bags, cans, buildings, utilities	Converts raw materials into finished goods	Pet food products
Hamburger stand	Meat, bread, vegetables, spices, supplies, personnel, utilities, machines, cartons, napkins, buildings, hungry customers	Transforms raw materials into fast-food products and packages	Satisfied customers and fast-food products
Automobile factory	Purchased parts, raw materials, supplies, paints, tools, equipment, personnel, buildings, utilities	Transforms raw materials into finished automobiles through fabrication and assembly operations	Automobiles
Trucking firm	Trucks, personnel, buildings, fuel, goods to be shipped, packaging supplies, truck parts, utilities	Packages and transports goods from sources to destinations	Delivered goods
Department store	Buildings, displays, shopping carts, machines, stock goods, personnel, supplies, utilities	Attracts customers, stores goods, sells products	Marketed goods
Accounting firm	Supplies, personnel, information, computers, buildings, office furniture, machines, utilities	Attracts customers, compiles data, supplies management information, computes taxes	Management information and tax services
Automobile body shop	Damaged autos, paints, supplies, machines, tools, buildings, personnel, utilities	Transforms damaged auto bodies into facsimiles of the original	Repaired automobile bodies
College or university	Students, books, supplies, personnel, buildings, utilities	Transmits information and develops skills and knowledge	Educated persons
City police department	Supplies, personnel, equipment, automobiles, office furniture, buildings, utilities	Detects crimes, brings criminals to justice, keeps the peace	Lower crime rates and peaceful communities
Department of Fisheries	Supplies, personnel, ships, computers, aircraft, utilities, office furniture, equipment	Detects offenders of federal fishery laws, brings them to justice, preserves fishery resources	Optimal stock of fish resources

Source: Norman Gaither, *Production and Operations Management*, Dryden Press. Reprinted by permission.

"YOU CAN HAVE EITHER COMFORT OR STYLE OR DURABILITY, BUT NOT ALL THREE."

The intent of the production process is to match products with consumer needs.

Sidney Harris

sharing is highly standardized, there is less standardization in such services as hair care, lawn services, and professional consulting. Whether the result of the process is a tangible good or an intangible service, both are created by the conversion of input into output.

This chapter describes and analyzes the process of producing products and services designed to create utilities.

Mass Production and the Assembly Line

Canada began as a colonial supplier of raw materials to Europe and evolved into one of the stronger countries of the world. A major factor in this remarkable change has been the application of the concept of mass production. **Mass production** is the manufacture of products in large amounts through the effective combination of three factors: specialized labour, mechanization, and standardization. The result of mass production is the availability of large quantities of products produced efficiently and sold at lower prices than could be dreamed of if such products were individually crafted.

mass production
Manufacture of products in large quantities as a result of standardization, specialized labour, and mechanization.

Specialization

specialization
Dividing work into its simplest components to permit concentration by workers or machines in performing each task.

A key factor in making mass production possible is **specialization**— the dividing of work into its simplest components in order that workers can concentrate on performing each task. The father of this approach was Frederick W. Taylor, whose efforts in the late nineteenth and early twentieth century were devoted to achieving industrial efficiency by reducing and simplifying jobs. Taylor's contemporary, Frank B. Gilbreth, carried this reduction of tasks to the ultimate. Gilbreth called the smallest possible time-and-motion unit for a given task a *therblig* (a term that comes from reversing the letters in his last name). He applied many of these production concepts to operating his household, and became famous to later generations in the book and film *Cheaper by the Dozen* written by two of his twelve children.

Mechanization

mechanization
Use of machines to perform work previously performed by people.

Once jobs were separated into smaller tasks, managers could consider the possibility of **mechanization**—the use of machines to perform work previously performed by people. Prior to the Industrial Revolution, work was performed primarily by people and animals. In 1850, the typical worker spent 70 hours per week on the job and produced an average of twenty-five cents' worth of goods per hour. In 1990, the average person works 40 hours a week or less and, with machines, produces goods almost 100 times the value of his or her counterpart of the mid-nineteenth century.

Standardization

standardization
Production of uniform interchangeable goods and parts.

The third component of a mass production system—**standardization**—involves the production of uniform, interchangeable goods and parts. Although production of virtually identical products is taken for granted today, this was not always the case. Prior to 1798, for example, each part of an army rifle was manufactured by hand. The result was that each part fitted only one gun. That year inventor Eli Whitney introduced a new method of forging and stamping out ''standard'' interchangeable parts. These parts were produced in quantity and then assembled into a finished rifle at a later stage of production. Availability of standardized parts makes possible the replacement of defective and worn-out components. Repairs of such products as automobiles are facilitated by the simple purchase of replacement parts at a local auto supply store. Without such standardization, each needed replacement would involve special machining at unacceptable expense.

Assembly Lines

In a logical extension of the factors of worker specialization, mechanization, and standardization, Henry Ford revolutionized the factory by using what he called the assembly line to assemble his automobiles. This manufacturing technique involved placing the product upon a conveyor belt which travels past a number of work stations where workers performed certain tasks such as welding, painting, installing a part, or tightening a bolt. The results were phenomenal. Prior to adding the assembly line, Ford's Model Ts were being assembled at the rate of one for each twelve-hour workday. The assembly-line technique slashed the number of work hours required to 1.5. Not surprisingly, dozens of other industries whose production consisted of assembling complex products quickly adopted the assembly-line technique.

Job simplification and routinization often result in extreme boredom, frustration, and carelessness. Although the assembly line continues to be a fixture in many manufacturing operations, a number of adjustments have been made in recent years. There is a growing trend to increase the scope of an employee's work in order to improve the quality of worklife. In many instances, workers have been given more control of the assembly line and have the authority to stop the line to correct problems. In addition, the use of machine robots has taken over some of the most boring tasks.

Focus 16-1

The Moving Assembly Line Revolutionized Modern Life

The year 1988 marked the 75th anniversary of the moving assembly line, arguably one of the pivotal inventions of the 20th century (other contenders for the title are the computer and the atom bomb).

The roots of the modern internal-combustion-engine-powered auto can be traced directly back to the 1880s, and in broader terms, far beyond that. But until 1913, when Henry Ford developed the assembly-line process, cars were hand-built, expensive toys for the few.

Within a few years of Ford's invention, assembly line techniques had spread far beyond his Highland Park, Michigan, plant and automobiles were rolling out to face the rutted roads of North America by the hundreds of thousands. Prices nosedived from thousands at the turn of the century to a few hundred dollars by 1920.

The impact of the automobile on society since has been well documented—starting with the freedom and mobility it gave the average person. The assembly line itself has also helped shape the modern consumer-driven world, making cheap, mass-produced goods possible.

By 1908, Henry Ford had developed the legendary Model T, for its time a practical and reliable transportation device. Its simplicity made it the ideal vehicle to put North Americans on wheels—but it cost too much.

In those days, car bodies were delivered to Ford's plant by

horse-drawn wagon, and assembly was carried out with the chassis mounted on sawhorses. Teams of runners distributed parts to the cars being built on the factory floor, and the assembly workers moved from car to car doing their particular jobs.

Ford historians don't actually credit Henry with the blinding-light discovery of the assembly line concept, but they do say he created the climate that brought about its development.

In seeking a solution to lower production cost, Ford surrounded himself with experts from fields as diverse as brewing, canning, steelmaking, and even meat-processing—Chicago slaughterhouses of the time had a "disassembly" system to break down carcasses.

"In later years he was glorified as the originator of the mass production idea. Far from it; he just grew into it like the rest of us," says Charles Sorensen, production chief at Ford for many years, in his autobiography.

The process apparently began with the move by the seven-year-old Ford Motor Co. into the new Highland Park factory in 1910. Improved machine tools increased parts output and precision, allowing true interchangeability (something pioneered by firearms makers in the early 1800s).

The first Ford assembly line was established in 1913 to build flywheel magnetos. The process, which employed 29 men, cut assembly time to 13 minutes per unit, compared to 20 minutes when they were assembled by one person.

On October 17, 1913, the concept was taken to the factory floor, with a rudimentary assembly line 45.7 metres long. A winch hauled the chassis down the line of 140 men. Parts had been stacked at intervals along the line, with the spacing based on the known time it took to install them. Time of the final assembly was reduced from 12 man-hours under the old stationary system to less than three.

The impact was immediate. In 1912, Ford produced only 82,388 Model Ts, with the touring car selling for US$600. By 1916, production of the T had risen to 585,000 and the price had dropped to US$360.

The principles weren't new, but until Ford and his people brought them together and made them work, nobody had ever tried to assemble consumer durable goods on a continuous-flow basis.

Ford's next major impact on North American industry, in January 1914, was the institution of the $5-a-day wage, an unheard-of amount in those days. One of Ford's goals was to reduce attrition, the other to avert a strike, but the move also boosted the standard of living of the working man, turning him in the process into a potential car buyer.

Seventy-five years later, the assembly line, branded as dehumanizing and worse, is giving way to more flexible, user-friendly systems, some using remotely guided vehicles to haul cars through the final assembly process. But it will certainly live on in some areas of assembly where robots are an ideal answer to dirt, danger, and drudgery.

Source: Robert English, "How 'Fordism' Drove the Car and Revolutionized Modern Life," *The Financial Post*, January 2, 1989, p. 14.

Classifying Production Processes

The methods used in producing a product or service can be classified by the means and the time used to create the product or service. The product or service results from the use of either an analytic or a synthetic system by either a continuing or an intermittent process.

An **analytic system** is one in which a raw material is reduced to its component parts in order to extract one or more products. In petroleum refining, crude oil is broken down and gasoline, wax, fuel oil, kerosene, tar, and other products are obtained. A meat-packing plant slaughters cattle and produces various cuts of meat, glue from the horns and hooves, and leather from the hides.

A **synthetic system** is the reverse of an analytic system. It combines a number of raw materials or parts into a finished product or changes raw materials into completely different finished products. On the assembly line, an automobile is produced from the combination of thousands of individual parts. Drugs and chemicals are produced by a synthetic system, as is stainless steel.

Continuous process production describes a manufacturing operation where long production runs turn out finished products over a period of days, months, or even years. The steel industry provides a classic example; its blast furnaces never completely shut down unless a malfunction occurs. Petroleum refineries and nylon and other chemical manufacturers also represent continuous process production. A shutdown can ruin equipment and prove extremely costly.

Intermittent process production describes a manufacturing operation where the production run is short and machines are shut down frequently or changed in order to produce different products. When intermittent production occurs in response to a specific customer order, it is called **job-order production**. When it is used for inventory, it is called **lot-order production**.

analytic system
A system in which a raw material is reduced to its component parts in order to extract one or more products.

synthetic system
A system that combines a number of raw materials or parts into a finished product or changes raw materials into completely different products.

continuous process
A manufacturing operation where long production runs turn out finished products over a period of days, months, or even years.

intermittent process
A manufacturing operation where the production run is short and machines are shut down frequently or changed in order to produce different products.

job-order production
Intermittent production that occurs in response to a specific customer order.

lot-order production
Intermittent production that occurs in response to inventory needs.

Computer-Aided Design/Computer-Aided Manufacturing (CAD/CAM)

Computer-aided design and computer-aided manufacturing have the potential to revolutionize the way Canadian industry designs and manufactures products. It also has the potential to give Canadian companies the edge they need to compete effectively with foreign manufacturers.

Engineers and designers use computer-aided design (CAD) to determine the best way to meet product specifications. Using a special electronic pen, engineers can sketch three-dimensional designs on a tablet connected to a computer. They then can use the computer to make major and minor design changes. When engineers are satisfied with their sketches, they instruct the computer to analyze the design for certain characteristics or problems. Completed designs become part of the computer's memory. They can be printed out for use away from the computer terminal or converted into a tape that is "read" by numerically controlled machine tools.

CAD is used by automobile manufacturers to evaluate new car designs even before prototypes of the designs are made. Using the computer, engineers put the structural components of each car through the paces of a simulated road test. If they find a problem with weight distribution, for example, they can make the necessary changes right on their computer terminal. Only when they are satisfied with all the structural characteristics of their design will they manufacture an actual car model. Aircraft designers use CAD for similar design purposes. Once an aircraft design is displayed on the computer screen, engineers can analyze the shape and strength of the fuselage and wings under various conditions. These instantaneous analyses leave few doubts about the integrity of the design.

Computer-aided manufacturing (CAM) picks up where CAD leaves off. This process enables manufacturers to use rapid-speed, automated equipment on jobs that require the production of small batches of goods. Bela Gold, an expert on manufacturing technologies and industrial productivity, sums up the value of CAM in this way:

> Although its benefits are not readily visible to the untrained eye, CAM offers the potential for a flexible manufacturing process in which a sequence of operations is directed by an integrated system of computer controls. By simply changing the programmed instructions guiding each machine, manufacturers can produce different sizes of a given part as well as a number of different parts within a given range.
>
> The degree of control made possible by a CAM system allows managers to route each part through the proper sequence of machines, to instruct each machine in the required sequence of operations for each part, and to allocate these tasks so as to optimize the working time available from all machines.

Thus, from initial design to completed product CAD/CAM systems enable engineers, designers, and manufacturers to make the best use of time and equipment. The results in all cases are more competitive products.

Automation and the Use of Robots

automation
Replacement of people with machines that perform work with little or no human assistance.

robot
Programmable machine capable of performing numerous tasks requiring programmed manipulations of materials and tools.

Continuous process production systems are typically highly mechanized and frequently utilize assembly lines. A logical extension of mechanization is **automation**—the replacement of people with machines that perform production processes with little or no help from humans. Once jobs are divided into specific tasks, it is often possible to design machines to perform such tasks, freeing humans from the repetitive, boring tasks that characterize many assembly-line operations. In an automated factory, people design the systems and occasionally monitor their operations and inspect the final output, but the actual work is performed by machines.

In other cases, machines handle both the production and the monitoring phases. In their attempts to increase factory productivity and to free humans from routine assembly-line tasks and potential dangerous assignments such as handling hazardous materials, many production managers are replacing blue-collar workers with "steel-collar" workers in the form or robots. A **robot** is a reprogrammable machine capable of performing a variety of tasks requiring programmed manipulations of materials and tools.[2]

Today's industrial robots look nothing like the androids of *Star Wars* fame, and they vary considerably in complexity and versatility. A pick-and-place robot is the simplest version, accounting for about one-third of all installations. Freedom of movement is usually limited to two or three directions as it picks something from one spot and places it in another. The most common industrial robot is the servo robot. The name comes from the servomechanisms that permit the arm and gripper to alter direction in midair without having to trip a mechanical switch. It can be taught a sequence of arm-and-gripper movements that is repeated indefinitely. A computerized servo robot can be taught new tasks through instructions that are transmitted electronically. In addition, some computerized robots have one or more artificial senses, typically sight or touch. The state of the art in industry is the automated factory—a flexible manufacturing system that permits adjusting assembly-line tasks to perform different work activities. The system consists of computer-controlled machining centres to produce metal parts, robots to handle the parts, and remote-controlled carts to deliver materials. All components are linked together by electronic controls that dictate what will happen at each stage of the manufacturing sequence, even automatically replacing broken or worn-out drill bits and other implements.[3]

The usefulness of robots in the factory has been demonstrated throughout the industrialized world. Robots don't take coffee breaks, call in sick, or demonstrate periods of fatigue depending on the time of day. As technology has reduced their prices and increased their flexibility, robots have become increasingly common in industry.

What Is Involved in Production and Operations Management?

production and operations management
Management of the use of people and machinery in converting materials and resources into finished products and services.

Obviously the process of converting input into finished goods and services must be managed. This, then is the task of **production and operations management**—to manage the use of people and machinery in converting materials and resources into finished products and services. To see more clearly how this is accomplished it is useful to visit a production facility. One such facility is familiar to every student although few have ever thought of it as a factory: McDonald's (see Focus 16-2).

Managers of the production function are responsible for three major activities. First, production managers must make plans for production input. This involves determining the necessary input required in the firm's operations and includes such decisions as product planning, plant location, and provision for adequate supplies of raw materials, labour, power, and machinery. These plans must be completed before the conversion process from raw material to finished product or service can begin.

Second, production managers must make decisions about the installation of the necessary input. These include the actual design of the plant, the best types of machines to be used, the arrangement of the production machinery, and the determination of the most efficient flow of work in the plant.

Third, production managers must coordinate the production processes—the routing of material to the right places, the development of work schedules, and the assignment of work to specific employees. The objective is to promote efficiency and effectiveness.

Production Planning

Henry Ford was obsessed with a burning question: could the motor car be converted from a plaything for the rich to a replacement for the horse used by the general public? In 1893, when Ford built his first horseless carriage, the price tag was $9,000. Every piece of the automobile was hand designed, and the emphasis was on high prices for limited production runs.

Ford saw a different strategy. If the horseless carriage could be mass produced, a firm could earn small profits on each car sold and reduce the price to fit the budgets of most families. But such a production revolution would require careful planning. These plans would have to deal with every component of the production process if Ford's low-price, mass-production strategy was to succeed.

Ford's plans resulted in a solution for the production cost problems. He decided to use vanadium steel for automobile bodies, and he added a fast-moving assembly line. Specialists were hired, trained, and assigned specific duties on the line. Worker morale was boosted tremendously through the adoption of an eight-hour workday. Ford shocked industry by paying his employees $5 a day, more than double the prevailing wages in similar industries. And his plan worked. By 1908 his Model T carried a price tag of $850. In 1926 the price had dropped to $284. By that time nearly 15 million Model Ts had been built and sold.

Focus 16-2

A Factory with Golden Arches?

A good place to start describing the production process at McDonald's is with the product itself. The McDonald's burger is a machine-stamped 45 g patty, 5.6 mm thick and 98.4 mm wide when raw; next comes 7 g of onion, a pickle slice, and splats of ketchup and mustard. All the ingredients rest on a 108 mm bun.

At every McDonald's outlet, blinking lights on the grills tell the counter-persons exactly when to flip over the hamburgers. Once done, the burgers can be held under infrared warming lights for up to ten minutes—no more. After that, any burgers that have not been ordered must be thrown away. Deep fryers continuously adjust to the moisture in every potato stick to make sure that french fries come out with a uniform degree of brownness; specially designed scoops make it almost physically impossible for an employee to stuff more or fewer french fries into a paper bag than headquarters specifies for a single order. The bun has a higher-than-normal sugar content for faster browning. The whole process is dedicated to speed—turning out a burger, fries, and a shake in fifty seconds.

Professor Theodore Levitt of the Harvard Business School described McDonald's as ''a machine that produces, with the help of totally unskilled machine tenders, a highly polished product. Everything is built integrally into the machine itself, into the technology of the system. The only choice available to the attendant is to operate it exactly as the designers intended.''

Product Planning

A firm's total planning begins with the choice of products it wants to offer its customers. Plant location, machinery purchases, pricing decisions and selection of retail outlets are all based on product planning. In a very real sense, the sole economic justification for the firm's existence is the production and marketing of want-satisfying products.

In most firms, product planning is the joint responsibility of the production and marketing departments. Because a product must be designed to satisfy consumer needs, market research studies are used to obtain consumer reactions to proposed products, to test prototypes of new products, and to estimate the potential sales and profitability of new products. The production department is primarily concerned with (1) converting the original product concept into the final product, and (2) designing production facilities to produce this new product as efficiently as possible. As Chapters 10 to 13 pointed out, the new product must not only be accepted by consumers; it must also be produced economically to assure an acceptable return on company funds invested in the project.

Service Planning

Planning the production of services involves the same considerations as planning the production of products described above. Services, like products, must be designed to satisfy consumer needs, and market research is also used to determine consumer reactions to a proposed service. The planning of the services, however, concentrates on the personnel who will provide them, rather than on the engineering specifications and technology that are needed to manufacture a product.

Facility Location

One of the major production decisions is the choice of a plant location. The decision typically represents a long-term commitment and a substantial investment. A poor location poses severe problems in attempting to compete with better-located competitors.

Many companies have managed to overcome location obstacles very effectively. They have used other advantages, such as superior product quality and aggressive marketing. For example, Triple E Manufacturing is located in Winkler, Manitoba, 177 kilometres south of Winnipeg. The company produces such high quality motor homes that European demand for the product overcomes the problem of their being produced in the centre of Canada. Similarly, Volvo successfully markets their cars around the world. Nevertheless, there are basic facility location principles which should be considered.

What Constitutes a Good Location?

Choosing a facility location is typically divided into two stages: (1) selecting a community in which the facility will be located, and (2) choosing a specific site within the community. The choice of a location should be made after considering such factors as proximity to raw materials and markets; availability of labour, transportation, and energy; local regulations; and community living conditions.

Favourable labour climate. One of the most important considerations in the location of production or service facilities is the cost and/or availability of a qualified labour force. One early problem facing oil exploration companies off the coast of Newfoundland was the lack of sufficient numbers of skilled workers. Many electronics firms are located in the Toronto area, which has a high concentration of skilled technicians. The same is true for Calgary (oil), Winnipeg (insurance), Hamilton (steel), and Montreal (aircraft).

When unskilled workers can be used, the manufacturer has a much greater choice of locations. Many manufacturing plants employing unskilled labour have located in areas where wage rates have historically been lower. In the worldwide search for inexpensive labour, a number of electrical equipment manufacturers have recently begun to manufacture parts in North America (mechanized production), ship them in unassembled form to the island of Taiwan, have them assembled there by low-cost workers, and then ship them back to North America for inclusion in a finished product.

Proximity to markets. If transportation costs for raw materials are not a significant part of total production costs, the plant is likely to be located near markets where the final products are to be sold. A nearby location allows the manufacturer to provide fast, convenient service for customers. Many automobile components manufacturers are located in close proximity to Ontario and Detroit auto manufacturers in order to provide quick service for auto assembly plants.

Sixty-two percent of Canada's population is concentrated in Ontario and Quebec. It is not too surprising that 71 percent of Canadian manufacturing is found near the St. Lawrence River and the Great Lakes. This provides the option of ready rail or truck transportation to much of the market, as well as water transportation to many distant destinations.

Many foreign manufacturers with large Canadian markets have set up production facilities in Canada. They include Xerox, Hyundai, Michelin, and others.

Facilities that provide services, such as dry cleaners, laundromats, banks, hotels, local government offices, and hospitals, must be located near the largest concentrations of their target customers. If, for example, dry cleaners were located too far from where people live, no one would patronize them.

Community living conditions. Quality of life is important in choosing a location. Factors considered here are the quality of the community, as measured by its school system, colleges, cultural programmes, fire and police protection, climate, spending levels of its citizens, and community attitudes toward the new facility.

Proximity to raw materials is an important consideration when selecting a location for a production facility. For example, production facilities that process trees into wood products are usually located near forests.

The decision on plant location should be based upon a careful evaluation of all the factors discussed here (summarized in Table 16-2.) Management must weigh each of these factors in the light of its own individual needs.

Proximity to raw materials. When raw materials are large and heavy, manufacturing firms often locate their plants near the source of these inputs. Production facilities for plasterboard are usually close to where the major ingredient, gypsum, is mined. (Mined gypsum must be dehydrated immediately in order to avoid transporting the water in it.) Trees are processed into wood products near forests, thereby eliminating the cost of transporting those parts of the log that become waste materials. Because 200,000 litres of water are required to produce one tonne of paper, paper mills must be located in areas where large quantities of clean, low-cost water are available.

Transportation. Transportation facilities are required to ship raw materials to the plant and finished products to customers. At most locations the producer can choose among several alternatives, such as trucks, railways, ships, and airplanes. Availability of numerous alternatives can result in increased competition and lower rates for transportation users.

Service facilities also must consider available transportation. Customers must be able to get to them by either public transportation or private automobile. If cars are the primary method of transportation, then adequate parking must also be provided.

Energy. While all production facilities are affected by both availability of adequate energy resources and their costs, factories producing goods tend to be more affected than service industries.

The aluminum industry developed in Kitimat, BC and Arvida, Quebec, because the manufacture of aluminum requires great amounts of electric power. The cheap hydro-electricity available at these sites allows aluminum to be produced at a competitive price. For industries such as aluminum, chemicals, and fertilizers, availability of inexpensive power supplies is a major consideration in plant location.

Local regulations. Another factor to consider in facility location is local and provincial taxes. Local and provincial governments typically impose real estate taxes on factories, equipment, and inventories. Sales taxes and income taxes may also be imposed. These taxes, which vary considerably from province to province and city to city, should be considered in making the location decision. Some provinces and cities attempt to entice manufacturers or service businesses into their areas by granting low taxes or temporary exemptions from taxation. However, low taxes may also mean inadequate municipal services. Taxes must be considered together with the availability and quality of needed city services.

Until recently, most communities actively competed in attracting industry, which they hoped would produce new jobs and population growth. In recent years, a countertrend has developed, as many communities reject the notion that all growth is beneficial. Most local officials are aware that more jobs also produce more demands on the public school system, more traffic congestion, increased likelihood of industrial pollution, and added pressures on police and fire departments. This awareness has resulted in numerous location constraints for manufacturers.

environmental impact study
Report that specifies the impact of a proposed plant location on the quality of life in a specific area.

An increasingly common requirement for firms desiring to locate a production facility in a particular area is an **environmental impact study**. It analyzes the impact of a proposed plant on the quality of life in an area. Regulatory agencies typically require the study to cover such topics as impact on transportation facilities; energy requirements; water and sewage treatment needs; effect on natural plant life and wildlife; and water, air, and noise pollution.

For example, community pressures in Manitoba were influential in preventing the construction of a giant aluminum smelter which would have created many jobs, but posed a risk of pollution. Pollution concerns likely will affect any further plant location decisions along the St. Clair and Niagara rivers in Ontario. Provincial and community attitudes thus often play a role in the facility location decision.

Table 16-2
Factors to Be Considered in Making the Facility Location Decision and Examples of Affected Businesses

Location Factor	Examples of Affected Businesses
Transportation	
Proximity to markets	Baking companies or manufacturers of other perishable products, dry cleaners and hotels or other services for profit
Proximity to raw materials	Mining companies
Availability of transportation alternatives	Brick manufacturers, retail stores
Human Factors	
Labour supply	Auto manufacturers, hotels
Local regulations	Explosives manufacturers, welding shops
Community living conditions	All businesses
Physical Factors	
Water supply	Paper mills
Energy	Aluminum, chemical and fertilizer manufacturers

Choosing a Site

Once a community has been selected, a specific site must be chosen. Before this can be done, a number of factors must be considered: zoning regulations; availability of sufficient land; cost of the land; existence of shipping facilities, such as railroad sidings, roads, and dock facilities; and construction costs.

industrial park
A planned site location that provides necessary zoning, land, shipping facilities, and waste disposal outlets.

Most cities have developed **industrial parks**—planned site locations that provide necessary zoning, land, shipping facilities, and waste disposal outlets. These are created to entice manufacturers to locate new plants in the area by providing maximum cooperation between the firm and the local governing bodies.

Proximity to customers or clients is often the determining factor in the location of service facilities. Service-oriented organizations as diverse as government services, health and emergency services, retailers, and profit-seeking service firms attempt to locate near their customers or clients.

Locating near population concentrations allows such facilities as hospitals, fire stations, and ambulance services to provide fast service and minimize loss of life and loss of property.

Design and Layout of Production Facilities

An efficient production facility is the result of careful consideration of all phases of production and the necessary input at each step of the process. A number of alternatives are available in selecting the most appropriate layout.

process layout
A manufacturing facility design that accommodates a variety of nonstandard products in relatively small batches.

The first three designs are common in manufacturing facilities. A **process layout**, as shown in Figure 16-2, is designed to accommodate a variety of nonstandard products in relatively small batches. Custom machine shops are typically organized in this fashion.

Figure 16-2
Process Layout

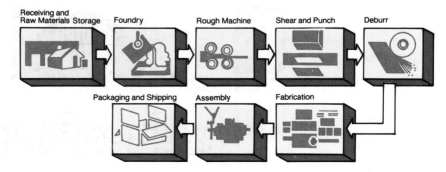

Receiving and Raw Materials Storage — Foundry — Rough Machine — Shear and Punch — Deburr

Packaging and Shipping — Assembly — Fabrication

Figure 16-3
Product Layout

product layout
A manufacturing facility design that accommodates only a few products in relatively large quantities.

fixed-position layout
A manufacturing facility design that locates the product in a fixed position, and workers, materials, and machines are transported to and from it.

customer-oriented layout
A service facility design where the arrangement facilitates the interaction of customers and the organization's services.

A **product layout** like the one in Figure 16-3 is designed to accommodate only a few product designs. In the automobile industry, this type of layout allows a direct material flow through the facility to the products. The figure illustrates the addition of various components to the unit until a complete car rolls off the assembly line.

Figure 16-4 illustrates a **fixed-position layout**, which locates the product in a fixed position, and workers, materials, and machines are transported to and from it. This approach is common in such operations as missile assembly, ship construction, large aircraft assembly, and bridge construction, where the product is very bulky, heavy, or fragile.

A **customer-oriented layout** is common in service facilities where the facility must be arranged to enhance the interactions of customers and the organization's services. The example of a hospital layout shown in Figure 16-5 illustrates this approach. From an operations management point of view, the customer-oriented layout may also reflect a process layout.

Figure 16-4
Fixed Position Layout

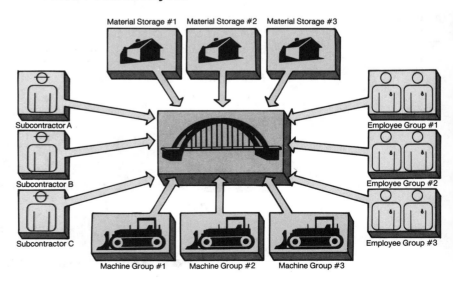

Figure 16-5
Customer-Oriented Layout

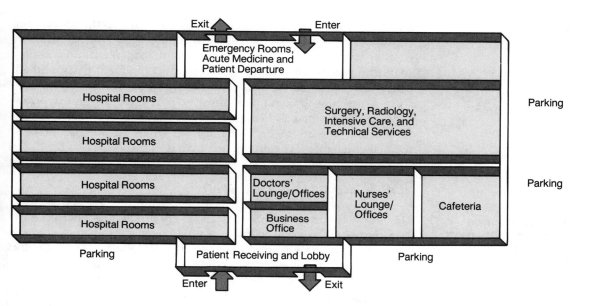

Focus 16-3

Technology and Modern Materials Eliminate Older Production Systems

Production systems come and go.

Canadian Tire Corp. recently had to close Cantire Products Ltd., a subsidiary devoted to the reconditioning of used auto parts.

Changing technology made new products cheaper than old ones reconditioned by the plant. Also affecting the decision were other factors such as rapid product obsolescence because of product change, and the increasing use of materials such as plastics that are not geared to re-use.

Source: Colin Laquedoc, "Canadian Tire Bites the Bullet in Closing Auto Parts Unit," *The Financial Post*, January 9, 1989, p. 20.

Putting the Production Plan into Operation

Once the product or service decisions have been made, the production facilities developed, the necessary machinery purchased, and the most efficient facility layout determined, management must implement the production plan. Raw materials, component parts, and all other goods and services that will serve as production ingredients, from paper clips to computers, must be purchased, inventory levels must be determined and controlled, and production schedules must be put into operation. Each of these activities will have to be performed efficiently if the production plan is to succeed.

The Make or Buy Decision

make or buy decision
Fundamental management decision of whether to manufacture a needed product or component, or to purchase it from an outside supplier.

One of the fundamental issues facing every producer is the **make or buy decision**: whether to manufacture a needed product or component or to purchase from an outside supplier. Rolls-Royce provides the engines for the Boeing 757 plane, while Boeing's own plant builds the nose and another outside supplier, Vought, manufactures the tail section. Like other auto companies, Ford Motor Company depends upon hundreds of suppliers to produce over half of the 12,000 different parts used in a typical Ford.

By contrast, some canners such as Heinz or Campbell's may manufacture their own cans at company-owned subsidiaries. Factors affecting the make or buy decision include the costs of purchasing parts from outside suppliers as compared with producing them in-house; the availability of outside suppliers and dependability of their shipments in the quality and quantity needed; the need for confidentiality; and whether the need for the commodity in question is short- or long-term. Even when the decision is made to purchase from outside suppliers, managers should maintain more than one supply source. Availability of an alternative supplier is important to assure availability of needed materials in the case of strikes, quality assurance problems, or other problems preventing one supplier from meeting its delivery commitments.

Focus 16-4

Murphy's Law

Managers who wonder why everything seems to go wrong during the production process need look no further than Murphy, the unknown author of the famous Murphy's Law and its numerous corollaries. Murphy said "If anything can go wrong, it will." The law's corollaries drum the point home. Here are just a few.

- Nothing is as easy as it looks.
- Everything takes longer than you think.
- If there is a possibility of several things going wrong, the one that will cause the most damage will be the one to go wrong.
- If you perceive that there are four possible ways in which a procedure can go wrong, and circumvent these, then a fifth way will promptly develop.
- Every solution breeds new problems.
- A fail-safe circuit will destroy others.
- A failure will not appear until a unit has passed final inspection.
- A purchased component or instrument will meet its specifications long enough, and only long enough, to pass incoming inspection.
- After the last of 16 mounting screws has been removed from an access cover, it will be discovered that the wrong access cover has been removed.
- After an access cover has been secured by 16 hold-down screws, it will be discovered that the gasket has been omitted.
- After an instrument has been assembled, extra components will be found on the bench.

Purchasing Decisions

The objective of purchasing is to buy the right materials in the right amounts at the right time for the right price. To achieve this goal, the purchasing department must (1) precisely determine the correct materials to purchase, (2) select the best supplier, and (3) develop an efficient ordering system. (See Focus 16-5.)

Too many people define the term quality as "high quality." But quality costs money, and the purchase of materials of a higher than necessary quality can adversely affect the ability of the company to price its products competitively. A minimum quality level is obviously necessary for the product to perform its functions. But the precise quality levels needed for materials to be purchased should be specified in order to assist in the purchasing process.

Selecting the Right Supplier

The choice of a supplier is usually made by comparing the quality, prices, availability, and services offered by competing companies. In many cases quality and price are virtually identical among suppliers, and the choice is based on factors such as the firm's previous experience with each supplier, speed of delivery, warranties on purchases, and other services.

Focus 16-5

Purchasing Raw Materials for the Telephone Is a Worldwide Job

Most people think of the telephone as a Canadian-made product, but it is a regular United Nations when it comes to the materials needed to make a phone.

To give you an idea of where the purchasing agent at the phone company has to look for needed materials, let's examine the telephone. The chromium used to make your finger stop on the dial comes from Africa. Indonesian or Malayan rubber finds several uses, including the phone's feet.

Of course, most of the materials are mined, grown, or made in Canada. Some of these include nickel used in springs, carbon for the mouthpiece, plastics that house the insides, and steel that forms a variety of parts.

Some of the materials seem a little unlikely for a telephone. Cotton (from the US) acts as an acoustical barrier in the handset. Wax fills capacitors and insulators. There is even a trace of gold and silver in the transmitter. And don't forget the paper your number is printed on. Other materials include aluminum, cobalt, copper, lacquer, lead, petroleum, rayon, silicon, tin, and zinc.

Where major purchases are involved, the period of negotiations between the purchaser and potential suppliers may take several weeks or even months, and the buying decision may rest with a number of persons in the firm. The choice of a supplier for industrial drill presses, for example, may be made jointly by the production, engineering, and maintenance departments as well as by the purchasing agent. These departments have different points of view that must be reconciled before purchasing decisions are made.

Raw materials and component parts are often purchased on a long-term contractual basis. If a manufacturer requires a continual supply of materials, a one- or two-year contract with a supplier ensures that they will be available as needed.

reciprocity
The practice of extending purchasing preferences to those suppliers who are also customers.

Reciprocity. A highly controversial practice in a number of industries is **reciprocity**—the extension of purchasing preferences to those suppliers who are also customers. Reciprocal agreements are particularly common in the chemical, steel, rubber, paint, and petroleum industries. Even though the purchasing department might prefer the freedom of using suppliers of its own choosing, guaranteed sales are stong incentives for reciprocity, particularly when the prices and quality of competing offerings are similar. The matter of reciprocity is thus a controversial issue with firms as well as from the wider viewpoint of the principles of open competition.

Inventory Control

inventory control
The balancing of the need to have industry on hand to meet demand with the costs involved in carrying the inventory.

Inventory control balances the need to have inventory on hand to meet demand with costs involved in carrying the inventory. Development of an efficient ordering system results from balancing two needs: (1) the need to have on hand sufficient supplies of raw materials and components to meet production needs and (2) the need to minimize inventory on hand in order to reduce the carrying costs.

The financial costs of carrying inventory are the funds tied up in it that cannot be used in other activities of the business. Among the expenses involved in storing inventory are warehousing, taxes, insurance, and maintenance. If the inventory on hand is excessive, these expenditures represent waste.

For example, if an automobile manufacturer were to run out of an import part, the financial impact could be major. Until a supply of the needed part could be obtained, assembly lines would have to be shut down, workers would be laid off, shipment schedules would not be met, relationships with dealers would be hurt, and so on. On the other hand, carrying too large an inventory of a specific part represents large costs to the firm because the purchase price would have to be financed through loans.

Firms lose business when they develop a reputation for inability to meet promised delivery dates or when their shelves are empty. On the other hand, bulging warehouses of unneeded goods cut into profits. These two costs must be balanced to produce acceptable inventory levels.

perpetual inventory
Continuously updated listings of items in inventory.

A commonly used technique of monitoring the amount and location of inventory is the maintenance of a **perpetual inventory**. This inventory control system continuously updates all major inventory items. The system is typically computerized and frequently will automatically determine orders to be made and print purchase orders at the appropriate times. The scanning devices used in many supermarkets are typically linked to perpetual inventory systems and are used in reordering needed merchandise. As a shopper's purchase is recorded, each item is subtracted from the inventory stored in the computer. Once inventory on hand drops to a pre-determined level, the merchandise is automatically reordered.

Just-In-Time Systems

It is well known that Japanese automobiles have made a significant impact on the world market. Japanese cars have been made better and produced more efficiently than many North American cars. This came about because of many differences from manufacturing processes in North America. However, at the core of Japanese productivity improvement is the just-in-time (JIT) system.

The essence of this system is the production (or receipt) of the right items in the quantities needed by subsequent production processes at the time needed. This organization of materials flow eliminates the buildup of inventories, and therefore saves the associated investment and storage costs. This system also strives to coordinate the final assembly rate with the customer demand rate to eliminate the need for finished goods inventory.

Most firms that have successfully implemented JIT have the following characteristics:[4]

- uniform assembly schedules
- group technology (parts with similar characteristics and machines are grouped in order to achieve high levels of repeatability)
- flexible work force
- short setup times
- low rates of machine failure
- low rates of yield loss or rework.

Materials Requirement Planning

In order to implement the production plan, an adequate amount of the raw materials, components, and operating supplies must be available when needed. For relatively simple products with few components provided by numerous suppliers in the immediate vicinity, this is a relatively simple process. A telephone call may be sufficient to secure overnight delivery of needed materials, and management enjoys the luxury of minimal investments in inventory and little risk of production downtime resulting from lack of needed materials.

This process of ensuring adequate amounts of materials and parts in the right amounts at the right times becomes much more complicated when complex products are involved. For a firm such as Ford Motor Company, the process of determining the efficient sequencing of precisely the exact amounts of materials at exactly the right times can be a nightmare. If the components are received too early, they must be stored until needed. If they arrive late, production is disrupted until they are available. In his book *American Made*, Harold Livesay describes a group of Chrysler Corporation workers using acetylene torches to cut holes in a locked railway car filled with bolts. Stopping the production line while assembly-line workers waited for the car to be unlocked would have cost Chrysler $40,000 per hour, so the plant manager insted opted to pay for the damaged rail car.[5]

materials requirement planning (MRP)
Computer-based production planning system for making certain that needed parts and materials are available at the right time and place and in the correct amounts.

Materials requirement planning (MRP) is a production planning system designed to ensure that a firm has the parts and materials needed to produce its products and services at the right time and place and in the right amounts. Production managers use special computer programmes to create schedules that identify the specific parts and materials required to produce an item, the exact quantities required of each, and the dates when orders should be released to suppliers and should be received for best timing within the production cycle.[6]

MRP is invaluable in systems involving complex products assembled with parts and materials secured from outside suppliers. It is even more important in major products such as the F-18 fighter plane, where entire subassemblies of the plane are produced by dozens of firms scattered across North America. MRP's computer programme coordinates the deadlines for each subassembly in addition to overall assembly.

Control of the Production Process

Throughout this chapter, production has been viewed as a process of converting input into finished products and services. First, plans are made for production input—the products to be produced, the location of facilities, and the sources of raw materials, consumers, labour, energy, and machinery.

Next, the production plans are implemented through the purchase of materials and equipment and the employment of a trained work force to convert the input into salable products and services. The final step in the production process is control.

What Is Production Control?

production control
A well-defined set of procedures for coordinating people, materials, and machinery to provide maximum production efficiency.

Production control is a well-defined set of procedures for coordinating people, materials, and machinery to provide maximum production efficiency.

Suppose that a watch factory has been assigned the production of 800,000 watches during the month of October. Production control executives break this down to a daily production assignment of 40,000 for each of twenty working days. The next step is to determine the number of workers, raw materials, parts, and machines needed to meet this production schedule.

Similarly, in a service business, such as a restaurant, it is necessary to estimate how many meals would be served each day and then determine the number of people needed to prepare and serve the food, as well as how much food must be purchased and how often. For example, meat, fish, and fresh vegetables might have to be bought every day or every other day to ensure freshness, while canned and frozen foods might be bought less often depending on storage space.

The Five Steps in Production Control

Production control can be thought of as a five-step sequence: planning, routing, scheduling, dispatching, and follow-up.

Production planning is the phase of production control that determines the amount of resources (including raw materials and other components) needed to produce a certain amount of goods or services. During the production planning process, a bill of materials is developed listing all parts and materials needed to produce a product or service. Comparison of the needed parts and materials with the firm's perpetual inventory allows the purchasing department to determine the additional purchases required to ensure availability of needed amounts. The MRP system establishes delivery schedules so that the needed parts and materials will arrive at regular intervals as required during the production process. Service-producing systems depend more on personnel than on materials.

Routing is the phase of production control that determines the sequence of work throughout the facility. It specifies where and by whom each aspect of production will be performed.

Scheduling is the phase of production control involved in developing timetables that specify how long each operation in the production process takes and when it should be performed. Efficient scheduling ensures that delivery schedules are met and productive resources are efficiently used.

Scheduling is extremely important for manufacturers of complex products with large numbers of parts or production stages. A watch contains dozens of component parts, and each of them must be available at the right place, at the right time, and in the right amounts if the production process is to function smoothly.

Scheduling practices vary considerably in service-related organizations. Such small services as local trucking companies or doctors' offices may use relatively unsophisticated scheduling systems and resort to such devices as "first come, first served" rules, appointment schedules, or take-a-number systems. Part-time workers and standby equipment may be used in handling demand fluctuations. On the other hand, hospitals typically use sophisticated scheduling systems that are similar to those of a manufacturer.

A number of methods have been devised for effective scheduling of complex products. A commonly used scheduling technique designed for such complex products as ships and new airplane designs is **PERT (Programme Evaluation and Review Technique)**. PERT, first developed for the military, was used to produce guided missiles for the Polaris nuclear submarine. But it was quickly modified for use by industry.

PERT has two basic concepts: (1) the structuring of a series of related activities and (2) associating time and/or costs with each activity in the network so as to determine the "critical path" or

production planning
The phase of production control that determines the amount of resources needed to produce a certain amount of goods or services.

routing
The phase of production control that determines the sequence of work throughout the facility.

scheduling
The phase of production control involved in developing timetables that specify how long each operation in the production process takes.

PERT (Programme Evaluation and Review Technique)
A scheduling technique (designed for complex products) to minimize production delays by coordinating all aspects of the production task.

sequence of activity completion. Figure 16-6 shows a simplified PERT diagram.

The first step is the development of the activity network. The main tasks in networking are to identify activities that must be performed *sequentially*, i.e., one must be completed before the next can begin, and to structure remaining activities so that they are carried out *concurrently*.[7] The required time can then be estimated for each.

PERT is designed to minimize production delays by coordinating all aspects of the production task. The line with dashes in Figure 16-6 shows the **critical path**—the sequence of operations in the PERT diagram that requires the longest time for completion. Other operations, which can be completed before they are needed by operations on the critical path, have some slack time and are therefore not critical. These operations can be performed early or delayed until later in the production process. Some workers and machinery can be assigned to critical path tasks early, then reassigned to the noncritical operations as they are needed.

There is therefore great value in critical path scheduling. The activity network shows that time can be saved by performing some activities concurrently. And the critical variables have now been identified. Efforts must be concentrated on keeping the schedule for these, while working on the other activities. Furthermore, the most desirable sequence of all is now identified.

critical path
The sequence of operations in the PERT diagram that requires the longest time for completion.

Figure 16-6
Critical Path Diagram for Constructing a House

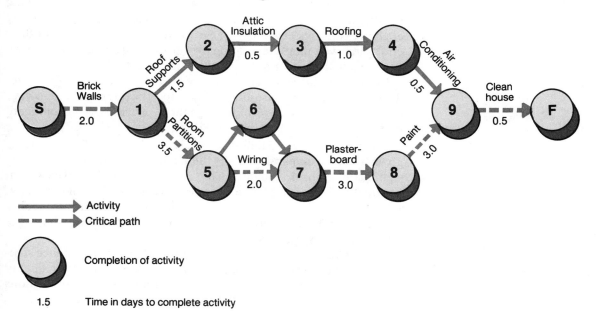

──────▶	Activity
----▶	Critical path

Completion of activity

1.5   Time in days to complete activity

In actual practice a PERT network may consist of thousands of events and cover months of time. Complex computer programmes are used in developing the network and in finding the critical path among the maze of events and activities.

dispatching
The phase of production control that instructs each department on what work is to be done and the time allowed for its completion.

Dispatching is the phase of production control that instructs each department on what work is to be done and the time allowed for its completion. The dispatcher authorizes performance, provides instructions, and lists priorities for each job.

Because even the best plans sometimes go awry, some means must be available to keep management aware of problems as they arise. **Follow-up** is the phase of production control that spots problems in the production process and informs management of needed adjustments. Problems come in many forms. Machinery malfunctions, delays in shipment of vital materials or in arrival of goods or supplies, and employee absenteeism can all result in production delays. These delays must be reported to production control so adjustments in production schedules can be made. A delay in the delivery of a particular component may require new assignments by the dispatcher to work areas affected by this delay.

follow-up
The phase of production control that spots problems in the production process and informs management of needed adjustments.

Quality Control

Few subjects have been more popular among Canadian organizations in recent years than that of quality. North American products have long held the reputation for good quality.

But at the same time that Canadian factories were improving quality, their Japanese counterparts were leapfrogging ahead by applying concepts developed in North America. The success of their efforts in developing a reputation for outstanding quality is evident by the inroads Japanese products have made in Canadian markets.

In many industries Canadians are turning to foreign made products. Some examples are automobiles, sports equipment, microwave ovens, videocassette recorders, pianos, bicycles, and outboard motors.

Japan's most coveted industrial award is the Deming Prize, which is given to the company and the individual who achieve the most significant gains in quality. The annual award is broadcast on national television in Japan. The prize is named in honour of W. Edwards Deming, an American statistician whose lectures on quality control in 1950 were largely ignored in the United States, but were implemented by Japanese managers.

Quality begins with product and service design. Performance standards are necessary prerequisites for the development of quality controls. Once these standards are set, various types of inspections can be made to provide quality assurance.

quality control
The measurement of products and services against established quality standards.

Quality control involves measuring products and services against established quality standards. Such checks are necessary to spot defective products and to see that they are not shipped to customers. Devices for monitoring quality levels of the firm's output include visual inspection, electronic sensors, and X-rays. Robots are particularly suited for many types of inspections since fatigue and inattention do not present problems. A high rate of rejected products can lead to necessary changes in equipment or raw materials or additional training for workers employed in the production process.

Quality Circles

quality circle
Voluntary group of employees from the same work area who meet on a regular basis to define, analyze, and solve quality and related problems in their area.

Researchers seeking to compare North American and Japanese firms discovered a widely used Japanese concept based upon the philosophy that the firm's work force is often the most qualified group to identify and solve work-related problems. A survey of 1566 Japanese firms revealed that 91 percent used quality circles. A **quality circle** is a group of employees from the same work area who define, analyze, and solve quality and related problems in their area. The groups usually number seven to ten people. They meet voluntarily and on a regular basis, typically once a week. A first-line supervisor or one of the workers usually serves as team leader to facilitate discussions and to keep management informed of the issues being addressed and the group's progress.

Production and Pollution

An undesirable output of many production processes is pollution, which takes many forms, including air pollution, water pollution, and noise pollution. Activities such as strip mining have produced extensive damage in Quebec, the Prairies, and BC. Major oil spills along the East Coast and in other parts of the world have killed thousands of fish and birds and damaged beaches. Discharges from chemical and pulp and paper plants also have meant death to fish. Atmospheric discharges of lead from a battery factory have endangered the health of nearby residents in Toronto. Acid rain caused by pollution from US and Canadian factories threatens many Canadian lakes. These undesirable outputs have resulted in the enactment of numerous provincial and federal laws designed to protect the environment. Efforts by manufacturers to stop pollution have involved the investment of billions of dollars in equipment. Buyers of new cars currently pay from $250 to $450 for air pollution abatement devices. A strong commitment to protection of the environment, coupled with investments in pollution control, will be an increasingly important component of production decisions during the remaining years of this decade.

Controversial Issue

Improving Productivity with Robots: Who Pays?

Canadian business needs a new management strategy to increase productivity and lower prices, says Geoffrey McKenzie, managing partner of international management consultants Currie, Coopers & Lybrand.

"The critical thing for Canadian business and industry in the next three to five years is to become more cost competitive," he says. "The name of the game is cost containment, cost reductions, and lowering the selling price. This is essential especially on world markets, which Canadian business must go after more aggressively than ever before.

"The days are gone when countries such as South Korea and Taiwan made second-rate products. Now their goods are pretty well equivalent to those in established manufacturing countries. We are now having to compete with third world countries who are becoming capable of pretty sophisticated manufacturing operations.

"Top management has to see the marketplace as being the world. We've been used to doing business in the US, but haven't done much business elsewhere."

In light of this challenge to become more productive and competitive, a number of solutions come to mind. One of these is to use robots in every possible manufacturing process. There are real concerns on the part of labour as to the effects of such automation on jobs. They might well argue, "Which is the greater evil: to be less competitive in world markets, or to have great numbers of people out of work because robots have taken over?"

Source: Bruce Gates, "Our Companies Must be More Cost Competitive," *The Financial Post*, January 5, 1985, p. 59.

Summary of Learning Goals

1. **Explain how production creates utility for a firm's customers.**

   Utility has been defined as the want-satisfying power of a product or service. Marketing activities result in the creation of time, place, and ownership utility. By converting human input, energy, raw materials, and component parts into finished products and services, production creates form utility.

2. **Explain the roles of standardization, specialization, and mechanization in mass production.**

   A major factor in the development of Canada as an industrialized country has been the application of mass production in the manufacture of products in large amounts through the effective combination of three factors. The first factor is specialization, the dividing of work into its simplest components so that workers can concentrate on performing each task. The second factor is

Divisible
— portable

Durable
Stable —
time value
Difficult to
Count

mechanization, the use of machines to perform work previously performed by people. The final factor is standardization, the production of uniform, interchangeable goods and parts. The results have been widespread availability of products at prices made possible by efficient production associated with these factors.

3. **Describe the contributions and problems involved with the use of assembly lines, automation, and robots in producing products and services.**

A special approach to manufacturing involves the assembly line. This technique involves placing the product upon a conveyor belt, which travels past a number of work stations where workers perform certain tasks. This approach resulted in increased speed of production as workers utilized the concepts of standardization, specialization, and mechanization. Automation is a logical extension of mechanization. In automation, machines perform specialized tasks previously performed by humans with little or no human interaction. The "child" of automation is the robot—a reprogrammable machine capable of performing a variety of tasks requiring manipulations of materials and tools. In addition to the reduced costs of automated equipment as a result of technological developments, robots can be assigned to perform boring, routine, repetitive, or dangerous work and free humans for more challenging assignments. In many instances, automation results in unemployment, thereby making retraining of displaced workers necessary.

4. **Identify the three components of production and operations management.**

Production management is responsible for three major activities: developing plans for production input; installing necessary production input and implementing production plans; and coordinating and controlling the production process. Production planning begins with a decision on which products or services will be produced. This is a major company decision because the firm fulfills its commitments to society by producing and marketing want-satisfying products and services. The manufacturing method may involve analytic or synthetic systems, and production runs may be continuous or intermittent.

5. **List the major factors involved in making plant location decisions.**

A number of factors must be considered in selecting a plant location. Among them are proximity to raw materials and to markets; availability of labour, transportation, and energy; local regulations; and community living conditions. An environmental impact study assessing the effect on the quality of life of locating the plant in a particular area may be required by regulatory authorities.

6. **Compare the alternative designs for production facilities.**
A number of alternatives are available in selecting the most appropriate layout for a production facility. Process layouts are used for nonstandard products produced in relatively small batches. When only a few product designs are involved, a product layout may be used. In situations involving very bulky, heavy, or fragile products, a fixed-position layout may be used. A customer-oriented layout is typically used for service facilities in order to enhance the interactions of customers or clients and the organization's service facilities.

7. **Identify the steps involved in the purchasing process.**
The make or buy decision results in a determination of which needed inputs will be manufactured by the firm and which will be purchased from outside suppliers. Those responsible for purchasing attempt to buy the right materials in the right amounts at the right time for the right price. Purchasing involves three steps:
   a) Precise determination of the correct materials to purchase.
   b) Selection of appropriate suppliers.
   c) Development of an efficient ordering system.

8. **Compare the advantages and disadvantages of maintaining large amounts of inventory.**
The task of inventory control is to balance two factors: the need to maintain adequate supplies to meet production requirements and the need to minimize funds invested in inventory. Excessive inventory results in increased expenditures for warehousing, taxes, insurance, and maintenance. Inadequate inventory may mean production delays, lost sales, and inefficient operations. Once quantity levels for parts and materials have been determined, suppliers are contacted and orders are placed. Many firms use perpetual inventory systems to continuously update the on-hand inventory of parts and materials. Such systems may be further automated to place orders when inventory levels reach a predetermined point.

9. **Identify each step in the production control process.**
Production control attempts to provide maximum productive efficiency through the coordination of people, materials, and machinery. The production control process consists of five steps: planning, routing, scheduling, dispatching, and follow-up, as well as quality control. Coordination of each of these phases should result in improved production efficiency and lower production costs.

Key Terms

form utility
production
mass production
specialization
mechanization
standardization
analytic system
synthetic system
continuous process
intermittent process
job-order production
lot-order production
automation
robot
production and operations management
environmental impact study
industrial park
process layout
product layout

fixed-position layout
customer-oriented layout
make or buy decision
reciprocity
inventory control
perpetual inventory
materials requirement
    planning (MRP)
production control
production planning
routing
scheduling
PERT
critical path
dispatching
follow-up
quality control
quality circle

Discussion Questions and Exercises

1. Give two examples of production facilities in your city or region that use each of the following manufacturing methods:
   a) analytic process.
   b) synthetic process.
   c) continuous process.
   d) intermittent process.
2. Why are standardization and mechanization necessary for a system of mass production? How can mechanization be distinguished from automation?
3. Identify the major advantages of specialization. What are the primary disadvantages? Suggest methods for reducing these disadvantages.
4. Relate the three components of production and operations management to each of the following businesses. Give specific examples of each component:
   a) major league sports facility in the Vancouver area.
   b) convenience food store.
   c) automobile brake repair shop.
   d) fish processing facility.
   e) colour television assembly plant.

5. Identify the alternative designs for production facilities and give two examples of firms that might use each alternative.
6. Name five factories and five service firms that are located in your community or a nearby city. Identify the factors likely to have led to the location of each. Explain your choices.
7. What factors are likely to be most important in the make or buy decision?
8. What costs must be considered in setting up an inventory control system? What contributions can materials requirement planning (MRP) make to an inventory control system? What types of firms are most likely to use perpetual inventory systems?
9. What are the chief methods of ensuring quality control? Suggest appropriate quality control techniques for use in the following firms:
   a) local bank.
   b) city hospital.
   c) amusement park.
   d) furniture factory.
   e) bottling plant.
10. Draw a Critical Path diagram for the product described below. Make any necessary assumptions. In order to become a BIC fresh-packed pickle, the cucumber undergoes a series of operations. Once the cucumbers arrive at the plant they are sized, sorted, washed, sliced, and packed into jars. Specially prepared brine containing spices is added to the sliced product, and the jars are closed. The pickle next undergoes a pasteurizing process, after which labels are affixed to the jars. The individual jars are next packaged into protective cases. The cases are combined on shipping pallets, and moved to a warehouse to await shipment to customers.

Case 16-1

Quality: Showing Pontiac the Way

At a Pontiac engine manufacturing complex, W. Edwards Deming, 82, the American statistician who taught the Japanese about quality three decades ago, is a genuine hero. When he visits the plants as a consultant, which he does about once a month, he gets as much attention as the chairman of GM. Hourly workers crowd around to get his autograph. Managers hang on their walls Deming's *14 Points* for improving quality and productivity.

The *14 Points* carry messages that can alter the way a company is run. The messages are backed by a relatively simple type of statistical control that pinpoints the sources of quality problems.

Before Deming, Pontiac had been struggling for years to improve quality. In 1980 William Hoglund, the general manager of Pontiac, and some of his staff happened to watch an NBC documentary, "If Japan Can...Why Can't We?" that explained how much Deming had helped the Japanese achieve their world-famous quality. "Why not invite Deming to Pontiac?" they asked each other. Deming started working with Pontiac early in 1981. "His message shook the foundations of our approach to quality," says Hoglund.

In Deming's system, simple changes can yield large results. Plant No. 18 was having a lot of trouble with the threads on the connecting-rod bolts it was buying from four different vendors, but amazingly, Pontiac had not arranged its records to show which vendors were performing poorly. Once the Deming statistical controls were established, it became clear that all of one vendor's shipments were being returned because they were faulty, and he was dropped.

A more sophisticated example involved the fit of the camshaft gear. The gear must be bored to an accuracy of a few ten-thousandths of an inch if it is to hold fast to the camshaft. If it doesn't hold fast, the whole engine has to be pulled out of the car, at a cost of at least $1,000. Before Deming, the job setter who ran the boring tool adjusted it whenever he thought necessary. A statistical analysis of the tool showed that if the borings on three successive gears were measured once an hour, the tool could always be kept within the tolerances. The job setter now keeps an hour-by-hour chart of the tool's performance, and the results are striking. The year before the change in procedure, 38 engines had to be pulled because the gear was loose. Well into the following year, none had to be pulled.

As statistical controls spread through Pontiac so does the rest of Deming's cure for productivity and quality ills—most notably, worker participation and training. Several workers and union officers recently helped design a new engine line; previously that would have been the exclusive responsibility of the process engineers. Hourly workers never used to get any training worth the name, but now they have a full-time, four-week course from which they emerge equipped with a calculator, a magnifying glass (to look at their tools more carefully), and a knowledge of statistical controls.

Deming dropped in on one recent class, and students and visitor were clearly in total rapport, alternately fascinating and amusing each other. Deming got one 35-year veteran to relate what happened in the old days when he found a tool was malfunctioning. Said the worker, "I'd tell the supervisor and he'd say 'Leave it for the second shift.' The second shift would leave it for the third shift and the third shift would leave it for me in the morning. Then my supervisor would say, 'Leave it for the weekend.' Well, now we've only got the day shift left, and if we don't do better there just ain't gonna be no day shift."

Unfortunately, the quality improvements are not necessarily apparent to Pontiac's customers because the engines are mixed with parts from other divisions that aren't on the same quality track.

The engine plants have at least shown the way. Says James Harbour, an auto industry consultant, "The Pontiac engine plants are a superb example of what can be accomplished when you decide that quality and productivity go hand in hand."

Questions:
1. Describe how individual worker participation has aided Pontiac in improving quality. Why does productivity increase as the level of quality improves?
2. General Motors utilizes approximately 3,500 suppliers to provide parts and materials for its automobiles. How can quality improvement attempts be expanded to include them?
3. Suggest methods by which Pontiac's top management can include quality as a factor in employee and manager evaluations and compensation.

Case 16-2

Inventory Kills

The predominant attitude in Japanese industry is that inventory wastes money and space, and covers up problems. As a result, Japanese manufacturers have gone to great lengths to pare inventory to the minimum necessary for work in process, and to set schedules to produce goods on a timely basis so that finished stock doesn't gather dust. For example, automaker Toyota has been refining a system called "kanban"—or "just in time"—for approximately ten years. The Toyota system requires suppliers to deliver only the number of parts needed to build a certain number of cars during a specific time. In some cases, suppliers may deliver parts several times a day. The goal is to eliminate buffer stock, which takes up space and is prone to damage.

One Toyota subsidiary has redesigned its plant so that suppliers can drive their trucks right to the assembly line where the parts are going to be used. There are no delays in receiving. Small parts are delivered in bins, each containing a fixed quantity, and packed regularly to minimize damage and make count checking easy.

The system is able to work because a great emphasis has been placed on perfecting the production-flow process and reducing machine set-up times to enable production of smaller batches with fewer defects. In North America, we have tended to increase the production speed and the efficiency of machines at the cost of long and expensive set-ups. Therefore it is necessary to run large batches to absorb the set-up costs economically. This leads to the need for high inventories in buffer stocks and work-in-process.

It takes four to eight hours to change body presses in North America, compared to just eight minutes at Toyota. On a machine that produces eight different types of parts, instead of producing them in batches over a period of several weeks, the Japanese will make all eight parts every day. By producing small batches without delays between processes, problems are identified immediately and can be corrected.

Source: Ken Musgrave and Colin Lockie, "Toyota Stays Ahead Via Inventory Route," *The Financial Post*, December 11, 1982, p. 22.

Questions:
1. How has an efficient inventory control system helped the Japanese save money and streamline their production systems?
2. Which type of production process is described in this case?
3. Discuss the quality of production planning in Japanese plants.
4. What are the implications for Canadian auto manufacturers of this highly efficient production process? Is it necessary that Canadians follow the same procedures?

Part Seven

Financing the Enterprise

Chapter 17

Money and Banking

Learning Goals

The lack of money is the root of all evil.
—*George Bernard Shaw*

1. To describe the characteristics of a good form of money and list the functions of money
2. To distinguish between money and near-money
3. To identify the major categories of financial institutions and the sources and uses of their funds
4. To introduce the Bank of Canada and how it acts to increase or decrease the money supply
5. To show the purpose and chief functions of the Canada Deposit Insurance Corporation
6. To distinguish between credit cards and debit cards
7. To explain the role of electronic funds transfer systems

Profile

John Crow—*Bank of Canada Governor Maintaining Monetary Stability*

He brings the same steady stride and single-minded determination to his anti-inflation crusade as he does to his morning run. The Governor insists that the bank's exclusive function is to maintain monetary stability. The goal is to maintain confidence in the value of the dollar.

Crow's unswerving confidence in his own judgement can enrage his critics. But it is also the guarantee, to investors inside and outside Canada, that John Crow is his own man; he will not let anybody push him around.

The only child of a school janitor, John Crow was born in one of the poorest districts of London, England. During the Second World War, when the German Luftwaffe bombed London, many of the Cockney kids from his area were evacuated from the city. After being evacuated twice, he has developed a self-sufficiency that serves him well in this position.

Crow has a reputation within the tight little world of the bank as an outstanding economist, an aggressive soccer player, and a tyrant to work for. And he has shown a similar lack of patience for politicians when he perceives that politics are being stressed over principle.

The crucial hours of Crow's working life are those at the start and finish of each day. First thing in the morning, senior managers brief the governor on how the internal money markets have behaved overnight, where interest rates are going, whether the bank will need to intervene to ensure dollar stability. After markets close in the afternoon, the governor is responsible for "cash-setting"—deciding how much money is left in the banking system for the next day.

Ten times a year, John Crow flies to Basle, Switzerland, for meetings of the most powerful, exclusive, and discreet club in the world—G10 central bankers. These people control the monetary policies of the ten major industrialized countries.

Even those who don't like John Crow's tight-monetary policy or his overbearing manner agree that there is an uncomprising consistency about Canada's chief money manager. They also admit that so far, his judgement has been vindicated.

Source: Charlotte Gray, "The Good Governor," *Canadian Business*, February 1989, pp. 25-28.

The fifteen people who staff the money market desk at the investment firm of Nesbitt Thomson Bongard Ltd. in Toronto arrive at their posts by 8 a.m. They immediately begin punching up numbers on their computer terminals, indicating how many millions worth of commercial paper—interest-paying notes issued by corporations—and government treasury bills are available for sale. Then, the money traders begin working the telephones. Their conversations are with their counterparts at institutions that want to borrow or lend money for short terms and are geared at establishing the nature of the investment and the rate of interest. If two parties agree on a price, which can be in the millions, a simple "done deal!" barked into a telephone seals the transaction. The scene is repeated dozens of times each working day in bank, financial and pension fund offices across the country as money managers trade billions in surplus cash. The amount of money available for trading is staggering. According to the Bank of Canada, there was $93.7 billion in outstanding treasury bills and commercial paper in the money market at the end of July. Billions of that changes hands every day.[1]

Money: Lubricant of Contemporary Business

Money is a lubricant of contemporary business. It is not only one of the 5*M*'s of management, it is a vital resource in the operation of any organization.

In analyzing the characteristics, functions, and different types of money, it is useful to begin by defining it. **Money** is anything generally accepted as a means of paying for goods and services.

Anyone asked to define *money* will probably respond something like this: "It's the coins in my pocket and the folding kind I wish I had in my wallet and whatever is currently in my chequing account." And bankers would agree: these are all money.

Money is one of the most fascinating subjects for both individuals and businesspeople. Everyone seems to need it:

> Money bewitches people. They fret for it, and they sweat for it. They devise most ingenious ways to get it, and most ingenious ways to get rid of it. Money is the only commodity that is good for nothing but to be gotten rid of. It will not feed you, clothe you, shelter you, or amuse you unless you spend it or invest it. It imparts value only in parting. People will do almost anything for money, and money will do almost anything for people. Money is a captivating, circulating, masquerading puzzle.[2]

This chapter analyzes the characteristics, functions and types of money. It discusses the operations of banks and other financial

money
Anything generally accepted as a means of paying for goods and services.

institutions, and examines the methods used by the Bank of Canada in regulating the Canadian financial system. Many related aspects of the system will be discussed, but the starting place for our analysis is with money.

Money Comes in Different Shapes and Sizes

Money has not always been the same to all people. Historically, objects of practical value were used as money. These objects can be referred to as "full-bodied" money, because they had a usefulness apart from this function. Cattle often were used this way: a cow was valuable because it could produce milk, butter, and cheese and eventually be converted into meat and hide, but its owner could also trade it for other goods. The list of products that have served as money is long, including such diverse items as wool, pepper, tea, fishhooks, tobacco, shells, feathers, salt (from which came "salary" and "being worth one's salt"), boats, sharks' teeth, cocoa beans, wampum beads, woodpecker scalps, and precious metals. For a number of reasons, precious metals gained wide acceptance as money. As early as 2000 B.C. gold and silver were used as money, and Canada still issues gold coins as legal tender.

What Characteristics Should Money Possess?

Most of the early forms of money possessed a number of serious disadvantages. A cow is not a very useful asset for the owner who wants to buy only a loaf of bread. To perform its necessary functions, money should be divisible, portable, durable, and difficult to counterfeit—and it should have a stable value.

Divisibility. The owner of a cow who found that a loaf of bread cost one-fiftieth of a cow was faced with a major dilemma. So were the owners of comparable items used as money. But gold and silver coins could be minted in different sizes with differing values in order to facilitate the exchange process.

Spanish gold doubloons were literally divided into pieces of eight. The dollar can be converted into pennies, nickels, dimes, and quarters. The pound sterling of the United Kingdom is worth 100 pence. A French franc is valued at 100 centimes. The German deutsche mark can be traded for 100 pfennigs. And all these forms of money can easily be exchanged for goods ranging from a pack of chewing gum to a car.

Portability. The inhabitants of the little island community of Yap in the South Pacific chose a unique form of money—huge round stones with as much of a mass as 40 kg each. Because the stone money was often placed at the door of its owner, the wealth of the inhabitant was known to every passerby. But Yap money lacked the important characteristic of portability. The process of trading the stones for needed goods and services was difficult at best.

Modern paper currency is lightweight, which facilitates the exchange process. Canadian paper money comes in denominations of $1, $2, $5, $20, $50, $100 and $1,000.

Durability. Durability is a third important characteristic of money. A monetary system using butter or cheese faces the durability problem in a matter of weeks. Although coins and paper currency wear out over time, they are replaced easily with shiny new coins and crisp new paper. Two-dollar bills have an average life of approximately 10 months and can be folded some 4,000 times without tearing.

Stability. A good money system should have a stable value. If the value of money fluctuates, people become unwilling to trade goods and services for it. Inflation is, therefore, a serious concern for governments. When people fear their money will lose much of its value, they begin to abandon it and look for safer means of storing their wealth. Where once they accepted dollars or francs, they may now demand gold coins or they may store their wealth in the form of land, jewellery, or other physical goods. In the case of runaway inflation, where the value of money may decrease 200 percent or more in a single year, people increasingly return to a barter system, exchanging their output for the output of others.

Difficult to counterfeit. If you hold a dollar bill to the light, you will notice small green dots (planchets) embedded in the mash when the paper was made. These planchets can be picked off real bills. Furthermore, the ink used in printing our money never completely dries; it can be smeared. The purpose of these devices is to make counterfeiting difficult. Theft of currency plates from government mints is a common plot of espionage novels and movies, because the production and distribution of counterfeit money could undermine a nation's monetary system by ruining the value of legitimate money. For this reason all governments make counterfeiting a serious crime and take elaborate steps to prevent it.

What Are the Functions of Money?

medium of exchange
The function performed by money in facilitating exchange and eliminating the need for a barter system.

Money serves primarily as a **medium of exchange**, facilitating exchange and eliminating the need for a barter system. Rather than follow the complicated process of trading wheat directly for gasoline or clothing (the barter system), a farmer can sell the wheat and use the money from the sale to make other purchases.

unit of account
The function performed by money in serving as the common denominator for measuring the value of all products and services.

store of value
The function performed by money in serving as a temporary store of accumulated wealth until it is needed for new purchases.

Money also functions as a **unit of account**—the common denominator for measuring the value of all products and services. A new car is worth, say, $12,500, a certain cut of beef $6, and a centre field ticket to the Grey Cup game $35. Using money as a common denominator aids in comparing widely different products and services.

Finally, money acts as a temporary **store of value**—a way of keeping accumulated wealth until it is needed to make new purchases. Wealth can also be held in the form of shares and bonds, real estate, antiques, works of art, houses, precious gems, or any other kind of valuable goods. The advantage of storing value in goods other than money is that they often produce additional income in the form of dividends, interest payments, rent, or increases in value. For example, paintings by Renoir, Monet, and van Gogh have greatly increased in value over the past 20 years. But money offers one substantial advantage as a store of value: it is highly liquid. An asset is said to be liquid if it can be obtained and disposed of quickly and easily.

A van Gogh painting may increase in value, but its owner can obtain money for it only after finding a purchaser. In order to exchange bonds for money, the owner must contract a broker and pay a commission. And the possibility always exists that the value of the bond may be less than when it was first purchased. The owner can then either hold the bond until maturity (at which time the corporation or government agency that issued it will pay the total amount of the bond and interest) or sell it at a loss in order to obtain the more liquid dollars. In addition to the liquidity problem, many non-money stores of value involve storage and insurance costs.

There are disadvantages in holding money, particularly in inflationary times. If prices double, all the dollar bills under the mattress will buy only half the clothes and movie tickets when they're pulled out to be spent. Also, unless it is held in the form of interest-bearing chequing/savings accounts, money earns nothing for its owner. Its chief advantage, then, is that it is immediately available to purchase products or pay debts.

Focus 17-1

Dollar Bills vs Dollar Coins

The ''loonie'' is now with us. The beautiful 11-sided bronze-coated gold-coloured coin has been received with mixed reactions. Because of negative reactions, and the loon design, the name ''loonie'' has stuck.

Why was it introduced? The mint hopes that the coin will reduce the demand on smaller circulation coins, and ultimately save money. Those with vending machines like it. On the other hand, it

Boom or your kent
Bust

costs financial institutions ten times more to handle and store the coins than it costs to deal with bills. It became obvious that the public would not use it regularly until bills were phased out. The most common complaints are that carrying several is too heavy, and that they wear out pocket and purse.

Here is a comparison of bills and coins:

Life expectancy of dollar bills	9 to 12 months
Life expectancy of dollar coins	20 years
Annual replacement of bills	270 million
Annual replacement of coins expected	50 million
Cost of bills	$39 for 1,000
Cost of coins	$170 for 1,000

Source: Andrew McIntosh, "If Coins Come, The Bills May Go," *The Globe and Mail*, June 11, 1985.

Composition of the Money Supply

The Canadian money supply is divided into the following categories: coins, paper money, demand deposits (chequing accounts), and chequing/savings accounts. About 3 percent of the total money supply is in the form of metal coins ranging from "copper" pennies to (partially) silver dollars. Another 6 percent is made up of paper money. These two components of the money supply are usually called **currency**.

currency
Two of the components of the money supply—coins and paper money

Demand deposits. A substantial proportion of the money supply is in the form of **demand deposits**, the technical name for chequing accounts at commercial banks and credit unions. Demand deposits are considered part of the money supply because they are promises to pay immediately to the depositor any amount of money requested—as long as it does not exceed the amount in the person's chequing account.

demand deposits
The technical name for chequing accounts at commercial banks and credit unions.

The majority of the dollar value of all financial transactions in Canada is conducted with cheques rather than currency. Canadians write and cash millions of cheques each day. There are several explanations for this frequent use of cheques:

1. A cheque is a more convenient form of payment for large or odd-numbered purchases. Writing a cheque for a $93.60 jacket is more convenient than handing the salesperson four $20s, a $10, three dollars, two quarters, and a dime.
2. Cheques reduce the possibility of theft or loss of currency.
3. Cheques make payment by mail easier and safer.

Even though an estimated 40 percent of the people in Canada deal almost exclusively in cash, the use of chequebook money offers the advantage of convenience and safety. In addition to chequebook money, many people also use credit cards as a substitute for cash.

Other forms of money. Because the depositor can write cheques on chequing/savings accounts, these accounts are also considered as part of the money supply. This type of deposit provides its owner with interest payments on deposited funds while also permitting immediate payment upon request.

Near-money. In addition to the money supply, a number of assets exist that are almost, but not quite, money. These include **time deposits**—the technical name for savings accounts—at chartered banks, trust companies, credit unions, caisses populaires, and Canadian government bonds. Such assets are called **near-monies** because they are almost as liquid as chequing accounts, but cannot be used directly as mediums of exchange. Such savings accounts permit the financial institution to require notice (usually seven days) prior to withdrawal, or to assess a penalty for early withdrawal in the form of losing some of the interest already accrued.

time deposits
The technical name for savings accounts.

near-monies
Assets that are almost as liquid as chequing accounts, but that cannot be used directly as a medium of exchange.

Plastic Money: A Substitute for Cash

The era of plastic money has arrived. With growing frequency, people are using credit cards as substitutes for cash. At least 6 million Canadians hold one or more credit cards. Many use three or more cards. At any point in time, consumers owe $3.6 billion on credit card accounts of all types. This amounts to 11.75 percent of all non-mortgage loans held by chartered banks. A major reason for the tremendous increase in credit card business is the convenience in making credit card transactions and the growing willingness of merchants throughout the world to accept them. New areas of credit card use are continually developing. More and more products can be purchased by simply making a phone call and listing a credit card number. Some charitable organizations and political parties hand out pledge cards with spaces for credit card numbers.

While the plastic card may function much like money in permitting the holder to make purchases, the monthly statement of card purchases is a tangible reminder that they are *credit* cards—not money. They merely represent a special credit arrangement between the holder and the organization issuing the card. The issuer—usually a bank—permits the cardholder to repay the outstanding balance at the end of the billing period or, in the case of bank cards and retail credit cards, to pay at least a stated minimum amount each month and pay interest on the outstanding balance until it is repaid.

In this era of plastic money, people often prefer to use credit cards because they are more convenient than carrying large amounts of cash.

The Canadian Chartered Banking System

At the heart of the Canadian banking system are the 12 Canadian-owned chartered banks, with their approximately 7,300 branches. There are also approximately 60 foreign-owned banks. These have all the powers of a Canadian bank but are restricted in size and number of branches.

chartered banks
Profit-making businesses that hold deposits of individuals and businesses in the form of chequing or savings accounts and that use these funds to make loans to individuals and businesses.

Chartered banks are profit-making businesses that perform two basic functions:
1. They hold the deposits of individuals and business firms in the form of chequing or savings accounts.
2. They use these funds to make loans to individuals and businesses.

Figure 17-1 shows how chartered banks perform these two functions. Another view of banks follows:

> Like frisbee manufacturers, bankers buy inputs, massage them a bit, burn a little incense, say the magic words, and out pops some output from the oven. If their luck holds, they can sell the finished product for more than it cost to buy the raw materials and process them through the assembly line.
> For a banker, the raw material is money. He buys it at a long counter he sets up in the store, then rushes around to the back, polishing it on his sleeve as he goes, sits down behind a huge desk (a little out of breath), and sells it as soon as he can to someone else....
> About the only way you can tell whether a banker is buying money or selling it is to observe him in his native habitat and see whether he's standing up or sitting down. For some unknown reason, probably an inherited trait, bankers always stand up when they buy money (take your deposit), but invariably sit down when they sell it (make loans or buy securities).[3]

Table 17-1 lists the largest banks in Canada.

Figure 17-1
The Operations of Chartered Banks

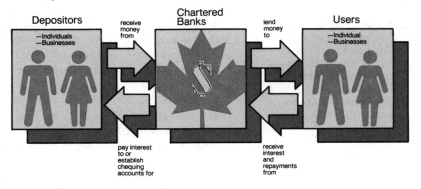

Table 17-1
The Largest Banks in Canada
Schedule A Banks

Rank 1988	Company	Assets $000
1	Royal Bank of Canada	110,054,340
2	Canadian Imperial Bank of Commerce	94,688,000
3	Bank of Montreal	78,908,911
4	Bank of Nova Scotia	74,674,837
5	Toronto-Dominion Bank	59,285,000

Schedule B Banks

Rank 1988	Company	Assets $000
1	Lloyds Bank Canada	5,145,847
2	Laurentian Bank of Canada	4,844,287
3	Hongkong Bank of Canada	4,832,290
4	Citibank Canada	4,142,127
5	Barclays Bank of Canada	2,206,106

Source: *Canadian Business 500*, June 1989.

Services Provided by Chartered Banks

"Full-service bank" is an accurate description of the typical chartered bank and the dozens of services it offers for its depositors. In addition to a variety of chequing and savings accounts and personal and business loans, chartered banks typically offer bank credit cards, safety deposit boxes, wire transfers that permit immediate payment by electronic transfers to distant banks, and some financial counselling. Most banks provide traveller's cheques at a small fee and many of them offer overdraft chequing accounts for some of their depositors. Such accounts automatically provide small loans at relatively low interest rates for depositors who write cheques exceeding the balances in their accounts. Another service is the bank's **automated teller machine (ATM)**, typically located outside the bank and at other convenient locations. Because of these and other services, chartered banks are considered the department stores of financial institutions.

automated teller machine
Electronic banking machine that permits bank customers to make cash withdrawals, deposits, and funds transfers on a twenty-four hour basis with the use of a special coded plastic access card.

Banks use deposits as the basis of the loans they make to individual and business borrowers. Because their income is derived from loans, banks lend most of the currency obtained from their chequing and savings account depositors to borrowers at interest rates higher than the rates paid to depositors. Approximately 10 percent of total demand deposits and 3 percent of notice deposits must be kept on

HERMAN®

Making loans to individuals and businesses is a key function for chartered banks in Canada.

"I don't want to borrow any, I just want to look at some."

hand at the bank or at the Bank of Canada to cover withdrawals; the remainder may be used for loans. The money kept on hand is known as **required cash reserves**, and is set by law in the Bank Act.

required cash reserves
The percentage of a bank's chequing and savings accounts that must be kept in the bank or on deposit at the Bank of Canada. This is set by law in the Bank Act.

The Need for a Central Banking Authority

What would happen if all the bank's depositors decided to withdraw their funds at once? The bank would be unable to return the depositors' money—unless it could borrow the needed funds from another bank. But if the demand for currency instead of chequing and savings accounts spread to other banks, the result would be a bank panic. Banks would have to close their doors until they could obtain loan payments from their borrowers. In the past such panics could result in a bank failure. Previous to 1985, the last bank failure in Canada was in 1923. In 1985 two banks failed, causing shockwaves through the country.

The Bank of Canada

Canada's central bank was created as a result of the Depression. Even though the Canadian chartered bank system was inherently more stable than the US commercial bank system, there was still a need for better monetary leadership. In 1934 Parliament passed the Bank of Canada Act, thereby creating a central bank for Canada.

In practice, the Bank of Canada is a banker's bank. The chartered banks are required to submit regular reports on their operations to the minister of finance and the Bank of Canada. Most importantly, they are required to keep reserve deposits with the Bank of Canada.

The Bank of Canada is expected to formulate and execute monetary policy for Canada. The work of the Bank is carried out through several departments, including Securities (to handle open-market operations), Research, and International Transactions. Through its nationwide network of offices and its role as the ultimate clearing agency, the Bank regulates monetary operations in the country.

Although a government agency, the Bank of Canada is designed to be fairly free from political interference. The governors of the Bank of Canada have tried to maintain a tradition of independence. Of course, the government, as the sole shareholder and as the body that is responsible for overall economic policy, has ultimate control over the Bank. There is regular, close consultation between the minister of finance and the governor of the bank, and in case of serious disagreement, it is clearly the minister who holds the upper hand.[4]

Focus 17-2

V.I.P. Banking Service

Imagine the day, a few years after graduation, when you are earning in excess of $125,000. You will find that you are now eligible for private banking—upscale service for upscale clients.

For example, the Canadian Imperial Bank of Commerce will provide you with a personal account manager. This specially trained person is your financial quarterback, able to handle a multitude of transactions—cash a cheque, arrange a loan, set up term deposits, or act as a liaison with other experts such as tax specialists or investment dealers.

You have the option of doing your banking in your account manager's plush office, or at your home or business. And your account manager is never more than a phone call away—day or night.

Private banking is part of a move by banks to more fee-based services to generate revenues. As well, banks are beginning to realize that their retail services are out of touch with the needs of their wealthier customers. Trust companies, who are now offering more bank-style service, have often done a better job of serving such clients. Banks realized they had to do something to stem the loss of wealthy clients.

Source: Paul Samyn, "V.I.P. Service: Private Banking Caters to Upscale Clients," *Winnipeg Free Press*, January 29, 1989, p. 10.

Control of the Money Supply: The Bank of Canada's Basic Function

The most essential function of the Bank of Canada is to control the supply of credit and money in order to promote economic growth and a stable dollar, both at home and in international markets. It performs this function through the use of three important tools: secondary reserve requirements, open market operations, and the discount rate.

Reserve requirements. The strongest weapon in the Bank of Canada's arsenal of tools to control the money supply is the **secondary reserve requirement**—the percentage of a bank's chequing and savings accounts that must be held in treasury bills. Treasury bills are promissory notes of the Government of Canada. They are the shortest term marketable debt instrument of the government and are one of the ways that the government borrows the money for its enormous needs.

secondary reserve requirement
The percentage of a bank's chequing and savings accounts that must be held in treasury bills.

By changing the percentage of reserves required from the chartered banks, the Bank of Canada can directly affect the amount of money available for making loans. For example, if it should choose to stimulate the economy by increasing the amount of funds available for borrowing, it may lower the reserve requirement.

Changing the reserve requirement is such a powerful means of affecting the money supply that it was seldom used before the unprecedented inflationary period of the late seventies and early eighties. Even a one percent variation in the reserve requirement means a potential fluctuation of billions of dollars in the money supply. Because of this the Bank seems to prefer to rely more often on the other two tools at its disposal—open market operations and changes in the bank rate.

Open market operations. The most common method used by the Bank of Canada to control the money supply is **open market operations**—the technique of controlling the money supply by buying and selling government bonds. When the bank decides to increase the money supply, it buys government bonds on the open market. The exchange of money for bonds places more money in the economy and makes it available to member banks. A decision to sell bonds serves to reduce the overall money supply.

open market operations
The technique of controlling the money supply through the purchase and sale of government bonds by the Bank of Canada.

Control of the money supply through open market operations is often exercised when small adjustments are desired. These operations do not produce the psychological effect that often results from announcements of changes in reserve requirements. Such announcements make newspaper headlines and are widely interpreted by banks, businesspeople, and the stock market as a signal from the Bank of Canada of "tighter" or "easier" money. Over the years, open market operations have been increasingly used as a flexible means of expanding and contracting the money supply.

bank rate
The interest rate charged by the Bank of Canada on loans to chartered banks.

The bank rate. Earlier, the Bank of Canada was referred to as a "banker's bank." When chartered banks need extra money to lend, they turn to the Bank of Canada, presenting either IOUs drawn against themselves or promissory notes from their borrowers. The interest rate charged by the Bank of Canada on loans to member banks is called the **bank rate**.

Chartered banks choose to borrow from the Bank of Canada when the bank rate is lower than rates charged by other sources of funds. A high bank rate may motivate bankers to reduce the number of new loans to individuals and businesses due to the higher costs of obtaining loanable funds.

The Bank of Canada may choose to stimulate the economy by reducing the bank rate. Because the rate is treated as a cost by chartered banks, a rate reduction encourages them to increase the number of loans to individuals and businesses.

The bank rate, therefore, has a controlling effect on the money supply and, indirectly, on the rate of inflation. Like the reserve requirement, it is a blunt instrument with considerable impact on such interest-sensitive industries as automobiles and housing. The bank rate is set weekly through a somewhat complicated process of auctioning of 91-day treasury bills each Thursday. The bid by the Bank for part of the amount offered offsets the average yield at tender; in this way, the Bank's interest rate intentions over the near term become known.

The bank rate communicates to banks and to the general public the attitude of the government concerning the money supply. An announcement of a reduction in the bank rate is interpreted as an

**Table 17-2
The Tools of the Bank of Canada and How They Affect the Economy**

Tools	Stimulate the Economy	Slow the Economy
Reserve requirement	Lower	Raise
Open market operations	Buy	Sell
Bank rate	Lower	Raise

indication that the money supply should be increased and credit should be expanded.

Table 17-2 shows how each of the tools of the Bank of Canada and federal government can be used to stimulate or slow the economy.

Setting the Bank Rate

The "life" of a treasury bill begins when Finance Canada and the Bank of Canada decide on the number and amount of bills to be issued. Although the amount depends primarily on the government's need for cash and on debt management policy, the total issue outstanding is watched closely. The Bank of Canada calls for bids (or tenders) one week in advance. The chartered banks, the larger investment dealers (about 13), and the Bank of Canada itself bid regularly at each weekly auction. Others may also submit tenders. Bids are usually submitted by telegraph. The highest bidder obtains all the bills it bid for at that price; the second and third highest bidders are then similarly accommodated and so on until the entire issue has been sold.

The process is quick. When the auction is over, calculations of allotments and of the average price and yield are made by computer. Bids may be submitted until noon, and by 2 p.m. successful bidders are informed by telephone, and the press release is circulated.

The bill rate is the key short-term rate from which other important rates, including the bank rate, are derived. This enables the federal monetary authorities to exert an important leverage on the entire spectrum of interest rates. Through increasing or decreasing the amount of its own holdings of treasury bills, the Bank of Canada can effect changes in its monetary policy through changes in short-term interest rates.[5]

Cheque Processing: The Canadian Payments System

cheque
A piece of paper addressed to a bank on which is written a legal authorization to withdraw a specified amount of money from an account and to pay that amount to someone.

Canadian Payments System
The system organized by the Canadian Payments Association, to process cheques between various banks and other financial institutions.

Cheque processing begins with a **cheque**—a piece of paper addressed to a bank on which is written a legal authorization to withdraw a specified amount of money from an account and to pay that amount to someone. (See Focus 17–3.) Because most business transactions are in the form of cheques, it is important to understand how they are processed, and the role played by the Canadian Payments Association (an agency of the banks and other similar financial institutions). The cheque processing system is known as the **Canadian Payments System**. In Figure 17-2, Jean Martin has purchased a new $75.00 car battery from Canadian Tire. Her cheque, in the amount of $75.00, has authorized the Royal Bank in Moncton to reduce her chequing account by paying this amount to Canadian Tire. If both parties have chequing accounts in the same bank, cheque processing becomes a simple matter of increasing the chequing account of Canadian Tire by $75.00 and reducing Martin's account by that amount.

But Canadian Tire has its chequing account in Toronto. In this situation the Canadian Payments System enters the picture to act as collector for intercity transactions. The system handles approximately 30 million cheques every week. Figure 17-2 shows the journey of Martin's cheque through the system. Whenever you receive a cheque with your monthly bank statement, you can trace the route it has taken by examining the endorsement stamps on the back of it.

Figure 17-2 A Cheque's Journey Through the Canadian Payments System

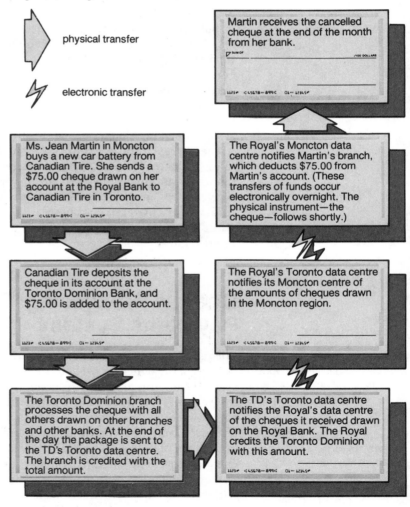

Source: Canadian Payments Association.

Focus 17-3

A Cheque Is a Cheque Is a Cheque Is a...

A cheque is an unconditional promise to pay, directing a bank to pay out a certain sum of money under specified conditions. The concept of cheques has been around for almost 3000 years, permitting us to do business without forcing us to handle currency. Almost all cheques are written on special chequebook paper, but they need not be.

Through the years, cheques have been written on many curious surfaces: on handkerchiefs, cigarette paper, calling cards, fragile valentines, and newspapers.

One written on a hard-boiled-egg shell was cashed without trouble by the Canadian Imperial Bank of Commerce. A western lumberman made out so many cheques on his own brand of shingle that his bank had to construct a special type of file cabinet for them. A contractor in Memphis once settled his weekly payroll by drawing on the banks with slabs of wood.

One story tells of a sailor who was plagued by his family back home with requests for money. He engraved a cheque on a piece of battleship plate with a blowtorch and sent it home, confident the annoying requests would stop. At the end of the month, though, the steel cheque came back with the rest of his cancelled cheques, with a proper endorsement—also made with a blowtorch.

Somewhat similar is the bizarre tale of a solid-steel cheque the size of a small headstone that was carried into the Cleveland Trust Company by two men in 1932. The teller handed over $7,500, then called bank guards, who carted the oversized cheque outside and cancelled it with submachine gun bullets! The cheque is now in the world-famous Chase Manhattan Bank Museum of Moneys of the World.

These wonderful pieces of paper, as we know them today, had their origin among the goldsmiths of London in the 17th century, although history records cheques as far back as the 9th century B.C. The first printed cheque was issued in 1762 by the House of Child, a firm that is still doing business in London.

The traveller's cheque was developed in 1891 by J. C. Fargo, then president of the American Express Company, after he returned from a trip to Europe exasperated by the difficulties of cashing letters of credit.

Electronic Funds Transfer Systems and Other Efficient Bank Services

In a single year, Canadian businesses handle more than a billion cheques. The huge costs associated with processing these cheques have led companies and the banking system to explore methods of reducing the number of cheques being written.

electronic funds transfer system (EFTS)
A computerized system of reducing cheque-writing through electronic depositing and withdrawal of funds.

The long-awaited "cashless society" may already have begun in the form of the **electronic funds transfer system (EFTS)**—computerized system of reducing cheque-writing through electronic depositing and withdrawal of funds. EFTS includes the automated teller machine. Automatic cash dispensers are now common in airports, in shopping centres and major department stores—where consumers write the greatest number of cheques. The cash dispenser is connected to the bank's computer, which checks the validity of the card, reduces the cardholder's chequing account total by the amount of cash requested, and provides the cash and a printed receipt. In addition, some stores may soon have point-of-sale (POS) terminals similar to cash registers. By inserting the customer's card into the terminal and punching in the data relating to a purchase, the amount of the purchase will be transferred via computer from the customer's account to the retail store's account. EFTS offers advantages for both businesses and consumers. Merchants can reduce their bad cheque losses, banks can save on paperwork costs, and consumers can get money instantly.

Many institutions are now interested in gaining access to shared automatic teller machine (ATM) networks. These networks could eventually lead to a major revolution in how individuals and institutions handle money.

In time—and probably not too many years away—point-of-sale **debit cards** will be in everyday use. These will enable stores to debit a customer's account directly when a purchase is made. No cheques change hands, and there is no need to process credit card slips. Customers may not be so keen about them as they will eliminate the grace period on payment offered by credit cards.[6]

debit card
Coded access card that allows the cardholder to make electronic transactions such as payments or transfers from one account to another, as well as cash withdrawals.

The largest shared teller system that has been set up is known as "Interac." The five largest Canadian banks along with the Caisse Centrale Desjardins and other banks and trust companies are members. Client confidentiality is ensured by a specially designed switching system that routes transactions from your card to your own bank.[7]

Other bank services also provide consumer convenience and improve the efficiency of banking operations. Employers, for example, can automatically deposit employees' cheques in their bank accounts. Also, for a number of years banks have enabled depositors to automatically make home mortgage and even insurance payments. With the depositor's preauthorization, such creditors bill the bank directly. The bank then reduces the depositor's chequing account total by the amount of the payments and sends the person a receipt at the end of the month showing the amount of each bill paid. With appropriate identification, consumers can also make deposits and withdrawals from any associated branch of their bank.

With competition for customers growing, many banks are initiating even greater convenience services for consumers. Many have modified banking hours to fit the needs of their clients, and Saturday banking is now commonplace.

Other Financial Institutions

A number of financial institutions other than chartered banks exist both as sources and as users of funds. These include trust and mortgage-loan companies, credit unions and caisses populaires, and consumer loan companies. They perform some, although not all, of the same functions that banks do. In particular, these institutions function as go-betweens for savers with funds to lend and investors with the need to borrow. For this reason they are considered financial intermediaries, as are banks.

These intermediaries are often called "near-banks." They accept deposits on which cheques can be written, but they are currently not subject to the reserve requirements set by the Bank of Canada. With some exceptions, they are subject to provincial regulations. In recent years, credit unions alone have made personal or consumer loans to Canadians in amounts that exceed 25 percent of the loans issued by chartered banks.[8]

Canada's 3,600 **credit unions (caisses populaires** in Quebec) trace their origin to the mutual savings banks in Europe of the eighteenth century and the People's Bank movement of the nineteenth century. They have traditionally stressed the virtues of mutuality and thrift, as well as the provision of deposit and credit facilities for the "common people." Credit unions serve as sources for consumer loans at competitive rates for their members. They are typically sponsored by companies, unions, and professional or religious groups; they pay interest to their member depositors.

Trust companies were originally set up to act as executors of wills, as administrators of estates for living people, as guardians of children, as trustees for bond issues, and so forth. In carrying out their duties to invest the funds in their care, they extended their activities into granting mortgages and other loans. In recent years their acceptance of funds "in trust" has developed into a deposit account system very like that of the chartered banks. Because their function as trustee falls under provincial jurisdiction, trust companies are usually incorporated provincially rather than federally.[9]

Other sources of funds include insurance companies and pension funds. **Insurance companies** provide protection for insured individual and business policyholders in return for payment of premiums. They are major sources of long-term loans for corporations, commercial real estate mortgages on major commercial buildings and shopping centres, and government bonds. These funds are generated through the premiums paid by policyholders. **Pension funds** are established to guarantee members a regular monthly income on retirement or on reaching a certain age. Total book value of assets of all private, provincial and local government pension plans is approximately $60 billion. Most pension funds invest surplus cash in corporate securities.

credit unions
Financial institutions typically sponsored by companies, unions, or professional or religious groups that pay interest to their member depositors and make loans to members.

caisse populaire
A type of credit union originated for parishioners of the Catholic church; found mainly in Quebec.

trust company
A firm that manages the estates of deceased persons and acts as a trustee for business transactions, as well as providing a number of financial services similar to banks.

insurance companies
Businesses that provide protection for individual and business policyholders in return for payment of premiums.

pension funds
Funds set up to guarantee members a regular monthly income on retirement or on reaching a certain age.

Providing Insurance for Depositors: The CDIC

Canada Deposit Insurance Corporation
A corporation that insures each bank deposit account up to a maximum of $60,000 and sets requirements for sound banking practices.

What if your bank fails? Most Canadians have paid little or no attention to the question until the failures of the Canadian Commercial and Northland banks in 1985. The previous bank failure was 1923. Several other financial institutions have also failed. This could create catastrophic results for depositors. Both individuals and businesses fear the loss of their deposits and have demanded means of protecting them.

The **Canada Deposit Insurance Corporation (CDIC)** is a federal government agency that insures depositors' accounts up to a maximum of $60,000 for all deposit accounts in one institution and sets requirements for sound banking practices. Insurable deposits include savings and chequing accounts, guaranteed investment certificates, debentures other than bank debentures, money orders, deposit receipts, and certified drafts or cheques. To be insurable, a deposit must be payable in Canada, in Canadian currency, and must be repayable on demand or on or before the expiration of five years. Types of uninsured instruments include stocks, bonds, mortgages, and mutual funds.

All chartered banks and trust and loan companies outside Quebec must subscribe to the CDIC. Members must display CDIC's official membership sign. In Quebec, deposits in all financial institutions other than the chartered banks are guaranteed by the Quebec Deposit Insurance Board.

The CDIC protects the safety of deposits in institutions insured with it in three ways: it examines and supervises the financial affairs and management of these institutions; it pays each depositor's claim on a failed institution up to a maximum of $60,000; and it may prevent an institution from failing by providing financial and management assistance.[10] Recent evidence shows that even such assistance may not be enough to save a bank that falls on hard times.

The CDIC was established in 1967. Despite the failures of 1985, deposit insurance is not of such vital importance to the survival of Canadian chartered banks. As any bank within the Canadian banking system is part of a huge national operation, it is unlikely that it would encounter the type of liquidity problems that would face a single-unit bank, which is common in the United States. In fact, deposit insurance is far more important to depositors in the smaller financial intermediaries—the trust companies and credit unions—and places these institutions in a more secure position in competing with the banks for the depositor's dollar.[11]

Controversial Issue

New Directions for Canadian Banking

In November 1988, a discreet order-in-council of the Canadian Government granted preliminary approval for American Express to be granted a foreign bank licence as a schedule B bank. Major schedule A, or home-based, banks objected vehemently, claiming this approval was granted because of political payoffs, among other things. The extent of their objection to the approval of another competitor entering the market was much greater than might be expected. What were they really objecting to?

Toronto Dominion President Robin Korthals criticized the government's move to shareholders. "By licensing Amex," he said, "the government would strike a major blow to its financial services policy. It is difficult to see how licensing Amex was consistent with the government's professed desire to prevent further industrial-financial co-mingling in this country." Korthals further complained that granting the licence would give a foreign institution powers now denied to Canadian banks. It would permit Amex to combine a bank and travel business under one roof.

Until now, most foreign banking licences have only been granted in cases where the parent is a full-fledged bank. Nick Mancini,

vice-president of American Express Canada, Inc., said that there was no immediate plan to open any branches or to take deposits. He indicated that American Express was more interested in becoming part of Canada's payments system, in giving American Express cardholders access to cash through the network of automatic banking machines and in gaining the right to issue cheques. This would help them to evolve their core business: cards.

From the Canadian bank client's viewpoint, this would do little to provide new competition to Canada's schedule A banks. There would be some advantage to holders of American Express cards.

The major question remains. If there will be no new competition at the retail banking level, do consumers benefit? And does allowing a link between commercial concerns and financial institutions add any advantages? This does seem to break Canadian banking tradition. Subsequent to this, schedule A banks began to say, "if they can do it, we want to do it too." Is this a direction in which Canadians want their financial institutions to go?

Sources: Sonita Horvitch, "Mulroney Denies Striking Amex Deal," *The Financial Post*, January 19, 1989; and "Why Amex Wants a Bank," *Winnipeg Free Press*, February 4, 1989, p. 18.

Summary of Learning Goals

1. **Describe the characteristics of a good form of money and list the functions of money.**
   In order to perform its necessary functions, money should possess the following characteristics: divisibility, portability, durability, stability, and difficulty of counterfeiting. These characteristics allow money to perform its functions as a medium of exchange, a unit of account (or common denominator of measuring the value of different products), and a temporary store of value.

2. **Distinguish between money and near-money.**

   Money is broadly defined as anything generally accepted as a means of paying for goods and services. The Canadian money supply is divided into the following categories: coins, paper money, demand deposits (chequing accounts), and chequing/saving accounts. Near-monies are assets that are almost as liquid as money, but cannot be used directly as a medium of exchange. Items such as time deposits (savings accounts) and Canadian government bonds are highly liquid and can be quickly converted into money.

3. **Identify the major categories of financial institutions and the sources and uses of their funds.**

   The major components of the Canadian financial system can be divided into two groups: deposit institutions and nondeposit institutions. Deposit institutions accept deposits from customers or members and offer some form of chequing or savings account. They include the nation's chartered banks and credit unions. These hold the deposits of individuals and business firms, and they use these funds to make loans. Nondeposit institutions include insurance companies, pension funds, and consumer and commercial finance companies. They represent sources of funds for businesses and provide considerable mortgage funds used in financing major commercial buildings and shopping centres. In addition, they invest funds into government bonds and securities of private corporations. Consumer finance companies make loans to individual borrowers.

4. **Describe the Bank of Canada and and how it acts to increase or decrease the money supply.**

   The regulation of the banking system is the responsibility of the Bank of Canada, which has three major tools in controlling the money supply: the secondary reserve requirement, open market operations, and the discount rate. Increases in the reserve requirement or the discount rate have the effect of reducing the money supply. Decreases in these rates have the opposite effect. Open market operations—the purchase and sale of government bonds—are the most commonly used tool. Purchases of government bonds by the Bank of Canada have the effect of placing more money in circulation. Sale of bonds acts to reduce the money supply.

5. **Discuss the purpose and chief functions of the Canada Deposit Insurance Corporation.**

   The Canada Deposit Insurance Corporation (CDIC) regulates the banking system. It establishes rules for sound banking practices and insures deposits up to a maximum of $60,000. The CDIC insurance programme and regulations apply to all banks and credit unions, except in Quebec where financial institutions other than chartered banks are guaranteed by the Quebec Deposit Insurance Board.

6. **Distinguish between credit cards and debit cards.**

   Credit cards function as temporary cash substitutes, but they are actually special credit arrangements between the issuer and the cardholder. The cardholder is billed periodically for purchases made with the card. Although debit cards closely resemble credit cards, they are access cards that allow the cardholder to make electronic transactions and cash withdrawals from his or her account. Transactions using a debit card result in an immediate deduction from the purchaser's bank account.

7. **Explain the role of electronic funds transfer systems**

   Electronic funds transfer systems (EFTS) are computerized systems of making purchases and paying bills through electronic depositing and withdrawal of funds. They are designed to increase the efficiency of the financial system by eliminating the paperwork involved in processing cheques.

Key Terms

money
medium of exchange
unit of account
store of value
currency
demand deposits
time deposits
near-money
chartered banks
automated teller machine
required cash reserves
secondary reserve requirement
open market operations

bank rate
cheque
Canadian Payments System
Electronic Funds Transfer System (EFTS)
debit card
credit unions
caisses populaires
trust companies
insurance companies
pension funds
Canada Deposit Insurance Corporation (CDIC)

Discussion Questions and Exercises

1. Identify the components of the Canadian money supply. What functions are performed by these components? Which money supply components are most efficient in serving as a store of value?

2. Explain the concept of near-money. Why is it not included as part of the money supply?

3. Distinguish between credit cards and debit cards. Are they part of the money supply? Why or why not?

4. Explain how the different types of financial institutions can be categorized, and identify the primary sources and uses of funds available from each institution.

5. Explain the functions of the Bank of Canada. Give an example of how each of the following tools may be used to increase the money supply or to stimulate economic activity:
   a) open market operations.
   b) reserve requirements.
   c) discount rate.

6. Why was the Canada Deposit Insurance Corporation created? Explain its role in protecting the soundness of the banking system. Outline the steps that may be taken by the CDIC to assist banks with financial problems. What actions are taken in case of bank failure?

7. Prepare a brief report on the most recent economic policy actions of the Bank of Canada. Your research should include recent newspaper and magazine accounts of Bank of Canada decisions.

8. What advantages do the use of debit cards offer banks? retail merchants? debit card users? Why would some purchasers choose not to use debit cards?

9. Outline the processing of cheques by the banking system in Canada.

10. How do you explain the existence of credit unions and caisses populaires in light of the many services offered by Canada's large chartered banks?

Case 17-1

A Higher Canadian Dollar

Canadians who travel to the United States and other foreign countries complain quite bitterly when the value of the Canadian dollar is low. They are pleased when the dollar strengthens. This can happen when the Canadian economy improves and foreign investors view it positively.

In 1988 this happened as prices for such commodities as nickel and forest products began to strengthen, and other parts of the economy grew as well. At the same time, interest rates in Canada were higher than in the United States, which attracted foreign investors who wanted a higher yield for their money. This external demand for Canadian currency gradually pushed the dollar up.

The dollar's rise against the US dollar makes most US imports cheaper. And Canadians vacationing in the US, or any country that uses the greenback as its prime currency, get more value for their dollar.

On the other hand, the increase in the dollar eventually makes it more difficult to sell Canadian goods because the stronger dollar makes these goods more expensive.

But some economists say that high rates of interest are not necessary to keep the dollar strong if the economy is strong. And, they argue, lower rates would stimulate domestic economic activity, keeping the dollar high.

On the other hand, lower interest rates might weaken the dollar if foreign investors begin looking for better returns elsewhere. If that happened, Canadians might experience higher inflation because they would have to pay more for imports as the dollar fell.

Question:
What would be the best policy for Canada to follow?

Case 17-2

"Will That Be VISA or Cashcard?"

Many observers have pointed out that Canada has become a credit-card economy. Consumer installment debt is counted in the billions, and the widespread use of credit cards continues to be an important feature of modern retailing.

Credit card companies charge retailers from 2 to 9 percent for handling their charge sales. This cost is then passed on to consumers in the form of higher prices—unless the retailer can generate enough added sales through the convenience of offering credit card service to cover the added costs. Both cash and credit card customers pay any higher prices that might occur.

Many people consider charging identical prices to both cash and credit card customers discriminatory. The result has been the formation of cash-discount organizations. These groups provide 3 to 10 percent discounts at participating retailers when the cardholder pays by cheque or in cash.

Questions:
1. Do you think charge cards result in discriminatory pricing?
2. Why might a retailer oppose a two-price system for cash and credit card customers?

Chapter 18

Financial Management

Learning Goals

Though my bottom line is black, I am flat upon my back. My cash flows out and customers pay slow. The growth of my receivables is almost unbelievable; The result is certain—unremitting woe! And I hear the banker utter an ominous low mutter, "Watch cash flow."
—*Herbert S. Bailey, Jr. with apologies to Edgar Allan Poe's "The Raven"*

What's a million?
—*attributed to C.D. Howe during the TransCanada Pipeline debate, 1956*

1. To identify the functions performed by a firm's financial manager

2. To explain how a firm uses funds

3. To explain how a financial manager can generate additional revenue from excess funds

4. To compare the two major categories of sources of funds

5. To identify the likely sources of short-term funds

6. To list the alternative sources of long-term funds

Profile

Don Low—*Financing a Dream through Sale of Shares*

Don Low owns a mining service company but lately he hasn't spent much time there. He's been consumed by a new dream: to turn his new venture, Flash Pack Ltd., into a household name by opening a minimum of 150 franchises across Canada within three years. Flash Pack specializes in custom foam packaging, crating, and shipping. In the same way that a travel agent arranges trips, the company finds the best way to send consumers' parcels anywhere. For example, it will ensure that a shipment of fine china to Aunt May in another city can be done safely, easily, and cheaply. It will do the same for business organizations.

Low realized that a great deal of capital would be needed to get the company off the ground and expanding quickly. He had already spent $650,000, and expected to need another $1 million in the next year. He decided to raise this by going public.

Going public means giving up a percentage of the ownership of the business and facing the pressure of shareholders. It is also expensive since a prospectus must be prepared and brokerage commissions must be paid. But the prospect of raising a lot of money outweighed the disadvantages. Many franchisors are content to open one or two stores at a time and grow slowly, but with American competitors already moving into Canada, Low had no time to waste.

His first step was to gain credibility by setting up two franchises. In addition to his own resources, he raised $500,000 privately through friends and investors. This paid for the franchises, and his cost of preparation for going public. One significant expense was $85,000 for a prospectus.

His next task was to find one or more stockbroking companies who would underwrite and sell the shares. This was not an easy task, as the recent stock market crash was fresh in everyone's mind. They had to be convinced that

the business idea was a good one, and would be attractive to the market.

By mid-June 1988, 1,050,000 shares were sold at 60 cents. This was down from the $1.00 a share that Low had hoped to raise before the market crash. Flash Pack was able to raise $550,000 after paying $74,000 in brokerage commissions.

Low was pleased that his company was able to complete the offering. "I'm very proud that we achieved it," he says. On the basis of the funds raised, expansion began with the opening of five Flash Pack stores in Toronto and one in Vancouver. Don Low is now optimistic about the spread of his business throughout the country.

Source: Tim Falconer, "Handle With Care," *Canadian Business*, October 1988, p. 115.

Credit management is a major part of a company's working capital management. The extension of credit is a valuable sales tool, but it may also create a considerable drain on a firm's financial resources, including its cash flow. As credit is extended, the time it takes to acquire the cash from a sale increases. This may cause the firm to increase its borrowings and thus its costs of financing. It also increases the costs of following through on overdue invoices. The ultimate costs in case of nonpayment may be very high.

To encourage prompt payment when credit is extended, many firms offer cash discounts for early payment and/or charge a financing fee for late payment. These are only a few of the considerations faced by the financial managers of many firms.[1]

What Is Finance?

finance
The business function of effectively obtaining and using funds.

Finance is the business function of effectively obtaining and using funds.

On numerous occasions this text has stressed the two primary functions that must be performed by a business to satisfy its customers: production and marketing of products and services. But a third—and equally critical—function must also be performed. Unless adequate funds are available for the purchase of materials and equipment and the hiring of production and marketing personnel, management may find itself in bankruptcy proceedings.

The Role of the Financial Manager

As business becomes more competitive, effective financial decisions are increasingly becoming synonymous with organizational success. As a result, the financial manager is emerging as one of the most important people on the corporate scene. The growing importance of this position is reflected in the number of chief executives who were promoted from financial positions. A recent study of major corporations revealed that nearly one in three chief executives has a finance or banking background.

financial manager
A manager who develops and implements a firm's financial plan and determines the most appropriate sources and uses of funds.

The **financial manager** is responsible for raising and spending money. Specifically, financial managers develop a financial plan for the firm and decide on the best sources and uses of funds. They also continually monitor the firm's cash, inventories, and unpaid bills to ensure that excessive funds are not tied up in these items. Although financial managers do not not directly control many of these areas, they must act as "watchdogs" over them to be sure that cash is being used efficiently.

financial plan
Document specifying the funds needed by the firm for a specified time period, the timing of inflows and outflows, and the most appropriate sources and uses of funds.

The organization's **financial plan** is a document specifying the funds needed by the firm for a specified time period, the timing of inflows and outflows, and the most appropriate sources and uses of funds. It is based on forecasts of production, purchasing, and expected sales activities for the period. Financial managers use the forecast to determine the specific amounts and timing of expenditures and receipts. The financial plan is built on answers to three vital questions:

1. What will the expenses be for the firm during the next period of operations?
2. How will the necessary funds be obtained?
3. When will additional funds be needed?

As Figure 18-1 indicates, the financial manager must consider these three equations carefully and then decide on the best sources of funds and how they should be used.

Figure 18-1
Key Ingredients of the Financial Plan

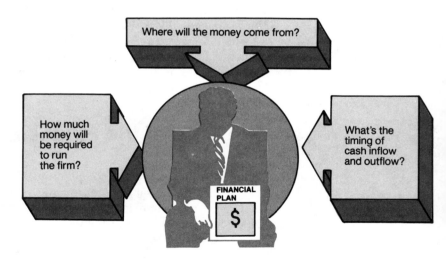

Some funds will be obtained through sale of the firm's products or services. But funds are needed in different amounts at different times, and the financial plan must reflect both the amount and the timing of inflows and outflows of funds. Profitable firms often face a financial squeeze as a result of the need for funds when sales lag or when customers are slow in making payments. The financial plan should indicate when the flows of funds entering and leaving the organization will occur and in what amounts.

Why Do Organizations Need Funds?

Organizations require funds for dozens of reasons. Some funds must be held in the form of cash to meet day-to-day requirements. If the firm permits customers to make credit purchases, funds must be available to prevent cash deficiencies during the period of time between the sale and the receipt of funds. Inventory used in producing products and services or stocked in a retail store costs money; and this money will not be recovered until the finished output is sold or the raw materials are converted into finished products and sold. Other funding requirements include making interest payments on loans; dividend payments to shareholders; and outlays for purchases of land, facilities, and equipment. The firm's financial plan will identify these specific cash needs and when these needs will be present. Comparing these needs with expected cash inflows from product sales, payments made by credit purchasers, and other sources will permit the financial manager to determine precisely how much additional funds must be obtained at any given time. If inflows exceed cash needs, the financial manager will invest the surplus to earn interest. Conversely, if inflows do not meet cash needs, the financial manager will seek out additional sources of funds. Figure 18-2 illustrates this process.

Figure 18-2
Financial Planning and Decision Making

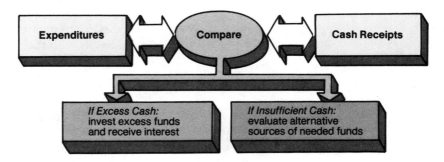

Day-to-Day Business Activities

Financial managers attempt to minimize the amount of funds held in the form of cash since this does not earn interest. However, some funds must be available each day in the firm's chequing account to pay bills and meet payrolls. Periodically, larger amounts of cash must be available to pay taxes, provide shareholders with dividends (if the firm is a corporation), or pay interest payments due on loans or mortgages. While the typical firm will use an interest-earning chequing account for these funds, such accounts earn considerably less interest than other investments.

The general principle underlying cash management is the minimization of the amount of cash required for business operations, thereby allowing a maximum amount of funds to be used in interest-producing investments. In order to minimize the firm's cash needs, the financial manager should pay bills as late as legally possible and collect money owed to the firm as quickly as possible. These actions lead to efficient cash management, as long as they do not damage the firm's credit rating or cost more than they save.

Credit Sales to the Firm's Customers

In order to keep their present customers and attract new ones, most companies find it necessary to allow at least some credit purchasing. For many firms, such purchases—labelled **accounts receivable** on the firm's financial statements—make up 15 to 20 percent of all assets. Accounts receivable reflect customer purchases of products and services not yet paid for. Because the seller has already rendered the service or invested funds in manufacturing the goods, accounts receivable represent another need for funds.

accounts receivable
Credit sales to customers for which payment has not yet been received.

Financial managers typically devote a great deal of attention to the efficient management of credit sales. The decision on whether to sell on credit to another firm is usually based on past dealings with that firm or on financial information provided by such credit-rating agencies as Dun & Bradstreet and Credit Bureau of Canada. When credit sales are involved, the financial manager must balance the need for prompt collection of accounts with the need to raise sales levels.

Inventory

For most firms—producers, wholesalers, and retailers—inventory requires considerable investment and represents a major use of cash. Because most firms hold inventory in order to satisfy consumer demand quickly, it represents a major dollar investment. Cash is continuously invested in raw materials, work in process (goods in various stages of production), and finished goods inventory. Although these investments are recouped by the firm when the products are sold, at any point in time substantial funds are tied up in unsold goods and raw materials.

The amount of money invested in inventory may vary during the year. Retail stores increase their inventory considerably just before the Christmas selling period, and reduce it beginning December 26. When the next selling season approaches, inventories are again increased.

Purchases of Land, Plant, and Equipment

Some businesses need short-term funding to meet seasonal inventory requirements

For many companies, particularly manufacturing firms, the major cash requirements involve the purchase of land, plant facilities, and equipment needed to produce salable products and services. These types of purchases were referred to in Chapter 15 as fixed assets.

Land owned by the firm is a fixed asset with an unlimited life. Since its value does not decrease over time, the firm receives no tax benefits from its ownership. Plant refers to buildings that belong to the firm. Because buildings are likely to deteriorate over time, the owners are allowed to deduct a certain percentage of the purchase price from income each year. These deductions, commonly called depreciation, result in lowering the firm's taxable income. Equipment refers to all items used in production, from drill presses to forklift trucks, and from typewriters to computers. Because equipment is also expected to deteriorate with use and become obsolete over time, business firms are permitted to depreciate it on their tax returns, again reducing their taxable income. Because land, plant, and equipment represent major purchases, the financial manager typically plays an important role in the decision process associated with their purchase.

Generating Revenue from Excess Funds

At some time or another, virtually every organization will find itself with more funds than it needs to meet its day-to-day obligations. A major sale or the signing of a licensing agreement with a foreign firm may produce major cash inflows. In such cases, the financial manager will attempt to utilize these excess funds to generate additional revenue for the firm.

Firms with substantial excess funds may decide to expand their realm of operations, to increase productive capacity, to modernize current facilities, or even to acquire other companies. As pointed out earlier, however, such uses of excess funds reduce liquidity. Capital expenditures for a new plant or the cash purchase of another firm means that the funds used for these purposes cannot easily be converted to cash should a need for additional funds arise quickly. Even though one company estimates its cash reserves at more than $500 million, the firm's management has chosen to maintain liquidity rather than making longer-term investments.

Focus 18-1

The Need for Venture Finance

He was 41 years old, a skilled sailor, and he had a plan. By plotting a new nautical trade route, he could bring back wealth in the form of gold, gems, drugs, and spices. He would also be honoured for the rest of his life. But the axiom "it takes money to make money" applied to his plan, and he would need at least $14,000 to finance the venture. His own meager savings were totally inadequate and no commercial lender would provide the funds. A formal request for funding from the Portuguese government was rejected.

Finally, almost in desperation, he dispatched his brother Bartholomew to London and Paris to seek financing from the English and French governments. He decided to handle personally the presentation of his proposal to the Spanish government. It took five years, but finally the leaders of the Spanish government accepted his ideas and consented to back the venture. They agreed to provide the necessary funds for the implementation of the plan, to grant him a percentage in any ensuing trade that might develop, to award him the title of Admiral, and to make him governor of any new lands he might discover.

He invested the $14,000 in hiring a crew, purchasing the necessary provisions, and preparing a fleet of three ships that would subsequently become famous: the flagship *Santa Maria*, and two smaller vessels, the *Nina* and the *Pinta*.

Although the venture did not prove to be a financial success for Christopher Columbus, his voyages to the West Indies rank among the most important events in history. And finance made them possible.

Marketable Securities as Substitutes for Cash

If a firm chooses to emphasize liquidity, the financial manager has several alternatives to cash. Although interest-bearing chequing accounts provide some interest, most financial managers will choose to invest the majority of a firm's excess cash in marketable securities because they pay higher interest. These are often considered near-money since they are, by definition, marketable and can be easily converted into cash. A number of different types of marketable securities are available for purchase. Three of the most common are treasury bills, commercial paper, and certificates of deposit.

treasury bills
Short-term Government of Canada borrowings that are issued each week on a competitive bid basis and are virtually riskless and easy to resell.

Treasury bills. Treasury bills are issued each week on a competitive bid basis to the highest bidder. Most of them are short-term Government of Canada borrowings, usually for 91 or 182 days. The smallest denomination of treasury bills is $1,000, and the largest, $1 million. Because treasury bills are issues of the Canadian government, they are considered virtually riskless. Because of their riskless nature and ease of resale, treasury bills are the most popular marketable security.

Commercial paper. Commercial paper, discussed later in the chapter, is riskier than treasury bills, and does not have as well developed a secondary market for resale prior to maturity. However, it does pay the purchaser a higher rate of interest. The secondary market is improving because some firms now include a call feature on the issue. This allows the buyer to return the paper to the issuer at any time with a loss of only about 0.25 percent of the quoted yield. The smallest block is generally $50,000, but most issues are $100,000.

certificate of deposit (CD)
A short-term, high-interest note issued by a chartered bank.

Certificates of deposit. A **certificate of deposit (CD)** is a short-term note issued by a chartered bank. The size and maturity date of a CD are often tailored to the needs of the investor. Normally, the smallest denomination is $10,000, and the minimum maturity is 30 days. CDs are easily resold, and their interest rate is typically higher than treasury bills but lower than commercial paper.

Sources of Funds

So far, we have focused on half of the definition of finance—the reasons organizations need funds and how they are used. But of equal importance to the firm's financial plan is the choice of the best sources of needed funds. Sources represent the financial means by which the firm can accomplish its overall objectives.

Funds needed to implement the organization's financial plan come from two major sources: debt and equity. **Debt capital** represents funds obtained through borrowing. **Equity capital** consists of funds from several sources:

debt capital
Funds obtained through borrowing.

equity capital
Funds provided by the firm's owners through plowing back earnings, additional contributions by the owners, contributions by venture capitalists, or share issues to the general investor public.

1. Revenues from day-to-day operations and plowing back earnings into the firm.
2. Additional contributions by the firm's owners.
3. Contributions by venture capitalists, who invest in the firm in return for a share of ownership.
4. Share issues to the general investor public.

These alternative sources are shown in Figure 18-3.

Figure 18-3 Sources of Funds

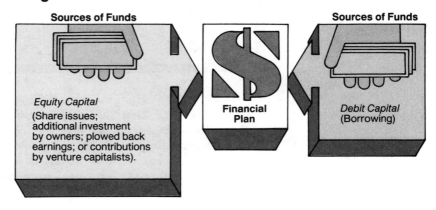

Sources of Funds

Equity Capital
(Share issues; additional investment by owners; plowed back earnings; or contributions by venture capitalists).

Financial Plan

Sources of Funds

Debit Capital
(Borrowing)

A major portion of the firm's day-to-day cash needs is generated from operating revenues. Sales, rentals, and other forms of revenue produce cash inflows that may be used to pay bills and operating expenses. In companies emphasizing growth as a major organizational objective, owners may choose to plow back earnings to finance future growth rather than withdraw profits in the form of bonuses or dividends. A growth-oriented company such as Mitel typically distributes less than 10 percent of its annual earnings in the form of dividends. On the other hand, mature companies such as Bell Telephone pay out as much as 80 percent of their profits in the form of dividends to shareholders.

As pointed out earlier, cash needs vary from one time period to the next and funds generated from daily operations may not be sufficient to cover required funds. Catalogue retail stores such as Consumers Distributing feature a variety of products—from luggage, small appliances, and gift items to sporting equipment, toys, and jewellery. Since these products are commonly purchased as gifts, catalogue retail outlets typically generate 80 percent of total annual sales during the Christmas season. Such a store will generate surplus cash for most of the year, but the buildup of inventory just before the Christmas season will require additional funds to finance it until it is sold. As sales occur during the Christmas season, the incoming funds can be used to repay the sources of the borrowed funds. Figure 18-4 describes this annual cycle of cash needs and cash inflows for the firm.

Figure 18-4
Seasonal Cash Inflows and Outflows
for a Catalogue Retailer

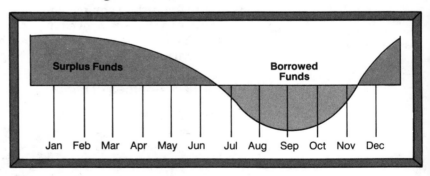

In addition to variations in the timing of cash inflows and outflows during the year, there are other reasons for needing extra funds. Newly formed firms require substantial funds to finance purchases of equipment, train a work force, make lease payments on buildings, and purchase needed raw materials and component parts. Even established firms may not be able to generate sufficient funds from operations to cover all costs of a major expansion into new geographic areas or a significant investment in new equipment and facilities. In all of these instances, the financial manager must evaluate the merits and potential problems of seeking funds by borrowing. The alternative to borrowing is equity capital, which may be raised in several ways. Table 18-1 compares debt capital and equity capital on the basis of maturity, claim on assets, claim on income, and right to a voice in the management of the firm.

Table 18-1
Comparison of Debt and Equity Financing

Factor	Debt	Equity
Maturity	Has a specific date when it must be repaid.	Has no maturity date.
Claim on assets	Company lenders have prior claims on assets.	Shareholders have claims only after claims to lenders have been paid.
Claim on income	Lenders have prior claim on a fixed amount of interest, which must be paid before dividends can be paid to shareholders. Interest payments are a contractual obligation of the borrowing firm.	Shareholders have a residual claim after all creditors have been paid. While common shareholders may receive large dividends when the company prospers, dividends are paid only when the board of directors of the firm chooses. Dividends are *not* a contractual obligation of the firm.
Right to a voice in management	Lenders are creditors, not owners. They have no voice in company affairs unless interest payments are not received.	Shareholders are the owners of the company, and most are given a voice in the operation of the firm. Common shareholders normally have voting rights, while preferred shareholders generally are not given this privilege.

Short-Term Sources of Funds

Short-term sources of funds typically finance current needs for cash or inventory at times when cash requirements exceed available funds. These sources must be repaid within a one-year period.

In contrast, long-term sources must be repaid over a period of one year or more. The four major sources of short-term loans for business firms are trade credit, unsecured bank loans, commercial paper, and secured short-term loans.

Trade Credit

trade credit
The short-term source of funds from making purchases on credit or open account.

Most firms not only sell on credit, they also make purchases on credit, or open account. These open account purchases, called **trade credit**, represent the major source of short-term financing by most business firms.

Trade credit typically does not involve a formal contract. The purchaser who accepts shipped merchandise in effect agrees to pay the supplier for the goods. The credit terms are stated on the supplier's invoice (or bill), which accompanies the shipment (see Focus 18-2).

Focus 18-2

Why Purchasers Should Take Advantage of Cash Discounts

The supplier's invoice includes credit terms; it lists the period of time for which credit is extended, the size of the discount offered if the purchaser pays cash, and the date the credit period begins. A cash discount is a reduction of the purchase price of products, provided the purchaser pays for the goods within a specific time period. These discounts are offered for the following reasons: when a seller ships products to customers, funds are tied up in the sale until payment is made. Consequently, purchasers are motivated to defer payment until the last possible moment. Because of this waiting cost and the additional costs of subsequent billings and possible use of collection agencies for delinquent accounts, a number of sellers use positive incentives to obtain speedy payments—that is, they give their customers a cash discount.

A typical supplier's credit terms may be stated as "2/10 net 30." The purchaser reads these terms as "a 2 percent discount will be allowed if I pay the invoice within 10 days. Otherwise the bill is due in 30 days." But why should the firm pay quickly in order to take advantage of the 2 percent discount? The following time line explains the dollars-and-cents reasons:

March 16
A local Pizza Hut is extended
credit terms of 2/10 net 30 on
a $1,000 paper supplies
purchase.

March 25
If the manager takes the
discount and pays within 10
days, the cost will be $980
($1,000 less 2 percent).

April 15
If the discount offer is
ignored, the cost will be
$1,000 on April 15.

The decision not to take the discount means that the manager is
paying $20 to keep the money for an extra 20 days (March 26 to
April 15). Because there are slightly more than eighteen 20-day
periods in a year, the interest cost—on an annual basis—amounts to
more than 36 percent. It is wise for the Pizza Hut manager (or any
other financial manager) to borrow money from the bank if
necessary to take advantage of cash discounts of this magnitude.

Unsecured Bank Loans

unsecured loan
A short-term source of funds
from a loan in which the
borrower does not pledge any
assets as collateral but is
given the loan on the basis of
credit reputation and previous
experience with the lender.

A second major source of short-term funds is **unsecured loans** from
chartered banks. These loans are called *unsecured* because the borrower firm does not pledge any assets (such as accounts receivable or
inventory) as collateral. Chartered banks make short-term loans on
the basis of previous experience in dealing with the firm and the
firm's credit reputation. They lend unsecured short-term funds in
three basic forms: promissory notes, lines of credit, and revolving
credit agreements.

promissory note
A traditional bank loan for
which the borrower signs a
note that states the terms of
the loan.

Promissory notes. A **promissory note** is a traditional loan agreement whereby the borrower signs a note that states the terms of the
loan. Promissory notes come in two basic forms. **Installment notes**
lay down a specific schedule of repayments by the borrower over a
fixed time period. This may be a few months or as long as 10 years,
depending on the circumstances. Installment notes are often used by
consumers to finance such items as vacations or new cars. **Demand
notes**, which set no time limits, are usually used by businesses that
expect to be able to repay the loan in one to three months. For
example, a retailer wishing to finance a temporary increase in inventory for the ''back to school'' sales season might sign a demand note
for the necessary funds. Figure 18-5 shows a typical demand note.

installment note
A promissory note that states
a specific repayment schedule
over a fixed time period.

demand note
A promissory note without a
stated date of repayment
often used by businesses as a
source of short-term funds.

The note will state the basis on which interest is payable. Sometimes a fixed rate of interest is given. More and more in these days of
fluctuating interest rates it is stated as so many percentage points
''above the bank's prime interest rate.''

Figure 18-5
A Demand Note

The First Canadian Bank
Bank of Montreal

1000 Major Ave, Cityville — Branch — July 6 19 9x $ 8,500.00

On demand we jointly and severally promise to pay to the order of The Bank of Montreal

the sum of eight thousand, five hundred xx/100 Dollars
and to pay interest monthly at a rate of 1.25 per cent per annum above the Bank of Montreal's prime interest rate per annum in effect from time to time, up to and after maturity and until actual payment at the above mentioned branch of the Bank of Montreal. At the date of this note such prime interest rate per annum is 11 per cent.
Value received.

Alice Business
Robert Partner

Prod. 1059207 - Form. 824 (3/80) Litho. CANADA-124698

prime interest rate
The lowest rate of interest charged by chartered banks for short-term loans.

For major business firms with high credit standings, the interest rate is at or near the **prime interest rate**—the lowest rate of interest charged by chartered banks for short-term loans. The prime rate shifts on the basis of availability of funds and demand for short-term funds, as well as on the basis of changes in the Bank of Canada bank rate. Each fluctuation of the prime rate makes news headlines, because it indicates the relative availability of funds.

line of credit
An agreement between a chartered bank and a business firm that states the amount of unsecured short-term credit the bank will make available to the borrower.

Line of credit. A **line of credit** is an agreement between a chartered bank and a business firm that states the amount of unsecured short-term credit the bank will make available to the borrower. A line of credit is not a guaranteed loan. It typically represents a one-year agreement that the bank will allow the firm to borrow the maximum stated amount of money. The presence of a line of credit speeds the borrowing process for both the bank and the borrowing firm because the bank does not have to examine the creditworthiness of the firm each time it borrows money. Lines of credit are available to individuals as well as businesses (see Focus 18-3).

Focus 18-3

Bank Credit Cards: Lines of Credit for Individuals

The chartered banks that issue MasterCard or VISA cards provide a service similar to a line of credit for individual cardholders. Each cardholder is allowed to make credit purchases of up to the authorized amount. The services even extend to the purchase of money from the bank that handles the bank card. Cardholders can automatically withdraw $50 to $100 without a credit check being made. In the climate of the nineties banks have become so competitive that new services continue to be offered. Personal lines of credit can now be arranged without the use of a credit card.

---

revolving credit agreement
A guaranteed line of credit.

Revolving credit agreement. A **revolving credit agreement** is simply a guaranteed line of credit. The bank guarantees that the amount shown in the credit agreement will be available to the borrower. For guaranteeing availability, the bank usually charges a commitment fee that applies to the unused balance of the revolving credit agreement.

Commercial Paper

commercial paper
Short-term promissory notes issued by major corporations with high credit standings and backed solely by the reputation of the issuing firms.

Commercial paper consists of short-term notes issued by major corporations with very high credit standings. It is backed solely by the reputation of the corporations, and it may have a maturity of anywhere from 3 to 270 days. It can be both a use of cash for firms with excess funds and a source of funds for major corporations attempting to raise money.

Because commercial paper is unsecured—backed only by the reputation of the issuing firm—only very large firms with unquestioned financial stability are able to issue it. Even with large companies, risk is present. Commercial paper typically has a maturity of one to three months. Using commercial paper to raise funds directly from large lenders is usually one or two percent cheaper than using short-term bank loans. The rates fluctuate daily with supply and demand conditions.

Secured Short-Term Loans

As a firm continues to borrow money, it soon reaches a limit beyond which no additional unsecured loans will be made. Indeed many companies, especially smaller ones, are unable to obtain any short-term unsecured money. For them, secured loans are the only source of short-term borrowed funds.

Secured loans require the borrower to pledge collateral such as accounts receivable or inventory. The agreement between lender and borrower lists the amount of the loan, the interest rate and due date, and the pledged collateral. A copy of the agreement is filed with the province. The filed agreement provides to future lenders information about which assets of the borrower are still free to be used as collateral.

Chartered banks and commercial finance companies usually extend loans backed by pledges of accounts receivable or inventory. Both assets are usually highly liquid and are therefore an attractive form of short-term collateral.

Factoring—Outright Sale of Accounts Receivable

factor
A financial institution that purchases at a discount the accounts receivable of firms such as furniture and appliance dealers.

Instead of using accounts receivable as collateral for loans, some firms sell them to a **factor**—a financial institution that purchases at a discount the accounts receivable of firms such as furniture and appliance dealers, for whom credit sales are common. Selling the accounts receivable to a factor means that every sale is a "cash" sale and the firm is thus free from the necessity of collecting payments from customers. In many instances, sales finance companies perform the role of a factor, as do some chartered banks.

Accounts receivable that are factored are sold at a discount, with the factor typically assuming all credit risks. Once the factor has purchased the accounts, customers are notified to make future payments directly to that company. Although factoring is an expensive method of raising short-term funds, it is often used in retailing because it reduces the need for major record keeping and for maintaining a collection department.

Floor-Planning—The Automobile Dealer's Friend

floor-planning
The assignment of inventory title (collateral) to financing agencies in return for short-term loans.

The automobile industry uses a special type of financing called **floor planning**—the assignment of inventory title (collateral) to financing agencies in return for short-term loans. This practice is commonly used by retailers who handle identifiable, expensive goods such as automobiles, furniture, and major appliances.

An auto dealer who receives a shipment of new cars may sign an agreement with a local chartered bank or other financing agency for a loan in the amount of the shipment. Title to the cars passes to the lender, but the cars themselves (the inventory) remain with the dealer. The lender periodically checks the dealer's inventory to make sure that all the required collateral is still in the borrower's hands. As cars are sold, the dealer pays a portion of the sales price plus interest to the lender.

Some automobile manufacturers allow their own financing subsidiaries to make floor-plan loans. The local Chevrolet dealer may have the alternative of floor-planning through a local chartered bank or through General Motors Acceptance Corporation (GMAC), the financial subsidiary of General Motors.

Long-Term Sources of Funds

While short-term sources of cash prove satisfactory in financing current needs for cash or inventory, major land, plant, and equipment purchases require funds for a much longer period of time. The business firm has three long-term financing sources available: long-term loans, bonds, and equity financing.

Long-Term Loans

Long-term loans are made by various financial institutions to business firms, primarily for purchasing machinery and equipment. They generally have maturities of up to five years. Long-term loans are made by financial institutions such as chartered banks, insurance companies, and pension funds; some are also made by the Federal Business Development Bank (FBDB). In some cases equipment manufacturers may allow their customers to make credit purchases over a period of several years.

The cost of long-term loans is generally higher than that of short-term loans due to greater uncertainty about the future. Long-term financing agreements include the length of time for repaying the loan, the interest rate, the timing of payments, and the dollar amount of the payments. Quarterly interest payments are normally required.

Bonds

bond
A certificate of indebtedness sold to raise long-term funds for corporations or government agencies.

A **bond** represents a method of long-term borrowing by corporations or government agencies. The corporate bond is issued according to the terms of a legal contract called the bond indenture, which contains the provisions of the loan—amount, interest rate, and maturity date. Figure 18-6 shows a corporate debenture, which is a common type of bond.

Bonds are typically sold in denominations of $1,000. They are purchased by chartered banks, insurance companies, pension funds, and even individuals. Like stocks, they are actively traded and can be bought and sold through any stockbrokerage firm. Their current market prices are quoted daily in the financial sections of newspapers. Issuing bonds to raise money is generally possible only for larger companies with regional or national reputations.

Equity Financing

equity funds
Funds obtained by selling stock in the company or by reinvesting company earnings.

Equity funds are obtained by selling shares in the company or by reinvesting company earnings. They differ from debt in that there is

**Figure 18-6
A Corporate Bond**

no maturity date. Sale of ownership shares (the subject of Chapter 19) is an important company decision. Such sales provide cash inflows for the firm and a share in ownership for purchasers. Because most shares are traded on organized security exchanges, shareholders can easily sell their shares. Retaining and reinvesting earnings can be used by all firms. Share sales can be used only by corporations. Each source of equity funds must be evaluated by the financial manager of a business.

Sale of shares. The sale of shares—both preferred and common—represents the true source of equity funds to the business firm. Shareholders are considered the real owners of the firm. However, they are not guaranteed dividend payments. Shareholders receive dividends only after bondholders of the company are paid. Even then, dividend payments must be decided by the firm's board of directors. Subject to certain legal requirements, any corporation can sell shares to raise new funds.

Retained earnings. Another source of funds is the reinvestment of earnings in the firm. A company may have funds available after paying all claims, including taxes. One choice is to distribute the earnings to shareholders in the form of cash dividends. But seldom are all earnings paid out as dividends; at least a portion is usually kept to finance future growth.

Attracting Venture Capital

venture capital
Funds invested in new, small, or struggling businesses with potential for rapid growth, by outside investors in exchange for an ownership share in the business.

As discussed in Chapter 4, **venture capital** refers to funds for new, small, or struggling businesses with the potential for rapid growth. It is usually provided by outside investors in exchange for an ownership share in the business. The venture capitalist may be a corporation, wealthy individual, pension fund, or major endowment fund. In exchange for funds, the venture capitalist receives shares of the corporation's stock at low prices and becomes a part-owner of the corporation. For taking the risks inherent in any struggling firm, the venture capitalist has the opportunity to earn substantial profit, should the firm become successful and issue shares of stock to the general public. Often, a venture capitalist provides a firm with management assistance as well as funds.

Venture capitalists typically receive dozens of proposals each month from businesses seeking funds. Most applications are rejected by these investors, who seek out soundly managed firms with unique products or services in rapidly growing industries. In recent years, venture capitalists have concentrated in high-tech industries such as medical technology, information processing equipment and software, robotics, and energy-related firms.

Focus 18-4

The Investor's Checklist

Before you invest, investigate. Hal Tennant suggests the following questions be asked:

QUESTIONS ABOUT MYSELF
- What's my purpose or goal in investing—immediate income, long-term capital growth, or some combination?
- Are my expectations realistic?
- Should I favour risk-free investments to preserve my capital, or am I able—by temperament and circumstance—to accept a degree of risk in return for the potential of greater gain? If so, how much risk is appropriate?
- Might certain investments be too worrisome or too much bother for me?
- Am I emotionally equipped to deal with an investment that turns sour?

Having completed that self-assessment, you'll be ready to evaluate various investments by seeking out the answers to these questions:

Equities

Stocks
- What assets does the company have? Has it grown over the past five years?
- Does it have enough cash flow to meet its obligations, expand its operations, and pay dividends? Was it profitable in the past quarter? Last year?
- Is the debt-equity ratio acceptable?
- What's the management's track record in growth, earnings, profits?
- Has the stock's price been moving up or down? How does its price-earnings ratio compare with those of other companies in the industry?
- Has the company been paying dividends regularly?
- Are there any special circumstances that warrant extra study? Is it, for example, a takeover target, or on the acquisition warpath?
- Am I interested enough in the industry in general to follow its ups and downs?

Mutual Funds
- How good is the management's record?
- Is there commission to pay? If so, how is it calculated? Do I pay going in (front-end load) or when pulling out (back-end load)?
- Is there an administration fee?
- Is the fund open-ended (redeemable only by the issuer) or closed-ended (traded among investors)?
- Considering my needs and my attitude toward risk, what kind of

investment focus is most appropriate (e.g. stocks, bonds, real estate, mortgages, gold, money market)?

- How often and how well does the fund report to unit-holders; how often does it declare capital gains or dividends?
- What has been the fund's average annual compound rate of return over the past five to ten years? How does this record compare with those of other funds of the same type?
- Has it outperformed risk-free investments, such as T-bills?

Real Estate

- What kind of real estate would help me meet my financial goal?
- How much of my own capital do I want to invest? How much capital should I borrow (e.g. through a mortgage)?
- Is the property already producing a good net return on investment?
- How much are the carrying costs (mortgage payments, taxes, maintenance)?
- Will the revenue cover these expenses and still provide a return on my investment? Is it enough to justify the risk?
- Is the building structurally sound? Will it need improving?
- What are the area's market trends?
- Is the area pleasant, healthy, and growing? Are radical changes or developments in prospect?
- What are the prospects for a capital gain when I sell?
- Is the property zoned for the use I have in mind?
- Am I prepared to accept the aggravations of being a landlord?

Private Ventures

- What exactly is the business? Is there a ready market for it? Is this a growth industry?
- Why is the money needed? How will it be used?
- Is this person mature, trustworthy and competent, with all the necessary skills and experience? What training or track record does he or she have? Who else is involved?
- Is there a proper prospectus or business plan? Or, if the business is already running, what does the balance sheet show?
- Will the deal be handled and documented in a businesslike manner?
- If my investment is in the form of a loan, how will it be secured?
- How and when will the principal be repaid?
- How much interest will be paid? How often? Is there enough cash flow to ensure steady payments?
- If my money is intended as equity, are there sound reasons for favouring this venture over other investments? How much say will I have in how the business is run?
- Does the proposition suit my financial needs?
- If the loan or investment is requested by a relative or good friend, what would happen to our personal relationship if the business failed?

Franchises

- What will I be getting for my money?
- Will the franchise package supplement my strengths by covering areas where I'm weak or deficient?
- Will the franchisor provide help when I need it?
- Can the franchisor produce hard numbers, including audited statements, to show the financial strength necessary for him to honour his end of the deal?
- What are the franchisor's projections for cash flow and profit (a) for his own business and (b) for the operation I would undertake? Do they support the claims he makes for the franchise?
- Do these projections show enough earnings to provide a fair return on my investment as well as a salary for my work as an owner-manager?
- Does the business involve a marketable service or product?
- Is the franchisor honest and decent?

Source: © 1989 Hal Tennant Associates Ltd. Adapted from "The Investor's Checklist," *Report on Business Magazine*, February 1989, p. 104.

Leverage: Increasing the Rate of Return

leverage
A technique of increasing the rate of return on investment through the use of borrowed funds.

Raising needed cash by borrowing allows the firm to benefit from the principle of **leverage**—a technique of increasing the rate of return on investment through the use of borrowed funds. Table 18-2 shows two identical firms that chose to raise money in different ways. The Leverage Corporation obtained 90 percent of its funds through issuing bonds. The Equity Corporation raised all its needed funds through

Table 18-2
Simplified Income Statements for the Leverage Corporation and the Equity Corporation

Leverage Corporation			Equity Corporation		
Common stock	$ 10,000		Common stock	$100,000	
Bonds (at 10% interest)	90,000		Bonds	0	
	$100,000			$100,000	
Earnings	$ 30,000		Earnings	$ 30,000	
Less bond interest	9,000		Less bond interest	0	
	$ 21,000			$ 30,000	
	$ 21,000			$ 30,000	
Return to shareholders	$ 10,000	= 210%	Return to shareholders	$100,000	= 30%

the sale of shares in the firm. Although each company earned the same profits, shareholders of the Leverage Corporation received a 210 percent return on their $10,000 investment—even after paying $9,000 in interest to bondholders. The $30,000 earned by the Equity Corporation represents only a 30 percent return on its shareholders' investment of $100,000.

As long as earnings exceed interest payments on borrowed funds, the application of leverage allows the firm to increase the rate of return on shareholders' investments. But leverage also works in reverse. If company earnings drop to $5,000 in the example, the Equity Corporation will earn a 5 percent return on its shareholders' investment. But because bondholders must be paid $9,000 in interest at the Leverage Corporation, what appears to be a $5,000 gain is actually a $4,000 loss for its shareholders.

Controversial Issue

Impossible Financing?

Can we afford to let farmers go broke? Dozens of policy papers have been written on the farm financial crisis since the bottom fell out of the markets in 1982, yet the industry is still far from a solution. Until then, prices for farm products were quite high, and farmers borrowed heavily. Banks and other financial institutions happily obliged.

The farm debt now stands at about $22.5 billion, of which $6 billion may never be recovered. At the Farm Credit Corporation, the federal agency in charge of farm lending, eighteen percent of the loans are six months in arrears, and half that number are three years behind. Five percent of all Canadian farmers have negative cash flow and a negative equity position. In other words, they are technically bankrupt. About 12,500 farmers are considered in severe financial difficulty.

Many schemes have been tried to restructure debts, and to try to find new capital for the industry. However, it seems that farming is just not a good investment, at least in the short term. The FCC manages a return of only three to four percent on its western grain properties,

and even the best farms provide less than a ten percent return.

In response to this, the free market proponent might respond, "So what? Farmers have the same right to go broke as any other business person who expanded at the wrong time and has run into interest and cash flow problems. Those farmers who have not been good financial managers should pay the consequences, just as any other small or large business."

On the other hand, the farm scene matters to all Canadians, for reasons that go beyond the fact that farmers put food on urban tables. Farming is a big base industry upon which many others are built. In a recent year it brought farmers more than $19 billion in revenue and earned Canada's economy $9.5 billion in exports. The industries of farm machinery, chemicals and transportation—not to mention food processing and retailing—all have a big stake in the health of this portion of the economy.

Source: Oliver Bertin, "Farm Debt Problem Would Baffle Solomon," *The Globe and Mail*, January 14, 1989, p. B4.

Summary of Learning Goals

1. **Identify the functions performed by a firm's financial manager.**

   The financial manager's major responsibility is to develop and implement a financial plan for the organization. This plan is based on a forecast of expenditures and receipts for a specified time period, and reflects the timing of cash inflows and outflows. It includes a systematic approach to determining needed funds during the period and the most appropriate sources for obtaining them. In short, the financial manager is responsible for both raising and spending money.

2. **Explain how a firm uses funds.**

   Funds are needed for a variety of reasons. Day-to-day operating requirements call for funds to pay bills, meet payrolls, make interest payments, and pay taxes. Additional funds are tied up in accounts receivable if the firm allows customers to buy on credit. Inventory—in the form of raw materials, work in process, or finished goods—also requires considerable funds. Major purchases of land, buildings, and equipment may involve sizable outlays of funds.

3. **Explain how a financial manager can generate additional revenue from excess funds.**

   When funds on hand exceed cash needs, the financial manager may choose to make a number of investments designed to earn interest. These include the purchase of treasury bills, commercial paper issued by major corporations, or certificates of deposit issued by commercial banks and brokerage firms. These investments generate revenue for the firm, but do not tie up funds for a long time.

4. **Compare the two major categories of sources of funds.**

   The two major sources of funds are debt capital and equity capital. Debt capital consists of funds obtained through borrowing. Equity capital refers to ownership funds provided by 1) revenues from day-to-day operations and plowed-back earnings, 2) additional contributions by the firm's owners, 3) contributions by venture capitalists who invest in the firm in exchange for a share of ownership, and 4) stock issues to the general public. In contrast to equity capital, which has no maturity date, debt capital has a specific date when it must be repaid. Lenders also have a prior claim on assets and a prior claim on income paid in the form of interest. Owners have only a residual claim on assets and income after lenders have been paid. Lenders, unlike owners, have no voice in the management of the firm unless interest payments have not been made.

5. **Identify the likely sources of short-term funds.**

   If funds provided by day-to-day operations are inadequate to cover cash needs, the financial manager must seek short-term sources of additional funds. These include the use of trade credit provided by suppliers, unsecured bank loans, and secured short-term loans. Major corporations can also consider issuing commercial paper. Secured loans are those backed by pledges of such company assets as accounts receivable or inventory. Some firms sell their accounts receivable directly to financial institutions called factors, which purchase the accounts at a discount. Retailers of furniture and appliances often sell accounts receivable to factors.

6. **List the alternative sources of long-term funds.**
   Long-term funds may be obtained from debt capital or equity financing. Debt capital includes the use of long-term loans or the issuing of bonds. Equity capital may be obtained by additional contributions by the original owners or, in the case of a partnership, investment by new partners in exchange for a share in the firm. In some cases, new, small, and promising firms with growth and profit prospects may be able to attract funds from venture capitalists who invest in the company in exchange for ownership shares. Finally, corporations may raise equity capital by issuing stock to the general public.

Key Terms

finance	demand note
financial manager	prime interest rate
financial plan	line of credit
accounts receivable	revolving credit agreement
treasury bills	commercial paper
debt capital	factor
equity capital	floor-planning
trade credit	bond
unsecured loan	equity funds
promissory note	venture capital
installment note	leverage

Certificate of deposit (CD)

Discussion Questions and Exercises

1. Explain the functions performed by the financial manager. What role does forecasting play in these functions?
2. Many firms offer cash discounts, such as a two-percent discount if the bill is paid within ten days of its receipt and total payment within 30 days (2/10 net 30). Why are such discounts offered? Should purchasers take advantage of these discounts? Defend your answer.

3. Identify the primary uses of cash in an organization.
4. Evaluate the major alternatives available to the financial manager in generating additional revenue from excess funds.
5. What role do firms like Dun & Bradstreet and the Credit Bureau of Canada play in financial management? What types of information could they provide for use in developing a credit risk assessment analysis?
6. What are the primary sources for short-term financing? Distinguish between unsecured and secured loans.
7. Distinguish between debt capital and equity capital on the basis of maturity, claim on assets, claim on income, and right to a voice in management. What are the primary sources of equity capital?
8. Explain how trade credit is used in financing expenditures. Is trade credit considered short-term or long-term financing?
9. Identify the sources for long-term financing. Explain how borrowed funds produce leverage.
10. Identify the basic principle underlying efficient cash management. What dangers exist if this principle is carried too far?

Case 18-1

Polaris Consulting Services Ltd.

Most boardrooms in downtown Toronto stay empty on Saturday mornings. But on November 10, 1987, ten managers of Polaris Computer Systems Ltd. assembled in the consulting firm's boardroom for a meeting that would launch them on a five-month emotional roller-coaster ride. As Mel Steinke, the company's general manager, entered the room he could feel the tension in the air. Earlier that week, he had learned that the parent company, Toronto's Crowntek Inc., planned to sell Polaris. Boldly, Steinke proposed a management buyout.

The nervousness dissipated as the managers responded enthusiastically. Steinke knew, however, that Crowntek was asking about $5 million for Polaris, a steep amount for the management group to raise. Quickly the mood of the meeting cycled from high to low when everyone realized that a successful bid would require selling personal stocks, bonds, and securities, mortgaging homes and even securing personal loans. Even then they would have to find an outside investor to fund a substantial portion of the bid. "Everybody was nervous about pledging their assets," recalls George Lecompte, vice-president of finance at Polaris. "But Mel carried the ball with the shareholders. He kept their confidence up."

When the management team submitted its offer on November 26, Crowntek was skeptical about the group's ability to get the necessary financing. "How do you take something seriously when there is nothing behind it?" said Ed Cannon, president of Crowntek.

Surprisingly, in the months that led to the bid for Polaris, Steinke discovered that his biggest challenge was not getting the money but managing negotiations. "You must have confidence in yourself and you must be persistent," he says. "Negotiating skills are important, but most important are the interpersonal skills to keep everyone involved."

Crownx Inc., which owns Crowntek, wanted to sell Polaris so it could concentrate on its insurance and health-care businesses. Twelve companies, including competitors such as SHL Systemhouse Inc. of Montreal, were interested in Polaris because of the impressive growth of the consulting firm—revenues rose from $1.8 million in 1983 to $11 million in 1987—and because of its foothold in six American cities. But the management team beat them all to the table.

Steinke and Lecompte knew that an early bid would strengthen their position. "The other purchasers wouldn't want to compete with the management buyout," says Steinke's lawyer, Sheldon Plener, because any successful outside bidder would need the support of Steinke and his executives. "Crowntek didn't fully understand how important the managers were to the success of the company," says Ian McCallum, Ottawa vice-president of Polaris.

By January 1988, Crowntek still hadn't made a decision and serious parties began dropping away, unable or unwilling to compete with the management group. When Winston Ling, Crownx's executive vice-president of finance, finally called in early February to say that the management team's offer had been accepted in principle, Steinke faced further tough negotiations. Several key issues had to be ironed out, including a determination of the company's assets, whether Crowntek's pension plan should be kept, and which side would be responsible for existing accounts receivable and the leases for the premises. Steinke had yet to ink an agreement for the 20 key personnel in the investors' group and he hadn't found a partner or investor.

Coopers & Lybrand, a Toronto-based accounting firm that wanted to expand its computer services practice, expressed interest in the deal. "We saw Polaris as a potentially attractive partner," says Rick Hossack, national partner with Coopers & Lybrand's information technology group. "Not many businesses could give us an enhanced market position." But talks broke down during the second week of February when Coopers decided that Polaris's operations simply were not a good fit.

Without a major investor, the buyout was in jeopardy. It was an embarrassing situation, as Coopers & Lybrand had been presented as financial backers. Steinke asked Cannon for a two-week delay while he explored other options. Small venture capital firms and brokerage firms were quickly ruled out because they wanted to take a bigger piece of the company than the buyers wanted. However, Steinke and Lecompte approached the Royal Bank Capital Corp., the venture capital arm of the Royal Bank. RBCC saw Polaris as a good investment opportunity. By the third week of February the RBCC negotiations were substantially complete.

After adding up the numbers, however, Steinke and Lecompte

realized they were $250,000 short of the purchase price. The investors were tapped to the limit and the RBCC couldn't put in any more cash without assuming a majority position, something neither side wanted.

Source: Wili Liberman, "Power to the People," *Canadian Business*, February 1989, p. 17.

Question:
What should Steinke and his partners do now? Give a rationale for your answer.

Case 18-2

Prestige Clothing, Inc.

Prestige Clothing, Inc. generates annual revenues of $7 million in a relatively stable business—tuxedos. Yet despite the stability of its market, Prestige faced a severe financial crisis in a recent year as a result of interest rates. Although the firm earned a profit of $480,000 from operations the previous year, its interest expenses reduced overall net income to a minuscule $26,400. The market price of the firm's shares skidded to only 25 percent of book value. A total of $2.9 million in outstanding loans was payable, equalling 40 percent of sales and 108 percent of shareholders' equity.

It appears that Prestige Clothing's financial problems were caused to a large degree by the fact that only 15 percent of its revenues were generated by direct retail sales. The remaining 85 percent came from credit sales to retail stores. Because most of these stores tended to be undercapitalized, Prestige provided them with 90-day credit at an annual interest rate of 4.8 percent. Such generous credit terms provided the necessary inducement for retail purchasers, but they were painfully expensive. Because Prestige was borrowing funds at the market rate, it found itself paying 2.5 times as much in interest as it was charging its retail customers.

Reducing interest expense was clearly the major challenge facing Prestige's management. In fact, their earnings per share would rise from a mere 13 cents to $1 if they could cut interest expenses in half.

Questions:
1. Relate the problems faced by Prestige Clothing's financial managers to the information presented in this chapter.
2. What recommendations would you make to the chief executive officer of Prestige Clothing?
3. Identify two or three other firms in different industries that face similar financial problems. What can be learned from these situations?

Chapter 19

Long-Term Financing: The Securities Markets

How to get rich in the stock
market: take all your savings
and buy some good stock and
hold it till it goes up and then
sell it. If it don't go up, don't
buy it.
—*Will Rogers*

Learning Goals

1. To describe the nature of securities: the major source of long-term financing

2. To describe the securities exhanges, and the steps involved for an investor to buy or sell shares

3. To show how to read the information included in stock and bond quotations

4. To identify the three basic objectives of investors and the types of securities most likely to accomplish each objective

5. To explain the role of mutual funds in the securities field

Profile

Russ Latham—*Building Profitability and Encouraging Investment*

Russ Latham spent the past three years rescuing Sherritt Gordon Ltd. from death's door. He successfully turned around the company and pointed it in better directions.

The onetime mining company jettisoned its tired mineral assets, the source of much of its woes. It also generated greater resources by welcoming aboard a new major shareholder, Vencap Equities Alberta Ltd. Vencap purchased an 11.2 percent interest in the company. Furthermore, profitability was returned to its income statements through other actions such as mercilessly chopping debt. From $240 million three years previously, long-term debt was reduced to $72 million.

The company's stock, after floundering around $5 for the previous two years, shot up 74 percent to $9½ in ten months, far outpacing the 3.6 percent gain in the Toronto Stock Exchange 300 index. Professional investment analysts were still cautious as to whether the turnaround would last, and whether to recommend increased investment in shares. Latham was confident, however. With strong earnings now occurring, he expected that earnings per share, which had languished at 10 cents for many months, would range around $2 for the next two years at least.

Investors were obviously pleased with the turnaround. Returns to current investors would be greatly improved. And it would be much easier to raise new money in the securities market because of the performance.

Source: Laima Dingwall, "Sherritt Gordon Plots New Path," *The Financial Post*, December 5, 1988, p. 21.

The previous chapter discussed a number of aspects of financial management. It was shown that the organization must manage funds at different phases of the business cycle. Sometimes there are short-term and sometimes long-term cash needs in the process of ultimately generating a positive profit flow. In this chapter we will consider the special nature of long-term sources of funding—the securities markets. The securities markets are such an important part of business and private investor life that this entire chapter will be devoted to their consideration.

Securities: Stocks and Bonds

The two sources of funding for long-term capital are equity capital and debt capital. Equity capital takes the form of stocks—shares of ownership in the corporation. Long-term debt capital exists in the form of corporate bonds. Stocks and bonds are commonly referred to as **securities** because both represent obligations of their issuers to provide purchasers with an expected or stated return on the funds invested.

When a corporation needs capital for plant expansion, product development, acquisition of a smaller firm, or for a variety of other legitimate business reasons, it may decide to make a stock or bond offering. A stock offering gives investors the opportunity to purchase ownership shares on the firm and to take part in its future growth in exchange for current capital. In other instances, a corporation or a government agency may choose to raise funds by issuing bonds.

Stocks: Shares of Ownership in the Corporation

Stocks are units of ownership, or shares, in a corporation. Although many corporations issue only one type of share, two types exist: common shares and preferred shares.

Common shares. The basic form of corporate ownership is **common shares**. Purchasers of common shares stock are the true owners of a corporation; in return for their investment they expect to receive payments in the form of dividends and/or capital gains resulting from increases in the value of their stock holdings.

Holders of common shares vote on major company decisions, such as the purchase of other companies or the election of the board of directors. They benefit from company success, and they risk the loss

securities
Stocks and bonds that represent obligations on the part of the issuers to provide purchasers with an expected or stated return on funds invested.

common shares
Shares whose owners have only a residual claim on the firm's assets but who have voting rights in the corporation.

par value
The value printed on the share certificates of some companies.

market value
The price at which a security is currently selling.

book value
The value of shares determined by subtracting a company's liabilities from its assets (minus the value of any preferred shares).

of their investment if the company fails. Creditors and preferred shareholders are paid before common shareholders. Common shares are sold on either a par or no-par value basis. **Par value** is the value printed on the share certificates of some companies. Because the par value is highly arbitrary, most corporations now issue no-par value shares. In either case, the total number of shares outstanding represents the total ownership of the firm, and the value of an individual shareholder's investment is based on the number of shares owned and their market price rather than on an arbitrary par value.

Sometimes confusion results over two other types of value: market value and book value. **Market value**—the price at which shares of stock are currently selling—is easily determined by referring to the financial page of the daily newspaper. It usually varies from day to day, depending on company earnings and investor expectations about future prospects for the firm. **Book value** is determined by subtracting what the company owes (its liabilities) from its assets minus the value of any preferred stock. When this net figure is divided by the number of shares of common stock, the book value of each share is known.

Figure 19-1
A Share Certificate

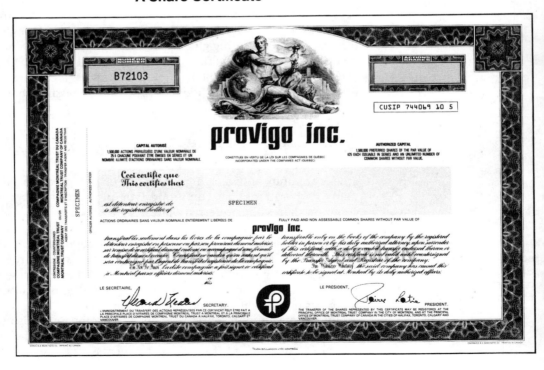

What happens when the corporation decides to raise additional long-term funds through the sale of additional shares of stock? In most cases current shareholders are given the opportunity to purchase a proportionate amount of new share issues—their **preemptive right**. Without this right a shareholder owning 6 percent of a company's stock would find his or her ownership of the company diluted to 3 percent if the firm decided to double the number of shares of stock. An illustration of a share certificate is shown in Figure 19-1.

preemptive right
The right of current shareholders to purchase proportionate amounts of new share issues.

Preferred shares. In addition to common shares, many corporations issue **preferred shares**—shares whose owners receive preference in the payment of dividends. Also, if the company is dissolved, preferred shareholders usually have a claim on its assets prior to any claim by common shareholders.

In return for this preference, preferred shareholders usually do not have voting rights. And even when they do exist, voting rights are typically limited to major proposals such as mergers, sales of company property, and dissolution of the company itself. Although preferred shareholders are granted certain privileges over common shareholders, they are still considered owners of the firm, and their dividends are therefore not guaranteed.

Preferred shares can be cumulative or noncumulative. In the case of **cumulative preferred shares**, shareholders must be paid a dividend for each year before dividends can be paid to common shareholders. If, for example, Alcan's board of directors decides one year to omit a $4 dividend to preferred shareholders because of poor earnings, it cannot pay any dividends to the common shareholders the following year until dividends of $8 are paid to each preferred shareholder. Omitted dividends accumulate automatically and must be paid before common shareholders can receive any dividends at all. Owners of **noncumulative preferred shares**, on the other hand, need be paid only the current year's dividend before common shareholders receive their dividends.

Preferred shares are often issued with a conversion privilege. These **convertible preferred shares** give shareholders the option of having their preferred shares converted into common shares at a stated price.

Preferred shares are usually issued to attract conservative investors, who want the margin of safety in having preference over common shares. Although preferred shares represent equity capital, many companies consider them a compromise between bonds and common shares. Figure 19-2 is an advertisement announcing a new issue of preferred shares.

preferred shares
Shares whose owners receive preference in the payment of dividends and have first claim to the corporation's assets after all debts have been paid but who usually do not have voting rights in the corporation.

cumulative preferred shares
Preferred shares whose owners are entitled to the automatic payment of accumulated dividends, when the company omits a dividend payment, before common shareholders can receive any dividends at all.

noncumulative preferred shares
Preferred shares whose owners are entitled only to the current year's dividend before common shareholders receive their dividends.

convertible preferred shares
Preferred shares whose owners have the option of converting their preferred shares into common shares at a stated price.

Figure 19-2
An Advertisement Announcing a New Share Issue

This advertisement is not to be construed as a public offering in any province of Canada of the securities mentioned herein. Such offering will be made only by a prospectus in those provinces where such prospectus has been accepted for filing by a securities commission or similar authority in such province.

New Issue

$270,337,500
12,150,000 Shares*

CANADIAN UTILITIES LIMITED
Cumulative Redeemable Second Preferred Shares Series H
Carrying the right to receive Warrants to purchase Class A Common Shares
of
TRANSALTA UTILITIES CORPORATION
*This offering may be increased, at the option of the Underwriters, by up to 821,900 shares.

Retraction Privilege

Retractable at the option of the holder by deposit on or before October 26, 1987 for redemption on November 1, 1987 at $22.25 per share.

Warrants

Holders of Series H Preferred Shares of record at the close of business on December 1, 1982 will receive one warrant for each Series H Preferred Share held, entitling the holder to purchase one outstanding Class A Common Share of TransAlta Utilities Corporation at a price of $22.25 per share on or before November 1, 1987.

Price: $22.25 per share to yield 9.00% per annum

The Series H Preferred Shares are offered pursuant to a prospectus dated October 18, 1982, copies of which may be obtained from such of the undersigned and other dealers who may lawfully offer these securities.

Richardson Greenshields of Canada Limited   **Pitfield Mackay Ross Limited**

Wood Gundy Limited   **Nesbitt Thomson Bongard Inc.**

Dominion Securities Ames Limited	**McLeod Young Weir** Limited	**Pemberton Securities** Limited
Burns Fry Limited	**Merrill Lynch, Royal Securities** Limited	**Midland Doherty** Limited
Walwyn Stodgell Cochran Murray Limited	**Bell Gouinlock** Limited	**Houston Willoughby** Limited
Lévesque, Beaubien Inc.	**Bache Halsey Stuart Canada** Ltd.	**McDermid, Miller & McDermid** Limited
Andras, Hatch & Hetherington Ltd.	**Moss, Lawson & Co.** Limited	**Odlum Brown** Limited
Scotia Bond Company Limited	**Tassé & Associés,** Limitée	**MacDougall, MacDougall & MacTier** Inc.

Molson Rousseau Inc.   **Peters & Co.**

October, 1982

How Money is Raised Through Sale of Shares

When a firm decides to raise money by selling shares in the market, it "goes public." The decision is a very significant one in that the owners are sharing their holdings with others. There is a formal process required to do so. It is controlled by provincial securities commissions in order to ensure a fair and honest offering to the public. First, there is a decision as to how many dollars are to be raised. Next, the type of securities to be offered (type of stocks, etc.) must be chosen. A prospectus describing the offering must be prepared. It must meet specified requirements. The firm wishing to sell shares also must find one or more brokerage firms to underwrite the offering. Underwriting involves an agreement to purchase the shares at an agreed-upon price or to work on a "best efforts basis" and bring the shares to the market. One or more underwriters will likely be involved. Shares are generally offered to the public the day after the issue is cleared by a provincial securities commission.

Bonds

Selling bonds is another way of raising long-term debt capital. Bondholders are creditors, not owners, of the organization. Since ownership is not transferred, bonds are also used as sources of funds for municipal, provincial, and federal governments. Except for Canada Savings Bonds, bonds are normally issued in larger denominations starting at $1,000 and ranging to $50,000. They indicate a definite rate of interest to be paid to the bondholder and the **maturity date**— the date at which the loan must be repaid. Because bondholders are creditors of the corporation, they have a claim on the firm's assets prior to any claims for preferred and common shareholders in the event of the firm's dissolution.

maturity date
The date at which a loan must be repaid.

Types of bonds. The potential bondholder has a variety of bonds from which to choose. Some bonds are **secured**—backed by specific pledges of company assets, including real property and personal property such as furniture, machinery, and even stocks and bonds of other companies owned by the borrowing firm. A company such as Canadian Pacific may raise a large proportion of its long-term funds through issuing bonds, often using equipment such as aircraft, locomotives, and rail cars as collateral.

secured bond
A bond backed by specific pledges of company assets.

Since bond purchasers are attempting to balance their financial returns with the risks involved, bonds backed by pledges of specific assets are less risky than those without such collateral. Consequently, a firm will be able to issue secured bonds at lower interest rates than would be possible if it had chosen to issue unsecured bonds.

debenture
A bond backed by the reputation of the issuing corporation rather than by specific pledges of assets.

However, a number of companies do issue such bonds. These unsecured bonds are called **debentures**—bonds backed by the reputation of the issuing corporation rather than by specific pledges of assets. Only major corporations with extremely sound financial reputations can find buyers for their debentures. Bell Canada has successfully raised millions of dollars from debentures. Bond purchasers have been willing to buy Bell Canada unsecured bonds because of their faith in the ability of the issuing company.

convertible bonds
Bonds that offer the option of being converted into a specific number of shares of common stock.

bond indenture
The legal contract containing all provisions of a bond.

In order to entice more speculative purchasers, **convertible bonds** are sometimes issued. These are bonds with the option of being converted into a specific number of shares of common stock. The number of shares of stock exchanged for each bond is included in the **bond indenture**—the legal contract containing all provisions of the bond. A $1,000 bond might be convertible into 50 shares of common stock. If the shares are selling at $18 when the bonds are issued, the conversion privilege has no value. But if the shares rise in price to $30, the value of the bond increases to $1,500.

How bonds are retired: Because bonds have a maturity date, the issuing corporation must have the necessary funds available to repay the principal when the bonds mature. The two most common methods of repayment are serial bonds and sinking-fund bonds.

serial bonds
A large number of bonds that are issued at the same time but mature at different times.

In the case of **serial bonds**, a corporation simply issues a large number of bonds that mature at different dates. If a corporation decides to issue $4.5 million in serial bonds for a 30-year period, the maturity dates may be established in such a manner that no bonds

Table 19-1
Types and Characteristics of Bonds

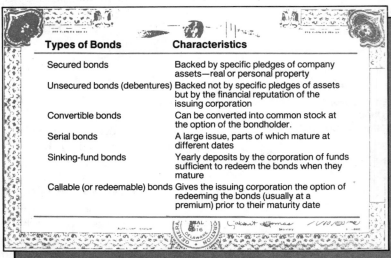

Types of Bonds	Characteristics
Secured bonds	Backed by specific pledges of company assets—real or personal property
Unsecured bonds (debentures)	Backed not by specific pledges of assets but by the financial reputation of the issuing corporation
Convertible bonds	Can be converted into common stock at the option of the bondholder.
Serial bonds	A large issue, parts of which mature at different dates
Sinking-fund bonds	Yearly deposits by the corporation of funds sufficient to redeem the bonds when they mature
Callable (or redeemable) bonds	Gives the issuing corporation the option of redeeming the bonds (usually at a premium) prior to their maturity date

Source: New York Stock Exchange, *Fact Book 1981*, p. 28.

mature for the first 15 years. Beginning with the sixteenth year, $300,000 in bonds mature each year until all the bonds are repaid at the end of the 30-year period. Serial bonds are often issued by city governments.

sinking-fund bonds
Bonds whose issuing corporation makes annual deposits of funds for use in redeeming them when they mature.

A variation of the concept of serial bonds is **sinking-fund bonds**. Under this plan, the issuing corporation makes annual deposits of funds for use in redeeming the bonds when they mature. These deposits are made with a **bond trustee**—usually a major bank with the responsibility of representing bondholders. The deposits must be large enough so that with accrued interest they will be sufficient to redeem the bonds at maturity.

bond trustee
An individual, major bank, or other financial institution that has the responsibility of representing bondholders.

Callable bonds have provisions that allow the issuing corporation to redeem them prior to their maturity dates if a premium is paid. For instance, a 20-year bond may not be callable for the first ten years. Between 11 and 15 years it can be called at a premium of perhaps $50, and between 16 and 20 years it can be called at its face value.

callable bonds
Bonds that have provisions allowing the issuing corporation to redeem them prior to their maturity date (ordinarily at a premium).

Table 19-1 summarizes the characteristics of the most important types of bonds.

The Securities Exchanges

stock exchanges
The locations at which stocks and bonds are bought and sold.

Securities exchanges are the marketplaces for stocks and bonds. They are commonly known as **stock exchanges**. All stock exchanges perform basically the same function: to provide a regulated marketplace for the buying and selling of securities.[1] Although corporations' securities are traded, the corporations themselves are not directly involved, and they receive no proceeds from the sales. The securities traded at organized exchanges have already been issued by corporations. The sales are between investors.

Only stockbrokers may trade on the stock exchanges. A stockbroker is a middleman who buys and sells securities for clients.

The Toronto Stock Exchange (TSE)

There are five Canadian stock exchanges, but when investors talk about the stock market, they are usually referring to the Toronto Stock Exchange. This is the largest stock exchange in Canada. In order to transact business on the TSE, a brokerage firm must be a member. There are usually about 80 member firms, each having purchased one or more "seats" on the exchange. Memberships have varied considerably in price, ranging from $12,000 in 1978 to $165,000 in 1982. Each seat entitles a member to send five representatives to trade on the floor of the exchange on behalf of the firm's clients. No member firm may have more than twenty traders on the floor. Each representative must meet certain basic qualifications of education and be accepted by the exchange management.

The Vancouver Stock Exchange

Virtually all the major publicly held companies are listed (traded) on the TSE. This means approximately 1,300 stocks and bonds issued by 850 companies. The daily average number of shares traded amounts to several million. Approximately 80 percent of the dollar value, and 45 percent of the total number of listed shares traded in Canada are traded on the TSE.

Other Canadian Stock Exchanges

The remainder of the trading on Canadian exchanges takes place at four regional and local exchanges. The largest of these is the Montreal Stock Exchange. The others are the Vancouver, Calgary, and Winnipeg exchanges. Often, companies listed on these exchanges are also listed on the TSE. These exchanges trade mainly in the shares of smaller firms operating within a limited geographic area. As well as the shares of larger companies, many smaller, more speculative stocks are often traded here.

Foreign Stock Exchanges

Stock exchanges are found around the world. The world's oldest exchange is the Amsterdam Stock Exchange, which began operations in 1611. The London Stock Exchange, which lists more than 10,000 stocks, goes back to the eighteenth century. The world's largest is the New York Stock Exchange. Other important foreign exchanges are located in Tokyo, Hong Kong, Paris, Zurich, Frankfurt, Johannesburg, Melbourne, and Copenhagen. Major Canadian corporations are frequently listed and traded on foreign exchanges.

The Over-the-Counter (OTC) Market

over-the-counter market
A method of trading unlisted securities outside the organized securities exchanges.

Individuals who are interested in investing in certain companies may not find their stocks listed on the Toronto Stock Exchange or on any of the other regional exchanges. There are about 2,100 securities traded in the **over-the-counter market (OTC)**. Actually, the OTC market is not a real place at all. It is simply a method of trading unlisted securities outside the organized securities exchanges. It is a network of securities dealers and brokers throughout Canada who buy and sell unlisted stocks and bonds by telephone. These brokers are in regular contact with one another, and the prices of the securities they trade are established by supply and demand.

Securities dealers in the OTC market often purchase shares in their own names. When a prospective buyer appears, they sell these shares at a profit. A broker who has none of the wanted shares in inventory will call other brokers to make purchases at the lowest possible price for resale.

The Futures Market

Actual securities are not the only items traded on the stock exchange. A buyer may also invest in futures contracts. Futures contracts guarantee the price at which the number of shares of some stock or amount of some commodity covered by the contract will exchange hands at some specified later date (see Focus 19-1).

Focus 19-1

Thrills and Chills in the Risky Futures Market

Unlike options contracts that give the buyer the right (or the option) to purchase or sell a stock, bond, currency, or amount of gold, futures contracts *commit* the holder to take delivery of commodities or financial instruments for a specified price, at some specified date in the future. Few investors actually do take delivery, of course. The game plan for futures players is to keep an alert eye on the price of, say, soybeans, pork bellies, or treasury bills and, if the price climbs— thus boosting the value of the contract—to unload the contract at a profit. If the price falls, the investor could easily end up in deep financial trouble.

But this is one of the few remaining corners of the investment supermarket where a tough-skinned, financially liquid speculator can hit the jackpot. Cash requirements for futures trading are low—a margin of 5 to 10 percent of the contract price, depending on the commodity or financial instrument and the broker. If you do pay, say, $3,000 down on a contract for 5,000 bushels of soybeans to be delivered at $6 a bushel next May, however, the margin required to maintain the contract could be raised far and fast if the price of the beans begins to soften. But then, soybeans could soar to $8 a bushel by spring, and your profit on the contract would turn out to be $2 a bushel or $10,000, minus your $3,000 down payment and commission.

The futures market isn't merely a playpen for speculators, though. Those who *sell* the primary contracts are invariably hedgers. A farmer who borrows cash to plant his corn crop could be asked by his bank to sell two futures contracts (5,000 bushels each) for September delivery at $2.54 a bushel. In other words, the farmer has locked in his price by selling his corn in advance and the bank's loan is guaranteed, even if the price of corn slumps to $2. The price of corn could soar by September, of course. But even so, the farmer is assured of his $2.54 a bushel, so he can repay his loan and turn a nice profit on his remaining crop.

The largest percentage of commodities futures trading in Canada is done on the Winnipeg Commodity Exchange. Trading in financial futures has been the exclusive preserve of the Toronto Stock Exchange and the Montreal Exchange.

Source: *Canadian Business*, February 1983, p. 37.

How Securities Are Bought and Sold

stockbroker
A middleman who buys and sells securities for clients.

If you decide to invest the $500 you earned in overtime on your summer job you first must contact a **stockbroker** (or investment dealer). If you do not already have a stockbroker, you should probably contact one of the stockbrokerage firms listed in the *Yellow Pages* of

Figure 19-3
How a Stock is Bought and Sold

your local telephone directory. Most cities have offices of major brokerage firms, such as McLeod Young Weir; Merrill Lynch Canada; Dominion Securities Pitfield; Richardson Greenshields of Canada; and Wood Gundy, as well as smaller firms.

Once you have contacted a broker, your next step is a discussion of your investment objectives. Then you and your broker can discuss a number of stocks and bonds that appear to meet your investment goals. When you have made your decision, the broker will place your order (see Figure 19-3).

If, for example, you have dual goals of income and growth, the shares of XYZ Company may suit you. Your broker can determine the current trading facts on the stock by punching in the stock's code symbol on a CANDAT machine. The CANDAT service is operated by the Toronto Stock Exchange.

Instantly, you and your broker have an exact, up-to-the-second quote on the stock, as well as the last trading price, the number of shares traded, net change, and the opening, high and low prices for the day, up to the time of the CANDAT enquiry. Suppose the information reads:

$$\text{XYZ} \quad 9\tfrac{1}{4} \quad 9\tfrac{3}{8} \quad 9\tfrac{3}{8} \quad 2{,}745 \quad + \quad \tfrac{1}{8} \quad 9\tfrac{1}{4} \quad 9\tfrac{1}{2} \quad 9\tfrac{1}{8}$$

This means: the bid on XYZ is $9.25 and the asking price $9.37. The last trade took place at $9.37 and 2,745 shares have been traded. The price is up 12 cents from the previous day's close. The stock opened, or first traded that day, at $9.25, but has subsequently traded as high as $9.50 and as low as $9.12. You decide to place an order with your broker to buy 100 shares at the best possible price, but no higher than $9.37.

Your order is then immediately relayed to the firm's telephone clerk, who is seated in one of the booths that surround the floor of the exchange. The clerk in turn gives it to one of the firm's floor traders, who goes to the post where XYZ is posted. Being one of the TSE's approximately 1,300 issues of some 850 listed companies, XYZ will appear on one of the 8 posts designated for the trading of securities located on the trading floor.

The floor trader announces your bid in a clearly audible voice, to attract the attention of a trader from another firm who may have an order to sell the stock. When the two traders have reached an agreement on the price, the selling trader makes out a "floor ticket" in triplicate. Both traders initial it. Each retains a copy, as the official receipt of the transaction. The third copy is given to the post clerk, an exchange employee, who time stamps it and relays it by electronic keyboard to the exchange's Trades Input Department, the official recording section of the exchange.

Here the details on the floor ticket are recorded by the computer that produces the ticker tape, and within a few seconds, the tape in brokerage offices across the country shows that 100 shares of XYZ have changed hands at $9\frac{3}{8}$. (The transaction is anonymous. There is no public record of your name.)

Thus the ticker tape publicly tells the latest price for XYZ that has been agreed upon in this completely open and free market. This is your guarantee that you have received the best available price at the time of your transaction.[2]

board lots
Quantities of 100 shares of stock purchased or sold.

odd lots
Purchases or sales of fewer than 100 shares of stock that are grouped together to make up one or more board lots.

bulls
Investors who expect stock prices to rise and buy securities in anticipation of the increased market prices.

bears
Investors who expect stock prices to decline and sell their securities in expectation of declining market prices.

Board lots and odd lots. Stock trading is conducted in quantities of 100 shares, called **board lots.** But because 100 shares of XYZ Company cost more than $900, how can you invest your $500 in XYZ? The answer is through **odd lots**—purchases or sales of fewer than 100 shares of stock that are grouped together to make up one or more board lots. The stocks are then distributed to the various odd-lot purchasers when the transaction is completed.

Bulls and bears. The two most frequently mentioned stock market terms refer to investor attitudes. **Bulls** are investors who expect stock prices to rise. They buy securities in anticipation of the increased market prices. When stock market prices continue to rise, market observers call it a bull market.

Bears are investors who expect stock prices to decline. They are likely to sell their securities because they expect market prices to fall. When market prices steadily decline, the market is labelled a bear market.

The Cost of Trading

Buyers and sellers of securities pay commissions to brokerage firms for their services. Commission charges currently are fixed and do not vary among brokers. They generally range from 1 to 3 percent of the total value of the stock transaction. A slightly higher fee is often charged when shares are traded in odd lots. The percentage charged typically declines as the dollar value of the transaction increases.

Focus 19-2

Stock Promoters' Hype Can Cost You Your Shirt

Promoters are a special breed of salespeople, and the Vancouver Stock Exchange has lots of them. But unless you want to lose your shirt, you had better know how they operate because there are no money-back guarantees.

Promoters fill the void between brokers, who are authorized to offer investment advice under the "full, true and plain disclosure" creed of their industry, and company management, which is charged with developing the business.

In theory, a promoter drums up investment for a company and sometimes acts as a market maker, usually in exchange for shares in the company.

Sometimes the theory works.

When two Ontario prospectors staked the Hemlo gold claim a few years ago, they got their drilling money by approaching a Toronto promoter. He brought the deal to Vancouver promoter Murray Pezim, who put the claims into one of his 70 or so VSE-listed companies. Hemlo turned out to be the biggest Canadian gold find in years, making money for a great many people.

But few VSE listings do that well. One study found that only about one in five issues actually increases in value over the long term, while many others fall into inactive oblivion. Many VSE promoters have discovered, for example, that it's often easier to convince the public they have found gold than it is to actually find it.

Not that the investors are blameless. Most of them are speculators looking for quick capital gains. They, too, are less interested in the company finding gold than they are in the market thinking it will find gold.

Stock promotion can, and often does, become a paper game where promoters go to great lengths to increase share prices and unload their stocks at or near the top of the market. It's called stock manipulation and many of the techniques are illegal, although hard to prove.

Rupert Bullock, the British Columbia Superintendent of Brokers, says the situation is improving. He believes that only a small percentage of the 1,700 companies trading on the VSE are grossly manipulated. Nevertheless, it's not uncommon for the price of some stocks to jump from a few pennies to a few dollars on little more than rumours. "Some of this is not necessarily done with malicious intent," Bullock says. "The promoters get excited about their own deals and get a little out of hand at times."

A broker who promises a client that a stock will double in price has broken industry rules and could be disciplined. However, a promoter who does the same thing is just an enthusiastic saleperson.

"Promoters are about the only people in the industry who are not licenced in some way, so they can be a real problem," Bullock says. "We have no way of disciplining them or controlling what they do."

According to Bullock, the VSE is particularly vulnerable to such practices because of the nature of its listings. For the most part, these are junior companies engaged in mining exploration—they either win big or lose completely.

He adds: "Secondly, the number of shares outstanding is relatively low (so that) you can get a little more control over it. And thirdly, the price is low. Those combinations make for ideal targets for somebody who wishes to manipulate stock."

Source: *The Globe and Mail*, July 5, 1985, p. B9.

Regulating Securities Transactions

Regulation of the sale of securities is under provincial jurisdiction. Provinces have enacted regulatory legislation, and each of the exchanges in Canada is incorporated under provincial law. The exchanges possess self-regulatory powers, and have developed extensive controls over their members through various bylaws and regulations. The basic objective of these controls is to protect investors from securities trading abuses and stock manipulations that have occurred in the past both in Canada and elsewhere by (a) assuring orderly markets; and (b) maintaining the financial responsibilities of member firms.

One important requirement for the protection of investors is that full disclosure of relevant financial information must be made by companies desiring to sell new stock or bond issues to the general public. This information is included in a booklet called a prospectus, which must be furnished to purchasers.

Reading the Financial News

Source: The *Financial Post*, October 9, 1982, p. 9. Reprinted by permission.

At least two or three pages of most major daily newspapers are devoted to reporting current financial news, which typically focuses on the previous day's securities transactions. Stocks and bonds traded on the TSE and other exchanges are listed alphabetically in the newspaper. Information is provided on the volume of sales and the price of each security.

Stock Quotations

Figure 19-4 is reproduced from the *Financial Times of Canada*. It shows a portion of the stock quotations as of March 2. To see how to read these, focus on the stock, Alberta Natural Gas. The highest price for that stock in the past year was $17.25 per share; the lowest was $13. The company paid dividends of $0.68. Over the last week the value of the stock was fairly steady. It closed at $15⅞, up ¼ over the week. There were 20,200 shares of Alberta Natural Gas traded on the Toronto Stock Exchange. Earnings per share were $0.85 as of December 1988.

price-earnings ratio
The ratio of current market price to annual earnings per share.

The **price-earnings ratio**—current market price divided by annual earnings per share—is given as 18.7 percent. The P/E ratio shows how much investors are willing to pay per dollar of reported profits.

Figure 19-4
Weekly Stock Summary

Highest and lowest price for the past 52 weeks. Prices are quoted in fractions; hence, 14¾ is $14.75

Most recent earnings per share, during the fiscal year. Hence, in August, after 9 months AGF has earned 61¢ per share.

Ratio of stock price to annual stock earnings

Number of shares traded in one week

Net change in the price of the stock since last week

Abbreviation indicates the name of the company

Earnings per share, as of most recent fiscal year ended

The most recent annual dividend paid to shareholders

pf = preferred stock. All other stock is common stock.

Price at the close of the week's trading

A

Close	Change on week	Volume 100s		12 mo. Hi Lo	Dividend	% Yield	Latest fiscal year earnings	Latest Interim earnings	P/E ratio
7¼	−⅛	533	AGF Pf f	9 5½	.44	6.1	Nov86.75	Aug9m.61	6.4
1.20		475	AHA Auto Tch	3.25 75	.00	0	Dec87.28	Sep9m.13D	
0.07		826	Abbey Expl	55 04	.00	0	Mar87.01D		
0.90	15	1720	Aber Res	2.10 55	.00	0		Oct9m.03D	
0.17		395	Abermin Corp	95 14	.00	0	Dec87.03D	Sep9m.03D	
20	−⅜	888	Abitibi-Prce	23⅛ 18½	1.00	5.0	Dec88 2.60		7.7
0.60	−10	591	Abitibi Wts	4.05 55	.00	0			
47	⅝	6	Abitib P17.5	49 46	3.75	8.0			
0.63	−.05	310	Acadia Mnl	3.05 57	.00	0			
1.05	20	191	Accgrph Cl A	1.85 45	.00	0	Aug88.77D	Nov3m.07D	
13¾	−⅝	47	Acklands	16¾ 13¾	.00	0	Nov87.64	Aug9m.45	21.8
0.27	02	25	Adenac Mng	33 15	.00	0			
3.15		105	Ageetz Res	4.00 3.10	00	0	Jun87.08D	Dec6m.25	
12⅜	−⅝	558	Agnice Eagle	20 11⅜	.30U	2.9	Dec87.69	Sep9m.12D	
7⅜		9	Agra Ind Cl A	8⅛ 6¼	.10	1.4	Jul88.43	Oct3m.08	21.1
7¼	−⅛	59	Agra Cl B f	7⅞ 6½	.12	1.7	Jul88.43	Oct3m.08	20.7
11¾	−⅛	10217	Air Canada	12½ 7	.00	0	Dec88.260		4.5
0.41	−.02	32	Akallch Ylk	73 40	.00	0	Dec87.01	Sep9m.02	
0.16	−.02	291	Albany Corp	47 15	.00	0	Dec87.00D	Sep9m.02D	
17⅛	¼	1101	Alta Energy	19½ 13⅝	.30	1.8	Dec88.52		32.9
26⅛	⅛	119	Alta En Pf 2	30 24½	1.94	7.4			
15⅞	¼	202	Alta Net Gas	17¼ 13	.68	4.3	Dec88.85		18.7
39⅛	−½	14415	Alcan Alum	42⅞ 32½	1.68U	5.1	Dec88 5.77		5.7
22¾		39	Alcan Pfd C	23⅜ 21¾	1.97	8.7			
22¾		18	Alcan Pfd D	24½ 21⅜	1.88U	8.3			
23	−¼	70	Alcan Pfd E	25 22⅝	2.16	9.4			
24¾	−⅜	9	Alcan 2.00 R	26 24⅝	2.00	8.1			
25	⅛	497	Alexis 7.4%	25⅜ 24½	1.85	7.4			
3.85	−.15	5	Algo Grp A	8 3.80	.25	6.5	Dec87.41	Sep9m.45	9.4
21⅝		11	Algoma Cnt R	24¾ 20	.80	3.7	Dec87 1.77	Sep9m 1.23	11.4
25¼		3	Algoma 8% Pf	25½ 23⅝	2.00	7.9			
24¾		83	Algoma 9.75%	25⅝ 24	2.44	9.9			

D—deficit; **f**—non-voting, subordinate-voting, or restricted-voting shares; **R**—dividends in arrears; **U**—dividends and earnings in U.S. funds (yields and P/E ratios are adjusted for currency-exchange differences); **X**—extra dividend declared during the past 12 months.

Stock Indexes

TSE 300 Composite Index
Stock averages based on the market prices of 300 stocks to provide a general measure of market activity for a given time period.

A feature of most daily newscasts is the report of current stock averages. The major Canadian stock average is the **Toronto Stock Exchange 300 Composite Index**. This index has been developed to reflect the general activity of the stock market.

The TSE 300 Composite Index is based on the market prices of 300 stocks listed on the Toronto Stock Exchange. These form a cross-section of major companies in the country. Individual stocks sometimes do not rise or fall with the index; however, it does provide a general measure of market activity for a given time period. The arbitrary starting level of the TSE 300 index in 1977 was 1000. Subindexes representing seventeen different industry sectors are also reported.

Dow Jones Industrial Average
An average based on the market prices of 30 industrial stocks that provides a general measure of market activity for a given period.

Another familiar stock average is the **Dow-Jones Industrial Average**. Dow-Jones actually produces three different indexes based on the market prices on the New York Stock Exchange of 30 industrial, 20 transportation, and 15 utility stocks.

Figure 19-5
Performance on the TSE

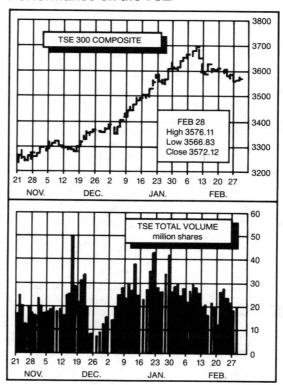

Source: *The Globe and Mail*, March 1, 1989 p. B15.

Watch Out for the LBO

Many firms have been taken over through a technique known as the LBO (leveraged buyout). The LBO is a simple concept whose roots date back to the late 1960s. In such a deal, a small group of investors, usually a combination of management and an LBO specialist, borrow big sums of money to take an undervalued company private.

The debt, often 90 percent or more of the purchase price, is paid off from the company's internal cash flow and by aggressive asset-stripping. Ross Johnson of Nabisco tried to take over the company this way by shedding the company's food divisions and retain its lucrative cigarette business.

Fortunes can be made if the target companies are worth more than the whole. On the other hand, others are worried about the effect of such a takeover. They argue that the new owners of a company that has been through an LBO are more concerned about short-term profits and paying down the debt than building long-term values that make the company competitive. Research and developments expenditures, for example, are often the first victims of a newly privatized company.

Source: Eric Reguly, ''The Year of the LBO Leaves Many Concerns,'' *The Financial Post*, December 26, 1988, p. 4.

Securities Purchasers: Who Are They and Why Do They Buy?

Types of Investors

institutional investor
Organization, such as an insurance company, pension fund, mutual fund, university, or bank, that invests its own funds or funds it holds in trust for others.

Two general types of investors exist: institutional investors and individual investors. An **institutional investor** is an organization that invests its own funds or those it holds in trust for others. Included in this definition are insurance companies, pension funds, mutual funds, universities, and banks. Institutional investors buy and sell large quantities, often in blocks of at least 10,000 shares per transaction. Such block trading represents a major part of total daily volume on organized securities exchanges, consistently in excess of 25 percent. Institutional investors account for approximately 60 percent of all trading volume.[3]

Although institutional investors are the most important force in today's securities market, the impact of *individual investors* cannot be overlooked. First, individual investors, typically purchasing in much smaller quantities than institutional investors, account for more than two out of every five dollars involved in securities markets. Second, many of the institutional investments reflect the demands of individual investors, who have chosen to allow such institutions as mutual funds and insurance companies to make securities market investments and then to purchase shares of the institutional investors. Consequently, the investment desires of individual investors cannot be ignored by the institutions. The importance of individual investors is likely to grow since only about 10 percent of Canadians currently invest in the stock market.

Investment Motivations

Why do people and institutions invest? For some investors (typically individual investors), the motive is speculation. Others seek growth, income, safety, or some combination of all three.

Speculation

speculation
Purchasing stocks in anticipation of making a large profit within a short period of time.

For some people the motivation for purchasing stocks is **speculation**—the hope of making a large profit on stocks within a short time period. Speculation may take the form of high-risk stocks, such as low-priced penny stocks (so called because they sell for less than a dollar per share). Shareholders hope that their 50-cent stock will soar to $5, giving them ten times the amount of their purchase price in return. Penny stocks include inactive uranium mining companies, exploration companies, and numerous small oil-drilling firms. Most of them show no current profits and have little prospect of future profits.

Investment

investment
The purchase of stocks and bonds with the hope of getting satisfactory dividends and interest as payment for the risk taken.

In contrast to speculation, **investment** is the purchase of stocks and bonds that assure some safety for the investment and that provide satisfactory dividends and interest as payment for the risk taken. Investors may also be interested in growth—increases in the value of a stock due to the company's success. The investor's objectives include one or more of these three goals: growth in the value of the investment, income, or safety.

Growth. Investors who choose growth as a primary goal will select companies whose earnings have increased and are expected to continue growing at a rate faster than that of other companies. They are likely to own shares of companies in industries such as electronics, pharmaceuticals, and energy, which typically pay out only small amounts in the form of dividends. Most of their earnings are reinvested in the company to finance further growth. Investors should benefit from this growth through increases in the value of their shares.

Income. Some investors use stocks and bonds as a means of supplementing their income. When income is the major goal, investors concentrate on the dividends of prospective companies. Because dividends are paid from company earnings, investors consider the company's past record for paying dividends, its current profitability, and its prospects for future earnings. Purchasers of income stocks are likely to own shares of companies in industries such as banking, insurance, and public utilities.

The income received from securities is called the investor's return, or **yield**. Yield is expressed as a percent. Assume that a potential investor plans to purchase $1,500 in stocks. She is interested in four companies: Bell Canada, Canadian Tire, Canadian Utilities, and Hudson's Bay Co. Their recent market prices and dividend rates are shown in Table 19-2.

yield
The rate of return on an investment; calculated by dividing dividends by market price.

The yield (annual dividend divided by current market price) for Bell is 7.9 percent, for Canadian Tire .67 percent, for Canadian Utilities 8.02 percent, and for Hudson's Bay Co. 2.4 percent. For the investor seeking immediate income from securities, a stock such as Canadian Utilities may be appropriate.

The yield from any particular security varies with the market price and the dividend payments. If the market price of Bell rises to $50, the yield for a prospective investor will be 3.9 rather than 7.9 percent.

Table 19-2
Market Price and Annual Dividend for Selected Companies

Company	Recent Market Price	Recent Annual Dividend
Bell Canada	$24.63	$1.94
Canadian Tire Corp.	35.88	.24
Canadian Utilities	53.00	4.25
Hudson's Bay	24.88	.60

Thus, even though the value of the dividend return remains the same, the yield changes.

Safety. In many cases investors are unwilling to risk the potential reverses of common stock. Neither their blood pressure nor their bank account is able to endure fluctuations such as those that occurred in recent years. In a single 12-month period during a recent year, Bow Valley Industries share prices fluctuated between 16 and 11⅝, Canadian Tire from 45 to 27¼, Ford of Canada from 178 to 115, Golden Terrace from 93 to 27 , and Stelco from 24⅝ to 21⅛. Investors whose primary objective is safety for their original investments are likely to purchase high-quality bonds and preferred shares. These securities offer substantial protection and are likely to continue paying a good return on the investment.

Most investors have more than one investment goal. Investors who emphasize safety of principal may buy preferred shares, hoping they will also grow in market value. Those who buy growth stocks may choose stocks paying at least a 3 percent yield in order to receive some short-term return on the investment. Table 19-3 is a useful guide for evaluating stocks and bonds in terms of the three investment objectives.

Table 19-3
Comparison of Securities with Investment Objectives

| Security | Investment Objective | | |
	Safety	Income	Growth
Bonds	Best	Very steady	Usually none
Preferred stocks	Good	Steady	Variable
Common stocks	Least	Variable	Best

Focus 19-4

Developing a Portfolio Strategy

Ninety percent of the problems investors will encounter in the next year are already in their portfolios.

That's because most of those so-called portfolios are just grab bags of securities, says Fred Marconi, vice-president and director of Cassels Blaikie & Co. Ltd. of Toronto. They are simply a collection of investments that lack direction.

Most investors cannot afford a professional portfolio manager, and time constraints and lengthy client lists limit how much assistance and review a registered representative can offer. An investor's failing is often not that the wrong security was purchased, but that it was not followed closely after it was purchased.

And Marconi says, following a stock does not mean simply

checking the stock listings in the morning to find out how it did the day before. It means watching the industry, changes in company management, new products, profits, and the economy in general. It means spending time and making timely decisions. There's no lack of information; it's a question of knowing what to do with it.

David West, supervisor of education with the Canadian Securities Institute, recommends following the same portfolio management procedure a stockbroker does—know the client; develop and implement the investment strategy; monitor the client, the market and economy; and measure and adjust the performance of the portfolio.

The first step is perhaps the most important. Why invest? Some people buy whenever they receive a hot tip. Others try to buy securities that match their needs, but don't bother to make any changes as the companies and their lives change. They forget that a strategy does not hold up forever. Children are born, salaries rise, spouses die, marriages break down, salaries fall, and all along taxes must be paid. Shrewd investors will keep in tune with the economy and with their personal needs.

The investment strategy should reflect lifestyle, income, tax bracket and temperament, among other factors. Investors under 35 will need cash and savings for emergencies, but they could also (temperament permitting) try higher risk growth securities. Between the ages of 35 and 50, one might wish to reduce one's savings levels and put more money into higher risk vehicles. The peak earning years of 50 to 65 would emphasize moderate risk and maximum income to prepare for retirement. Post-65 investments would be risk-adverse and emphasize safety and income.

After defining their goals and determining what types of securities will help achieve them, investors should examine a list of their current assets and evaluate the balance and mix of securities they hold. Is there too much interest income? Are there too many stocks from the same industry? Is there room for growth?

The best advice is to keep the investments that work toward the new goals and get rid of others. From now on, buy only securities that fit into the investment plan and fall within the limits of comfortable risk.

Source: Cathyrn Motherwell, "Close Attention Needed to Develop Portfolio Strategy," *The Globe and Mail*, July 22, 1985, p. B9.

Mutual Funds—Another Approach to Investing

mutual funds
Companies that sell shares of their own stock in order to raise money to invest in the securities of other firms.

Many investors recognize that they have neither the time nor the knowledge to analyze stock market developments continually. These people often concentrate their investments in **mutual funds**—companies that pool investment money from purchases of their own securities and use the money to buy a diversified portfolio of securities of other firms. In so doing, investors obtain diversification in their portfolio of stocks and the professional management of the mutual fund. Investors who buy shares in a mutual fund become part owners of a large number of companies, thereby spreading the risk.

Mutual funds are managed by trained, experienced professionals whose careers are based on success in analyzing the securities markets and specific industries and companies. Mutual funds attempt to accomplish for the individual investor what he or she might do with enough time, inclination, background, experience, and money to spread the investment among many businesses. Over 500,000 Canadians currently own shares in one or more of the approximately 275 mutual funds.[4] Mutual funds have become Canada's fastest growing investment vehicle.

Just as individual investor goals differ, so do the objectives of mutual funds. Growth funds emphasize the purchase of growth companies. Income funds emphasize high dividends. Balanced funds diversify their holdings by purchasing all types of securities—common and preferred shares and corporate bonds. Money market funds emphasize returns to investors through investment in short-term debt instruments such as certificates of deposit, commercial paper, and treasury bills. Specialty funds concentrate on particular industries such as gold, real estate, or banking.

Controversial Issue

Mentally Deficient Clients—What is a Broker's Responsibility?

The broker was perplexed. An elderly woman had always been a responsible client. Now she had Alzheimer's disease, and simply would not give anyone power of attorney to handle her affairs. Worse, she was becoming increasingly paranoid. The broker was afraid she would empty her account, convert the brokerage cheque to cash and literally hide tens of thousands of dollars.

Another broker tells of an Alzheimer's patient who was pressing her children to convert all her assets to cash so she could count the dollar bills.

Such stories are bound to become more common in a population becoming older and more susceptible to Alzheimer's. The Alzheimer Society of Canada estimates 300,000 Canadians have the incurable disease. The number is expected to reach 500,000 by the year 2000.

The disease, which begins with short-term memory failure, progressively destroys the patient's judgement and the ability to communicate even the most basic ideas. Such people eventually become fully dependent on other people. In addition to problems created for family members, it poses tough problems for brokers and financial advisors.

These individuals must consider what some of the possible solutions are and what, if any, responsibilities they have.

Source: Bruce Cohen, "Alzheimer Era Raises Legal, Ethical Maze," *The Financial Post*, January 9, 1989, p. 1.

Summary of Learning Goals

1. **Describe the nature of the securities market.**

   Securities are issued in the form of shares or bonds. Shares are units of ownership in a corporation and may be either common or preferred. Owners of preferred shares receive preference in the payment of dividends and have first claim on the corporation's assets after all debts have been paid, but usually do not have voting rights in the corporation. Although common shareholders have voting rights, they have only a residual claim on the firm's assets, after creditors and preferred shareholders. Bondholders are creditors—not owners—of a corporation, nonprofit organization, or governmental unit. Bonds provide the most safety and common shares the least. Bonds usually do not grow in value, but they do provide a steady income. Common shares are likely to be purchased by investors seeking growth. Many investors consider preferred shares a compromise investment between common shares and bonds.

2. **Outline the steps involved for an investor to buy or sell shares on the organized securities exchanges.**

   Common and preferred shares and the bonds of most major corporations are traded through organized securities exchanges. Securities purchases and sales are handled by a trained specialist called a stockbroker. Once the broker receives a customer's order, it is conveyed to the stock exchange through a communications terminal. The firm's floor broker executes the sale and a confirmation is communicated to the broker. The broker then notifies the customer that the transaction has been completed and charges a commission for handling the transaction.

3. **Describe the information included in stock and bond quotations.**

   Stock quotations typically include the following information: highest and lowest market prices for the security during the previous 52 weeks; whether the stock is common or preferred; annual dividend; yield; price-earnings ratio; number of shares traded; high, low, and closing prices for the day; and changes in the closing prices as compared with the closing price on the previous day. Bond quotations typically provide the following information: maturity date and interest rate stated on the bond certificate; current yield; volume, high, low, and closing prices for the day; and comparison of the closing price with that of the previous day. In addition, the quotation identifies convertible bonds.

4. **Identify the three basic objectives of investors and the types of securities most likely to accomplish each objective.**

   Speculators purchase securities in the hope of making large profits in a short time. Investors purchase securities to achieve one or

more of the following objectives: growth in the value of the
original investment, income, and safety. Bonds satisfy the safety
objective while simultaneously producing a very steady income.
However, they typically provide no opportunity for growth other
than through interest payments. Common shares are typically the
best alternative for accomplishing growth objectives but they rank
last among the three alternatives in safety. Preferred shares fall in
the middle, with steady income and reasonable safety, but with
limited growth opportunities.

5. **Explain the role of mutual funds in the securities field.**

   Investors who are unwilling or unable to spend the necessary time
   to analyze individual companies, and who want to spread their
   investment risks by owning shares in a number of different companies, may choose to purchase shares of mutual funds. These are
   professionally managed investment companies that own shares in
   a large number of different companies. The investor who purchases shares in a mutual fund has partial ownership of many
   companies.

Key Terms

securities
common shares
par value
market value
book value
preemptive right
preferred shares
cumulative preferred shares
noncumulative preferred shares
convertible preferred shares
maturity date
secured bond
debenture
convertible bonds
bond indenture
serial bonds
sinking-fund bonds

bond trustee
callable bonds
institutional investor
speculation
investment
yield
stock exchanges
over-the-counter market
stockbroker
board lots
odd lots
bulls
bears
price-earnings ratio
TSE Composite Index
Dow-Jones Industrial Average
mutual funds

Discussion Questions and Exercises

1. What are common shares? Explain the alternative methods for
   evaluating common shares.
2. Explain the major types of bonds issued by corporations and
   governmental units. What are the primary methods used in
   retiring bonds?

3. Identify the three major goals of investors and suggest an appropriate mix of securities to achieve these goals.

4. Assume that you have just inherited $20,000 from your aunt, and her will stipulates that you must put all the money into investments until you have completed your education. Prepare an investment plan for the $20,000 inheritance.

5. How does the Toronto Stock Exchange operate? Compare the TSE operations with that of the over-the-counter market.

6. Assume that you are an investment counsellor who has been asked to set up some general investment goals for the following individuals, each of whom has adequate current income and about $30,000 to invest. Prepare a short report outlining the proposed investment goals for each person with general suggestions of an appropriate mix of securities:

   a) a 56-year-old retired army officer.

   b) a 40-year-old divorced woman with two children.

   c) a 19-year-old college student receiving $200 weekly for the next ten years in survivors' insurance benefits.

   d) a 26-year-old unmarried person earning $24,000 annually.

7. How does an investor go about placing an order for common shares?

8. Discuss the purchase of shares in mutual funds as an alternative to purchasing stocks and bonds.

9. Under what jurisdiction are laws affecting securities transactions? What is the primary purpose of the legislation governing the securities industry?

10. Record for 30 days the daily price movements of a group of three to five common stocks. At the end of this period prepare a brief report on what you think influenced the price movements in these issues.

Case 19-1

Choosing a Stock for Harry and Susan Jacobs

Harry Jacobs graduated two years ago from Ryerson and accepted a retailing position at Simpsons. At 28, Harry earns $26,000 a year while his wife Susan earns $400 monthly in a part-time job. The Jacobses have two small children and a savings account of $5,000. They have decided to invest in shares and have agreed upon an investment goal of balancing growth in the market value of their shares with at least a steady return in the form of dividends. The Jacobses have narrowed their choice of shares to five and have assembled the following data from the past three years.

Year	Company Designation	Average Price per Share	Earnings per Share	Average Dividend per Share
1988	A	$ 60	$ 5.12	$ 2.70
	B	268	13.35	10.00
	C	42	2.17	.05
	D	6	.12	.08
	E	30	3.06	1.70
1989	A	59	7.98	2.80
	B	275	15.94	10.00
	C	45	2.72	.06
	D	8	.22	.10
	E	29	3.20	1.80
1990	A	72	9.00	3.00
	B	320	17.50	10.00
	C	60	3.40	.10
	D	11	.80	.12
	E	42	3.75	2.00

Questions:
1. Calculate the dividend yield and price-earnings ratio for each stock for each of the three years.
2. On the basis of the data, evaluate the potential risk of each of the five securities. Use graph paper to plot the data for each stock over the three-year period shown. Use the data in matching each security with a specific investment objective.
3. Based upon your analysis of the five stocks and the risks and rewards involved, recommend one of the five stocks for the Jacobses to purchase.

Case 19-2

Slide Charts International Corp.

Richard Slaven was looking for an angel. After five years his Toronto company, Slide Charts International Corp., had expanded out of his basement into a 743-square-metre plant in an industrial area north of the city. With two employees making slide charts—three-piece laminated cardboard devices that are used by bankers, druggists, and mortgage companies to make fast calculations—Slaven's company had revenues of $400,000 in 1987. But Slaven needed precision-gluing tables, die-cutting presses and other equipment in order to make more of the charts, which he sells for 65 cents each. "I want to grow," he says, "and I didn't want to deal with conventional banks. There's no point in having all these assets and pledging everything I own to a bank to pay for them."

Through his accountant, Slaven got wind of the Ontario government's Small Business Development Corp. (SBDC) programme. It encourages small private investors—known as "angels" because of the aid they give to small companies in need— to provide venture capital to firms such as Slide Charts International. Slaven approached Ontario's SBDC administrators last April. The SBDC office in Oshawa, Ont., searched its list of about 1,000 registered SBDCs, and sent a description of the company to the investors who matched.

Heaven was smiling on Slaven. The investor who called him liked the company. By June, he had purchased treasury shares worth $75,000, and by September he had increased his investment to $100,000. Slaven's backer, whom Slaven will not identify, fits the description of most angels. He lives close to Slaven's factory, runs his own business, and is secure enough to make an investment without demanding an immediate return.

Source: Bruce McDougall, "The Angel Who Hears the Little Guys' Prayers," *Financial Times of Canada*, October 10, 1988, p. 15.

Question:
Evaluate this type of financing compared with issuing stocks or bonds, or borrowing from a bank.

Risk Management and Insurance

Learning Goals

1. To explain the meaning of risk and to distinguish between the two types of risk faced by individuals and businesses

2. To explain each of the four methods of dealing with risk

3. To analyze the law of large numbers and how it makes insurance possible

4. To identify the several types of property and liability insurance and to describe their importance to a business

5. To analyze each of the types of life insurance a firm might offer its employees

Profile

Herb Beiles—*Working With Olympic Athletes to Ease Consequences of Injury*

Herb Beiles and his team from Crown Life recognized that athletes participating in world-class events required a Life and Health package that would remove worries related to the financial consequences of injury, and permit them to focus on the task at hand. They saw such events as an opportunity to demonstrate the high calibre of its Life and Health products, and of its service delivery capabilities.

The company has been the official insurer of the Canadian team for all Olympic games since the 1980 Winter Games held in Lake Placid, New York. Most recently, it was the official insurer for the Canadian team at the 1988 Seoul Olympics.

The company developed a system to make it easier for those involved in the Olympics coverage to obtain hassle-free medical services. To do this, it developed a Preferred Provider Organization (P.P.O.). This was made up of ten area hospitals and clinics which offered such advantages as the prior establishment of a fee schedule and of medical capability.

As well, the P.P.O. made it possible to put in place procedures both for instant recognition and treatment of all the athletes, and for billing directly to Crown Life so that the athletes were never out of pocket for expenses.

The Olympics experience has led Beiles and his team to strive to become the official insurer of world-class events. Included among the successes in this field was the provision of coverage to 25 million visitors to Expo '86 in Vancouver.

Serving this unique market niche has benefited the company through pride instilled in its employees, and the contacts and experience gained.

Source: W.J. McGill, "Crown Life: An Official Insurer of Major Events," *Canadian Insurance/Agent and Broker*, October 1988, p. 46.

In golf, a hole-in-one brings a golfer considerable prestige. In Japan, however, that distinction can cost a winning golfer the equivalent of $1,200 to $2,000 in gifts, food and drinks, according to a report in the *International Insurance Monitor*.

One such incident involved golfer Tashiro Yoshitaka. When Yoshitaka shot a hole-in-one, after the game he had to buy drinks for his partners, a celebration feast for his friends, gifts of monogrammed sports towels for acquaintances, a memorial tree planting at the hole, and a tip for his caddy. But he was prepared. The achievement cost Yoshitaka's insurer $1,600. There are about 50,000 golfers at the club, and almost all of them carry hole-in-one coverage.[1]

The Concept of Risk

Risk is a daily fact of life for both individuals and businesses. Automobile accidents take the lives of nearly 5,000 people in Canada each year. Fires also take their toll in lives and property damage. A spring flood in southern Manitoba in 1979 resulted in payments of over $18.8 million for damages. In 1982 the oil drilling rig *Ocean Ranger* sank off the coast of Newfoundland, killing all 84 crew members. Five months later, 31 lawsuits worth $226 million had been launched. Recently, one ten-minute hailstorm in Calgary resulted in damage amounting to $150 million.

Businesses face these catastrophes and more. They run the risk of injury to their employees in job-related accidents, of changing consumer tastes transforming their profits into losses, and of faulty products causing lawsuits and loss of business.

If managers are to carry out their responsibilities of achieving organizational objectives, they must understand the types of risks they face and develop methods for dealing with them. One important method of dealing with risk is to shift it to specialized firms called insurance companies. This chapter will discuss the concept of insurance, the types of insurance available for various perils, and the role played by insurance in individual firms. The starting point for this discussion is to define the meaning of risk.

Types of Risk

risk
Uncertainty about loss or injury.

Risk is uncertainty about loss or injury. The business firm's list of risk-filled decisions is long. The Los Angeles Kings paid a great deal for Wayne Gretzky. What if he were injured and couldn't play? The warehouse faces the risk of fire, burglary, water damage, and physical deterioration. Accidents, judgements due to lawsuits, and nonpayment of bills by customers are other risks. Two major types of risk exist: speculative risk and pure risk.

speculative risk
A type of risk where the firm or individual has the chance of either a profit or a loss.

Speculative risk. In the case of **speculative risk** the firm or individual has the chance of either a profit or a loss. Purchasing shares of stock on the basis of the latest hot tip can result in profits or in losses. Expansion of operations in a new market may mean higher profits or the loss of invested funds. Karl Wallenda's performances on the high wire exposed him to the risk of death as the price for failure—and in 1978 that risk became a reality as Wallenda plunged to his death while walking a wire stretched between two buildings during high winds. But his years of risk taking had brought him lucrative earnings and admiration as rewards for his successes.

pure risk
A type of risk involving only the chance of loss.

Pure risk. **Pure risk** involves only the chance of loss. Automobile drivers always face the risk of accidents. If they occur, the drivers (and others) may suffer financial and physical loss. If they do not occur, however, there is no gain. Insurance is often used to protect against the financial loss resulting from pure risk.

Dealing with Risk

Because risk is an unavoidable part of business, management must find ways of dealing with it. Recognition of its presence is an important first step. Once this occurs, the manager has four methods available for dealing with it: avoiding the risk, reducing the frequency and/or severity of the risk, self-insuring against the risk, or shifting the risk to insurance companies.

Avoiding Risk

Chapter 19 dealt with different types of investors. Some are willing to take high risks as the price for potentially high rewards, and others are not. The same is true for companies. Some firms are, for example, unwilling to risk the costs involved in developing new and untried products. They may know that Dupont's attempt to develop a leather substitute called Corfam resulted in losses of more than $100 million, and that Ford's unhappy experiences with the Edsel cost over $200 million.

Companies unwilling to assume risk are content to produce and market products that have a stable demand and offer an adequate profit margin. This strategy ensures profitability, but it stifles innovation. Companies whose managers seek to avoid most risk are rarely leaders in the industry. Even though Corfam was a market failure, the overall Dupont product development record is an enviable one, with such contributions as cellophane, nylon, Dacron, and Teflon.

Reducing Risk

Many types of pure risk can be reduced or even eliminated through minimizing hazards. Safety programmes are often used to educate employees about potential hazards and the proper methods of performing specific tasks. Safety glasses and safety shoes may be required for workers performing certain activities. Danger areas within a factory may be marked with red lines or special caution signs.

Other steps can be taken to reduce risk. Guard dogs and 24-hour security patrols may cut down burglaries. Installation of fire-retardant building materials and an automatic sprinkler system can help protect a warehouse from fire. Preventive maintenance lessens the risk of defective machinery. To reduce speculative risk, adequate credit checks allow managers to make careful decisions on which customers should be extended credit.

All these actions can reduce the risk involved in business operations; they cannot, however, eliminate it. Preventive maintenance greatly reduces the possibility of plane crashes due to mechanical problems, but such disasters still occur. The risk of loss—although decreased—is still there. (See Focus 20-1.)

Requiring workers to wear special safety equipment while performing certain jobs is one method companies use to reduce the risk of accidents.

Focus 20-1

Risks International

With concern rising among world corporations about the safety of their executives who travel and work overseas, Risks International fills a modern business need. Based in Alexandria, Virginia, the firm publishes and sells special reports about worldwide terrorist activities. Through its monthly *Executive Risk Assessment* reports, the company discusses the level of risk to executives working in various parts of the world and explains the reasons behind terrorist activities. The reports also provide a detailed chronology of all the terrorist incidents that occurred during the month. To the several hundred oil companies, banks, high-tech manufacturing firms, and government agencies who spend $1,260 a year for these reports, this information is invaluable and is frequently used in corporate planning.

All too often Risks International's predictions of increasing terrorist activity are accurate. In November 1982 and again in January 1983, for example, the firm predicted that kidnappings were on the increase in Colombia, South America. Within one month after the January warning, Kenneth Bishop, Texaco Oil Company's manager of operations in Colombia, was kidnapped. In October 1981 Risks International also predicted that the southern command of NATO would be a target for terrorist activities. Within two months American Brig. Gen. James Dozier, in charge of logistics for the southern command, was kidnapped.

Risks International also provides consulting services to individual corporations on a wide range of security topics, including corporate security planning, executive protection, and the physical security of office and manufacturing facilities. "We advise corporations where, when, and how their executives should travel," said Walter J. Burns, one of Risks International's founders. "We warn them of dangers in an area and work with them to avoid problems before they occur."

Risks International can also arrange for personal security escorts to travel with executives during their overseas stays. These escorts are recruited from the company's worldwide network of personal protection associates.

During a crisis such as a kidnapping, Risks International's help can be crucial. Says Col. Roy Tucker, another Risks International founder, "I put the company in touch with the expert in their area whom I would want to arrange the release if I were the victim."

Self-Insuring Against Risks

Instead of purchasing insurance against certain risks, some multiplant, geographically scattered firms accumulate funds to cover

self-insurance
The practice of some multiplant, geographically scattered firms of assuming risk by developing a system, such as accumulating funds, in order to absorb possible losses.

losses. This is called **self-insurance**. Firms that self-insure set aside cash reserves on a periodic basis to be drawn on only in the event of a financial loss resulting from the assumption of a pure risk.

The federal government owns and rents hundreds of properties and automobiles. Rather than purchase fire insurance, the government has chosen to self-insure. It is also self-insured against liability in automobile accidents. Similarly, grain companies have come together to create a fire reserve fund to insure the many grain elevators around the country. They believe that this type of self-insurance is cheaper than paying insurance premiums.

The use of self-insurance may be appropriate in instances where a firm faces similar risks and the risks are spread over a broad geographic area. The self-insurance alternative may be a realistic choice for large multiplant companies, because the likelihood of several fires is small, and the likelihood of one can be calculated. For the single-plant firm, one fire can prove disastrous, and contributions to a reserve fund for large potential fire damage can be prohibitively high. As a result, small firms with concentrated facilities and the possibility of being forced out of business by a major fire or accident usually shift the risk to others through the purchase of insurance.

Shifting the Risk to Insurance Companies

insurance
The process by which a firm for a fee agrees to pay another firm or individual a sum of money stated in a written contract if a loss occurs.

Although steps can be taken to avoid or reduce risk, the most common method of dealing with it is to shift it to others in the form of **insurance**—the process by which a firm (the insurance company) for a fee (the insurance premiums) agrees to pay another firm or individual (the insured) a sum of money stated in a written contract (the policy) if a loss occurs. The estimated annual cost of insuring with Lloyds of London that hockey star Wayne Gretzky is fit to play with the Los Angeles Kings is $599,000.[2] Thus, insurance is the substitution of a known loss (the insurance premium) for a larger unknown loss that may or may not occur. In the case of life insurance, the loss (death) is a certainty; the uncertainty is the date of occurrence.

The Importance of Insurance Companies

The importance of insurance companies in dealing with risk is best illustrated by a single statistic: total premiums paid to commercial insurance companies by individuals and businesses for casualty and property insurance coverage is now approximately $6 billion annually.[3]

The premiums accumulated by insurance companies are designed to cover eventual losses. However, these funds are carefully invested to generate additional returns for the company. The returns from insurance company investments may be utilized in reducing premiums, generating a profit for those companies organized as profit seeking, or both. Insurance companies represent a major source of long-term financing for other businesses.

Insurance Basics

Insurance companies are professional risk takers. They serve society, for a fee, by accepting the risk of loss or damage to businesses and individuals. Three basic principles operate in insurance: the concept of insurable interest, the concept of insurable risks, and the law of large numbers.

Insurable Interest

insurable interest
An insurance concept wherein the policyholder must stand to suffer financial loss due to such occurrences as fire, accident, or lawsuit.

In order to purchase insurance, an applicant must demonstrate that he or she has an **insurable interest** in the property or life insured. That is, the policyholder must stand to suffer financial loss due to such occurrences as fire, accident, or lawsuit. However, for life insurance, a blood relative may have an insurable interest even though no financial loss occurs in the event of the insured's death.

A businessperson can obtain fire insurance for property. An individual can purchase life insurance for herself or himself or for family members. Because top managers are important assets to a firm, the corporation can purchase key-executive insurance. But a business cannot collect on insurance to cover damage to the property of competitors when no insurable interest exists. Nor can an individual purchase an insurance policy on the life of a stranger. In these two cases an insurable interest is not present.

Insurable Risks

insurable risk
The requirements that a risk must meet in order for the insurance company to provide protection against its occurrence.

An **insurable risk** must meet a number of requirements in order for an insurance company to provide protection against its occurrence:

1. The likelihood of loss should be predictable. Insurance companies know approximately how many fires will occur each year, how many people of a certain age will die, how many burglaries will occur, and how many traffic accidents and job-related injuries will take place. Knowledge of the numbers of such losses and of their average size allows the insurance company to determine the amount of premiums necessary to repay those companies and individuals who suffer losses.

2. The loss should be financially measurable. In order to determine the amount of premium income necessary to cover the costs of losses, the dollar amount of losses must be known. For this reason

life insurance policies are purchased in specific dollar amounts, which eliminates the problem of determining the value of a person's life. Many accident insurance policies list the dollar value for specific losses, such as that of an eye or a hand.

3. The loss must be accidental, happening by chance and not intended by the insured. The insurance company is not required to pay for damages caused by a fire if the insured is guilty of arson. Similarly, life insurance policies typically exclude the payment of proceeds if the insured commits suicide in the first year of the policy's coverage.

4. The clients of an insurance company should be spread over a wide geographic area. An insurance company that concentrates its coverage in one geographic area risks the possibility of a major catastrophe affecting most of its policyholders. A major Nova Scotia hurricane, British Columbia earthquake, or Alberta hailstorm might bankrupt the company.

5. The insurance company has the right to set standards for accepting risks. It may refuse insurance coverage to individuals with heart disease or to those in dangerous occupations—such as fire fighters, test pilots, and crop dusters, or it may choose to insure these people at considerably higher rates. In the same manner, fire insurance rates may be different for residences and commercial buildings.

The Law of Large Numbers

Insurance is based on the law of averages (or statistical probability). Insurance companies have studied the occurrence of deaths, injuries, lawsuits, and all types of hazards. From their investigations they have

law of large numbers
A probability calculation of the likelihood of the occurrence of perils on which premiums are based.

developed the **law of large numbers**—a probability calculation of the likelihood of the occurrence of perils on which premiums are based. They also use actuarial tables to predict the number of fires, automobile accidents, plane crashes, and deaths that will occur in a given year.

The use of the law of large numbers in calculating insurance premiums can be described in the following example. A small city has 50,000 homes. Previously collected statistical data indicate that the city would experience an average of 500 fires in a year, with damages totaling an average of $30,000 per occurrence. What is the minimum annual premium that an insurance company would charge? To simplify the calculations, assume that the premiums charged would not produce profits or cover any of the insurance company's operating expenses. In total the claims would be $15 million (500 homes damaged × $30,000). If these losses are spread over all 50,000 homes, each homeowner would be charged annual premiums of $300 ($15 million divided by 50,000 homes). In reality, the insurance company would set the premium at a higher figure to cover its operating expenses and earn a reasonable return.

Table 20-1 is an actuarial table indicating the number of deaths per thousand persons that will occur this year for each sex and age category, and the number of additional years people in each category are expected to live. For 33-year-old males, deaths average slightly less than two per thousand, and people in this age group are expected to live another 40 years. In the case of females of the same age, deaths average slightly less than one per thousand, and life expectancy is an additional 46.6 years.

Table 20-1
Mortality Table for Males and Females Through Age 50*

Age	Male Deaths per 1,000	Expectation of Life (Years)	Female Deaths per 1,000	Expectation of Life (Years)
0	13.37	70.2	10.58	77.8
1	1.01	70.1	0.71	77.6
2	0.75	69.2	0.56	76.7
3	0.59	68.3	0.46	75.7
4	0.49	67.3	0.38	74.8
5	0.43	66.3	0.33	73.8
6	0.40	65.4	0.29	72.8
7	0.37	64.4	0.26	71.8
8	0.33	63.4	0.23	70.8
9	0.28	62.4	0.21	69.9
10	0.24	61.5	0.19	68.9
11	0.24	60.5	0.18	67.9
12	0.33	59.5	0.21	66.9
13	0.51	58.5	0.26	65.9
14	0.77	57.5	0.34	64.9
15	1.06	56.6	0.44	64.0
16	1.33	55.6	0.52	63.0
17	1.55	54.7	0.58	62.0
18	1.69	53.8	0.61	61.1
19	1.78	52.9	0.61	60.1
20	1.85	52.0	0.61	59.1
21	1.93	51.1	0.61	58.2
22	1.96	50.2	0.61	57.2
23	1.93	49.3	0.61	56.2
24	1.87	48.4	0.62	55.3
25	1.79	47.5	0.62	54.3
26	1.72	46.5	0.62	53.3
27	1.66	45.5	0.62	52.4
28	1.62	44.7	0.64	51.4
29	1.61	43.8	0.66	50.4
30	1.60	42.8	0.69	49.5

31	1.60	41.9	0.72	48.5
32	1.63	41.0	0.76	47.5
33	1.68	40.0	0.80	46.6
34	1.76	39.1	0.85	45.6
35	1.86	38.2	0.90	44.6
36	1.99	37.2	0.98	43.7
37	2.13	36.3	1.07	42.7
38	2.29	35.4	1.19	41.8
39	2.47	34.5	1.33	40.8
40	2.68	33.6	1.49	39.9
41	2.93	32.6	1.66	38.9
42	3.22	31.7	1.85	38.0
43	3.58	30.8	2.06	37.1
44	3.99	29.9	2.28	36.1
45	4.44	29.1	2.52	35.2
46	4.93	28.2	2.78	34.3
47	5.48	27.3	3.06	33.4
48	6.08	26.5	3.34	32.5
49	6.73	25.6	3.65	31.6
50	7.46	24.8	3.98	30.7

* The numbers in this table are for white males and females. For blacks and others, the number of expected deaths per 1,000 is somewhat higher, and the expectation of life is somewhat lower.

No one can predict which two persons per thousand will die; the insurance companies only know that an average of two per thousand will do so. Armed with this knowledge, the company can determine the size of premium necessary to pay the beneficiaries of its policies when claims arise. The longer the life expectancy, the lower the premiums. The same type of calculation is also made to determine premiums for automobile (see Focus 20-2) or fire insurance. The law of large numbers is the basis of all insurance premium calculations.

Matching Premiums to Different Degrees of Risk

Although the law of large numbers is used by insurance companies in designing policies, they often divide individuals and industries into different risk categories and attempt to match premiums to the risk involved. A good example is automobile insurance.

Insurance claims statistics reveal that drivers under 30 are involved in far more accidents than older drivers. Although only one driver in three is under 30, fully 50 percent of all drivers involved in an accident are in this age group. Drivers in the 20 to 24 year age group have the highest risk of an auto accident and the greatest chance of being involved in a fatal crash. As a result, youthful drivers—especially males—pay the highest insurance premiums.[4]

The Law of Adverse Selection

law of adverse selection
Insurance principle stating that persons with actual or potential health problems and those in dangerous occupations are more likely to purchase and renew health and life insurance policies than are others.

The **law of adverse selection** states that persons with actual or potential health disabilities and those in dangerous occupations are more likely to purchase and renew health and life insurance policies than are others. This tendency, referred to by insurance companies as *antiselection*, can result in high claim costs to the insurer since such policyholders are more likely than others to become ill or die. Insurance companies that fail to guard against antiselection may discover that the premiums they collect are too small to cover policyholders' claims.

This is an especially serious problem for health insurers, since evidence of insurability—good health—is only required when the policy is first issued. In addition, insurance companies offering guaranteed renewable term life insurance policies face similar problems. In both cases, policyholders who develop health problems after purchasing insurance are more likely to renew these policies than are policyholders in general.

Health and life insurance companies attempt to protect themselves from the costly effects of the law of adverse selection by requiring applicants to submit detailed medical and personal histories and by submitting each application to a thorough risk-appraisal process. A risk appraiser evaluates the insurability of the applicant and makes one of three recommendations: (1) acceptance with normal premiums, (2) acceptance with higher than average premiums because of medical or occupational factors, or (3) rejection. In addition, insurance firms charge higher premiums for guaranteed renewable term insurance policies than they do for comparable nonrenewable policies.

Focus 20-2

Insurance Companies: Reflecting Different Degrees of Risk in Premiums Charged

Ontario statistics reveal that drivers under 25 years of age are involved in collisions much more frequently than more mature drivers. Although young female drivers have greater involvement in collisions than older women, even young women have many fewer accidents than young men. As a result, youthful male drivers pay the highest insurance premiums.

In an attempt to inform the motoring public of the rationale for differing rates, an insurance association recently initiated an advertising campaign. The message shown below appeared in a number of general-interest magazines.

Some people feel...	That's why we want you to know...
"So what if I'm young. I've never had an accident or even gotten a ticket. Why should I pay the highest insurance rates?" 	We understand how you feel. You've got a good driving record, and that's great. And you don't expect to have an accident. No one does. But the fact is that good drivers as well as bad have accidents. That's why insurance protection exists. No one can predict which <u>individual</u> is going to have an accident. But we can predict the accident potential for <u>groups</u> of drivers who share similar characteristics. This is the only way possible to make auto insurance rates. Insurance companies set their rates to reflect how often they have to pay claims of insured groups and how much those claims cost. This is done for each state and for each rating territory within the state. Year after year, without exception, statistics show a consistent pattern: <u>younger</u> drivers have more accidents than <u>older</u> drivers. Young <u>males</u> have more accidents than young females. And young <u>unmarried</u> males have more accidents than young <u>married</u> men. The fairest way to distribute accident costs is for each driver to pay an insurance rate that reflects as closely as possible the exposure to loss of his or her group. Of course, differences within the groups also are taken into account. Among them are the age and type of car and how the car is used (whether for business, pleasure or commuting). But take heart. If you have a good driving record, you will pay less than others in your group who have been involved in serious accidents or who have been guilty of major traffic law violations. And, as you get older, the accident potential of your group will decline, and so will your rates. **We're working to keep insurance affordable.**

Sources of Insurance

Although the term "insurance company" is typically associated with private companies, a vast amount of insurance is provided by federal and provincial governments. Governments provide such things as health, unemployment, old age and automobile insurance.

Types of Insurance Companies

Insurance companies are typically categorized by ownership. Two types of companies exist: stock companies and mutual companies.

Stock Companies

stock insurance company
An insurance company operated for profit. It has share capital in which management is directed partly by shareholders.

Stock insurance companies are insurance companies operated for profit. Stockholders do not have to be policyholders. They invest funds in the stock company in order to receive dividends from company earnings. Profits earned by the company come from two sources: (a) insurance premiums in excess of claims and operating costs, and (b) earnings from company investments in stocks, bonds, and real estate.

Mutual Companies

mutual insurance company
An insurance company owned by its policyholders, without shareholders, in which management is directed by a board elected by policyholders rather than shareholders.

A **mutual insurance company** is actually a type of cooperative; it is owned by its policyholders. The mutual company is chartered by the province and governed by a board of directors elected by the policyholders.

Table 20-2
The 15 Largest Life Insurance Companies
Ranked by Assets

Rank 1988	Life Insurance Companies	Assets $000
1	Manufacturers Life Insurance	23,888,315
2	Sun Life Assurance of Canada	23,188,813
3	Great-West Life Assurance	17,257,730
4	Confederation Life Insurance	13,599,085
5	Canada Life Assurance	11,365,518
6	Mutual Group	10,967,000
7	London Life Insurance	9,332,000
8	Crown Life Insurance	8,988,809
9	Imperial Life Assurance of Canada	5,999,878
10	Prudential Insurance of America	5,563,513
11	Standard Life Assurance	5,406,318
12	Metropolitan Life Insurance	4,528,102
13	North American Life Assurance	3,569,978
14	Prudential Assurance Group	2,998,172
15	Industrial-Alliance Life Insurance	2,913,015

Source: *Canadian Business*, June 1989. Reprinted by permission.

Unlike stock companies, a mutual company earns no profits for its owners. Because it is a nonprofit organization, any surplus funds remaining after operating expenses, payment of claims, and establishment of necessary reserves are returned to the policyholders in the form of dividends or premium reductions.

Mutual companies are found chiefly in the life insurance field. They account for 54 of the approximately 175 life insurance companies in Canada, and they sell 61 percent of all the life insurance in force.[5]

The major difference between stock and mutual companies is that shareholders seek profits from stock insurance companies. Even so, there is no clear indication that the insurance premiums of stock companies are greater than those of mutual companies. Although mutual companies dominate the life insurance field, the majority of all other types of insurance is written by stock companies. The efficiency of a particular company appears to depend on its management ability.

Insurance companies—whether stock or mutual companies—are interested in minimizing the premiums necessary to cover operating expenses and to pay for personal or property losses. Accident claim data are studied carefully in an attempt to spot problem areas and to adjust coverage costs accordingly. Such data provide expected reasons for accidents—excessive speed, alcohol, equipment malfunction, and inattentiveness, among others (see Focus 20-3).

Focus 20-3

"Did You Hear the One about the Invisible Car?"

The explanations for accidents given by Metropolitan Life Insurance Co. auto insurance claimants were sometimes bizarre:

"An invisible car came out of nowhere, struck my car and vanished."

"The other car collided with mine without warning me of its intention."

"I had been driving my car for 40 years when I fell asleep at the wheel and had the accident."

"As I reached an intersection, a hedge sprang up obscuring my vision."

"I pulled away from the side of the road, glanced at my mother-in-law, and headed over the embankment."

"The pedestrian had no idea which direction to go, so I ran over him."

"The telephone pole was approaching fast. I attempted to swerve out of its path when it struck my front end."

"The guy was all over the road. I had to swerve a number of times before I hit him."

"The indirect cause of this accident was a little guy in a small car with a big mouth."

Types of Insurance

Although literally hundreds of different types of insurance policies are available for purchase by individuals and businesses, they can be conveniently divided into two broad categories: (a) property and casualty insurance, and (b) life insurance.

Property and Casualty Insurance

Nine types of property and casualty insurance exist: fire insurance; automobile insurance; burglary, robbery, and theft insurance; workers' compensation insurance; health insurance; marine insurance; fidelity, surety, title, and credit insurance; public liability insurance; and business interruption insurance. Table 20-3 describes the purposes of each.

Fire insurance. Every 6 minutes a fire that will cause serious damage starts somewhere in Canada. Fires will cause more than $1 billion in property losses this year. Many businesses and individuals purchase **fire insurance** to cover losses of this type.

fire insurance
Insurance coverage for losses due to fire—and with extended coverage— windstorms, hail, water, riot, and smoke damage.

Fire insurance rates vary according to the risks involved. Homes and buildings located in cities with adequate fire protection have lower rates than those in rural areas. Frame buildings have higher rates than brick or metal structures.

Standard fire insurance policies protect only against damage by fire or lightning; therefore, policyholders commonly purchase added coverage to protect them against perils such as windstorms, hail, water, riot, and smoke damage. This supplementary coverage is called extended coverage.

coinsurance clause
An insurance policy clause requiring that the insured carry fire insurance of some minimum percentage of the actual cash value of the property (usually 80 percent) in order to receive full coverage of a loss.

Because most fires result in less than total destruction, many businesspeople insure their property for less than its total value. For example, a $100,000 building may carry insurance of $80,000. Because insurance companies extend coverage on the entire building and receive premiums on only a fraction of the value of the building, they protect themselves by including a **coinsurance clause** in the policy. This clause requires that the insured carry fire insurance of some minimum percentage of the actual cash value of the property (usually 80 percent) in order to receive full coverage of a loss.

Many businesspeople purchase fire insurance to cover losses due to fire, smoke damage, and other hazards.

Table 20-3
Types of Property and Liability Insurance and Their Functions

Type of Insurance	Protection Against
Fire insurance	Losses due to fire
Automobile insurance	Losses due to automobile theft, fire, or collision; claims resulting from damage to other property due to collision or injury or death of another person resulting from an automobile accident
Burglary, robbery, and theft insurance	Losses due to the unlawful taking of the insured's property, either by force or by burglaries
Workers' compensation insurance	Medical expenses and partial salary payments for workers injured on the job
Health insurance	Medical and surgical expenses not covered by provincial plans, and lost income due to sickness or accidents
Marine insurance	Losses to property that is being shipped from one location to another
Fidelity, surety, and credit insurance	Misappropriation of funds (fidelity bond); failure to perform a job (surety bond); failure to repay loans (credit insurance)
Public liability insurance	Claims against property owner for injuries or damage to property of others caused by falls, malpractice, negligence, or faulty products
Business interruption insurance	Losses occurring when a fire or other disaster causes a business to close temporarily

The coinsurance clause works this way. If the owner of a $50,000 building suffers a $20,000 fire loss, the amount the insurance company will repay depends on the value of the fire insurance policy. Should the owner have $30,000 in fire insurance, the insurance company will pay only three-fourths of the damage. Why? Because the coinsurance clause requires the owner to have a minimum of $40,000 insurance (80 percent of the $50,000 actual cash value of the building), the $30,000 policy amounts to 75 percent of the required insurance. The insurance company calculates its share of the loss as:

$$\frac{\text{Amount of Insurance Carried}}{\text{Amount of Insurance Required}} \times \text{Loss} = \frac{\text{Insurance Company's}}{\text{Share of the Loss}}$$

$$\frac{\$30,000}{\$40,000} \times \$20,000 = \$15,000$$

The remaining $5,000 of the loss must be absorbed by the insured. In many provinces the coinsurance clause applies to residential property.

Business interruption insurance. Fire insurance with extended benefits provisions would reimburse the owner of a factory for losses to the equipment, raw materials and inventory on hand, and smoke and water damage to the building. But if the owner is forced to close the business until repairs can be made, new raw materials ordered, and new inventory purchased or manufactured, the business will suffer a serious loss. As a result, many businesses attempt to protect against this possibility by purchasing business interruption insurance. **Business interruption insurance**, which is frequently purchased as an additional provision of a basic fire insurance policy, is designed to cover losses resulting from temporary business closings as a result of a fire or other specified property damage. This type of insurance may pay the costs of leasing equipment or temporary facilities; salaries and wages of employees; taxes; mortgage and note payments; other fixed expenses; and normal profits the owners would have earned during the reconstruction period.

business interruption insurance
Type of insurance designed to cover losses resulting from temporary business closings as a result of a fire or other specified property damage; typically purchased as an additional provision of a basic fire insurance policy.

A similar type of insurance aimed at insuring against loss of earning power is called *contingent business interruption insurance*. This type of policy is intended to cover the possible losses incurred by a firm should the business of a major supplier or customer be damaged by fire. Such a fire is likely to result in financial losses to the insured due to unavailable supplies or the loss of the customer's business even though the insured suffers no physical damage.

Automobile insurance. The Canada Safety Council regularly advertises to inform the public of the risk involved in driving automobiles—with good reason. Every 2.4 minutes someone is injured in an automobile accident; every 2 hours someone dies in one. The automobile injury toll in a recent year was approximately 200,000.[6]

automobile insurance
Insurance coverage for losses due to automobile theft, fire, or collision and for claims resulting from damage to the property or person of others involved in an automobile accident.

Most **automobile insurance** includes coverage for losses due to theft, fire, or collision and claims resulting from damage to the property or person of others involved in an automobile accident. The automobile owner protects against these risks through the purchase of comprehensive fire and theft, collision, and liability insurance.

Comprehensive coverage protects the insured's car against damage caused by fire, theft, hail, falling objects, and a variety of other perils. Contents of the car are usually covered if the car is locked. In recent years insurance companies have been forced to exclude stereo tape decks and CB radios (or to issue special policies at a separate premium) due to the ease of their detachment from the car and their attractiveness to thieves.

Collision insurance pays for damage caused by collision with another vehicle or a stationary object. Most policies list a deductible amount ranging from $50 to $200 or $300 that the insured must pay. Most automobile insurance policies provide both comprehensive and collision coverage for a single premium.

Liability insurance covers both property damage and bodily injury. Each province has legislated minimum coverage required, varying from $50,000 to $200,000. Property damage liability insurance covers any damage to other automobiles or property caused by the insured's automobile. Liability insurance also typically includes a medical payments endorsement, which pays hospital and doctor bills up to a specified amount for any persons injured in the insured's car. Such payments for medical expenses are usually deemed to be for expenses in excess of medicare benefits. Virtually all provinces require that insurance policies include a provision that innocent victims will be indemnified for losses where the driver at fault is uninsured. This is known as uninsured-motorist insurance. This may be paid from a government fund collected from uninsured motorists when renewing licenses, or it not available, by the victim's own insurance company.

As automobile insurance premiums soar and the delays of settling claims lengthen, some provinces have begun to look for new ways to insure motorists. **"No-fault" insurance** has been legislated by British Columbia, Saskatchewan, Manitoba, and Quebec. This requires that payment be made to the insured person and others involved in accidents without determining the degree of fault. "No-fault" is somewhat of a misnomer in that liability *is* apportioned in accidents, but this does not affect the benefits available to any person involved in the accident. In some jurisdictions victims are limited in their right to sue for damages. In others the right is retained.

Such insurance is still controversial. One of the major advantages is that persons involved in an accident receive much quicker satisfaction with the no-fault system than they would if they had to go to court and sue. Proponents also argue that this system will lead to lower premiums. Others argue the opposite.

At one time most provinces in Canada had similar insurance laws and car insurance policies that were quite uniform. Legal requirements for no-fault insurance, however, have sent the provinces concerned in different ways in their approach to insurance. British

no-fault insurance plan
An insurance plan, created by law, that requires claims payments to be made by the policyholder's insurance company without regard to fault.

Columbia, Manitoba, and Saskatchewan have established compulsory government insurance which has basically displaced private insurance companies. In the latter two provinces, private companies are allowed to sell insurance for amounts of coverage above that offered by government plans. Quebec's insurance system is split: personal injury claims are covered under a government scheme, while private insurance companies provide physical damage coverage for accidents that occur within the province and full liability insurance when traveling elsewhere. All other provinces and territories have private insurance company plans in effect.

burglary insurance
Insurance coverage for losses due to the taking of property by forcible entry.

robbery insurance
Insurance coverage for losses due to the unlawful taking of property from another person by force or the threat of force.

theft insurance
Insurance coverage for losses due to the unlawful taking of property.

Burglary, robbery, and theft insurance. Although burglary, robbery, and theft are all crimes, each has a different meaning, and the insurance rate for each crime is different. The act of taking property from an unlocked building is theft, not burglary. **Burglary insurance** provides coverage for losses due to the taking of property by forcible entry. **Robbery insurance** provides coverage for losses due to the unlawful taking of property from another person by force or threat of force. **Theft** (or larceny) **insurance** gives coverage for losses due to the unlawful taking of property. Theft insurance provides the broadest coverage and is, therefore, the most expensive of all insurance coverages for crime.

workers' compensation insurance
Insurance provided by employers under provincial law to guarantee payment of medical expenses and salaries to employees who are injured on the job.

Workers' compensation insurance. **Workers' compensation insurance**—insurance provided by employers under provincial law to guarantee payments of medical expenses and salaries to employees who are injured on the job—exists in all 10 provinces. Premiums are based on the company's payroll, and rates depend on the hazards present on the job and the safety record of the employer. Payments are usually set at a fraction of the employee's regular wage (usually one-half to two-thirds). In addition, workers' compensation typically reimburses the injured worker for rehabilitation expenses. A waiting period of a few days to two weeks is usually provided to discourage claims for minor accidents.

health insurance
Insurance coverage for losses due to sickness or accidents.

Health insurance. The cost of medical care has steadily increased over the years until it is widely recognized that some type of **health insurance** coverage is necessary for every person. In Canada it has been felt that these costs are a public concern. Consequently, each province has provided some type of universal health insurance scheme. Private insurers such as Blue Cross sell additional insurance to increase the availability of benefits such as better hospital rooms, and dental care.

ocean marine insurance
Insurance that covers shippers for losses of property due to damage to a ship or its cargo while at sea or in port.

Marine insurance. Marine insurance is the oldest form of insurance, dating back at least 5,000 years. It is used as a means of insuring ships and their cargoes. **Ocean marine insurance** protects shippers

inland marine insurance
Insurance coverage for losses of property due to damage while goods are being transported by truck, ship, rail, or plane.

from losses of property due to damage to a ship or its cargo while at sea or in port. **Inland marine insurance** covers losses of property due to damage while goods are being transported by truck, ship, rail, or plane.

Fidelity, surety, and credit insurance. **Fidelity bonds** protect employers from employees' dishonesty. They are commonly used by banks, loan companies, and other businesses to cover cashiers and other employees who handle company funds. The employer is guaranteed against loss up to the amount of the policy.

fidelity bonds
Bonds that protect employers from employees' dishonesty.

Surety bonds are designed to protect people or companies against losses resulting from nonperformance of a contract. A building contractor who agrees to construct a new city library may be required to furnish a surety bond that the library will be erected according to specifications and completed within the time limit of the contract.

surety bonds
Bonds that protect people or companies against losses resulting from nonperformance of a contract.

Credit insurance protects lenders against losses from bad debts. Most credit insurance policies do not protect against all unpaid debts, because the premiums would be too expensive. Instead they usually define normal losses from bad debts and cover any in excess of the norm.

credit insurance
Insurance protection for lenders against losses from bad debts.

Title insurance protects real estate purchasers against losses that might be incurred because of a defect in the title to the property. It eliminates the purchaser's need to investigate legal records in order to determine the true owner of the property and the presence of any claims against it. This insurance is often purchased by a person buying a new home.

title insurance
Insurance protection for real estate purchasers against losses that might be incurred because of a defect in the title to the property.

Public liability insurance. **Public liability insurance** is designed to protect businesses and individuals against claims caused by injuries to others or damage to the property of others. Most homeowners' insurance policies include liability coverage for claims such as those by people injured in falls or bitten by pets. Businesses purchase this insurance to cover possible injuries to customers in their stores or arising out of their operations. Many professionals, such as doctors, purchase **malpractice insurance** to protect themselves against charges of incompetence or negligence. Because of recent large claims liability insurance premiums have skyrocketed to the point that it has become virtually unaffordable for some.

public liability insurance
Insurance protection for businesses and individuals against claims caused by injuries to others or damage to the property of others.

malpractice insurance
Insurance designed to protect a practitioner against liability for professional misconduct or lack of ordinary skill in the performance of a professional act.

Product liability insurance (which comes under the general heading of public liability insurance) is designed to protect businesses against claims for damages resulting from the use of the company's products. It covers, for example, a druggist being sued by a customer who claims that a prescription was prepared improperly, or a manufacturer accused of producing and selling unsafe products. Product liability insurance has become increasingly necessary in recent years. The number of product liability cases has increased in the late seventies and eighties. In this day of clearly articulated consumer

product liability insurance
Insurance protection for businesses against claims for damages resulting from the use of the company's products.

rights, insurance for product claims is vital. Premiums for product liability insurance are rising steadily, and in some cases coverage may be hard to obtain.

Focus 20-4

Dealing with AIDS Insurance

North American Life Assurance Co. has become the first Canadian life insurer to formally establish a special provision to cover the costs of paying acquired immune deficiency syndrome (AIDS) claims.

The company wrote off a $10 million AIDS provision against its 1988 profit. Even after the special provision it was a very profitable year for the company. Toronto-based North American Life saw its profit rise 40.5 percent to a record of $35.8 million.

"We decided to bite the bullet and to take the hit in the current year and get it over once and for all," William Bradford, President, said in an interview.

He said the move stemmed from a desire to protect the future benefits of policy holders, not from the company's experience with AIDS claims, which has been fairly good.

North American Life had 22 AIDS claims last year, resulting in payment of $2 million in benefits, and 25 claims with payments totalling $1.3 million in 1987.

Similar announcements of special AIDS provisions or reserves can be expected from other insurers. The federal Office of the Superintendent of Financial Institutions has instructed senior actuaries in each company to follow the recommendations of the Canadian Institute of Actuaries in establishing such provisions or reserves.

The Institute last year designed a model that actuaries are to use in determining the number of AIDS claims that can be expected over the next 30 years. For example, the model incorporates the assumption there will be 1.2 AIDS deaths for each 1,000 thirty-year-olds in the next year. There are similar statistics for each age and sex group.

Source: Angela Barnes, "North American Life Sets AIDS Provision," *The Globe and Mail*, February 15, 1989, p. B1.

Relative importance of each type of property and casualty insurance. Each type of property and casualty insurance has been developed to protect individuals and businesses against specific types of losses. As Figure 20-1 indicates, automobile insurance, which once accounted for more than half of the Canadian general insurance market, has now diminished to about 45 percent. Property insurance premiums have grown steadily over the years and now are approaching automobile insurance totals.

Life Insurance

Life insurance is different from all the other types of insurance coverage described in this chapter. It deals with a calamity that is certain—death. The only uncertainty is when it will occur. Life insurance is a common fringe benefit in most firms because its purchase provides financial protection for the family of the policy-holder and, and in some instances, an additional source or retirement income for employees and their families. An immediate estate is created by the purchase of a life insurance policy. Because the need for financial security is great in most families, more than half the people in this country are covered by life insurance. Some 14 million people are covered by $740 billion of insurance. The average amount of life insurance coverage per insured individual in 1985 was $51,500. The average amount owned per household was $80,500—nearly four times the figure in 1970.

Group or individual insurance. Life insurance policies can be purchased on an individual basis for almost any amount. Unlike property and casualty insurance, the life insurance purchases are limited only by the amount of premiums people can afford to pay—provided that purchasers qualify medically. Insurance companies have paid as much as $8 million in death benefits on a single policy.

Most businesses purchase employee life insurance on a group basis as a company fringe benefit. Employees may be required to contribute a portion of the cost of the insurance, or the employer may pay the

Figure 21-1
Property and Casualty Insurance Premiums by Class

Approximate split of 1984 premiums
by percentages

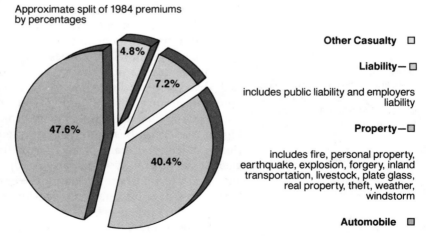

Other Casualty ☐

Liability—☐

includes public liability and employers
liability

Property—☐

includes fire, personal property,
earthquake, explosion, forgery, inland
transportation, livestock, plate glass,
real property, theft, weather,
windstorm

Automobile ☐

Source: Facts of the General Insurance Industry, 13th ed. (Insurance Bureau of Canada) p. 7.

group life insurance
Life insurance for company employees that is typically written under a single master policy.

total cost. **Group life insurance** for company employees is typically written under a single master policy, and covered employees are not normally required to undergo medical examinations. Because selling costs and administrative expenses are much lower for group insurance, this type is usually much cheaper than individual insurance.

mortality table
The table, based on past experience, predicts the number of persons in each age category who will die in a given year.

The mortality table. The **mortality table**, first introduced in Table 20-1, is based on past experience with large numbers of policyholders. It is used to predict the number of people in each age category who will die in a given year. Once this is known, the premiums for a life insurance policy can be calculated to provide sufficient income to pay death benefits, company operating expenses, and profits (if the company is a stock company).

Insurance premiums for a 40-year-old are usually greater than for a 20-year-old, because the number of deaths per thousand increases from 0.61 to 1.49. As the age of the insured increases, the length of expected life decreases and life insurance premiums rise.

key executive insurance
Life insurance designed to compensate the organization for the loss of the services of an important executive and to cover the costs of recruiting and training a successor.

Key executive insurance. The death of a sole proprietor, partner, or a key executive in a larger organization is likely to result in financial losses to the organization. **Key executive insurance** is life insurance designed to reimburse the organization for the loss of the services of an important executive and to cover the expenses of securing a qualified replacement. Such insurance may very well prevent the liquidation of a sole proprietorship upon the death of its owner. Although a partnership is automatically dissolved upon the death of a general partner, key executive insurance may enable the surviving partners to purchase the deceased's interest in the firm. In the case of larger organizations, key executive insurance may lessen the reduction in earning power that might result following the death of a company president or senior executive.

Types of life insurance. The four basic types of life insurance are term, whole life, limited payment, and endowment. A company can choose one type or a combination of them as part of its total fringe benefit package for its employees.

term insurance
Insurance coverage protecting the individual for a specified period of years that has no value at the end of that period.

Term insurance provides protection for the individual for a specified period of years, but it has no value at the end of that period. It is "pure" insurance with no savings features. Some term policies give the policy holder the right to convert to whole life insurance at a higher rate. Term insurance is most often purchased by young married couples who want protection in the early years of marriage against the possibility of an early death of one partner. Term insurance offers low-cost protection for the one or two decades before the family can develop financial security through savings and investments.

In some instances, term policies are written to provide reduced amounts of protection over the life of the policy. This type, called *decreasing term insurance*, is often appropriate for young families seeking large amounts of low-cost insurance protection for a few years and gradually reducing the amount of protection as the financial assets of the household grow and as the working members of the households are promoted to higher-paying positions.

A special form of term insurance, **mortgage** or **credit life insurance**, is often purchased by persons buying a home or other major item. It repays the balance owed on these items if the policyholder dies, thereby protecting both the family and the lender. Such life insurance decreases in value as the loan is repaid.

Whole life insurance is a combination of protection and savings. It provides protection for the individual, who pays premiums throughout a lifetime, and also builds up a cash surrender value in the policy. This **cash surrender value** is the savings portion of a life insurance policy: it can be borrowed by the policyholder at low interest rates or paid to the policyholder if the policy is canceled.

Several variations of whole life insurance exist. Many companies offer **limited payment life insurance**—whole life insurance for which the policyholder pays all premiums within a designated period such as 20 or 30 years. An extreme variation is the **single payment policy**, which consists of a large premium paid in a lump sum at the time the insurance is purchased.

Endowment policies place more emphasis on savings than do whole life policies. The purchaser of an endowment policy gets coverage for a specified period, such as 20 years or until the age of 65. After this period the face value of the policy is refunded to the policyholder. Endowment insurance is considered forced saving and is commonly used as a portion of a family's retirement income plan.

Which type of life insurance policy is best? Individuals must carefully study their personal situation with the aid of a qualified insurance agent. It is important for consumers to understand the

mortgage or credit life insurance
Term insurance purchased by persons who are buying a home or other major item that repays the balance owed on these items if the policyholder dies.

whole life insurance
Provides both protection and savings for the individual who pays premiums throughout life and builds up a cash surrender value in the policy.

cash surrender value
The savings portion of a life insurance policy that can be borrowed by the policyholder at low interest rates or paid to the policyholder if the policy is canceled.

limited payment life insurance
Whole life insurance for which the policyholder pays all premiums within a designated period such as 20 or 30 years.

single payment policy
Whole life insurance that consists of a large premium paid in a lump sum at the time the insurance is purchased.

endowment policy
A type of insurance policy that provides coverage for a specified period after which the face value is refunded to the policyholder.

Table 20-4
Comparison of Sample Annual Premiums per $1,000 in Insurance

Bought at Age	Straight Life	Limited Payment (20 Years)	Endowment (20 Years)	Renewable-Convertible (5 Years)
18	$13.72	$21.40	$45.66	$ 2.18
20	14.18	22.26	45.56	2.18
25	16.09	24.79	45.38	2.30
30	19.32	28.23	45.70	2.36
40	30.09	37.61	48.02	4.18
50	48.42	51.21	53.97	10.24

Source: *Stone & Cox Life Insurance Tables*, 1986, pp. 126, 158.

various types of insurance and what their particular needs are. In addition to determining the appropriate type, they must also decide upon both the amount and the source of such insurance coverage. Factors such as costs, the insured's age, family responsibilities, health, and future expectations must be considered. Each person must determine the proper balance between savings and protection that is best for the household. Table 20-4 provides an illustration of cost comparisons among the different types of life insurance.

Controversial Issue

When is the Individual, Not the Company, Liable?

When, on what grounds, and to what extent do we or should we hold individuals responsible for their own actions in product liability cases?

In June 1980, Richard Hogard, a pipe insulation worker at a naval shipyard, won a judgement of $250,000 against Johns-Manville and Raybestos, two manufacturers of asbestos materials. Some facts concerning the case are:

- Hogard began to work there after publication of the dangers of asbestos. He, the union, and the manufacturer were aware of the hazards.
- At the shipyard, the industrial hygienist offered classes on asbestos, and the union also spread information to workers.
- Hogard failed to use a respirator despite regulations to the contrary.
- Hogard, a long-time cigarette smoker, continued to smoke fairly heavily despite the information that smokers had a much higher incidence of asbestosis.
- Hogard received hazard pay for working with asbestos.

Despite these factors, Hogard won a quarter of a million judgement from the courts.

The costs of this kind of judgement are borne by the rest of society through product and

insurance costs. The case raises some real questions. As a society, how much protection can we provide consumer/users without seriously jeopardizing our economic health? How much responsibility should we demand from individual consumer/users? Should we differentiate more carefully between different kinds of product situations? For example, at one end of the continuum there may be no individual responsibility when consumers may not be able to assess the quality of complex technology like fuel, brake, and steering systems in automobiles. At the other end of the continuum could be such things as mountain climbing or skydiving, where risk is great and substantial responsibility for use and maintenance of equipment rests on the user. Or should we generally hold manufacturers liable since they have the resources to insure that victims are compensated (the deep pocket), and since they are best equipped to prevent or correct a problem?

Source: William W. May, "Product Liability: When Does the Individual Assume Risk?" in Chris Whipple and Vincent T. Covello, eds. *Risk Analysis in the Private Sector* (New York: Plenum Press, 1985), pp. 209-211.

Summary of Learning Goals

1. **Explain the meaning of risk and distinguish between the two types of risk faced by individuals and businesses.**

   Risk is part of the daily life of both the individual and the business firm. It comes in different forms: property damage, dishonesty, death, injury to employees or customers, sickness, lawsuits, and nonpayment of debts. The two types of risks are speculative risk, in which the firm or individual has the chance of either a profit or loss; and pure risk, which involves only the chance of loss.

2. **Explain each of the four methods of dealing with risk.**

   Once the presence of risk has been acknowledged, a manager has four methods available for dealing with it. Some firms may choose to avoid risk entirely; others cannot completely avoid risk but can reduce much of the risk through risk-reduction programmes designed to eliminate hazards, detect problems, and encourage employees to practice safe work procedures. Other firms may choose to self-insure by creating self-insurance funds. For many organizations and individuals the method of dealing with risk is to shift the risk to insurance companies.

3. **Analyze the law of large numbers and explain how it makes insurance possible.**

   Insurance is based on the concepts of insurance interest, insurable risks, and the law of the large numbers. Insurance companies are professional risk takers who operate by charging premiums that are large enough to repay insurance claims and cover operating expenses. The law of large numbers is based upon statistical probability and is used to predict the likelihood of the occurrence of perils—the number of fires, automobile accidents, earthquakes, or deaths that will occur in a given year.

4. **Identify the types of property and liability insurance and describe their importance to a business.**

   Insurance can be divided into three categories: property and liability insurance, health insurance, and life insurance. Property and liability insurance provides protection against fire losses; loss of income due to fires or other property damage (business interruption insurance); automobile accident losses; and burglary, robbery, and theft losses. Other types of property and liability insurance include marine insurance; fidelity, surety, title, and credit insurance, and public liability insurance.

5. **Analyze each of the types of life insurance a firm might offer its employees.**

   Life insurance is a common part of most employee fringe benefit programmes. In addition, many organizations purchase key executive insurance to reimburse the organization for the loss of the services of an important executive and to cover the expenses involved in acquiring and training a replacement. Although life insurance can be purchased by individuals, employers who purchase on a group basis can usually secure coverage at lower rates. Four basic types of life insurance are available. Term insurance provides protection for a specific period of time. Whole life insurance provides a combination of protection and savings for the policyholder, who pays premiums throughout a lifetime. Limited payment insurance is similar to whole life, except that the policyholder pays all premiums within a designated time period. Endowment life insurance policies are a type of forced savings; they provide protection for a specified time period and then return the face value of the policy to the policyholder.

Each type of life insurance has merits and shortcomings. The choice of the best type or types must be made by the individual, who should consider factors such as age, family responsibilities, personal health, and future job expectations.

Key Terms

risk	health insurance
speculative risk	ocean marine insurance
pure risk	inland marine insurance
self-insurance	fidelity bonds
insurance	surety bonds
insurance interest	credit insurance
insurable risk	title insurance
law of large numbers	public liability insurance
law of adverse selection	malpractice insurance
stock insurance company	product liability insurance
mutual insurance company	group life insurance
fire insurance	mortality table
coinsurance clause	key executive insurance
business interruption insurance	term insurance
automobile insurance	mortgage or credit life insurance
no-fault insurance plan	whole life insurance
burglary insurance	cash surrender value
robbery insurance	limited payment life insurance
theft insurance	single payment policy
workers' compensation insurance	endowment policy

Discussion Questions and Exercises

1. Identify and give an example of each of the four methods of dealing with risk.

2. Discuss the concept of self-insurance as it relates to each type of insurance. Give an example of a firm that might be a candidate for self-insurance for each general category of insurance.

3. Discuss the three basic principles of insurance. What requirements are necessary for an insurable risk?

4. Assume that a small town of 10,000 homeowners is considering developing its own nonprofit insurance company to provide fire insurance. Historical data reveal that an average of 120 fires occur annually, with average damages of $20,000 per fire. Although the new company will be nonprofit, it was decided to add 10 percent to total premiums paid to generate cash reserves and funds to pay expenses. What is the minimum annual premium that would be charged each homeowner?

5. Give an example of the role each type of property and liability insurance plays in the operation of a business.

6. Insurance companies typically charge higher automobile insurance rates for people under 25 than they do for older drivers. Do you think this is a fair policy? Explain. Can you think of any situations in which younger people receive more favourable insurance rates than older ones?

7. How is life insurance different from other types of insurance? Identify and describe the four basic types of life insurance.

8. Develop an insurance plan for a small family-owned bakery. Make any necessary assumptions.

9. Why does group insurance cost less than individual insurance?

10. Explain the concept of risk as it relates to business.

Case 20-1

Lloyd's of London

The concept of insurable risk and the law of large numbers are rules to live by for most insurance companies. The typical insurance company requires that the likelihood of a loss be predictable, that the risk be spread over a wide geographic area, and that standards of acceptable risk be established. But Lloyd's of London is hardly a typical insurance company. In fact, it is actually not an insurance company at all, but an association of individual insurers who agree to insure risks that are not acceptable to more conventional insurance companies. The association has a colourful history that spans nearly three centuries since its beginning in a London coffeehouse in 1689. Today, Lloyd's is comprised of more than 400 separate risk-taking syndicates who share profits in good years and divide losses in bad years. The syndicates, in turn, are made up of from 20 to 3,000 mostly nonprofessional investors out of the ranks of 20,000 members, known as "names"—individuals who must have at least $200,000 in personal wealth before they can invest. Names, who must put up at least $10,000, include tennis star Virginia Wade, champion jockey Lester Piggott, members of the rock group Pink Floyd, and numerous Americans, Arabs, and members of the British aristocracy.

Although the traditional emphasis at Lloyd's has been on marine insurance, it is best known throughout the world for providing insurance against extremely unusual risks. Lloyd's has insured body parts such as Jimmy Durante's nose, Marlene Dietrich's legs, Gene Simmons' tongue, and Glenn Gould's hands. It has agreed to pay $2 million if the Loch Ness monster is captured. The International Olympic Committee purchased a $5 million policy to cover possible cancellation of the 1984 Winter Olympics in case of a tremor in earthquake-prone Sarajevo, Yugoslavia.

For three centuries, names—including more than 500 currently from Canada—have placed their entire fortunes on the line in joining syndicates at Lloyd's. Unlike a corporation, there is no limit on the liability of individual members.

With generous tax write-offs in losing years and the ability to take out special stop-loss insurance against outsized claims, members generally have fared well.

In July 1988 the Piper Alpha oil rig disaster accounted for the biggest payout in Lloyd's history. Already $1.4 billion (US) has been paid, and more claims are pending. This added to the existing worries of some of the Lloyd's names about the desirability of a continuing association.

Among these are a reduction in tax rates, which strips away some of the protection against money-losing years, the growing difficulty of getting so-called stop-loss coverage and, especially, the long shelf-life of US environmental cases. For example, even after three years, cases concerning asbestosis and toxic waste dumps could not be closed, and it was impossible to estimate what liabilities might still roll in.

"Nothing is more disturbing to names than the prospect of being haunted by old insurance policies for 20 or 30 years," says Lloyd's chairman, Murray Lawrence. "The whole insurance business is getting riskier."

No one has learned that lesson more than the 1,600 members of the Outhwaite syndicate, who each stand to lose at least $540,000 (US) for losses incurred in writing various forms of reinsurance for other Lloyd's syndicates. The policies covered claims on exposure to asbestosis, and pollution in the United States, and nobody knows how high the bill might go for the disastrous 1982 year.

Although Lloyd's admits that its only responsibility is to provide professional underwriters to assess the risks and establish policy premiums, members of many syndicates argue that more internal controls should be established.

Syndicate members were considering suing Lloyd's, arguing that it wasn't vigilant enough in ensuring that syndicate operators did not exceed limits on writing this high-risk type of insurance.

As far as Lloyd's is concerned the aggrieved names simply came out on the short end of what is, after all, a risky game.

Mr. Lawrence was fairly nonchalant about names dropping out of Lloyd's. For the most part, he thinks the departees are weaker links in the underwriting chain—skittish people on the bottom rung of the wealth ladder.

Lloyd's is better supervised and regulated today than it was when many of the current problems originated, he said. Better regulation aside, those with weak stomachs probably are not suited for the commercial direction in which the Lloyd's market is drifting. Finding it difficult to compete with domestic insurers for smaller, more predictable policies, Lloyd's increasingly has become the provider of coverage against major catastrophes.

Even with the best of names, everybody associated with Lloyd's recognizes that today's commercial challenges are potentially more damaging than the highly publicized scandals of the early 1980s, which for all their drama actually affected few members.

As it is, the 300-year-old institution can withstand an outflow of names for a while longer as it seeks to adjust to current insurance realities.

Lloyd's underwriters currently are not doing enough business to cover even two-thirds of their insurance capacity. Besides being uncompetitive in many bread-and-butter areas, they have decided that after being burned once it is best to be shy when it comes to environmentally related policies in the United States.

Source: Edward Greenspon, "Lloyd's Fraternity Losing Members," *The Globe and Mail*, January 7, 1989, p. B1.

Questions:
1. How can an organization such as Lloyd's ignore such concepts as the law of large numbers and insurance risk and expect to earn profits? Upon what principles would such an organization be based?
2. What types of industries are likely to purchase insurance from such an organization?
3. Recommend some possible reforms that would allow Lloyd's to continue to operate while reducing the risk exposure of its affiliates.

Case 20-2

The Insurance Crisis

The crisis struck municipalities, companies, and clubs across the nation. In Ottawa, the Canadian Ski Association declared that it might pull its national teams off the World Cup circuit because it could not obtain liability insurance—at any price. In Saint John, NB, the nonprofit Cherry Brook Zoo reopened when its directors finally found a company willing to provide coverage. To pay the $8,900 premium—up 1,483 percent from last year's $600—mayor Elsie Wayne organized a raffle. As dozens of groups scrambled to find more money for less coverage, the political outcry mounted.

In Ottawa, ten MPs demanded an inquiry under the Combines Investigation Act into what they called a "conspiracy" among companies selling liability insurance. However, property and casualty insurers insist they are as hard-pressed as their clients. Industry experts say that companies are losing money on liability insurance because the number of claims—and the size of court-ordered awards—has increased dramatically.

International insurance companies, which reinsure the policies of Canadian insurers, usually examine the record of claims for *all* of North America. That means that the liability record of the United States—with its numerous claims and expensive settlements—is driving up the rates paid by Canadian companies. As well, many reinsurance firms are staggering from the financial impact of catastrophe claims like some of those made after several air disasters in 1985. As a result, they are either withdrawing from the North American market altogether or offering less reinsurance for more money to primary insurance companies.

Faced with reluctant reinsurers and reinsurance price increases of up to 1,000 percent, many Canadian insurance firms have stopped offering liability insurance—or have raised their prices for reduced coverage. There are now only a handful of companies in Canada even willing to touch liability insurance.

That aversion is the result of a discouraging financial record. In 1984, companies paid out $1.16 for every dollar earned. They also added to their own losses when they became locked in a vicious price war. When some companies began cutting liability premiums by up to 80 percent in order to attract money for investment purposes, the entire industry followed suit. Policies were sold on price and the degree of risk was ignored.

When competition finally lessened during 1985 and insurance firms raised their rates to reflect costs, the impact on their clients was staggering. If a policy price had fallen by 50 percent, it had to double to return to its previous level. As well, some insurance companies are now trying to make premiums—instead of the traditional combination of premiums and premium income—pay for claims and expenses.

The sudden high rate increases also reflect insurers' concern that Canadian courts will match high American awards. For instance, in 1985 the city of Brampton in Ontario was ordered to pay $6.3 million to a youth who became a quadriplegic at 14 when he rode his dirt bike at full speed around a blind curve in an abandoned quarry owned by the city and crashed into another bike. The court found the city guilty of negligence because it had not posted trespassing signs. That award is now under appeal.

The Brampton judgement also worried industry experts because it underlined the changed attitude toward risk. In the past, individuals had to prove negligence on the part of others to win damages. Now, said Helen Gagné, senior counsel for the Toronto-based Insurance

Bureau of Canada, that traditional theory of risk has eroded and "the individual is being protected in spite of his own stupidity."

But the insurance crisis may also force many Canadians to re-examine the whole concept of responsibility. Faced with costly court awards, many institutions have tried to improve their services—and reduce damages. Ann MacIntosh, for one, the risk management director at Halifax's Victoria General Hospital, has instituted procedure checks to "prevent patient harm from happening in the first place." The hardest adjustment, say many insurance executives, may involve changing social attitudes toward insurance. "It is the psychology of entitlement—if someone is injured, sue everyone in sight, even if it is your own fault," says Edward Belton, president of the Toronto-based Insurance Advisory Organization. "But society is waking up to the fact that this aberration in the civil justice field is costing us a lot of money."

Source: Mary Janigan, "The Insurance Crisis," *Maclean's*, January 27, 1986.

Question:
In light of the foregoing, what would you do:
a) if you were an insurance company executive?
b) if you were a manufacturer of children's toys?

Additional Dimensions

Chapter 21

International Business

Learning Goals

No nation was ever ruined by trade.
—*Benjamin Franklin, 1779*

Free trade, they concede, is very well as a principle, but it is never quite time for its adoption.
—*Ralph Waldo Emerson, 1876*

The call for free trade is as unavailing as the cry of a spoiled child for the moon. It never has existed; it never will exist.
—*Henry Clay, 1832*

Trade is in its nature free, finds its own channel, and best directeth its own course; and all Laws to give it rules and directions, and to limit and circumscribe it, may serve the particular ends of private men, but are seldom advantageous to the public.
—*Charles Davenant, 1697*

1. To introduce the concept of globalization of business
2. To show the importance of international business in the Canadian economy
3. To define the basic concepts of international trade
4. To describe the different levels of involvement in international business
5. To identify the various obstacles to effective international business
6. To explain the role of the multinational corporation

Profile

Garry Steiman—*Building on International Business*

Garry Steiman knows that exporting pays. From the very beginning of Gemini Fashions of Canada Ltd. in 1971 he and his partners were aware of the importance of exports to a company. "As a former chartered accountant, I could count," says Steiman. "However, you learn very quickly in business that if you don't sell your product you will have nothing to count. We saw the world as our marketplace, and as much as a third of our total output has been exported."

Gemini has become one of Canada's leading outerwear manufacturers. Production is split evenly between children's and ladies' outerwear. The product range incorporates fashion, quality, warmth, and durability. Its Gem Tots collection, for example, has been conceived with infants and toddlers in mind to the satisfaction of new mothers and the wants of grandmothers. The company's Ski-Gem collection was developed for the 3 to 12 age group as the result of research and interviews with children and their mothers.

As well, the firm markets a collection of ski fashions under the brand name of Mobius which is designed specifically for the active skier. The Mobius collection is sold exclusively through ski shops in Canada and the United States.

For the haute couture market, Gemini Fashions offers the Sachet collection appealing to the fashion requirements of ladies' specialty fashion stores.

The company has the full capability to style, manufacture, service and sell their products to all of their selective markets. Production is supported by state-of-the-art technology.

Mr. Steiman has found that exporting has paid off in several ways. In addition to providing a great deal of additional sales it was found that customers in other parts of the world were prepared to buy merchandise at times that fitted into Gemini's normal production valleys. This made the operation more competitive and profitable. "An extreme example," says

Steiman, "was Australia where we had some large customers. Because their winter season was different than ours, we were able to extend our winter production by as much as 10 days by producing Australian orders for winterwear at the tail end of our domestic order production."

The company also discovered that retailers in different parts of the world called for shipments of winterwear later than the Canadian and American retailers. Americans require their winterwear shipments in June, Canadian retailers in July and August, and European customers in September and October. "Apparently, Europeans have grown accustomed to retailing winterwear in season, unlike North Americans who sell ahead of season," says Steiman.

Gary Steiman cautions that "it takes effort, time, investment, talent, and luck to achieve success in the export market. It is there for those who are willing and able to pay the price." The success of his firm provides evidence of the effectiveness of his leadership in this dynamic area.

Source: Myron Love, "Gemini Shines in the Western Sky," *Style*, March 25, 1986, p. K14.

globalization
The process of focusing the resources and objectives of an organization on global opportunities in marketing and production.

International trade has existed since people began to buy and sell commodities. There have always been adventurers who were willing to go beyond the bounds of their current region to explore. Inevitably, new products were discovered, and introduced back home. The search for better trade routes for spices and silks led to the discovery of North America.

Statistics show that Canada has been very successful in exporting her products, as well as being a major importer. Despite this, there is a general consensus that we need to do more. This emphasis on the need for more trade is the same the world over. Its growth has led to the trend toward **globalization**, a trend that will alter the map of world business.

In boardrooms across the country executives are considering where to build the factories of the future. Will it be Windsor, Ontario; Seoul, South Korea; Minneapolis, Minnesota; Chiang Mai, Thailand; or Richmond, BC?[1] The view of business has changed. The concept of exporting or importing from or to our country is evolving into a global view of the world. A garment may be designed in Winnipeg, partially manufactured in Malaysia, and finally made ready for the market in Montreal. Computers and cars are made of parts manufactured in many parts of the world.

The concern is with total efficiency and opportunity wherever it is found. It is clear that Canada cannot compete with cheaper labour countries in certain types of manufacturing. On the other hand, we are much more able to perform other business activities such as sophisticated marketing planning, or those based on information technology. Firms are learning to manage and think in a global context.

The process of broadening business horizons is illustrated in the recognition of nations that freer trade between them is desirable. In 1989, the Canada-United States Free Trade Agreement was signed. It provided for a gradual elimination of obstacles to trade between the two nations. This trend is also exhibited in the prospect of a fully integrated common market in Europe by 1992.

The Canada-US Free Trade agreement has forced many firms to think on a continental rather than a Canadian basis. Moreover, many have utilized the stimulus of the agreement to formulate global strategies. Gillette, for instance, has closed plants in Montreal and other parts of the world, to centralize operations in Boston where the company had unused plant capacity.

On the other hand, Du Pont Canada, 75 percent owned by E.I. du Pont de Nemours & Co. of the US, invested heavily in plants in both Canada and the United States, each of which could be world-competitive. Other foreign companies have set expectations that their Canadian subsidiaries will serve specific market niches on a global basis.[2]

Free Trade agreement or not, the marketplace has changed. Canadian companies will suffer or benefit from the realities of global competition. It is to Canada's advantage if firms recognize and respond to these challenges and opportunities.

The Importance of International Business

Evidence of the growing importance of world business is everywhere. Canada is both a seller and a purchaser in the world marketplace. Many Canadian firms, like their counterparts elsewhere, have experienced tremendous growth since they began to view the world as their market.

Some Canadian companies depend heavily on their ability to sell their products overseas. Half the companies listed in Table 21-1 receive more than 50 percent of their revenues from abroad. Inco received at least 50 percent of its revenues from the US.

exporting
Selling domestic goods abroad.

importing
Buying foreign goods and raw materials.

Foreign trade is important to Canada from two viewpoints—**exporting**—selling goods abroad—and **importing**—buying foreign goods. The US has long been Canada's best trading partner, and in 1988 provided 69 percent of Canada's imports. Americans bought 74 percent of Canadian exports. Canada's leading trading partners are shown in Table 21-2.

World business allows a nation to sell abroad products that are not needed domestically and to import goods that are not produced or are in short supply locally. Some leading Canadian exports and imports are shown in Table 21-3. Except for the motor vehicles and parts that flow across the border under the Canada-US auto pact, machinery is the leading import, and wheat and paper products are the leading exports.

Table 21-1   The Top 50 Exporters in Canada

Rank 1988	Canadian exports $ million	Company	Exports as % of sales	% change in exports vs 1987
1	11,435	**General Motors Canada**	59%	+22%
2	8,079	**Ford Motor Canada**	51%	+20%
3	3,487	**Noranda**	39%	+10%
4	3,116	**Canadian Pacific**	26%	+8%
5	3,087	**Alcan Aluminium**	29%	+43%
6	2,959	Inco	74%	+142%
7	2,147	**Canadian Wheat Board**	75%	−11%
8	1,470	Nova	37%	+58%
9	1,446	**Mitsui & Co. (Canada)**	46%	+39%
10	1,352	**IBM Canada**	37%	+36%
11	1,228	**Abitibi-Price**	37%	+8%
12	1,067	**Falconbridge**	50%	+48%
13	1,048	**Cominco**	63%	+43%
14	1,031	**Bombardier**	71%	+29%
15	931	**Magna International**	64%	+21%

Rank 1988	Canadian exports $ million	Company	Exports as % of sales	% change in exports vs 1987
16	906	Sumitomo Canada	70%	+1%
17	889	Pratt & Whitney Canada	84%	+10%
18	886	Fletcher Challenge Canada	60%	+7%
19	870	Mitsubishi Canada	71%	+8%
20	804	Repap Enterprises	78%	+40%
21	755	Royal Canadian Mint	85%	−9%
22	715	Consolidated-Bathurst	30%	+5%
23	682	Canadian Commercial Corp.	100%	−12%
24	653	Rio Algom	33%	+24%
25	628	Canfor	58%	−18%
26	545	TransCanada PipeLines	17%	+34%
27	537	Amoco Canada Petroleum	27%	+11%
28	526	Seaboard Lumber Sales	100%	+5%
29	517	Quebecor	40%	+434%
30	500	Agro Co. of Canada	95%	+25%
31	498	Canpotex	100%	+31%
32	497	Weldwood of Canada	56%	+51%
33	497	Donohue	77%	+31%
34	492	Domtar	18%	+14%
35	480	Dofasco	16%	+30%
36	477	McDonnell Douglas Canada	100%	+23%
37	456	George Weston	4%	−2%
38	423	Stelco	16%	−19%
39	400	Ivaco	18%	+19%
40	399	Digital Equipment of Canada	41%	+53%
41	394	Cansulex	100%	+15%
42	388	Mobil Oil Canada	31%	−30%
43	368	Cargill	33%	−49%
44	346	Hydro-Québec	7%	−22%
45	317	Ford Electronics	95%	−6%
46	300	Eurocan Pulp & Paper	89%	+2%
47	300	Petro-Canada	6%	−20%
48	277	Rockwell Int'l. Canada	51%	−6%
49	276	General Electric Canada	17%	−13%
50	275	Groupe Lavalin	31%	−8%

Source: *Financial Post 500*, Summer 1989.

Table 21-2
Canada's Leading Trading Partners
(millions of dollars)

Major Trading Areas	Exports	Imports	Balance of Trade
United States	101,581	87,992	13,589
United Kingdom	3,485	4,721	−1,236
Other E.E.C.	7,259	10,608	−3,349
Japan	8,222	7,920	302
Other O.E.C.D.	3,047	3,618	−571
Other Countries	13,514	12,653	861
Data for 1988			

Source: *Canadian Economic Observer*, Statistics Canada, June 1989, No. 11-010.

Table 21-3
Leading Canadian Exports and Imports

Exports	(millions of dollars)
Consumer goods	2,783
Energy products	11,828
Agriculture and fish products	13,178
Machines and equipment	21,320
Forest products	21,386
Industrial goods	29,222
Automobile products	35,356
Total	135,073

Imports	(millions of dollars)
Forest products	1,296
Energy products	5,287
Agriculture and fish products	7,560
Consumer goods	13,606
Industrial goods	24,461
Automobile products	33,229
Machines and equipment	40,385
Total	125,824

Data for year 1988
Source: *Canadian Economic Observer*, Statistics Canada, June 1989, No. 11-010.

Basic Concepts in International Trade

International business activity is the result of several factors—some economic, others political or traditional. To understand international business it is essential to understand the concepts of balance of trade and balance of payments.

Balance of Trade

balance of trade
The relationship between a country's exports and imports.

A country's **balance of trade** is determined by the relationship between its exports and its imports. A favourable balance of trade, or export surplus, occurs when exports exceed imports, because, other things being equal, new money flows into the economic system. An unfavourable balance of trade, or import surplus, occurs when imports exceed exports, because, other things being equal, the net money flow is outward. In 1982, Canada had a trade surplus of $17.8 billion.[3]

Balance of Payments

balance of payments
The relationship between a country's inward and outward money flows.

A country's balance of trade plays a key role in determining its **balance of payments**—the flow of money into or out of the country. A favourable balance of payments means a net flow into the country, while an unfavourable balance of payments means a net outflow.

But balance of payments is affected by other factors, too, such as tourism, military expenditures abroad, investment abroad, and foreign aid. A money outflow caused by these factors may erase the money inflow from a favourable balance of trade and leave a country with an unfavourable balance of payments. See Table 21-4 for the current account trade for a 29-year period between 1960 and 1988.

The Exchange Rate

devaluation
The reduction in value of a country's currency in relation to gold or to some other currency.

revaluation
An upward adjustment in the value of a country's currency.

exchange rate
The rate at which a country's currency can be exchanged for other currencies or gold.

floating exchange rate
An exchange rate that varies according to market conditions.

The value of a nation's currency is sometimes changed by a government action or by market conditions. **Devaluation** is the reduction in value of a country's currency in relation to gold or to some other currency. Devaluation of the dollar would have the effect of lowering the cost of Canadian goods abroad and making trips to Canada cheaper for foreign tourists. **Revaluation**, a less typical case, is the upward adjustment in value of a country's currency. In either situation, the country adjusts its **exchange rate**—the rate at which its currency can be exchanged for other currencies of gold. Most nations, including Canada, have now adopted a **floating exchange rate** which is allowed to vary in accordance with market conditions.

Exchange rates can have considerable impact on trade flows. As the Canadian dollar has declined in relation to currencies in other countries, prices of our products are cheaper for Germans, Japanese or Swiss, to name a few. This makes it easier for Canadians to export into those countries.

Dumping

Just a few years ago almost no one knew what the term *dumping* meant. Now dumping is viewed as a threat to our economic system. **Dumping** is selling goods abroad at a price lower than that used for the domestic market.

If foreign goods sell in Canada at prices substantially lower than those offered by local producers, the result will be lost jobs for

dumping
Selling goods abroad at a price lower than that charged in the domestic market.

Table 21-4
Canada's Current Account Trade, 1960 to 1988
(Balance of Payments Basis)

Year	Merchandising Trade Exports	Imports	Trade Balance	Non-Merchandising Trade Receipts	Payments	Total Current Account Balance
	(millions of $)					
1960	5,392	5,540	−148	7,215	8,448	−1,233
1961	5,889	5,716	173	7,904	8,832	−928
1962	6,387	6,203	184	8,548	9,378	−830
1963	7,082	6,579	503	9,416	9,937	−521
1964	8,238	7,537	701	10,887	11,311	−424
1965	8,745	8,627	118	11,648	12,778	−1,130
1966	10,326	10,102	224	13,600	14,762	−1,162
1967	11,338	10,772	566	15,303	15,802	−499
1968	13,537	12,162	1,288	17,464	17,561	−97
1969	14,832	14,007	825	19,425	20,342	−917
1970	16,751	13,845	2,882	21,932	20,826	1,106
1971	17,788	15,533	2,255	23,051	22,620	431
1972	20,129	18,272	1,857	25,483	25,869	−386
1973	25,461	22,726	2,735	31,776	31,668	108
1974	32,591	30,902	1,689	40,352	41,812	−1,460
1975	33,511	33,962	−451	41,840	46,597	−4,757
1976	37,995	36,607	1,388	47,110	50,952	−3,842
1977	44,253	41,523	2,730	54,103	58,404	−4,301
1978	53,054	49,047	4,007	64,577	69,512	−4,935
1979	65,275	61,157	4,118	79,182	84,144	−4,962
1980	76,772	68,284	8,488	93,615	94,711	−1,096
1981	84,480	77,112	7,368	100,628	107,946	−5,766
1982	84,577	66,239	18,338	101,438	99,863	3,017
1983	91,268	73,227	18,041	108,181	107,488	1,577
1984	111,330	91,493	19,838	24,432	41,575	2,695
1985	119,070	102,669	16,400	27,009	45,345	−1,935
1986	119,889	110,079	9,810	29,185	49,492	−10,496
1987	126,125	115,149	10,976	30,529	52,081	−10,576
1988	137,106	127,512	9,594	38,596	59,451	−11,262

Source: *Canadian Economic Observer*, Statistics Canada, June 1989, No. 11–010.

Canadians. The Anti-Dumping Tribunal investigates any complaints related to dumping. The Tribunal has the power to impose extra duties and tariffs in order to protect Canadian employment.

While dumping is viewed by many people as an unfair business practice, it is a difficult charge to prove. Japanese steel firms, for instance, have balked at providing cost data essential to investigations in that industry. Furthermore, dumping complaints can take a long time to resolve. Although Canada remains committed to a free-trade philosophy, pressures exist to protect basic industries from unfair foreign competition, sometimes from firms actually owned by foreign governments. Another worry is that dumping complaints may lead to extensive trade warfare. It seems certain that the question of dumping will remain a vital public issue as long as Canada suffers from relatively high unemployment, economically threatened industries, and related economic ills.

Government policy and public opinion on imports have varied over time. Relatively high unemployment usually leads to calls for higher tariff walls and severe import restrictions to protect Canadian industry and its employees. This economic protection argument has been voiced by both corporate management and labour union executives. The import market has often been used to accomplish economic and political objectives. For example, the Australian government once revalued its dollar upward to attract cheaper imports in an attempt to combat severe inflation.

It appears likely that imported goods will continue to grow in importance in Canada. The long-run trend is toward increased international trade. Eastern countries are trading more too, realizing that they are better off with increased trade.

Countertrade. Sometimes it is difficult to tell who is selling and who is buying in international trade. For example, Spar Aerospace is selling Brazilian-made Volkswagen Beetle spare parts in the US and mangoes in Toronto. Why is an aerospace company selling such products? The reason for this surprising behavior is **countertrade**, or international bartering agreements. This practice has grown considerably in the past few years. It is estimated that it now affects approximately 10 percent of world trade. In a recent year it is estimated that countertrade, in one form or another, affected approximately $600 million worth of exports from Canada.[4]

countertrade
Selling to a foreign buyer and accepting goods in lieu of money.

A typical countertrade agreement requires the seller to also purchase something from the buyer. For example, Versatile Farm Equipment might sell sugar cane harvesters to Cuba from their plant in Australia. However, in order to get the business, Versatile could be required to purchase an equivalent value of sugar from Cuba. Versatile would then have to use an agent to sell the sugar to another country before it could receive remuneration in the form of currency. Countertrade is a common feature of East–West trade. It is not always easy to implement, and adds extra work to consummating a deal.

Countertrade was the key that unlocked major export deals in Europe for two Ontario manufacturing companies. In Poland, Vulcan Equipment secured a $1 million order for tire repair equipment with a countertrade deal for coal through a Danish trading house. The coal was sold in Denmark and funds were then released to Vulcan. Normal after-sales service and training were arranged by the company on a regular commercial basis.

In the German Democratic Republic, Capsule Technology Corp. made a breakthrough with the sale of a hard gelatin capsule manufacturing plant for use in that country's pharmaceutical industry. In return for the order, Capsule Technology has agreed to buy back some of the products produced by its capsule machinery in that country and some other related equipment.

Specialization Among Countries

New Zealand has a climate and terrain ideally suited to raising sheep, while Hong Kong's estimated 6 million people live in a small area that has become one of the most urbanized territories in the world. Hong Kong is a world trader as well as a source of foreign exchange for the People's Republic of China. Kuwait has rich oil fields but few other industries or resources.

These situations suggest that countries can specialize in certain products or commercial activities. By doing what they do best, they are able to exchange products not needed domestically for foreign-made goods that are needed. This allows a higher standard of living than would be possible if the country tried to produce everything itself. The concepts of absolute and comparative advantage explain this.

Absolute Advantage Concept

absolute advantage
The situation where a country has a monopolistic position in the marketing of a product it produces at the lowest cost.

A country has an **absolute advantage** in the marketing of a product if it has a monopolistic position or if it produces the item at the lowest cost. Examples of absolute advantage are rare, because few countries are sole suppliers and because economic conditions rapidly alter production costs.

Comparative Advantage Concept

comparative advantage
One country can produce a good or service relatively more cheaply than another country.

A more realistic approach to international specialization is that of comparative advantage. A country has a **comparative advantage** in an item if it can supply that item more efficiently and at a lower cost than it can supply other products. Nations usually produce and export those goods in which they have the greatest comparative advantage or least comparative disadvantage. Countries tend to import those items in which they have the least comparative advantage or greatest comparative disadvantage.

Consider the following example. Suppose with 1 unit of resources the US can produce 10 tonnes of soybeans or 1 kg of wheat. Similarly, with 1 unit of resources Canada can produce 15 tonnes of soybeans or 3 kg of wheat.

	Soybeans		**Wheat**
US—1 unit of resources produces	10 t	or	1 kg
Canada—1 unit of resources produces ...	15 t	or	3 kg
Total Output	25 t		4 kg

It is obvious that Canada would have an absolute advantage in both areas of production. Using 1 unit of resources it can produce more soybeans and wheat. This might imply that Canada should specialize in both and the US in neither. It might also lead one to ask—how could Canada benefit from trade with the US if it has an absolute advantage in producing both products?

The key to the answer is comparative advantage. The theory of comparative advantage was initially developed by the British economist **David Ricardo**, back in the early 1800s. His theory illustrated that two countries can benefit from trade (even if one country is better than the other at producing all items) if each country specializes in its areas of comparative advantage.

Ricardo theory
Two countries can benefit from trade if each country specializes in its areas of comparative advantage.

Comparative advantage simply means that one country can produce a good or service relatively more cheaply than the other. The theory of comparative advantage states that a country should specialize in the production of those goods and services in which it has a comparative advantage. In this case, the US should specialize in soybeans and Canada in wheat.[5]

Tables 21-3 and 21-4 suggest how the comparative advantage concept has evolved in Canada. The export commodities tend to be those in which Canada has a comparative advantage over its trading partners. Being an industrialized nation with good natural and agricultural resources, Canada tends to export manufactured items, food products, and natural resources such as wood. By contrast, countries with low-cost labour often specialize in products that require a significant amount of labour such as shoes and clothing.

Specialization and trade benefit countries by enabling more production and generating more income. They also benefit the world economy because they result in more production and can help to lower prices.

Focus 21-1

Oddities in Country Specialization

Specialization by countries sometimes produces odd situations. For example, Cherry Valley Duck Farms, a British firm, has a long-term contract to provide Peking ducks to the People's Republic of China. The British ducks grow and breed faster than their Chinese counterparts, so they will be used to upgrade the local variety of Peking duck. Water-poor Saudi Arabia once spent $1 million on a feasibility study on hauling Antarctic icebergs to one of their ports. The Saudis and other Middle Eastern nations are now buying fresh water from Japan: tankers bringing oil to Japan are loaded with water for the return trip.

The Self-Sufficiency Argument

Some countries refuse to specialize their productive efforts because they want to be self-sufficient. The communist nations have typically followed this pattern, as has Israel. Other countries subscribe to the self-sufficiency viewpoint only for commodities that they regard as strategic to their long-run development, such as energy in Canada.

In most cases, countries that seek to be self-sufficient do so for reasons of military preparedness, fear of economic reprisal from other countries, and nationalism. They see noneconomic advantages as being more important to the national welfare than the economic advantages of specialization.

Foreign licensing permits a product to be produced and sold abroad in exchange for a share of the profit.

Levels of Involvement in International Business

International business involvement is an evolving process for many firms. A company usually starts exporting on a small scale, then expands its efforts abroad as management gains confidence and the ability to operate well in other countries. (See Focus 21-2 for a discussion of adapting to other cultures.) Because of the national economic importance of maintaining a favourable balance of payments, the federal government offers a number of services to those who wish to do business abroad.

There are five levels of involvement in world business: casual or accidental exporting, active exporting, foreign licensing, foreign marketing by the firm, and foreign production and foreign marketing.[6]

Focus 21-2

Cracking the Global Market

Looking for new export opportunities? If so, your best resource is probably the network of over 400 Canadian trade officers, scattered across 102 cities worldwide, whose primary function is to help Canadian exporters start or expand sales in international markets. Trade commissioners can:

- identify market opportunities
- promote your company to local customers
- recommend appropriate technical experts to help you negotiate a deal
- help you find good translators and interpreters
- help you select effective agents
- maintain your liaisons with your agents and encourage them
- advise you on the settlement of overdue accounts
- advise you on situations and circumstances affecting travel to and within a country.

How can exporters take advantage of the services of Canadian trade commissioners? A good first step would be to call Info Export, toll-free, at 1-800-267-8376. The people there can advise you on which of the many federal and provincial services are best for your company. Before contacting Canadian missions abroad, discuss your plans with a trade officer in one of the International Trade Centres across Canada.

What does a trade commissioner need to know about your company in order to help you? Put yourself in the place of a Canadian trade commissioner located in a foreign country offering your company's products or services to a local buyer, then imagine what information you would need. The trade commissioner is marketing your products or services and has to make a sales pitch that explains what your company does, describes your products or services, highlights your reputation, and lists your key reference accounts. The better this presentation, the better are your company's chances of securing a good agent or making a sale.

Once you have developed your export marketing plan and are ready to contact Canadian trade offices abroad (embassies, high commissions, or consulates), be sure your letters explain clearly and in detail the assistance you require. The first time you contact a trade commissioner you should provide:

- your name and title
- the full name and address of your company
- your telephone and facsimile number with area code
- your telex number with answerback
- a precise description of your product(s) and how it is used (avoid using abbreviations that could be confusing)
- your marketing plan and target markets
- your company's export experience
- five copies of your product literature, preferably in colour and with multilingual copy, included with your letter.

Source: "Cracking the Global Market," *Manitoba Business*, Jan./Feb. 1989, p. 36.

Casual or Accidental Exporting

Some firms sell goods abroad without being aware of it. Buyers for foreign firms often purchase the goods in Canada and then ship them overseas, but the Canadian company considers the transaction a domestic sale. Canadian purchasers of a supplier's goods sometimes export them for inclusion in an item manufactured overseas. Casual exporting is thus quite common, but it is not a real commitment to international trade.

Active Exporting

Once a firm decides to enter the export market, it must invest two company resources—capital and managerial effort. The export operation may be handled within the organization by an "export manager," or the company may elect to engage an outside firm that specializes in this activity. Active exporting is distinguished from casual exporting by the company's commitment to seek foreign sales. In some cases active exporting may evolve from a casual exporting experience. The foreign transactions of such resource-based companies as Inco, Noranda, and Abitibi are mainly active exporting.

Foreign Licensing

Another approach is to license foreign manufacturers to produce an item rather than to export it. Licensing is often selected because of high shipping costs, tariff barriers or trade restrictions, or nationalistic markets. Sometimes it is chosen because the licensee can provide considerable marketing expertise.

Foreign Marketing by the Firm

Foreign marketing involves setting up a foreign sales organization. While the goods may come from a variety of sources—including the firm's own plants, licensees, or contract manufacturers—foreign marketing is controlled directly by the parent company operating abroad. The BMW is marketed in Canada by a foreign sales organization. The cars are produced in West Germany.

Foreign Production and Foreign Marketing

joint venture
The sharing of a foreign operation's costs, risks, and management with a partner firm in the host country.

Total international business involvement exists when a company starts or acquires both a foreign manufacturing organization and a foreign marketing organization. In either case the firm is totally committed to doing business abroad. One popular way to accomplish overseas production is through a **joint venture**: the sharing of a foreign operation's costs, risks, and management with a partner in the host nation.

Obstacles to International Business

Various barriers to effective world business exist. Some are minor and can be overcome easily; others are nearly impossible to bridge. But either way, business executives must expect and learn to handle a multitude of problems in attempting to reach international markets. (See Focus 21-2.)

Economic, Social, and Cultural Obstacles

Numerous economic, social, and cultural obstacles can interfere with a firm's attempt to sell its product in countries other than Canada. Consumer buying preferences differ from country to country, and can hold many surprises for the unwary Canadian businessperson. In France, men use almost twice as many cosmetics as women. In Italy, children like to eat a bar of chocolate between two slices of bread as a snack.

Canadian products do not always meet the needs of foreign consumers. Massey-Ferguson designed a large horsepower tractor with a standard 190-cm gauge between the treads and virtually failed to penetrate the US market of corn farmers. The reason: American corn farmers plant in 75-cm rows and the wheels would have trampled every third row.[7]

Similarly, ways of conducting business differ across national borders. For example, Japanese business executives rarely say "no" outright. Canadian businesspeople become frustrated because they don't know where they stand. Conversely, Canadians tend to come to the point quickly in business negotiations; the Japanese find this approach offensive.[8]

These examples suggest the importance of economic, social, and cultural factors in the success of international business. Business managers who want to operate in an international market should consider these factors before beginning their ventures. See Focuses 21-3 and 21-4 for discussions of doing business in the Orient.

Focus 21-3

Doing Business the Japanese Way

There's no doubt about it: they do things very differently in Japan, and anyone who wants to break into that market is well advised to do a little homework first. Here are some useful tips for doing business successfully and surviving, from westerners who've found out the hard way how to operate:

• *Building relationships*. The Japanese like to set up relationships and get to know you before they sign a contract. This means that at a first meeting, they are likely to discuss general topics, such as the state of the world economy. They may even take you out to a restaurant or to the golf course, a very fruitful place for meetings. One place you're unlikely to go is home with them to meet the family.

Once things feel more comfortable, they'll start to talk business. From this fact follows the advice that it's better for the same people to do all the negotiating—even if it takes several years—as did Northern Telecom Inc. negotiations for the Displayphone contract.

- *Business cards* translated into Japanese are essential. Bilingual cards are available in Canada from Canadian Pacific Airlines and Japanese Airlines for a minimal fee, and take about two weeks to order.

  Cards are exchanged at the beginning of a meeting—remember to offer yours, Japanese-side-up, and to wait to see whether they wish to shake hands or bow. Do not write on cards you have just been given as this is considered highly impolite.

- *Scheduling meetings*. It is important to set up appointments in advance because the Japanese don't like "cold" calls—part of their credo of no surprises. But because many people commute long distances from their offices, it's difficult to fit in more than three meetings a day. Breakfast gatherings are not popular, nor are after-work get-togethers unless they invite you.

- *Negotiations*. One feature that can be absolutely bewildering is being confronted by a phalanx of negotiators. It helps to sort out who's who by arranging the business cards always exchanged at these meetings to reflect the seating order. What's even harder is figuring out who's the head individual, who often may be the person who says nothing. Equally, the silent one could be a neophyte who is at the meeting only to gain experience and is expected to say nothing.

  The slowness of Japanese decision-making (the famous consensus) can be frustrating for the Western businessperson who is used to jetting in and out and arriving at decisions quickly in between. However, it probably evens out in the end, as once a contract has been signed, most of the hard work is over.

  During negotiations, don't take silence as a criticism. It may simply be that your suggestions are being considered and evaluated before a reply is made. There's probably no need to sweeten the deal by adding concessions you may later regret. Similarly, listen to everything that is said to you before responding. A sentence that starts off, "Yes..." may well contain a "but" further on.

- *Using an interpreter*. Good interpreters cost about $150 to $250 a day, plus expenses, and can be arranged by your hotel. Make sure they are briefed thoroughly on any difficult technical terms you might be using and that they know something about your line of business.

  When conducting a meeting through an interpreter, speak slowly and clearly. Break your thoughts down into simple but self-contained sentences so that what you say can be translated point by point. If you are going to be involved in hard negotiations that last all day, you will probably need two translators who will work in shifts.

- *Getting around*. Taking a cab is obviously the least painful method, provided you don't mind spending a lot of time stuck in traffic jams (you're charged extra for such time, by the way). Your hotel will write out your destination in Japanese and instruct the cab driver. Be warned, however, of Tokyo's extraordinary address system, aptly described as blindman's bluff. Few streets have names, although some of the biggest have recently been labelled.
- *Eating*. If you insist on nothing but Western food, that's easy enough to find, but don't let your inability to speak a word of the language prevent you from sampling the local cuisine. Almost all restaurants display realistically coloured plastic models of their food in the front window. No one will be the slightest bit surprised if you indicate what you want by pointing. Incidentally, if you're on a tight budget, such eating spots will be much cheaper than the restaurants in your hotel. They're also considerably more interesting.

Source: Araminta Wordsworth, "How to Conduct Business the Japanese Way," *Financial Post Special Report*, June 9, 1984, p. S7.

Focus 21-4

Doing Business the Chinese Way

"Selling to the Chinese is a tough job," says Robert Ferchat, president of Northern Telecom International Ltd.

Speaking recently at a China trade and investment conference in Toronto sponsored by the Canada-China Trade Council and Bank of Montreal, Ferchat outlined Nortel's experience in China, and offered some advice to exporters.

- *Be patient*. Negotiating with the Chinese government takes time, energy, and commitment.
- *Do your homework*. Know which authority makes the buying decisions in your sector.
- *Be aware of government priorities*. For instance, Beijing wants technology transfers, training, and steady economic growth. If you keep these priorities in mind, your selling job will be easier.
- *Make it clear that you are in for the long haul*. Demonstrating long-term commitment will give your company an edge.

Ferchat had some specific advice about the telecommunications sector, too. He thinks the field is "promising," pointing out that "needs are enormous" in China. Comparing Chinese and Canadian geography, he suggests Nortel's experience providing telecommunications services at home, where long distances, rivers, mountains, and poor transportation systems are the norm, has prepared the company to offer similar services in China. Since China has only 0.4 telephones per 100 population (versus 87 per 100 in North America), the potential market "is huge by any standards."

All this doesn't make it any easier to sell to China. Ferchat figures companies must rely on old-fashioned hard work and an understanding of the customers and their needs.

Of course in China, the "customer" is still the government, despite recent reforms aimed at decentralizing power and economic decision-making. The Ministry of Post & Telegraphs is the major government purchaser and supplier of telecommunications equipment, although the Ministry of Electronics Industry is still an important supplier to the non-government "end-user." Nortel has separate agreements with some provincial governments and special economic zones, as do companies from Italy, Belgium, Japan, Sweden, the US and the Netherlands. But in each of these deals, the goals of the Chinese national government are paramount.

Foreign companies need to be aware of national priorities, says Ferchat. China is "determined to become independent," and doesn't just want to buy turn-key systems. As in all sectors of the economy, China is interested in technological transfer and joint-ventures, not simply in "briefcase technology" and 100 percent foreign direct investment.

One result: companies wanting to do business with China have to consider options like buy-backs and counterpurchase, two favourite Chinese devices for protecting foreign currency reserves and enhancing local industrial capabilities.

Ferchat also believes you have to develop "a long-term strategy" in China to prove your good intentions. Chinese officials will ask that "products be competitively priced," and that the supplier be "committed to keeping products at the cutting edge of technology through ongoing research and development projects." And, as in any sector, you "have to approach the market with care and diligence," over the long term.

Source: Mathew Horsman, "The Do's and Don'ts of Dealmaking," *Financial Post Special Report*, July 13, 1985, p. S10.

---

tariffs
Taxes levied against products from abroad.

revenue tariffs
Tariffs designed to raise funds for the government.

protective tariffs
Tariffs designed to raise the retail price of imported products to the level of products produced domestically.

Tariffs. Tariffs are taxes levied against products imported from abroad. Some are a set amount per kilogram, litre, or other unit; others are figured on the value of the imported product. Tariffs can be classified as either revenue or protective. **Revenue tariffs** are designed to raise funds for the government. **Protective tariffs**, which are usually higher than revenue tariffs, are designed to raise the retail price of imported products. In earlier days it was believed that a country should protect its "infant industries" by using tariffs to keep out foreign-made products. Although some foreign goods would enter the country, the high tariff payment would keep domestic products competitive. Periodically some groups argue that such tariffs should be used to protect employment and profits in domestic Canadian industry.

General Agreement on Tariffs and Trade (GATT)
An international trade accord that has sponsored various tariff negotiations leading to cuts in the overall level of tariffs throughout the world.

Multinational Trade Agreements. The **General Agreement on Tariffs and Trade (GATT)** is an international trade accord among 88 countries that together generate about 85 percent of the world's trade. In this accord tariffs have been gradually negotiated downward through a series of negotiation "rounds" (the Geneva Round, Dillon Round, Kennedy Round, and Tokyo Round). The effects on tariff levels have been very significant. For example, tariffs on most industrial goods are generally less than 8 percent in the most advanced western countries. The most recent round, the Uruguay Round, has faced real obstacles to agreement on new reductions, especially in the area of agricultural subsidies.

While the general movement has been toward tariff reduction, economic downturns and local industry problems bring calls for protection of threatened industries. In numerous instances the successes of GATT in reducing general tariff barriers have been undermined by a multitude of restrictive trade agreements that have sprung up outside the framework of GATT. These include such restrictions as quotas, voluntary export restraints, and similar measures. An example is Canada's establishment of "voluntary quotas" on the number of Japanese cars shipped to our country. The quota is "voluntary" in that if Japan were not to comply, Canada would legislate perhaps more severe and long-lasting restrictions.

This development is often described as "managed trade," and now covers a broad range of industries, including textiles, clothing, steel, automobiles, machine tools, and consumer electronics. There seems to be a growing consensus that such restrictions have put the multilateral trading system at risk. The developed countries show a growing understanding that the best route to improved competitiveness is through positive adjustment within an open international trading system. The Uruguay Round of GATT is currently struggling with these problems and opportunities. The decisions are not easy, because while there is agreement that freer trade is necessary, internal industries and markets cry out for protection.

Sylvia Ostry, Canada's ambassador for Multilateral Trade Relations, says, "Canada's ability to compete in a rapidly changing and increasingly tough world environment depends to a large degree on open trade. In many industries, our domestic market is too small to permit optimum plant size and product specialization. That is why we are deeply concerned with maintaining and enhancing the GATT system."[9]

import quotas
Limitations on the number of products in certain categories that can be imported with the objective of protecting domestic industries and preserving foreign exchange.

Trade restrictions. There are also other forms of trade restrictions. **Import quotas** set limits on the number of products in certain categories that can be imported. The objective of such quotas is to

embargo 禁止
A complete ban on certain imported products.

protect domestic industries and their employees and preserve foreign exchange. Sometimes the threat of mandatory import quotas causes a nation to change its export policies. The Japanese agreed to limit textile exports to Canada in face of such a threat. The ultimate quota is the **embargo**—a complete ban on certain products. In 1980, Canada temporarily prohibited the importation of products from Iran to protest that government's handling of the hostage-taking crisis involving US consular personnel.

exchange control
The allocation, expansion, or restriction of foreign exchange according to existing national policy.

Foreign trade can also be regulated by exchange control through a central bank or government agency. Under **exchange control**, firms must buy and sell foreign exchange through the central bank or government agency. The government can allocate, expand, or restrict foreign exchange according to existing national policy.

Focus 21-5

The Pros and Cons of Tariffs

Very few economic choices—maybe none—can be explained in clear black-and-white terms. Tariffs as protection against lower-priced imports raise an issue of some dispute in Canada.

Consumers would benefit from the lower priced competition. It means more choices and lower prices. But businesspeople would probably see things differently. They would see potential business going to foreign competitors, meaning lower sales, less revenue and hence less profit or a loss. Workers at Canadian companies trying to compete with these cheaper imports might become unemployed if enough business was lost to foreign competitors.

Tariffs have the effect of raising the price at which foreign companies must sell their products in Canada to make a profit, which gives Canadian firms an advantage. The issue of tariff protection for Canadian businesses is a crucial one. Here are some of the points made on either side of the debate.

Major Points of Those Arguing for Tariff Protection:
- Tariffs are necessary to protect Canadian jobs. If Canadians buy lower priced imports, Canadian production falls and some workers will lose employment.
- Tariffs are necessary to protect certain Canadian businesses (if not entire industries) from lower priced imports. Other countries may be able to produce more cheaply because of lower wage costs, cheaper resources, etc. As such, they may be able to underprice Canadian producers and put them out of business.
- There are many areas in which Canada does not have a comparative advantage. Tariffs help broaden the areas in which Canadians can compete. This can increase business opportunity and jobs.

Major Points of Those Arguing Against Tariff Protection:
- Tariffs raise prices for Canadian consumers.
- Tariffs protect inefficient industries—those that can't compete on equal terms with foreign producers. They should be forced to compete or allowed to fail. If they fail, the resources invested can be redirected to a business that can compete. Companies that can compete more effectively and employ more workers should be supported.
- Levying a tariff encourages other countries to retaliate with their own tariffs on Canadian goods. This hurts the sales of Canadian exporting firms. Production and employment fall and opportunities for economies of scale are lost. Hence, prices of Canadian-produced goods rise.

Political and legal obstacles. Political factors certainly influence international business. For example, Colgate's popular Irish Spring soap was introduced in England with a political name change. Britain knows it as Nordic Spring.[10]

Many nations try to achieve political objectives through international business activities. Like it or not, firms operating abroad often end up involved in or influenced by international relations. US companies have been boycotted, burned, bombed, and banned by people who object to American foreign policy. A dynamic political environment is a fact of life in international business. Canadian businesses are perhaps fortunate that this country has a fairly low international profile.

There have been important events and dates in Canada's history of international business and trade relations. These are shown in Table 21–5.

Table 21–5
Important Dates in Canada's Trade History

1846	British adoption of free trade brings an end to Canada's privileged position with Great Britain's old colonial system of tariff preferences and shipping markets. British-American merchants seek to obtain comparable preferential treatment with the United States.
1854	Reciprocity Treaty negotiated. Colonies that will form Confederation enjoy free trade with the United States in certain natural resource and agricultural products.
1866-1876	Canada seeks better terms of access to both United States and British markets, with disappointing results.
1873	World-wide depression.

1879	Sir John A. Macdonald's National Policy—Canada adopts a high tariff policy, as did most trading countries. Canada unsuccessfully tries to persuade Britain to discriminate against non-imperial sources.
1892	Founding of the Trade Commissioner Service.
1897	Canada grants British goods preferential access, which later becomes the system of Commonwealth preferences. Britain does not reciprocate, and because Canada's trade with emerging trade partners was previously negotiated by Britain for Canada, countries such as Germany retaliate against the British preferential access by imposing a maximum tariff on Canadian goods.
1907	Canada adopts a tariff structure that provides for three levels of duty: • the British preferential tariff, enjoyed by British and Commonwealth goods, which has the lowest rates. • the intermediate tariff, with rates lower than the general tariff, which could be extended to any country by order-in-council. • the general tariff, which has the highest rates, applied mainly to imports from the United States, even though the United States is fast becoming Canada's best customer.
1910	A renewed effort to obtain reciprocity with the United States results in a trade agreement similar to the one in 1854 but is rejected in the Canadian election of 1911.
1919	Britain gradually retreats from its adherence to free trade by selectively introducing preferences favouring Commonwealth countries.
1920s	Canada continues negotiations with non-Commonwealth countries, notably France, offering access to the Canadian intermediate tariff in exchange for most-favoured-nation (MFN) status or similar treatment by the other party.
1930s	World-wide depression.
1930	Smoot-Hawley Tariff in the United States brings in large tariff increases and other barriers to trade. Britain follows suit with other Commonwealth members at a trade conference in Ottawa in 1932.
1934	The United States introduces the Reciprocal Trade Agreements Act and enters into most-favoured-nation (MFN) agreements through a series of bilateral trade negotiations. A limited Canada-US agreement is concluded in 1935.
1937-1938	In return for US tariff reductions, Canada and Britain further reduce their tariffs to the United States in exchange for access to the US MFN rate and concessions affecting some principal Canadian exports. For the first time since 1866, Canada-US trade is fully restored to MFN status with the exception that Canada retains its Commonwealth preferences.

1948	The disruption of the world trading system in the thirties and forties leads to the creation of a new world trading order as espoused by the General Agreement on Tariffs and Trade (GATT). Canada is a major participant.
1950s	Priority is given to reducing foreign barriers to Canadian exports of industrial materials, foodstuffs, and selected manufactured goods, while making reciprocal reductions in selected tariff-protected Canadian secondary industries.
1960s	Canada gives high priority to obtaining improved access for fully manufactured products, while protection given to secondary industries in Canada is gradually reduced. Multilateral trade liberalization through successive GATT negotiations is supplemented by two important bilateral deals with the United States: the Automotive Products Trade Agreement and, to a lesser extent, the Defence Production Sharing Arrangements. Commonwealth preferences diminish in importance.
1970s	Bilateral non-preferential trade and economic cooperation agreements are concluded with the European Community (EC) and with a number of other countries. The Tokyo Round of GATT talks produces large decreases in global tariff barriers.
1980s	As a result of the Tokyo Round, tariffs continue to decrease. Use of non-tariff barriers are on the rise. With increasing Canadian exports to the United States, debate heats up on Canada-US free trade proposals and other trade options for Canada. The new Uruguay Round of GATT commences.
1989	The Canada-United States Free Trade Agreement is signed. This sets in motion a gradual elimination of tariffs over the next ten years.

Source: Gary Rabbior, *Export Canada: Opportunities and Challenges in the World Economy,* 1984, pp. 42, 43.

Legal requirements also complicate international business. India controls the amount of money a firm (or person) can take out of the country. The Netherlands requires that candy commercials on television carry tooth decay warnings. Many nations have local laws specifying the portion of a product that must come from domestic sources. These examples suggest that managers involved in international business must be well versed in legislation affecting their industry.

The legal environment for Canadian firms operating abroad consists of three dimensions: Canada law, international law, and the legal requirements of host nations.[11] Firms in Canada are subjected to comprehensive Canadian business legislation. International operations are also subject to various regulations, tax laws, and import-export requirements.

friendship, commerce, and navigation treaties
Treaties with other nations that include many aspects of international business relations such as the right to conduct business in a treaty partner's domestic market.

International Monetary Fund
A fund established to lend foreign exchange to countries that require assistance in conducting international trade.

International law can be seen in the various agreements existing among nations. Canada has many **friendship, commerce, and navigation (FCN) treaties** with other nations. Such treaties include many aspects of international business relations such as the right to conduct business in the treaty partner's domestic market. The **International Monetary Fund (IMF)** was established to lend foreign exchange to countries that require assistance in conducting international trade. This facilitates the entire process of international business. Other international business agreements concern standards for products, patents, trademarks, reciprocal tax treaties, export control, international air travel, and international communications.

The legal requirements of host nations often affect foreign marketers. Japan, for example, is cited as having complex import requirements. Other nations, including Canada, limit foreign ownership in their business sectors.

The majority of international businesspeople realize the importance of obeying the laws and regulations of the countries within which they operate. Violations of these legal requirements are setbacks for international business as a whole and should be carefully avoided.

Multinational Economic Communities

Several multinational economic communities have been formed since World War II.[12] The European Economic Community (EEC)—also known as the common market—is the most widely publicized of them. Some of the participants in such regional associations (shown in Table 21-6) have strong political as well as economic ties.

Three basic formats for economic integration exist: the free trade area, the customs union, and the common market or economic union. Within the **free trade area**, participants agree to allow trading among themselves without any tariffs or trade restrictions. Under the **customs union**, a free trade area is established for member nations, with a uniform tariff imposed on trade with nonmember nations. The **common market** or economic union maintains a customs union and seeks to bring all government trade rules into agreement. The EEC, the best example of a customs union, has not yet become a true common market, but is moving in that direction.

free trade area
Participants agree to allow trading among themselves without any tariffs or trade restrictions.

customs union
A free trade area is established for member nations and a uniform tariff is imposed on trade with nonmember nations.

common market
A customs union that seeks to bring all government trade rules into agreement.

Regardless of their approach, it seems certain that multinational economic communities will play a significant role in international business during the next decade. Multinational economic integration is forcing management to adapt its operations to meet the requirements of the economic associations.

Table 21-6
Regional Economic Associations

Name	Membership	Date of Origin
ANCOM: Andean Development Corporation (also called the Andean Common Market)	Bolivia, Colombia, Ecuador, Peru, Venezuela	1969
Council of Arab Economic Unity	Iraq, Jordan, Kuwait, Syria, Egypt, Sudan, Libya, Mauritania, Palestine Liberation Organization, Somalia, United Arab Emirates, Yemen Arab Republic, Yemen People's Democratic Republic	1964
ASEAN: Association of Southeast Asian Nations	Indonesia, Malaysia, Philippines, Singapore, Thailand	1967
Benelux	Belgium, Luxembourg, the Netherlands	1960
CACM: Central America Common Market	Costa Rica, El Salvador, Guatemala, Honduras, Nicaragua	1960
CARICOM: Caribbean Common Market	Antigua, Barbados, Dominica, Belize, Grenada, Guyana, Jamaica, Montserrat, St. Christopher-Nevis-Anguilla, St. Lucia, St. Vincent and the Grenadines, Trinidad, and Tobago	1973
CEAD: Communauté économique de l'Afrique de l'ouest (West African Economic Community)	Ivory Coast, Mali, Mauritania, Niger, Senegal, Upper Volta (observers are Benin and Togo)	1974
CMEA: Council for Mutual Economic Assistance (also called COMECON)	Bulgaria, Czechoslovakia, East Germany, Hungary, Mongolian People's Republic, Poland, Romania, USSR, Cuba, Vietnam	1949
EEC: European Economic Community (also called the Common Market)	Belgium, France, West Germany, Italy, Luxembourg, the Netherlands, Denmark, Ireland, United Kingdom, Greece, Portugal, Spain	1958
ECOWAS: Economic Community of West Africa States	Benin, Cape Verde, Gambia, Ghana, Guinea, Guinea-Bissau, Ivory Coast, Liberia, Mali, Mauritania, Niger, Nigeria, Senegal, Sierra Leone, Togo, Upper Volta	1975
EFTA: European Free Trade Association	Austria, Norway, Sweden, Switzerland, Iceland, Finland (associate member)	1960
ALADI: Asociación latino-americana de integración (Latin American Integration Association)	Argentina, Bolivia, Brazil, Chile, Colombia, Ecuador, Mexico, Paraguay, Peru, Uruguay, Venezuela	1980
OCAM: Organisation commune africaine et mauricienne	Central African Republic, Ivory Coast, Mauritius, Niger, Rwanda, Senegal, Togo, Upper Volta, Benin	1965

Name	Membership	Date of Origin
RCD: Regional Cooperation for Development	Iran, Pakistan, Turkey	1964
UDEAC: L'union douanière et économique de l'Afrique centrale (Customs and Economic Union of Central Africa)	Cameroon, Central African Republic, Congo, Gabon	1964

Source: Compiled by Professor Paul F. Jenner, Institute of International Business, Georgia State University, from information in *The Europa Year Book 1981. A World Survey*, Vol. 1 (London: Europa Publications Ltd., 1981).

The Multinational Corporation

multinational corporation
Corporation that operates production and marketing facilities on an international level and considers the world its market.

It is useful to distinguish between an international firm and a multinational corporation. An **international firm** is one that sells in international markets. This could be done either through exporting or overseas sales outlets. By contrast, a **multinational corporation** operates production and marketing facilities on an international level, in several countries. The corporation often tries to standardize its product lines to maximize efficiency. Parts are usually manufactured where it is most economical and sales efforts are concentrated where the market is growing fastest. The multinational corporation considers the world its market.

Alcan Aluminum is an example of a multinational corporation. Alcan is headquartered in Canada, but its products can be found around the world. The company has branches in many world markets. With approximately 80 percent of its sales originating outside of the country, the company must think in global rather than domestic terms as it develops strategy and manages the business.

Focus 21-6

Mistakes People Make in International Business

Many marketing experts insist that advertising methods used in the sophisticated markets of Western countries can often be applied to the third world: believing this has gotten many an advertiser into a heap of trouble.

Underdeveloped nations have little of the complex data—demographics, psychographics, Nielsens, etc.—that make North American marketing and research departments tick. Finding out how many people live in a third world city, how old they are, and how many can read is often a mind-boggling task. Advertisers are frequently unprepared to deal with differences of culture, language, and morality in third world countries. Being so unprepared, they confront problems undreamed of back home.

Esperanto, Anyone? Not long ago the residents of a Middle Eastern country saw an auto ad about a new suspension system that, in translation, said the car was "suspended from the ceiling." Since there are at least thirty different dialects in the eighteen Arab countries, there is plenty of room for error. Not even print ads are free from the dialectics of dialect; by making a wrong choice in calligraphy styles, for example, an advertiser could offend a conservative Moslem nation.

Only Men Need Apply. Ranging from the glamour of Revlon's Lauren Hutton to symbols of conventional domesticity like Betty Crocker, women play a large role in North American advertising. In a number of nations, however, one must tread cautiously. In Saudi Arabia, for example, advertisers were recently told they could no longer portray women in their ads—veiled or unveiled.

Hold the Pickles, Hold the Lettuce, Hold the Hamburger. As the Armour meat-packaging company found when it tried to open a branch office in Goa, India, one cannot kill a sacred cow. Cultural taboos vary from nation to nation; it is imperative that advertisers learn about them and avoid transgressions.

You Can't Fight City Hall. In Bahrain, an independent state in the Persian Gulf, outdoor advertiser Poster Projects Company learned the hard way that feuds with the government are bad for business. During a dispute with Poster Projects over the imposition of the world's biggest outdoor advertising tax, Bahrain municipal officials sneaked out at the crack of dawn one morning and tore down every billboard that Poster Projects had erected a week earlier. The company capitulated, ending the dispute. One might complain that "there oughtta be a law," but there usually isn't.

Blondes Have More Fun. . .or Do They? North American advertising is heavily populated with fair-haired, freckle-faced children and lanky Caucasian adults with year-round tans. In the third world most people have black hair, brown eyes, and skin tones that range from black to brown to yellow. Imagine for a moment switching on your television and discovering that all the men in the commercials are wearing turbans. This is precisely the jarring effect a typical North American commercial has on a resident of the third world.

Source: *Grey matter*, Grey Advertising, 1981, Vol. 52, No. 1, p. 2.

---

world product mandate
Responsibility given to a subsidiary of a multinational corporation to supply the international market with a specialized product.

Efficiency of production has led to the growth of a simple yet appealing concept—the **world product mandate**. Under such a mandate the multinational corporation gives a subsidiary the responsibility to supply the international market with a specialized product without competition from other subsidiaries of the firm. For example, Canada has a relatively small domestic market for electric frying pans; however, Canadian General Electric, a subsidiary of General Electric, has increased production of electric frying pans from 50,000 to 600,000 under a world product mandate from the company's headquarters. The power of the parent firm will be used to market the Canadian product on a world-wide basis.

Many multinational corporations such as Exxon, Mobil, and Ford are American. There are, however, some Canadian multinationals, mainly in resource-based industries. Inco heads the list, followed by Noranda, McMillan-Bloedel, and Consolidated Bathurst.

Multinational corporations have become so dominant in some markets that they are now the object of close political and economic scrutiny. These firms have been criticized for their profit margins, investment policies, employment practices, market positions, and the like.

The Challenge for Canadian Business

A Canadian businessperson might read the numerous concepts in this chapter and conclude that business in Canada is enough of a challenge in itself. This is a big country, with many opportunities without looking beyond our borders. Many firms have done this successfully.

However, today's trends are gradually making confining operations to Canada a less desirable option. The facts of globalization have created a situation where the local business is competing with international competitors right in the home market. The economies of scale that such international competitors bring to the market can make it very difficult for the firm with a small localized market base.

On the other hand, the fact that so many Canadian firms have been successful in the international marketplace is a great incentive to others to become involved. The opportunities for the firm are multiplied many times. International business is exciting and can be very rewarding. The issue is not one of ability, but one of vision.

Reprinted by permission of Chronicle Features

How Much Attention Should We Pay to Japan?

In 1988 and 1989 Canada's national energies were concentrated on the debate about free trade between Canada and the United States. A recent report issued by the Canada Japan Trade Council argues that Canada is "being euchred out of representation in the only other market we must penetrate to prosper as a nation: the Pacific Rim in general and Japan in particular." The author, Charles J. McMillan, argues that we are tied into a triangle. "The Japanese understand the US market, and the Americans are doing their best to learn about that market. The Japanese are clearly present in Canada. But how much are we tied into the Japanese market? Hardly at all—our presence there is piecemeal and static. Why, for example, do we maintain something like 600 people at our London high commission—where businessmen don't really need much advice to establish contacts—while our embassy in Tokyo is staffed by only 80? We do more business with South Korea than with France and yet we have 400 at the embassy in Paris and 45 in Seoul," he says.

McMillan recommends that Canada must undertake long-term research in areas where Japanese interest is high—human biology and aging, robotics, artificial intelligence, computer translation, marine manufacturing, and biotechnology.

While Japan and the US remain the only technological superpowers, Canada is lagging so far behind that we are in real danger of being counted out of contention. Japan is currently spending about four percent of its gross national product on research and development (compared with Canada's 1.3 percent) and, unlike most North American research, which is defence-related, nearly all of Japan's funds go to projects with commercial applications. One Tokyo agency translates each issue of 20,000 foreign technological journals, and Japan has 50 times more young people studying in North America than vice versa.

The most revealing statistic is in the essential field of robotics, the computer-based automated equipment at the leading edge of most production technologies. More than two-thirds (93,000) of the world's robots have Japanese passports, while the United States is a poor second (20,000), and Canada ranks last among the major industrialized nations, with only 1,032 robots sporting the maple leaf.

Most Canadian businesses still view Japan as just another trading partner, rather than as Asia's leading industrial power and the window to the Pacific Rim. They seem to feel that it will be much more profitable to concentrate on the lucrative and close US market.

Source: Peter C. Newman, "The Risks of Kissing Off the Japanese," *Maclean's*, April 11, 1988, p. 38.

Summary of Learning Goals

1. **Discuss the concept of globalization of business.**
   Globalization is a trend that will alter the map of world business. Global management is the process of focusing the resources and objectives of an organization on global opportunities in marketing and production.

2. **Evaluate the importance of international business.**

   International business is growing in importance. Many Canadian firms depend heavily on exports. Canada is already one of the leading international traders, and our government is trying to increase our share of exports even more.

3. **Define the basic concepts of international trade.**

   The basic concepts of international business include the *balance of trade* (the relationship between exports and imports) and *balance of payments* (the difference between inward and outward cash flows); *countertrade* (agreements to trade products instead of paying for them) and *dumping* (the selling of goods abroad at a price lower than they are sold domestically).

   Countries usually benefit if they specialize in certain products or commercial activities. A country has an absolute advantage in marketing a product if it holds a monopolistic position or produces the item at lower cost. It has a comparative advantage if it can supply the product more efficiently or at lower cost than it can supply other products to a trading partner.

4. **Describe the different levels of involvement in international business.**

   The five levels are casual or accidental exporting, active exporting, foreign licensing, overseas marketing by the firm, and foreign production and foreign marketing.

5. **Identify the various obstacles to effective international business.**

   The three primary obstacles are economic, societal, and cultural obstacles; tariffs and trade restrictions; and political and legal obstacles.

6. **Discuss the role of the multinational corporation in world business.**

   An international firm is one that sells in markets beyond its own borders. A multinational corporation operates production and marketing facilities on an international level in several countries.

Key Terms

exporting
importing
balance of trade
balance of payments
devaluation
revaluation
exchange rate
floating exchange rate
absolute advantage
Ricardo theory

comparative advantage
tariffs
globalization
import quotas
embargo
exchange control
friendship, commerce, and
   navigation treaties
International Monetary Fund
joint venture

free trade area
customs union
common market
multinational corporation
world product mandate
revenue tariffs
protective tariffs

General Agreement on Tariffs
 and Trade (GATT)
subsidiary P. 8 7
Investment Canada P. 668
dumping
countertrade

Discussion Questions and Exercises

1. Is it possible for a nation to have a favourable balance of trade and an unfavourable balance of payments? Explain.
2. Distinguish between the concepts of absolute advantage and comparative advantage.
3. Identify the five levels of involvement in international business and give an example of each.
4. Explain the difference between a revenue tariff and a protective tariff. What type is Canada most concerned with in the 1990s? Why?
5. Describe the three basic formats for multinational economic integration. Should the United States, Canada, and Mexico set up similar arrangements? Defend your position.
6. What is meant by countertrade? Why do you think this has become such an important part of international business?
7. Discuss the growing importance of international business.
8. What types of products does Canada export? What types does it import?
9. Prepare a report on the use of protective tariffs by Canada from its founding to the present.
10. Many people believe that we should limit imports of automobiles and other products which compete with those we produce here in Canada in order to protect the jobs of Canadian workers and restore domestic manufacturers to profitability. On the other hand, limiting imports could increase consumer costs substantially. Whom should we protect—Canadian workers or Canadian consumers?

Case 21-1

Dicon Systems Ltd.

Dicon Systems Ltd. was founded in 1976 by partners Steve Chepa and John Mallory to produce and market smoke detectors. Sunbeam Corp. liked the prototype, based on a new design, and ordered 20,000 units (worth $390,000). This contract was a turning point for the fledgling company as it provided a steady cash flow. Other retailers, such as Sears Canada, also began to purchase Dicon's smoke detectors.

However, the owners believed that they should go after more than the Canadian market. At first their target was the US, and by 1978, 20 percent of sales were flowing south. Unfortunately, competition from 40 other manufacturers was so heated that the following year Dicon decided to abandon the US market. "Spending money to maintain a market share was not a good option for us," Chepa says.

It was a controversial decision as the company floundered for the next three years—1981 sales were only 40 percent of those in 1979, and the number of employees dropped to 80 from 240. Because of its international outlook, the company continued to look for export markets. They found a market in Sweden, traditionally first off the mark in Europe as a follower of North American trends. Their entrance into this market coincided with the Swedish insurance industry encouraging policyholders to install smoke detectors. From Sweden they engaged agents to represent them in Norway, Denmark, and Finland.

The company has been lucky in its chance encounters. For instance, its Swedish agent was acquired as a result of a meeting at a security show in London, which Dicon attended as part of an Ontario government promotion. Thanks to this agent's contacts, Dicon was able to secure the Swedish insurance industry's approval of its products. A Chicago show turned up the Norwegian agent, while those for Finland and Denmark were the result of personal recommendations.

The company also faced competition in Europe. However, Chepa says, "We found the same competitors, General Electric for instance, but at least we were both on foreign soil, so we were more equal."

Dicon's experience was less happy in Britain where the company failed to get official support from the insurance industry. The firm also felt that operating there was too expensive. However, they have not abandoned this market and are considering what to do next to penetrate it.

Source: Olivier Baube, "Business Caught Fire after Smoke Detector Hit World Markets," *The Financial Post*, March 9, 1985, p. 46.

Questions:
1. Evaluate this firm's approach to international business.
2. What should they do to break into the British market?
3. Recommend an approach which they might take in planning to enter the French and German markets.

Case 21-2

Schwartz Diabrasive International

Alexander Schwartz was enthusiastic about the new product development. In fact, he was so optimistic, he did not think that the Canadian market was large enough for it, and wanted to get into the international marketplace as soon as possible.

The product which seemed to have so much potential to Schwartz was his firm's new method for turning industrial diamonds and bullet-proof Kevlar into the 1990s answer to heavy-duty sandpaper.

Traditional products are softer and less durable silicon carbide abrasives (including conventional sandpaper). These are used by many industries for grinding or polishing glass, stone, ceramics, and metal. Diamonds are the ultimate abrasive. However, because they are difficult to incorporate with flexible materials, their use has been restricted to rigid tools such as drill bits, saw blades, and grinding wheels. Schwartz's attempts to develop durable backing that could withstand the stress generated by a diamond-based abrasive forced his two-year-old company into several major design and production overhauls in the past year.

However, Diabrasive seems to have the product working correctly now. Customers report productivity gains of 500 percent to 600 percent when Diabrasive's belts, discs, and pads (which last two to four times longer than conventional products) are substituted in their operations. They are pleased with the new product despite having to pay at least 20 times more for the Diabrasive product.

Because of its revolutionary nature, the company has already made significant sales overseas. Ninety percent of Diabrasive's $1.6 million revenues came from customers in Europe, the US, and Japan. However, Schwartz wants to move into the international market quickly and extensively in order to meet his growth plans. He and his managers feel that their small company will not have the technological lead long before the industry's dominant players, Minnesota Mining and Manufacturing Co. and Norton Co., enter the market with competing products.

By setting out to establish themselves internationally, Diabrasive's managers are betting the company can translate its current technological lead into maximum market share before the heavyweights catch up. They feel that the more entrenched their product becomes, the easier it will be to hold their ground.

For a lot of young companies, an international sales base might seem like too much to shoot for all at once. But Tony Krystofik, Diabrasive's vice-president of international operations, thinks that this will make them harder to dislodge.

The company plans to team up with abrasive and diamond-tool distributors and manufacturers that might wish to add Diabrasive's products to their portfolios in other countries. Once that is done, the Montreal company plans to concentrate on manufacturing what is essentially a raw material. Once these other firms begin to build the Diabrasive material into their products, the company feels that the base will have been established, and that "we can just sort of stand back and watch it happen," says Krystofik.

Source: Brian Banks, "When Diamonds Aren't Forever," *Canadian Business*, June 1988, pp. 19–20.

Questions:
1. Do you think that it is too soon for this young company to be counting so heavily on going international?
2. Evaluate their strategy of having others produce the various abrasive products, and sticking to production of the basic abrasive.
3. Suggest precise steps as to how they might accomplish this.
4. What other strategies might they have followed to get the product distributed internationally?

Chapter 22

Business and the Legal System

Learning Goals

The more you allow the courts to clarify things the worse you make them!
—*Henri Bourassa in H. of C., 1935; Method of Amending the BNA Act 10.*

I never knew there was so much law in the world as I find in Canada.
—*John Anderson, fugitive slave from Missouri, on being discharged from a murder charge, by Court of Common Pleas of Upper Canada, Feb. 18, 1861.*

1. To explain the meaning of law and the nature of business law
2. To differentiate between the various types of law
3. To outline the current status of bankruptcy law
4. To discuss negotiable instruments
5. To differentiate between patents, trademarks, and copyrights
6. To describe how competition is regulated in Canada

Profile

Garfield Emerson—*Hired Gun*

Garfield Emerson is top gun among Canada's elite posse of securities lawyers. His specialty: mergers and acquisitions. From the courtroom to the boardroom, he is considered by corporate Canada to be the best at the bar.

The roster of full-time securities practitioners is tiny, from 50 to 100 with half or more located in Toronto. Corporate lawyers used to take charge of a takeover or financial placement for their clients once it landed on the Street. But now securities law and public market approaches have multiplied, and when big money is at stake, corporate customers are inclined to retain an expert such as Emerson.

Emerson and his firm, Davies Ward and Beck of Toronto, are known to clasp the work ethic dearly. "He was on all kinds of committees and he was always prepared, always had his answers," recalls Henry Knowles, who was Ontario Securities Commission (OSC) chairman from 1980 to 1983. "I used to think he was working 24 hours a day."

When a series of mighty takeovers hit the market around the mid-80s, Emerson and his firm scored some coups, sharpened their skills and rode the wave. These days, he directs his energies into little else but mergers and acquisitions.

One client firmly in Emerson's pocket attracts particular envy among securities lawyers: the Reichmann brothers used Emerson for the legal work when Olympia & York Developments Ltd. acquired Gulf Canada Ltd. in 1985. Since then, he and his firm have been in on five major market actions for the Reichmanns, including Gulf's ill-fated move on Hiram Walker Resources Ltd.'s distillery arm.

In Emerson's business, however, today's client can be tomorrow's opponent. And vice versa. In 1981 he worked for First City Financial Corp. Ltd. in its bid against Genstar Corp. for control of Canada Permanent Mortagage Corp. Next time around, Genstar used him to ram home a hostile bid for Canada Trustco

Mortagage Co., with rival Manufacturers Life Insurance Co. selling out its holdings after Emerson shackled it with an injunction. Genstar rolled the two trusts together and, three years later, again tapped Emerson when Imasco Ltd. came calling with a chequebook. He helped to lever the offer to Genstar up to $58 a share. At that stage, he recalls, "We said, 'Hey, it's yours, give us our cash.' "

Source: Kim Lockhart, "Hired Guns," *Canadian Business*, January 1989, pp. 33–34.

law
The body of rules or conduct prescribed by controlling authority and having binding legal force.

Law is the body of rules or conduct prescribed by controlling authority and having binding legal force. In Canada, our complex body of law arises from our history as a French and a British colony, leading up to the creation of the confederation of Canada. Canada was created by the British North America Act (BNA Act), an act of the British parliament that came into effect on July 1, 1867. The BNA Act was patriated to Canada in 1982 as the Constitution Act. In 1984 the Canadian Charter of Rights and Freedoms became incorporated into the legal framework of this country.

The Constitution Act divides legislative powers between the federal and provincial governments. Some of the major powers given to the federal government relating to business law are the regulation of trade and commerce, the power of taxation, banking, currency, bills of exchange, bankruptcy, interest, patents and copyrights, as well as "general and residual authority in relation to all matters not coming within the classes of subjects assigned exclusively to the Legislatures of the Provinces."

The powers given to the provincial legislatures include all matters relating to property and civil rights in the province, direct taxation within the province in order to raise revenue for provincial purposes, local works and undertaking, and "generally all matters of merely local or private nature." In the area of business law, matters such as contract, torts, sale, leasing, partnership, property law, and security arrangements fall within provincial legislative jurisdiction.

Sources of Law

The broad body of legislative jurisdiction of the federal government and of all provinces except Quebec is based on the principles of English **common law**. The common law is the body of unwritten law based on court decisions of early England. However, while common law plays an important role in Canada's legal system, more emphasis is placed on **statutory laws**, those written and enacted by legislative bodies.

common law
The body of law arising out of judicial decisions related to the unwritten law of England.

statutory law
Written laws enacted by legislative bodies.

Civil Code (Code civil)
System of law used in the province of Quebec based on the system used in France.

In Quebec, the law falling within provincial jurisdiction is based on its **Civil Code**. This code stems from the same laws that form the *Code civil* of France. The Canadian Charter of Rights and Freedoms has affected provincial legislation since its incorporation in 1984. (See Focus 22-1.)

Courts are frequently called on to determine whether or not a particular statute is "constitutional"—that is, whether the enacting legislature has the authority to legislate on this matter in accordance with the Constitution Act. The interpretation of a particular statute can be the central issue in many court cases. Statutes must be worded in a precise, reasonable, and unambiguous manner so that they will be enforceable.

Business must operate within the framework of federal, provincial, and local legislation; thus, business law plays an important role in the operation of many enterprises. Executives are not expected to be lawyers, but they should be aware of the legal requirements that affect their management decision making.

Law changes as society changes. No system of law, written or unwritten, is permanent. Laws reflect the beliefs of the people they regulate, and both courts and legislatures are aware of this fact. Laws are constantly being added, repealed, or modified as the requirements of society and government dictate.

Focus 22-1

The Charter Meets Big Biz

In April 1987, the Supreme Court of Canada dropped a legal bomb on organized labour. The Court held that Ottawa's 1982 wage- and price-control policy, which froze collective agreements, did not violate freedom of association, a right enshrined in the Charter of Rights and Freedoms. Writing for the majority, Mr. Justice Gerald Le Dain said: "The modern rights to bargain collectively and to strike are not fundamental rights and freedoms." Both strikes and collective bargaining were still legal, but they were not protected by the Charter from legislated curbs. Says Allan Hutchinson, a professor at Osgoode Hall Law School in Toronto: "Labour, you could say in a nutshell, lost when it tried to use the Charter to protect itself from government legislation."

Now, the nation's highest court is preparing to render decisions that could have a similar impact on corporate Canada. Two pending decisions will likely determine whether commercial speech— advertising—is protected by the Charter from legislative regulation. The subject of the two judgements: Quebec's Bill 101, the French-only sign law, due to be ruled on this week, and the Irwin Toy case, concerning the Quebec law banning advertising aimed at children, for which no date has been set. Says Peter Russell, an expert in constitutional law at the University of Toronto: "This is the first time we will hear from the Supreme Court on commercial speech and the Constitution. These will be among the biggest decisions for business."

The rulings will throw the Court under the spotlight. At issue: the way the Court metes out Charter protection to business and labour interests. Some legal scholars, citing the earlier decisions affecting labour, contend that the Court has already shown an anti-labour bias. Most others say it's unfair to suggest a Court bias—that it's too soon to keep a scorecard. They say that observers should wait for rulings on business regulations before attempting to measure a Court bias. Says Russell: "Labour has been up before the Court ahead of business and has taken a drubbing under the Charter. Now it's very important to see how far the Charter is going to prevent government from regulating business."

Some experts say the rulings could leave the impression that the Court has been politicized. Russell believes it has, so far, remained impartial, but suggests politicization is inevitable. Before long, he says, one interest group will begin to believe it has been shortchanged by the Court and will fight for new judicial appointments to correct the bias. "Eventually," says Russell, "if the Court does lean in a clear direction, say on the Charter, there will be a large group in Canadian society who don't like the way it's leaning. And if that group captures power in Ottawa they will try to turn it around. It certainly happened in the United States." But Jacob Ziegel, a law professor at the University of Toronto, asserts that if rulings appear to favour business, for instance, it's probably the Charter that contains the bias. Says Ziegel: "It's not because the Court is biased in one direction or the other."

Osgoode's Hutchinson argues that politicization has already occurred. Many Court members, he says, have a conservative mentality that works to the benefit of business. "When you are laying things on the constitutional scales," he says, "business get on the scales and sometimes they'll be outweighed. The unions don't even get on the scales." Hutchinson cites two rulings that helped business but hurt labour. A 1984 decision on a combines case that involved a raid on a newspaper office effectively said that corporations were entitled to Charter protections in much the same way as individuals. The case, which involved Southam Inc., was beneficial to corporations, giving them the ability to encase themselves in the Charter's armour to fend off legislative arrows. And a 1986 ruling on secondary picketing by striking workers established that there is no constitutional guarantee of workers' right to picket private employers. Says Hutchinson: "Business gets all the rights—which is more than unions have—then they are told that nobody can challenge what they're doing."

So far, the Court has issued few major rulings on business issues. But the Bill-101 decision, while it will be watched mostly for its political fallout in Quebec, could have important implications for business nationally. The Court must decide whether the law banning English on signs in the province violates freedom-of-speech guarantees in the Charter. But it could also have a serious effect on corporate advertising. Says John Whyte, Dean of Law at Queen's University in Kingston, Ont.: "It's actually a case about the extent to which commercial speech is protected."

While the Bill-101 decision is not guaranteed to establish definitive bounds for commercial speech, the Irwin Toy case has a better chance. The Court must rule on whether to uphold a lower court's decision striking down a Quebec advertising regulation that attempted to ban advertisements directed at children under 13 years. Russell says that if the Court upholds the lower court, it will be extending the Charter protections on freedom of speech to commercial speech. Such a ruling, he believes, would indicate a bias in the Court. Says Russell: "If commercial speech is fully protected by the Constitution, it will mean the Court is more pro-business than pro-labour, because it will be saying business activities—advertising—enjoy Constitutional status and protection, but striking and collective bargaining by labour don't.'' The U. of T.'s Ziegel cautions that it is dangerous to read too much into Court decisions. Still, he says, ''I would regard the judgement as being an important signpost as to how far the Court is willing to push freedom of speech.''

The implications could be enormous. The ruling, if it goes against Quebec, would cast a shadow over restrictions on advertising by lawyers and dentists. It could even place in question the federal law approved earlier this year that curbs tobacco advertising and promotions. Says Russell: ''Both the Quebec sign case and Irwin Toy have this major issue at stake: is the right of business to advertise protected by the Charter so that government restrictions and regulations on advertising are going to be cut down by the courts?''

Source: Adam Corelli, ''The Charter Meets Big Biz,'' *Financial Times of Canada*, December 12, 1988, p. 13. Reprinted by permission.

The Nature of Business Law

business law
Those aspects of law that most directly and specifically influence and regulate management of various types of business activity.

In a broad sense all laws apply to business, because any business entity—however it is organized—is subject to the entire body of law in the same manner as citizens are. But in a narrower sense, **business law** consists of those aspects of law that most directly and specifically influence and regulate the management of various types of business activity.

The term business law includes all law that is of concern to business, although particular areas of legal emphasis vary widely from business to business and from industry to industry. Laws affecting small firms are different from those governing large corporations. The legal interests of the automobile industry differ from those of real estate developers.

Laws have different applications. Some, such as the Income Tax Act enacted by the federal government, have universal application. However, some federal statutes regulate only one industry, such as oil and gas or television communications. Still other statutes control only certain businesses or business activities. The Lord's Day Act, which regulates the extent to which business—particularly retailers—can operate on Sunday, is an example of this kind of narrow control. Provincial statutes, such as workers' compensation laws that govern payments to workers for injuries incurred on the job, regulate all business conduct within the province regardless of the size or nature of the enterprise. Municipal bylaws, backed up by provincial regulations (and often by federal incentive programmes) control decisions made by the construction industry on where and what to build.

Law is important to all aspects of business. No owner, manager, or employee can conduct any type of business activity without reference to some laws. All business decisions must take into account the legal consequences. Some decisions must involve legal planning and review in depth, while others need have only an implied or sub-conscious adherence to the law.

Business decision makers gain experience and expertise in applying legal standards to their decisions in much the same manner as they develop any other management skill—through constant use and refinement. When legality cannot be determined through the experience and judgment of the businessperson, other professionals—such as lawyers, government employees, and elected officials—must be consulted. Generally, the more complex the business objective, the more complex is the role of law. Focus 22-2 highlights the need for and advantages associated with having in-house lawyers.

Focus 22-2

Keeping Counsel

Over the past five years, in-house counsellors have become permanent fixtures in many large Canadian companies. These days, the corporate bar accounts for about 7 percent of Canada's roughly 40,000 lawyers. But most of these captive counsellors were put in place to control legal costs; only recently have top executives twigged to their greater benefit—the ability to provide day-to-day management of legal affairs that can anticipate problems and help legal-proof the firm.

"The greatest contribution that the in-house lawyer can make is to ensure that the company keeps out of trouble," says Patrick Burns, Confederation Life's CEO. "For too many years, the legal department sat behind its glass door and was confronted *after* a problem emerged. They should be part of the whole management team—offering a service, like personnel or the computer—rather than being seen as the court of last resort."

That's exactly how it works at Confederation Life where vice-president Mark Edwards manages a staff of 15 lawyers. In addition to helping out on potential fraud cases, they counsel personnel managers on ways to avoid wrongful dismissal suits, and they advise the investment division on regulations governing mortgages and other types of investments.

According to Edwards, the real beauty of Confederation Life's system is that it breeds effective informal contacts. "It may be down in the lunchroom, where a manager might casually say to the lawyer, 'Could I take a few moments to talk to you?'" he says.

This kind of preventive teamwork is becoming more common. At Steinberg Inc. of Montreal, for example, preventive law techniques are focused on advertising and marketing regulations, says Marcelin Laurin, the company's vice-president, general counsel and corporate secretary. Another major Montreal firm, Dominion Textile Inc., uses its staff of four lawyers to negotiate contracts with suppliers. Such preventive law tactics can be applied to problems that afflict all businesses.

At Confederation Life, where the number of potentially troublesome legal concerns has jumped to about 500 from 200 a year in the early 1970s, Edwards says in-house counsel is saving the company more than $1 million a year, mainly by reducing the billing by outside law firms. "It's the difference between the cost of inside counsel and the cost of retaining a good outside counsel who charges anywhere from $100 to $300 an hour," he says. The cost of in-house service ranges anywhere from one-fifth to one-half the rate charged by outside counsel.

That's the kind of economy that pleases upper management. But just when a company should add lawyers to its staff depends on the corporate cost structure. According to Derek Hayes, senior vice-president and general counsel at the Canadian Imperial Bank of Commerce (CIBC), the magic moment is when annual legal fees surpass $200,000. "Below that," he says, "it's not really cost-effective unless you are in a highly regulated industry." Confederation Life's Edwards provides a simpler rule of thumb: "The legal problems must occur regularly to justify bringing the expertise in-house."

Source: Liss Jeffrey," Keeping Counsel," *Canadian Business*, January 1987, pp. 68 and 70.

The Court System

judiciary
The branch of government charged with deciding disputes among parties through the application of laws.

The **judiciary**, or court system, is that branch of government charged with deciding disputes among parties through the application of laws. The judiciary is comprised of several types and levels of courts, each with specific jurisdiction. Administrative agencies often have the authority to render decisions without recourse to a court. Their decisions, however, usually can be appealed to a court.

Provincial Courts

Within each province there are several levels of courts. Although the titles of these courts may differ from province to province, their functions are approximately the same. Unless a case is assigned by law to another court or to an administrative agency, general trial courts hear most cases, both criminal and civil. Courts of appeal within each province hear appeals from the general trial courts. An appeal is usually filed when the losing party believes that the case may have been wrongly decided. The appeal process allows a higher court to decide whether or not to review a case. The higher court can change or overturn a ruling.

The provincial judiciary systems also have a wide range of courts of specific jurisdiction. County or district courts have jurisdiction to hear smaller disputes and lesser criminal offenses. Probate courts settle the estates of deceased persons. Small claims courts allow persons to represent themselves in suits involving claims for damages. Family courts handle marital disputes and matters involving children.

Federal Courts

The federal courts decide civil suits brought against the Crown in federal affairs. Cases mainly involve revenues of the Crown, ships and navigation, and some matters arising out of federal legislation, such as copyright and patents. There is a separate tax review board for cases involving taxation.

Supreme Court of Canada

The Supreme Court is the highest court in Canada. It decides to hear appeals from provincial appellate courts and from the federal courts.

Administrative Agencies

administrative agencies
Government boards and commissions whose powers are restricted by statute.

Administrative agencies—also known as boards or commissions— exist at most levels of government. One example is a workers' compensation board. Agencies' powers and responsibilities are derived from statutes. Technically, they conduct hearings or inquiries rather than hold trials. But the parties are often represented by lawyers, evidence and testimony are included, and the agencies issue binding decisions based on the regulations involved.

In some cases, the decision of an administrative agency is final and cannot be appealed. The courts may review any decision that has violated the principles of justice.

Examples of provincial administrative agencies are public utility commissions, rent review agencies, boards that govern the licensing of various trades and professions, securities commissions, and liquor boards. At the local level are zoning boards, planning commissions, and boards of appeal. Some major federal regulatory agencies are described in Table 22-1.

Most businesses have regular contact with federal, provincial, and local administrative agencies, even though they have almost no contact with the court system.

Table 22-1
Canadian Federal Regulatory Agencies

Anti-Dumping Tribunal (1968) Rules on whether a foreign country is selling its goods in Canada at prices well below production costs. Anti-dumping laws allow the government to impose duties on these imports to balance the price between the foreign and domestic goods.

Atomic Energy Control Board (1946) Regulates the nuclear industry in both commercial/domestic and military applications, and markets the Canadian Candu reactor. As concern over nuclear industry increases so will the importance of this board.

Canadian Radio-television and Telecommunications Commission (1976) Licenses all radio and television stations (including cable and pay TV). Charged with the responsibility of developing and maintaining a bilingual Canadian broadcast system in all electronic media, the CRTC regulates Canadian content, as well as setting the rates that can be charged by cable companies, telephone, and telegraph operations. The CRTC also monitors broadcasting in Inuktitut in the Arctic.

Canadian Transport Commission (1970) Regulates and controls the transportation system in Canada. Striving for efficiency in operations and adequate service for all parts of the country, the CTC monitors motor, air, and water transport, railways, and non-oil-and-gas pipeline transportation.

Energy Supplies Allocation Board (1974) Established after the Arab oil embargo of 1973, this board is responsible for the establishment and administration of resource allocation programmes during times of scarcity and emergency. This control board ensures, for example, that hospitals will have enough oil, and ambulances enough gasoline to continue functioning during any crisis.

Investment Canada (1985) Encourages investment in Canada and reviews takeovers and the establishment of new businesses in Canada by foreign controlled corporations, governments, or individuals.

National Energy Board (1959) Mandated to regulate the oil, gas, and electric utilities industries in Canada for the public interest, and to advise the government on the development and use of energy resources. The NEB authorizes oil and gas exploration operations, distribution, and exports and sets domestic and export prices.

National Harbours Board (1936) Finances and operates major ports in Canada (15 ports handling 25 percent of international trade). New legislation (effective January 1, 1983) increased the local autonomy of NHB ports, with the aim of making them more efficient and accessible to the public.

Important Aspects of Business Law

Most laws affect business in some manner, whether directly or indirectly. But certain laws are so vital to business enterprises that every businessperson should understand their roles in the legal framework.

contract law
The legal foundation on which normal business dealings are constructed.

contract
An agreement between two or more parties regarding a specified act or thing that the law will enforce.

Contract Law

Contract law is important because it affects most aspects of any business operation. It is the legal foundation on which normal business dealings are constructed.

A **contract** is an agreement that the law will enforce.[1] The key element is that there must be an agreement between the parties as to the act or thing specified. In order for such an agreement, or contract,

consideration
The value or benefit that one party provides to those with whom a contract is made.

to be valid and enforceable through the courts, **consideration**—the value or benefit that a party provides to the others with whom the contract exists—must be furnished by each party to the contract. Legal consideration for a contract exists when, for example, A agrees to work for B and B agrees to pay A a certain salary. The contract is just as valid if B actually pays A at the time A agrees to work. Similarly, valid consideration exists even if no promises are exchanged but A works for B and B pays A for the work.

In addition to consideration, an enforceable contract must involve a legal and serious agreement. An agreement between two competitors to fix the prices for their products is not enforceable as a contract, because the subject matter is illegal and because the performance of the agreement will violate the law. Agreements made in a joking manner or relating to purely social matters are not enforceable as legal contracts.

capacity
The legal ability of a party to enter into contracts.

The last element of a legally enforceable contract is the capacity of each party to make the agreement. **Capacity** is the legal ability of a party to enter into agreements. The law does not permit certain persons, such as those under age, or judged to be insane, to enter into legally enforceable contracts.

Contracts are used in almost all types of business activities. Generally, they are created and executed by firms with little notice or concern on the part of the contracting parties. Examples of valid contracts are purchase agreements with suppliers, labour contracts, group insurance policies for employees, franchise agreements, and sales contracts. Many contracts are on standard forms.

The Law of Sale

law of sale
An offspring of contract law that involves the sale of goods or products for money or on credit.

The law of sale is an offspring of contract law. A sales agreement, or sales transaction, is a special kind of contract that is entered into millions of times each day throughout the economic system. The **law of sale** concerns the sale of goods or products for money or on credit. As an economic transaction, sales can be of services or real estate as well as goods, but the law of sale is concerned only with the transfer of tangible personal property. The law involved with intangible personal property and real estate will be examined later in the chapter.

Executives must be concerned not only with the body of general contract law but also with the specifics of law of sale.

The law of sale falls within provincial jurisdiction. The common law provinces (all provinces except Quebec) have each enacted a substantially similar sale of goods act, based on the long-standing customs of merchants as expressed in English common law. The parties must intend to create a valid, binding contract. A contract for the sale of goods is concluded by the express or implied acceptance by one party of an express or implied offer made to him or her by the other party. A sales contract may be concluded verbally (except in British Columbia). However, in most provinces, the statute of frauds laws require that a contract for the sale of goods over a certain dollar amount ($40 in Ontario, New Brunswick, and Nova Scotia) must be in writing if it is to be enforceable by law. Even then, any ambiguities in the contract, or the absence of certain terms (such as a date) will not keep a sales contract from being enforceable. Should either party take the matter to court, the court will look to past dealings, commercial customs and other standards of reasonableness in evaluating the existence of a legal contract.

These variables will also be considered by a court when either the buyer or the seller seeks to enforce his or her rights against the other party where the sales contract has not been performed or has been only partially performed or where performance has been defective or unsatisfactory. A sale of goods act defines the rights of the parties to have the contract specifically performed, to have it terminated, and to reclaim the goods or have a lien placed against them. In case of breach of a contract, the parties can settle out of court or the injured party can sue the other. The remedy in lawsuits consists of an order for specific performance (to do as the contract stated) or monetary damages awarded to the injured party.

Other provisions of the sale of goods act of each province govern the rights of acceptance, rejection, and inspection of the goods by the buyer; the rights of the parties during manufacture, shipment, delivery, and the passing of title to goods; the legal significance of sales documents such as bills of lading; and the placing of the risk of loss in the event of destruction or damage to the goods during manufacture, shipment, or delivery.

The laws regarding sale in the province of Quebec are contained in its Civil Code. The seller and the purchaser need only consent in order to conclude a sale; neither delivery nor a written contract are necessary to perfect a sales agreement. However, where the object of the sale is valued at more than $500, proof of the sale must be made in writing unless the buyer has already received at least part of the goods. In most other aspects, sale of goods for Quebec contracts is similar to that of the common law provinces.

Warranties. A warranty is a statement that certain facts are true. In commerce a warranty is a seller's statement that the merchandise sold has a specific fitness and performance. There are two basic types of warranties. **Express warranties** are specific representations made by the seller regarding the goods. **Implied warranties** are those legally imposed on the seller. Generally, unless implied warranties are disclaimed by the seller in writing, they are automatically effective. Implied warranties are covered by each provincial sale of goods act. Implied warranties can be negated by a disclaimer clause, but this must appear right on the manufactured good.

express warranties
Warranties with specific representations made by the seller regarding the goods.

implied warranties
Warranties legally imposed on the seller and, generally, automatically effective unless disclaimed by the seller in writing.

The Law of Property

property
Something for which someone has the unrestricted right of possession.

tangible personal property
Physical property, such as goods and products.

intangible personal property
Property most often represented by an instrument in writing.

real property
Land and whatever is permanently attached to that land.

Property describes something for which someone has unrestricted right of possession. Property can be divided into two main categories: personal and real. Personal property can be tangible or intangible.

Tangible personal property consists of physical goods and products. Every business is concerned with this kind of property, which includes equipment, supplies, and delivery vehicles.

Intangible personal property is property that is most often represented by a document or other instrument in writing, although it may be as vague and remote as a bookkeeping or computer entry. Certain intangible personal properties such as personal cheques and money orders are well known. Others, although less widespread or well known, are important to the businesses or individuals who own and utilize them. Examples are shares, bonds, treasury bills, letters of credit, and warehouse receipts. Even ideas can be intangible personal property.

Real property, or real estate, refers to land and whatever is permanently attached to that land, such as buildings and structures. All firms have some concern with real estate law, because of the need to own or occupy the space or building where business is conducted. The real estate needs of national retail chains or major manufacturing companies are considerable. Some businesses are created to serve the real estate needs of others. Real estate developers, builders, contractors, brokers, mortgage companies, and architects are all concerned with various aspects of real property law.

The law of property falls within the exclusive legislative jurisdiction of each province. In the common law provinces, the law of property is based on the common law of England modified and formalized by Canadian statutes. In Quebec, the laws regarding property are found in its Civil Code.

The Law of Agency

agency
A legal relationship between two parties, principal and agent, who agree that one will act as a representative of the other.

principal
The person who, wishing to accomplish something, hires an agent to act on his or her behalf.

agent
The person employed to act on the principal's behalf.

Agency describes a legal relationship in which two parties, the principal and the agent, "agree that one will act as a representative of the other. The **principal** is the person who wishes to accomplish something, and the **agent** is the one employed to act on the principal's behalf to achieve it."[2]

While the agency relationship can be as simple as one family member acting on behalf of another, the legal concept is most closely associated with business relationships. This is true because all types of firms conduct business affairs through a variety of agents—among them partners, directors, corporate officers, and sales personnel.

The law of agency is based on common law principles and case decisions. In Quebec, the law of agency is contained in the Civil Code.

Relatively little agency law has been enacted into statute. The law of agency is important because the principal is generally bound by the actions of the agent.

The legal basis for holding the principal liable for acts of the agent is the Latin maxim of *respondeat superior* ("let the master answer"). In cases involving agency law, the courts must decide the rights and obligations of the various parties. Generally, the principal is held liable where an agency relationship existed and the agent had some general authority to do the wrongful act. The agent in such cases is liable to the principal for any damages caused to that person. Principals have no responsibility for the acts of persons who are not their agents.

The Law of Torts

tort
A civil wrong inflicted on other persons or their property.

Torts, the French word for "wrongs," has come to have a more specific meaning in law. It refers to civil wrongs inflicted on other persons or their property.[3] In Quebec such wrongs are referred to as delicts and are dealt with in its Civil Code. The law of torts is closely related to the law of agency because the business entity, or principal, can be held liable for the torts committed by its agents in the course of business dealings. Tort law differs from both criminal and contract law. While criminal law is concerned with crimes against state or society, tort law deals with compensating injured persons who are the victims of noncriminal wrongs. For example, the Elliot-Hamil Funeral Home of Abilene, Texas, filed a $311,000 lawsuit against Southwestern Bell, when the telephone company listed the mortuary under "Frozen Foods—Wholesale" in the *Yellow Pages*, causing a rash of crank calls.

intentional torts
Civil wrongs purposely inflicted on other persons or their property, such as assault, embezzlement, slander, or libel.

Many torts, such as assault, are intentional actions carried out by the wrongdoer (although sometimes the person argues that while the actions were intentional the damages were not). Examples of **intentional torts** are embezzlement, trespass, slander, libel, and fraud. Business can become involved in such cases through the actions of both owners and employees. The supermarket clerk who handles a suspected shoplifter and holds the suspect in the manager's office for questioning may have committed a tort if the conduct is excessive or otherwise unjustified. Under agency law, the store owner can be held liable for any damage or injury caused to the suspect.

negligence
A tort based on careless rather than intentional behaviour that causes injury to another person.

The other major group of torts is **negligence**. This type of tort is based on careless (rather than intentional) behaviour that causes injury to another person. Under agency law, businesses are held liable for the negligence of their employees or agents. The delivery truck driver who kills a pedestrian while delivering goods creates tort liability for the employer if the accident is a result of negligence. Similarly, an airline is liable if a plane crashes because of faulty maintenance, pilot error, or other negligence.

products liability
An area of tort law developed by both statutory and case law to hold business liable for negligence in the design, manufacture, sale, and use of products.

An area of tort law known as **products liability** has been developed by both statutory and case law to hold business liable for negligence in the design, manufacture, sale, and use of products. Thus a court might award damages to a man who had drunk over half a soft drink before discovering that the bottle also contained a dead rat.

Principles of negligence in Quebec have extended the theory of tort or delict to cover injuries by products regardless of whether the manufacturer is proven negligent. Under this legal concept, known as **strict products liability**, the injured party need only show that the product was defective, that the defect was the immediate cause of injury, and that the defect caused the product to be unreasonably dangerous.

strict products liability
A legal concept that extends the tort theory to cover injuries caused by products regardless of whether the manufacturer is proven negligent.

Careful supervision of employees and careful conduct by employees in their duties are the best means of avoiding most tort liability. However, with damages in this area running higher and higher, most firms have turned to liability insurance for protection.

Bankruptcy Law

bankruptcy
The condition that exists when the debts of someone or of a business cannot be paid.

Bankruptcy is the condition that exists when a person or a business cannot pay debts as they are or become due. Bankruptcy law in Canada falls within federal jurisdiction and is contained in the Bankruptcy Act. This act provides for the distribution of the assets of a bankrupt person or business proportionately among the creditors.

An insolvent debtor may voluntarily go bankrupt by way of an assignment into bankruptcy, or may be forced into it by a receiving order made by the court following a petition by a creditor who is owed at least $1000. A receiving order names a trustee to place a business in receivership. The trustee can sell the business and pay off the creditors.

An insolvent debtor may also make a proposal to its creditors, agreeing to pay them back a certain percentage of the money owing them, for example, 50 cents on the dollar, and specifying the time in which it will be paid. If the creditors refuse to accept the proposal, the debtor becomes retroactively bankrupt to the date of the filing of the proposal.

In all cases of bankruptcy, the property of the bankrupt is administered by a trustee. Certain personal property of the bankrupt is exempt and is not subject to the claims of the creditors, such as some furniture and clothing and some tools necessary for carrying on his or her trade.

The trustee oversees the distribution of the assets of the bankrupt to the creditors. The secured creditors such as mortgage holders will be paid off by realization of their security on the property which the bankrupt had given the creditor in guarantee of payment of the debt.

Certain creditors, known as preferred creditors, are entitled to be paid off first—such as the trustee (for his or her fees), the government (for unpaid taxes), and a landlord, if there is one. The ordinary creditors rank last and, in most cases, there is little left of the bankrupt estate to satisfy their claims. Many small companies have been pushed to bankruptcy themselves when a major customer declared bankruptcy and left them with large uncollectible accounts receivable.

Negotiable Instruments

negotiable instruments
Forms of commercial paper that are transferable among individuals and businesses.

Negotiable instruments are forms of commercial paper that are transferable among individuals and businesses. The most commonplace example of a negotiable instrument is a cheque; drafts, certificates of deposit, and notes are also sometimes considered negotiable instruments.

The Bills of Exchange Act specifies that a negotiable instrument must be written and must:

1. Be signed by the maker or drawer.
2. Contain an unconditional promise or order to pay a certain sum in money.
3. Be payable on demand or at a definite time.
4. Be payable to order or to bearer.

Cheques and other bills of exchange payable to order are transferred when the payee signs the back of the instrument, a procedure known as **endorsement.** The three basic kinds of endorsement are:

endorsement
The procedure that renders commercial paper transferable when the payee signs the back of the instrument.

1. Blank endorsement, which consists only of the name of the payee. All that is required to make a blank endorsement is to sign the instrument. This makes it payable to the bearer. A blank endorsement should not be used if the instrument is to be mailed.
2. Special endorsement, which specifies the person to whom the instrument is payable. With this kind of endorsement, only the person whose name appears after "Pay to the order of..." can further the negotiability of the instrument.
3. Qualified endorsement, which contains wording that the endorser is not guaranteeing payment of the instrument. The qualified endorsement of "without recourse, (signed)...." will limit the endorsee's liability in the event the instrument is not backed by sufficient funds.
4. Restrictive endorsement, which limits the negotiability of the instrument. One of the most common restrictive endorsements is "For deposit only." This restriction is of great value if an instrument is lost or stolen, because it means that the instrument, usually a cheque, can only be deposited to the indicated account; it cannot be cashed.

Patents, Trademarks, and Copyrights

Patents, trademarks, and copyrights come under personal property law, and lie within exclusive federal jurisdiction. They are important legal protection for key business assets that should be carefully guarded by their owners.

According to the Patent Act, a **patent** allows an inventor exclusive rights to his or her invention for a period of 17 years, provided a patent has been granted by the Patent Office. The owner of the patent then has the exclusive right to make, construct, and use the patented invention as well as to license the use of the patent to others for a fee.

A **copyright** permits an artist and artist's heirs to have exclusive rights to literary, musical, and artistic works. The copyright prevents others from copying or reproducing such works. The current Copyright Act provides the term of copyright for a particular work to be the artist's lifetime plus 50 years. The Act is undergoing revision to deal with technical advancement in photocopying.

A **trademark** is defined by the Trademark Act as a registered mark that is used to distinguish wares or services manufactured or sold by a person or business from those manufactured or sold by others. A trademark may be a word, logo, symbol, or other designation used by a business to identify its product. A trademark may be registered for a period of 15 years, subject to renewal every 15 years indefinitely. However, if a trademark becomes the generic term for a class of products, then the registrant loses this important protection. Aspirin, nylon, kerosene, linoleum, shredded wheat, and milk of magnesia were once the exclusive properties of their manufacturers, but they became generic terms, and now anyone can use them.

Trademarks can become very valuable assets. Fabergé reportedly paid $200,000 to a California cosmetic firm in order to be able to use the trademark Macho for a new men's cologne.[4]

patent
Guarantees to inventors of exclusive rights to their inventions for 17 years, provided the inventions are accepted by the Patent Office.

copyright
The exclusive right of an artist to literary, musical or artistic works.

trademark
The words, logo, symbol, or other designation that distinguishes one manufacturer's goods from others.

Regulation of Competition

The legal framework influences and regulates business in many areas, including that of competition. Effective and ongoing competition is essential to our economic system. An overconcentration of economic power in a few hands could lead to monopolies in certain basic industries.

The federal Combines Investigation Act lists agreements and conspiracies that lessen competition; mergers and monopolies; price discrimination and price maintenance; misleading advertising; and other unfair selling practices as offenses punishable by fine, imprisonment, or both. The Act is administered by the Bureau of Competition Policy of Consumer and Corporate Affairs Canada.

Other practices may also reduce effective competition. The Restrictive Trade Practices Commission has authority to review certain trade practices such as refusal to deal, consignment selling, exclusive dealing, tied sales and market restrictions, and may order an offender to change its ways of doing business. Failure to obey such an order is an offense punishable by fine, imprisonment, or both.

regulated industries
Industries in which competition is either limited or eliminated altogether, and close government control substitutes for the market controls of free competition.

In **regulated industries,** competition is either limited or eliminated altogether, and close government control is substituted for the market controls of free competition. Examples of regulated industries are the public utilities and other industries that are closely tied to the "public interest." In these industries, competition is restricted or eliminated because it tends to become wasteful or excessive. In Canada, only one telephone company is permitted to serve a given geographical area or market. The large capital investment required to construct a pipeline or electric transmission line over great distances, or to build and operate a nuclear power plant makes this type of regulation economically reasonable. But the lack of competition can sometimes cause deterioration in services and performance. The administrative agencies responsible for regulating these industries are supposed to prevent such deterioration. Focus 22-3 provides an example of what is covered under the Act.

Focus 22-3

Federal Watchdog Warns Imperial

Imperial Oil Ltd. will proceed at its peril if it closes its $5 billion purchase of Texaco Canada Inc. before the federal government's Bureau of Competition Policy gives its blessing.

Consumer groups and opposition politicians are enraged by the transaction, which will reduce the number of major gasoline retailers in Canada from four to three. Imperial Petro-Canada, and Shell would be the three remaining dominant gasoline retailers. They hope the Competition Bureau will prove to be the reef on which the deal founders.

"Companies would be taking a chance were they to close a deal before the competition board has had the opportunity to conduct a full and thorough investigation," said Calvin Goodman, the bureau's director. "I will not hesitate to take whatever action is required to protect competition in the Canadian marketplace."

The Imperial-Texaco deal, announced early in 1989, was the third multibillion-dollar merger or acquisition to confront the Competition Bureau in just three days. A few days earlier, Molson Companies Ltd. and Elders IXL Ltd. announced a merger of their North American brewing operations. They were followed by PWA

Corp.'s agreement to buy control of Wardair Inc. from entrepreneur Max Ward.

The Competition Bureau has to be satisfied that there is no "substantial lessening" of competition before it approves a deal. If it is not satisfied, it can refer a transaction to the Competition Tribunal, which would hold public hearings, and has the power to overturn a deal. The tribunal is rarely used, however. The bureau usually tries to negotiate with the companies involved in a takeover to find ways in which anticompetitive concerns may be alleviated— perhaps through the sale of certain assets.

Imperial has made it clear it is willing to cooperate in such a process. The company says it has already given the bureau undertakings that it will "divest service stations and bulk terminals and other assets if necessary." Still, Imperial acknowledges that Goldman has "the unrestricted right to apply to the Tribunal to dissolve the merger in whole or in part." Goldman also has the power to try to block the deal even before it closes. If he is sufficiently worried by it, he can apply for an interim injunction, as he has done once before.

Source: David Hatter, "Federal Watchdog Warns Imperial," *The Financial Post*, January 23, 1989, p. 5.

Other Business Regulations

Since earliest times an important function of government has been the regulation of weights and measures. Citizens have always wanted to know that a merchant would give them the expected length of cloth, whether it was measured by the cubit, ell, or metre, or the usual quantity of vegetables, whether weighted by the mina, pound, or kilogram. Because weights and measures are so vital to the business dealings of Canadians both at home and abroad, their regulation is a responsibility of the Canadian government. Like most other nations, Canada uses the International System of Units (or SI for Système Internationale), commonly known as the **metric system.** The government of John A. Macdonald first permitted the use of the metric system in 1871, but it was not until a century later that Canada began to convert completely from the older imperial system of measurement.

metric system
The standard of weights and measures based on the decimal system.

In more recent times citizens have demanded that their governments become concerned with a wide variety of issues affecting such matters as health and safety. As a result, businesses that deal in products and services for the general public tend to be fairly heavily regulated. For example, businesses in Canada are required to comply with the following acts passed by the federal government and administered by the Department of Consumer and Corporate Affairs:

Hazardous Products Act
Textile Labelling Act
Consumer Packaging and
   Labelling Act
Weights and Measures Act
Canada Agricultural Products
   Standards Act

Precious Metal Marking Act
Food and Drug Act
Fish Inspection Act
Maple Products Industry Act
Canada Dairy Products Act
Motor Vehicle Safety Act

Controversial Issue

Sexual Harassment—Employers are Liable

Until recently, it was possible for an employer to defend a sexual harassment action by claiming that he could not be held responsible for harassment committed by an employee. This was so because sexual harassment was generally deemed to involve interaction between two individuals as opposed to between an employer and an individual.

Both the Supreme Court of Canada and the Quebec Superior Court have recently had a chance to render decisions on the question of an employer's responsibility for acts of sexual harassment committed by an employee.

On July 29, 1987, the Supreme Court of Canada rendered judgement in the case of Robichaud vs Canada (Treasury Board). Ms. Robichaud was employed by the Department of National Defence as a cleaner in 1977. Shortly thereafter, she complained to the Canadian Human Rights Commission that she had been sexually harassed by her supervisor.

Treasury Board claimed that, as an employer, it was not responsible for the acts of its supervisor since harassment is not something an employee is hired to do.

Mr. Justice Gerald La Forest, writing for the Court, decided against the position put forward by the Treasury Board. He described section 7 of the Canadian Human Rights Act as being almost constitutional in nature—incorporating within it certain basic goals of society, including the removal of discrimination. Given

this objective, the legislation should be interpreted in a broad fashion and an employer should be responsible for the acts of its employees.

In the case of Foisy vs Bell Canada (1984), Madam Justice Mailhot was called upon to interpret section 16 of the Quebec Charter of Human Rights. Ms. Foisy had been dismissed by her supervisor at Bell following her refusal to accede to his sexual advances, and this notwithstanding a favourable evaluation she had received.

Madam Justice Mailhot decided that section 16, although it does not specifically refer to sexual harassment, was broad enough to encompass sexual harassment. This is consistent with the reasoning of the Supreme Court. It was held that Bell Canada was responsible for the moral damages which Ms. Foisy had suffered due to psychological trauma.

Given this jurisprudence, the problem of sexual harassment of an employee by a supervisor can no longer be swept under the carpet by an employer on the basis that it is a personal problem between two employees.

Quite the contrary, it is a problem which affects the employer and for which the employer may be held responsible.

Source: Thomas Davis, "Employers Liable for Sexual Harassment," *This Week in Business*, March 12, 1988, p. 14.

Summary of Learning Goals

1. **Explain the meaning of law and the nature of business law.**

   Law can be defined as the body of rules or conduct prescribed by controlling authority and having binding legal force. Business law consists of those aspects of law that most directly and specifically influence and regulate the management of various types of business activity. It is administered through a series of courts and administrative agencies that exist at all levels of government.

2. **Differentiate between various types of law.**

   Contract law is the legal foundation on which normal business dealings are constructed. The elements of enforceable contracts are acceptance, consideration, legality and seriousness of the agreement, consent, and the parties' capacity to make the agreement.

   Sales law is an offspring of contract law. It involves the sale of goods or products for money or on credit. The law of sale falls within provincial jurisdiction. It also sets forth the law of warranty. The two basic types of warranties are express and implied.

   Property law is a key feature of the legal system. Property can be divided into two main categories: personal property (both tangible and intangible) and real property. Law of property falls within the exclusive legislative jurisdiction of each province.

   Agency law is based primarily on common law principles. An agency is a relationship in which two parties, the principal and the agent, agree that one will act as a representative of the other. The principal in any agency relationship is responsible for the actions of the agent.

   The law of torts deals with compensating injured persons who are the victims of noncriminal wrongs. It is closely related to the law of agency. The three major areas of this area of law are intentional torts, negligence, and products liability.

3. **Outline the current status of bankruptcy law.**

   Bankruptcy law provides for an orderly handling of bankruptcies by the federal court system. Two types of bankruptcies are recognized—voluntary and involuntary.

4. **Discuss negotiable instruments.**

   Negotiable instruments are forms of commercial paper that are transferable between individuals and businesses. The Bills of Exchange Act gives specifications for negotiable instruments and describes the three basic kinds of endorsement for them: blank, qualified, and restrictive.

5. **Differentiate between patents, trademarks, and copyrights.**

   Patents guarantee inventors exclusive rights to their inventions for a period of 17 years. Trademarks are registered words, symbols, or other designations used to identify products. When registered they give their owner protection for an unlimited time period.

Copyrights give exclusive rights to artistic works to the artist or the artist's heirs during the artist's lifetime plus 50 years.

6. **Describe how competition is regulated in Canada**.

In Canada, government regulation of competition is necessary by either limiting or eliminating it in order to regulate the country's economy. This regulation takes two broad forms—regulation of industry, and enactment of statutes concerning competition. Current legislation includes the Combines Investigation Act. The Restrictive Trade Practices Commission is the agency responsible for regulation of competition. Many other statutes have been drafted to regulate business further. Other statutes cover a number of business areas, and an interested businessperson will soon become familiar with many of them. However, it is almost impossible to find out about all the rules and regulations created by the various levels of government; when in doubt, one should consult a lawyer.

Key Terms

law
common law
statutory law
Civil Code
business law
judiciary
administrative agencies
contract law
contract
consideration
capacity
law of sale
express warranties
implied warranties
property
tangible personal property
intangible personal property

real property
agency
principal
agent
tort
intentional torts
negligence
products liability
strict products liability
bankruptcy
negotiable instruments
endorsement
patent
copyright
trademark
regulated industries
metric system

Discussion Questions and Exercises

1. Trace how law has evolved in Canada.
2. Describe the organization of the Canadian Court System.
3. A representative of organized crime has just issued a contract on a rival gangster. The hit man was offered $10,000 for completion

of the contract. Under a strict legal interpretation, is this a valid contract. Why or why not?

4. A local delivery firm's driver became intoxicated over a long lunch with a friend at a local pub. The driver then struck another truck as he left the pub's parking lot. Is the delivery firm responsible for the actions of its driver? Discuss the legal concepts involved here.

5. A Saskatchewan jury awarded over $200,000 in damages to two men who were severely injured when an industrial laundry dryer that they were using blew up. A 128-pound hot-air balloon had been put in the dryer, and the manufacturer claimed that the dryer was not built to handle this type of load. What legal concepts would be involved in this case?

6. An air conditioning repair firm has refused to accept a third party cheque endorsed by Fred Bates. The cheque was from Sandra McKinney in the correct amount and payable to Bates. He endorsed it to the repair firm with the notation "without recourse." Why did the firm refuse the cheque?

7. Discuss the law of sale.

8. Explain the difference between the two types of personal property. Give examples from business.

9. What is meant by the law of agency?

10. How is competition regulated in Canada?

Case 22-1

Sleeping Pill Linked to Memory Loss

The most widely prescribed drug in Canada has been associated with amnesia in hundreds of patients and Quebec doctors have been warned to "think twice" before prescribing it.

A committee of Quebec physicians and pharmacists says hundreds of reports associated the sleeping pill Halcion with amnesia. Canadian doctors wrote out about 4 million prescriptions last year for the pill, marketed by Toronto-based Upjohn Co. of Canada.

"We want doctors to think twice about to whom they prescribe Halcion and the dosage and duration of use they select," says Dr. Pierre Biron, a Université de Montréal pharmacology professor. "Amnesia can very well occur in the first dose."

Biron coordinates th five-member steering committee of Le Programme conjoint de pharmacovigilance, formed in 1986 to track new and unexpected drug side-effects. It is composed of doctors' and pharmacists' associations and the university.

Last summer, the company took its 0.5-mg tablet off the market, retaining the weaker tablet strengths of 0.25 mg and 0.125 mg. The move came soon after countries such as West Germany, Italy, and

France suspended the 0.5-mg dosage when it came to be increasingly associated with reports of side-effects such as confusion and hallucinations.

About 300 reports have been sent to the federal Health Protection Branch in Ottawa, including about one dozen cases of amnesia associated with the 0.5-mg and 0.25-mg strength tablets.

Upjohn official Paul Fitzhenry said his company can't control how doctors prescribe the drug and how patients use it. He said his company acted responsibly in withdrawing the strongest tablet strength and "we're trying to inform doctors to begin with the lowest effective dosage."

Source: Nicholas Regush, "Popular Sleeping Pill Linked to Memory Loss," *The Gazette*, January 29, 1989, p. A-1.

Questions:
1. Under which act can the situation described above be located? Explain.
2. Had the company not acted responsibly, what legal recourse may users have to base their case on? What potential problems may arise? Discuss.

Case 22-2

The Asbestos Industry—Making Pits Safe a Major Concern

Making the mining pits safe is a key concern for the asbestos industry.

"The problem began during the Second World War," says Dimitry Poutiatine, vice-president for international sales in JM Asbestos Inc., "when asbestos was carelessly sprayed on warships to make them fireproof. Today, you can walk into an asbestos mine in a navy blue suit and you won't even have a dust particle on you when you leave."

Part of the solution has been automation, and the remainder was engineered by providing air-tight compartments in trucks and mills for workers.

"The health of all our employees is followed very carefully and the situation is well under control," notes Jean-Marc LeBlanc of LAB Chrysotile Inc. LAB is a management and marketing consortium of all asbestos producers in Quebec except JM. It was set up three years ago to revive the sagging asbestos market. About the same time, the federal and provincial governments funded the Asbestos Institute to study health issues and give asbestos a safer image.

Asbestosis is a form of lung cancer caused by breathing asbestos fibres. Most cases have been detected among miners and processing workers.

According to Claude Forget of the Asbestos Institute, the industry certainly learned its lesson well. "Asbestosis is on the way out. In another 20 years, it will be in the medical books as a curiosity."

Leblanc admits, however, that asbestos sales have disintegrated in North America due to the difficulty in obtaining product liability insurance, suggesting that the industry may be convinced about safety but many others are not.

Source: Hyman Glustein, "Asbestos Industry on the Rebound," *This Week in Business*, January 14, 1989, p. 11.

Questions:
1. Under which act can the situation described above be located? Explain.
2. Despite all their efforts to safeguard employee health and safety, why do companies in the asbestos industry face continuing problems getting insurance? Discuss.
3. How does industry history regarding safety reflect societal changes? Explain.

Chapter 23

The Future of Canadian Business

Learning Goals

1. To describe the recent major changes in the way Canadians live and work and why it is difficult to predict future changes
2. To analyze the accelerating pace of change
3. To explain the role of high technology in Canada's future and to identify the problems associated with high technology

I believe the choice is still open to us, that we can still decide, you and I and our fellow citizens, whether we want to return to the path that made this the great land of opportunity for millions of people or whether instead we want to continue down the road toward a destruction of both liberty and prosperity.
—*Milton Friedman*

The future is beyond knowing, but the present is beyond belief.
—*Wm. Irwin Thompson*, At the Edge of History, 1971, p. 163

Profile

People and Technology are Key for the Future—*Michael Cornelissen*

The recession of the early eighties had a profound influence on organizations. Companies whose profits were ravaged by high interest rates and the people whose careers were affected learned some sobering lessons. Another adjustment has been to the explosion in microtechnology: new technology is everywhere; computer literacy is expanding rapidly; and the ability to use technology appropriately is increasingly critical to meeting business objectives.

Yet another major factor is the abundance of employable people as the Baby Boomers move through Canadian organizations; many of them are well-educated and ambitious. This excess of qualified individuals makes the mid-eighties a buyer's market. Organizations can be increasingly selective in promoting and hiring, thus creating strong internal pressures for performance.

Faced with the changing climate of human resources. Royal Trust president and chief executive Michael Cornelissen has drawn some important conclusions about the future:

- The focus on productivity will increase. Organizations will be more skillful in managing their human resources.
- The demand for effective performance from managers will intensify. Managers will have to deliver results, or be replaced.
- Concerns over organizational culture and performance will become more focused. Multi-disciplinary management teams will introduce change more quickly, more frequently and with much more determination.

At Royal Trust, dramatic shifts towards technological sophistication have traced trends in the mid-eighties. No longer is technology relegated to the back room or to teams of specialists; rather, the trend is toward management at all levels making joint decisions on important technological issues. Products could not be implemented, policies could not be changed, and customer requirements could not be met without consideration of the capabilities and limitations of the Information Systems function. In this business, technology is a strategic tool, without which Royal Trust cannot be master of its own destiny. Without technology, Royal Trust cannot meet its customers' changing requirements.

Source: Michael Cornelissen, "Management Trends: People and Technology are Key," *Business Quarterly,* Spring 1985, pp. 84, 85, 87.

Business must be able to predict the future extent and direction of economic, societal, and technological change if it is to successfully meet the industrial challenges of the eighties and nineties. But it is difficult to predict change since it seems to be occurring at an escalating pace.

Business cannot assume that what happened yesterday or today will be true tomorrow. The pact of change has clearly quickened. For example, in 1970 Alvin Toffler's *Future Shock* pointed out that human-kind's last 50,000 years of existence can be divided into 800 "life-times" of about 62 years each. The first 650 of these lifetimes were spent in caves. Writing has existed for only the past 70 lifetimes. Most of the products used today have been developed within the present lifetime.

Changes in the Way We Live and Work

In Toffler's next classic book, *The Third Wave*, he argued that the economies of developed nations are now entering a third era. According to Toffler, the first wave in history occurred when permanent settlements replaced nomadic lifestyles. The second wave was marked by the Industrial Revolution, when work shifted out of the home and into factories and offices, changing family structures in the process. This second-wave or nuclear family, as Toffler labels it, was characterized by a breadwinning husband, housekeeping wife, and two children.

third wave
The term coined by author Alvin Toffler to describe the shift of industrialized societies to a home-based, service-oriented economy.

Toffler points out that the nuclear family is no longer the norm, now accounting for only 7 percent of the population. The best-selling author cites the tremendous increase in single-person households, the popularity of childless marriages, and the growth of a service-oriented economy as some of the causes of the **third wave** in human history. Toffler also concludes that work, often computer-based, will begin to shift back into the home, similar to the pattern that existed in the first wave. Most children will grow up in a home that doubles as a workplace; and this changed work/living environment will impact male-female relationships. Nonfamily members will join households as part of the new work organizations, forming a new version of the extended family.

Many of Toffler's predictions have already come true. The work-force, once dominated by men who held one job throughout their working lives, now reflects the changing status of women, the accept-ance of career shifts for both men and women, and the oversupply of workers skilled in yesterday's jobs. This oversupply has forced busi-ness, governments, and labour to take a hard look at the current Western economic situation and at what they perceive as the future of the industrial base.

W. J. Lomax, general manager for personnel, policy and planning at the Bank of Nova Scotia, gave an address at the 1979 graduation ceremony of the Institute of Canadian Bankers in Rothesay, New Brunswick. In his speech he stressed that everyone must be concerned with the future, but the margin of error in predicting it is often wide and deep.

How many silk mills survived the challenge of nylon, he asked. How many major radio manufacturers survived the introduction of television? How many watch companies in Switzerland anticipated the threat of digital timekeeping? Only a few still survive. Maybe some of these survivors—the winners—had incredible foresight. Mostly, however, they were flexible: when changes came, they adapted.

In 1905, Henry Ford built his mass production automobile plant, and his success became a model for generations of industrialists. Ford was no fool in anticipating the demand for cars, but the art of prediction is more complicated now and the stakes are higher. In Ford's day it took only six months from the signing of the first contract for materials, to the first car reaching the market—not time enough for a significant change in market conditions or the development of a serious competitive threat. A lot more foresight was required 61 years later, when it took three years from designing the Mustang to producing it. That first black Model A was produced by the cooperative efforts of 125 individuals in a company with $150,000 in authorized capital. The styling costs for the Mustang were $9 million, production costs were $50 million, and the Ford Motor Company employed 317,000 people by that time.

Wooing the "Woopies"

Since "volume" is the key word in sales success, some groups are, from an advertiser's point of view, needier than others. Until recently, few advertisers focused on consumers aged 50-plus. That will change. As baby boomers turn grey, old will be gold.

"By 2000, 40 percent of adults will be 50-plus. We cannot afford to ignore them," says Marion Plunkett, director of research for Ogilvy & Mather Advertising (Canada) Ltd. Ad gurus are already formulating catchy labels: the successors to yuppies may be "woopies"—well-off older people.

"Many in the 50-to-65 age bracket, their nest-building finished, have more time and money for leisure, clothing and cars," notes Prudential-Bache Securities Canada Ltd. "The boomers are used to prosperity and will carry their free-spending habits into old age."

Ads in the 1990s will increasingly target the older consumer's interests. Food ads will emphasize low cholesterol. Car ads will tout ease of getting in and out. Ad dollars will shift more toward print. "With increasing age and education levels, there is greater propensity to read,'' explains Stephen Rosenblum, vice-president with admen Young & Rubicam Ltd. Still, the boomers are a TV generation, and alongside lifestyle programming in the Golden Girls mould, TV will surfeit on elderly wisdoms about reliable brands.''[1]

The innovation in the late 19th century was technology. The revolution facing us today is no less dramatic: our most precious resources will be people and knowledge. The goal will be to bring those individuals to a common task, and mine that knowledge productively through planning, organization, and innovative thinking.

Mostly, what we need to know is that what we knew yesterday may no longer be true tomorrow.

As individuals, managers cannot afford to fail to anticipate and adapt to change. The cost of failure will be high, both in personal and career terms. The cost of failure in corporate terms is just as high. The most obvious result of our failure to anticipate and to adapt to change will be reduced competitive status, and ultimately business failure.

The Problems of Prediction

It is important to stress how difficult it is to predict trends. If society cannot correctly assess broad economic, social, and cultural movements, how can business managers forecast future directions?

The North American auto industry sadly missed the mark on its forecast of small-car demand. When small-car sales captured more than half the total automobile market, the car manufacturers admitted that their predictions had been inadequate. Since then, because of their failure to recognize changing consumer tastes, they have had to take drastic action to get smaller cars on the market. The trend toward smaller cars actually began in the mid-sixties, but it received a big push by the energy crisis.[2] Later, the downsizing—the industry term for the designing of smaller cars—became necessary because of government mandates on increasing fuel efficiency.

Businesspeople are often required to predict future conditions for their industries and companies. No one should underestimate the problems involved in this important task or the speed at which such predictions must be made.

Current Trends Affecting Business

Several social trends are currently influencing business. Effective managers must recognize these trends, determine how they affect their businesses, and develop appropriate strategies for dealing with the changed environment.

The transformation of Canada's economy imposed by more rapid technological change and tougher competition from overseas has generated human costs that are impossible to calculate. ''The number of people unemployed in Canada for 1988 averaged over 1 million. While the total unemployment rate for Canada has been decreasing consistently since 1983, this figure will grow as North America goes through a cyclical economic slowdown.''[3] In addition to those who have actually been out of work, there are countless thousands who have been forced to accept shorter hours, a lateral transfer, or a cut in pay to keep their jobs.

Our lives and our expectations for the future are being reshaped by the irresistible pressures of the marketplace. Those changes are traumatic for the individuals who are the victims of unemployment or involuntary job change, but they also come as a shock to managers who must make and announce the hard decisions about how a company or institution adapts.

The forces at work include:

- The emergence of low-cost new resource suppliers in developing countries make some mines and mills uneconomical to operate.
- The arrival of low-cost imports of high quality goods forces fabricating and finishing plants to undertake major changes in products, processes or obtaining of materials. It may even be necessary to relocate some aspects of the operation to a low-cost area overseas.
- The introduction of new technologies, such as banking machines and other automated devices, forces companies to completely rethink their way of serving clients and using their employees.
- The slowdown in population growth and tax revenues forces governments not only to curtail the growth in public-sector employment but also to seek ways to deliver public services at lower cost.

The scope of macroeconomic and marketplace changes that are in play is underlined by a comparison of the growth in employment by industry in the period 1985-1988 (when the economy grew by 7.9 percent) with what happened in 1981-1984 (when it grew by 3.3 percent). The effects of the 1981-82 recession are apparent through the wide-ranging loss in employment across most industries. The period from 1981-1984 showed a marked slowdown in job creation in all the basic industries, depite an increase in economic growth of 3.3 percent.

In contrast, the period from 1985-1988 showed a marked increase in job creation across all industries as the economy recovered from the recession and industries adapted to the changes in the marketplace. In all, over 1 million jobs were created in the period. Community, business and personal services alone accounted for 454,000 jobs (see Table 23-1).

Not only has growth been slower in the eighties, but pressures from technology, import competition, and slower population growth have forced employers in those industries to find ways to produce more with fewer people. Some people call this process **jobless growth**.

At the same time, there also have been dramatic changes in the nature of jobs within the workplace. The introduction of computers

jobless growth
The way in which industry produces more output with fewer people.

Table 23-1
Changing World of Work

Jobs Gained or Lost	1981-1984	1985-1988
Agriculture	− 9,000	n.a.
Forestry, fishing, mining	− 31,000	+ 5,000
Manufacturing	−154,000	+216,000
Construction	− 79,000	+102,000
Transportation	− 54,000	+ 18,000
Trade	+ 45,000	+219,000
Finance	+ 37,000	+ 87,000
Community Services	+216,000	+454,000
Public Administration	+ 23,000	+ 14,000
Economic growth over period (rise in real GNP)	+ 3.3%	+ 7.9%

Source: *Economic Observer*, a monthly publication of the Minister of Regional Industrial Expansion and the Minister of State for Science and Technology, Ottawa: Supply and Services Canada, Catalogue #11-010, March 1989 (vol. 2, no. 3), Table 2-8, p. 5-30.

and advanced electronic equipment is blurring the distinction between clerical and technical staff, and between technical staff and production workers. Changes in distribution systems have reduced the need for workers in shipping, storing, and receiving. Middle- and even senior-management jobs are being eroded as new management information systems evolve and companies adopt leaner organizational structures. The daunting fact is that the transformation process is only beginning. Canadian firms are in the early stages of the modernization and adaptation programmes needed to compete in the markets of the eighties.

What hope does all this offer the unemployed and those who will be entering the labour force? For the young, there are some promising signs. For one thing, the growth in the labour force will soon slow dramatically, to about half the increase that occurred in the late seventies.

The numbers of people aged 15 to 24 will decline over the next few years by more than 400,000, to about 2.6 million in 1990. So, to the extent that a stable number of entry-level jobs remain, there will be a sharp decline in the numbers vying for each opening. People in this age group also have the advantage of adapting their educations to suit the changing industrial and occupational structure. What they lack in experience and bargaining power they can make up in flexibility and good training.

In contrast, the older generations face two severe handicaps. First, the competition for jobs will be fierce, particularly in the 25 to 34 age group, which is by far the largest group because of the fifties baby boom. Second, most of these people have long since finished their formal preparation for the work force, and must find ways to re-educate themselves if they want to acquire skills that are more in demand than those they possess. Some will get help from their employers, but many will not.

The smallest, and in many respects the most disadvantaged, group is made up of those over the age of 55. They are being forced off the payroll now by various forms of early retirement and they are probably the ones who find it most difficult to train or adapt (see Table 23–2).

By 2000, Canada's workforce of 15.4 million (up from 12.4 million today) will toil increasingly in the service sector, will comprise a growing number of females, and will be notably older—so much older, in fact, that economic survival will hinge on an influx of newcomers from abroad.

Primary industries and manufacturing, which have declined in relative importance since 1980, will continue to do so, while the service sector will mushroom to control more than 70 percent of employment. The 1.25 million jobs created since 1985 are virtually all in the service sector. Services can proliferate regardless of automation: employment in the banking sector rose from 162,618 in 1985 to 166,967 in 1988, despite the spread of computerized accounts and automatic teller machines.

Most new jobs in the 1990s will be service sector, and most will be filled by women. The Institute for Policy Analysis in Toronto judges that participation of females aged 25 to 54 in the workforce will reach about 85 percent by the late 1990s. The rate for males the same age has been consistently around 94 percent since the 1960s. Incidentally, 67 percent of all Canadians over age 15 participate in the workforce. DRI Canada projects more than 70 percent participation by 2000, a figure that is striking when compared with the 56 percent rate of the early 1960s.

Within the foreseeable future, there may be more work than we can handle. Labour shortages will inhibit economic expansion. Canada's population, just 25 million in 1986, will barely pass 27 million by 1996. Since the birth rate (1.7 children per family) is below replacement level, the working-age population will shrink. Already, as today's tradesmen retire, apprentices are lacking to replace them. A Statistics Canada sampling in April 1988 found a record 8 percent of manufacturers complaining that skill shortages were impairing production. Stores and restaurants, especially in southern Ontario, are stymied trying to tap their usual source of workers, the now-dwindling 18 to 24 age bracket.

To help fill the gap, many older people may choose work over retirement—and governments will make that easier to do. A 1988 Commons committee urged the abolition of mandatory retirement and a national campaign against "ageism"—discrimination against older job applicants.[4]

The labour market in Canada for the next decade will be characterized by more competition between generations—primarily between

Table 23-2
Canada's Jobless and the Future

Age and Sex	Unemployed in 1988	Change in Labour Force* 1984-1990
Both sexes, 15-24	326,000	−411,000
Men, 25-54	312,000	+627,000
Women, 25-54	316,000	+459,000
Both Sexes, 55+	77,000	+178,000
Total	1,031,000	+853,000

*With participation rate remaining at 1984 levels.

Source: Statistics Canada, *Labour Force Annual Averages 1981–1988*, Ottawa: Supply and Services Canada, Catalogue #71–529, March 1989. Table 1, p. 15.

those in their thirties who are pushing ahead and older workers trying to hold on to what they have. That competition will mean stress (if not economic hardship) for some senior managers, who will find themselves being asked to leave just at the point where they had expected to sit back and enjoy the respect and privileges that go with a senior executive position. (See Focus 23-1.)

Focus 23-1

Little Room at the Top for Baby Boom Workers

The generation that overpopulated schools in the 60s, couldn't find work in the 70s, and created a housing boom in the 80s has spawned a new problem.

Baby boomers are clogging up the corporate hierarchy as they move into lower and middle management. There are now thousands of them waiting to move up the ladder, but few openings at the top, says demographics expert David Foot, an economics professor at the University of Toronto.

Unemployment among 35- to 44-years-olds will leap by 43.4 percent between 1981 and 1991, Foot says. Meanwhile, fewer young people are entering the work force, lowering unemployment among 15- to 24-year-olds by 20 percent during the same period.

"The corporate structure that has served us so beautifully until now is no longer appropriate," Foot says. The perfect match between the age of the population and the typical corporate hierarchy occurred in 1979-80, when the bulk of the population was at the corporate entry level. Now, the upper end of the baby boom is age 42, and the largest baby boom group is 27.

Foot warns that the career path of the baby boomers is about to hit a plateau. "Opportunities for promotion will be severely limited throughout the 1990s."

As a result, companies will have an increasingly tough time keeping employees motivated and happy.

"Companies are going to have to find ways to give people a new challenge—and pay them for it," Foot says. "If companies want to stop the dissatisfaction that is starting to brew at the front end of the baby boom, the notion of salaries related to hierarchy within the corporation has got to go."

Making matters worse, companies cut out layers of management and consolidated job descriptions during the recession. Layoffs and early retirement programmes made corporations lean and mean, but they also cut into promotion opportunities.

Many companies are tackling the problem with the psychological approach—getting employees to lower their expectations rather than changing compensation strategies.

"The concept of moving up from one level to another is on the way out," says Anne Lackie, manager of human resources at the Royal Bank of Canada in Montreal. "We talk more about career paths these days, rather than a career ladder."

At least one employer has taken more drastic steps. In late 1986, the Ontario government implemented its "strategy for renewal" programme to cope with the dearth of new recruits and bulge in middle management. The programme includes a voluntary exit option, with incentives for people to quit at all levels of its ministries.

"You lose some of the good ones in the process, but it improves the corporate hierarchy," says George Podrebarac, former assistant deputy minister of Ontario's Human Resources Secretariat.

Foot says employers are going to have to get even more innovative in the 1990s. To keep good employees, they'll have to offer rewards for moving laterally, more generous education leaves, and better vacation packages. Promotions, power, and seniority are on the way out.

"The employee is going to have to have a value to the company, not the position," Foot says. "An employee has to be rewarded in whatever position he's in."

Source: Barrie McKenna, "Baby Boom Workers Finding There's Little Room at the Top," *The Financial Post*, May 16, 1988, p. 9.

There also will be more competition between the sexes, as both men and women get crowded out of certain stereotyped occupations (there are now fewer opportunities in both the female-dominated retail trade, service, and clerical positions, and male-dominated production-line, transportation, and construction jobs). This may be a setback for women, whose employment in the past 10 to 15 years has been enhanced by the rapid growth of service-sector jobs.

There will be a growing need for retraining of employees to help them adapt, which will offer a rapidly expanding market for post-secondary education services, a market that many colleges and universities still are ill-equipped to serve.

The best odds for survival in the coming job market will be with those who have power, seniority, adaptability, or a good level of technical/computer literacy. Inevitably, many individuals will find their lives disrupted by corporate reorganization. That is the human side of a process with major consequences for our economic future.

Canada's growth prospects for the nineties will depend heavily on how well we manage the economic transformation from an economy based on resources and a narrow line of manufactured goods. Decisions made now will determine not only whether we can produce efficiently but also whether we produce the range of products that people want to buy. The challenge is to emerge trim and fit, equipped with the right skills and products.

High technology is not just another buzzword, like "industrial strategy" or "concentration." It has become the key to survival for many, if not most, Canadian industries.

Underlying economic pressures are forcing Canada to transform the impetus for economic growth from the exploitation of physical resources—land and labour—to the mobilization of intellectual knowledge. In the past, Canada's growth has been generated primarily by extracting more raw materials from the land, employing more workers, and increasing the amount of capital invested in plant and equipment. A small but significant proportion of growth was generated by doing things in smarter ways—exploiting advances in knowledge, improving the skills of the work force and the quality of capital equipment, and achieving economies of scale.

The fundamental economic challenge of the next decade is to shift the balance more in the direction of smarter solutions. One reason we must do this is that it is becoming increasingly difficult to achieve growth in resource industries. Big chunks of our resource sector are on the decline, for these reasons:

- A number of developing countries have a low-cost resource base that can be developed using low-cost labour: coal in Colombia, copper in Chile and pulpwood in Brazil, for example. During the seventies, those countries made major commitments to develop their resources. Many of the companies involved are government-owned or controlled, while the invested capital has come mainly from foreign lenders and development agencies.

- Major industrial projects to develop resources take a long time between plan and reality, especially in remote areas. Policies in the late sixties and early seventies (when we were worried that the "limits to growth" would cause shortages of raw materials) turned to the opening of new mines and processing facilities in the late seventies.

- That burst of new capacity coincided with a marked slowing of global economic growth as the inflation bubble led to two severe recessions back-to-back, in 1980 and 1981-82.

- The new projects also added to global production capacity of such commodities as copper, nickel, and iron ore at a time when those minerals began to encounter increasing competition from novel industrial materials—a side effect of new technologies. Copper is being replaced in electrical circuitry by fibre-optic products that offer greater capacity, speed, and flexibility in many key uses. Iron ore and nickel are falling in demand as steel becomes replaced by plastics and light metals such as aluminum in many applications.

- Commodity exports are the sole source of foreign exchange earnings for many developing countries—their only means of raising the money needed to pay interest on foreign debts and buy essential imports. Accordingly, producers in those countries are not driven by the profit motive, but continue to export regardless of market conditions to keep gross revenues steady. If prices are depressed because of weak demand, such producers may even increase output to try to maintain a given level of export earnings.

Many Canadian resource companies therefore face exceptionally tough competitive conditions. Global excess capacity, at a time when materials substitution is causing significant and unpredictable erosion of demand, has depressed market prices. The weakness in prices has been aggravated by competition from new resource producers that are often insensitive to short-term fluctuations in price. In this global context, many existing Canadian production facilities look unprofitable. Some are being closed permanently (such as iron mines in northern Quebec) because they have no hope of competing with other countries where reserves are of high quality and can be exploited at lower cost. Some are being scaled back and investments are being made to reduce unit production costs in the hope that the facility will become competitive again when markets improve (as is the case with nickel producers at Sudbury and sawmills in British Columbia). Some have been closed temporarily until world demand has a chance to catch up with global supply (such as coal mines in Alberta and British Columbia).

The unavoidable conclusion is that resource development will not be the engine of economic growth in Canada that it has been in the past. It will be some time before new capacity is needed. And, when that time comes, there will be low-cost reserves in other countries competing for the development opportunities.

Canada's comparative advantage at one time was that the resources existed here and they could be reliably developed and produced (with significant help from foreign investors). Now other countries are attracting that development activity more easily.

This does not mean we should write off the whole resource sector. There will be segments of strong growth, especially in the energy field, and sales from existing facilities will increase as economic growth gradually brings demand and supply back into balance. In short, most existing mines and mills will continue to operate and may eventually be expanded or replaced. The missing element will be the drive to develop new reserves and add substantial amounts of new capacity. That development activity has been an important engine of growth in Canada throughout the country's history, but has been slowing relative to other sectors for several decades. As Table 23-3 shows, exports of food (mainly wheat) and crude and fabricated materials accounted for 84 percent of Canada's exports in 1965, but only 56 percent in 1987. The sector that was most dynamic was automobiles and parts; those exports increased from 15 percent of the total in 1965 to 43 percent in 1987, because of the integration of North American production facilities after implementation of the auto pact. The share of both machinery and consumer goods also increased slightly.

The erosion of our comparative advantage in resource exports forces Canadian industry to shift the focus of production into goods (and services) with a higher value added; i.e., where more technical, managerial and marketing skills are required to produce the end product.

What Table 23-3 shows is that in 1965 Canadians were highly dependent on their ability to hew wood and draw water—extracting and fabricating materials from the land. The major shift since then has been into mass production of relatively homogeneous end products such as autos, parts, machinery, consumer goods, and so on. That type of a activity, however, is also experiencing vigorous competition from newly industrialized countries such as South Korea (whose Hyundai Excel and Sonata cars are selling so well in Canada).

Table 23-3
Composition of Canadian Exports (%)

Exports	1965	1985	1987
Live animals	0.9	0.4	0.3
Food, feed, beverages, and tobacco	19.1	7.9	8.4
Crude materials	20.7	16.7	13.8
Fabricated materials	43.7	31.7	34.4
End products (inedible)	15.2	42.9	42.7
Special transactions	0.3	0.3	0.3

Source: Exports Table, *Canada Facts 1989*, An Annual Statistical Profile of Canada's Business Environment. Ottawa: Prospectus Investment and Trade Partners Inc, 272 Clarence Street, Ottawa, K1N 5R3, p. 31.

As with resources, Canadian firms can, by using the most modern technology to reduce unit costs, preserve a share of the market for mass-produced goods. The real challenge, though, is to carve out a niche in areas where Canadians have a unique touch, offering one of these things:

• A special quality (as in high-fashion clothing);
• A unique combination of skills (such as engineering services);
• The application of leading-edge ideas (such as the Canadarm used on recent space shuttle missions).

In effect, economic success in the developing countries is forcing Canadian industry out of its traditional market niche and into activities where it must make creative use of new technologies to carve out a market position for the nineties.

Population Changes

population explosion
The rapid growth in the world's population.

It has been estimated that global population will rise to 6.1 billion by the year 2000, compared to its current 4.7 billion. The so-called **population explosion** is a well-documented fact. In 1750 the world's population stood at about 800 million. It doubled by 1900 and doubled again by 1964. Probably it will stabilize at 10.5 billion.[5]

Economically disadvantaged nations traditionally have higher birthrates. The population of less developed countries is rising at a rate faster than that of economically advanced nations such as Canada, the United States, the United Kingdom, the Federal Republic of Germany, Japan, France, and the USSR.[6] But people in developed nations typically have longer life expectancies. For example, a male in Canada is expected to live to 70.2 years and a female to 77.8.[7] By contrast, in India men are expected to live to 41.9 and women to 40.6,[8] and in Bangladesh both men and women have a life expectancy of 47.[9]

Population growth in Canada and elsewhere has always meant expanding markets for business. The 1981 census set Canada's population at 24,343,181.[10] It is expected to hit 30 million by 2001.[11] But the composition of the Canadian population will change even more significantly.

A lowered birthrate means that Canada will have an aging population. In 1976, half of the population was less than 27.8 years old, but by 2001, half of all Canadians will be older than 36 years old, and during the same period the mean age of the population will increase from 31.9 to 36 years old.[12] An older population will produce several effects: increased financial pressure on private and government pension plans, possible labour shortages, and marketing's gradual move away from youth-oriented advertising. The increasing numbers of elderly people will represent a larger proportion of the Canadian voting population. They will command more public attention as well as exerting more influence on economic, political, and social policies.

Lifestyle Changes

lifestyle
The way a person lives, including work, leisure time, hobbies, and personal philosophy.

Lifestyle is the way a person lives; it includes work, leisure time, hobbies, other interests, and personal philosophy. One person's lifestyle may be dominated by work, with few social activities. Another's may revolve around hobbies, recreation, or a personal philosophy.

There is little doubt that lifestyles are changing and that these changes will have an impact on the way business operates in the years ahead. Several factors are causing lifestyle changes in Canadian society.

First, there is more leisure time than ever before. The workweek is now less than 40 hours, as compared with 70 hours a century ago. Some experts believe it will be 25 hours or less before the year 2000.[13] Several firms have adopted four-day workweeks with more hours per day, while others have cut the number of hours worked each week. Reduced work schedules mean increased leisure time.

Second, families have fewer children than before—and young couples are postponing childrearing until later in their marriages. This trend has forced many businesses to modify their competitive strategies. Gerber Product Company used to advertise ''babies are our business—our only business.'' Now Gerber's product line has expanded to include infant and toddler clothing, stuffed animals, and accessories such as bottles, bassinets, and baby powder.[14]

Third, more people are better educated and prosperous now. These advantages bring with them the freedom to question current lifestyles and examine new ones, sometimes leading to personal lifestyle changes. Today's youth are not only better educated but more independent and individualistic than past generations.

Fourth, more women, both single and married, with and without children, are working full time outside the home. Between 1951 and 1971 the number of women in the labour force increased over 160 percent, and continues to grow.[15] This trend is certainly important for business. As the needs of working women and their families change, the products and services to meet these needs are also changing.

Lastly, it is important to consider older Canadians who are more socially active, more financially secure, and healthier than ever before. Growing old is not what it used to be. Focus 23-2 explores these golden lifestyles and the implications for our future.

Business is only beginning to realize how people's lifestyles can influence their behaviour as employees, consumers, and members of society.

Focus 23-2

Golden Lifestyles

In many respects, there's little difference between older and younger Canadians: seniors are a diverse collection of citizens who go to restaurants and movies, vote in elections, earn money, pay taxes, watch television, and help others. There is, though, a major difference between the older and younger sets: since seniors participate considerably less in the labour force, they have much more free time to follow whatever pursuits they desire—perhaps

buying a camper and hitting the road, going to school, or starting a
new career. Obviously, aging does not necessarily mean decline and
dependency.

When it comes to quality of life, chronological years mean
virtually nothing; what counts at any age is health and well-being.
Most older Canadians fend for themselves very nicely, and most also
report they are in good health and happy. Older Canadians are just
as committed as anyone else to leading active and independent
lives—which is precisely what the vast majority of them are doing.

The employment level of older Canadians has declined markedly
in the past 30 years. In the mid-1950s, nearly 20 percent of the
65-plus population were employed; however, only 7 percent were
working in 1986. Employment among Canadians aged 55 to 64 has
also been in decline; for example, 84 percent of men had jobs in
1956, compared with 64 percent in 1986. With fewer teenagers and
more seniors in our population, some service-industry companies
are courting older Canadians as employees. McDonald's, for
instance, employs hundreds of "McMasters"—the fast-food
company's term for workers over 50.

Part-timers: Thirty percent of employed men and 45 percent of
employed women 65 years and older worked part-time in 1986; in
contrast, only 3 percent of employed men and 22 percent of
employed women between the ages of 25 and 64 worked part-time.
Most older workers preferred it that way: 85 percent of men and
79 percent of women working part-time said they did not want
full-time work. Nationwide, nearly 40 percent of the jobs in Canada
are in small, independent businesses; but these businesses employ
52 percent of the seniors who are in the work force.

Source: "Golden Lifestyles," *Royal Bank Reporter*, Winter 1989, p. 12.

Dual-Career Couples

The traditional couple was characterized by a clear division of roles:
the woman was responsible for keeping house and the man worked to
provide the family's economic necessities. Undoubtedly, this division
of roles continues to apply to many couples. However, there is a
tendency toward change, due to the increasing proportion of married
women in the labour market.

More and more Canadian women are working outside the home.
Figures published by Statistics Canada indicate that this was especially the case for women aged 25-54 years. Their participation rate
went from 39.3 percent in 1968 to 56.6 percent in 1978 and 73.4 percent in 1988. This increase is all the more striking for single and
divorced women between the ages 25 and 44, whose participation
rates increased to an all-time high of 84.7 percent and 76.8 percent
respectively.[16]

This influx has had several consequences. First, since both spouses are wage earners, working couples earn a higher income. Second, the assignment of household chores changes. Third, the fact that both spouses are gainfully employed seems to affect the husband's commitment to his career. And finally, decisions on the number of children and the best time to have them are affected.

Thus, the phenomenon of dual-career couples constitutes a new social issue. On the one hand, the couples concerned must make some necessary adjustments; on the other hand, companies are also affected, and some have taken steps to deal with the specific problems that can arise.

Two-career couples may have an impact on the following personnel management activities: internal communications, geographic transfers, recruitment and selection, training, and benefits (including hours of work).

Dilemmas can arise in handling confidential information where the same company employs both members of the couple. There is a serious risk that information available to an employee in his or her work may be disclosed to his or her spouse in another section.

Occasionally, companies need to transfer employees or executives from one location to another simply for effectiveness. We can see the problem that arises when a transfer involves a member of a two-career couple. Some individuals might decline a transfer because it would have too great an impact on their spouse's career; others might accept it unwillingly, bowing to pressures from the organization. In both cases, the efficient operation of the organization may be affected. The company would then be obliged to transfer another person, hire a new employee, or both.

What then, are the alternatives an organization has in dealing with this problem? One approach is to take these circumstances into account in the company's human resource planning. In defining their human resource requirements, managers must ask themselves whether a particular transfer is absolutely necessary. Alternatively, they could identify the circumstances of employees who are members of a two-career couple, regarding them as unavailable for given positions or available only under certain conditions.

Where transfers are indeed necessary, another solution is to offer incentives to those who accept. By giving enough advance notice and meeting with the spouse of the transferee at a fairly early stage, the company can offer to help him or her find another satisfactory job in the new location.

Two-career couples can also pose the following problem in terms of recruitment and selection. Because of geographic isolation, some companies will have more trouble attracting candidates for available jobs. Since urban centres offer more varied employment opportunities, they are better suited to two-career couples. Therefore, such couples will tend to rule out isolated or rural areas as possibilities. One member may still apply for a job out of personal interest or some other reason, but later decline because no satisfactory position can be found for the spouse.

A business must continually be able to find human resources to meet its needs: without access to these resources, it risks a loss of effectiveness. Such a company has several alternatives. First, it must ask itself how much importance it attaches to filling particular positions. Where the cost of attracting candidates outweighs the expected benefits, it may be inadvisable to bother.

The firm should act only when the position in question appears essential. In terms of recruitment, this may mean that the company must offer better salary conditions or a range of benefits more suited to the needs of two-career couples. Where the hesitant member of a two-career couple would be a valued employee, the company should make additional efforts. To avoid a refusal on the part of a candidate, a company would do well to involve the other spouse in the hiring process at the most opportune time.

In training and development, a conflict arises between the philosophy espoused by two-career couples and that of most organizations.

People know they cannot reach position D without first spending time in positions A, B, and C. They also know that a particular training programme or assignment is needed for position D. This organizational philosophy is based on two assumptions: that organizational objectives are more important than individual objectives and that employees will be loyal to their employer.

Two-career couples pose something of a challenge to these two assumptions, serving as a reminder that what's good for an organization is not necessarily good for individuals or their families. The clash between these two philosophies can undoubtedly cause problems for an organization, if it cannot assign people where it feels they belong. However, this can also act as an opportunity for a company to review certain policies or practices. For example, it could re-examine its need for requiring some employees or executives to move frequently. Does one become a better vice-president of finance for having spent two years in the human resource department, or vice versa? Is the mandatory training programme for all new recruits really necessary? Could the same result not be achieved locally through simulations, management games and case studies? Could a promising young executive not be given orientation training other than being assigned to a given location for a six-month period?

These questions show that two-career couples can have a positive effect on human resource management by raising issues that lead to reviewing or changing organizational policies.

The challenges for the future presented by two-career couples can be met. They can even allow human resource managers to introduce innovations that improve organizational behaviour, policies, and practices. Thus, instead of being regarded as one more obstacle to the efficient operation of a company, two-career couples can help to introduce a less "reactive" and more "proactive" forward-looking style of human resource management.[17]

Economic Changes

The past decade has witnessed sweeping economic changes that have altered the course of Canadian business. Oil boycotts, inflation, unemployment, recession, currency fluctuations, and energy resource allocation have all had profound impacts.

People are becoming more conscious than they were a decade ago about how economic factors affect everyday life. Some are alarmed by the high unemployment and double-digit inflation of recent years. Others fear economic domination by American, Japanese, or German firms or the oil-rich Arab states. But Canada is still a wealthy nation and an effective competitor in the world marketplace.

Still, the economic changes noted above indicate the importance of businesspeople's thorough understanding of the competitive system. No firm is far removed from the basic economic changes that occur in society, and effective managers must be aware of current economic events affecting their businesses.

The restructuring of the USSR economy excites the Canadian imagination as much as the Soviet—maybe more. Enthusiasts foresee soaring investment in Soviet ventures and Canada–USSR trade reaching several billion dollars annually by 2000. But like China, which opened to trade and investment in the early 1970s, the Soviet market will develop slowly.

On the one hand, the USSR, out of sync with global economic progress, can't afford failure. To overcome domestic shortages and improve international competitiveness, the Soviets are encouraging joint ventures with western firms that can introduce modern methods and technologies. Canadians on the bandwagon in 1989 included McDonald's Restaurants of Canada Ltd. (up to 20 outlets planned for Moscow); Magna International Inc. (25 percent ownership of an auto-parts factory in the Ukraine); Canadian Foremost Ltd. of Calgary (participation in a heavy machinery manufacturing venture); and Toronto-based Seabeco Group Corp. (helping finance a US $150-million theatre, office, and hotel complex in Moscow).

But since the ruble is not yet convertible into hard currency, it is difficult for westerners to patriate profits. Alternatively, Magna may take its profit in Soviet machinery for its own use or re-sale.

Canada sent $800 million in goods to the USSR in 1987 and imported only $35 million. The Soviets cannot afford such lopsidedness, given the low price of oil, their hard-currency staple. But they'll buy more from us if we buy more from them. Besides machinery and vodka, Canadian firms are negotiating to import Soviet construction and grain-handling technology, low-priced clothing, sports equipment, and musical instruments.

Like any market, the USSR needs nurturing. Firms involved in joint ventures will have an inside track on trading contracts in the next decade as the Soviets shop for tools to modernize their economy, particularly transportation, high tech, and oil and gas equipment. "The Soviets stick with people they've dealt with before."

Success in economic relations will naturally hinge on the international political climate. But business's advance guard has the satisfaction of knowing that commercial ties bring East and West closer together.[18]

From classroom to boardroom, the basic unit of economic study in the 1990s will be the globe. Global trends promise to make business a tougher and more exciting calling—and a major contributor to the uniting of the planet.

The Global Marketplace

Globalization is a necessary response to a world market made smaller by telecommunications and larger by a more balanced division of wealth. In 1960 the US accounted for 40 percent of global GNP; nowadays, the US share is 20 percent, Europe has 22 percent, and East Asia 22 percent.

As a result, we'll see more trans-border joint ventures and mergers as corporations seek global hookups. On the airways, Japan Air Lines Co. Ltd. bought into Hawaiian Airlines Inc. Scandinavian Airlines System has linked with Texas Air Corp. We'll see global niche consolidation. Canada's CAE Industries Ltd. in 1989 bought the four military simulation divisions of the Link Co. in the US and became the world's largest simulator-maker. There will be a predatory wave as trading blocs produce giant corporations—Europe's common-market plans have inspired mergers and takeovers there—that attempt overseas acquisitions, forcing potential target firms to expand on the eat-or-be-eaten principle. The rash of mergers in the Canadian economy in the early part of 1989 is just an early tremor in a global shake-up.[19]

Technological Changes

technology
The innovations, methods, practices, systems, equipment, and related operational knowledge applicable to the industrial setting.

Technology is the innovations, methods, practices, systems, equipment, and related operational knowledge applicable to the industrial setting. New technology is being introduced at a rate far faster than that of a decade ago.

Technological changes lead to other changes. Production methods must be updated, employees retrained, and management thinking restructured. Knowledge acquired in school is outdated within ten years of graduation, and certain jobs become obsolete. Society has thus begun to emphasize lifelong education and training so people can remain productive for more than a few years.

Technology is a driving force of our civilization, as nations compete to develop the tools and techniques that will fashion tomorrow's economies. Canada, however, is barely in the race, with R & D spending stagnant at just above a paltry 1.3 percent of GDP since 1983. But even with our mightiest effort, we couldn't keep up with larger nations. For example, the US spent $50 million in 1989 on the first stages of a potential $3-billion 15-year effort to pinpoint the 100,000 genes on human chromosomes—information that will provide the ability to shape human destiny. Three billion dollars on a biology project!

The massive cost of crossing technological frontiers makes international cooperation mandatory. Canada has an aggressive export-oriented high-tech community ($13.6 billion in annual exports), but with government support weak, companies may increasingly latch on to international ventures, imitating the success of our aerospace industry, a participant in both the US and European space programmes.[20]

high technology firm
Companies whose research and development expenditures and number of technical employees are twice as great as the average for all manufacturing firms.

High technology firms are companies whose research and development expenditures and number of technical employees are twice as great as the average for all manufacturing firms. These firms are expected to experience major growth in the future Canadian economy as they have made an impact in Kanata, Ontario, which is Ottawa's Silicon Valley.

Attracting high-tech industries is a current issue, with many provinces and communities now offering incentives to such firms to locate in their regions. It is important to note that affordable labour is the most attractive factor.

Problems associated with high tech include:

• shifting the unemployed and unskilled from smokestack industries to high technology,
• the loss of high-tech jobs to foreign countries,
• the risks associated with high-tech entrepreneurship,
• restrictions on high technology transfer.

technology transfer
The provision of technology processes, materials, and know-how to another nation.

Technology transfer can be defined as the provision of technological processes, materials, and know-how to another nation.

Some people worry that technology is out of control. A few even believe that humans will some day be the slaves of computers or of "super machines." Most business executives, however, believe that technology has been and will continue to be a way of improving the standard of living and the quality of life. But they also point out that technological improvements will fail to win public support if they are too expensive.

Social Changes

"Just how long have you been with the firm, Owens?"

Source: From the *Wall Street Journal*—Permission, Cartoon Features Syndicate.

Many social changes affecting business involve either social responsibility or the quality of life. People want socially responsible decisions from executives and have begun to protest actions that are not in line with this thinking. Canadian citizens have filed lawsuits against producers of poor products, picketed supermarkets, boycotted manufacturers, and demanded stronger legislation to control certain business practices.

They also are increasingly concerned about the quality of life. While most people still seek material possessions, there is now a greater interest in living fuller, more personally rewarding lives. Individuals must decide on the lifestyle that is right for them, which includes work and personal styles.

Biotechnology

Although its triumphs to date have been mostly in the pharmaceutical domain, biotechnology's greatest impact in the 1990s will be in a field of vaster economic potential—agriculture, worth $22 billion in annual cash receipts in Canada alone.

Agricultural biotech is creating new plants and animals by gene manipulations or transfers. Work is underway to make wheat frost-resistant by importing into its DNA a fish's antifreeze gene. The earth's entire genetic heritage, human included, may be mixed to produce commercially useful creatures such as meatier livestock or faster-growing crops. In fact, crops could be preset to a desired shape and size to reduce waste at the processing stage.

"We are far from transferring a few genes and then, presto, you have corn that grows in a desert. But in the 90s, we should see engineered plants that resist disease and have greater nutritive value."

Several hundred new plants, animals, and microbes have already been created—Monsanto Co. of St. Louis, Mo., has produced pest-resistant tomatoes, for instance—but there is still much to learn. When US researchers implanted a human growth hormone gene into pigs, for example, the animals developed side effects including lameness and internal bleeding.

And there are hazards: the unwitting release of a destructive organism into the environment would be the biotech equivalent of the Chernobyl disaster. In the US, groups of Rifkinites, named for ecological activist Jeremy Rifkin, have opposed the commercialization of altered microbes and, moreover, have contested Harvard University's 1988 patent on a drug-test mouse—the world's first patented animal—genetically designed to contract cancer.

"Some people oppose patenting lifeforms because it might one day be extended to humans. But farmers own plants and animals, whereas if you own humans, that's slavery. Can't we distinguish along those lines?'' The short-term answer is yes: watch for Canada, following the US example, to stimulate R & D by allowing lifeform patents. Federal funding plus industrial spending here add up to only $400 million annually on biotech, including manufacturing, compared to US $5 billion on R & D alone south of the border [21]

Focus 23-3

Discovering New Ways to Run Your Business

Over the past two years, Dome Advertising B.C. Ltd. has grown at a furious clip. A few months ago, one of the problems that plagues any fast-growing business hit Dome. ''We realized,'' says account executive Paula Heal, ''that we were hiring an awful lot of secretaries'' to handle the exploding output.

With a consultant's help, nine personal computers were bought and linked in a network. The staff was so enthusiastic that Heal ordered more computers; everybody who wanted one could have one. Things have worked out well for Dome. According to Heal, ''the amount of material being produced is incredible.''

Toronto consultant Don Kaplan, of DM Kaplan Concept Innovation, has seen it happen time and again: companies such as Dome Advertising upgrade their technology to solve a specific office bottleneck and end up discovering a whole new way of running their offices. Over the past five years, he has specialized in helping companies use office automation to do their work faster and better.

According to Kaplan, most typical businesses think of upgrading only in terms of replacing typewriters with word-processing equipment. But the challenge for most farsighted businesses is to look beyond that. ''I encourage my clients to look far more deeply into the issue of how the office operates.''

In short, companies should think about the long term, even if they do take a step-by-step approach. Kaplan explains: ''Think about a fully integrated office and leave the pathway open so you can get there by evolution. Pick a technology that is going to be compatible to a long-term development programme.''

Fully automated offices use technology to do two fundamental things. First, individual tasks are automated. Secondly, individuals are tied together so they can communicate with one another electronically. Both increase efficiency in the workplace.

Once these efficiencies have been attained, completely rethinking the way the office operates will yield still more benefits. ''How can we change this or that reporting activity,'' asks Kaplan, ''so that, given the electronic facilities, we can avoid certain steps, enhance others, speed up others and economize on the elapsed time taken to get the document through the office?''

Going down this path to systems nirvana needn't send the company to the poor-house either, says Gordon Adair, systems consultant with Deloitte Haskins & Sells in Vancouver. ''Fortunately the price of personal computers is such that companies can start down the path very cheaply. They can experiment and see the benefits for themselves." The growth of the PC market, the competition, and the number of people that write material for PCs are expected to drive the price down and the flexibility and usability up.

Source: Terry MacDonald, "Discovering New Ways to Run Your Business," *Financial Times of Canada*, March 7, 1988, p. A3.

Business Strategy Changes

Changes in business strategy over the years have had a direct effect on how firms operate today (see Focus 23–3). Some of these changes include:

1. Computer-based management information systems (MIS). An efficient MIS is one that gets the appropriate data (and only the appropriate data) to the responsible decision maker in time for a considered decision. It is estimated that by 1990 computer related business will generate over $20 billion of revenue.[22]

2. **Automation**—the replacement of people with machines that can perform tasks faster or cheaper than humans. Most experts point out that because workers are required to make the new machines, the labour force is not significantly reduced. The problem is that the displaced workers may not be qualified to handle the new jobs.

3. More extensive cost control programmes, within which accountants and other managers find new ways to hold down the rising costs of doing business. These programmes are very important, especially during periods of inflation or sales decline.

4. New ways of acquiring the energy and materials necessary to operate business. The importance of this change is obvious, because shortages of energy and raw materials have been experienced by Canadian businesses recently.

5. Management awareness and understanding of the attitudes and problems of workers. The labour force is composed of a multitude of different groups requiring different managerial approaches. Management must be sure that leadership styles match the work situation.

automation
The replacement of people with machines that can perform tasks faster or cheaper than humans.

Electronic Breakthroughs

Ten years from now, you'll consider your home a dumb place to live. Oh, you'll smarten it up with timing and control devices, but ultimately you'll concede that the Jones' darling new Smart House has a higher IQ.

In the Jones' house, a single cable distributes power, telecommunications and audio/video signals, eliminating separate wiring for cable television, phones, stereo speakers, alarms, and appliances. Smart appliances for Smart Houses communicate with one another: the microwave triggers a message on the television, for example, to inform Mr. Jones his dinner is ready.

It will be possible to phone any electrical device in the smart home. "Suppose your washer is on the blink. Rather than send a repairman, the manufacturer will use the phone to get into the appliance and find the problem."

The Smart House has been under development in the US since 1984, sponsored by the National Association of Home Builders and several high-tech and appliance companies. Two trailer trucks roam the US exhibiting smart rooms to the public, and construction of the prototype got underway in October 1988. Although the Smart House consortium is in a leading position to shape tomorrow's home, "the Japanese and Europeans are pursuing the same idea, and even in the US different firms are developing their own systems," notes Norm Aspin, president of the Electrical and Electronic Manufacturers Association of Canada, which in November 1988 joined with Ontario Hydro, Hydro-Québec, Bell Canada, and the National Research Council to champion the automated house concept in this country.[23]

The greatest computer-related triumph in the 1990s will be the spread of artificial intelligence (AI) software. AI programmes known as expert systems make humanlike inferences by drawing from data bases containing facts, paradigms, and precepts relating to particular fields of expertise. Linked to sensors and robots, expert systems will lead an industrial transformation.

Among early AI applications is an expert system developed by Canadian Pacific Ltd. that analyses lubricant samples from diesel locomotives, then indicates which engine parts need maintenance. Ultimately, AI computers, feasting on data streaming from sensors, will make thousands of such decisions to run automated plants. Mining giant Noranda Minerals Inc., for example, is developing an expert system to control milling processes.

In the US, where firms such as Boeing Co. and GM have invested in AI companies, market researcher Frost & Sullivan Inc. of New York estimates that suppliers' revenue from AI software will catapult from US $200 million in 1989 to US $1.6 billion in 1993. "In five to ten years expert systems will come to the fore," says Gordon MacNabb, president and CEO of Precarn Associates Inc. of Nepean, Ont., a 34-company AI and robotics research consortium. "We will depend on this technology to compete with the rest of the world."

AI will enable robots with vision systems to locate specific items in complex environments. The US military is experimenting with an AI robot vehicle ultimately intended to recognize obstacles and geographical features. Consumer spin-offs will include robot vacuum cleaners and lawn mowers. "AI's potential is almost unlimited," says George Sekely, CP vice-president for computers and communications. "Whatever can be quantified can be done."[24]

Balancing the Positive and Negative Aspects of Change

Assessments of the future of business often assign more importance to negative influences than to positive ones.[25] Indeed, many factors and circumstances may well have an adverse impact on forecasts: inflation, unemployment, and bureaucratic red tape are but a few. Still, there are favourable situations balancing the negative inputs to assessments of our future, including:

1. Recognition of the importance of continued capital investment is strong. Some recent tax proposals illustrate this vital concern.
2. Communist nations, such as China and the Eastern European bloc, are viewed as excellent spots for future business investments and marketing efforts.
3. New research efforts concerning energy and various raw materials are quite hopeful. Many people believe that by the nineties Canada will be considerably more self-sufficient in these areas than it is now.[26]
4. Canada, with a leading position in both data communications and word processing industries, has an opportunity to play a major role in office automation.[27]
5. The decline in the value of the Canadian dollar has brought total compensation per hour to about 10 percent below United States rates after adjusting for exchange rates.
6. Tariff and non-tariff barriers on manufacturing products in other countries are being reduced under the Tokyo Round. The net effect of these changes is to reduce tariff rates in most of the major industrialized countries to the lowest levels in the present century.[28]

Tomorrow's Challenges

Many of today's challenges will be present tomorrow. But management must also watch for the new challenges that will appear. Some of today's vexing situations may seem minor when compared with the compexities to be faced in the future.

Tomorrow's challenges require today's preparation. Business executives must learn to adapt to events that may be unheard of now. Management must be flexible, prepared to meet new situations with strategies designed for the future—an approach requiring a sound education. Qualified executives must have a solid understanding of the business system and must be able to adapt to change.

The only thing constant about Canadian business, in fact, is change! It is a vital part of everyday business life. Change was yesterday's challenge. It is today's challenge. And it will be tomorrow's challenge.

One critical question remains: What will be your role in facing tomorrow's challenges? Virtually every sector of society and every career field is influenced by contemporary business—directly or indirectly. And business offers exciting opportunities for a rewarding future. Now that you have an overview of the business system, in the next chapter you will learn about where you fit in it.

The space industry, somnolent since the 1986 Challenger tragedy, will soar once again in the 1990s. Construction of a manned, US-led international space station will begin in the late 1990s. Canada's contribution, a $1.2-billion mobile robotic arm system, will help assemble the station. Much space investment will come from private companies or consortia.

Already US firms are planning their own rocket launches. Sooner or later they will make extra bucks by delivering capsules of cremated ashes into orbit (proposed by the Celestis Group Inc. of Florida) or huge orbital billboards.

The benefits of space activity will go beyond the development of new alloys, semiconductor crystals and medicines in zero-gravity labs. Space and moon bases will constitute a colonial market dependent on Earth for goods from plumbing to paint. Space folks will need minigyms to keep in form, cookbooks to tempt their palates, entertainments to enliven long tours of duty. Zero-gravity clothes washers, toilets, and showers have been a constant problem, although NASA may replace showers with mist sprays and suction systems. We don't think much about soap foam on Earth, but in space that foam quickly fills waste tanks. "Space products must be compatible with on-board water and atmosphere recyling," says Bill Seitz, former head of systems development in NASA's man-systems division, which looks to "task out" elements of its space habitation project.[29]

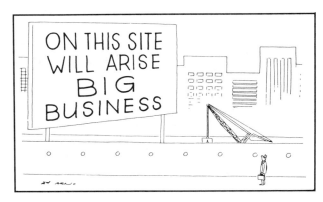

Drawing by Ed Arno;
© The New Yorker
Magazine, Inc.

Sure, the earth is afflicted with acid rain and toxic chemicals, chlorofluorocarbons (CFCs) attack the ozone layer, a miasma of CO^2 slowly stews us. But let's suppose, for once, that we will control our environmental problems. The question is: what will make that possible? Answer: a change in the social psyche that will affect industry, consumers, retailers, and governments.

In the midst of the 1988 election, Brian Mulroney suddenly called for a national commitment to protect the environment, and his government lickety-split advanced deadlines for the elimination of leaded gas and PCBs. Why? Surveys revealed a surprising amount of support among voters for environmentalism.

"Polls say 80 percent of the population is worried. The environment will be a mainstream concern in the next decade," predicts Colin Isaacs, executive director of Toronto's Pollution Probe, whose role until recently was to bemoan public apathy.

The antismoking laws of the 80s were a foretaste of government attempts to alter our bad habits. Governments will toughen pollution laws and increasingly tax products—such as throwaway items—that sully the environment. In June, the feds plan to begin granting seals of approval for environment-friendly products, including those made from recycled materials or enclosed in biodegradable packaging.

Industry will take matters into its own hands. Already, most Canadian producers have ceased to use CFCs as propellants in aerosol cans, aside from medical sprays. US chemical giant E.I. du Pont de Nemours & Co. has announced a complete withdrawal from CFC production by 2000, and last year the company spent more than US $30 million seeking replacements for the CFCs used in solvents and refrigeration systems.

"There's a greening of corporate board rooms. Industry won't push the environment to the edge any more. Aside from the moral concern, there are the financial liabilities.

"Industry was often blamed for environmental problems. Now we see economic growth as the engine for improving conditions. We have to bring jobs and knowledge to the Third World." Third World poverty has led to the destruction, for economic gain, of the CO^2-absorbing forests that are our best resistance to the greenhouse effect.

The new economic watchword, however, will be "sustainable development"—signifying that current growth should not undermine future growth by impairing the environment.

Waste recycling is here to stay, not because it's lucrative—although one day it may be—but because the number of cheap, safe, and politically acceptable dump sites has dwindled. Many North American communities now require residents to recycle. By the end of 1988, 91 Ontario municipalities, harbouring half the province's population, had blue-box programmes, which encourage residents to place newspapers, bottles, and cans in curbside boxes for recycling.

Although such programmes often depend on government and private-sector subsidies, recycling will become financially attractive as Earth's rising population makes greater demands on energy and materials.

The potential of recycling will be maximized with monetary incentives. Other provinces may imitate Alberta's recycling depots that reimburse people for glass, metal, or plastic containers. Depot operators earn fees from the companies whose containers they collect. Nonrefillable glass bottles are crushed and shipped to a glass plant. Metal is sold as scrap. Plastics go to a recycler who makes them into household items such as flower pots. Alberta's 120 depots are licenced and guaranteed an exclusive territory to ensure their financial viability. ''The depots make money, judging by how actively licences are sought.''

A conserver society need not be a poorer society. It will simply be smarter. ''Japan has had spectacular growth yet cut its energy and materials input about 60 percent in 11 years,'' notes the Canadian Environmental Advisory Council. Besides, a conserver society will mean new entrepreneurial and job opportunities. There's lots of cleaning up to do.[30]

Focus 23-4

Tomorrow's Big Sellers and Services

Here are the products that will fly in the coming decade:

- *Home security*: An aging but technologically hip population increasingly vulnerable to crime will fortify with electronic sensors, automatic light-timers and security cameras.
- *Home automation*: Computerized control systems will govern home energy use. Fridges with microchips will track grocery requirements and, at a smarter stage, phone the order to the foodmart. And (at last!) a robot lawn mower.
- *Home entertainment*: Tomorrow's high-tech home entertainment centres will feature videotex information systems, audio equipment including programmable multiple CD players, high-resolution VCRs and TV receivers with surround-sound stereo and, sold separately, flat, wall-sized high-definition screens.
- *Lap-top computers*: Essential as pens for business travellers and, with declining prices, even students. They could be second computers for two-computer families.
- *Smart cards*: A single plastic card with embedded microchips will store volumes of information including bank balances, debit and credit transactions, medical history and other personal data—and could double as library card, transit pass, and house key.

- *Videophones*: Once phone companies install integrated services digital networks (ISDN), it will be possible to accompany calls with video images at relatively low cost. Expect a new generation of telephone hardware. Already Panasonic, perhaps preparing the market, has introduced a picture-phone that transmits still photographs over regular lines.

Here are the services that will bud in the nineties and bloom in the new millennium:

- *Home information*: Interactive telecommunications technology will bring into the home, via the phone line, direct marketing, business, and entertainment text services including romantic "chat" lines, electronic mail, correspondence courses, classified ads, home shopping and financial information. Bell Canada and CETI Inc. of Montreal have launched interactive systems and together expect to place a million terminals in Canada by 1995.
- *Home shopping and delivery*: With husband and wife busy advancing their careers, there's no time left for necessities. Home shopping over cable TV or home telecommunications systems will thrive— especially at wholesale prices and when products (such as packaged brands) do not require on-site inspection.
- *Financial service centres*: The merging of banks, insurers, and brokerages opens the path to under-one-roof financial service marts. Independent brokerages long cloistered in skyscrapers may have to open storefront locations just to keep up with the action.
- *Temporary employment agencies*: As employers pursue workforce flexibility and reduce benefit commitments by contracting-out and hiring part-time help, specialized agencies will help freelance workers market their talents and coordinate their part-time and temporary assignments. By the end of the century, the proportion of part-time workers will reach as high as 19 percent of total employment.
- *Travel services*: By 1996, 50 percent of the population will be over 34 years old and 28 percent will be over 50. People who have passed the nest-building stage of the life cycle have more time and money for leisure pursuits and a pent-up desire to sample foreign climes. Crowded skies and the threat of air terrorism could mean increased emphasis on land and sea junkets.
- *Services for seniors*: As the population grows older, there will be more of a demand for services dealing with the phenomenon of aging, including anti-aging treatments. Seniors wishing to prove themselves fit as fiddles will visit geriatric Club Meds. Those oriented toward personal development will seek spiritual approaches to age and death.

Source: Ian Allaby, "The Future Now! Priming Your Business for the 1990s," *Canadian Business*, March 1989, p. 60.

Controversial Issue

Social Responsibility—Disposing of Hazardous Waste

To be effective in the future, managers must recognize social trends, determine how they affect their businesses, and develop appropriate strategies for dealing with the changed environment.

Over the past few years, many social changes affecting business have involved either social responsibility or the quality of work life. People want socially responsible decisions from executives and have begun to protest actions that are not in line with this thinking.

No issue facing the government and business community is as politically sensitive or pressing as the necessity for some form of programme aimed at disposing toxic waste—in particular, PCBs.

Thus far, both government and business have tended to be reactive in their response rather than preventive. No issue exemplifies so well the pitfalls of setting environment policy in the wake of disaster.

Twice in the past four years, accidents with hazardous polychlorinated biphenyls (PCBs) have caused a national outcry and laid bare the environmental anxieties of Canadians.

A PCB spill in 1985 on the TransCanada Highway near Kenora, Ontario, led to tougher rules on transporting chemical waste. In August 1988, a raging PCB warehouse fire in St. Basile-le-Grand, Quebec, produced an ambitious but muddled plan to phase out the use of PCBs. The most controversial aspect of this plan involved the imposition of a deadline for taking PCBs out of use—before a plan for destroying them was in place.

Julia Langer, executive director of the environmental lobby group Friends of the Earth, says that, without a detailed incineration plan, the idea of phasing out PCBs and putting them on storage is pure "PR."

Langer agrees with most industry representatives that PCBs are safer where they are until a way of destroying them is found.

"Most of the hazard with any hazardous waste is in handling and shipping."

A more methodical plan to dispose of PCBs is needed.

Breaking out of the pattern of setting regulations as a reaction to crises is seen as a key to improving environmental policy and planning. Langer says business may be leading government when it comes to advance planning on pollution control. The high cost of cleaning up after a disaster should persuade the industry to look for ways to prevent expensive environmental mistakes.

"When businesspeople start believing their calculators, they see that they can actually benefit financially from changing their ways," Langer says. Complying with the federal PCB phase-out plan, for example, will cost Canadian companies using and storing the substance an estimated $500 million over five years.

There are signs that the federal government is moving towards less costly, preventive policies.

According to Victor Shatora, the federal official in charge of the PCB programme, "We're going to be publishing a list of the top priority chemicals that we think are of concern. By doing that, we hope to get out of the reactive mode—we'll know the chemicals are of concern, and industry and public will be alerted to that."

The ministry would prepare the assessment reports on the health and safety risks associated with the chemicals. Regulations on handling and controlling the chemicals would follow. Companies introducing new chemicals will have to "prove conclusively that they are not going to create a problem," says Shantora. "If PCBs were introduced today, they would be subject to tough scientific testing before going into mass production."

In other words, businesses should take note.

Source: John Geddes, "PCB Disposal Plan Ambitious but Flawed," *The Financial Post*, February 10, 1989, p. 11.

Summary of Learning Goals

1. **Describe the recent major changes in the way Canadians live and work and why it is difficult to predict future changes.**

   Alvin Toffler has pointed out that we are now entering a third wave of industrialization, dominated by a home-based, service-oriented type of economy. However, these trends are very difficult to predict because of the accelerating rate of change in the way North Americans live and work.

2. **Analyze the accelerating pace of change.**

   It is difficult to predict the future of Canadian industry. We often miss even broad economic, social, and cultural changes that will affect businesses. Prediction is also difficult because of the accelerating pace of change and trends such as population changes, lifestyle changes, economic changes, technological changes, and business strategy changes.

3. **Explain the role of high technology in Canada's future and identify the problems associated with high technology.**

   High-technology firms are those whose research and development expenditures and number of technical employees are double those of other manufacturers. High-tech firms are expected to experience major growth in the future Canadian economy. However, their growth is not expected to completely offset the loss of jobs experienced by smokestack industries.

   Various problems are associated with the development of high-tech industries. One is the difficulty of shifting the unemployed from blue-collar labour to high-tech employment. Another is that many high-tech jobs are lost to foreign operations. Increased competition in many industries means that it is often difficult for an entrepreneur to succeed. Finally, restrictions on high-technology transfer can be an obstacle to many organizations in this field.

Key Terms

third wave
jobless growth
population explosion
lifestyle
technology

high technology
firm
technology transfer
automation

Discussion Questions and Exercises

1. Cite some examples that support Toffler's argument that a third wave has taken place in history.
2. Why is it difficult to predict the future course of Canadian business?
3. What can be learned about predictions from the failure of the North American auto industry to forecast small car demand?
4. Identify the current trends affecting business.
5. Why are population changes particularly significant for the less developed nations?
6. Assume you are leading a negotiating team for the United Auto Workers. What would your position be on robots in the plant?
7. What business strategy changes have occurred in recent years?
8. What positive factors are likely to affect the future of Canadian business and the private enterprise economic system?

Case 23-1

The Technology Trap

When Michael Landry made the decision to automate the management audit group at Hubbard Life Insurance Co., he thought the new technology would be the answer to all his problems. Landry was concerned about the inefficiency of his staff and the deteriorating quality of their work.

The audit group at Hubbard has about 100 white-collar and pink-collar (clerical) employees. Their job is to audit the other parts of the organization, to monitor their compliance with company procedures, and determine how well they are maintaining financial and management controls. Auditors divide their time between field visits and report-writing in the office.

Before the office was automated, clerks, typists, and secretaries were located close to the field auditors and project coordinators they reported to. Work loads varied. Landry believed that word-processing equipment would make the division of work more equitable and his department more productive.

Landry set up a project team led by himself to manage the switch to computers. The other two members of the team were a technical person and an administrative manager, both Hubbard employees from outside the audit group.

After reviewing the work loads of the group, they decided to reorganize the support staff into separate units, each with its own supervisor. Three supervisors would report to one coordinator. Typists received training to become word-processing operators and the entire department moved to new quarters.

Job descriptions changed as a result of the automation. Whereas previously the audit group had clerks, typists, and secretaries, it now has clerical staff, word-processing operators, and administrative assistants. The clerical staff are further divided into receptionists, file clerks, and mail clerks. Word-processing operators are centralized in one area and clerical staff in another.

Many of the support staff had been with the company for close to 15 years. Until Landry decided it was time to join the computer revolution, electric typewriters were the highest technology they knew. Landry expected a major change to meet with some griping because people were used to doing things the old way. In the audit group, this reaction was especially pronounced. To Landry's dismay, the complaints haven't subsided in the three months since the changeover. So far, he hasn't seen the increase in productivity he had expected. Turnover, previously almost non-existent, is high and morale has plummeted.

One reason could be that there is less flexibility now and less chance for career advancement. There is also less interaction among staff. Despite the training they received before the changeover, the operators weren't able to match their previous output until much later. Efficiency in other areas, such as phone answering and filing, has been reduced as a result of the centralization and specialization of clerical work. Clerks who used to have a diversity of tasks are now confined to one job.

The only members of the audit group who seem satisfied are the administrative assistants, because they have dropped the clerical duties they had as secretaries and now handle more senior tasks. Their morale is high because they feel upgraded. Unlike the clerks and typists, they have not been grouped together in a separate area.

But everyone else is unhappy. Some have left, others are transferring away. The computer screens are affecting some operators' health; they complain of skin rashes, sore muscles, and eye strain. Sick leave and absenteeism are up.

The audit group was the first department at Hubbard to adopt word-processing equipment. Its experience was seen by top management as a pilot project. Based on the results so far, other departments are in no hurry to follow Landry's example.

Source: Daniel Stoffman, "The Technology Trap," *Canadian Business*, October 1987, pp. 171, 173.

Questions:

1. What was wrong with Landry's project to improve productivity through new technology? What might he have done differently? Explain.
2. What should Landry do now? What does this imply about a more employee-oriented style of management? Discuss.

Case 23-2

The 21st Century Workplace

Regardless of where North Americans work in the 21st century, their jobs will be less toilsome, thanks to computers and advanced automation.

Tomorrow's factories will be smaller, cleaner, and much more attractive than the teeming industrial caverns of the 19th and 20th centuries. Computerized robots will perform most tasks, from transporting materials in and around the plant to the assembly, inspection, and packaging of finished products.

Already there are over 6,000 industrial robots at work in North American factories, according to the Robot Institute of America. By 1990, some 200,000 will be in place; by the turn of the century they will number more than 1 million.

Some plants will run with as few as 10 workers on hand to maintain equipment and monitor operations by closed-circuit television. In another 50 years, production will be controlled by computer commands flashed directly from corporate headquarters to robots on the assembly line, thus making product changes both easy and inexpensive to accomplish.

Fewer workers will mean less space set aside for lunchrooms, offices, locker rooms, parking, and the like. There will be less call for safety equipment and climate control, such as systems to filter dust. The cleaner and more compact factories of the future will be built in places that would never allow today's noisy sprawling facilities.

Some automated factories will even operate in outer space, where zero gravity will enhance the production of items such as bearings, biogenetic products and semiconductor chips. Robots and computers will become office fixtures, too. They will do everything from preparing coffee to delivering mail, freeing employees for more creative assignments.

Paper will be almost nonexistent; so will typewriters. Nearly all communications will take place through electronic means.

Computers will speak, listen, recognize voices, translate words into other languages, send and take messages, schedule appointments—and even make phone calls.

Executives will dictate letters to computerized voice machines that will type, proofread, and correct. The messages then will be distributed to the appropriate electronic "mailboxes." When hard copies are desired, machines will print and duplicate documents in a fraction of a second on reusable paper.

With so much information stored in computers—rather than in workers' heads—employees will be valued not for possessing information but for their ability to analyze and use it.

By the year 2000, workers in a variety of occupations—from engineers to secretaries—will perform many of their daily tasks at home. Computer networks linked by satellite will enable workers using home terminals to communicate with fellow employees and company headquarters, write reports, and have access to records stored in a central computer. Business travel also will be reduced through widespread use of "teleconferences." Engineers will send their product designs electronically to the factory. Even salespeople will do substantial portions of their work at home by computer. The result will be less drudgery and greater levels of productivity in almost every field.

"The high-tech applications in the factory, home, and office will be in full bloom by the year 2000," predicts Jerome Rosow, president of the Work in America Institute. "As a result, work will be much more pleasant and rewarding."

Source: Reprinted from "Ahead: Work without Drudgery?" *U.S. News & World Report*, May 9, 1983, p. A26. Copyright, 1983, U.S. News & World Report, Inc.

Questions:
1. With which of the above predictions do you agree and with which do you disagree?
2. What factors could potentially change this scenario?
3. How would an automated, 21st century workplace affect employment opportunities?
4. Would government action be required to protect employment if this scenario were to unfold? Discuss.

Chapter 24

Your Career in Business

Learning Goals

To most men, there should come a time for shifting harness, for lightening the load one way and adjusting it for greater effort in another. That is the time for the second career, time for the old dog to perform new tricks.
—*Wilder Penfield, address, Canadian Club, Montreal, December 1959.*

1. To explain the concept of an occupational cluster and how it helps one establish a career in business

2. To describe the challenges facing nontraditional students seeking a business career

3. To explain why knowing yourself is vital for career development

4. To analyze the steps in the job search process

5. To outline the special problems of women choosing business careers

6. To explain how women can overcome career barriers

Profile

Heather Reisman—*Strategic Change Specialist*

Since Heather Reisman feels "compelled by the whole issue of change," it is fitting that she went through a few changes herself on the way to launching one of the country's most innovative management consulting firms. Reisman, 38, studied psychology at McGill University, did social work for Montreal's Children's Service Centre, and helped her brother with his computer business before joining Montreal's Intergroup Ltée, where she first encountered the concept of strategic-change consulting.

That was in 1975. By 1977 Reisman and Marc Gerstein, a colleague at Intergroup, had formed Gerstein & Associates, the forerunner of Paradigm Consulting Inc. Today, what began as a two-person office in Montreal with four clients is a Toronto-based operation with an active client roster of 25. That's enough to keep eight consultants and four support staff busy, and while Reisman won't reveal Paradigm's current revenues, she does confidently predict they will hit $7.5 million by 1990.

What sets Paradigm apart is its unusual approach.

In contrast to most management consulting firms, which provide a broad spectrum of services to a certain sector, Paradigm advises *all* types of firms on a single issue: how they can most effectively adapt to internal or external changes. Current or former clients value this specialization.

Terry Jackson, executive vice-president with investment dealer Nesbitt Thomson Deacon, a former Paradigm client and part-owner from 1985-86, praises the firm's workshop-based approach. "With traditional consultants, you give them your problem and they go away and bring back solutions," he says. "Paradigm works with executives to define the problem, develop solutions and put them into practice." Or as Reisman says, "We supply the process,

the executives do the thinking."

It was an approach that took a long time to catch on. But catch on it did. And Reisman was able to garner many admirers in the process. Gerald Pencer, chairman of Financial Trustco Capital Ltd., appointed Reisman to the board of Financial Trustco in 1984—now one of seven boards she sits on, including Magna International Inc. and the Toronto Stock Exchange. He touts Reisman, who advised both the federal and provincial Liberals on policies, as "the best candidate for our first lady prime minister."

Source: Catherine Dowling-Smont: "Heather Reisman: Consultant as Quick-Change Artist," *Canadian Business*, August 1987, p. 55.

Jeanne Picard had planned to study journalism, but she became a commerce student at Concordia University instead.

In her final year of high school, Jeanne decided that her future career should offer variety and a chance to meet people. Journalism was her choice, until she attended a province-wide meeting of school newspaper editors that led her to conclude the field was too crowded. She then considered a teaching career in French or the humanities.

The next fall, Jeanne enrolled in Vanier College in Montreal, a CEGEP. A friend mentioned the availability of career guidance at the Canada Employment Centre serving the campus. The centre led to CHOICES, a system that adds a computer to the team of counsellor and client. CHOICES is a service of the Occupational and Career Analysis and Development Branch of the Canadian Employment and Immigration Commission.

CHOICES has been designed as a dual file system to allow users to access information on occupations, on educational and training institutions, or on both. Through a linkage system, users can move easily between the Occupations File and the Education and Training File. With this system one can access related programmes of study for a selected occupation and vice versa. At the same time, CHOICES provides users with a process for selecting personally relevant information that will help them now and later in their career history. This double file makes CHOICES a very comprehensive source of career and vocational information for Canadian users.

People can search occupations through such topics as interests, aptitudes, educational level, future outlook, earnings, or hours of work and travel.

Jeanne used CHOICES while at Vanier, to search for an occupation that met her chosen criteria, and a university that would prepare her for that occupation. Jeanne Picard's experience with CHOICES was most helpful. She became a commerce student at Concordia University and later on a junior manager in a retail chain.[1]

Career Clusters and Employment Trends

entry-level job
The first permanent kind of employment after leaving school.

How should you approach your career in business, especially your first **entry-level job**—that is, your first permanent kind of employment after leaving school? First, you should become aware of employment projections and trends. Suppose you are interested in teaching. You should know that many areas of this field are faced with an oversupply of trained people.

In an employment area where the supply of workers exceeds the demand, some qualified individuals will still be able to obtain employ-

career cluster
A group of related jobs.

ment, but others will have to accept alternative jobs. Therefore, students should select and prepare for a group of related jobs—a **career cluster**—that offers positive employment opportunities.

In most colleges and universities, the business curriculum is organized around the key courses of accounting, management, marketing, business law, finance, economics, statistics, and computers. These courses deal with the common knowledge required in any meaningful entry-level business position. Students then acquire more specialized knowledge by taking advanced classes in each area. This background, along with a positive attitude, provides the initial flexibility needed for many kinds of business jobs. More knowledge can be acquired at any time by anyone valuing personal and professional improvement. Many business jobs are in high demand, but people who have a good understanding of the basic business subjects can gain entry-level employment in several areas.

Focus 24-1

Retraining Programmes Needed to Fill Holes in the Workplace

Many employers—big and small—are finding that they must invest more time and resources in staff training than ever before. Despite the lineups at employment offices, recruting people for even entry-level jobs has become a growing challenge.

Michel Gagne, a training supervisor at Pratt and Whitney Canada Inc., blames this shortage of skilled workers on the school system, vocational advisers and general attitudes in our society—all of which, he contends, are lagging behind trends in the labour market and perpetuating a bias against "blue-collar" jobs. Most students are directed towards office work and the professions, Gagne comments. But many of them are unable to find jobs that pay well, and they must then be "rethreaded" through the employment system.

Meanwhile, the shortage of skills has become pervasive in today's economy.

In a recent survey by the Canadian Federation of Independent Business, 52 percent of small and medium-size business respondents reported that the shortage of qualified labour was a "significant problem" for their companies. And a recent report by the Economic Council of Canada pinpoints "mismatching" between job vacancies and job seekers as one of the most important and pressing issues in the economy.

This phenomenon is global and goes far beyond the training of youth. It reflects the drastic shift to computers and other information-age technology, and calls for extensive retraining of older workers.

"We're experiencing a dramatic industrial restructuring that is yielding a shift from the goods-producing sector to the service industries," says Keith Newton, senior research director for

Ottawa's Economic Council. "And while Canada has done well in terms of job creation since the 1981-82 recession, we still have high unemployment. And the age profile of the unemployed is growing higher."

Many industrial workers lose their jobs as a result of extensive modernization and restructuring. Quebec, with high capital spending, has undergone drastic employment shifts over the past eight years. This hard push to modernize, combined with inadequate training in the schools and a high illiteracy rate in the province, has taken a toll.

"Since 1981-82, we've seen a lot of modernization, a lot of advanced technology—computers and robotics," explains Gilles Rheaume, an economist with the Ottawa-based Conference Board of Canada. "Now, we need trained individuals to work with central computers. The forest products and mining industries have seen such modernization. Much of the work done by computer used to be manual jobs."

The same is true in service sectors like financial services, where computer literacy has become essential.

"In labour negotiations, job training and retraining is becoming more and more of an issue," Rheaume notes. "In terms of priority, it's hand in hand with job security."

Source: Nancy McHarg, "Retraining Programs Needed to Fill Holes in the Workplace," *This Week in Business*, February 11, 1989, p. 3.

Employment Trends

Today's students are following on the heels of the baby boomers, who are crowding the first rungs of the management ladder. Unfortunately, the economy hasn't been growing fast enough to absorb them, let alone the recent crop of graduating students, so the unemployment rate among the young is soaring well above the national average.

David Foot, a University of Toronto professor who has written extensively on demographics, believes the challenge of the nineties will be the creation of more than two million jobs for future labour market entrants. Automation threatens to reduce the number of employment openings, as does the decline in certain uncompetitive industries. See Figure 24-1 for projected 21st century careers.

In the annual demographic roundup of *Tomorrow's Customers*, the management consultant firm Woods Gordon suggest the service sector will continue to increase faster than other areas, four times faster than manufacturing. Government employment, on the other hand, is likely to "slow dramatically as budgetary restrictions limit hiring." Transportation, communication, and utilities are in for the slowest growth this decade. Focus 24-1 details the increasing need for employers to institute more training in the workplace as recruiting people becomes a growing challenge.

Figure 24-1   A Sample of Emerging Careers for the 21st Century

Professional

Cable TV auditor
Career counsellor
Career change counsellor
Certified alcohol counsellor
Certified financial planner
Child advocate
Communications specialist
Computer designer
Computer scientist
Computer security specialist
Computer systems analyst
Data base designer
Data base engineer
Divorce mediator
Documentation specialist
Ecologist
EDP auditor
Energy auditor
Engineering geologist
Environmental engineer
Ethicist
Family mediator
Forecaster
Forensic scientist
Fusion engineer
Gene splicing worker
Geneticist
Genetic counsellor
Geriatric nurse
Health physicist
Hibernation specialist
Human services expert
Image consultant
Information broker

Information research scientist
Lead system analyst
Licensed therapeutic recreation
  specialist
Marine geologist
Mineral economist
Molecular biologist
Neutrino astronomer
Ombudsman
Oncology nutritionist
Phobia therapist
Planetary engineer
Planetary scientist
Professional ethnicist
Public affairs psychologist
Robot engineer
Robotic scientist
Security engineer
Selenologist
Sex therapist
Software writer
Solar architect
Solar designer
Solar energy consultant
Space colonist
Space botanist
Sports psychologist
Strategic planner
Thanatologist
Theoretical chemist
Underwater archeologist
Volcanologist
Wind prospector

Paraprofessional

Exercise technician
Family and planning midwives
Home health aide
Hotline counsellor
Lawyer's aide
Library aide

Licensed psychiatric technician
Medical aide
Sex counsellor
Social work aide
Teacher's aide
Veterinary aide

Managerial and supervisory

Complaints manager
Data base administrator
Data base manager
Director of human resources
Director of software developments

International sales and
  marketing manager
International systems director
New product manager
Site selector specialist

EDP audit systems manager
Employee relocation
  services director
Executive VIP for international
  product planning
Halfway house manager
Information coordinator
Information manager

Space launch director
Systems analysis manager
Technical services manager
Telecommunications marketing
  director
Transplant coordinator
Underwater hotel, pavilion
  or observatory director

Sales

Cable TV salesperson
Computer salesperson
Digital radiography sales
  representative
Distributor of new business
  equipment
Phonovision salesperson

Robot salesperson
Salesperson for talking
  encyclopedias
Sales trainer
Software salesperson
Telecommunication salesperson
Telephone salesperson

Small business

Aquaculture
Artist (graphic)
Book club sales
Catering and fast food
Child daycare service
Computer games developer
Consultant
Electric car service station
Financial consultant
Financial planner
Fish farmer
Freelance writer
Home correspondence courses
Information salesperson
Inventor

Manufacturer of talking signs
Music store
New health foods
Orthotist
Picture framer
Plant and pet service
Publishing
Self-employment
Shrimp and trout fish farming
Specialized food services
Telephone answering service
Training services
Truffle nursery
Tutor
Videodating services

Skilled

Asteroid miner
Bioconversion technologist
Biomedical technician
Bionic medical technician
Computer assisted design
  (CAD) technician
Computer assisted manufacturing
  (CAM) specialist
Computer axial tomographer
  (CAT) technologist
Computer programmer
Computer service technician
Cryogenic technician
Cyborg technician
Diagnostic medical sonographer

Holographic inspection specialist
House husband and house wife
Industrial robot technician
Laser technician
Lunar miner
Materials utilization technician
Mechanic for hydrogen powered
  automobiles
Medicine aid technician
Microbiological mining technician
Nuclear fuel technician
Nuclear reactor technician
Positron emission tomograph
  (PET) technician
Rehabilitation housing technician

Dialysis technician   Space mechanic
Exotic welder   Solar engineering technician
Fibre optic technician   Telecommunications technician
Hazardous waste technician   Underwater culture technician
Hibernation technician

Semi-skilled	**Unskilled**
Battery technician	Home companion
Bio-gas technician	House pet and plant sitter
Computer graphics assistant	TV monitor (guard)
Courier	
Paramedics	

Focus 24-2

Where the Jobs Will Be

How many and what types of new jobs will be created in Canada into the nineties are still matters of broad conjecture, clouded by economic uncertainty and the impact of technology in the workplace.

Informetrica Ltd., the Ottawa forecaster, predicts 1.25 million new positions or about 1.6 percent annual growth between now and the end of 1990. But Data Resources of Canada, another major consultant, feels that 1.95 million or 2.4 percent more jobs a year will be brought on over the same period. That's a forecasting gap of 50 percent, a discrepancy that hinders planners.

What both forecasts suggest is that the country is in for tighter employment markets than during the seventies, when new jobs were being created at a rate of 3.1 percent annually.

Informetrica's projections say that service industries and those in trade, finance, and insurance, will produce relatively more jobs than others during the rest of the decade. Although some economists claim that manufacturing will rebound, others feel that the high cost of North American labour has exported great numbers of manufacturing jobs for good.

Informetrica says that manufacturers will create 31,000 new jobs a year for an average annual increase in employment of 1.1 percent over the rest of the eighties. That compares with 34,300 jobs or gains of 1.8 percent a year during the seventies. Service industries, on the other hand, will boost their workforces by 75,000 a year between now and the end of 1990—for 2.3 percent annual employment growth. Leading the sector in job creation will be the finance, insurance and real estate industries. Another great hope will be high technology. This industry says it expects to add 50,000 jobs each year.

However, Murray Hardie, executive director of a 1981 parliamentary task force on employment opportunities in the eighties, notes that balanced against the industry forecast, is "the coming impact of industrial technology, whose effect has yet to be felt in any extensive way."

Montreal economics professor Jeannine David McNeil also argues that the so-called microelectronic revolution hasn't altered society yet to the extent that it will. "Offices will have an hour-glassed organization," she says. "A lot of people at the bottom, very few in the middle and a great number at the top."

Serge Bertrand, the federal employment department chief of labour demand analysis, says workers with only medium skills—spot welders or computer programmers, for example—could find their jobs eliminated either as a result of robots or grade school computer courses. However, more demand is expected for high-skilled workers and those with technical skills.

Bertrand says it's getting harder to predict what skills will be in demand later in the decade. A two-year-old federal research project, the Canadian Occupational Projection System, has made a stab at predicting the demand for 500 different occupations. While he can't reveal specifics, Bertrand warns job seekers not to get carried away by the lure of high technology. "Despite the new technology, almost 40 percent of new jobs will be in the traditional areas, such as secretarial or bookkeeping. Many new high-tech jobs, such as electrical engineers or systems analysts, will grow very rapidly, but they won't account for a big chunk of employment."

Source: Times staff, "Where the jobs will be," *Financial Times*, March 26, 1984, p. 24.

Occupational Cluster: Opportunities for Alternative Careers

The rationale for an occupational cluster is straightforward. Changes in technology and demand for goods and services make it difficult to forecast specific employment opportunities, and a significant portion of the nation's future labour force will work in jobs relating to products and services not yet in existence. Many will switch occupations at least once by the year 2000—and job obsolescence will be the key factor. This startling prediction suggests that it is easier to estimate job trends in a cluster or related occupations than job by job.

Because each entry-level job requires specific skills and knowledge, students are wise to select a primary interest. But they should also acquire the broad base of knowledge and skills associated with an overall occupational cluster, to allow for greater flexibility.

The Canadian Employment and Immigrant division has identified about 20 occupational clusters, including administrative and managerial, marketing and sales, natural sciences and mathematics, and health and other technologies. Many of these clusters are based on business knowledge and skills.

Any senior college instructor can recount how students have changed over the years. Most can recall when colleges and universities served a market of primarily 18- to 22-year-olds. This age group then sought out the entry-level jobs described earlier.

Nontraditional Students

Clearly, Canada's university student body is aging. This is the most distinguishing feature of what has been called the nontraditional or the mature student.

Who Are the Nontraditional Students?

nontraditional student
Any student who does not fall into the 18- to 22-year-old age group, historically the traditional clients of higher education.

The term **nontraditional student** can be defined as any student who does not fit into the 18- to 22-year-old age group, the "traditional" clients of higher education. To some, the term is already inaccurate, since older students have become the norm on many campuses. In any case, nontraditional students have two other characteristics: they work, either full-time or part-time; and university is often only one of their daily responsibilities. Many are married, and many, regardless of marital status, have children.

Most nontraditional students come from one of the following groups.

displaced homemaker
Full-time homemaker who returns to school or joins the work force because of divorce, widowhood, or economic reasons.

1. The **displaced homemaker**—a full-time homemaker who returns to school or joins the work force because of grown children, a change in marital status, or economic reasons.
2. The veteran—another major segment of nontraditional students, many of whom lack practical job skills.

technologically displaced worker
Worker whose job is lost due to automation or to the decline of the industry in which the worker was previously employed.

3. The **technologically displaced worker**—one whose job was lost to automation or to the decline of the industry in which he or she was previously employed.
4. The older, full-time employee—someone who seeks additional education to enhance career prospects or for personal satisfaction.

Problems and Advantages for Nontraditional Students. Most nontraditional students face two primary disadvantages as they seek career opportunities in business: the ways in which the skills they are attempting to acquire differ from what they are accustomed to, and the burden of their other responsibilities. A steelworker seeking to become a computer analyst, for example, has to adopt a whole new set of behaviours. This switch is often very difficult for older students.

As rapidly changing technology alters the job-market, workers will need to be re-educated.

Going to university part-time, often in the evening, is exhausting. Most nontraditional students juggle the responsibilities of work, school, and maintaining a household. Some also have responsibilities to a spouse or children. Studying may have to be accomplished at odd times—during meals, at coffee breaks, while commuting, or late at night while the rest of the family sleeps.

But nontraditional students have one extremely important advantage: they have *experience*, even if it is in an alien field. Technologically displaced workers and returning students know how businesses operate. Displaced homemakers know about human relations skills from managing a household and from previous civic activities. And veterans can describe organizational foul-ups by the hour.

Nontraditional students need to take inventory of their personal experiences, and try to relate these activities to business careers. This analysis will point out the individual's strengths and weaknesses. The weaknesses may be remedied with courses at a local college, while the strengths can be featured in one's résumé. Like traditional students, older students need to look at employment trends and how to organize a job search.

Knowing Yourself Is Part of Career Development

In order to become successful in a particular job, a person needs to enjoy and value the tasks required by that job. It makes sense for most people to select a line of work that provides such satisfaction.

In addition to analyzing the demand for employment, people must understand themselves. The process of doing so will enhance their career development. Following are some questions aimed at generating this self-understanding:

1. What motivates you to do something?
2. What type of lifestyle do you want?
3. What do you want to be 15 years from now?
4. What do you like and dislike?
5. What do you fear?
6. What personal values do you hold?
7. What is your honest opinion of yourself?

Finally, people must understand the requirements of a job if they are to do well in it. The goal of career development, in fact, is to match individuals with compatible jobs. That is what CHOICES did for Jeanne Picard.

Most people need help in both self-analysis and job analysis. Students can find considerable information and personal assistance at the library, at a Canada (or Quebec) Employment Centre, and at career guidance or placement offices. During recent years there has been a major trend toward career education. Most schools now have materials explaining how to analyze your strengths and weaknesses, personal value structures, and job interests.

Obtaining the Right Position

What is the best way to find the right job for you? While there is no single approach, there are some general principles that can be followed.

The job search process is hard work. Good entry-level positions are highly sought after, so there is a lot of competition. The best first step is to locate available positions that interest you. Be resourceful. Your success depends on gathering as much information as possible. Then go after a job. Prepare a good résumé and have ready other materials that might convince a company that you will help further its goals. Be ready to write a lot of letters, make a lot of phone calls, and suffer a lot disappointments. When you are asked to an interview, put plenty of time and energy into preparing yourself. The job search is work in itself—work that can pay off for you.

Preparing Your Job Search Materials

Most prospective employers will want the same general kinds of information, so it is worthwhile setting up a folder with materials you have obtained or prepared in advance. You need the following information: (a) letters of recommendation from professors, employers, and others; (b) transcripts of your academic work to date; (c) personal data on yourself; and (d) a statement of career goals. The last two items are often combined in a **résumé**—a written summary of your personal, educational, and professional achievements.

résumé
A written summary of one's personal, educational, and professional achievements.

Many prospective employers will require you to produce much or all of this information on their own application forms, but preparing it ahead of time on your own has several advantages. First, it gives you time to assemble all the information you need, to consider carefully what you want to include, to remember or check facts you may have forgotten. (You want to avoid sitting in a personnel office struggling to remember the address of the fast-food restaurant you worked in four summers ago.) Second, it gives you time to write several drafts, to let other people read and criticize it, and to prepare a neat, perfectly typed final copy. Third, it ensures that you already have a résumé to use in seeking other employment interviews. Fourth, it encourages you to assemble your references and transcripts, both of which can take time.

Your résumé. For your job search, you must learn how to develop and use a résumé. The résumé is a very personal document, covering your educational background, work experience, career preference, major interests, and other personal information. It should also include basic information, such as your address and telephone number. Human rights legislation in your jurisdiction probably forbids employers to discriminate against you on the basis of age, marital status, or mother tongue (as well as many other grounds), but although this information in not compulsory you may include it if you think doing so will help you.

The primary purpose of a job résumé is to highlight your qualifications. In general, a résumé for a person seeking entry-level employment should be only one page long. The information should therefore be as concise as possible. An attractive layout will facilitate the employer's review of your qualifications.

There are several acceptable ways of preparing a job résumé. Some use narrative sentences to explain job duties and career goals; others are in outline form. Remember that your résumé must be designed

Figure 24-2
A Sample Résumé

```
PERSONAL INFORMATION
Alice W. Belskus                    Date of Birth:  30.10.64
901 North Elm                       Excellent health:  160 cm, 53 ka
Scarborough, Ontario                Fluently bilingual
M1C 4L9
(416) 388-2222


CAREER OBJECTIVE
To obtain a challenging position in industrial accounting in the Toronto area.


EDUCATION
Niagara College of Applied Arts and Technology—Associate of Arts in Business
(1984) York University—Bachelor of Business Administration (1987)
B+ average.


EXTRACURRICULAR ACTIVITIES
Accounting Club 1983-84
Glee Club 1984-86
Accounting Honorary Society 1985-87


BUSINESS EXPERIENCE
Room Clerk, Town Centre Motel, Downsview, Ontario 1983-84
Accounts Payable Clerk, Doctors' Hospital, Toronto 1984-86
Earned 80 percent of my educational expenses: balance was in part from OSAP loans.


REFERENCES
Mr. Edward Van Allan                Professor C. Carson Jones
Business Division                   Department of Accounting
Niagara College                     York University
St. Catharines, Ont.                4700 Keele Street
L2M 4A2                             Downsview, Ontario
                                    M3J 1P3


Mrs. Helen Steinmetz
Manager, Town Centre Motel
2046 Hinsdale Road
Downsview, Ontario
M1C 3V4
```

around your own needs and objectives. Figure 24-2 shows a very simple example.

References. Letters of recommendation are very important. Be selective in securing them, and try to include a business professor in your list of references. The people you ask for recommendations should be familiar with both your strengths and your career goals. But remember that these people are usually busy and cannot be expected to meet short deadlines. Allow them adequate time to prepare their letters; then follow up on missing ones.

Always ask people personally if they will write a letter of recommendation for you. Be prepared to give them a brief outline of your academic preparation, along with information concerning your job-seeking preferences and your career objectives. This will help them prepare the letter and may enable them to respond more quickly.

Finding Employment Sources

Even when job markets are tight, people do get hired every day. The trick is to find out about employers that have openings or might have openings. Sources for this information include (but are certainly not limited to) public and private employment agencies, your campus guidance office, advertisements, and word of mouth. You can also create your own sources by writing to likely employers.

Canada Employment Centres. The Canada Employment and Immigration Commission operates 438 regular Canada Employment Centres (CECs) plus 105 special centres at universities and colleges. (See Figure 24-3.) Quebec has its own provincially operated employment centres, as well as CECs. Unfortunately, because CECs are involved in processing unemployment insurance claims, some students think they provide services only for semiskilled and unskilled workers. In fact, they list many professional positions and provide a full range of guidance services. People who underrate CECs probably don't realize that residents of other countries envy Canadians' public employment system.

Private employment agencies. Private employment agencies can also be useful in your job search. These agencies, which often specialize in certain types of jobs, may have established good relationships with employers who are looking for particular types of workers. They also can offer candidates valuable counselling on how to "market" skills to employers.

If you use a private employment agency, be sure you understand its financial arrangements. Some are nonprofit organizations (an example is the Technical Service Council, an industry-sponsored service specializing in technical positions). Most, however, are in business for a profit, and someone has to pay their fees. Some Canadian jurisdictions forbid charging the job seeker; others do not. Be sure you know whether you or the employer will pay if the agency finds you a job. Avoid agencies that charge a fee whether they find you a job or not.

Campus placement offices. Your school's placement office is a valuable source of help for your job hunt. It offers guidance, reference materials, and probably assistance in writing your résumé. It arranges interviews with employers who recruit on campus. (These employers are often especially good prospects; after all, they clearly want

Figure 24-3
Summary of Employment Programmes and Services

Keep this chart as a handy reference. It shows how Employment and Immigration Canada's programmes and services can work for you. If you are interested in one of the items listed here, speak to a counsellor at your local Canada Employment Centre.

Program/ Service	What It Does	Who Can Use It
Canada Employment Centres (CEC)	• provide information about jobs, counselling, training • make referrals to jobs and training • process UI claims	• anyone who needs help to find a job, or to apply for training or UI
Canada Employment Centres on Campus (CEC-OC)	• provide employment related counselling and job placement services	• post-secondary students
Canada Employment Centres for students (known as Hire-A-Student in Alberta)	• provide a summer job placement service for students and job-hunting tips	• students (most centres are open from April to September only)
Outreach Projects	• provide in-depth counselling, referral and employment services for people who have problems finding and keeping a job • provide employment-related services in isolated areas	• some projects are set up especially for certain groups such as women, Native people, disabled individuals, and young people
Women's Employment Counselling Centres	• provide counselling, testing, training and referral services • some centres also place women in jobs	• women
Specialized Youth Units (SYUs)	• provide special services to help youth enter the work force	• people aged 15 to 19 who have major problems finding work
Canada Farm Labour Pools	• provide an agricultural recruitment service	• farmers and farm workers
Job Finding Clubs	• provide material and support for effective job searches	• anyone looking for a job
Native Employment Counsellors	• provide employment counselling and referral to testing, training or employment	• Native people
CHOICES	• a computerized career information system available in some CECs and in many schools, career centres, and community agencies, that can help you zero in on occupations that best suit you	• people not sure about the type of work they want to do • you must be referred by a counsellor

National Institutional Training Program	• classroom training that teaches you the skills required to do specific jobs	• generally, people no longer required by law to attend school in the province in which they live
National Industrial Training Program	• *Critical Trade Skills Training* provides on-the-job training in high-skill occupations where there is a shortage of workers • *General Industrial Training* provides on-the-job training in other occupations	• workers affected by new technology or whose jobs are otherwise threatened • unemployed people • women interested in jobs traditionally done by men • Natives • disabled people • people with special employment needs
Other training	• various courses are available to help you set employment goals, acquire basic working skills, and find a job	• ask your CEC counsellor if you are eligible
Job Corps	• a combination of short-term work experience and in-depth counselling to prepare you for a permanent job	• people who have problems finding a job because they lack education, training or work experience
Career-Access Programme	• subsidizes employers to give you on-the-job experience • provides 6-18 week summer internships, to give students work experience related to their fields of study	• people who have been unemployed for at least five months and are unlikely to find employment without the help of the programme • special arrangements are available for Native people, disabled people and those not fluent in the language of the area • full-time students who plan to continue their studies in the fall
Canada Works Programme	• creates jobs lasting from 6-52 weeks in communities where unemployment is high • creates summer jobs, lasting 6-18 weeks, for students, in projects of benefit to the community	• people who have been unemployed for at least eight weeks • full-time students who intend to continue their studies in the fall
Local Employment Assistance and Development (LEAD)	• provides funds to organizations and associations to create jobs in areas with high unemployment	• people registered at CECs are eligible for jobs created through LEAD funding
Financial help	• unemployment insurance, mobility assistance and training allowances may be available	• requirements vary—consult your CEC counsellor

Source: *Jobs Canada*, Vol. 1, No. 1, Winter 1984, p. 25.

employees without years of experience.) It may also maintain a list of available positions, and its staff certainly hear about others.

Other sources. Other sources that can help in identifying job openings are: (1) newspaper employment advertisements (metropolitan newspapers are often a rich source of job leads); (2) trade journals or magazines; (3) professors and school administrators; (4) community organizations, such as the local chamber of commerce; and (5) friends.

Unsolicited inquiries. Another approach to the job search is to identify all the organizations you think you would like to work for, then send an inquiry to each. To get your list—which may have as many as a hundred names—consult the University and College Placement Association's *Career Planning Annual*. Your librarian can also help you find the standard reference books that list Canadian companies. Another source of information about companies is trade associations in the appropriate field (for a list of trade associations, consult your librarian again or use a Canadian almanac). Use your imagination to find more sources—for example, if you want to work for an insurance company in British Columbia, the Vancouver and Victoria yellow pages would be a good starting place.

Once you have your list, arm yourself with a stack of neatly photocopied résumés. Mail along with a word-processed or individually typed letter of inquiry to each company. The letter should highlight one or two points from your résumé and ask briefly about employment opportunities in a particular line of work. It should also ask for a personal interview. If possible, direct your letter to a specific person, preferably one who has the authority to hire.

Studying Your Employment Opportunities

You should carefully study the various employment opportunities you find. Obviously you will prefer some over others, but as you assess each job possibility you should consider a variety of factors including: (1) the actual job responsibilities, (2) industry characteristics, (3) the nature of the company, (4) geographical location, (5) salary and advancement opportunities, and (6) the job's contribution to your long-term career objectives.

Too many graduates consider only the most striking features of a job—perhaps the location or the salary. However, a comprehensive review of job openings should provide a balanced perspective of the overall employment opportunity, including long-term as well as short-term factors.

A number of information sources are useful in ranking job prospects. Annual reports, financial summaries, and other data can usually be obtained from libraries, stockbrokers, and placement offices. In addition, your placement office or employment agency may be familiar with the companies on your list. If possible, try to visit each of these companies for firsthand impressions. Ask your friends and associates what they know about any companies you are studying.

The Personal Interview

The initial objective of a job search is to obtain an appointment with prospective employers. Once this has been accomplished, you should begin planning for the interview. You will want to enter the interview with a good understanding of the company, its industry, and its competition. Preparation includes obtaining essential information about the company, including:

1. How was the company founded?
2. What is its current position in the industry?
3. What is its financial status?
4. Which markets does it compete in?
5. How is the firm organized?
6. What is its competition?
7. How many people does it employ?
8. Where are its plants and offices located?

This information is useful in several ways. First, it helps you gain a feeling of confidence during the personal interview. Second, it can keep you from making an undesirable employment choice. Third, it can impress interviewers, who often try to determine how much applicants know about the company as a way of assessing their interest level. Candidates who do not make the effort to obtain such information are often eliminated from further consideration.

Where do you get this preinterview information?

1. Check with your placement office or employment agency. It should be able to tell you something about the company and to provide published material.
2. Check with business instructors at your school.
3. Go to the library and investigate the company in the standard business information guides. (Many of these are the same sources you may have used in making a list of companies to send unsolicited inquiries to.) If necessary, ask your librarian for help.
4. Contact a stockbroker and ask for information about the company.
5. Ask friends who have dealt with the company either as customers or as workers.
6. Contact the local chamber of commerce office.

These techniques should produce all the information you will need.

Interviewers report that many students fail during the interview process for two reasons: inadequate preparation for the interview, and lack of confidence. Both factors prevent effective communication. Remember that the interviewer will first determine whether you can communicate effectively. You should be specific in answering and asking questions and should express your concerns clearly and positively. Notice the importance that is assigned to communications in the sample interviewing rating sheet in Figure 24-4.

Most people who conduct initial employment interviews work in the personnel division of organizations. They are in a staff position, which means that they can make recommendations to other managers about which individuals should be employed. Line managers get involved in interviewing at a later stage of the hiring process. In many instances the decision is made jointly by personnel people and the immediate supervisor of the prospective employee; in other cases by the immediate supervisor alone. Rarely does the personnel department have sole hiring authority.

Ralph Dunagin/Orlando Sentinel Star

Although a good résumé is necessary for job-hunting, the impression made during an interview is equally important.

"YOUR RESUME IS VERY IMPRESSIVE, MR. FINWICK, BUT THE JOB CALLS FOR SOMEONE WITH A LITTLE MORE SELF-CONFIDENCE."

open-ended interview
An interview designed to study the thought processes of interviewees by forcing them to open up and talk about themselves and their goals.

Interviewers use a number of techniques to elicit information. A common one is to get the interviewee to talk as much as possible during the interview. This type of **open-ended interview** is designed to study your thought processes, forcing you to open up and talk about yourself and your goals. If your appear unorganized, the interviewer may eliminate you as a possible employee. When faced with this type of situation, be sure to express your thoughts clearly

Figure 24-4
A Sample Interview Rating Sheet and Often Asked Sample Questions

Name of Candidate _____

Interview Rating Sheet

Candidate: "For each characteristic listed below there is a rating scale of 1 through 7, where "1" is generally the most unfavourable rating of the characteristic and "7" the most favourable. Rate each characteristic by *circling* just *one* number to represent the impression you gave in the interview that you have just completed."

1. Appearance
   Sloppy   1   2   3   4   5   6   7   Neat
2. Attitude
   Unfriendly   1   2   3   4   5   6   7   Friendly
3. Assertiveness/Verbal Ability
   A.   Responded Completely to Questions Asked
   Poor   1   2   3   4   5   6   7   Excellent
   B.   Clarified Personal Background and Related to Job Opening and Description
   Poor   1   2   3   4   5   6   7   Excellent
   C.   Able to Explain and Sell Job Abilities
   Poor   1   2   3   4   5   6   7   Excellent
   D.   Initiated Questions Regarding Position and Firm
   Poor   1   2   3   4   5   6   7   Excellent
   E.   Expressed thorough Knowledge of Personal Goals and Abilities
   Poor   1   2   3   4   5   6   7   Excellent
4. Motivation
   Poor   1   2   3   4   5   6   7   High
5. Subject/Academic Knowledge
   Poor   1   2   3   4   5   6   7   Good
6. Stability
   Poor   1   2   3   4   5   6   7   Good
7. Composure
   Ill at Ease   1   2   3   4   5   6   7   Relaxed
8. Personal Involvement/Activities, Clubs, etc.
   Low   1   2   3   4   5   6   7   Very high
9. Mental Impression
   Dull   1   2   3   4   5   6   7   Alert
10. Adaptability
    Poor   1   2   3   4   5   6   7   Good
11. Speech Pronunciation
    Poor   1   2   3   4   5   6   7   Good
12. Overall Impression
    Unsatisfactory   1   2   3   4   5   6   7   Highly satisfactory
13. Would you hire this individual if you were permitted to make that decision right now? YES   NO

and keep the conversation on target. Talk for about ten minutes; then ask some specific questions of the interviewer. Listen carefully to the responses. Remember that if you are prepared for a job interview, it will involve a mutual exchange of information.

If you are interested in a job as a supervisor or salesperson, a few companies use an interview technique that creates a pressure situation—the stress interview. The interview may begin with a harsh criticism of your academic record or lack of practical experience. You may also be faced with a series of rapid-fire questions about how you would handle a hypothetical situation. It is important to retain your composure and communicate in a clear and precise manner.

If the initial interview is satisfactory, you will probably be invited to come back for another. Sometimes you will also be asked to take a battery of intelligence or aptitude tests.

The Employment Decision

Now let's consider the actual hiring interview. By this time the company knows a lot about you from your résumé, references, application form, and initial interview. You should also know a lot about the company. The primary purpose of the second interview is to determine whether you can work effectively with your potential superior and with your peers.

If you create a positive impression during your second interview, you may be offered employment. Again, your decision to accept the offer should depend on the closeness of the match between career opportunities and career objectives. If there appears to be a good match, your work is just beginning.

Make the best entry-level job decision you can; then get on with your career plan. Learn your job responsibilities as quickly and thoroughly as possible; then start looking for other ways to improve your performance and that of your company. Remember...your first promotion is just around the corner, so be sure not to miss the opportunity in your lifelong career development plan.

The Special Problems of Women Choosing Business Careers

Women now account for over 40 percent of the Canadian labour force,[2] and this proportion is expected to continue to grow. While the number of employed women has increased substantially over the years, women are only now opening the doors to executive office suites. See Focus 24-3 for a discussion of barriers and problems.

Traditionally, women entered professions such as teaching, nursing, and secretarial slots. While many were truly oriented to these careers, others may have selected them because of social and family pressure and outright bias against them in other fields. The situation is now changing considerably, with women entering many fields previously closed to them. Business administration classrooms, for instance, are full of women aspiring to high-level careers in private enterprise. Focus 24-3 discusses why some of the best women in business are tired of the problems and barriers that confront them in the corporate world.

Retailing has long been a favourite industry for women seeking business careers. Other choices have included consumer goods and service industries. Now these traditional areas are being shunned by some women who are performing well in industrial sales, public accounting, and the like. In increasing numbers, women are running their own businesses.

Personnel is another favoured area. A survey by a professional personnel association reveals that most women in management are hired in this area, although many are also being hired in sales, accounting, data processing, and engineering.[3]

In large companies, relatively few women hold top management jobs. This situation can be explained in part by the fact that relatively few women have acquired the experience necessary to assume such posts. It is reasonable to believe that as today's young businesswomen progress in organizations, many will eventually become corporate officers. However, they will probably face many career obstacles that cannot be overlooked if contemporary business is to reach its goal of equal employment opportunity.

What are some of the special problems that face women choosing a business career? Heidrick & Struggles, management consultants, asked 148 female corporate officers about the factor that most impeded their careers. The largest number, 48.5 percent, cited discrimination. When asked what factor most contributed to their own success, 48 percent of the respondents answered "hard work," another 21 percent said "ability," and 10 percent named "luck."[4]

Women often lack the sort of career development model that is commonplace for men. Young women entering industry today are often their family's first generation of female businesspeople and lack the career perspectives often provided to their sons. In the past, women tended to enter business with non-business educational backgrounds such as elementary education and home economics. Finally, the limited number of female executives provide few career models for young women advancing in a company, so they must break new ground at each stage of their careers.

Male coworkers can also create special problems. Unaccustomed to working with women of equal or higher managerial rank, men are sometimes ill at ease in such situations. Some even attempt to disregard or circumvent directives or suggestions by female executives. As more women enter executive ranks, these incidents are expected to decline.

A married woman may encounter dilemmas created by her spouse's career aspirations and her own family responsibilities.

Mothers face many special problems, ranging from finding care for infants to juggling office hours against an older child's need for attention. These problems should become easier to solve as more husbands and wives consider both careers in making their decisions, as child care facilities expand, and as more companies introduce flexible hours and other schedule adjustments compatible with parenting. Today all these situations do force difficult choices, but successful female executives are coping with the problems and pursuing professional goals. Success in any field has always required hard work and tough decisions.

Despite these obstacles, the survey conducted by Heidrick & Struggles found that the vast majority of female officers were optimistic about the future of women in business. Three out of four believe that female managers and professionals will travel the path to corporate power at a faster rate in the eighties than they did in the previous decade.

Focus 24-3

Women in Business—Thanks, But No Thanks

When Deborah Lawton earned her MBA from the University of Western Ontario in 1978, she assumed she was bound for the top. She expected a lot of hard work and obstacles. But she figured she was equal to the task. After all, if you could survive the MBA grind, you could survive anything that life could dish out.

Lawton and her colleagues belong to a new elite: businesswomen whose credentials match their will to advance. Corporate Canada's most esteemed degree made them fledgling members of the same high-powered club as CEOs C. Richard Sharpe (Sears Canada Inc.), Rhys Eyton (Canadian Airlines International), and Ken Harrigan (Ford Motor Company of Canada Ltd.). The club had been a male preserve until 1958, when Western's MBA programme produced a lone female graduate. But by 1978, the barriers were crumbling. Lawton's class included 33 women whose minority status— 15 percent of the class—made them prize recruits for forward-looking employers newly conscious of the sexual skew in management.

Now, ten years' experience has brought them to that critical stage, beginning in the mid-30s, when fast-trackers either break into senior management or lose their momentum.

Back in 1978, the obstacle in the way of women's progress seemed fairly straightforward: chauvinistic men who doubted women's skills and called them ''girls.'' Hardly anyone mentions chauvinists any more. Blatant discrimination has been eclipsed by subtler problems less easily solved through preparation and persistence. Husbands who may champion full equality in marriage still leave childrearing worries to their wives. Male bosses who cheered women on through middle-management can't be relied on to back their next move. And women themselves are asking whether the perks and power at the top are worth the personal sacrifices required—and the loneliness—along the way.

If the standard of success is having power and money, most of these women still have a long way to go. While a determined few may yet reach the top, many have abandoned that goal. They are short of energy after a decade of slogging in a world where men still call the shots. And time is running out. Their peak ladder-climbing years are also their last chance for motherhood.

Women executives' exhaustion may be attributable to the contradictory expectations they face. On the one hand, they must demonstrate such ''masculine'' traits as toughness and independence. But if they go too far, their lack of ''feminine'' submissiveness will unnerve coworkers.

In a ground-breaking study, Ann Morrison, Randall White, and Ellen Van Velsor of the Center for Creative Leadership in San Diego compared 76 women at or near the general management level with male managers. They interviewed not only the managers themselves, but ''insiders'' who control access to top jobs in their companies. It turned out that women, to be viewed as successful, had to meet nearly *twice* as many standards as men.

Whether because of discouraging messages from the top or simply because of past socialization, high-achieving women are less willing than men to be corporate slaves. They want friends and families as well as mentors, hobbies as well as promotions. It all adds up to a new definition of success: a balanced life.

Recent studies by Dorothy and Alexander Mikalachki comparing male and female MBA graduates from Western found that women are far more likely than men to say that career had become less important than family as the focus of their lives. Yet many men considered business more important than ever. And while the women often agonized about their relationships with their children, even the most family-oriented husbands did not.

First-generation female managers tended to resolve the work-family conflict by foregoing marriage and motherhood; now baby-boom women want to drive a harder bargain. And more often than not, they still lose out on something: either a jump on competitors at work or precious time with their kids. In the absence of private or public initiatives aimed at reducing this dilemma, child care remains the family's worry—which usually means the wife's. As a result, the choices confronting the female manager remain the same: either admit that her children come second, or interrupt her career, with no assurance that she will ever make up for lost time.

Source: Rona Maynard, ''Thanks, But No Thanks,'' *Report on Business Magazine*, February 1988, pp. 26, 28, 29, 31.

A Final Note...The Authors' View

We believe that choosing a career is the most important, and often the toughest, decision you will ever have to make. There is little room for error; your future happiness depends on a wise, thoughtfully considered choice.

Do not procastinate or trust others to make this decision for you. Make your own decision. Follow the steps outlined here or in other sources. Your instructors, parents, friends, and advisers will be willing to help in a multitude of ways. But the bottom line is your own personal decision.

We hope this textbook has opened a panorama of business- and management-oriented careers for you. Probably many of your classmates will work for a business firm when they leave school. But whatever your own decision, be sure it is right for you. As the old saying goes, "You pass this way only once." Enjoy!

Controversial Issue

Help Wanted: The Need for More Educational and Training Programmes

The signs are everywhere. Small businesses and franchises in Canada's major cities are signalling a desperate need for workers. Optimists are calling it a short-term cyclical problem. Others are not so sure. They read the signs as evidence of massive structural changes in the economy.

By the early decades of the next century, members of the Paris-based Organization for Economic Cooperation and Development (OECD) will experience labour shortages. The aging of the baby boom generation, combined with lower birth rates, means that the percentage of the working-age population will shrink considerably.

Ironically, most OECD countries have also been plagued for more than a decade by high unemployment levels. The average jobless rate:

8.25 percent. Canada and the US have bucked the trend in recent years because their expanding service sectors have provided opportunities in low-wage, low-skilled occupations. According to a report by the Ontario Premier's Council, these gains are deceptive: politicians focus too much on job creation and not enough on policies that address fundamental problems in the economy. Without such direction, lower unemployment rates will only be temporary.

How can there be labour shortages and high unemployment at the same time?

Participants at an OECD conference in 1988 on education and the economy agreed that a major cause of unemployment is structural—many are unemployed because world economies are changing so rapidly that their training and skills no longer apply. Innovations in technology, especially in the communications and manufacturing industries, are putting constant pressure on workers to upgrade their skills.

Employers and employees are finding it increasingly difficult to build a working marriage, for reasons ranging from poor motivation and lack of basic numeracy and literacy skills to inadequate training for specialized high-skill jobs. The aging of the workforce will only exacerbate the situation, resulting in reduced productivity, higher unemployment, and massive social costs.

In an effort to deal with the shortage and unemployment problems, the OECD council has outlined structural plans that emphasize wealth creation rather than just job creation. To lay the groundwork for this strategy, the council has placed education and training at the top of its agenda.

One well-known solution to meeting the challenge is the integration of work and training (learning for life). Most European nations and Japan are well ahead of Canada in dealing with the issue. The reason: other OECD countries have rejected the prevalent North American notion that labour is the major cost that's inhibiting growth and productivity.

The reluctance to appreciate the human value of productivity is built into a traditional model of industrial production, which measures wealth largely in material terms. But the model is outmoded in an information-based economy, where a nation's most valuable resource is not goods and machinery but the knowledge and skills of workers. In the new economy, the education and well-being of the workforce translate directly, if not immediately, into increased productivity.

In order to achieve those gains, however, business and labour must work together. One possibility is paid educational leave (PEL), a system for allocating funds and resources in the workplace to ensure retraining for all employees at regular intervals without loss of pay or job security.

While the business, labour, and government representatives on Canada's federal skill-development-leave panel agreed absolutely that PEL is necessary, they disagree about how to make it a reality.

"There is a bad climate among the social partners in Canada—social equity and economic inefficiency are seen as incompatible goals," says Kjell Rubenson, director of the Centre for Policy Studies in Education at the University of British Columbia. This shortsightedness leads to constant buck-passing on the implementation of socioeconomic legislation. When it comes down to who pays, business is against legislation, labour says business should pay, and both want the government to take the lead.

If private enterprise is truly the source of the country's economic growth and well-being—not to mention its major risk-taker and bill-payer—then it must act. And it must do so quickly. The useful lifespan of job skills is shortening. Significant investments in time and money must be made to keep the skills and knowledge of workers and management competitive. In the absence of government action, business must take the initiative.

If it doesn't, the overemphasis on the creation of low-wage, low-skill occupations will continue. But even increases in low-skill labour may not be enough for the mushrooming service sector. Information technology has upgraded job prerequisites in many occupations that previously could be filled by people with fewer skills. In Toronto and other urban centres, service-sector employers cannot find suitable applicants for clerical, sales, and warehousing jobs that require greater literacy and numeracy skills than before.

Labour-starved retailers and small businesses think that waiting for new educational and economic policies to address their current crisis is an exercise in futility. They want bodies now, and for many the solution is increased immigration quotas. However, experiences in Europe have dissuaded other OECD countries from the immigration option. According to Kjell Rubenson, European countries that have traditionally relied on immigration to solve the shortage problem realize that retraining is the only way to keep themselves competitive.

The problem with the immigration option is that it addresses only the labour shortage dilemma and ignores the problem of unemployment. Similarly, Employment and Immigration Canada's attack on unemployment through the Canadian Job

Strategy (CJS) ignores the fundamentals of labour shortage. The CJS reflects federal views that educating for the economy is best left to market forces.

More than 75 percent of the CJS budget is allocated to job entry and job development programmes. Both are aimed at helping the unemployed enter or re-enter the labour force. The budget makes little provision for retraining in the context of long-term economic training.

Large corporations are much better equipped, both in attitude and resources, to take advantage of the CJS. High-tech industries especially have long recognized that competition demands they keep up-to-date. These companies have concluded that

retraining ultimately yields a profit, not a loss.

Technological advances, whether they occur in the manufacture of product or in administration, do not by themselves mean higher productivity. Many companies have brought in new technology without recognizing that machines are only as useful as their masters. Companies must explore all the social implications of technological change in order to get the most out of it. Exploring these social implications can mean a fundamental reassessment of the human dynamics within an organization.

Source: Mark Czarnecki, "Help Wanted," *Canadian Business*, June 1988, pp. 62, 249, 251, 255.

Summary of Learning Goals

1. **Explain the concept of an occupational cluster and how it helps one establish a career in business.**

   When approaching a career in business, students should become aware of projected employment trends and should prepare for a group of related jobs—an occupational cluster—that offers good employment and career opportunities. A good business background along with a positive attitude will pave the way for many entry-level jobs. Students should also acquire business-related experience either through part- or full-time employment, cooperative education programmes, or participation in campus activities.

2. **Describe the challenges facing nontraditional students seeking a business career.**

   Nontraditional students are any students who do not fall into the 18- to 22-year-old age group, the traditional clients of higher education. Many nontraditional students are displaced homemakers, veterans, technologically displaced workers, and full-time employed persons seeking education for career enhancement or personal satisfaction. All face two primary problems: the challenge of adopting new, unfamiliar behaviours, and balancing their school responsibilities with other ones.

3. **Explain why knowing yourself is vital for career development.**

   Besides analyzing the demand for people in certain areas, students should learn about themselves. Help is available from school libraries, counselling centres, and career guidance and placement offices and CECs. They need to critically assess their motivations, lifestyle preferences, career ambitions, personal tastes and values, and so forth.

4. **Analyze the steps in the job search process.**

Obtaining the right job is difficult. Some ways to begin the search are:

- Locate available jobs that interest you.
- Prepare a job-seeking file, including letters of recommendation from instructors and others who know you well; transcripts of your academic work; and a résumé containing factual information about yourself and a statement of career goals.
- Seek out job sources such as public and private employment agencies and campus placement offices. Look at newspaper ads and trade journals and magazines. Talk to your professors and to school administrators, community organizations, and friends. Write directly to companies that interest you.
- Study your employment opportunities and consider many factors in assessing them, rather than only the most striking features.
- Be well prepared for the personal interview with a prospective employer. Know as much as you can about the company, its industry, and its competition. Be confident and communicate effectively.
- Make your employment decision.

5. **Outline the special problems of women choosing business careers.**

Women lack the kinds of career development models that have been commonplace for men, and they may be discriminated against by male coworkers. In addition, married women may be caught in the dilemma of allocating priorities amongst their husband's aspirations, family responsibilities, and their own career goals.

Key Terms

entry-level job
career cluster
nontradional student
displaced homemaker

technologically displaced worker
résumé
open-ended interview

Discussion Questions and Exercises

1. What is meant by the occupational cluster concept? Why is it so important in personal career planning?
2. Why do many people switch careers several times?
3. Discuss how nontraditional students prepare for a business career.

4. Discuss the job search process. What steps are involved and how should one approach each of them?

5. Construct your own résumé following the procedure outlined in this chapter. Ask your instructors, friends, family, and associates to criticize it. What did you learn from this exercise?

6. What employment sources are available to you?

7. What are the special career development problems facing women?

8. Explain how education and re-training programmes can fill many gaps in the Canadian economy.

Case 24-1

Access 51—Moving Women Up

In 1987, the Montreal Chamber of Commerce launched a computerized programme to help women executives break into the top echelon of Quebec's business community. The data bank, dubbed Access 51, started with a mere 60 names. Word of its existence has since spread afar and the list has grown to more than 425 names.

All names belong to women who are eminently qualified to sit on boards of directors, economic advisory committees, or task forces. The programme does not compete with head-hunters or placement personnel. "We simply believe that women have been under-represented and need to be promoted," says Paule Dore, the Chamber's general manager. At the center of Access's beliefs is the feeling that a growing number of organizations and government agencies actually want to appoint women to senior positions, but don't know where and how to find them.

There is a special significance to Access's name. In Quebec, women make up 51 percent of the population, yet they hold only 2 percent of the directors' positions with provincial companies. The few who have penetrated Quebec's so-called inner circle of power tend to sit together on several boards. The same names return to the same directorships over and over again.

As names trickle in, businesses have begun to draw on them for some of their appointments. Most women are recommended for the programme by executives who already hold senior posts. Each woman's name, and the full range of her qualifications and experience, comprise a confidential computer file. Organizations, companies or governments use the Access 51 data bank by telling the Chamber, as precisely as they can, the kind of women they seek—and for what post.

The backgrounds of those women listed in the data bank are then compared to the kind of candidate being sought. Once the names of the most suitable women are available, they are contacted so that meetings can be arranged between them and the requesting firm or organization.

The programme has received more than 150 inquiries about the data bank, of which 115 have been serious attempts to recruit women. These have come from 70 different enterprises, six of them large corporations, but most of them small and medium sized businesses and non-profit organizations. So far, 64 women have been considered for posts and 35 of them have been appointed. Concedes Dominique Groleau, the programme's coordinator, "Access 51 has really begun to address an issue that has gone on for far too long."

Source: Adrian Waller, "Access 51 Helps Women Executives to Move Into Circle of Influence," *This Week in Business*, April 23, 1988, p. 15.

Questions:
1. What are some of the problems confronting women who choose business careers? Explain.
2. How do programmes such as Access 51 help to circumvent some of these problems? Explain.

Case 24-2

The Professional Dream. . .or Dilemma

A few years ago, Paul Raymond decided to become an architect. He based his choice on his academic results, his natural inclination toward drawing, the information he had about the profession, and his knowledge of himself. He was also considerably impressed and influenced by the lifestyle of his uncle George Talbott, a distinguished architect who had received two awards from the Governor General. With youthful confidence in himself and in life, he entered Laval University's School of Architecture with only a beautiful professional dream in his pocket.

At his graduation, Anne Durand, his longtime girlfriend and now fiancée, was by his side. She was supportive, ambitious, and was studying for her own career as a research chemist. Together, their professional futures seemed bright.

A few weeks after graduation, Paul began looking around for a position. In response to the interview question, "What can you do for us?" he could only present the new diploma clutched in his hand, average grades, and the enthusiasm and energy of someone of 24.

As luck would have it (and perhaps with a helping hand from Uncle George), Paul was accepted into the second architectural office he visited. He started his first day there full of enthusiasm and bright ideas. His employer introduced him around, then set him to work to redraw (not create), under the supervision of the section chief, some plans for a cottage. Nothing out of the ordinary, and not even an expert architect but an old-style industrial designer to guide him!

Somewhat taken aback by this first brush with the real world, Paul thought to himself that they hadn't led him to expect this at university. Next he had to do research on different types of mortar on the market and draw up a list of provincial building code requirements—not a thing that called upon his creative talents. He was even reprimanded when he dared to suggest moving the doors of a gymnasium, although he knew he was right. Paul found himself far from the world of office design and décor that he had dreamed of, and still farther from any awards from the Governor General.

But his recent marriage to Anne helped him put up with these professional doldrums. Anne found a promising starting position in the R&D section of a major petrochemical manufacturing firm, and their joint salary allowed them to buy a condominium. Apart from their lesser experience, their situation compared favourably with those of their parents.

A few months after the celebration of Paul's being accepted into the Society of Architects, Philip was born. For the proud young parents, the feeling was of having really become somebodies: positions in reputable firms, professional recognition, a growing family, and a home of their own.

On Philip's first birthday, however, the home atmosphere was tense. Paul received an attractive offer from another firm. But to take it, he would have to leave Ottawa for Edmonton.

The decision was difficult for Paul and Anne, since they had only three days in which to make it...three days to clarify their values, identify their needs, take stock of those things that mattered. Which came first? Their professional lives, their family lives, or their social and community lives? How would Anne's career be affected? Did they both want the same things and to the same extent? Were they motivated by the same values—money, power, security, prestige? What kind of retirement did they look forward to? What would give them a sense of success in life?

Three days to find the answer to these questions—first, singly as individuals, then together as a couple. How far was each prepared to go in sacrificing one grand dream for that of the other? And could any compromise be satisfactory to both? Where would the needs of their baby enter into this? Would he go to a day-care centre or have a sitter at home to look after him? Or would Anne herself stay home, or could both parents coordinate their schedules to look after him? In a very short time, Philip, like the typical middle-class Canadian child, would have to be driven to hockey practice, to music lessons, to Saturday movies. Meanwhile, both Paul and Anne might be working overtime. This glimpse into the future made them both aware that their present priorities would perhaps have to be reconsidered in a few years.

Three days to consider the mortgage that would be due next year and that breaking the contract would be costly; that their pension fund wasn't transferable; that they might not want to rent their Ottawa house; that the cost of housing in Edmonton was out of sight; and that Anne would have to start job hunting in a new environment with a young baby and a husband who was also adjusting to a new position. And in considering this, Paul came to realize that his professional success depended to a great extent on his mobility. Large office complexes aren't built in small cities, and even in big cities, the competition is steep. To follow his career might mean the disruption of his entire family life. Question after question rose to the surface, and the answers took on an unsuspected dimension.

Source: Serge Rainville, "Career Planning. . .What's it all about?" *Opinions*, Auditor General of Canada, Vol. 2, April/May 1984, pp. i, ii, iii.

Questions:

1. How is it possible that a career such as Paul Raymond's, reasonably well chosen according to the rules, could give rise several years later to the dilemma he faces both professionally and personally?
2. What would you suggest Paul Raymond now do so that he is not faced with the same dilemma at the next phase of his career?

Careers in Selected Aspects of Business and Its Environment

Business is the primary employer in our private enterprise system. *Contemporary Canadian Business* introduces the reader to a wide range of future business careers. The career sections of this appendix accompany each major part of the text, featuring employment opportunities in each particular functional area. The careers discussed here are in selected aspects of business and its environment. Several business-related careers currently available appear below.

Lawyer. Most legal firms are extensively involved in business problems. Some lawyers work directly for a firm, but most are independent contractors. Because so much of most lawyer's work is in business law, it is advisable for them to have a business as well as a legal education.

Banker. The term *banker* applies to a number of people in banking positions. Most top bank executives have had experience in all aspects of bank management and operations. Banking is a prestigious, rewarding career field.

Owner/manager. The ownership and management functions are often performed by the same person in a small business, where people are "their own bosses." This is a rewarding experience for many people.

Accountant. Accountants are businesspeople who provide accounting services to firms and individuals. They have an independent business or work within a firm. These services range from setting up accounting systems to preparing tax forms. Professional certification for accountants is indicated by the title Chartered Accountant (CA), Certified Management Accountant (CMA), or Certified General Accountant (CGA).

Sales representative. Sales representatives are the people who handle the personal selling aspects of the firm's marketing programme. They call on prospective buyers, explain the firm's products, and secure orders. They are also responsible for seeing that customers are satisfied with their purchases and become repeat buyers.

Supervisor. A supervisor is a manager of a particular work area within a plant. This person directly supervises employees such as assembly line workers, welders, cutters, warehouse workers, and others. The supervisor is at the first level of management in a factory.

Systems analyst. Systems analysts are well-trained computer experts who develop the various computer-based information systems needed in an organization. They determine which information is required and how best to obtain it.

Careers in Management

Management offers an exciting array of career opportunities for the person who has the leadership qualities and professional preparation to deal with the complex problems facing the modern executive. Effective managers have numerous career paths available to them, because they can move from one industry or economic sector to another. Good industrial executives, for example, can effectively apply their abilities in service industries, government agencies, and hospitals.

Most management positions require considerable practical experience. Management is not a beginning job; it is one to work toward as you acquire experience.

General Manager. After obtaining substantial practical experience, some people move into general management positions. Titles can range anywhere from president to vice-president to general manager. These positions involve the management of activities that cross functional areas. For example, a general manager of an automobile dealership has overall responsibility for sales (new and used vehicles), leasing, service, finance, and personnel.

Department head. A department head is a manager of an organizational unit. Office managers, marketing managers, and production managers are all department heads. These people usually have experience in the areas that are to be managed.

Supervisor. Supervisors are managers of part of a department. They are the first level of management, and they directly supervise employees.

Public administrator. A public administrator is a manager of a government department, bureau, agency, or other division, or of a unit in a hospital or other nonprofit institution. Many local governments have been employing professional public administrators to manage their operations.

Administrative assistant. Administrative assistants are staff personnel who work directly for general management. They often hold the title "Assistant to..." Sometimes the position of administrative assistant is used as a training ground for people expected to advance to higher management positions in the firm.

Careers in Human Resource Management

Human resource management involves people management. Admittedly, all managers must deal with people, regardless of the functional areas with which they are associated. But executives directly involved in human resource management have primary responsibility for the administration of people-related activities such as employment, wages and salaries, health, and safety. Several of the careers available in these areas appear below.

Human resource management has become a growth activity during the last four years. In an effort to contain or reduce turnover, employers have hired additional specialists in compensation, benefits, and training. The growth of this occupational group has provided unrivaled opportunities for women, many of whom are now in supervision or management.

Demand will continue for experienced generalists as well as specialists in compensation, training, and recruitment. Most industrial openings for managers of personnel and industrial relations will go to candidates who have strong labour relations and negotiating experience.

Personnel manager. A personnel manager has overall responsibility for the personnel function. This includes recruitment, hiring, training, wage and salary administration, health, and safety. The personnel manager is usually the chief executive involved in human resource management. Sometimes this person has the title of vice-president of personnel.

Director of industrial relations. The director of industrial relations is usually management's representative in dealings with labour unions. He or she is often the chief representative for management during collective bargaining. In some firms this person also performs the duties of the personnel manager.

Union executive. Many labour unions are starting to employ people with a management education as union executives. While most union leaders still come from the rank and file, more professional managers are entering this field. A labour union career provides many interesting challenges in human resource management.

Wage and salary administrator. Wage and salary administrators are in charge of the compensation plans used in the organization. They are responsible for setting them up, administering them, and studying their effectiveness, so timely revisions can be made as needed.

Industrial counselor or psychologist. Many large firms have added industrial counselors or psychologists to their personnel departments to counsel employees and management on work, career, and personal problems. Such counselors also help determine selection procedures for new employees. Many counselors are qualified industrial psychologists; others hold degrees in guidance and counseling or social work. To be effective, industrial counselors must have a firm business background so they can understand and deal with problems they encounter.

Careers in Marketing

Marketing includes many exciting, dynamic fields, such as advertising, market research, personal selling, and physical distribution management. These are all areas of growing employment. Many beginning marketers start as sales personnel, then move into other positions as they gain experience. Others remain in sales roles. Still others begin their careers in different areas such as advertising or market research. Several of the marketing careers currently available appear below.

Marketing manager. The marketing manager, or marketing director, has overall responsibility for all phases of the marketing function. This person holds the highest position within the marketing area.

Advertising director. The advertising director is the person responsible for all aspects of the firm's advertising programme. When part of the programme is handled by outside agencies, the director is responsible for the contractual relationship with the agencies.

Advertising account executive. The account executive works for an advertising agency and is assigned to handle one or more of its accounts. This person is in charge of all advertising plans submitted to the clients.

Market researcher. Market researchers analyze information and data on consumers and on buying behaviour. They identify facts and trends that might be relevant in developing an improved competitive strategy.

Sales manager. Sales managers are in charge of a group of sales representatives or the entire sales force. In some cases they also are involved in selling to big accounts. But the sales manager's primary job is seeing that the firm's sales personnel perform effectively.

Sales representative. Sales representatives are the people who handle the personal selling aspects of the firm's marketing program. They call on prospective buyers, explain the firm's products, and secure orders. They are also responsible for seeing that customers are satisfied with their purchases and become repeat buyers.

Physical distribution manager. Sometimes called the traffic manager, the physical distribution manager is responsible for seeing that the firm's physical distribution function is performed effectively. Duties include transportation, shipping, warehousing, and the like.

Buyer. Buyers procure merchandise for retail stores. They usually specialize by product or department.

Operations manager. The operations manager is the person responsible for the nonmerchandise-related activities of retailing. Duties include supervision of the receiving, shipping, delivery, service, security, and inventory control departments.

Careers in Production, Computers, Research, and Accounting

Accounting, computers, production, and research offer considerable career opportunities for business students. People with accounting training are in high-level positions throughout most organizations. Entry-level jobs are plentiful and provide real challenges for graduates. Computers require professional personnel to assure that management gets the information needed for critical decisions. Production management positions are available in a diverse array of industries. Business researchers are also important in several areas of business: they secure and analyze the data on which decisions are based. Several of the currently available careers in these areas appear below.

Chartered accountant. Chartered accountants are independent businesspersons who provide accounting services to firms and individuals. These services range from setting up accounting systems to preparing tax forms.

Auditor. An auditor is an accountant who checks the accuracy and validity of accounting records and procedures. If they conform to recognized standards, the auditor certifies them in a public statement.

Cost accountant. Cost accountants are involved in accounting for the costs of producing the firm's product and operating the enterprise. They gather, analyze, and report on cost data for management.

Production manager. The production manager is responsible for the actual manufacturing of a product. This includes engineering, production control, quality control, and other areas of administration. The production manager is sometimes referred to as the plant manager.

Programmer. A programmer is a person who gives commands to a computer through specialized computer languages and selects meaningful information out of the data stored in a computer.

Systems analyst. Systems analysts are well-trained computer experts who develop the various computer-based information systems needed in an organization. They determine which information is required and how best to obtain it.

Statistician. Statisticians apply statistical procedures to data in order to assess their validity and reliability and to analyze, predict, and evaluate in such areas as quality control, marketing research, production control, and finance.

Supervisor. A supervisor is a manager of a particular work area within a plant. This person directly supervises employees such as assembly line workers, welders, cutters, and others. The supervisor is at the first level of management in a factory.

Actuary. Actuaries calculate insurance risks. Using statistical methods, they determine the likelihood of death at a certain age or the possibility of casualty loss under given circumstances. Once these risks are calculated actuaries help determine the insurance rates necessary to cover the risks.

Careers in Banking, Finance, Investments, and Insurance

All enterprises and many individuals require financial services. This means that there is a wide array of potential career fields for people interested and qualified in the area of finance. These careers are exciting and challenging, and they provide excellent advancement possibilities into top management. Several of the careers currently available in these areas appear below.

Finance director. The finance director is the chief financial officer of any organization, with the responsibility for all aspects of the finance function. This position usually carries the title of vice-president of finance or treasurer.

Financial analyst. A financial analyst is someone who studies and analyzes data, then prepares reports for management that outline various financial strategies that can be taken by the firm. Financial analysts are very important in any enterprise.

Banker. The term *banker* applies to a number of people in banking positions. Most top bank executives have had experience in all aspects of bank management and operations. Banking is a prestigious, rewarding career field.

Stockbroker. Stockbrokers are agents in the purchase and sale of securities—generally common and preferred stocks and bonds. They work for brokerage houses, providing information and advice to clients about their investments. Stockbrokers execute the buy and sell orders for securities.

Portfolio manager. Portfolio managers are financial consultants to investors. They supervise investments and often have legal authority to buy and sell securities for a client. Individuals, pension funds, banks, trust funds, colleges, insurance companies, and private foundations all employ portfolio managers.

Underwriter. Underwriters evaluate insurance applications to determine the risks involved for the insurer. They specialize in various types of insurance, such as life and casualty. After assessing the insurance application, the underwriter assigns the proper rate (price) to the new policy. If the risks are too great for the insurer, the underwriter rejects the application.

Insurance agent. Insurance agents are insurance consultants and sales representatives. They evaluate people's insurance needs and recommend the best type of coverage. If the prospect agrees, they complete the sales transaction. Insurance agents can either work for a particular company or represent several companies as independent agents.

Careers in International Business, Business Law, and Selected Industries

International business, business law, and certain industries all offer career opportunities. International business includes many careers, both at home and abroad. Lawyers assist management and often become actively involved in the operation of a firm. Some work directly for companies, but most contract their services out. Several of the careers available in these areas appear below.

Lawyer. Most attorneys are extensively involved in business problems. Some work directly for a firm; others are self-employed.

International Banking Officer. International banking officers must be knowledgeable in foreign financial systems and the trade relations between nations. They are the bank's representatives in all its international dealings.

Import-Export Manager. Import-export managers plan and supervise the flow of goods to and from other nations. They are important contributors to international business.

International Manager. Companies typically set up a separate international unit to handle their overseas affairs. The international manager is the chief executive for this unit and has overall responsibility for its operation.

Notes

Chapter 1

[1]David Bercuson, "It's a Hit," *Report on Business Magazine*, Aug. 1987, pp. 62-64.
[2]The term "five *M*s of management" was first suggested by L. T. White, a leading small business proponent. See U.S. Small Business Administration, *Strengthening Small Business Management: Collections from the Papers of L. T. White*, Joseph C. Schabacker, ed. (Washington, D.C.: Government Printing Office, 1971), p. 21.

Chapter 2

[1]These examples are from William Guttmann, "You Can't Beat Inflation," *The Age*, Sept. 28, 1974, p. 11.
[2]Rosemary Speirs, "Hydro Sale Will Kill Lakes, Energy Probe," *Globe and Mail*, Nov. 14, 1981.
[3]Reported in Edward M. Syring, "Realizing Recycling's Potential," *Nation's Business*, Feb. 1976, pp. 68, 70.
[4]R. Crawford and H. Gram, *Canadian Management, Responses to Social Issues* (McGraw-Hill Ryerson, 1981) p. 103.
[5]*The Age*, Aug. 13, 1974, p. 1.
[6]R. Crawford and H. Gram, op. cit., p. 117.
[7]*The Financial Post*, Sept. 8, 1978.
[8]Alan Bayless, "Ottawa's Crystal Ball Suggests Leaner Times Ahead For Energy," *Financial Times of Canada*, Dec. 12, 1988, p. 15. Reprinted by permission.
[9]*The Crude Petroleum and Natural Gas Industry, 1987*, Statistics Canada, Industry Division, Energy Section, Ottawa: Supply and Services Canada, Tables 7 and 8, pp. 30-36.
[10]*An Energy Policy for Canada, 1976*, Energy, Mines and Resources, p. 149.
[11]This study is discussed in Max Ways, "Business Faces Growing Pressure to Behave Better," *Fortune*, May 1974, p. 316.

Chapter 3

[1]J. E. Smith, D. A. Soberman, *The Law and Business Administration in Canada*, 4th ed. (Toronto: Prentice-Hall, 1983), p. 606.
[2]Peter H. Fuhrman, *Business in the Canadian Environment* (Toronto: Prentice-Hall, 1982), pp. 105-106.
[3]Max Ways, "Business Faces Growing Pressure to Behave Better," *Fortune*, May 1974, p. 316.

Chapter 4

[1]Based on Marianne Teft, "College Pro Shows the Way to Go," *The Financial Post*, July 24, 1982, pp. 1-2. Reprinted by permission.
[2]"From Car Rentals to Coffee to Drugstores," *The Financial Post*, Aug. 25, 1984, p. 57.
[3]Guy A. Lavigueur, "In Praise of Entrepreneurs," *Business Life*, Jan. 1982, p. 16. Reprinted by permission.
[4]Statistics Canada, *Small Business in Canada: A Statistical Profile 1981-1983*, Minister of Supply and Services Canada, Ottawa, Catalogue #65-521, Tables 1 and 2, Oct. 1986, pp. 22, 42, 53, 55.
[5]Dina Lavoie, *Women Entrepreneurs: Building a Stronger Economy*, Background Paper, Ottawa: Canadian Advisory Council on the Status of Women, Feb. 1988, p. 1.
[6]These features are suggested in *Meeting the Special Problems of Small Business* (New York: Committee for Economic Development, 1947), p. 14.
[7]Based on W. Jennings, *Entrepreneurship: A Primer for Canadians* (Toronto: Canadian

Foundation for Economic Education, 1985), pp. 21-23.

[8]*Small Business in Canada: A Statistical Profile* (Minister of State, Small Business and Tourism, 1981), p. 18 and Statistics Canada Cat. 71-001, Nov. 1982. Reprinted by permission.

[9]"Have Idea Will Travel," *The Financial Post*, Oct. 30, 1982, p. 14.

[10]"Doyle Hoyt Survives Bankruptcy, Succeeds Second Time Around," *Wall Street Journal*, Nov. 29, 1977.

[11]"Reporting Burdens and Business Restrictions Survey Results," *Canadian Federation of Independent Business*, Dec. 4, 1980, p. 1.

[12]Bruce Gates, "Fast Food Still a Big Winner," *The Financial Post*, Aug. 25, 1984, p. 51.

[13]"Canadian Women Owners/Managers," *Small Business Secretariat*, Jan. 1982, p. 1.

[14]Taxation Statistics, Revenue Canada, Table 12, various years.

[15]Gary L. Cohen, Statistics Canada, *Enterprising Canadians: The Self-Employed in Canada*, Minister of Supply and Services, Ottawa, Catalogue #71-536, Oct. 1988.

[16]"Canadian Women Owners/Managers," op. cit., p. 11.

Chapter 5

[1]Fred Feidler, *A Theory of Leadership Effectiveness* (New York, McGraw-Hill, 1967).

Chapter 6

[1]The immense organizational tasks involved in landing an astronaut on the moon are described in *Man and the Organization* (New York: Time-Life Books, 1975), pp. 88-99.

[2]C. Northcote Parkinson, *Parkinson's Law and Other Studies in Administration* (Boston: Houghton Mifflin, 1957), p.2.

[3]Ibid., pp. 7-11.

[4]Ibid., pp. 4-7.

[5]Frederick W. Taylor, *The Principles of Scientific Management* (New York: Harper & Bros., 1916).

[6]A thorough discussion of the matrix organization structure is contained in Stanley M. Davis and Paul R. Lawrence, *Matrix* (Reading, Mass.: Addison-Wesley, 1977).

[7]Robert Townsend, *Up the Organization* (New York: Knopf, 1970), p. 134.

[8]Keith Davis, *Human Relations at Work* (New York: McGraw-Hill, 1972), pp. 261-273.

Chapter 7

[1]From Bowen Northrup, "More Swedish Firms Attempt to 'Enrich' Production-line Jobs," *Wall Street Journal*, Oct. 25, 1974.

[2]Stuart Chase, *Men At Work* (New York: Harcourt, Brace & World, 1941), pp. 21-22.

[3]Abraham H. Maslow, "A Theory of Human Motivation," *Psychological Review*, July 1943, pp. 370-396.

[4]Robert Louis Stevenson, *Familiar Studies of Men and Books* (1882).

[5]Douglas McGregor, *The Human Side of Enterprise* (New York: McGraw-Hill, 1960), pp. 33-34.

[6]Ibid., pp. 47-48.

[7]Frederick Herzberg, *Work and the Nature of Man* (Cleveland: World Publishing, 1966).

[8]Peter Drucker, *The Practice of Management* (New York: Harper & Bros., 1954), pp. 128-129.

[9]Charles R. Walker and Robert Guest, *Man on the Assembly Line* (Cambridge, Mass.: Harvard University Press, 1952), p. 19.

[10]William J. Paul, Jr., Keith B. Robertson, and Frederick Herzberg, "Job Enrichment Pays Off," *Harvard Business Review*, March-April 1969, p. 61.

[11]"The New Industrial Relations," *Business Week*, May 11, 1981, pp. 85-98 and "Workers Don't Give A Damn? Chrysler Thinks They Do, If—," *Ward's Auto World*, June 1972, p. 43.

[12]Personal interview with Randy Castelluzzo, manager of personnel services, General Foods Corporation, May 1981.

[13]Robert N. Ford, *Motivation Through the Work Itself* (New York: American Management Association, 1969).

[14]M. D. Kilbridge, "Do Workers Prefer Larger Jobs?" *Personnel*, September-October 1960, pp. 45-48.

[15]William E. Reif and Peter P. Schoderbek, "Job Enrichment: Antidote to Apathy," *Management of Personnel Quarterly*, Spring 1966, pp. 16-23.

Chapter 8

[1]Lee Lescage, "Anyone Who Answers This Job Ad Probably Won't Get the Position," *Wall Street Journal*, April 10, 1984, p. 31. Reprinted by permission.

Chapter 9

[1]The Polish government-union disputes are discussed in "In Poland, Solidarity Walks a Tightrope," *U.S. News & World Report*, Jan. 12, 1981, pp. 31-32; "Solidarity Wins a Round," *Newsweek*, Nov. 24, 1980, pp. 74, 76; and "The Government Gets Tough," *Time*, Jan. 26, 1981, pp. 42-43.

Chapter 10

[1]Gail Chiasson, "Canadelle Starts Market Revolution, *Marketing*, Oct. 22, 1984, p. 1.
[2]Committee on Definitions, *Marketing Definitions: A Glossary of Marketing Terms* (Chicago: American Marketing Association, 1960) p. 15.
[3]*Annual Report* (New York: General Electric, 1952), p. 21.
[4]"Pizza Huts Assert Presence in Lunch Market," *Marketing News*, April 29, 1983, p. 4.
[5]James F. Engel and Roger D. Blackwell, *Consumer Behavior*, 4th ed. (Hinsdale, Ill.: Dryden Press, 1982), p. 9.
[6]Jo Marney, "Seminar Helps Advertisers Rethink Markets," *Marketing*, Jan. 7, 1985, p. 17.
[7]Committee on Definitions, *Marketing Definitions*, p. 17.

Chapter 11

[1]Bill Abrams, "Despite Mixed Record, Firms Still Pushing for New Products," *Wall Street Journal*, Nov. 12, 1981.
[2]Terms first suggested by Melvin T. Copeland in *Principles of Merchandising* (New York: McGraw-Hill, 1924). Later commentary in Richard H. Holton, "The Distinction between Convenience Goods, Shopping Goods, and Specialty Goods," *Journal of Marketing*, July 1958, pp. 55-56.
[3]David R. Rink and John E. Swan, "Product Life Cycle Research: A Literature Review," *Journal of Business Research*, September 1979, pp. 219-42.
[4]Committee on Definitions, *Marketing Definitions*, pp. 9-10.
[5]Kenneth Uhl and Carl Block, "Some Findings Regarding Recall of Brand Marks: Descriptive Marks vs Non-descriptive Marks," *Southern Journal of Business*, October 1969, pp. 1-10.
[6]"How Coke Protects Its Good Name," *Business Week*, Nov. 4, 1972, p. 66.
[7]"For Those Who Can Afford It, There's a New Rolls-Royce Out," *Seattle Times*, Oct. 4, 1980, p. C4.
[8]Peter Vanderwicken, "P & G's Secret Ingredient," *Fortune*, July 1974, p. 78. According to a P & G spokesperson, Tide was still its best-selling brand as of June 1, 1981.

Chapter 12

[1]Adapted from Robert McLeod, "Stakes High in Retail Store Shakeup," *The Winnipeg Free Press*, Sept. 27, 1985, p. 35.
[2]Robert McLeod, "Dominion Biggest Loser," *The Winnipeg Free Press*, Sept. 27, 1985, p. 35.
[3]*Handbook of Canadian Consumer Markets*, 3rd ed. (Ottawa: The Conference Board of Canada, 1984), p. 201.
[4]The wheel of retailing, originally proposed by M.P. McNair, is discussed in Stanley C. Hollander, "The Wheel of Retailing," *Journal of Marketing*, July 1960, pp. 37-42. Some of the material in this section is based on the Hollander article.
[5]*Transport Review: Trends & Selected Issues*, 1981 (Ottawa: Canadian Transport Commission, Research Branch, 1981), pp. 13-69.
[6]Ibid.
[7]Inventory control's impact on profitability is discussed in Lewis Bemon, "A Big Payoff from Inventory Controls," *Fortune*, July 27, 1981, pp. 76-80.

Chapter 13

[1]Rona Maynard, "Blitzing the Media," *Report on Business*, June 1986, p. 70.
[2]This rule is noted in Harold C. Cash and W. J. E. Crissy, "The Salesman's Role in Marketing," *Psychology of Marketing*, vol. 12, Personnel Development Associates.
[3]"Antifreeze Marketers Set Major Winter Ad Campaigns," *Advertising Age*, Sept. 16, 1974, p. 2.
[4]"A Report on Advertising Revenues in Canada" (Toronto: Elliott Research, 1981).
[5]*Maclean's*, Feb. 28, 1983, pp. 28-29. Reprinted by permission.
[6]The discussion of various advertising media is adapted from S. Watson Dunn and Arnold M. Barban, *Advertising: Its Role in Modern Marketing*, 5th ed. (Hinsdale, Ill.: Dryden Press, 1982), pp. 512-91.
[7]"Labor Letter," *Wall Street Journal*, Sept. 14, 1971.
[8]Walter Gaw, "Specialty Advertising," *Specialty Advertising Association*, 1970, p. 7.

Chapter 14

[1]Hoo-Min D. Toong and Amar Gupta, "Personal Computers," *Scientific American*, Offprint, Dec. 1982, p. 3.
[2]Susan Gittens, "Networking Know-How Strained to Meet Corporate Data Demands," *The Financial Post*, Nov. 14, 1988, p. 51.

Chapter 15

[1]Henry Dauderis, Albert Slavin, Isaac N. Reynolds, *Basic Financial Accounting* (Toronto: Holt, Rinehart and Winston of Canada, 1982), pp. 12-13.

Chapter 16

[1]Kenneth Harrigan, "Making Quality Job One—A Cultural Revolution," *Business Quarterly*, Winter 84/85, pp. 68-70.
[2]Robert Kreitner, *Management* (Boston: Houghton Mifflin, 1983), p. 84.
[3]Gene Bylinsky, "The Race to the Automatic Factory," *Fortune*, Feb. 21, 1983, p. 53.
[4]Lee J. Krajewski and Larry P. Ritzman, *Operations Management, Strategy and Analysis* (Reading, Pa.: Addison-Wesley, 1987), pp. 574-75.
[5]Harold C. Livesay, *American Made* (Boston: Little, Brown, 1979), pp. 20-21.
[6]Richard B. Chase and Nicholas J. Aquilano, *Production and Operations Management: A Life Cycle Approach* (Homewood, Ill.: Richard D. Irwin, 1981), p. 516.
[7]Keith K. Cox and Ben M. Enis, *The Marketing Research Process* (Goodyear Publishing Company, Inc., 1972), p. 200.

Chapter 17

[1]Michael Salter, "The High Cost of Money," *Maclean's*, Nov. 4, 1985, p. 50.
[2]"Creeping Inflation," *Federal Reserve Bank of Philadelphia Business Review*, August 1957, p. 3. Quoted in Campbell R. McConnell, *Economics* (New York: McGraw-Hill, 1975), p. 289.
[3]Lawrence S. Ritter and William L. Silber, *Principles of Money, Banking and Financial Markets* (New York: Basic Books, 1974), pp. 385-386.
[4]Edwin G. Dolan and Roy Vogt, *Basic Economics* (Toronto: Holt, Rinehart and Winston of Canada, 1981), pp. 192-193.
[5]"Treasury Bills—What They Are and How the Weekly Auction Works," *Canadian Bankers' Association Bulletin*, April 1980. Reprinted by permission.
[6]Richard Blackwell, "Computers Have A Way With Money," *The Financial Post*, Nov. 9, 1985, p. C1.
[7]Ann Shortell, "Banks, Stores Jump On Auto Debit Bandwagon," *The Financial Post*, Nov. 9, 1985, p. C1.
[8]Edwin G. Dolan and Roy Vogt, *Basic Economics* (Toronto: Holt, Rinehart and Winston of Canada, 1981), p. 196.
[9]Gordon F. Boreham, *Money and Banking*, 2nd ed. (Toronto: Holt, Rinehart and Winston of Canada, 1979), pp. 356-359.

[10]H. H. Binhammer, *Money, Banking and the Canadian Financial System* (Toronto: Methuen, 1977), p. 113.

[11]Edwin H. Neave, *Canada's Financial System* (Toronto: John Wiley & Sons, 1981), p. 84.

Chapter 18

[1]Calvin M. Boardman and Kathy J. Ricci, "Defining Selling Terms," *Credit & Financial Management*, April 1985, p. 31.

Chapter 19

[1]Vancouver Stock Exchange advertisement, *The Globe and Mail*, Feb. 15, 1989, p. B5.

[2]The Toronto Stock Exchange, *Ticker Tape and All That*, pp. 4-5.

[3]Frank K. Reilly, *Investments* (Hinsdale, Ill.: Dryden Press, 1982), p. 85.

[4]Deborah Read, "Mutual Funds Seek New Buyers," *Winnipeg Free Press*, Feb. 23, 1983, p. 28.

Chapter 20

[1]"Hole-in-One Covered in Japan," *Canadian Insurance/Agent And Broker*, April 1985, p. 42.

[2]Allan Gould, *Report on Business Magazine*, April 1989, p. 116.

[3]*Facts of the General Insurance Industry of Canada*, 9th ed. (Toronto: Insurance Bureau of Canada, 1981), p. 4.

[4]*Insurance Facts* 1982-83 (New York: Insurance Information Institute, 1983) p. 60.

[5]*Facts of the General Insurance Industry of Canada*, op. cit., p. 18.

[6]Ibid.

Chapter 21

[1]David Estok, "Firms Restructuring for a Global Market," *The Financial Post*, Jan. 9, 1989, p. 11.

[2]Ibid.

[3]*The Gazette* (Montreal), Feb. 5, 1983.

[4]*Canada Export*, Vol. 2, no. 22 (Dec. 1985), p. 1.

[5]Gary Rabbior, *Export Canada: Opportunities and Challenges in the World Economy*, 1984, pp. 4, 5.

[6]From Vern Terpstra, *International Marketing*, 2nd ed. (Hinsdale, Ill.: Dryden Press, 1978), p. 11.

[7]Diane Francis, "Bailing out the Titanic," *Canadian Business*, June 1981.

[8]Philip Kotler and Gordon J. McDougall, *Principles of Marketing*, Canadian ed. (Scarborough: Prentice-Hall, 1983) p. 514.

[9]Sylvia Ostry, "In Praise of GATT—and a Warning on the Long-Term Implications of Protectionism," *The Financial Post*, March 9, 1985, p. 48.

[10]"Off the Record," *Detroit News*, Feb. 28, 1975.

[11]Based on information from Terpstra, *International Marketing*, Canadian ed.

[12]Ibid., pp. 41-46.

Chapter 22

[1]Rate A. Howell, John R. Allison, and Nate T. Henley, *Business Law: Text and Cases*, 2nd ed. (Hinsdale, Ill.: Dryden Press, 1981), p. 140.

[2]Ibid., p. 503.

[3]Ibid., p. 115.

[4]Joseph J. Joyce, "How to Select and Protect a Trademark," *Product Marketing*, May 1979, p. 28.

Chapter 23

[1]Ian Allaby, "The Future Now! Priming Your Business for the 1990s," *Canadian Business*, March 1989, p. 59.

[2]An excellent update is contained in William Serrin, "Detroit Strikes Back," *New York Times Magazine*, Sept. 14, 1980, p. 26.

[3]*Canadian Economic Observer*, A monthly publication of the Minister of Regional Industrial Expansion and the Minister of State for Science and Technology, Ottawa: Supply and Services Canada, Catalogue #11-010, March 1989 (Vol. 2, no. 3), Table 2.1, p. 5.24, and Unemployment Rate Chart, p. 5.27.

[4]Ian Allaby, ibid., p. 58.

[5]Warren Talbot, "Next Century Offers Chance for Man to Soar or to Stumble," *Sentinel Star*, Nov. 25, 1979, p. 1-D.

[6]See, for example, data in *World Bank Atlas* (Washington, D.C.: World Bank, 1975), p. 6.

[7]Statistics Canada, *Canada Year Book 1980-81* (Ottawa: Ministry of Supply and Services, 1981), p. 150.

[8]*The World Almanac & Book of Facts 1981* (New York: Newspaper Enterprise Associates, Inc., 1981), p. 544.

[9]"If You Live in Bangladesh and Want Some 40 More Years," *Forbes*, July 6, 1981, p. 24.

[10]Statistics Canada, *Federal Electoral Districts*, Catalogue 95-901, vol. 3, Profile Series A, 1982, p. 1.

[11]Statistics Canada, *Population Projections for Canada and the Provinces, 1976-2001*, 1979, p. 36.

[12]Ibid., p. 13.

[13]Ella Mae Howay, "Business in the Year 2000," *Carroll Business Bulletin*, Fall 1974, pp. 18-19.

[14]"Gerber Products Grows Up With Infant-related Interests," *Detroit News*, June 18, 1978.

[15]Statistics Canada, *Canada's Female Labour Force*, one of a series from the 1976 Census of Canada, 1980, p. 3.

[16]Statistics Canada, Historical Labour Force Statistics, Ottawa, Supply and Services Canada, Catalogue #71-201, January 1989, p. 256 and Statistics Canada, Labour Force Annual Averages, 1981-1988, Ottawa: Supply and Services Canada, Catalogue #71-529, March 1989, Table 3, p. 63.

[17]Jean Yves Le Lovarn, "Two Career Couples and Human Resource Management," *Dialogue*, July 1984, Vol. 8, no. 4, pp. 7-9.

[18]Ian Allaby, ibid., pp. 54, 55.

[19]Ibid., p. 54.

[20]Ibid., p. 56.

[21]Ibid., p. 57.

[22]*The Financial Post*, Jan. 24, 1981, p. 51.

[23]Ian Allaby, ibid., p. 56.

[24]Ibid.

[25]Noted in William Lazar, "The 1980s and Beyond: A Perspective," *MSU Business Topics*, Spring 1977, p. 21.

[26]Charles J. Lapp, "Future Needn't be Dismal; Key Lack: Investment Capital," *Marketing News*, Sept. 23, 1977, p. 4.

[27]*Canada Year Book*, p. 528.

[28]*Canadian Business Review*, The Conference Board of Canada, Vol. 9, no. 3, Autumn 1982, p. 10.

[29]Ian Allaby, ibid., p. 58.

[30]Ibid., p. 62.

Chapter 24

[1]*Computerized Career Selection Systems, 1982* (Ottawa: Employment and Immigration Canada, 1982), pp. 7-8. Reprinted by permission of the Minister of Supply and Services.

[2]Statistics Canada, *Canada's Female Labour Force*, one of a series from the 1976 Census of Canada, 1980.

[3]"Where Women Work," *Wall Street Journal*, Nov. 1, 1977.

[4]"Women Still Struggle in Work World," *Detroit News*, Sept. 24, 1977.

Photo Credits

The publishers thank the following sources of reprint photographs used in this textbook. We have attempted to trace the ownership of copyright for all photographs used, and will gladly receive information enabling us to rectify any errors in references or credits.

Chapter 1

Photograph page 4 courtesy of Quebecor Incorporated. Photograph page 20 courtesy of Canadian Pacific.

Chapter 2

Photograph page 38 Courtesy of MacDonalds of Canada. Photograph page 48 by Grant Heilman.

Chapter 3

Photograph page 72 courtesy of SNC Group. Photograph page 74 by Gisele Beauvais. Photograph page 76 copyright © by Susan Dobson. Photograph page 77 copyright © Raphael Macia/Photo Researchers Inc.

Chapter 4

Photograph page 102 courtesy of Zenon Environmental Inc. Photograph page 106 courtesy of Mac's Convenience Stores.

Chapter 5

Photograph page 128 courtesy of Ultramar Canada. Photograph page 142 courtesy of Toronto Symphony.

Chapter 6

Photograph page 156 courtesy of John Labatt Inc.

Chapter 7

Photograph page 188 courtesy of General Motors Corporation.

Chapter 8

Photograph page 220 courtesy of Bank of Montreal.

Chapter 9

Photograph page 254 courtesy of Government Consultants International. Photograph page 256 courtesy of Culver Pictures Inc. Photograph page 271 courtesy of Canada Wide Features Service Ltd.

Chapter 10

Photograph page 286 courtesy of mmmuffins Inc. Photograph page 293 by Peter Southwick/Stock Boston.

Chapter 11

Photograph page 308 courtesy of Sun Ice Designs. Photograph page 324 copyright © Paul Sequeira/Photo Researchers Inc.

Chapter 12

Photograph page 343 copyright © Donald Dietz 1980/Stock Boston. Photograph page 353 Canada Wide Features Services Limited.

Chapter 13

Photograph page 370 courtesy of Loblaws Inc. Advertisement page 378 courtesy of the Canadian Pulp and Paper Association. Advertisement page 379 courtesy of the Insurance Bureau of Canada. Advertisement page 381 courtesy of 3M Canada Inc.

Chapter 14

Photograph page 402 courtesy of Statistics Canada.

Chapter 15

Photograph page 428 courtesy of Maclean Hunter.

Chapter 16

Photograph page 464 courtesy of Palliser Furniture.

Chapter 17

Photograph page 506 courtesy of The Bank of Canada. Photograph page 512 by Gisele Beauvais.

Chapter 18

Photograph page 532 courtesy of Flash Pack Ltd.

Chapter 19

Photograph page 560 courtesy of Sherritt Gordon Ltd. Photograph page 567 courtesy of Vancouver Stock Exchange.

Chapter 20

Photograph page 590 courtesy of Crown Life. Photograph page 593 copyright © Josephus Daniels/Rapho/Photo Researchers Inc. Advertisement page 601 courtesy of American Insurance Association. Photograph page 605 copyright © Ronny Jacques/Photo Researchers Inc.

Chapter 21

Photograph page 626 courtesy of Gemini Fashions Ltd. Photograph page 636 copyright © Joe Munro/Photo Researchers Inc.

Chapter 22

Photograph page 660 courtesy of Davies, Ward and Beck.

Chapter 23

Photograph page 686 courtesy of Royal Trustco Ltd.

Chapter 24

Photograph page 722 courtesy of Paradigm Consulting Inc.

Index

Those terms and page references appearing in boldface type indicate the location of the margin glossary definitions.

To the Owner of
This Book:

We are interested in your reaction to **Contemporary Canadian Business third edition**. Through feedback from you, we can improve this book in future editions.

1. What was your reason for using this book?
   _____university course   _____continuing education course
   _____college course   _____personal interest

2. Approximately how much of the book did you use?
   _____1/4_____1/2_____3/4_____all

3. What is the best aspect of the book?

4. Have your any suggestions for improvement?

5. Is there anything that should be added?

Fold here